People
in the News
1994

People in the News 1994

David Brownstone

Irene Franck

MACMILLAN PUBLISHING COMPANY
NEW YORK
Maxwell Macmillan Canada
TORONTO
Maxwell Macmillan International
NEW YORK   OXFORD   SINGAPORE   SYDNEY

Acknowledgments for illustrative materials are on pp. 411–413, which shall be considered a continuation of the copyright page.

Macmillan Publishing Company   Maxwell Macmillan Canada, Inc.
866 Third Avenue   1200 Eglinton Avenue East, Suite 200
New York, NY 10022   Don Mills, Ontario M3C 3N1

Macmillan Publishing Company is part of the Maxwell Communication Group of Companies

Printed in the United States of America

Printing number

1   2   3   4   5   6   7   8   9   10

ISBN: 0-02-897057-8

Library of Congress Cataloging-in-Publication Data
The Library of Congress has cataloged this serial as follows:

Brownstone, David M.
    People in the news / David Brownstone and Irene Franck.
        p.   Cm.
    Includes bibliographical references and index.
    Summary: Presents clear, up-to-date biographical information on a wide selection of the most newsworthy people in the world.

Annual
Began with issue for 1991.

ISSN 1062-2713
    1. Celebrities—Biography.   2. Biography—20th century.   [1. Celebrities.
2. Biography.]   I. Franck, Irene M. II. Title.
CT120.B76   1991
920—dc20   91-14962
                                                                   CIP

The paper used in this publication meets the minimum requirements of American National Standard for Information Sciences—Permanence of Paper for Printed Library Materials. ANSI Z39.48–1984 ⊗ ™

Contents

Preface

In this fourth edition of **People in the News**, we have again developed current profiles of a wide selection of the world's most newsworthy people—the presidents, prime ministers, generals, musicians, film stars, directors, scientists, doctors, sports figures, business leaders, spies, criminals, victims, writers, judges, and the rest who are the main stuff of day-to-day reportage on screen, on radio, and in print throughout the year. The profile for each person first stresses 1993 activities, then presents a concise biography, and finally offers a further reading list for those who want to dig deeper into the person's current and past history. Each obituary offers a capsule overview of the person's life, also with a further reading list.

As in the 1992 and 1993 editions, we have included a cumulative alphabetical index and a cumulative occupational index, covering the first four editions of **People in the News**. These make it possible for readers to reach quickly and easily the whole set of people covered in any edition of **People in the News**. Each individual volume is also self-indexed by alphabet.

We should note that approximately 75–80 percent of the material in this edition of **People in the News** is completely new, even though the majority of the entries cover people previously profiled. That will always be so, and stems from the nature of the work, for in each such entry material from the previous year has been merged into the biographies, leaving room for the entirely new material comprising the current and usually largest portion of the entry. Entries on living people are current to the end of 1993, and sometimes later. So are suggestions for further reading; these have also been updated, with newer bibliographic citations added and older ones dropped. Note that for people with massive bibliographies, such as Bill Clinton, we include periodical references only for 1993; readers seeking older material can check previous editions.

This edition of **People in the News** once again covers approximately 700 people in all, including 200 key obituaries, with photographs of over

200 people. As is our pattern in this work, we have added many news-worthy people and dropped others, and some from earlier editions are back in this edition or will return in future editions, as their newsmaking activities warrant. The 1993 edition includes somewhat fewer political figures than the 1992 edition, partly because the presidential transition is past and a new administration has settled into Washington. This edition also includes somewhat more literary figures, music people, and (by popular request) sports notables, and slightly more movie people, as Hollywood (along with the rest of the country) begins to pull out of the recession. Overall, we have a somewhat higher proportion of wholly new people than in previous editions.

Our thanks once again to Philip Friedman, president and publisher of Macmillan Reference; his assistant, Ruth Mannes; managing editor Andy Ambraziejus; and Sabrina Bowers, Tom Hroncich, Angelo Zurica, and Nancy Cohen who have so capably seen this book through the publishing process. We also again thank the staff of the Chappaqua Library—Director Mark Hasskarl; the expert reference staff, including Martha Alcott, Teresa Cullen, Carolyn Jones, Paula Peyraud, Mary Platt, and Carolyn Reznick; and the circulation staff, including Marilyn Coleman, Lois Siwicki, and Jane McKean—and their colleagues throughout the northeastern library network, who have once again been so helpful in fulfilling our research needs. Our thanks also to our expert photo researcher, visual resources consultant Susan Hormuth, and to Mary Racette for her invaluable assistance in organizing the bibliographies.

David Brownstone
Irene Franck
Chappaqua, New York

People
in the News
1994

Abbott, Jim (James Anthony Abbott; 1967–) Even non-baseball fans knew something notable had happened when New York Yankee lefthander Jim Abbott pitched a no-hitter in a 4–0 win against the Cleveland Indians on September 4, 1993. This first Yankee no-hitter since 1983, and before that 1956, was an achievement in itself, but the more so because Abbott was born with no right hand, only stubs for fingers. New York City is a tough town, and its baseball fans had given Abbott a hard time after his December 1992 trade to New York; Abbott himself was unhappy about the trade, had lost a bitter salary arbitration battle in February, and, up to the no-hitter, had a record of only 9–11. That no-hitter seemed to bring the fans and pitcher together with dreams of future championships, though the Yankees lost a late-season pennant race, and Abbott himself ended the season 11–14, with a 4.37 earned run average, up from 2.77 the previous year. In October, he was honored with the Freedom Forum's Free Spirit Award, donating the $100,000 to Amigos de los Ninos, a California organization providing aid for children.

Born in Flint, Michigan, Abbott graduated from the University of Michigan, where he won the U. S. Baseball Federation's Golden Spike award as best amateur player (1987) and was named to the *Sporting News* Collegiate All-American team (1988). Also in 1988, he became the first baseball player to win the Sullivan Award for best amateur athlete, and pitched a 5–3 win over Japan to give the U.S. baseball team the gold medal at the Seoul Olympics. He then became a pitcher for the California Angels, in Anaheim (1989–92), and was named to the All-Star Team in 1991. He is married to Dana Abbott.

FURTHER READING

" 'Courage is so much . . .' " STEVE MARANTZ. *Sporting News*, July 19, 1993.
Jim Abbott (All-American Pitcher). HOWARD REISER. Melmont, 1993.
Jim Abbott. RICHARD RAMBECK. Child's World, 1993.
Sports Great Jim Abbott. JEFF SAVAGE. Enslow, 1993.
Jim Abbott, Pitcher. GREG LEE. Rourke, 1993.
Jim Abbott: Star Pitcher. BILL GUTMAN. Houghton Mifflin, 1992; Millbrook Press, 1992.
Jim Abbott. JOHN ROLFE. Lerner, 1991.
Jim Abbott: Sports Illustrated Kids. JOHN ROLFE. Little, Brown, 1991.
Jim Abbott: Beating the Odds. RICK L. JOHNSON. Macmillan, 1991.
"Jim Abbott. . . ." SAM BLAIR. *Boys' Life*, Mar. 1990.
Jim Abbott Against All Odds. ELLEN E. WHITE. Scholastic, 1990.

Abdel Rahman, Omar: See **Rahman, Omar Abdel.**

Abdul, Paula (1962–) Singer, dancer, and choreographer Paula Abdul in 1993 issued the music video *Under My Spell*, filmed in Japan during her 1992 Asian tour. Much-discussed

and Tracey Ullman, winning an Emmy for her choreography of the "Tracey Ullman Show." In 1988, her career took an entirely new turn, as her first album, *Forever Your Girl*, hit the top of the best-seller charts, with such hits as "Straight Up," "(It's Just) The Way That You Love Me," "Knocked Out," "Forever Your Girl," "Cold-Hearted," and "Opposites Attract." "Straight Up" was named the most performed song of 1989 by ASCAP (American Society of Composers, Authors and Publishers). Abdul also won a 1990 Emmy for her choreography of the American Music Awards. Her second hit album was *Shut Up and Dance (The Dance Mixes)* (1990), and her third was *Spellbound* (1991). She attended California State University.

FURTHER READING

Paula Abdul: Straight Up. M. THOMAS FORD. Dillon/Macmillan, 1992.
"Abdul, Paula." *Current Biography*, Sep. 1991.
Magic of Paula Abdul: Straight Up to Spellbound. DEVRA NEWBERGER. Scholastic, 1991.
"The many talents of. . . ." LYNN NORMENT. *Ebony*, May 1990.
"Paula Abdul." *People*, Spring 1990.
"Straight up. . . ." JEANNIE PARK. *People*, Mar. 12, 1990.
Paula Abdul: Forever Yours. GRACE CATALANO. New American Library-Dutton, 1990.

plans for her next album were put on hold, after an announcement that it would be forthcoming in 1994. Forthcoming on the video side, however, were two fitness tapes, one a dance and aerobic video, the other a children's video.

In September, Abdul and Arsenio Hall hosted a second AIDS-awareness television special, *In a New Light*, a sequel to their acclaimed 1992 special. The show aimed to help develop public understanding of the disease and public help for its victims. A wide range of celebrities participated, among them Elizabeth Taylor, Pat Benatar, Elton John, Barry Manilow, Lily Tomlin, Rosanna Arquette, Angela Bassett, Dustin Hoffman, Hulk Hogan, Kate Jackson, Sally Jessy Raphael, Geraldo Rivera, and Joan Rivers.

On the legal side, a Los Angeles jury ended a two-year-long lawsuit, deciding that Abdul herself sang the lead vocals solo on her album *Forever Your Girl*, and rejecting singer Yvette Marine's claim that she had co-sung the leads on two songs.

Of Syrian, Brazilian, and French Canadian descent, California-born Abdul studied tap and jazz dancing as a child, performing summers in a traveling group. She began her work as a choreographer during her six-year engagement as one of the Laker Girls, cheerleaders at the Los Angeles Lakers basketball games. In 1984, she also began to choreograph for Michael Jackson and his brothers, then for Janet Jackson and other entertainment figures, including the Pointer Sisters, Eddie Murphy in *Coming to America*,

Abe, Kobo (1924–93) A leading Japanese novelist, playwright, and screenwriter, Abe was best known at home and abroad for his surreal novel *The Woman in the Dunes* (1962) and for his film adaptation of that work (1964), directed by Hiroshi Teshigahara. Son of a surgeon, Tokyo-born Abe grew up in Japanese-occupied Manchuria, opposed Japanese imperialism and was, for a time after World War II, a communist; he left the Communist Party in 1956. A prolific and highly regarded short story writer from the 1940s, his works also included such novels as *The Road Sign at the End of the Road* (1949) and *The Box Man* (1973). He was survived by his wife, Machiko, and by a daughter. (d. Tokyo; January 22, 1993)

FURTHER READING

Obituary. *Current Biography*, Mar. 1993.
Obituary. *The Times* (of London), Jan. 25, 1993.
Obituary. *New York Times*, Jan. 23, 1993.

"Sand and tendrils." *Economist*, Aug. 3, 1991.
"Abe, Kobo." *Current Biography*, July 1989.

Abravanel, Maurice (1903–93)

Salonika-born Maurice Abravanel, a leading 20th-century conductor, grew up in Lausanne, Switzerland, moved to Berlin in 1922, and emerged as a conductor in Weimar Germany. In 1930, he conducted Kurt Weill's *Mahoganny* at the Kassel Opera, winning his first international recognition. He fled Nazi Germany in the early 1930s, and in 1933, as musical director of the George Balanchine Ballet company, conducted the world premiere of Weill's *Seven Deadly Sins*. He was a staff conductor with New York's Metropolitan Opera (1936–38), then moving to Broadway, where he conducted several premieres, including those of Weill's *Knickerbocker Holiday*, *Lady in the Dark*, *One Touch of Venus*, and *Street Scene*. Abravanel was musical director of the Utah Symphony (1947–1979). He was also a prolific recording artist, perhaps most notably for his Mahler cycle. He was survived by his third wife, Carolyn, and by two sons. (d. Salt Lake City, September 22, 1993)

FURTHER READING

Obituary. *The Times* (of London), Oct. 22, 1993.
Obituary. *New York Times*, Sep. 23, 1993.

Adams, Diana (1926–93)

Virginia-born Diana Adams studied dance in Memphis and New York, making her debut with Agnes De Mille in *Oklahoma!* (1943). Joining the Ballet Theatre in 1944, she emerged as a soloist, most notably creating the mother's role in De Mille's *Fall River Legend*. She was a leading dancer with the New York City Ballet (1950–63), creating roles in such works as the George Balanchine-Igor Stravinsky *Agon*, Anthony Tudor's *Lady of the Camellias*, Frederick Ashton's *Picnic at Tintagel*, Jerome Robbins's *The Pied Piper*, and several other Balanchine ballets. Her films included Gene Kelly's *Invitation to the Dance* and Danny Kaye's *Knock On Wood*. She later taught at the School of American Ballet and the Kansas City Ballet. She was survived by a daughter. (d. San Andreas, California; January 10, 1993)

FURTHER READING

Obituary. *Current Biography*, Mar. 1993.
Obituary. *The Times* (of London), Feb. 4, 1993.
Obituary. *Variety*, Jan. 18, 1993.

Aiello, Danny (Danny Louis Aiello, Jr.; 1935–)

Turning from his highly regarded portrait of Lee Harvey Oswald's assassin, Jack Ruby, in *Ruby* (1992), Aiello focused on a modern show business story in 1993. In *The Pickle*—a film written, produced, and directed by Paul Mazursky in 1991, which opened in 1993—Aiello played director Harry Stone, facing a career crisis after having made a series of box office disasters. Stone, knowing that he has for the first time sold out all his artistic ideals, makes a straight commercial science-fiction exploitation movie aimed at the teenage market, and finds that his career crisis has turned into a major personal crisis, as well. Aiello also starred as a con artist in *Me and the Kid*, produced and directed by Dan Curtis, and in Bill Duke's Pittsburgh-set *The Cemetery Club*, opposite Ellen Burstyn and Esther Moskowitz, with screenplay by Ivan Menchell, based on his play of the same title. On stage, Aiello toured in the off-Broadway hit *Breaking Legs*.

New York City-born Aiello played modest supporting roles on stage and screen from the early 1970s, appearing in such films as *The Godfather Part II* (1974), *The Front* (1976), *Fort Apache, the Bronx* (1981), and *The Purple Rose of Cairo* (1984), then emerged in substantial roles in the late 1980s, with leads opposite Cher in *Moonstruck* (1987) and Eddie Murphy in *Harlem Nights* (1989). Aiello won a best supporting actor Oscar nomination and Chicago and Los Angeles film critics awards for his role as Sal, the Italian pizza parlor owner in a racially troubled Brooklyn neighborhood, in Spike Lee's *Do the Right Thing* (1989). Recent films include the poorly received *Hudson Hawk*, *The Closer*, and *Jacob's Ladder* (all 1991), and *Ruby* and *Mistress* (both 1992). He married Sandy Cohen in 1955; the couple have four children.

FURTHER READING

"Broadway Danny. . . ." GAVIN SMITH. *Film Comment*, July-Aug. 1991.
"Danny Aiello." LORENZO CARCATERRA. *People*, Feb. 19, 1990.
"His bus came in." MICHAEL NORMAN. *New York Times Magazine*, Jan. 21, 1990.

Aikman, Troy (1966–) The year 1993 could not have been better for Troy Aikman. The talented young quarterback led his equally young and talented Dallas Cowboys through the Conference playoffs in the National Football League, and on into the Super Bowl. There they bested the Buffalo Bills 52–17, and Aikman himself was named the game's most valuable player, completing 22 of 30 passes for 4 touchdowns and no interceptions. Under the circumstances, Aikman's old contract, which had two years to run and made him only the 31st highest paid quarterback in the NFL, was replaced in late 1993 after some considerable negotiation by a new 8-year, $50 million contract, making him the highest-paid player ever in football history (though not in all of team sports, baseball, basketball, and hockey all having a player earning more). In fact, the contract can even be worth more, for special provisions call for additional payments for Pro Bowl and championship games, and assure that he will be paid at least as much as the average of the five highest-paid quarterbacks in the league. Clearly both Aikman and the team intend that he should be with the Cowboys for the rest of his career.

For the 1993 regular season, Aikman guided his team to a division-leading 12–4 record. Aikman himself ended the season with a 69.1 completion percentage, and a 99.0 rating, just a shade behind top-ranked Steve Young, whose San Francisco 49ers Aikman and the Cowboys defeated in the January 1993 Conference cham-

pionships and again in January 1994 en route to the Super Bowl. Aikman was named NFL offensive player of the month for October 1993 and was named to the Pro Bowl. At the previous Pro Bowl, in February 1993, Aikman was fined $10,000 for leaving before the game ended.

Born in California, and raised there and in Oklahoma, Aikman spent two years at Oklahoma University, then transferred to UCLA, where he led his team to wins at the 1988 Aloha Bowl, when he was named Collegiate All-American, and 1989 Cotton Bowl; his 64.8 percent completion record, for 5,298 yards and 41 touchdowns with only 17 interceptions, made him the third-highest-rated passer ever in NCAA history. He was the top pick of the NFL college draft and of the Dallas Cowboys in 1989, and he has been named to the Pro Bowl three times (1991–1993).

FURTHER READING

"A rude awakening. . . ." PAUL ATTNER. *Sporting News*, Nov. 15, 1993.
"Troy's triumph." PAT JORDAN. *Playboy*, Oct. 1993.
"Troy Aikman. . . ." WALTER ROESSING. *Boys' Life*, Oct. 1993.
"Hero." JEFF WEINSTOCK. *Sport*, July 1993.

Akebono (Chad Rowan; ca. 1970–) After three centuries of tradition in the Japanese form of wrestling called *sumo*, Hawaiian-born Chad Rowan, whose professional name is Akebono (Rising Sun), was named the first non-Japanese *yokozuna*, or grand champion, in January 1993. Though the rules of promotion are vague, Akebono had won two 15-day tournaments in a row and three of his last five (eclipsing the records of many former grand champions), and also showed honor to tradition by exhibiting the dignity (*hinkaku*) and adopting the spartan lifestyle considered appropriate in sumo tradition.

Had Japan's Yokozuna Promotion Council not promoted Akebono to the position of champion, they would have faced charges of racism. Earlier, in 1992, a Samoan-born sumo wrestler, Konishiki (born Salevaa Atisanoe), appeared to be in line for promotion to yokozuna, but had not been promoted; charges of racism were raised at that time, but Konishiki lost his next match, so the question was moot. The 6′ 8″-inch, 466-pound Akebono became the 64th yokozuna in sumo history, the only one still active, reaching the position in the record time of only five years, even though his height and relatively thin legs would seem to put him at a disadvantage, where champions traditionally have exhibited a low center of gravity. The sport itself is fought in a clay ring (*dohyo*), with the two semi-naked wrestlers tussling and grappling with each other until one falls or is pushed out of the ring, leaving the other the winner. Akebono's coach is Kuhaulua, the first non-Japanese ever to win a sumo tournament, in 1972.

Akebono caused some additional controversy in March, when he adopted a new design in the ceremonial apron worn before a wrestling bout; his apron had his name, which is traditional, and the Hawaiian state flower, the hibiscus, while the aprons of his two attendants bore Japan's rising sun and America's stars and stripes, respectively, the first time non-Japanese symbols have appeared in the sumo ring. Konishiki wears a football and helmet on his ceremonial apron.

Born in Honolulu, Hawaii, Akebono earlier played baseball and basketball. After dropping out of college, he moved to Tokyo, where he became interested in sumo wrestling

FURTHER READING

"Prince of whales. . . ." *People Weekly*, Feb. 22, 1993.
"Sumo Yankee." GINA BELLAFANTE. *Time*, Feb. 8, 1993.
Bulled. . . ." SALLY GUARD. *Sports Illustrated*, June 1, 1992.

Albright, Madeleine Korbel (1947–)

U.S. Ambassador to the United Nations, Madeleine Albright spent much of her first year in office trying to deal with a series of "hot spots," in which American policies were not at all successful. Chief among these were the unresolved conflicts in Bosnia and Somalia, and the tenacious military dictatorship in Haiti. On Bosnia, she spoke again and again in support of the Muslim position, sharply criticizing other western nations for failing to support the Muslim call for more land in the stalled peace talks. Albright also conveyed repeated and apparently empty Clinton administration threats of air strikes on the Serbs.

On Somalia, she hailed the planned changeover from United States to UN peacekeeping forces in the spring of 1993, and scrupulously defended failed American and UN policies in that country as the year wore on. In her role as American spokesperson at the UN, she also defended such American actions as the June missile attack on Iraq, while successfully urging the UN to maintain its sanctions against Iraq, Serbia, and Libya.

Albright's 1959 B.A. was from Wellesley College; she also attended the Johns Hopkins School of Advanced International Studies (1962–63), and earned her M.A. and Ph.D. at Columbia University's Department of Public Law and Government. In 1976, she began her Washington career, as a staff assistant to Senator Edmund Muskie, and from 1978 worked on the White House National Security Council staff. She was Research Professor of International Affairs and Director of Women in Foreign Service at Georgetown University's School of Foreign Service (1982–92); president of the Center of National Policy (1989–92), and as well as a foreign policy advisor in the Mondale, Dukakis, and Clinton presidential campaigns. Her books include *The Role of the Press in Political Change: Czechoslovakia 1968* (1976) and *Poland: the Role of the Press in Political Change* (1983). Albright is divorced and has three daughters.

FURTHER READING

"Albright. . . ." *Washington Post*, Dec. 7, 1992.
"Woman on top. . . ." MOLLY SINCLAIR. *Washington Post.* Jan. 6, 1991.

Alda, Alan (1936–)

Veteran screen star Alda went back to the movies, after his major 1992 Broadway success in the Tony-nominated title role of Neil Simon's comedy *Jake's Women*, his first Broadway appearance in 20 years. In 1993, he starred as Ted, the bachelor writer friend of Woody Allen and Diane Keaton in the comedy *Manhattan Murder Mystery*, written and directed by Allen, with a cast that included Anjelica Huston, Jerry Adler, and Lynn Cohen. Alda also starred as controversial scientist Robert Gallo in *And The Band Played On*, Arnold Schulman's screen adaptation of Randy Shilts's book about AIDS; directed by Roger Spottiswoode, the cast also included Matthew Modine, Phil Collins, David Dukes, Richard Gere, Glenne Headly, Anjelica Huston, Swoosie Kurtz, Steve

Martin, Ian McKellen, and Lily Tomlin. Alda was also host of the public television series "Scientific American Frontiers." Forthcoming was a starring role opposite John Candy and Rhea Perlman in the comedy *Canadian Bacon*, written and directed by Michael Moore.

New York-born Alda, the son of actor Robert Alda, appeared on the New York stage from the late 1950s, in such plays as *Purlie Victorious* (1961), *The Owl and the Pussycat* (1964), and *The Apple Tree* (1966). He became a television star in the 1970s, in *The Glass House* (1972), and then as Korean War surgeon Benjamin Franklin "Hawkeye" Pierce, in the long-running series "M*A*S*H" (1972–83). He has also starred in such films as *The Moonshine War* (1970), *California Suite* (1978), *Same Time Next Year* (1978), and *The Seduction of Joe Tynan* (1979), and appeared in many other films, including *Crimes and Misdemeanors* (1989), for which he won the Directors Guild of America's award for best supporting actor, and *Whispers in the Dark* (1992). Alda wrote, directed, and starred in the films *The Four Seasons* (1981), *Sweet Liberty* (1986), and *Betsy's Wedding* (1989). Alda attended Fordham University. He married Arlene Weiss in 1957, with whom he wrote *The Last Days of M*A*S*H* (1984); they have three children.

FURTHER READING

"Memories of M*A*S*H." CRAIG TOMASHOFF. *People*, Nov. 25, 1991.

Alexander, Jane (Jane Quigley; 1939–)

In August, President Bill Clinton nominated Jane Alexander to head the National Endowment for the Arts, and with that nomination brought one of America's leading theater figures to the front and center of American cultural life. With Alexander's nomination, the often-controversial agency, which some conservatives had long sought to abolish, became an entirely different cultural phenomenon, for Alexander carried with her an enormous body of prestige, almost as if she *were* Eleanor Roosevelt, the role with which she is most popularly identified. In September, she was unanimously confirmed by the Senate Labor and Human Resources Committee, in a hearing that took only a little more

than an hour, with committee conservatives just as complimentary as liberals. She went on to overwhelming confirmation in the Senate, and immediately went about the task of restoring the somewhat battered arts endowment's programs and beginning a further reach into cultural education, which she stressed in early interviews. Her own acting career now on hold, Alexander's admirers waited for her return to the theater.

Alexander played in regional theatre in the mid-1960s. She emerged as a major dramatic actress on Broadway in 1968, in her Tony-winning role opposite James Earl Jones in *The Great White Hope*. Some of her most notable stage roles were in *6 Rms Riv Vu* (1972), *Find Your Way Home* (1974), *The Heiress* (1976), *First Monday in October* (1978), *Hedda Gabler* (1981), *Old Times* (1984), *Night of the Iguana* (1988), *Shadowlands* (1990), and *The Sisters Rosenzweig* (1993). On screen, she was nominated for a best actress Oscar for the film version of *The Great White Hope* (1970), and she also appeared in such films as *All the President's Men* (1976), *Kramer vs. Kramer* (1979), *Testament* (1983), and *Glory* (1989). She has also made several telefilms, most notably *Eleanor and Franklin* (1976) as a classic Eleanor Roosevelt, *Playing For Time* (1980), *Calamity Jane* (1984), and *A Marriage: Georgia O'Keefe and Alfred Stieglitz* (1991). Alexander attended Sarah Lawrence College and the University of Edinburgh. Previously divorced, she married Edwin Sherin in 1975, and has one child.

FURTHER READING

"Jane Alexander. . . ." GREG MILLER and DIANE HAITHMAN. *Los Angeles Times*, Aug. 8, 1993.

Alexandra of Yugoslavia (1921–93)

The widow of Peter II of Yugoslavia, Athens-born Alexandra of Yugoslavia was the daughter of Alexander and Aspasia of Greece; her father died in 1920, while Alexandra and her mother went into exile, returning to Greece in 1935. They went into exile again after the Germans took Greece in World War II. Alexandra of Greece married Peter of Yugoslavia in London in 1944, while both were in exile. He was deposed in 1945 by the postwar Greek republican government;

the couple then lived in exile until his death in 1970. She was survived by her son, Alexander, who made an unsuccessful claim to the Yugoslavian throne in the early 1990s. (d. London; January 30, 1993)

FURTHER READING

Obituary. *The Times* (of London), Feb. 2, 1993.
Obituary. *New York Times*, Feb. 1, 1993.

Allen, Marcus (1960–)

Allen, Marcus (1960–) If ever there was an argument for free agency—for athletes' ability to go where their talents will be used and appreciated—it is Marcus Allen. In his career with the Los Angeles Raiders, he rushed for 8545 yards (becoming the team's all-time rushing leader), caught over 400 passes for 3938 receiving yards, and scored 98 touchdowns, but he ran afoul of Raiders' owner, Al Davis. After a 1989 contract dispute and especially after Allen joined the football players' free agency suit in 1991, he was largely relegated to the sidelines. In the 1992 season, he was a third-string running back with the Raiders, used for only 67 plays, generally on third downs. He was so frustrated that, in a December 1992 television interview, Allen charged Davis with trying to ruin the latter part of his career. When free agency was won in 1993, he quickly left.

In 1993, Allen moved to the Kansas City Chiefs, where his new coach, Marty Schottenheimer, made it clear from the start that Allen was his "go-to guy" in short-yardage situations. Allen responded by rushing for 764 yards on 206 carries, and making a league-leading 12 touchdowns: 10 rushing, 2 receiving. On December 5th, against Seattle, he scored three touchdowns in one game, and by season's end he had moved into fourth place in all-time career touchdowns and was 11th on the career rushing list. Football fans also had the pleasure of seeing Allen and new quarterback Joe Montana—both "oldtimers" in their 30s—take the Chiefs to a division-leading 11–5 record, and into the Conference finals, before finally being stopped by the Buffalo Bills. Allen was personally honored by being named once again to the Pro Bowl as a starting running back.

Born in San Diego, Allen attended the University of Southern California, taking USC's football team to four bowls, including two Rose Bowls, and winning football's prestigious Heisman Trophy as top college player in 1981. After joining the Los Angeles Raiders in 1982, he was named *Sporting News* Rookie of the Year for the National Football League (NFL). In 1984, when the Raiders won the Super Bowl, Allen was named most valuable player, gaining a then-Super-Bowl-record total of 191 yards and scoring two touchdowns, one a 74-yard run from scrimmage, still an NFL record. In his best year, 1985, he led the NFL with 1759 rushing yards; gained 2314 combined yards (rushing and receiving), also an NFL record; scored 14 touchdowns; and was named the NFL's most valuable player, also setting an NFL record by gaining over 100 yards in 11 consecutive games over the 1985–86 seasons. Allen has been named to the Pro Bowl six times.

FURTHER READING

"Rush job. . . ." RICK WEINBERG. *Sport*, Aug. 1991.
"Allen tackles Davis. . . ." CHRIS MORTENSEN. *Sporting News*, July 22, 1991.

Allen, Tim

Allen, Tim (Tim Allen Dick; 1953–) Television comedian Tim Allen hit the top in 1993, when his prime-time situation comedy "Home Improvement," in its third season, reached number one in the ratings. It had been the highest-rated new series of the 1991–92 television season, in the fifth spot, building to third place in the 1992–93 season. It hit number one occasionally in spring 1993 and consistently during 1993 summer reruns and on into the 1993–94 season. On the show, Allen and Patricia Richardson play Tim and Jill Taylor, Detroit-based parents of three boys; Tim Taylor's job as host of a cable home-improvement show, "Tool Time," somehow does not prepare him for dealing with everyday situations at home, forming the basis of much of the series humor. "Home Improvement" was named television's best comedy series in the 1993 People's Choice Awards. In December 1992, Wind Dancer Productions, which produces "Home Improvement," signed a multiyear contract with ABC, calling for three more years of the series, through at least the 1995–96 season. Meanwhile, the popular Allen continued working live, as at Los Angeles's Universal Amphitheatre in October 1993, and was making a film, *The Santa Clause*, directed by John Pasquin.

Denver-born Allen attended Central Michigan University and received his B.A. in television production from Western Michigan University in 1976. On graduating, he worked in a sporting good store, moving to the store's advertising agency. He made his first public appearance in 1979 at Detroit's Comedy Castle; then, after some months of imprisonment for selling cocaine, he built a career as a stand-up comedian, working live and in radio, television, and film, including commercials. He first came to wide attention on cable, notably with his Showtime specials *Men Are Pigs* (1990) and *Tim Allen Rewires America* (1991), winning an ACE award in 1991. Working with co-creator Matt Williams from Allen's own idea, he then developed the television series *Home Improvement* (1991–   ), as star, co-writer, and co-producer. He is married to Laura Allen; they have one daughter.

FURTHER READING

"Home for the holidays. . . ." RUSSELL MILLER. *Ladies Home Journal*, Dec. 1993.
"Tim Allen." *Playboy*, Feb. 1993.
"Tim Allen's. . . ." JEFF ROVIN. *Ladies Home Journal*, Dec. 1992.
"Caution. . . ." MICHAEL LEAHY and HOWARD GENSLER. *TV Guide*, Nov. 9, 1991.

Allen, Woody (Allen Stewart Konigsberg; 1935–   ) In a departure from the more serious tone of some of his recent films, Allen in 1993 wrote, directed, and starred in the very well-received light comedy *Manhattan Murder Mystery*, opposite Diane Keaton as his wife (a role originally intended for Mia Farrow), in a cast that included Anjelica Huston, Alan Alda, Jerry Adler, and Lynn Cohen. Allen also won a best screenplay Oscar nomination for *Husbands and Wives* and was set to direct and star in a forthcoming television film version of his 1966 play and 1969 film *Don't Drink the Water*. Forthcoming was a new film, untitled at year's end, written and directed by Allen, and starring John Cusack, Mary-Louise Parker, Jennifer Tilly, Chazz Palmintieri, Dianne Wiest, Carl Reiner, Tracey Ullman, Alan Arkin, and Jack Warden.

A new book, *The Illustrated Woody Allen Reader*, written with Linda Sunshine, was also published in 1993.

On the personal side, the long, highly-publicized custody case involving Allen, Farrow, and their three children ended in June, with custody awarded to Farrow, and only limited visitation rights won by Allen. In September, a Connecticut state's attorney announced that he would not press charges against Allen for alleged sexual molestation of his daughter, most unusually coupling his statement with an attack on Allen and a claim that he had "probable cause" to prosecute. Allen in turn attacked the state's attorney for his statement. At year's end, the case had left the headlines, and the lawyers and media who had helped create the massive story had gone on to other cases.

A New Yorker, Allen emerged as a leading television comedy writer in the late 1950s, and during the 1960s also worked in cabaret and theater, beginning a long series of hit films as the writer and star of *What's New Pussycat?* (1965). He then became one of the leading filmmakers of his time, with such films as his Oscar-winning *Annie Hall* (1977), *Manhattan* (1979), *Hannah and Her Sisters* (1984), *Crimes and Misdemeanors* (1989), *Scenes from a Mall* (1991), *Shadows and Fog* (1992), and *Husbands and Wives* (1992). Allen attended City College and New York University. Formerly married to Louise Lasser, Allen had a long-term relationship with Farrow (1980–1992); though they never married, they had three children: their biological son Satchel, an adopted daughter Dylan, and an adopted son Moses. Their breakup and subsequent custody suit was complicated by disclosure of Allen's affair with Farrow's 21-year-old adopted daughter, Soon-Yi Farrow Previn.

FURTHER READING

"All stick, no shtick." JOHN EPHLAND. *Down Beat*, Oct. 1993.
"Woody Allen. . . ." ANTHONY DeCURTIS. *Rolling Stone*, Sep. 16, 1993.
The Films of Woody Allen. SAM B. GIRGUS. Cambridge University Press, 1993.
Everything You Always Wanted to Know about Woody Allen: The Ultimate Quiz Book. FRANK WEIMANN. Shapolsky, 1993.
"Everything you always. . . ." PHOEBE HOBAN. *New York*, Sep. 21, 1992.

"Bananas. . . ." ROGER ROSENBLATT. *New Republic*, Sep. 21, 1992.

"Woody working. . . ." STEVEN DALY. *Entertainment*, Sep. 18, 1992.

"Love and fog." JESS CAGLE. *Entertainment*, Sep. 18, 1992.

" 'But she's not part of my family.' " JACK KROLL. *Newsweek*, Aug. 31, 1992.

" 'The heart wants what it wants.' " WALTER ISAACSON. *Time*, Aug. 31, 1992.

"A family affair." TOM GLIATTO. *People*, Aug. 31, 1992.

Brooklyn Is Not Expanding: Woody Allen's Comic Universe. ANNETTE WERNBLAD. Fairleigh Dickinson, 1992.

"Woody Allen. . . ." ERIC LAX. *Vogue*, May 1991.

"Woody and Mia. . . ." ERIC LAX. *New York Times Magazine*, Feb. 24, 1991.

Woody Allen: A Biography. ERIC LAX. Knopf, 1991; Random, 1992.

Woody Allen Encyclopedia. MARK A. ALTMAN. Movie Publications, 1991.

Woody Allen: His Films and Career. DOUGLAS BRODE. Carol, 1991.

Loser Take All: The Comic Art of Woody Allen, expanded ed. MAURICE YACOWAR. Continuum, 1991.

Woody Allen. GRAHAM MCCANN. Basil Blackwell, 1990.

Love, Sex, Death, and the Meaning of Life: The Films of Woody Allen, rev. ed. FOSTER HIRSCH. Limelight, 1990.

Allende, Isabel

Allende, Isabel (1942–　) Though her family name first became internationally known through the political life and 1973 murder of her uncle, Chilean President Salvador Allende, Isabel Allende has been making her own name as a novelist and is considered by many critics to be the finest contemporary Latin American woman writer. Her fourth novel, *The Infinite Plan*, the first set in the United States, where she now lives, and the first with a male central character, follows the life of Gregory Reeves, from his birth just after World War II as a lone Anglo in a Los Angeles barrio through the cataclysmic changes of the 1960s. The book was well-received, though some regretted that she had traded in the "magical realism" of her earlier novels for social realism. During 1993, Allende's first and still most celebrated novel, *The House of Spirits*, was being filmed by director Bille August, starring Jeremy Irons, Meryl Streep, and Glenn Close.

Born in Peru to a Chilean family, Allende was raised in Chile, Bolivia, Europe, and the Middle

East, following family diplomatic postings. Married at 19 to Miguel Frias, she had two children, and worked as a journalist beginning in 1967. Forced to leave Peru after the 1973 military coup, Allende lived with her family in exile in Venezuela, continuing work as a journalist, in print and on television. Her career as a novelist began in 1982 with the publication of *The House of Spirits*, a much-praised multigenerational family chronicle set in Chile, and continued with *Of Love and Shadows* (1984) and *Eva Luna* (1989); other works included the short story collection *The Stories of Eva Luna* (1990) and the children's story *La Gorda de Porcelana* (1984). Later divorced, Allende married San Francisco attorney William Gordon in 1988.

FURTHER READING

"Keeper of the house of spirits." KATE KELLAWAY. *Observer*, Mar. 7, 1993.

"The shaman and the infidel." MARILYN BERLIN SNELL. *New Perspectives Quarterly*, Winter 1991.

Critical Approaches to Isabel Allende's Novels. SONIA R. ROJAS and EDNA A. REHBEIN. P. Lang, 1991.

Beyond the Border: A New Age in Latin American Women's Fiction. NORA ERRO-PERALTA and CARIDAD SILVA-NUNEZ, eds. Cleis, 1991.

Interviews with Latin American Writers. MARIE-LISE GAZARIAN GAUTIER. Dalkey Arch, 1989.

Narrative Magic in the Fiction of Isabel Allende. PATRICIA HART. Fairleigh Dickinson, 1989.

Landscapes of a New Land: Fiction by Latin American Women. MARJORIE AGOSIN, ed. White Pine, 1989.

Alley, Kirstie (1955–)

As the long run of "Cheers" ended, television star Kirstie Alley again won the respect of her peers. In January, she received a Golden Globe nomination as best actress in a television musical or comedy and in July won an Emmy nomination as best lead actress in comedy series, both for her role as Rebecca Howe, opposite Ted Danson as bartender Sam Malone in the long-running series. The series ended its 11-year run on NBC in May, with top ratings for its final episodes.

Although she might have preferred to stay on in "Cheers," had Danson been willing, Alley's future career was assured; in March, she signed a multiyear film development contract with Universal Television and Universal Pictures. Late in the year, she starred, again opposite John Travolta, in the third of their "Look Who's Talking" films, this one entitled *Look Who's Talking Now.*

Kansas-born Alley worked as an interior decorator before taking up an acting career in the early 1980s. Her most notable early work was her role as Lieutenant Saavik in *Star Trek II: The Wrath of Khan* (1982), which was followed by supporting roles in several other theatre and television films. She made her major breakthrough in 1987, when she joined the cast of "Cheers." Her film breakthrough came opposite John Travolta in the film comedy *Look Who's Talking* (1989) and *Look Who's Talking Too* (1990). She went on to star in the 1990 film comedies *Madhouse* and *Sibling Rivalry.* Alley attended Kansas State University. She is married to actor Parker Stevenson; they adopted a baby son in 1992.

FURTHER READING

"And baby makes 35." ALESSANDRA STANLEY. *Redbook,* May 1993.
"Kirstie Alley. . . ." JEFF ROVIN. *Ladies Home Journal,* Jan. 1993.
"What she did. . . ." JEFF ROVIN. *Ladies Home Journal,* June 1992.
"Kirstie Alley." MARK MORRISON. *US.* Feb. 1992.
"What's hot. . . ." KATHLEEN NEUMEYER et al. *Ladies Home Journal,* Oct. 1991.
"Feisty, funny Kirstie Alley." GREGG KILDAY. *Cosmopolitan,* Dec. 1990.
"The tears behind the Cheers." J.D. REED. *People,* Oct. 29, 1990.
"Kirstie Alley." RICHARD BLAINE. *Good Housekeeping,* Mar. 1990.
"Chez Alley." FRED ROBBINS. *Saturday Evening Post,* Jan.-Feb. 1990.

Robert Altman (right) and Annie Ross

Altman, Robert (1925–)

Film director Altman was honored by his peers in 1993, winning Academy Award, Golden Globe, and Directors Guild nominations as best director for his 1992 film *The Player.* He also won an Emmy nomination as best director in a variety or music program for his *Black and Blue* show on public television's "Great Performances."

Altman's major film of 1993 was his very well received *Short Cuts,* based on eight stories and a poem by Raymond Carver, and adapted for film by Altman and Frank Barhydt. The large cast included Tim Robbins, Fred Ward, Anne Archer, Robert Downey, Jr., Jennifer Jason Leigh, Jack Lemmon, Andie MacDowell, Matthew Modine, Lily Tomlin, and Tom Waits.

Altman directed in television and films from the late 1950s, emerging as a major film director in the 1970s, with such films as *M*A*S*H* (1970), *Brewster McCloud* (1971), *McCabe and Mrs. Miller* (1972), *California Split* (1974), *Nashville* (1975), and *Buffalo Bill and the Indians* (1976). He received best picture and best director Oscar nominations for *M*A*S*H* and *Nashville.* But his film career sagged as the

American film industry moved toward the theatre of spectacle, and away from his kind of social commentary. During the 1980s, he directed a variety of films, plays, and telefilms, most notably *Come Back to the Five and Dime, Jimmy Dean, Jimmy Dean* (1982), *Streamers* (1983), *Vincent and Theo* (1990), and (with Garry Trudeau) the innovative pseudo-documentary series, *Tanner* (1988). In 1992, he made a major comeback, with the film *The Player*. Altman attended the University of Missouri. He has been married three times and has five children.

FURTHER READING

"Altman. . . ." ROBERT KILDAY and ALAN GRAISON. *Entertainment Weekly*, Oct. 29, 1993.
"Two for the road. . . ." BILL VAN PARYS. *Rolling Stone*, Oct. 14, 1993.
"Robert Altman. . . ." GRAHAM FULLER. *Interview*, Oct. 1993.
"Hollywood's last angry man." ZOE HELLER. *Vanity Fair*, Oct. 1993.
"Short Cuts." TOM JENKS. *Esquire*, Sep. 1993.
"Seeking the 'rotten core.'" JACK KROLL. *Newsweek*, Aug. 23, 1993.
"Game boy squares the circle." RICHARD COMBS. *Observer*, June 21, 1992.
"Robert Altman gives. . . ." JACK KROLL. *Esquire*, May 1992.
"Robert Altman. . . ." DAVID BRESKIN. *Rolling Stone*, Apr. 16, 1992.
"Home movie." JEANIE KASINDORF. *New York*, Mar. 16, 1992.
Inner Views: Filmmakers in Conversation. DAVID BRESKIN. Faber & Faber, 1992.
"Altman '91." BEVERLY WALKER. *Film Comment*, Jan.-Feb. 1991.
Robert Altman's America. HELENE KEYSSAR. Oxford University Press, 1991.
Robert Altman: Jumping Off the Cliff. PATRICK MCGILLIGAN. St. Martin's, 1989.

Altman, Roger Charles (1945–) Deputy Treasury Secretary Roger C. Altman was a key Washington figure throughout the Clinton administration's first year, developing and campaigning for the administration's position on the whole range of economic issues that dominated Clinton's first year. Those efforts were not always successful; key early economic policy defeats were the economic stimulus package and the broad-based energy tax. A major win came with passage of the Clinton budget by the narrowest possible margin; Altman's highly publicized role in the budget fight included his "war room" in the Old Executive Office Building, which coordinated the day-by-day budget campaign. He also played a considerable role in the North American Free Trade Agreement (NAFTA) campaign, and was active in other foreign trade matters, as well. As temporary head of the Resolution Trust Corporation, the agency set up to liquidate savings-and-loan crash properties taken over by the federal government, he temporarily froze all transactions early in the year, charging bidding irregularities, and in April changed bidding rules so that smaller investors, who had been frozen out of the bidding, could competitively bid on properties offered.

Altman is an investment banker, with strong Wall Street credentials and much prior government service. He began his financial career in 1969, as a Lehman Brothers associate, and was very much a "whiz kid" at the firm, becoming its youngest post-World War II general partner (1974). In 1977, he moved to Washington as a Carter administration Assistant Treasury Secretary for domestic finance, playing a substantial role in the bailouts of Chrysler and New York City. With Republican victory in 1980, he returned to Lehman Brothers, and was one of three managing directors of the firm when it was sold in 1984. He was chairman of New York City's Public Development Corporation (1985–89), and in the early 1990s was a key economic advisor to mayor David Dinkins. Altman's 1967 B.A. was from Georgetown University, and his M.B.A. from the University of Chicago. He is married to documentary filmmaker Jurata Kazakis; they have three children.

FURTHER READING

"Unholy trinity. . . ." JOHN B. JUDIS. *Mother Jones*, Mar.-Apr. 1993.
"Head to head." S.C. GWYNNE and STEPHEN KOEPP. *Time*, Oct. 12, 1992.

Ameche, Don (Dominic Felix Amici; 1908–93) Wisconsin-born Ameche began his professional career in repertory in Madison, Wisconsin, and made his Broadway debut in 1929 and in radio in 1930. He became one of the best known radio stars of the 1930s, as star of "The First Nighter Program" (1930–36), then moving

to Hollywood, where he starred in such films as *Ramona* (1936); *Alexander's Ragtime Band* (1938); opposite Claudette Colbert in the classic comedy *Midnight* (1939); in the title role of *The Story of Alexander Graham Bell* (1939); and *Heaven Can Wait* (1943). His film career waned after that, although he then successfully moved to television in a wide range of roles. He made a very notable film comeback late in his career, with *Cocoon* (1985), for which he won a best supporting actor Oscar. He went on to appear in *Harry and the Hendersons* (1987), *Coming to America* (1988), *Things Change* (1988), *Cocoon II: The Return* (1988), *Oddball Hall* (1990), *Oscar* (1991), and *Folks* (1992); and completed shooting *Corrina, Corrina* just before his death. He was survived by two daughters, four sons, two sisters, and a brother. (d. Scottsdale, Arizona; December 6, 1993)

FURTHER READING

" 'Gimme the Ameche.' " SARA GROSVENOR. *U.S. News & World Report*, Dec. 20, 1993.
Obituary. *Variety*, Dec. 20, 1993.
Obituary. *The Times* (of London), Dec. 8, 1993.
Obituary. *New York Times*, Dec. 8, 1993.

Ames, Leon (Leon Waycoff; 1903–93) Portland-born Ames began his long stage and screen career in 1925, touring in repertory. He made his Broadway debut in *It Pays to Sin* (1933), later appearing in several other plays. Ames began his long film career with *Murders in the Rue Morgue* (1932), and played a wide variety of roles in more than 100 movies, among them *Meet Me in St. Louis* (1944), *The Postman Always Rings Twice* (1946), *Peyton Place* (1957), *On a Clear Day You Can See Forever* (1970), and his last film, *Peggy Sue Got Married* (1986). He starred in the television series "Life With Father" (1953–56) and "Father of the Bride" (1961–62), also playing in many other television roles. Ames was a founding member of the Screen Actors Guild, which he and 18 other actors organized secretly in 1933, was on the Guild board of directors (1945–75), and was union president in 1957. He was survived by his wife, Christine. (d. Laguna Beach, California; October 12, 1993)

FURTHER READING

Obituary. *Variety*, Oct. 25, 1993.
Obituary. *New York Times*, Oct. 15, 1993.

Anderson, Marian (1897–1993) One of the most celebrated singers of the 20th century, Philadelphia-born Marian Anderson was also a major figure in the American civil rights struggle. The contralto, whose voice was described by Arturo Toscannini as one that could be heard "once in a hundred years," found her career blocked by American racial discrimination in the 1920s and went to Europe, there beginning her long recording career and becoming one of the leading singers of her time. She emerged as a major figure in the United States in the 1930s. In 1939, she was denied, because of her race, the use of Washington's Constitution Hall by the Daughters of the American Revolution (DAR). Eleanor Roosevelt then powerfully intervened, sponsoring Anderson's Easter Sunday concert at the Lincoln Memorial, attended by 75,000–100,000, a landmark event in American history. Even so, it took another 16 years for New York's Metropolitan Opera to break its color line; on January 7, 1955, she became the first African-American to sing on that stage, as Ulrica in *Un Ballo in Maschera*. There were no direct survivors. (d. Portland, Oregon; April 9, 1993)

FURTHER READING

Obituary. *Opera News*, July 1993.
Obituary. *Current Biography*, June 1993.
"She let freedom sing. . . ." KATRINE AMES. *Newsweek*, Apr. 19, 1993.
"Lift every voice. . . ." STEVEN V. ROBERTS. *U.S. News & World Report*, Apr. 19, 1993.
Obituary. *Variety*, Apr. 19, 1993.
Obituary. *The Times* (of London), Apr. 9, 1993.
Obituary. *New York Times*, Apr. 9, 1993.
"Marian Anderson. . . ." ROSALYN M. STORY. *American Visions*, Dec.-Jan. 1992.
One More River to Cross: Twelve Black Americans. JIM HASKINS. Scholastic, 1992.
Marian Anderson: A Great Singer. PATRICIA MCKISSACK and FREDRICK MCKISSACK. Enslow, 1991.
Marian Anderson. ANNE TEDARDS. Chelsea House, 1988.
Marian Anderson. CHARLES PATTERSON. Watts, 1988.

Anderson, Terry (1947–) He lost nearly seven years of his life—2454 days—from March 16, 1985 to December 4, 1991. During that time his father and young brother died, his daughter was born, and another daughter grew from age 9 to 15. Longest held of the Western hostages in Lebanon, Terry Anderson came to symbolize all

and television news in Des Moines, Iowa, while studying at Iowa State University, graduating in 1974. He joined the Associated Press (AP), working in Detroit, Louisville, and New York, before becoming an overseas correspondent, based first in Japan, then in South Africa. He covered the Israeli invasion of Lebanon in 1982, and returned to Beirut in early 1983 as news editor and then chief Middle East correspondent. In 1992, Anderson received the Overseas Press Club's President's Award; later that year he resigned from the Associated Press, saying he wanted to find ways to help people more directly. He accepted a fellowship at the Columbia University's Media Studies Center, where he wrote his book. He also became co-chair of the Vietnam Memorial Association, which wishes to honor the two million Vietnamese killed in their civil war, and, not ruling out a career in politics, helped found the Alliance for New York Renaissance, a grass-roots organization aimed at reforming New York State government.

FURTHER READING

"The world is fresh. . . ." DAVID AIKMAN. *Time*, May 18, 1992.
"Terry Anderson. . . ." *People*, Dec. 30, 1991.
Forgotten: A Sister's Struggle to Save Her Brother, America's Longest Held Hostage. PEGGY SAY and PETER KNOBLER. Simon & Schuster, 1991.
Pity the Nation: The Abduction of Lebanon. ROBERT FISK. Simon & Schuster, 1991.
Holding On. SUNNIE MANN. Trafalgar Square, 1991.
America Held Hostage: From the Teheran Embassy Takeover to the Iran-Contra Affair. DON LAWSON. Watts, 1991.

those taken by Hezbollah (Party of God), the Iranian-supported fundamentalist Islamic terrorist group.

In 1993, Anderson told of his hostage experiences in *Den of Lions: Memoirs of Seven Years.* The book tells of his own ordeal—of the squalor, fear, uncertainty, waste, and humiliation of his imprisonment, and of how he (and his fellow hostages) learned to deal with it, in his case including his return to Catholicism. Also included are recollections of waiting and rescue negotiations from Madeleine Bassil, the woman who, at the time of his abduction, was pregnant with his child. When kidnapped, Anderson was engaged to Bassil, a translator, but still in the process of being divorced from his first wife, Miki (Mihoko); he and Bassil married in May 1993.

In February 1993, HBO aired a television movie, *Hostages*, with Jay O. Sanders playing Anderson and Kathy Bates as Peggy Say, Anderson's sister, a tireless fighter for his freedom. Though Anderson and others originally complained about its being made, he praised it after seeing it, and said he hoped that the NBC movie being made from his own book would be as well done.

Born in Lorain, Ohio, and raised in Batavia, New York from age 7, Anderson served in the Marines for six years, as a combat correspondent in Vietnam, and then for the Armed Forces Radio and Television Service in Japan, as reporter, anchorman, and then station manager. After discharge as a staff sergeant, he worked in radio

Andrews, Bert (1929–93) Chicago-born Bert Andrews, who grew up in New York City's Harlem, was a leading photographer of the African-American theater. He was a singer, dancer, and songwriter before moving into photography in the 1950s, and in the decades that followed reportedly photographed more than 1,000 shows, such as *Ma Rainey's Black Bottom, Eubie, A Soldier's Song,* and *Bubblin' Brown Sugar,* and such theater luminaries as James Earl Jones, Denzel Washington, Diana Sands, Raymond St. Jackques, and Ciceley Tyson. He was also a photographer for Actor's Equity. Sadly, a 1985 fire destroyed the greater part of his work, including tens of thousands of negatives. He reconstituted some portion of his work, and 3,000 of his photographs are collected at Manhattan's Schomburg Center for Research in Black Culture. He published *In the Shadow of the Great White Way: Images from the Black Theater* (1990), with text by Paul C. Harrison. There were no survivors. (d. New York City; January 26, 1993)

FURTHER READING

Obituary. *Variety*, Feb. 1, 1993.
Obituary. *New York Times*, Jan. 27, 1993.

Angelou, Maya (1928–) As the world watched the inauguration of President Bill Clinton, millions of people were struck by Maya Angelou's delivery of her new poem "On the Pulse of the Morning," which then became a best-seller as a 16-page paperback, as did the audio version read by Angelou. She was the first inaugural poet since Robert Frost at John F. Kennedy's inauguration. Late in 1993, Angelou was back on the best-seller lists with another new work, *Wouldn't Take Nothing for My Journey Now*, a collection of brief personal essays, some originally published as "Lessons in Living" in *Essence* magazine. Angelou herself read the audio version of the book.

After this, and a July guest spot on Oprah Winfrey's afternoon talk show, new interest was sparked in Angelou's other works, all of which were reprinted; her first book, *I Know Why the Caged Bird Sings*, never out of print since its 1970 publication, was on the paperback best-seller list for much of 1993, with 2.5 million copies in print. A third new work was another poem, *Life Doesn't Frighten Me*, illustrated as a children's book. Also in 1993, her fifth play, *And Still I Rise*, opened in Washington, D.C. Another new book, *How Sheba Sings the Song*, was scheduled for 1994 publication.

As an actress, Angelou appeared on film as Aunt June in John Singleton's *Poetic Justice* and on television in *There Are No Children Here*, playing Lelia Mae, mother to Oprah Winfrey's LaJoe Rivers, a story about children in a Chicago housing project, based on a non-fiction work by Alex Kotlowitz.

St. Louis-born Angelou became a national figure in 1970, with publication of her autobiographical *I Know Why the Caged Bird Sings*, dealing with her life as a Black woman, and by extension with the lives of many other Black women in the United States. Her works, largely autobiographical, include such books as *Just Give Me a Cool Drink of Water B'fore I Die* (1971), *Georgia, Georgia* (1972), *Gather Together in My Name* (1974), *Singin' and Swingin' and Gettin' Merry Like Christmas* (1976), *The Heart of a Woman* (1986), and *All God's Children Need Traveling Shoes* (1987). Angelou teaches American studies at Wake Forest University, in North Carolina. A sometime actress, playwright, director, and producer, Angelou also played Kunta Kinte's grandmother in the television miniseries *Roots* (1977). She has one child.

FURTHER READING

"Maya Angelou. . . ." KARIMA A. HAZYNES. *Ebony*, Apr. 1993.
Maya Angelou: Woman of Words, Deeds, and Dreams. STUART KALLEN. Abdo & Daughters, 1993.
Writers Dreaming—Dreamers Writing: 25 Writers Discuss Dreams and the Creative Process. NAOMI EPEL. Crown, 1993.
"Maya Angelou. . . ." MARCIA ANN GILLESPIE. *Essence*, Dec. 1992.
Order Out of Chaos: The Autobiographical Works of Maya Angelou. DOLLY McPHERSON. Trafalgar, 1992.
Double Stitch: Black Women Write about Mothers and Daughters. PATRICIA BELL-SCOTT, ed. Beacon, 1991; HarperCollins, 1993.
Writers at Work. GEORGE PLIMPTON. Viking Penguin, 1992.

"Maya Angelou. . . ." NANCY CALDWELL SOREL.
Atlantic, Sep. 1990.
Conversations with Maya Angelou. JEFFREY M.
ELLIOTT, ed. University Press of Mississippi, 1989.

Annenberg, Walter Hubert (1908–)

Philanthropist and retired publisher Walter Annenberg made several massive gifts to educational organizations in 1993, through his family foundation. In June, he announced four major gifts: $100 million to New Jersey's Peddie School, a preparatory school he attended; $25 million to Harvard University; $120 million to the University of Southern California; and $120 million to the University of Pennsylvania. The latter two gifts were to be used to fund communications schools named after him. In October, he gave $25 million to Northwestern University.

On December 17, at a White House ceremony attended by President Clinton and Secretary of Education Richard W. Riley, Annenberg announced that he would give $500 million more to education over a 5-year period, as matching grants. Of that sum, $50 million was to go to the Coalition of Essential Schools, at Brown University; $50 million to the New American Schools Development Corporation; and the remaining $400 million to a wide range of organizations not yet selected

Milwaukee-born Annenberg is the son of publisher M. L. (Moe) Annenberg, who founded Triangle Publications, the large publishing company that Walter Annenberg built into an even larger communications empire. He has also been a very active Republican Party fundraiser and contributor, an intimate friend of presidents Nixon and Reagan; Annenberg was U.S. Ambassador to Britain (1969–75). He is also a major philanthropist, most notably as the founder of the Annenberg School of Communications at the University of Pennsylvania. After selling his interest in Triangle Publications to Rupert Murdoch for approximately $3 billion, he further developed his philanthropic interests. His major gifts include $50 million to the United Negro College Fund and $60 million to the Corporation for Public Broadcasting. His largest single gift came in 1991, when he made a bequest of his collection of more than 50 French Impressionist and Post-Impressionist paintings, valued at more than $1 billion, to New York's Metropolitan Museum of Art. Annenberg attended the Peddie School, the University of Pennsylvania, and its Wharton School. He has been married twice, and has one child.

FURTHER READING

"One man's gift. . . ." THOMAS TOCH. *U.S. News & World Report,* Nov. 1, 1993.
"Walter H. Annenberg." *Facts on File,* July 1, 1993.
"Walter Annenberg. . . ." *Connoisseur,* Feb. 1991.
"Strength of vision." HUNTER DROHOJOWSKA. *Harper's Bazaar,* Apr. 1989.

Antall, Jószef (1932–93)

Hungarian premier Jószef Antall, a librarian, archivist, teacher, and museum director, was active in the right-of-center Smallholders Party before the 1947 Communist takeover, was mostly out of politics until 1956, and was arrested after joining the failed Hungarian revolution against Soviet domination. He stayed in Hungary after the revolution, and in 1964 became director of the Semmelweis medical history museum, library, and archives in Budapest, though he was barred from travel abroad until 1973. He moved back into politics as Hungary shook off Soviet domination, became chairman of the Hungarian Democratic Forum in 1989, and after electoral victory in 1990 became the premier of Hungary, succeeding Socialist Miklos Nemeth. His tenure was marked by growing economic problems and the resurgence of Hungarian fascism and anti-Semitism. He was survived by his wife and two sons. (d. Budapest; December 12, 1993)

FURTHER READING

Obituary. *The Times* (of London), Dec. 13, 1993.
Obituary. *New York Times,* Dec. 13, 1993.
"Antall, Jószef, Jr." *Current Biography,* Sep. 1990.

Anthony, Joseph (1912–93)

A leading figure in the American theater, Milwaukee-born Joseph Anthony was an actor, writer, and dancer before emerging as a theater and film director in the 1950s. From 1955 to 1963, he directed many highly successful plays, among them *The Lark, The Most Happy Fella, The Marriage-Go-Round, The Best Man, Mary, Mary, Rhinoceros,* and *The Rainmaker,* which he also directed as a film in

1956. Among his other films were *The Match-maker* (1958), and *Captive City* (1963). Anthony was also active in professional affairs, as a board member of the Screen Directors Guild, an officer of Actors' Equity, and in several other capacities. He also taught theater at several colleges and universities, helping inaugurate the theater curriculum at the Purchase campus of the State University of New York. He was survived by his wife, actress Perry Wilson, a daughter, and a son. (d. Hyannis, Massachusetts; January 20, 1993)

FURTHER READING

Obituary. *New York Times*, Jan. 22, 1993.

Arafat, Yasir (1929–) On September 13, 1993, Palestine Liberation Organization (PLO) chairman Yasir Arafat and Israeli prime minister Yitzhak Rabin shook hands on the White House lawn, approving the historic declaration of principles that had a few minutes earlier been signed by their respective ministers, Mahmoud Abbas and Shimon Peres, which established a basis for Palestinian self-rule, beginning in the Gaza Strip and Jericho. The agreement was the product of a series of negotiations initiated by Rabin soon after becoming prime minister, in August 1992, and had been preceded by four months of secret negotiations in Norway, mediated by Norwegian foreign minister Johan Jorgen Holst. A preliminary agreement had been announced by both sides on August 30–31.

For Arafat, the event was a partial culmination of much of his life's work; it was also yet another major comeback in a career full of ups and downs, for in 1992 he had seemed to lose much of his political strength, having backed Saddam Hussein against his Arab allies in the Persian Gulf War and subsequently lost much of the PLO's funding and his main military base at Sidon to Syrian-backed Lebanese army forces. With the historic peace agreement, he was once more ascendant, beating off all challenges within the PLO and emerging yet again as the main Palestinian leader and spokesperson.

However, the agreement was still only a set of principles at year's end; though progress had been made, no full agreement on implementation had been achieved, and Israeli troops still occupied the Gaza Strip and Jericho. Nor was the agreement one that all Israeli governments would necessarily honor; a Likud government seemed quite likely to repudiate the agreement if it were to come to power in the near future.

Jerusalem-born Arafat was a founder of Al Fatah (1956) and of its guerrilla army (1959). He has headed the PLO and been the top leader of the Palestinian national movement since 1969. He suffered major personal defeats when his forces were expelled from Jordan (1970–71), and from Lebanon (1983). In the mid-1980s, he moved toward negotiation and publicly renounced terrorism, and seemed for a time all but overwhelmed by the more extreme terrorist elements within his own movement. In late 1988, he forced Palestine National Council and PLO acceptance of key United Nations resolutions 242 and 338. On November 15, 1988, he issued a Palestinian declaration of independence, and the proclaimed Palestinian state has since been recognized by more than 50 countries. Arafat attended Cairo University, and was an engineer before becoming a full-time political leader. He married Suha Tawil in 1992.

FURTHER READING

" 'There is no turning back.' " RICHARD Z. CHESNOFF. *U.S. News & World Report*, Nov. 8, 1993.
"Arafat's burden." BARRY RUBIN and JUDITH COLP RUBIN. *New Republic*, Oct. 4, 1993.
" 'This is a step. . . .' " DEAN FISCHER. *Time*, Sep. 27, 1993.
"Arafat. . . ." SHYAM BHATIA. *Observer*, May 2, 1993.
"Who pays Arafat?" BRIAN DUFFY and RICHARD Z. CHESNOFF. *U.S. News & World Report*, Apr. 26, 1993.
"Better without the boss?" LISA BEYER. *Time*, June 15, 1992.
"Arafat talks. . . ." TOM POST. *Newsweek*, May 4, 1992.
Behind the Myth: Yasser Arafat and the Palestinian Revolution. ANDREW GOWERS and TONY WALKER. Interlink, 1992.
"Yasir Arafat. . . ." *Time*, Oct. 21, 1991.
Arafat and the Palestine Liberation Organization. DIANA REISCHE. Watts, 1991.
Arafat: In the Eyes of the Beholder. JANET WALLACH and JOHN WALLACH. Carol, 1990; Prima, 1991.
Arafat: A Political Biography. ALAN HART. Indiana University Press, 1989.

Ardolino, Emile (1943–93) New York City-born Emile Ardolino, a leading film director, began his career as a dancer and actor, but quickly moved into film direction, at first as a

documentarian, and then as editor, director, and producer of a wide range of films, with an accent on but by no means limited to dance films. Among his early works were the films for New York production of *Oh! Calcutta!*, for which he won an Obie, and the co-production of the "Dance in America" television series. He emerged as a Hollywood director with the "sleeper" low-budget dance film *Dirty Dancing* (1987), and went on to make the films *Chances Are* (1988), *Three Men and a Little Lady* (1990), and *Sister Act* (1992), as well as directing several television movies, the last being *Gypsy* (1993). Ardolino, who died of complications caused by AIDS, was survived his companion, Luis M. Rodriguez-Dilla, and three sisters. (d. Los Angeles; November 20, 1993)

FURTHER READING

Obituary. *The Times* (of London), Nov. 23, 1993.
Obituary. *New York Times*, Nov. 22, 1993.
Obituary. *Variety*, Nov. 22, 1993.

Aristide, Jean-Bertrand (1953–) For exiled Haitian president Jean-Bertrand Aristide, 1993 was a year of great promise, seeming victory, and then hopes deferred. On July 3, protracted negotiations with Haiti's military rulers, whose coup had forced him to flee abroad in 1991, resulted in an agreement to end the military government, the safe return of Aristide to Haiti and his presidency, and the re-installation of democratic government. In August, the United Nations suspended its oil and arms embargo on Haiti. But after the agreement, a reign of terror against Aristide supporters continued in Haiti, and on October 11, unarmed U.S. and Canadian engineers sent to Port-au-Prince in conformance with the agreement were denied landing by armed irregulars, with the open approval of the military government led by General Raoul Cedras. On October 13, the UN embargo was renewed, while the Clinton administration deplored the military government moves but refused to take military action. On October 16, a UN naval blockade of Haiti began, although no effort was made to block land access from the Dominican Republic. The reign of terror continued, as did UN and U.S. pressure on Haiti, while Ariside remained in exile.

Haitian-born Aristide, an orphan, was raised by the Catholic Salesian order, was ordained a

Catholic priest in 1982, and soon became a leading and much-admired worker among the poor in his very poor country. At the same time, he became a leader in the fight against Duvalier and the Tonton Macoutes, and for Haitian democracy, surviving several attempts on his life. One of the young priests who brought liberation theology to Latin America, he was a source of great discomfort to conservative Catholic leaders, and was expelled from the Salesian order in 1986. In 1987, a massive popular street protest stopped Church hierarchy attempts to transfer Aristide out of Haiti.

On December 17, 1990, Rev. Aristide was elected President of Haiti, in his country's first democratic election. Aristide won close to 70 percent of the vote, in an election monitored by a 33-member observers group, under former U.S. president Jimmy Carter. Aristide, a Catholic liberation theologian long hailed by the Haitian poor, campaigned on an anti-U.S., anti-foreign aid program, calling for the prosecution and destruction of the repressive Tonton Macoutes organization, which had flourished during the hated 29-year Duvalier dictatorship, while Haiti became the poorest country in the Americas.

With army support, Aristide survived a quick January 1991 coup attempt, and did attack the Tonton Macoutes, prosecuting many, and replacing Macoutes throughout the government and army, as well as replacing older with younger officers. On September 29 and 30, 1991, he was deposed by an army coup, and fled abroad. Many countries expressed disapproval and took economic action against the new government, but no military action against it was seriously contemplated. Aristide continued to call for his reinstatement from abroad, while the military tightened its hold on Haiti, and the exodus of the "boat people," illegal immigrants trying to reach the United States, once again began. Among his written works are *In the Parish of the Poor: Writings from Haiti* (1990) and *Aristide: An Autobiography* (1992).

FURTHER READING

"Aristide. . . ." TIM MCCARTHY. *National Catholic Reporter*, Feb. 21, 1992.
"Haiti and Aristide. . . ." ANTHONY P. MAINGOT. *Current History*, Feb. 1992.
"Interview with. . . ." BISHOP EMERSON J. MOORE. *America*, Oct. 12, 1991.
"President Jean Bertrand Aristide." ANNE-CHRISTINE D'ADESKY. *Interview*, Oct. 1991.

"The oppositionist. . . ." AMY WILENTZ. *New Republic*, Oct. 28, 1991.

" 'I am president of Haiti'." *Time*, Oct. 14, 1991.

"Haitian priest-president. . . ." THOMAS HARTMAN. *National Catholic Reporter*, May 17, 1991.

"Aristide, Jean-Bertrand." *Current Biography*, May 1991.

"Haiti takes a new turn. . . ." CAROLE CLEAVER. *New Leader*, Jan. 14, 1991.

"An avalanche for democracy. . . ." GUY GARCIA. *Time*, Dec. 31, 1990.

Arnold, Roseanne Barr (1952–)

As her hit comedy series "Roseanne" completed its fifth season, Roseanne Arnold won an Emmy as best lead actress in a comedy series, and also a Golden Globe nomination as best actress in a television musical or comedy. In addition to "Roseanne," she starred in the made-for-television film *The Woman Who Loved Elvis*, as a welfare mother who notoriously cheats the welfare system, having undeclared sources of income, and who turns her home into a shrine dedicated to Elvis Presley. The film, directed by Bill Bixby, also starred her husband Tom Arnold, Sally Kirkland, and Cynthia Gibb. During the year, Arnold also developed a highly publicized estrangement with ABC, which did not renew Tom Arnold's series "Jackie Thomas." In mid-November, Roseanne and Tom Arnold signed a long-term production contract with Warner Television. Her autobiography, *My Lives*, was scheduled for 1994 publication. On the personal side, the Arnolds announced plans to marry—apparently jointly—their assistant, Kim Silver.

Salt Lake City-born Arnold began her career as a stand-up comedian in variety in the late 1970s. A decade later, she emerged as the star of the very popular television series "Roseanne" (1988–), which was generally at or near the top of the ratings from 1989. Propelled by her personal style, she also emerged as a major celebrity. Her first feature film was *She-Devil* (1989), and her first television film, *Backfield in Motion* (1991). An animated series "Little Rosey," based on the Roseanne character, aired during the 1990–91 television season. She has published *Roseanne: My Life as a Woman* and *Stand Up!*. In 1991, speaking to an incest survivors group, Arnold went public with charges that she had been sexually abused as a child, a charge her parents denied. She has been married twice, and has four children, one of whom she bore as a teenager and gave up for adoption.

FURTHER READING

"Strange bedfellows." FRANK SWERTLOW. *Redbook*, June 1993.

"Roseanne and Tom Arnold." *Playboy*, June 1993.

"The uncensored. . . ." SCOTT A. HUNT. *Christopher Street*, May. 1993.

"Two against the world." TOM GLIATTO. *People*, Mar. 29, 1993.

"Roseanne Arnold. . . . " LEO JANOS. *Cosmopolitan*, Feb. 1993.

Roseanne Arnold: Comedy's Queen Bee. KATHERINE E. KROHN. Lerner, 1993.

"Everything's coming up Rosie." BOBBIE KATZ. *First for Women*, Nov. 9, 1992.

"The King's biggest fans." MELANIE BERGER. *Ladies Home Journal*, Nov. 1992.

"Lady in waiting." *TV Guide*. Aug. 29, 1992.

"Roseanne!" LESLIE VAN BUSKIRK. *US*, May 1992.

"Roseanne Arnold." ED DWYER. *Los Angeles*, Mar. 1992.

"The Roseanne report." MARY MURPHY and FRANK SWERTLOW. *TV Guide*, Jan. 4, 1992.

"A star cries incest. . . ." VICKIE BANE. *People*, Oct. 1991.

Roseanne Barr. ROBERT ITALIA. Abdo & Daughters, 1991.

"Barr, Roseanne." *Current Biography*, May 1989.

Ashe, Arthur Robert, Jr. (1943–93)

A victim of AIDS-related illness, tennis star and writer Arthur Ashe "went public" in April 8, 1992, making a major contribution to public understanding of the disease, which he had probably contracted from the blood in transfusions connected with his 1979 or 1983 heart operations. After telling his story, he became active in fundraising for AIDS research and worked to help victims of the disease.

Richmond-born Ashe, a trailblazing African-American tennis player, was an amateur champion during his college years, and went on to become a leading professional. He was the first African-American to be named to the U.S. Davis Cup team (1963), win the U.S. Amateur title (1968), win the U.S. Open (1968), win the Australian Open (1970), and win at Wimbledon (1975). He retired from play in 1979, after three heart attacks, then becoming a sports consultant and holding several corporate positions. Always active in equal rights struggles, he was an early and highly visible opponent of South African apartheid. He was also an active author, whose major work was the three-volume *A Hard Road to Glory: The History of the African-American Athlete* (1988). His other works include *Arthur Ashe: An Autobiography* (1970); *Portrait in Motion* (1973), with Frank Deford; *Off the Court* (1981); and *Days of Grace: A Memoir*, with Arnold Rampersad (1993). Surviving was his wife, Jeanne-Marie Moutoussamy Ashe, a professional photographer who published a photo essay of Ashe's final year with their daughter, Camera, in a book titled *Daddy and Me* (1993), designed also to help parents explain AIDS to their young children. (d. New York City; February 6, 1993)

FURTHER READING

Arthur Ashe and His Match with History. ROBERT QUACKENBUSH. Simon & Schuster, 1994.
"Daddy and me." CLAUDIA GLENN DOWLING and JEANNE MOUTOUSSAMY-ASHE. *Life*, Nov. 1993.
"Unforgettable Arthur Ashe." CHARLES PASARELL. *Reader's Digest*, Sep. 1993.
"Ashe reaches the end. . . ." MATTHEW S. SCOTT. *Black Enterprise*, Apr. 1993.
"Lessons in living." BARRY LORGE. *Tennis*, Apr. 1993.
"Arthur Ashe. . . ." WALTER LEAVY. *Ebony*, Apr. 1993.
Obituary. *Current Biography*, Mar. 1993.
"Arthur Ashe. . . ." *Jet*, Feb. 22, 1993.
"Lessons from a friend. . . ." FRANK DEFORD. *Newsweek*, Feb. 22, 1993.
"Man of grace and glory." MARY HUZINEC et al. *People*, Feb. 22, 1993.
"He did all he could." KENNY MOORE. *Sports Illustrated*, Feb. 15, 1993.
"A man of fire and grace." PAUL A. WITTMAN. *Time*, Feb. 15, 1993.
"A debt of gratitude." MICHAEL KNISLEY. *Sporting News*, Feb. 15, 1993.
Obituary. *The Times* (of London), Feb. 8, 1993.
Obituary. *New York Times*, Feb. 7, 1993.
Arthur Ashe. TED WEISSBERG. Holloway, 1993.
Arthur Ashe: Champion of Dreams and Motion. STUART A. KALLEN. Abdo & Daughters, 1993.
Arthur Ashe: Black Americans of Achievement. TED WEISSBERG. Chelsea House, 1992.
Arthur Ashe. ED WEISSBERG. Chelsea House, 1991.

Aspin, Les (1938–)

On December 15, 1993, Secretary of Defense Aspin suddenly resigned, the first high level casualty of the Clinton administration. He had faced a series of very difficult issues during his term in office. Early in the year, perhaps the most highly visible problem was the controversy over the military's ban on gays, which incoming President Bill Clinton failed to upset, ultimately agreeing to a compromise "don't ask, don't tell, don't pursue" policy that Aspin helped negotiate. In April, Aspin removed the ban on women flyers in combat, but kept the ban on women in ground combat.

Pursuing his long-term commitment to cut military costs, Aspin in March proposed massive base and other military facility closings in the United States, in May abandoned the Strategic Defense Initiative (SDI), and in September proposed major cuts in military personnel and hardware, including nuclear weapons, as well as cuts in weapons systems in development. But in late autumn Aspin took the Pentagon's side in a major dispute with Leon Panetta over $50 billion in requested cuts, and went public with his disagreement.

Even more damaging was Aspin's refusal to supply requested tanks to field commanders in Somalia, just before the firefight that cost the lives of 19 lightly armed American soldiers, an action for which Aspin publicly apologized. Ultimately, Clinton asked for and received Aspin's resignation; whether for cause or because a scapegoat was needed for failed Clinton policies in Somalia, Bosnia-Herzegovina, and Haiti was a matter that was hotly debated by partisans of both sides.

On the personal side, Aspin, who has a heart condition, in late February suffered breathing problems after Army doctors preparing him for a trip to Somalia used a typhoid immunization agent known to cause such a problem in many people, apparently because a safer and entirely available agent cost $1.55 more.

Milwaukee-born Aspin began his long Congressional career in 1970. During the 1980s, he emerged as a leading Wisconsin Democrat, with powerful influence on military appropriations through his House committee memberships and then as chairman of the House Armed Services Committee. He was cautious at first, and then fully supported the 1991 Persian Gulf War, but after the war and through the 1992 Presidential campaign strongly attacked Bush administration defense policies and called for far greater military spending cuts than those proposed by the Pentagon, hoping to create a "peace dividend." In November 1992, he was reelected by a landslide, winning 58 percent of the vote in his district. In December 1992, he was appointed

Secretary of Defense by incoming President Bill Clinton.

Aspin's 1960 B.A. was from Yale University, his 1962 M.A. from Oxford University, and his 1965 Ph.D. from the Massachusetts Institute of Technology. He taught economics at Marquette University (1969–70). He has published the *Aspin Papers: Sanctions, Diplomacy and War in the Persian Gulf* (1991).

FURTHER READING

Les Aspin: Secretary of Defense. Bob Italia. Abdo & Daughters, 1993.
"The Aspin papers. . . ." Morton Kondracke. *New Republic*, Apr. 27, 1992.

Assad, Hafez al (1928–   ) Syrian President Assad continued to pursue established objectives during 1993. With Lebanon now firmly a protectorate, he directly faced Israel across that border, while at the same time continuing to seek return or at least neutralization of the Israeli-occupied Golan Heights. Although Syrian-Israeli peace talks had stalled early in 1993, after Israeli expulsion into Lebanon of 400 Palestinian fundamentalists, reports persisted throughout the year that Israeli and Syrian negotiators were moving toward solution of the Golan Heights question. In early August, Syrian and Lebanese forces cut off some of the weapons flow from Iran to Hezbollah militants in southern Lebanon, after Israeli air strike reprisals for Hezbollah guerrilla attacks had sent 300,000 refugees fleeing north toward Beirut. Assad also supplied and encouraged Kurdish forces in Turkey; his role regarding parallel Kurdish insurgencies in Iraq and Iran was not clear. His role in Syria, however, was completely clear: despite reported moves toward political liberalization, he remained undisputed leader of a single-party authoritarian state.

Assad began his political and military career as a Baath Party activist and air force officer. He became an air force general after the 1963 Baathist coup, and air force commander in chief and minister of defense in 1966. He took power in 1970 and was named President of Syria in 1971. During the Cold War, he was closely allied with, and his armed forces were supplied by, the Soviet Union. His forces were badly defeated by Israel in the fourth Arab-Israeli (Yom Kippur) war of 1973. Since 1976, his forces have partially occupied Lebanon; although they were defeated again by the Israelis in Lebanon in 1976. By the end of the long Lebanese Civil War, Assad had established a de facto Syrian protectorate over Lebanon. During the Iran-Iraq war of the 1980s, he supported Iran against Iraq, a long-time enemy. During the Persian Gulf War, he supported the anti-Iraq coalition, and after the war courted the United States, as his former Soviet supporters and suppliers had vanished. Assad attended Syria's armed forces colleges. He is married, and has five children.

FURTHER READING

"A hill screaming in Golan." James Gaffney. *America*, Nov. 27, 1993.
"Hope is as scarce. . . ." Raymond A. Schroth. *National Catholic Reporter*, Sep. 3, 1993.
"Hafez Assad. . . ." *Time*, Nov. 30, 1992.
"Syria's game. . . ." Judith Miller. *New York Times Magazine*, Jan. 26, 1992.
"Trouble in Damascus." Alan Cowell. *New York Times Magazine*, Apr. 1, 1990.
Hafez al-Assad. Matthew Gordon. Chelsea House, 1989.

Attenborough, Richard (1923–   ) British actor, producer, and director Attenborough in 1993 was active as all three. He produced and directed the acclaimed film *Shadowlands*, adapted by William Nicolson from his own hit play, with Anthony Hopkins as C.S. Lewis in the role played by Nigel Hawthorne on the New York stage, and Debra Winger as Joy Gresham in the Jane Alexander role.

Attenborough also starred in the Steven Spielberg blockbuster commercial hit, the special effects science-fiction film *Jurassic Park*, about modern genetically engineered dinosaurs that break free from a theme park and become a danger to humanity. Michael Crichton and David Koepp wrote the screenplay, based on Crichton's novel; Sam Neill, Jeff Goldbum, and Laura Dern co-starred.

Attenborough began his long and varied career on stage, in 1941, and made his West End debut in *Awake and Sing* (1942) and his film debut *In Which We Serve* (1942). He appeared on stage into the late 1950s, although film became his main focus. His major films as an actor include *Brighton Rock* (1947; he had appeared in the 1943 stage production), *The Magic Box* (1951), *Private's Progress* (1955), *The Great Escape* (1963), and *Séance on a Wet Afternoon* (1964; he also produced), *The Sand Pebbles* (1966), *David Copperfield* (1969), and *Conduct Unbecoming* (1974). His directorial career included *Oh! What a Lovely War* (1969), *Young Winston* (1972), *A Bridge Too Far* (1976), *Magic* (1978), *A Chorus Line* (1985), and *Cry Freedom* (1987). He directed and produced the epic *Gandhi* (1982), which won 8 Oscars, including best picture and best director, as well as many other awards. He also directed and produced *Chaplin* (1993). His written works include *In Search of Gandhi* (1982), and several books accompanying films, including *Richard Attenborough's Chorus Line* (1986; with Diana Carter), *Cry Freedom, A Pictorial Record* (1987), and *Chaplin* (1992).

He is married to Sheila Beryl Grant Sim, and has 3 children.

FURTHER READING

"Richard Attenborough." CHRIS VIELER-PORTER. *UNESCO Courier*, Aug. 1989.
Filming with Attenborough. DONALD WOODS. Holt, 1987.

Atwood, Margaret (1939–) Canadian novelist Margaret Atwood was back with a notable new work in 1993, *The Robber Bride*. The book focuses on the lives of three Toronto women, and how a fourth—the beautiful, bewitching maneater, Zenia, a modern but mysterious Lady Macbeth—uses and betrays them over the years. Critics generally lauded Atwood's style and confidence, in this dark but humorous version of the battle between the sexes, with women attacking other women, though some suggested that, at the end, Atwood's foray into magical realism did not entirely work. Even before Atwood began her three-nation publicity tour—United States, Canada, and the United Kingdom—the book appeared to be her best-selling effort to date. Many buyers are reading groups, for whom Doubleday also published *The Book Group Companion to "The Robber Bride"*. Atwood was also one of several authors courageous enough to supply some of their juvenile writings for a collection called *First Words: Earliest Writings from 42 Favorite American Authors*, edited by Paul Mandelbaum.

Atwood is a versatile poet, novelist, short story writer, essayist, and editor, whose other works include *The Edible Woman* (1969), *Surfacing* (1973), *Life Before Man* (1979), *Murder in the Dark* (1983), *The Handmaid's Tale* (1986, basis for the 1990 film), *Cat's Eye* (1989), *Wilderness Tips* (1991), and a children's environmental work, *For the Birds*. She is married to Graeme Gibson; they have one child. She attended the University of Toronto and Harvard University.

FURTHER READING

Margaret Atwood's Fairy-Tale Sexual Politics. SHARON R. WILSON. University Press of Mississippi, 1993.
Margaret Atwood: Mirrors, Reflections and Images of Power. SHANNON HENGEN. InBook, 1993.
"A heroine of the struggle casts a cool eye on women." LESLEY WHITE. *Sunday Times* (of London), Aug. 16, 1992.
"Margaret Atwood: 'Respectability can kill. . . .'" CLAUDIA DREIFUS. *Progressive*, Mar. 1992.
Margaret Atwood: Conversations. EARL G. INGERSOLL, ed. Ontario Review Press, 1991.
Margaret Atwood: A Reference Guide. JUDITH McCOMBS and CAROLE L. PALMER. G.K. Hall, 1991.

Auger, Arleen (1939–93) California-born Arleen Auger, a leading soprano, began her working life as an elementary school teacher, beginning her musical career in the mid-1960s. Her debut came with the Vienna State Opera in

1967; she quickly moved into leading soprano roles. Leaving the company in 1974, she thereafter toured in recital, largely in Europe, pursued her recording career as a major interpreter of art songs, and taught at the Frankfurt Academy. Her New York debut was a song recital at Alice Tully Hall in January 1984. In the years that followed, she became a major concert and recording star in Europe and America. She was survived by her parents and a brother. (d. Amsterdam, the Netherlands; June 10, 1993)

FURTHER READING

Obituary. *Opera News*, Oct. 1993.
Obituary. *Current Biography*, Aug. 1993.
Obituary. *The Times* (of London), June 12, 1993.
Obituary. *New York Times*, June 12, 1993.
"Center stage. . . ." JAMIE JAMES. *Stereo Review*, Oct. 1992.
"Arleen Auger." JAMES M. KELLER. *Musical America*, July 1990.
"Auger, Arleen." *Current Biography*, Feb. 1989.

Aung San Suu Kyi, Daw (1945–) During 1993, world human rights figure Aung San Suu Kyi remained the prisoner of the military dictatorship in Myanmar (Burma). It was her fifth year of house arrest; she has been held without charge or trial at her family home at Yangon, near Rangoon, because she continues to defy the dictatorship's demands that she renounce politics and the cause of Burmese democracy as the price of her freedom. That she has not otherwise been directly harmed is a tribute to the strength of her continuing presence as a symbol of democracy in Myanmar; perhaps the military is wary of international opinion, as well; she was the recipient of the 1991 Nobel Peace Prize.

In February, six Nobel Peace Prize winners, led by Archbishop Desmond Tutu, met in Thailand to urge her release; they were denied entrance into Myanmar by the military. They were joined by representatives of Amnesty International and the American Friends Service Committee; several other Nobelists sent messages of support. On May 20, President Clinton called for Aung San's release. But on July 20, the military junta extended her imprisonment for another year, as the campaign for her release continued.

Rangoon-born Daw Aung San Suu Kyi is the daughter of the founder of modern Burma (now Myanmar), Aung San (1914–47), who became Burma's first prime minister in 1947, and was assassinated on July 19, 1947. She grew up in Burma, leaving her country in 1960, when her mother became Burmese ambassador to India. Educated in India and at Oxford University, she married archeologist Michael Aris in 1972; they have two sons. She lived at Oxford with her husband and children until 1988, during those years publishing a biography of her father, *Aung San* (1984); she then returned to Burma to nurse her sick mother, who died later in 1988.

Although her reasons for returning to Burma had nothing to do with politics, she arrived during a revolutionary period, often called the Burmese Spring, with hundreds of thousands involved in massive street demonstrations against the 26-year-old military dictatorship of army leader Ne Win. She soon became a leader of the democratic opposition, heading the nonviolent National League for Democracy, and was in 1988 placed under house arrest and forbidden to run for office.

Ne Win resigned in July 1988, but remained in control of the army, while demonstrations continued. A democratic government briefly ruled in August and September 1988, but was overthrown by an army coup, in which thousands were killed. The military dictatorship that then took over Burma was led by General Saw Maung.

Aung San Suu Kyi, under house arrest, stayed on in Burma to lead the democratic opposition to the military dictatorship. When the military, facing powerful democratic opposition, promised and held democratic elections in May 1990, her party swept the election. The military then refused to honor the election results, and tightened its control, publicly attacking her for marrying a foreigner and at the same time trying to convince her to leave the country by making the terms of her imprisonment more difficult and keeping her family from visiting her. Various of her writings were published in 1992 under the title *Freedom from Fear*, edited by Aris.

FURTHER READING

"Extraordinary people." HERBERT BUCHSBAUM. *Scholastic Update*, Dec. 3, 1993.
"Burma's Gandhi." DAVID S. TOOLAN. *America*, Feb. 8, 1992.
"Aung San Suu Kyi." *Current Biography*, Feb. 1992.
"The wages of courage." *People*, Oct. 28, 1991.

Aykroyd, Dan (Daniel Edward Aykroyd; 1952–) Film star Aykroyd reached back to his early days in television in 1993, recreating his 1970s "Saturday Night Live" role as Beldar Conehead in a new film, *Coneheads*, opposite Jane Curtin, who recreated her role as Prymaat Conehead, and Michelle Burke, as Connie Conehead. Steve Barron directed the film, which was not very well received by the critics. Aykroyd also reached back, but only for two years, for his starring role in Howard Zieff's forthcoming film *My Girl II*, opposite Jamie Lee Curtis and Richard Mazur. On the personal side, he and Donna Dixon had a daughter, Belle Kingston, born June 9.

Canadian-born Aykroyd became a star in television comedy as one of the original members of the "Saturday Night Live troupe" (1975–79); he also wrote for the program. He and John Belushi created the Blues Brothers for the show, then starred in the film, *The Blues Brothers* (1980), which Aykroyd wrote. He went on to star in many other films, including *Neighbors* (1981), *Trading Places* (1983), *Ghostbusters* (1984), *Spies Like Us* (1985), *Dragnet* (1987), *The Great Outdoors* (1988), *My Stepmother Is an Alien* (1988), *Ghostbusters II* (1989), *Loose Cannons* (1990), *Nothing But Trouble* (1991; he also wrote and directed), *My Girl* (1991), *Chaplin* (1992; as Mack Sennett), *This is My Life* (1992), and *Sneakers* (1992). He won an Oscar nomination for best supporting actor as the son in *Driving Miss Daisy* (1989). Aykroyd attended Ottawa's Carleton College. He has been married twice, and has three children.

FURTHER READING

"Playboy interview. . . ." *Playboy*, Aug. 1993.
"Resident alien." BRIAN D. JOHNSON. *Maclean's*, July 26, 1993.
"Architectural Digest visits. . . ." SUSAN CHEEVER. *Architectural Digest*, Aug. 1992.
"Aykroyd, Dan." *Current Biography*, Jan. 1992.

Aylwin Azócar, Patricio (1919–) During his final year in office, Chilean President Aylwin continued to stabilize Chile's democracy and economy although the economic legacy of the 1980s remained, with unemployment, poverty, and foreign debt still very much problems that remained to be successfully addressed. Aylwin's government, still in uneasy co-existence

with the military, successfully brought Chile through four years of democracy, culminating in the free elections of November 11, 1993, which elected Eduardo Frei Ruiz-Tagle as Aylwin's successor. Frei, the son of former Chilean president Eduardo Frei Montalva (1964–70), won by a landslide 58 percent of the popular vote, his runner-up in the multiparty elections winning only 22 percent. Frei was expected to stress an expansion of social services, while continuing Aylwin's emphasis on the development of a competitive market economy. He was also expected to come into sharper conflict with Chile's military, their reaction remaining to be seen.

In a major victory for Aylwin and Chilean democracy, two high-ranking Chilean army officers were in November sentenced to prison terms for ordering the 1976 Washington, D.C. assassination of Chilean democratic leader Orlando Letelier.

Aylwin, a lawyer and Christian Democrat, became a senator in 1965 and leader of his party in 1973. He opposed the socialist Allende government in the early 1970s. In the early years he did not openly oppose the Pinochet dictatorship, but did join other lawyers in defending some of those imprisoned by the government, and later more openly opposed military rule. Aylwin led the democratic coalition that replaced military dictator Pinochet, and was elected to the Chilean presidency in December 1989. In power, he played a major role in restoring Chilean democracy, quickly freeing many of Chile's political prisoners, and setting up a national commission to study and report on the human rights violations of the Pinochet government. In March 1991, the commission reported that over 2,000 cases of murder, disappearance, and torture had occurred during the Pinochet years, including the long-charged murder of folksinger Victor Jara and the 1976 car bombing murders in Washington, D.C., of former cabinet minister Orlando Letelier and Ronni Moffitt. Aylwin Azócar married Leonor Oyarzun in 1948; they have five children.

FURTHER READING

"Chile. . . ." NATHAN GARDELS and ABRAHAM LOWENTHAL. *New Perspectives Quarterly* , Fall 1993.
"Seeking a free trade agreement." JEAN A. BRIGGS. *Forbes*, May 11, 1992.
"Chile's uncommon way." JONATHAN KANDELL. *Town & Country*, Oct. 1991.
"Aylwin Azocar, Patricio." *Current Biography*, Aug. 1990.

Azinger, Paul (1960–) For years a high-ranked golfer, Paul Azinger had never won a major tournament. That "huge burden," as he described it, was "lifted off his shoulders," when he won the Professional Golfers Association (PGA) championship at Inverness in Toledo, Ohio, in August 1993. With birdies on four of the last seven holes to tie with Greg Norman, whom he then beat in a two-hole playoff, his yearly winnings at that point totaled more than $1.3 million. Also in 1993, Azinger had two other wins on the PGA tour, at the Memorial Tournament and the New England Classic, and was a member of the successful Ryder Cup Team. Azinger's wins in 1993 kept alive the longest current winning streak on the PGA Tour, with a win in each of the last seven seasons.

In December, pain in Azinger's right shoulder was diagnosed as lymphoma; he was expected to miss at least six months of competition while undergoing therapy for the localized cancer; in 1991 he had an operation on the same shoulder to treat infection in the bone, with no cancerous tissue being revealed at that time.

Born in Sarasota, Florida, Azinger attended Broward Junior College and Florida State University. He turned professional in 1981 and by 1986 had moved into 29th position on the Professional Golfers Association (PGA) Tour, but his first notably successful year was 1987, when he won three tournaments (Phoenix, Las Vegas, and Greater Hartford), was second on the money list, and was named PGA Player of the Year. He had a win on the PGA Tour in each of the next six years (Bay Hill, 1988; Greater Hartford, 1989; Tournament of Champions, 1990; Pebble Beach National Pro-Am, 1991; Tour Championship, 1992), as well as winning Germany's BMW Open (1990; 1992). He is married to Toni Azinger and has two daughters.

FURTHER READING

"Critic's choice." KEN VENTURI. *Golf Magazine*, Feb. 1992.
"Child's play." JOHN GARRITY. *Sports Illustrated*, Mar. 12, 1990.

B

Babbitt, Bruce Edward (1938–) Secretary of the Interior Bruce Babbitt's first year in office reflected his strong environmental commitment, although a good many of his initiatives were stalled and some even reversed by administration compromises, and by negotiations on other issues—as when the much higher grazing fees on public lands, announced on August 9, 1993 and greatly opposed by western ranchers and legislators, were drastically scaled down shortly afterward as part of a deal for western votes in President Clinton's fight for the North American Free Trade Agreement (NAFTA). Babbitt was also active in shaping plans that allowed developers and loggers to encroach on previously protected habitats while promising to participate in the preservation of other portions of those habitats—as in the instance of the California gnatcatcher habitat, which served to some extent as a model for the July 1, 1993 Clinton compromise proposal on the northern spotted owl, the loss of the northwestern forest to logging, the loss of northwestern salmon habitat because of erosion caused by logging, and the return to timber cutting on federal land. Babbitt reportedly largely supported environmentalist positions during the northwestern dispute, which continued. The administration's compromise approach also extended to the wetland preservation policies announced on August 24. Babbitt also continued active on international environmental matters, as in attempts to save rhinoceros and elephant populations, threatened by the illegal rhinoceros horn and ivory trades.

Babbitt practiced law in Phoenix (1965–74), and again in Phoenix and Washington (1988–92), focusing largely in environmental matters, water, and natural resources. He began his political career as Arizona attorney general (1975–78), and was governor of Arizona (1978–87), becoming chairman of the Democratic Governors Association in 1985. In 1988, he made an unsuccessful run for the Democratic presidential nomination. He has been national president of the League of Conservation Voters, chairman of the National Groundwater Policy Forum, and served on the presidential commission set up to investigate the nearly catastrophic 1979 Three Mile Island nuclear accident. His books include *Color and Light: The Southwest Canvases of Louis Akin* (1973) and *Grand Canyon: An Anthology* (1978).

Babbitt's 1960 B.A. was from the University of Notre Dame, his 1962 M.S. in geophysics from Britain's University of Newcastle, and his 1965 LL.B. from Harvard Law School. He is married to the former Hattie Coons; they have two children.

FURTHER READING

"Bruce Babbitt. . . ." FRANCIS WILKINSON. *Rolling Stone*, July 8, 1993.
"Banking on Bruce?" JEFFREY ROSEN. *New Republic*, June 28, 1993.
"America's landlord." BETSY CARPENTER. *U.S. News & World Report*, May 17, 1993.
"Interior views. . . ." ROGER COHN and TED WILLIAMS. *Audubon*, May-June 1993.
"The land lord." TED GUP. *Time*, Mar. 8, 1993.

"Babbitt's feast. . . ." JACOB WEISBERG. *New Republic*, Mar. 8, 1993.

Laboratories of Democracy. DAVID OSBORNE. Harvard Business, 1988.

Zoë Baird (left) and Bill Clinton

Baird, Zoë (1952–) On December 24, 1992, President-elect Bill Clinton named Zoë Baird to be United States Attorney General; she was to be the first woman ever to hold that post. At first, her nomination seemed likely. However, confirmation prospects diminished sharply on January 14 when the *New York Times* reported that she and her husband, Yale law professor Paul D. Gewirtz, had in violation of the law hired a Peruvian couple who were illegal immigrants to work in their home, and had not paid Social Security taxes for them. Although they paid the required back taxes in January, plus a fine, the damage to the Baird nomination was done; it was withdrawn on January 22, in a major defeat for the incoming administration, after Democratic support for Baird dropped sharply during Senate confirmation hearings.

New York City-born Baird was a government lawyer during the Carter administration, first with the Justice Department's Office of Legal Counsel and then as an associate counsel on the White House legal staff. After the 1980 Republican victory, she joined Warren Christopher's firm, O'Melveny and Myers; she and Christopher had worked together on Iran hostage matters.

She became a partner at O'Melveny and Myers, left Washington to join the General Electric Company legal staff in Connecticut, and in 1990 became a Senior Vice-President and General Counsel of the huge Hartford-based Aetna Life and Casualty Insurance Company. Baird's 1974 B.A. was from the University of California at Berkeley, as was her 1977 J.D. Baird and Gewirtz have one child.

FURTHER READING

"Adventures in Babysitting." SIDNEY BLUMENTHAL. *New Yorker*, Feb. 15, 1993.

" 'I'm sorry about this'. . . ." RAE CORELLI. *Maclean's*, Feb. 1, 1993.

"Danny and Zoë. . . ." JEFFREY ROSEN. *New Republic*, Feb. 1, 1993.

Time, Feb. 1, 1993. "How it happened." JILL SMOLOWE. "Thumbs down." NANCY GIBBS.

"Mr. President. . . ." KENNETH T. WALSH et al. *U.S. News & World Report*, Feb. 1, 1993.

"Zoë Baird's briefcase. . . ." LISA DRISCOLL. *Business Week*, Dec. 23, 1991.

Baldwin, Alec (Alexander Rae Baldwin, 3rd; 1958–) Versatile stage and screen star Baldwin, fresh from his Tony-nominated triumph as Stanley Kowalski on Broadway in 1992 revival of Tennessee Williams's *A Streetcar Named Desire*, turned fully again to films in 1993. He starred as a brain surgeon in the college town-set mystery *Malice*, opposite Nicole Kidman, George C. Scott, Bill Pullman, and

Bebe Neuwirth; Harold Becker directed. Baldwin also starred in *Sliver*, directed by Phillip Noyce and adapted from Ira Levin's novel by Joe Eszterhas, opposite Sharon Stone and Tom Berenger. Long-time environmentalist Baldwin also was one of the many stars who did readings for the film *Earth and the American Dream*. Forthcoming was a starring role as a jailed criminal in the film *The Getaway*, opposite his wife, Kim Basinger, who organizes his escape; Roger Donaldson is slated to direct.

On the personal side, Baldwin received his B.A. from New York University in May; he had dropped out of school 4 credits short of graduation in 1980. Baldwin and Basinger married in August, at East Hampton, New York.

Long Island-born Baldwin starred in the television series "Knots Landing," and in the New York theater in such plays as *Serious Money* and *Prelude to a Kiss*, for which he won an Obie award. He became a film star in the late 1980s, in such films as *She's Having a Baby* (1988), *Beetlejuice* (1988), *Married to the Mob* (1988), *Talk Radio* (1988), and *Working Girl* (1988), making his major breakthrough in *The Hunt for Red October* (1990). His films also include *Miami Blues* (1990), *Alice* (1990), *The Marrying Man* (1991), *Glengarry Glen Ross* (1992), and *Prelude to a Kiss* (1992). Baldwin attended George Washington University (1976–1979), and studied theater at New York University and the Lee Strasberg Institute (1979–80).

FURTHER READING

"Baldwin, Alec." *Current Biography*, July 1992.
"Kim and Alec. . . ." ELIZABETH SPORKIN. *People*, Apr. 22, 1991.
"Not just another hunk." CATHLEEN MCGUIGAN. *Newsweek*, Apr. 23, 1990.
"The hunk from 'Hunt'." PETER TRAVERS. *Rolling Stone*, Apr. 5, 1990.
"Smart Alec." STEPHANIE MANSFIELD. *GQ—Gentlemen's Quarterly*, Feb. 1990.

Barkley, Charles Wade (1963–) The bad boy of basketball, Charles Barkley, thought he could win it all in 1993—and he came close. Third-best in the National Basketball Association (NBA) Pacific Division the previous season, the Phoenix Suns in Barkley's first season went right to the top, posting the best record in the league. Barkley himself was named the NBA's

most valuable player for the first time, edging out two strong contenders, Hakeem Olajuwon and three-time winner Michael Jordan; Barkley was also named a starting forward on the All-Star team.

But it was Jordan who foiled Barkley's dearest wish: an NBA championship. The Suns made it to the NBA finals, but then disastrously lost the first two games at home against the Chicago Bulls. The Suns came back with a stirring triple-overtime win, led by Barkley despite a sore elbow, and went on to win two games themselves, but finally lost the championship series 4–2 in a heartbreaker for Barkley and the Suns.

In the 1993–94 season, with some strong new players and more experience, Barkley and the Suns were ready to try again. In October, in the Munich Macdonald's Open, the Suns defeated the Bologna Bucklers, with Barkley as the game's MVP, receiving the Drazen Petrovic trophy honoring the European-born Nets guard killed earlier in the year. Scheduled for 1994 publication was *Sir Charles: The Wit and Wisdom of Charles Barkley*, written with Rick Reilly.

Barkley, his team, and his fans all received a scare in October, when during sprints he collapsed with numbness in his legs, due at least partly to a back injury. He was able to resume play shortly, but back problems and the feeling that his best years were past led Barkley to say that, whether or not the Suns win a championship, he was "99.9 percent" sure that the

1993–94 season would be his last. In a change of pace, brash-talking Barkley opened the season of television's "Saturday Night Live," as guest host in September 1993.

Born in Leeds, Alabama, Barkley emerged as a nationally recognized player during his years at Alabama's Auburn College (1981–84). Although often overweight and at odds with his coaching staff, he was the leading rebounder in the Southeastern Conference and a strong scorer during all three of his college seasons. He failed to make the 1984 U.S. Olympic team, but was a first round choice in the NBA draft after his junior year, going to the Philadelphia 76ers. There he became a fixture, one of the league's leading rebounders and scorers, and a perennial All-Star forward, on the second team (1986–87), then on the starting team (1988–92 for the East; 1993 for the West), and most valuable player in the 1991 All-Star game, but never winning an NBA championship. Barkley was a notable part of the gold-medal-winning "Dream Team" at the 1992 Barcelona Olympics. The always quotable Barkley published an autobiography, *Outrageous* (1992), written with Roy Johnson, Jr., and in 1992 began a local television show in Phoenix with the Suns' general manager Cotton Fitzsimmons. Barkley is married and has one child.

FURTHER READING

"Who are you calling hero?" VERN E. SMITH and ARIC PRESS. *Newsweek*, May 24, 1993.
"Chuck." MARK JACOBSON. *Esquire*, May 1993.
"Charles Barkley." TOM BOSWELL. *Playboy*, May 1993.
"Prodigal Sun. . . ." WILLIAM PLUMMER. *People*, Feb. 22, 1993.
"Rebel yell. . . ." JEFF WEINSTOCK. *Sport*, Feb. 1993.
"Hot head." RICK REILLY. *Sports Illustrated*, Nov. 9, 1992.
"Charles Barkley." RICK REILLY. *Sports Illustrated*, Mar. 9, 1992.
"Has mouth, will shoot." MIKE LUPICA. *Esquire*, Mar. 1992.
Sports Great Charles Barkley. GLEN MACNOW. Enslow, 1992.
"Headstrong." JEFF COPLON. *New York Times Magazine*, Mar. 17, 1991.
"Barkley, Charles." *Current Biography*, Oct. 1991.
"Sir Charles." RICHARD REGEN. *Interview*, June 1990.

Barr, Roseanne: See Arnold, Roseanne Barr.

Barry, Dave (ca. 1947–) Writer Dave Barry was in the unusual position of seeing his life as a Miami-based humor columnist portrayed on television by someone else, in this case Harry Anderson, when the prime-time television series "Dave's World" opened on CBS in fall 1993. The series is based on Barry's books, although instead of his actual one child the series has two, but only one dog, rather than the two—Earnest and Zippy—familiar to Barry fans. Barry himself appeared briefly in a walk-on part as a tourist in an early episode. Meanwhile, the real life Barry went on a May eight-city Massachusetts-to-Miami bus tour with an all-author rock band called the Rock Bottom Remainders, including Amy Tan, Stephen King, Barbara Kingsolver, Robert Fulghum, and Barry on lead guitar. The group is publishing a book about themselves, *Mid-Life Confidential*, due in 1994. Another new Barry book, *Dave Barry Is Not Making This Up*, was scheduled for 1994.

Born in Armonk, New York, Barry received his B.A. from Haverford College. He began his career in journalism as a reporter and editor for the West Chester, Pennsylvania, *Daily Local News* (1971–75), and then worked for the Associated Press out of Philadelphia (1975–83). He moved to Miami as a columnist for the *Miami Herald* (1983–), winning a writing award from the Society of Newspaper Editors (1987) and a Pulitzer Prize for commentary (1988). He emerged a widely read author in the early 1980s, with books such as *Taming of the Screw: Several Million Homeowner's Problems Sidestepped* (1983), *Babies and Other Hazards of Sex* (1984), *Dave Barry's Bad Habits: A One Hundred Percent Fact-Free Book* (1985; 1993), *Stay Fit and Healthy Until You're Dead* (1985), *Dave Barry's Guide to Marriage and/or Sex* (1987), *Claw Your Way to the Top* (1987), *Dave Barry's Greatest Hits* (1988), *Homes and Other Black Holes: The Happy Homeowner's Guide* (1988), *Dave Barry Slept Here: A Sort of History of the United States* (1989), *Dave Barry Turns 40* (1990,) *Dave Barry Talks Back* (1991), *Dave Barry's Only Travel Guide You'll Ever Need* (1991), and *Dave Barry Does Japan* (1992). He is married to Beth (Elizabeth) Barry, an editor of the *Miami Herald*'s Sunday magazine, and has one son.

FURTHER READING

"When Harry met Barry." RICK MARIN. *TV Guide*, Oct. 9, 1993.
"Sharp sting of a waspish wit." SIMON HOGGART. *Observer*, May 2, 1993.
"2–4—6–8 he doesn't want to renovate!" FRED BERNSTEIN. *Metropolitan Home*, Oct. 1990.
"Barry funny." MICHAEL KIEFER. *Ladies Home Journal*, Oct. 1990.
"Playboy interview: Dave Barry." FRED BERNSTEIN. *Playboy*, May 1990.
"Madcap airs all. . . ." JESSE BIRNBAUM. *Time*, July 3, 1989.

Basinger, Kim (1953–) Although her career was somewhat in eclipse, Basinger did star in 1993 as a bank robber in *The Real McCoy*, a film directed by Russell Mulcahy, and co-starring Val Kilmer. She also appeared in a strong supporting role in *Wayne's World 2*. Forthcoming was a starring role in *The Getaway*, as a woman who organizes the escape of her friend, a jailed criminal, played by her husband, Alec Baldwin; Roger Donaldson was set to direct. She and Baldwin married in August, in East Hampton, New York.

On March 25, Basinger was ordered by a Los Angeles court to pay a settlement of $7.4 million to the producer of *Boxing Helena*, for violating an oral contract to appear in the film. She later filed for bankruptcy.

Georgia-born Basinger worked as a New York model in the mid-1970s, then moved into television, most notably in *Katie—Portrait of a Cen-* terfold (1978), and in the 1979 remake of *From Here to Eternity*. On screen, she starred in *Hard Country* (1980) and *The Man Who Loved Women* (1983), and became one of Hollywood's leading sex symbols of the 1980s as Domino in Sean Connery's last James Bond film *Never Say Never Again* (1983) and opposite Mickey Rourke in *9 1/2 Weeks* (1986). She also starred in *The Natural* (1984), *Fool for Love* (1985), *Batman* (1989), and *Final Analysis* (1992). Basinger attended New York's Neighborhood Playhouse. She had a previous marriage.

FURTHER READING

" 'Boxed' in by deadline?" KATHLEEN O'STEEN. *Variety*, Mar. 8, 1993.
"Kim up close. . . ." JONATHAN VAN METER. *Vogue*, May 1991.
"Kim and Alec. . . ." ELIZABETH SPORKIN. *People*, Apr. 22, 1991.
"Basinger, Kim." *Current Biography*, Feb, 1990.

Bates, Kathy (1948–) In a performance praised for its stark realism, Bates in 1993 starred in the film *A Home of Our Own*, set in 1962, as Frances Lacy, a widow who quits her Los Angeles job after being sexually harassed by her boss, and heads east in an old car, with her six children and very little money, getting as far as Idaho and an old shack in which she creates a new life; the film was directed by Tony Bill.

Bates also played a strong supporting role as the sister of hostage Terry Anderson in the highly controversial and very well-received HBO television film *Hostages*, which recreated the capture, imprisonment, and final release of British and American hostages in mid-1980s Lebanon. Jay O. Sanders was Anderson, in a cast that included Colin Firth, Natasha Richardson, Ciaran Hinds, and Harry Dean Stanton; David Wheatley directed. The film opened in Britain in 1992 and in the U.S. in 1993.

Forthcoming was a starring role in *North*, directed by Rob Reiner, in a cast that includes Bruce Willis, Elijah Wood, Jon Lovitz, Julia-Louis Dreyfus, and Jason Alexander. Also forthcoming was a starring role in *Curse of the Starving Class*, opposite James Woods and Louis Gossett, Jr., directed by Michael J. McClary.

Memphis-born Bates began her acting career in New York in 1970, often working in children's and regional theater, with occasional small film roles, as in Milos Forman's *Taking Off* (1971) and Dustin Hoffman's *Straight Time* (1978), and guest spots on television series and telefilms. Her first lead was in the Off-Broadway play *Vanities* (1976), and she originated the role of Lenny McGrath in Beth Henley's Pulitzer Prize-winning play *Crimes of the Heart* (1979). Her breakout stage role was as the suicidal Jessie Cates in Marsha Norman's Pulitzer Prize-winning *'Night Mother* (1983), for which she won the Outer Critics Circle Award and a Tony nomination. This was followed by a string of leading stage roles, including *Come Back to the Five and Dime, Jimmy Dean, Jimmy Dean* (1982) and *Frankie and Johnny in the Claire de Lune* (1987) for which she won an Obie Award.

She began to play supporting roles on film after her 1985 move to Los Angeles, as in *Arthur 2 On the Rocks* (1988) and *Dick Tracy* (1990). She won a best actress Oscar for *Misery* (1990), and also starred in *At Play in the Fields of the Lord* (1991), *Fried Green Tomatoes* (1991), *The Road to Mecca* (1992), *Shadows and Fog* (1992), *Prelude to a Kiss* (1992), and *Used People* (1992). Bates graduated from Southern Methodist University in Dallas. She married actor Tony Campisi in 1991.

FURTHER READING

"Kathy Bates. . . ." MELANIE BERGER. *Ladies Home Journal*, Jan. 1993.
"Kathy Bates. . . ." WAYNE MILLER. *First for Women*, June 8, 1992.
"Kathy Bates. . . ." BROOK HERSEY. *Glamour*, Feb. 1992.
"Bates, Kathy." *Current Biography*, Sep. 1991.
"Kathy Bates." MICHAEL LASSELL and TIMOTHY GREENFIELD-SANDERS. *Interview*, Aug. 1991.
" 'I never was an ingenue'." DAVID SACKS. *New York Times Magazine*, Jan. 27, 1991.
"Wallowing in Misery. . . ." MARY H.J. FARRELL. *People*, Dec. 24, 1990.

Baudouin I of Belgium (1930–93)

Belgium's King Baudouin I was the son of Leopold III, who surrendered his country to the Germans without a fight in 1940. In 1950, although a referendum favored the return of the monarchy, civil war threatened in anticipation of Leopold's return. He abdicated in favor of his son, Baudouin, who became king in 1951, on his 21st birthday. The new constitutional monarch presided over the dissolution of Belgium's imperial holdings, and spent much of his reign not very successfully attempting to mediate the long-standing and growing Fleming-Walloon controversy that increasingly threatened to break his country in two. He was survived by his wife, Queen Fabiola. (d. Motril, Spain; July 31, 1993)

FURTHER READING

Obituary. *Current Biography*, Oct. 1993.
Obituary. *The Times* (of London), Aug. 2, 1993.
Obituary. *New York Times*, Aug. 1, 1993.

Bauza, Mario (1911–93)

Havana-born Afro-Cuban jazz trumpeter, saxophonist, and bandleader Mario Bauza considerably influenced the introduction of Afro-Cuban music into American jazz. There was a classical dimension, as well; he was a clarinettist with the Havana Symphony before moving to New York in 1931. He was first trumpeter and then orchestra director with Chick Webb (1933–38), and introduced Dizzy Gillespie to Afro-Cuban rhythms (1939), when they were both trumpeters with Cab Calloway. Bauza and his brother-in-law, Machito, formed a Latin big band in the early 1940s, though he continued to work in Afro-Cuban jazz as well. He was survived by his wife Lourdes and a daughter. (d. New York City; July 11, 1993)

FURTHER READING

"Mario Bauza. . . ." DIANE GORDON. *Down Beat*, Oct. 1993.

"Cubano bopper. . . ." LARRY BIRNBAUM. *Down Beat*,
   June 1993.
Obituary. *The Times* (of London), Aug. 13, 1993.
Obituary. *New York Times*, July 12, 1993.

Bazelon, David Lionel (1909–93)
Wisconsin-born David Bazelon, a major figure in
the American federal judiciary for more than
three decades, began his practice of law in Chicago in 1931; a New Deal Democrat, he was an
assistant U. S. attorney in Illinois (1935–40) and
an assistant U. S. Attorney-General (1946–49).
President Harry S. Truman appointed him to
the powerful U. S. Court of Appeals for the District of Columbia in 1949; he became Chief
Judge of that court in 1962. He became a major
figure during the McCarthy period, strongly resisting the witchhunting congressional committees of the period, and contributed heavily to the
growing body of decisions recognizing the constitutional rights of defendants to due process
and diligent representation. In October 1973, it
was Judge Bazelon who ruled that President
Richard M. Nixon must disgorge the Watergate
tapes, paving the way for the Nixon resignation.
Among his other major decisions were the 1971
banning of DDT and cases involving the Internal Security Act, Fifth Amendment violations,
and communications industry monopolistic practices. His written works include *Questioning
Authority* (1987). Bazelon was survived by his
wife, Miriam, and two sons. (d. Washington,
D. C.; February 19, 1993)

FURTHER READING

Obituary. *Current Biography*, Apr. 1993.
Obituary. *The Times* (of London), Feb. 25, 1993.
Obituary. *New York Times*, Feb. 21, 1993.

Beck, Dave (1894–1993) Teamsters union
leader Dave Beck worked as a laundry driver in
Seattle before World War I, joined the Teamsters Union in 1914, and began his long union
career after serving as an aerial gunner during
World War I. He organized Seattle laundry driv-
ers for the Teamsters during the postwar period,
and moved up in the union in the decades that
followed, becoming Teamsters national executive vice president in 1947. He was Teamsters
president (1952–57), becoming a millionaire on
his modest salary, and in 1957 defied the Senate's McLellan Committee, which was investigating corruption in his union, repeatedly
pleading the Fifth Amendment. He was jailed on
federal tax evasion and state embezzlement
charges for 30 months in the early 1960s, leaving prison in 1964, and pardoned in full by President Gerald Ford in 1975. He was survived by a
son. (d. Seattle; December 26, 1993)

FURTHER READING

Obituary. *New York Times*, Dec. 28, 1993.

Beers, Katie (Katharine Beers; c. 1983–   )
On December 28, 1992, at Nesconset, New York,
in eastern Long Island, 10-year-old Katie Beers
was reported missing by 43-year-old John Esposito, a family friend who said that she had
disappeared while on a shopping center outing
with him. A highly publicized and entirely unsuccessful search began, with national attention
focused on the case by massive television and
print media coverage. On January 13th, 16 days
later, Esposito—always the chief suspect in
the case, whose home had previously been
searched—led police to a 6′ x 7′ cell under his
home at Bayshore, Long Island, where the child
was found in good health after her long period of
solitary confinement. Media attention intensified, as the troubled backgrounds of those closest
to Katie Beers became public knowledge, with
multiple child molestation charges and a bitter
custody fight in progress prominently featured.
Some of the principals quickly found themselves
interviewees on popular national television
shows, while film companies and publications
vied for the right to commercially exploit the
child's tragedy. At year's end, Katie was in a
foster home and undergoing counseling, while
the various adults fought over her legal custody.
Esposito was in jail on $1.1 million bail.

FURTHER READING

"Katie's a survivor." *People*, Dec. 27, 1993.
"Rescued." JOE TREEN. *People*, Feb. 1, 1993.
"Little house of horrors. . . ." MELINDA BECK.
   Newsweek, Jan. 25, 1993.
"A little girl buried alive." RICHARD LACAYO. *Time*,
   Jan. 25, 1993.
*My Name is Katharine: The True Story of Little
   Katie Beers*. MARIA EFTIMIADES.

Lloyd Bentsen (right) and Bill Clinton

Bentsen, Lloyd (Lloyd Millard Bentsen, Jr.; 1921–) Secretary of the Treasury Lloyd Bentsen seemed a moderate-to-conservative influence in the Clinton administration during his first year in office, especially in tax and budget matters, as when he announced the dropping of the proposed and highly-controversial BTU energy tax from the budget in early June. In the main, he strongly supported the President's tax and budget measures at home, and pursued established American free trade policies abroad, with special attention to the long-standing attempt to break through discriminatory Japanese trade barriers to correct existing imbalances in American-Japanese trade. Bentsen also strongly supported the North American Free Trade Agreement (NAFTA). On a non-financial matter, he initiated an investigation of the Treasury-supervised Bureau of Alcohol, Tobacco, and Firearms after siege and disaster of David Koresh's Waco, Texas Branch Dravidian compound.

Bentsen began his long political career in 1948. A much-decorated B-24 bomber pilot during World War II, and a practicing lawyer after the war, he was a Hidalgo County, Texas judge (1946–48), winning election to House of Representatives in 1948. He served three terms in the House, and left to go into the financial business in Houston for 16 years, as president of Lincoln Consolidated. He returned to politics in 1970, making a successful Democratic primary run as a conservative against liberal Democratic Senator Ralph Yarborough. Bentsen then defeated Republican George Bush in the senatorial race, winning the first of his four successive terms in the Senate.

In the Senate, Bentsen ultimately became a very powerful figure. As chairman of the Senate Finance Committee, he exercised great influence on a wide range of matters very important to other legislators and to large numbers of Washington lobbyists, and was able in one period to run a series of $10,000-per-plate "power breakfasts" for lobbyists, for whom the $10,000 campaign funds contribution to Bentsen was just the beginning of a complicated and, for them, often very rewarding game. As a Senator, Bentsen was responsive to the interests of his constituents, especially on oil, gas, and real estate tax matters. In 1988, he was the Democratic vice-presidential candidate on the Dukakis ticket.

Bentsen's 1942 LL.B. was from the University of Texas. He is married to the former Beryl Ann Longino; they have three children.

FURTHER READING

"Bentsen, Lloyd." *Current Biography*, Apr. 1993.
"A supply sider. . . ." PAUL CRAIG ROBERTS. *National Review*, Feb. 1, 1993.
"Last of the line." PAUL BURKA. *Texas Monthly*, Feb. 1993.
"The eyes of Texas are upon them." *Life*, Feb. 1989.

Bérégovoy, Pierre (1925–93) French trade unionist and Socialist Party leader Pierre Bérégovoy was a railway worker who, as a member of the Resistance, sabotaged German operations in France during World War II. He became a Socialist Party activist after the war, in the mid-1960s beginning his long association with François Mitterrand, then emerging as party leader. On Mitterrand's election in 1981, he appointed Bérégovoy as Elysée Palace secretary general; in 1982, he became social affairs minister, the first of several cabinet-level appointments, and also became a member of the National Assembly. He succeeded Edith Cresson as prime minister on April 2, 1992, serving until the Socialist electoral defeat in March 1993. His tenure was marred by a series of financial charges and countercharges, which persisted after he left office. He committed suicide. He was survived by his wife Gilberte, two daughters, and a son. (d. Paris; May 1, 1993)

FURTHER READING

Obituary. *Current Biography*, July 1993.
Obituary. *The Times* (of London), May 3, 1993.
"Beregovoy, Pierre." *Current Biography*, Feb. 1993.

Tom Berenger (left) and Stephen Lang

Berenger, Tom (1950–) Actor Tom Berenger starred in the 1993 film *Sliver*, directed by Phillip Noyce, written by Joe Eszterhas, based on the Ira Levin novel. Sharon Stone and William Baldwin co-starred as offbeat lovers, with Berenger's character part of the triangle at the center of the murder mystery. Berenger also starred in the film *Sniper*, directed by Luis Llosa and co-starring Billy Zane, as a Marine sniper in Panama. A third major screen role was as General James Longstreet in Ted Turner's Civil War epic film *Gettysburg*, directed and written by Ronald F. Maxwell, and co-starring Martin Sheen, Richard Jordan, and Stephen Lang. In 1993, Berenger also won an Emmy nomination as best guest actor in comedy series for his role in *Cheers*. Forthcoming was a starring role opposite Dennis Hopper in the film *Chasers*, directed by Hopper.

Chicago-born Berenger began his career on stage, appearing in several off-Broadway productions in the early 1970s; he also appeared in the daytime soap "One Life to Live." He made his film debut in *Beyond the Door* (1975). His emerged as a star in his breakthrough film, *The Big Chill* (1983), then starring in such films as *Platoon* (1986; he received an Oscar nomination), *Someone to Watch Over Me* (1987), *Born on the Fourth of July* (1989), and *At Play in the Fields of the Lord* (1991), also starring in several television films. Berenger attended the University of Missouri.

FURTHER READING

"Terrific good old boy. . . ." SUSAN SPILLMAN. *Cosmopolitan*, Nov. 1991.

Bergman, Ingmar (1918–) The American Film Institute honored Ingmar Bergman in the year of his 75th birthday, by dedicating to him the closing night of the annual AFI fest, at which were shown *Sunday's Children (Söndagsbarn)*, a 1992 film written by Bergman and directed by his son Daniel, and *Wild Strawberries*, Bergman's own classic 1957 film. He continued his work with Stockholm's Royal Dramatic Theater, bringing his Swedish-language production of *Peer Gynt* for a brief stay at the Brooklyn Academy of Music in May, as he had done with three productions in 1991. Also in 1993, Bergman directed an opera based on Euripedes's *The Bacchants*, first for stage, then for television.

Bergman's first novel, *The Best Intentions*, was also published in English in 1993; based on the courtship of Bergman's parents and seen as a companion piece to *Fanny and Alexander*, the film of the work—direction and screenplay by Bille August—had premiered on Scandinavian television, then won the Golden Palm at Cannes. A totally new book was *Images: My Life in Film*, the second installment of his autobiography, a sequel to *The Magic Lantern* (1987); it was scheduled for publication in English translation in 1994, as was *Sunday's Child: A Novel*.

Bergman is a central figure in world film history and at the same time a major figure in the Swedish theater. From the mid-1950s, he created a series of film masterworks that have been tremendously important to all who followed, including such classics as *Smiles of a Summer Night* (1955), *Wild Strawberries* (1957), *The Magician* (1958), *The Virgin Spring* (1960), *Through a Glass Darkly* (1961), *Scenes From a Marriage* (1974), *After the Rehearsal* (1984), and *Good Intentions* (1989). In 1990, he received the D.W. Griffith award from the Directors Guild of America, for lifetime contribution to film. Since 1991, he has directed primarily for the theater and for television. Bergman attended Stockholm University. He has been married six times, and has eight children. His son, Daniel Bergman, is also a film director, while his sister, Margareta Bergman, is a novelist.

FURTHER READING

Film and Stage Work of Ingmar Bergman. ROBERT E. LONG. Abrams, 1994.
Ingmar Bergman: The Art of Confession. HUBERT I. COHEN. Macmillan, 1993.
"Ingmar Bergman." JOHN CLARK. *Premiere*, Sep. 1992.
Ingmar Bergman: A Critical Biography, rev. ed. PETER COWIE. Limelight, 1992.
The Poet at the Piano: Portraits of Writers, Filmmakers, and Performers at Work. MICHIKO KAKUTANI. Random, 1988.
Ingmar Bergman: A Guide to References and Resources. BIRGITTA STEEN. G.K. Hall, 1987.

Bernstein, Sidney Lewis (1899–1993)

British film and television entrepreneur Sidney Bernstein began his long career in his family's small group of movie theaters, inheriting the four-theatre London chain at the age of 22. He built it into a substantial chain during the 1920s, also moving into theatrical production, while at the same time becoming a Labour Party local councillor. He became a major figure in British film distribution during the 1930s, in that period also becoming a leading British anti-fascist. He served as a government film advisor during World War II. Bernstein also moved into film and television production during the post-war period, and in 1956 founded Granada Television. In the decades that followed, he became a major international figure, developing a communications-based conglomerate of which Granada was only a small part. He became a life peer (a lord, though the title does not pass to his heirs) in 1969. He was survived by two daughters and a son. (d. Ilford, Essex; January 30, 1993)

FURTHER READING

Obituary. *The Times* (of London), Feb. 6, 1993.

Bhutto, Benazir (1943–)

Making an extraordinary comeback, Benazir Bhutto and her Pakistan People's Party won a plurality in the October 6 general elections, and went on to make a strong showing in the October 9 provincial elections. On October 19, a 121–72 parliamentary vote elected Bhutto Prime Minister, at the head of a coalition government. In her early weeks in office, she took a considerably more conservative approach than she had during her 1988–90 period in the office, stating that Pakistan would continue to develop its nuclear program despite American protests, expressing support for the long Muslim insurgency in the Indian province of Kashmir, and questioning tax policies aimed at the Pakistani rich. Her views seemed to reflect a set of new arrangements between Bhutto and Pakistan's military and landholding elites, formerly her bitter opponents.

She had supported president Ishaq Khan's dismissal of the Nawaz Sharif government in April, and entered the succeeding government. It was Ishaq Khan who had dismissed her own government in 1990, and imprisoned her husband, Asif Ali Zardari. Her husband was released from prison in February, and in April was made a government minister by Ishaq Khan. In May, Pakistan's Supreme Court reversed the dismissal of the Nawaz Sharif government as unconstitutional, leading ultimately to the July resignations of both Nawaz Sharif and Ishaq

Khan, and setting the stage for the October elections.

In power, the questions of Islamic fundamentalism and the long, bloody relationship with India faced Bhutto, as they did every Pakistani leader, as did to a lesser degree the questions of Afghanistan and relations with China and the states of the former Soviet Union. Bhutto also ran into a rather unique personal-political question; her younger brother, Murtaza Bhutto, long exiled in Syria (1977–93), returned to Pakistan, and was in November arrested by his sister's government, on current insurgency charges and on airplane hijacking charges dating back to 1981. His mother, Pakistan People's Party (PPP) chairperson Nusrat Bhutto, supported him against her daughter, Benazir, and was dismissed from her PPP position by her daughter, precipitating a split in the party that was escalating at year's end.

On the directly personal side, Benazir Bhutto gave birth to her third child in February.

Bhutto's father, Zulfikar Ali Bhutto, had been Pakistan's prime minister (1972–77); he was executed in 1979 by Zia's military government. After the coup that deposed him, Bhutto and her mother were under house arrest in Pakistan (1977–84). She left Pakistan in 1984, returned for the funeral of a brother in 1985, and was rearrested and expelled from her country. She returned again in 1986, as head of the Pakistan People's Party, and led the opposition to the government.

After the death of military dictator Zia Ul-Haq in an August 1988 plane crash, Bhutto was elected prime minister of Pakistan in the free election of December 2, 1988, the second Bhutto to become prime minister. In office, Benazir Bhutto was hailed as one of the world's leading women; but at home, she faced increasing opposition from the Pakistani army and fundamentalist religious leaders. On August 6, 1990, she was removed from office by president Ishaq Khan, acting with the support of the military; she was charged with corruption, her husband and many supporters were arrested, and she was forbidden to leave the country. She and her party were defeated in the October 24, 1990 elections, which she called fraud-ridden.

Bhutto attended Harvard University and Lady Margaret Hall, Oxford University. In 1989, she published *Daughter of Destiny: An Autobiography*. She married Asif Ali Zardari in 1987; they have three children.

FURTHER READING

"Bent on preserving a dynasty." *Independent*, Oct. 16, 1993.
"Bhutto's fateful moment." MARY ANNE WEAVER. *New Yorker*, Oct. 4, 1993.
Benazir Bhutto. DIANE SANSEVERE-DREHER. Bantam, 1991.
Benazir Bhutto. KATHERINE M. DOHERTY and CRAIG A. DOHERTY. Watts, 1990.
From Prison to Prime Minister: A Biography of Benazir Bhutto. LIBBY HUGHES. Dillon, 1990.
Women and Politics in Islam: the Trial of Benazir Bhutto. RAFIG ZAKARIA. New Horizons, 1990.
"Dynasty's daughter." TARIQ ALI. *Interview*, Feb. 1989.

Biden, Joseph Robinette, Jr.

(1942–) Senate Judiciary Committee Chair Biden once again faced a Supreme Court vacancy and nomination in 1993. But this time there was no confirmation fight; instead, the August 3, 1993 Senate confirmation of Ruth Bader Ginsburg to replace retiring Justice Byron R. White, was by a 96–3 vote, following a unanimous July 29 approval by his committee. That committee now included senators Dianne Feinstein and Carol Moseley-Braun, energetically recruited by Biden at the start of the new session; he had been deeply embarrassed as the head of an all-male committee during the Anita Faye Hill-Clarence Thomas confrontation. Biden did face some confirmation fights, however, took a strong position regarding possible adverse public reaction, and was a factor in the withdrawal of the Zoë Baird, Kimba Wood, and Lani Guinier nominations. He also played a major role in passage of the Brady gun control law, defeating the Republican filibuster.

Pennsylvania-born Biden, a four-term Senator and a leading Senate liberal, became a Democratic senator from Delaware in 1972, later moving into a key position as head of the Senate Judiciary Committee. In 1986, he played a major role in the rejection of President Ronald Reagan's nomination of Robert Bork to the Supreme Court. He was a leading candidate for the 1988 Democratic presidential nomination, but withdrew after allegations that he had plagiarized some of material in his campaign speeches from the speeches of British Labour leader Neil Kinnock. In early 1990, he survived two brain operations, both for aneurysms, then resumed his Senate career. He was highly visible at the center of the 1991 firestorm that was the Anita Faye Hill-Clarence Thomas confrontation before his committee and a worldwide audience. He received his A.B. from the University of Delaware and his J.D. from Syracuse University. He was previously married to Neilia Hunter, and married Jill Tracy Jacobs in 1977. He has had four children, including two sons from his first marriage, who survived the 1972 automobile accident that killed their mother and infant sister.

FURTHER READING

"Biden is also reborn." MARGARET CARLSON. *Time*, Sep. 12, 1988.

Bigelow, Albert Smith (1906–93) An architect and World War II U. S. Navy lieutenant commander on destroyer duty in the Pacific, Albert Smith Bigelow became a Quaker and an advocate of nonviolence in 1954, then becoming a leading anti-war and pro-civil rights activist. He and three other Quaker pacifists drew worldwide attention in 1958, on February 10 setting out of San Pedro, California in the 30-foot ketch *Golden Rule* to try to stop scheduled nuclear tests at Eniwetok atoll. Their unsuccessful demonstration became an important part of the soon-successful campaign to stop atmospheric nuclear testing. Bigelow and several companion Freedom Riders were beaten by racists at Rock Hill, South Carolina in 1961. He was survived by his wife, Sylvia Weld, and two daughters. (d. Walpole, Massachusetts, October 6, 1993)

FURTHER READING

Obituary. *The Times* (of London), Oct. 18, 1993.
Obituary. *New York Times*, Oct. 8, 1993.

Billington, James Hadley (1929–) Librarian of Congress is not normally a high-profile position, but the current holder of the post, James Billington, found himself in the news over several issues during 1993. Most notable was the controversy over his decision, after Thurgood Marshall's death in January, to open to the public the former Supreme Court Justice's

papers, deposited at the Library. Marshall had directed that the papers be made available to researchers and scholars at the library's discretion. Many critics thought that the library should have excluded journalists from access to the files, especially since the papers included material on many still-sitting Justices, and Marshall's family had requested that the files be closed. At House hearings in June, some speakers expressed concern that justices might be less free in deliberation in the future if they knew their colleagues might be taking notes that could soon be made publicly available. But others noted that journalists are normally considered researchers, and Billington said he was following Marshall's directions. Whether future donations of documentary materials would be threatened was unclear; Chief Justice William Rehnquist, for one, threatened that he would not deposit his papers at the library.

Consultants hired by the House of Representatives criticized the Library of Congress for making insufficient efforts to improve minority hiring and promotion, and being slow to implement a 1992 court decision partially settling a class action suit by library employees charging a discriminatory hiring system. In congressional hearings, Billington charged that many problems stemmed from the time of his predecessors, and promised to appoint a deputy librarian to overhaul and oversee hiring and promotion practices, to make them more equitable.

In February, Billington proposed charging

user fees for electronic information services, though he stressed that other services would remain free of charge; it would be the first time that the 193-year-old library ever sold information to the public. The proposal was received coolly on Capitol Hill.

Born in Bryn Mawr, Pennsylvania, Billington received his 1950 B.A. from Princeton, where he was valedictorian, and his 1953 D.Phil. from Oxford University's Balliol College, as a Rhodes Scholar. After Army service (1953–56), he taught history at Harvard (1957), the Russian Research Center (1958–61), and Princeton (1961–73), and lectured widely in the United States and abroad. He was active on the Board of Foreign Scholarships (1971–76), as Chairman from 1971, and was director of the Woodrow Wilson International Center for Scholars from 1973, before becoming Library of Congress head (1987–   ). A longtime editorial advisor of *Foreign Affairs*, his books include *Mikhailovsky and Russian Populism* (1958), *The Icon and the Axe: An Interpretative History of Russian Culture* (1966), *The Arts of Russia* (1970), *Fire in the Minds of Men: Origins of the Revolutionary Faith* (1980), and *Russia Transformed: Breakthrough to Hope, Moscow, August 1991* (1992). Billington is married to Marjorie Anne Brennan; they have two daughters and two sons.

FURTHER READING

"Billington, James Hadley." *Current Biography*, May 1989.

Bird, Larry Joe (1956–   )

In February 1993, basketball great Larry Bird, forced by a bad back to retire, was honored at a special televised 2 1/2-hour "Larry Bird Night," at Boston Garden, attended by numerous basketball luminaries, including his old friend and rival, Earvin "Magic" Johnson. Bird's old number 33 was retired, alongside those of 18 other Celtic greats. Along with special radio and newspaper coverage in Boston, sculptor Armand LaMontagne created a larger-than-life-size 7-foot, 275-pound wooden sculpture of Bird that was sent on a six-week tour of New England, and Leroy Neman created a portrait of Bird, with 1,033 reproductions of it sold. The celebratory events raised over $1 million for local charities.

Bird continued his affiliation with the Celtics, as special assistant scouting new talent for the team, and also ran a mini-camp in July. From 1992, he was also a member of the board of directors of USA Basketball, helping to select players for future international competitions, including the 1994 world championships in Toronto and the 1996 Olympics in Atlanta.

In March 1993, doctors performed a fusion operation on the back that had forced Bird's August 1992 retirement, and had severely impeded his play for at least two years before then. In June 1991, Bird had an operation on a disk in his lower back. Also during 1993, Bird and his wife, Dinah, adopted a baby girl, their second child.

Indiana-born Bird was the high-scoring star forward of the Indiana University team (1976–79), named Collegiate Player of the Year by AP, UPI, and the National Association of Coaches (1978–79). He led the team to the 1979 National Collegiate Athletic Association (NCAA) championship round, there ultimately losing to Earvin "Magic" Johnson's Michigan State team. Bird and Johnson became basketball's two major stars from then on, their friendly rivalry being considered largely responsible for the widened popularity of the sport. Joining the Boston Celtics in 1979, Bird was named National Basketball Association Rookie of the Year in 1980, the league's most valuable player (MVP) three times (1984; 1985; 1986), and an All-Star 12 times, as a starter for nine straight years (1980–88); he was named most valuable player of the All-Star game 1982. He led the Celtics to three championships (1981; 1984; 1986) and was named playoff MVP twice (1984; 1986), as well as being NBA scoring leader (1984) and winning the first three of the popular three-point shot contests held on All-Star weekend. Bird ran into a series of injuries in the late 1980s, and was sidelined for long periods during the 1990–91 and 1991–92 seasons, returning only for limited periods. He ended his career as 11th among all-time NBA scoring leaders, with 21,791 points, though his old teammate Robert Parish moved past him in November 1993, dropping him to 12th place. He and Johnson were co-captains of the U.S. "Dream Team" that won the 1992 Olympic basketball gold medal at Barcelona. His autobiography, *Drive: The Story of My Life*, written with Bob Ryan, was published in 1989. Bird married Dinah Mattingly in 1989; they have two adopted children. He also has a daughter from a previous marriage.

FURTHER READING

The Big Three. PETER MAY. Simon & Schuster, 1994.
"Larry Bird." BOB RYAN. *Sport*, June 1993.
"The two and only." BOB RYAN. *Sports Illustrated*, Dec. 14, 1992.
"The brother from another planet." CHARLES P. PIERCE. *Esquire*, Feb. 1992.
Larry Bird. BOB ITALIA. Abdo & Daughters, 1992.
Sports Great Larry Bird. JACK KAVANAGH. Enslow, 1992.
"Guts and glory. . . ." J. DAVID MILLER et al. *Sport*, July 1991.
Magic Johnson Larry Bird. BRUCE WEBER. Avon, 1986.

Bixby, Bill (1934–93)

San Francisco-born Bill Bixby starred in several television series. He was best known to worldwide television audiences as gentle scientist David Banner, who turned periodically into an extraordinarily violent green monster (played by Lou Ferrigno) in the series "The Incredible Hulk" (1978–82). Bixby had previously starred in the television series "My Favorite Martian" (1963–66) and "The Courtship of Eddie's Father" (1969–72). He later starred opposite Mariette Hartley in the series "Goodnight Beantown" (1983–84), and also appeared in many television films, then turning largely to direction in his later years. His theatrical films included *Lonely Are the Brave*, *Irma La Douce*, and *Kentucky Fried Movie*. He also appeared in several plays, among them *Under the Yum-Yum Tree* (1964). He was survived by his wife Judith Kliban. (d. Century City, California; November 21, 1993)

FURTHER READING

"Bill Bixby. . . ." DEBORAH STARR SEIBEL. *TV Guide*, Dec. 4, 1993.
Obituary. *The Times* (of London), Nov. 24, 1993.
Obituary. *New York Times*, Nov. 23, 1993.
Obituary. *Variety*, Nov. 23, 1993.

Blackmun, Harry Andrew (1908–)

Now in his mid-80s, once-conservative Blackmun during 1993 played a major role as the leading dissenter in a far more conservative Court than the one he had entered in 1970. He wrote dissenting opinions in several major cases, very notably in *Herrera v. Collins*, which sharply limited the ability of those on death row to gain stays of execution on the basis of alleged later discovery of new evidence. He also wrote a dissenting opinion in *Zobrest v. Catalina Foothills School District*, ruling that local governments could pay for special services to the disabled in parochial schools, as compliance with federal equal educational opportunities for the disabled laws. He was the sole dissenter in *Sale v. Haitian Centers Council*, which ruled that Haitian refugees could be intercepted in international waters and forcibly returned to Haiti without violating American and international law. He also joined the minority in *Bray v. Alexandria Women's Health Clinic*, which allowed abortion protestors to legally block abortion clinics; *Shaw v. Reno*, which made it possible to challenge "bizarrely" shaped voting districts formed to provide minority representation as unconstitutional; *Alexander v. Reno*, which ruled that the First Amendment did not protect $25 million of books and movies destroyed, many of them not obscene, after a seller had been convicted as a pornographer for selling 4 obscene magazines and 3 obscene videotapes; and *St. Mary's Honor Center v. Hicks*, ruling that workers must provide proof of specific discrimination against them to claim protection of civil rights laws, sharply altering the previous burden of proof.

Blackmun did vote with the majority in several notable cases, including the landmark *Harris v. Forklift Systems*, in which the Court ruled unanimously that workers need not prove that they had suffered psychological damage or were unable to perform their tasks to successfully charge sexual harassment, instead applying the rule of "workplace equity;" *Lamb's Chapel v. Center Moriches Union Free School District*, in which the Court ruled unanimously that religious groups had equal access to school facilities with other organizations in the community; *Church of the Lukumi Babalu Aye v. City of Hialeah*, in which a unanimous Court ruled unconstitutional three city ordinances banning ritual animal sacrifice; and a unanimous *Wisconsin v. Mitchell*, ruling that states could prescribe increased sentences for hate-motivated crimes. In a rare move for a sitting Justice, Blackmun also granted an extensive televised interview to Ted Koppel and Nina Totenberg.

Nashville-born Blackmun practiced and taught law in Minneapolis during the 1930s and 1940s, and was then counsel to the Mayo Clinic (1950–59). He was named to the Eighth Circuit of the U.S. Court of Appeals in 1959 and was appointed by President Richard Nixon to the Supreme Court in 1970. His course in the liberal Warren Court of the time was thought to be moderately conservative; but in later years Blackmun's unwavering commitment to what were seen by most as a set of liberal positions on civil and personal rights placed him with the liberal minority in a more conservative Court. His 1929 B.A. and 1932 LL.B. were from Harvard University. He married Dorothy Clark in 1941; they have three children.

FURTHER READING

Harry Blackmun. BOB ITALIA. Abdo & Daughters, 1992.
"A new day in court." LAUREN TARSHIS and JAMES EARL HARDY. *Scholastic Update*, Nov. 1, 1991.

Bolton, Michael (1953–) Singer, songwriter, and guitarist Bolton was honored by his peers in 1993; at the 20th annual American Music Awards, he was named favorite male pop/rock artist and favorite adult contemporary artist of the year, and at Broadcast Music Inc.'s 41st Annual Pop Awards Dinner he and Mariah Carey were named the year's top songwriters.

In late October, Bolton issued the well-received single "Said I Loved You . . . But I Lied," and in late November issued the equally well-received album *The One Thing*, for which the sin-

gle was a preview; it included such songs as the title cut, "Completely," "Lean On Me," and "Soul Of My Soul." His albums *Time, Love and Tenderness* and *Timeless (the Classics)* continued to sell well. He also participated in the Pediatric AIDS Foundation recording *For Our Children: The Concert*, singing "You Are My Sunshine."

Bolton toured during much of 1993, as always playing softball at every opportunity. He also did the video "Michael Bolton's Winning Softball: Hit Harder, Play Smarter."

Bolton began his career in the late 1960s, while still a teenager in New Haven, Connecticut. He emerged as a leading lyricist in the mid-1980s, as co-writer of "How Am I Supposed To Live Without You" (1983), and as a popular singer in 1987, singing his own "That's What Love Is All About." His albums also include *The Hunger* (1987), *Soul Provider* (1989; he won a Grammy for best male vocal), *Time, Love and Tenderness* (1991), and *Timeless (The Classics)* (1992). He was formerly married, and has three children.

FURTHER READING

"Bolton, Michael." *Current Biography*, Aug. 1993.
"Michael Bolton. . . ." LAURA MORICE. *McCall's*, Aug. 1993.
"Michael Bolton." LAURA MORICE. *Us*, Feb. 1993.
"Nine million Michael Bolton fans. . . ." MICHAEL ANGELI. *Esquire*, Jan. 1993.
Michael Bolton: Time, Love, and Tenderness. LEE RANDALL. Simon & Schuster, 1993.
"The power source. . . ." STEVE DOUGHERTY. *People*, Dec. 7, 1992.
"Michael Bolton. . . ." DAVE DiMARTINO. *Entertainment Weekly*, Oct. 23, 1992.
"Michael Bolton." *Teen Magazine*, Aug. 1990.
"Once just a name. . . ." CYNTHOA SANZ. *People*, Apr. 23, 1990.

Bonds, Barry Lamar (1964–) San Francisco Giants left-fielder Barry Bonds was named the National League's most valuable player for the third time in four seasons. Only seven other players have ever been named league MVP three times—Stan Musial, Roy Campanella, Mike Schmidt, Jimmie Foxx, Joe DiMaggio, Yogi Berra, and Mickey Mantle—but none in just four years. And it was almost four in a row, for Bonds narrowly missed the MVP award in 1991. Legendary outfielder Willie Mays, Bonds's godfather, presented the 1992 MVP trophy to Bonds before the April 13, 1993 game.

Bonds had joined the Giants in 1993 with the richest baseball contract ever—$43.75 million for six years; by contract, he received a $100,000 bonus for being named MVP. He had led his previous team, the Pittsburgh Pirates, to three Division Championships, and almost did the same for the Giants, starting off the season with a home run, batting .431 in April, and taking his team to first place by May; but the Giants were squeezed out at the end by the Atlanta Braves, partly because Bonds had a mid-September slump, though he came on strong in the last 16 games. For the season, he had a .336 batting average, 46 home runs, and 123 runs batted in, all career highs, and led the league in several categories, including home runs, RBIs, on-base percentage, slugging percentage, extra-base hits, total bases, home run/at bat ratio, and RBI/at bat ratio.

California-born Bonds attended Arizona State University, and was named to the *Sporting News* Collegiate All-America team (1985). He spent his first years in the major leagues with the Pittsburgh Pirates (1986–92). His father is former major league player Bobby Bonds, who is also the Giants' batting and first base coach.

FURTHER READING

Barry Bonds: Baseball's Complete Player. MILES HARVEY. Childrens, 1994.
"Family of Giants." JOHNNY DODD. *People*, Oct. 4, 1993.
"Barry Bonds. . . ." WALTER LEAVY. *Ebony*, Sep. 1993.
"Barry Bonds' big bat. . . ." *Jet*, Aug. 9, 1993.
"Barry Bonds." *Playboy*, July 1993.
"Barry at the bat." BRUCE SCHOENFELD. *Sporting News*, June 14, 1993.
"The importance of being Barry." RICHARD HOFFER. *Sports Illustrated*, May 24, 1993.
"Barry Bonds." JEFF WEINSTOCK. *Sport*, Apr. 1993.
"30/30 vision. . . ." HANK HERSCH. *Sports Illustrated*, June 25, 1990.

Boulding, Kenneth (1910–93) Liverpool-born Kenneth Boulding, an Anglo-American economist, philosopher, author, and Quaker peace activist, was educated at New College, Oxford and did his graduate work at the University of Chicago. He taught at Edinburgh University (1934–37) before beginning his long career in the United States with a teaching position at Colgate University (1937–41); in 1948, he became an American citizen. He taught at Fisk University, Iowa State College, McGill University, the University of Michigan, and from 1967 at the University of Colorado. He also worked as an economist at the League of Nations in the early 1940s, and was director of the University of Michigan's conflict resolution center during the 1960s, in that period becoming a leading academic opponent of the Vietnam War. A prolific writer, his works included hundreds of books and articles. He was survived by his wife, Elise, and four sons. (d. Boulder, Colorado; March 19, 1993)

FURTHER READING

Obituary. *Current Biography*, May 1993.
Obituary. *The Times* (of London), Mar. 22, 1993.
Three Scientists and Their Gods: A Search for Meaning in an Age of Information. ROBERT WRIGHT. Random, 1988.

Bourgés-Maunoury, Maurice (1914–93) Former French prime minister Maurice Bourgés-Maunoury began his career in 1935, as an army officer. He was captured by the Germans during the World War II Battle of France (1940), imprisoned, and released in 1941, then becoming active in the Resistance. As "Polygone," he became a chief Resistance leader in southwestern France. He went into politics after the war, becoming a Radical Party national assembly deputy in 1946, served in a series of cabinet-level posts from 1947, and was defense minister during the 1956 Suez crisis. He served as prime minister during the summer and early autumn of 1957, one of a long series of ineffective pre-De Gaulle French leaders. His public life largely ended after the loss of his assembly seat in 1958, and he then pursued a business and financial career. He was survived by a daughter and two sons. (d. Paris; February 10, 1993)

FURTHER READING

Obituary. *The Times* (of London), Feb. 20, 1993.

Boutros Ghali, Boutros (1922–) During his second full year as United Nations Secretary General, Egyptian diplomat and lawyer Boutros Boutros Ghali continued his attempt to expand UN peacekeeping operations throughout the world, and ultimately to develop a UN "army" devoted to peacekeeping. He found little

support for the UN army concept, but during 1992 was able to mount very substantial operations in several countries, adding these to more than four decades of peacekeeping operations around the world, as on the India-Pakistan border, Iraq, the Israeli borders, Cyprus, and El Salvador. Perhaps the most successful of these was the Cambodian force, at its peak numbering 22,000 and by the end of 1993 almost all withdrawn from free Cambodia.

But several operations mounted or expanded by Boutros Ghali ran into serious trouble in 1993, most notably those in the former Yugoslavia, Somalia, Angola, and Haiti. Boutros Ghali was especially firm in his resolve to keep the UN in Somalia, engaging in a major dispute with the Clinton administration in an effort to keep American troops there, even after withdrawal dates had been announced by President Clinton, who had barely managed to extract a few more months in Somalia from a very reluctant Congress. Ultimately, Boutros Ghali found the UN less and less responsive to new pleas for peacekeeping intervention, and re-evaluating its peacekeeping role as demands mounted, while funds and the will to intervene dwindled.

Cairo-born Boutros Ghali attended Cairo University and the University of Paris. He was a professor of international law and head of the political science department at Cairo University, and has long been active in international law, political studies, and human rights organizations. He was Egypt's Minister of State for Foreign Affairs (1987–91) and became deputy prime minister in 1991. On January 1, 1992, Boutros Ghali began his five-year term as the sixth United Nations Secretary General, following Javier Pérez de Cuéllar, whose second five-year term expired on December 31, 1991. Boutros Ghali had campaigned long and hard for the job; an experienced mediator who played a significant role in negotiating the 1978 Camp David Accords and the 1979 Egypt-Israel peace treaty, he was thought by many to be a logical choice to continue the expanded worldwide UN mediating role developed so successfully by Pérez de Cuéllar. Boutros Ghali is married to Leila Nadler.

FURTHER READING

"Great expectations." ANDREW BILSKI. *Maclean's.* Aug. 30, 1993.
"Alboutros. . . ." MICHAEL LIND. *New Republic,* June 28, 1993.
"United notions?" INA GINSBURG. *Town and Country,* Mar. 1993.
"A secretary-general. . . ." AHMED MURSI. *World Press Review,* Oct. 1992.
"North/south squaring off. . . ." CAROLE COLLINS. *National Catholic Reporter,* Sep. 25, 1992.
" 'Give me the battalions. . . .' " HARVEY MORRIS. *Independent,* Aug. 3, 1992.
"Challenge for the new boss." BONNIE ANGELO. *Time,* Feb. 3, 1992.
"The new boss will work. . . ." DIETER BUHL and FREDY GTSEIGER. *World Press Review,* Feb. 1992.
"New U.N. chief. . . ." CAROLE COLLINS. *National Catholic Reporter,* Jan. 10, 1992.
"Hello, Ghali." *Nation,* Dec. 16, 1991.
"A man for all nations." BONNIE ANGELO. *Time,* Dec. 2, 1991.

Bowe, Riddick (1967–) World heavyweight champion Riddick Bowe suffered his first defeat in the ring on November 7, 1993, losing his title to Evander Holyfield, from whom he had taken it a year earlier, on November 13, 1992. It was a hard-fought contest, with fighting sometimes continuing after the bell and with over 600 punches landed, though no knockdowns.

In a bizarre turn, a man in a motorized paraglider descended from the air into the edge of the ring outside Caesar's Palace, Las Vegas, stopping the fight for 20 minutes early in Round 7. The man, whose equipment became tangled in the lights, was pummeled by spectators, then arrested. Nearby, Bowe's pregnant wife, Judy, fainted and was hospitalized, though a sonogram revealed no damage to her or the fetus; his 82-year-old trainer, Ed Futch, was also removed for medical attention.

Earlier in the year, Bowe had defended his title against a February challenge by Michael Dokes, winning with a technical knockout just 2:19 into the first round at New York's Madison Square Garden, and another in May by Jesse Ferguson, who was knocked out 17 seconds into the second round at Washington D.C.'s RFK Stadium. A contest with WBC heavyweight champion Lennox Lewis was much discussed, but did not eventuate. Bowe had made a six-fight deal with HBO that could have earned him as much as $100 million, but that was contingent on his retaining his title.

In February and March, Bowe had also visited South Africa, where he met Nelson Mandela, and Italy, where he met the Pope. In August, for the Arthur Ashe Tennis Challenge to benefit the Arthur Ashe Foundation for the Defeat of AIDS, Bowe had acted as chair umpire for a doubles match pairing Holyfield and Magdalena Maleeva against New York Mayor David Dinkins and Gigi Fernandez, the victors. In September, Bowe brought Holyfield with him to visit Frederick Douglass Junior High School, in Washington, D.C., as part of his attempt to inspire inner-city young people. He also appeared in a public service rap video "Whatcha Gonna Do About Hate."

Born in the Brownsville section of Brooklyn, Bowe was the youngest boy of 13 children raised by an abandoned mother, and was the family's only high school graduate, from Thomas Jefferson High, in 1986. Inspired by Muhammad Ali, he started training at the Bedford Stuyvesant Boxing Association in 1981, and won four New York Golden Gloves titles, going on to win a silver medal at the 1988 Seoul Olympics, losing to British boxer Lennox Lewis, after a controversial fight stoppage. He turned professional in 1989, and built a record of 34 wins and no losses before the November 1993 loss to Holyfield. He was world champion for nearly a year after winning a memorable November 13, 1992 contest over Holyfield, named "Fight of the Year." Bowe then held a unified heavyweight title, but in an argument involving Lennox Lewis, he threw away his WBC belt, with Lewis then becoming WBC champion by default. Bowe and his wife Judy grew up in the same neighborhood and married in 1986; they have three children.

FURTHER READING

"Wild night." PAT PUTNAM. *Sports Illustrated*, Nov. 15, 1993.
"Float like a butterfly. . . ." JANICE C. SIMPSON. *Time*, Nov. 8, 1993.
"Riddick Bowe." NELL SCOVELL. *Vanity Fair*, Nov. 1993.
"This Bowe knows boxing." WILLIAM PLUMMER. *People*, Feb. 8, 1993.
"Big bopper." CHRIS SMITH. *New York*, Feb. 8, 1993.
"Three minutes to history. . . ." KATHERINE DUNN. *Esquire*, Feb. 1993.
"The other kid from Brownsville. . . ." MIKE LUPICA. *Esquire*, Feb. 1993.
"The family man." STEVE HYMON. *Sports Illustrated*, Nov. 30, 1992.
"Riddick Bowe." JEFF RYAN. *Sport*, July 1992.

Bowie, David (David Robert Jones; 1947–)

Multifaceted rock star, songwriter, and actor David Bowie issued his first solo album in six years in 1993: *Black Tie White Noise*, co-produced with Nile Rodgers. The album's most popular song, "Jump They Say," was issued as a cassette single in March, before the April album release, and also appeared in video form. Other notable cuts from the album were "Pallas Athena," and the title song. Bowie also wrote and played the soundtrack of the British television series "The Buddha of Suburbia," adapted from the Hanif Kureishi novel. In addition, he issued a major retrospective of his work: *Bowie— The Singles Collection*. Although Bowie had no films during the year, he did contribute commentary to an expanded videodisc version of his first film, the science fiction classic *The Man Who Fell to Earth* (1976), as did director Nicolas Roeg. Bowie continued to support AIDS research, contributing several works to a silent auction of celebrity artworks, to benefit the American Foundation for AIDS Research.

Bowie became a leading rock singer and songwriter in 1969, with publication of his first song, "Space Oddity," followed by such albums as *The Man Who Sold the World* (1970), *Hunky Dory* (1971), *The Rise and Fall of Ziggy Stardust and the Spiders from Mars* (1972), *Pin Ups* (1973), *Young Americans* (1975), *Lodger* (1979), *Let's Dance* (1983), *Tin Machine* (1989), *Sound + Vision* (1989), and the retrospective *Changesbowie* (1990), which added seven songs and 27 minutes to the original 1976 *Changesonebowie* album. As an actor, Bowie also starred as the alien in the film *The Man Who Fell to Earth* (1976), and appeared in such films as *Merry Christmas Mr. Lawrence* (1983) *The Last Temptation of Christ* (1988), and *The Linguini Incident* (1992), and on Broadway in *The Elephant Man* (1980). Among his written works are *David Bowie in His Own Words* (1981), *David Bowie: Tonight* (1984), and *David Bowie Anthology* (1985). Previously married to Angela Barnett (1970–80), Bowie married the model Iman in 1992; he has one child.

FURTHER READING

"Station to station." DAVID SINCLAIR. *Rolling Stone*, June 10, 1993.
"Bowie light." JERRY STAHL. *Esquire*, May 1993.
"Savage dreams of Bowie Glory." KEVIN ZIMMERMAN. *Variety*, Apr. 5, 1993.
Backstage Passes: Life on the Wild Side with David Bowie. ANGELA BOWIE and PATRICK CARR. Putnam, 1993.
"A session with David Bowie." JIM JEROME. *Life*, Dec.1, 1992.
"Architectural Digest visits. . . ." CHRISTOPHER BUCKLEY. *Architectural Digest*, Sep. 1992.
Alias David Bowie. PETER GILLMAN and LENI GILLMAN. Holt, 1987.
Stardust: The David Bowie Story. TONY ZANETTA and HENRY EDWARDS. McGraw-Hill, 1986.
Bowie. JERRY HOPKINS. Macmillan, 1986.

Bradley, Bill (1943–) New Jersey Senator and former basketball star Bradley emerged further in 1993 as one of the Senate's leading Democratic liberals. Although he strongly supported the North American Free Trade Agreement (NAFTA), which was almost universally opposed by organized labor, he also called for the development of an "economic security platform" for all Americans, which would include universal health insurance, pensions, and education. He also strongly called for conclusion of the stalled GATT (General Agreement on Tariff and Trade) negotiations, seeking enhancement of world trade and job creation, and for the adoption of such community and job-building innovations as community stimulus banks and neighborhood reconstruction corps. The former Olympic star also sponsored a Senate resolution opposing award of the 2000 Olympic Games to Beijing, because of continuing Chinese human rights violations. In his home base, New Jersey, Bradley campaigned for defeated Democratic gubernatorial candidate James Florio, and continued to build his own support in anticipation of future Republican challenges.

Missouri-born Bradley received his 1965 B.A. from Princeton University and his 1968 M.A. from Oxford University, which he attended as a Rhodes scholar. He was a highly successful professional basketball player with the New York Knicks (1967–77), a mobile forward with an outstanding long shot, who helped his team to two National Basketball Association (NBA) championships (1970 and 1973). He served with the U.S. Air Force Reserves (1967–78). On his retirement from sports, Bradley moved into politics, as a Democratic senator from New Jersey (1979–), and quickly emerged as a leading Senate liberal, active on the finance and energy committees, as well as on the select committee on aging. Although often mentioned as a potential presidential or vice-presidential candidate, he decided not to make a run for either post in 1992, instead making one of the three Democratic convention nominating speeches for Bill Clinton and campaigning actively for the Clinton-Gore ticket. He is also a member of the National Advisory Council on Rights of the Child and the National Commission to Prevent Infant Mortality. Among his written works are the autobiographical *Life on the Run* (1976), *The Fair Tax* (1984), and (with several co-authors) *Implications of Soviet New Thinking* (1988). Bradley married Ernestine Schlant in 1974; they have one daughter.

FURTHER READING

" 'This was not what you'd call . . .' " STEPHEN B. SHEPARD et al. *Business Week*, Aug. 16, 1993.
"Senator Lazarus. . . ." MORTON KONDRACKE. *New Republic*, Sep. 2, 1991.
"Bill folds. . . ." JOHN B. JUDIS. *New Republic*, Jan. 28, 1991.
"Bradley's time." GERRI HIRSHEY. *Rolling Stone*, June 14, 1990.
"Sharing a dream with. . . ." DAWN GRAFF-HAIGHT. *Current Health*, Feb. 1990.

Brady, James (1944–) and Sarah Kemp Brady (1942–) In 1993, Sarah and James Brady won a major victory in their long battle for gun control. On November 11, the Brady gun control bill passed in the House of Representatives. But in the week that followed, the opposition of some Republican Senators

hardened, spurred by last-ditch lobbying by the National Rifle Association; led by Minority Leader Bob Dole, Senate Republicans began a filibuster, which the Democrats were unable to break. Ultimately, however, faced with massive popular support for the Brady bill, powerfully led by President Clinton, the Republicans ended their filibuster. Clinton signed the Brady Handgun Control Law on November 30.

James Brady, President Ronald Reagan's press secretary, was seriously wounded during John Hinckley's March 31, 1981 presidential assassination attempt, shot with a cheap $29 handgun; he remains partially paralyzed. After the incident, Sarah Kemp Brady, his wife, became an extraordinarily effective crusader for gun control, her work continuing and expanding throughout the 1980s and into the 1990s. She is chairman of Handgun Control, Inc. James Brady joined her in the fight for gun control after leaving his job as Reagan's press secretary in 1988.

The Bradys had seemed to score a major victory in 1991, with Congressional passage of the Brady Handgun Violence Prevention Act, the "Brady Bill," as part of the 1991 Crime Bill, with the help of former President Reagan and the seeming agreement of then-President George Bush. But ultimately Bush threatened to veto the entire Crime Bill, and without enough votes to overturn a veto, no gun control law was enacted.

The Bradys came back in 1992, in January joining Maryland Governor William Schaefer in his attempt to ban military-style assault weapons, and campaigned again very effectively during the presidential campaign. Still pressing for passage of the Brady Bill, Handgun Control, Inc. ran ads featuring President Reagan endorsing handgun control, and campaigned for congressional passage throughout the year. And on October 18, three weeks before the presidential election, Sarah Brady, a lifelong Republican, strongly endorsed Bill Clinton, calling Bush a president "fearful of crossing special interest gun lobbies."

Grand Rapids-born James Brady practiced law in Michigan (1969–77), and was a U.S. attorney in western Michigan (1977–81), then becoming presidential press secretary. He attended the University of Western Michigan and Notre Dame. Sarah Kemp Brady is an experienced political professional, who worked for the Republican Congressional Committee in the late 1960s and then was an administrative assistant

to two Republican congressmen (1970–74) and an administrator with the Republican National Committee (1974–78). James and Sarah Brady have one son; he also has a daughter from a previous marriage.

FURTHER READING

"Brady, James S." *Current Biography*, Oct. 1991. *Thumbs Up: The Jim Brady Story*. MOLLIE DICKENSON. Morrow, 1987.

Branagh, Kenneth (1960–) Multitalented British stage and screen figure Branagh adapted, directed, co-produced, and starred as Benedick in a very well-received new film version of Shakespeare's *Much Ado about Nothing*, released in 1993, and published an accompanying book, *Much Ado About Nothing: The Making of the Movie*. His co-stars were Emma Thompson as Beatrice, Denzel Washington as Don Pedro, and Michael Keaton as Dogberry. Branagh also appeared in the quite different Disney film *Swing Kids*, in an uncredited role. He also added another honor to his growing list, winning an Oscar nomination for his 23-minute film "Swan Song," a theater piece starring John Gielgud.

Forthcoming was another major film, a Francis Coppola-produced remake of the classic *Frankenstein*, based on the Mary Shelley novel, with Branagh directing and starring as Victor Frankenstein, opposite Robert DeNiro as the monster, in a cast that includes Helena Bonham-Carter, Tom Hulce, Aidan Quinn, John Cleese, and Ian Holm.

Belfast-born Branagh was one of the most promising theater people to come out of the 1980s. After attending the Royal Academy of Dramatic Art (RADA), he debuted in London in *Another Country*, then quickly became a notable Shakespearean actor, starring on stage as *Hamlet* and *Henry V* (at age 23) and directing and producing *Romeo and Juliet*, all in Britain. In 1987, he starred in the highly regarded television series "The Fortunes of War," co-starring Emma Thompson, and in the film *A Month in the Country*. After a notable split with the Royal Shakespeare Company, he founded the Renaissance Theatre Company (1987), and two years later brought to the United States stage productions of Shakespeare's *Midsummer Night's Dream* and *King Lear*, and Ibsen's *Ghosts*, starring in the latter two; *Ghosts* also appeared on television. In 1989, he also made his directorial debut and starred in a new film version of Shakespeare's *Henry V*; he won the Directors Guild of America's D. W. Griffith Award for best director, the movie was named the British Film Institute's best film, and both he and the film gained Oscar nominations. His first American film was *Dead Again* (1991). His films also include *Peter's Friends* (1992). Branagh published an autobiography, *Beginning*, in 1990, at age 28; he had earlier written and produced a play, *Public Enemy*. He married Emma Thompson in 1989.

FURTHER READING

"Much ado about Shakespeare." *Economist*, Oct. 2, 1993.
"Much ado about Branagh." DINITIA SMITH. *New York*, May 24, 1993.
"Baby grand old man." PAUL DONOVAN. *Sunday Times*, Apr. 19, 1992.
"Branagh. . . ." *Cosmopolitan*, Oct. 1991.
"Vaulting ambition. . . ." F.X. FEENEY. *American Film*, Sep.-Oct. 1991.
"Stratford on Sunset. . . ." JOHANNA SCHNELLER. *GQ-Gentlemen's Quarterly*, Sep. 1991.
"Renaissance man." GEORGINA HOWELL. *Vogue*, Sep. 1991.
"L.A. bard." *Esquire*, Sep. 1991.
"The man who would be king. . . ." KIM HUBBARD. *People*, Feb. 12, 1990.
"A rising star enlivens Shakespeare." GARY ARNOLD. *Insight*, Jan. 15, 1990.

Brandon, Henry (Oscar Henry Brandeis; 1916–93)

Czech-British journalist Henry Brandon began his long career as a sportswriter in Prague in the late 1930s; after taking refuge in London from the Nazis, he began his distinguished career in British journalism, working as a freelancer for London's *Sunday Times*, until joining the paper as a war correspondent in 1943. After the war, he was the highly-respected *Sunday Times* Washington correspondent (1949–83), becoming a major figure in British and American journalism. He also wrote a weekly column for *The Saturday Review* (1961–71), and contributed articles to a wide range of other publications. From 1983 until his death, he was a Brookings Institution guest scholar. His books included *As We Were* (1961), *In the Red* (1967), *The Retreat of American Power* (1971), *Special Relationships: A Foreign Corre-*spondent's *Memoirs from Roosevelt to Reagan* (1989), and *In Search of a New World Order: The Future of U.S.-European Relations* (1992). He was survived by his wife, Mabel Hobart Wentworth, a daughter, and two stepdaughters. (d. London; April 20, 1993)

FURTHER READING

"Lifetime of scoops. . . ." HAROLD EVANS. *Sunday Times* (of London), Apr. 25, 1993.
Obituary. *The Times* (of London), Apr. 22, 1993.
Obituary. *New York Times*, Apr. 21, 1993.

Braun, Carol Elizabeth Moseley

(1947–) Illinois Democratic Senator Carol Moseley Braun was the first African-American woman to become a U.S. Senator and during 1993 was the only African-American in the Senate. On entering that body, she and also-new Senator Dianne Feinstein became members of the Senate Judiciary Committee, actively recruited by committee chair Senator Joseph Biden, who had been extremely embarrassed by his leadership of the then-all-male committee during the Anita Faye Hill-Clarence Thomas confrontation. She also joined the Banking Committee.

Braun played a highly publicized and quite unusual role in what was to some a minor and for others a major and historic reversal in the Senate on July 22. The Judiciary Committee had voted 13–2 against renewal of the United Daughters of the Conferacy (UDC) design patent on a logo incorporating the design of the flag of the Confederate States of America. The full Senate, on an amendment to another bill, introduced by Senator Jesse Helms, was about to renew the patent. Braun rose, spoke passionately against the action, as insulting to African-Americans, told the Senate she was ready to mount a lone filibuster against the action, and won the majority of Senators to her position. The patent was defeated 75–25, generating a considerable national dialogue.

Chicago-born Braun's 1967 B.A. was from the University of Illinois, and her 1972 J.D. from the University of Chicago. She was an assistant district attorney (1973–77), a member of the Illinois Assembly (1979–89), and Cook County Recorder of Deeds (1990–92). She had not originally planned to run for the Senate, but had been appalled by the treatment of Anita Faye

Hill by the then-all-male Senate Judiciary Committee, as had many other women who then decided to run for office in 1992. In the Democratic primary race, she defeated lawyer Alfred Hofeld and incumbent Senator Alan J. Dixon, who had voted for the Supreme Court nomination of Clarence Thomas. She won election to the Senate by a landslide 55 percent of the vote, over her opponent, Republican Richard S. Williamson. She was formerly married to lawyer Michael Braun and has one child.

FURTHER READING

Carol Moseley-Braun: Breaking Barriers. MELLONEE CARRIGAN. Childrens, 1994.
"A star is born. . . ." RUTH SHALIT. *New Republic*, Nov. 15, 1993.
"Carol Moseley-Braun. . . ." DONNA BRITT. *Glamour*, Nov. 1993.
"Carol Moseley Braun. . . ." *NEA Today*, Mar. 1993.
"Carol Moseley Braun. . . ." *Jet*, Nov. 23, 1992.
"Behind the Braun phenomenon." GRETCHEN REYNOLDS. *Chicago*, Oct. 1992.
"A woman's place is in the house. . . ." LYNN SWEET. *Self*, Oct. 1992.
"Carol Moseley Braun. . . ." JILL NELSON. *Essence*, Oct. 1992.
"Woman of the year?" JOHN R. COYNE, JR. *National Review*, Sep. 14, 1992.

Bridges, Beau (Lloyd Vernet Bridges, III; 1941–)

Film and television star Bridges was joined by his father, veteran actor Lloyd Bridges, in a new prime-time hour-long television series "Harts of the West," about a family that moves to Nevada. He also won an Emmy as best supporting actor in a miniseries or special for his role in the television film *The Positively True Adventures of the Alleged Texas Cheerleader-Murdering Mom*, starring Holly Hunter as a Texas mother who allegedly arranged to kill the mother of her eighth-grade daughter's cheerleading rival.

On film, Bridges starred opposite Stockard Channing in *Married to It*, an ensemble film about the marital troubles and adjustments of three couples, directed by Arthur Hiller and co-starring Robert Sean Leonard, Mary Stuart Masterson, Cybill Shepherd, and Ron Silver. He also starred opposite Chuck Norris in the film *Sidekicks*, directed by Aaron Norris.

On the personal side, Wendy and Beau Bridges became the parents of their third child, Ezekiel.

As a child, Beau Bridges appeared in such films as *Force of Evil* (1948) and *The Red Pony* (1949). From his late teens, he emerged as a Hollywood star, in such films as *Gaily* (1969), *The Landlord* (1970), *Lovin' Molly* (1974), *The Other Side of the Mountain* (1975), *Norma Rae* (1979), *Heart Like a Wheel* (1983), *The Iron Triangle* (1989), and *The Fabulous Baker Boys* (1989), and in such telefilms as *The Child Stealer* (1979), *The Runner Stumbles* (1979), *Witness for the Prosecution* (1984), *Space* (1985), *Women and Men: Stories of Seduction* (1989), *Without Warning: The James Brady Story* (1991), and *Wildflower* (1991). Los Angeles-born Bridges is the son of actor Lloyd Bridges and the brother of actor Jeff Bridges, his co-star in *Baker Boys*. Bridges attended the University of California at Los Angeles. Previously divorced, he is married to Wendy Bridges; he has five children.

FURTHER READING

"Alas, this Beau knows guns. . . ." TOM GLIATTO. *People*, July 1, 1991.
"On a movie set. . . ." KAREN DE WITT. *New York Times*, Dec. 18, 1990.

Bridges, James (1935–93)

Writer and director James Bridges began his career as an actor, appearing in several television series during the 1950s; in that period also moving into television scriptwriting, most notably for the "Alfred Hitchcock Hour." He moved into theatre direction with Jack Larson's *The Candied House* (1966). He co-wrote several screenplays in the late 1960s, including *The Appaloosa* (1966), and began the major portion of his career by writing and directing the theatrical film *The Baby Maker* (1970). His first commercial hit was *The Paper Chase* (1973), which he wrote and directed. His recognition as a major filmmaker came with *The China Syndrome* (1979), starring Jane Fonda, Jack Lemmon, and Michael Douglas, which he wrote and directed. Among his other films were *Urban Cowboy* (1980; as writer and director), *Bright Lights, Big City* (1988; as director), and *White Hunter, Black Heart* (1990; as writer). He was survived by his companion, Jack Larson. (d. Los Angeles; June 6, 1993)

FURTHER READING

Obituary. *The Times* (of London), June 8, 1993.
Obituary. *New York Times*, June 8, 1993.

Jeff Bridges (right) and Isabella Rossellini

Bridges, Jeff (1949–   ) In yet another powerful character role, Jeff Bridges starred in 1993 as San Francisco architect Max Klein, who emerges from an airplane crash physically untouched but in fact vastly changed by the experience, in the film *Fearless*, directed by Peter Weir, and adapted by Rafael Yglesias from his own novel. Isabella Rossellina and John Turturro co-starred.

In a change of pace, Bridges also starred as the villain in *The Vanishing*, opposite Kiefer Sutherland and Sandra Bullock; George Sluizer directed. Forthcoming was yet another change of pace—a starring role in the action film *Blown Away*, as the head of a bomb squad, opposite Tommy Lee Jones as the bomber who is out to kill him; Stephen Hopkins was directing.

Bridges continued to be active in social causes as well, with Valerie Harper organizing a sympathy celebrity hunger strike to support the hunger strike of Ohio Democratic Representative Tony P. Hall, to protest the abolition of the House Select Committee on Hunger.

Los Angeles-born Bridges is one of the leading American film actors of the last two decades, in such films as *The Last Picture Show* (1971; and

its 1990 sequel *Texasville*); *Hearts of the West* (1975); *Starman* (1984); *Tucker* (1989); *The Fabulous Baker Boys* (1989), opposite his brother, Beau Bridges; *The Fisher King* (1990); and *American Heart* (1992). Jeff and Beau Bridges are the sons of actor Lloyd Bridges; Jeff played his first screen role at the age of eight, in his father's television series, "Sea Hunt." He is married to photographer Susan Geston; they have three children.

FURTHER READING

"The reluctant star." JANET MASLIN. *New York Times Magazine*, Oct. 17, 1993.
"What I learned from love." TOM SELIGSON. *Parade*, July 11, 1993.
"Jeff Bridges." TIM CAHILL. *Esquire*, Oct. 1991.
"Jeff Bridges." JOHN CLARK. *Premiere*, May 1991.
"Bridges, Jeff." *Current Biography*, Mar. 1991.
"Lone star Bridges." MARTHA FRANKEL. *American Film*, Oct. 1990.

Briseno, Theodore J.: See King, Rodney.

Broderick, Matthew (1962–   ) In 1993, Matthew Broderick starred opposite Annabella Sciorra in the film comedy *The Night We Never Met*, written and directed by Warren Leight; they play two of the three unrelated, time-sharing tenants of a city apartment, from which the featherweight plot develops. Broderick also starred opposite Jack Lemmon in the far more serious television film, *A Life in the Theatre*, adapted by David Mamet from his own play and directed by Gregory Mosher. Forthcoming was the film *Mrs. Parker and the Roundtable*, written and directed by Alan Rudolph, and co-starring Jennifer Jason Leigh, Campbell Scott, Sam Robards, Martha Plimpton, and Matt Malloy.

New York City-born Broderick, the son of actor James Broderick, emerged as a leading young stage and screen actor in the early 1980s. On stage, he won a Tony for *Brighton Beach Memoirs* (1983), and also appeared in such plays as *Torch Song Trilogy* (1981), *Biloxi Blues* (1985), and *The Widow Clare* (1986). On screen, he appeared in several popular films, including *Wargames* (1983), *Ladyhawke* (1985), *Ferris Bueller's Day Off* (1986), *Project X* (1986), *Torch Song Trilogy* (1988), *Biloxi Blues* (1988), *The Freshman* (1989), *Family Business* (1989), *Glory* (1989), and *Out on a Limb* (1992).

FURTHER READING

"In step with. . . ." JAMES BRADY. *Parade*, May 16, 1993.
"Glory days." JOHN SEDGWICK. *GQ—Gentlemen's Quarterly*, Jan. 1990.

Brokaw, Tom (Thomas John Brokaw; 1940–) In 1993, Tom Brokaw celebrated his 10th anniversary as anchor of "NBC Nightly News." During the summer he signed a new three-year contract, suggesting that those might be his last in the nightly news slot. He continued his occasional hour-long prime-time documentaries, "Brokaw Reports," in a July show focusing on lack of jobs for young people, in *The Lost Generation*. In May, he held a one-on-one televised interview with President Bill Clinton, *A Day at the White House*. But earlier his news organization had been embarrassed, and Brokaw forced to publicly apologize, over usage of misleading video footage.

For the 1993 fall season, seeking to boost its sagging prime-time line-up, NBC introduced a new weekly news program, "Now with Tom Brokaw and Katie Couric," pairing Brokaw with "Today" show co-host Couric. "Now" premiered strongly in August, its first show taking the sixth

spot in the weekly Nielsen ratings. Toward year's end "NBC Nightly News" was in second place in the ratings race among the top three networks, pulling slightly ahead of third-place CBS.

South Dakota-born Brokaw began his long career in broadcasting in 1962, and anchored news shows in Atlanta and Los Angeles during the mid-1960s, before becoming NBC White House correspondent in 1973. He became a nationally known figure as the host of the "Today" show (1976–82), and has anchored the "NBC Nightly News" since 1982, as one of the three chief American reporters and interpreters of the news. His B.A. was from the University of South Dakota. He married Meredith Lynn Auld in 1962; they have three children.

FURTHER READING

"Tom Brokaw. . . ." PETER ROSS RANGE. *TV Guide*, Oct. 2, 1993.
"50/50: happy birthday. . . ." JOANNA ELM. *TV Guide*, Feb. 3, 1990.
Anchors: Brokaw, Jennings, Rather and the Evening News. ROBERT GOLDBERG and GERALD J. GOLDBERG. Carol, 1990.

Brooks, Garth (1962–) His recording and touring career still very much in high gear, Garth Brooks was declared the world's best-selling country artist of the year at the 1993 World Music Awards. The year saw another hit album, his sixth: *In Pieces*, issued in September with such songs as "American Honky Tonk Bar Association," which appeared as a hit single in January, "Standing Outside the Fire," "The Night I Called the Old Man Out," "The Red Strokes," "Kickin' and Screamin'," "The Cowboy Song," "One Night a Day," and "Ain't Going Down ('Til the Sun Comes Up)," previously issued as a single in July. *In Pieces* spent 5 weeks at the top of the Billboard 200 list. He also issued the hit singles "Learning to Live Again" and "That Summer." During 1993, Brooks was judged by Billboard to be top artist of the year for combined singles and album in pop and country music. He was also top male pop album artist for the third straight year. Brooks also toured widely during 1993, and was scheduled to begin a European tour in March 1994. In January, Brooks contributed $1 million to Los Angeles, to help speed rebuilding after the spring 1992 riots.

Oklahoma-born Brooks began his career singing country music in cabaret. He and his wife made an unsuccessful bid to enter the Nashville country music world in 1985, but soon went home to Oklahoma. A second bid, in 1987, worked spectacularly well, resulting in his first country album *Garth Brooks* (1989), with the hit singles "If Tomorrow Never Comes" (his signature song), "Much Too Young," "The Dance," and "Not Counting You." The album sold more than 2 million copies, and Brooks became a star. His second album *No Fences* was equally successful, and contained such hit singles as "The Thunder Rolls" and "Friends in Low Places." That year saw his induction into Grand Ole Opry, and a long string of country music awards, including the Academy of Country Music and Country Music Association entertainer of the year awards, as well as best record awards for *No Fences* and "Friends in Low Places." He went on to issue the hit albums *Ropin' the Wind* (1991), *The Chase* (1992), and his Christmas album *Beyond the Season* (1992). Brooks's B.A. was from Oklahoma State University. He is married to the former Sandy Mahr, and has one child.

FURTHER READING

"The country craze." MARY NEMETH and DIANE TURBIDE. *Maclean's*, Nov. 8, 1993.

"A new world. . . ." MARJIE McGRAW. *First for Women*, June 28, 1993.

"Ropin' the wind. . . ." ANTHONY DeCURTIS. *Rolling Stone*, Apr. 1, 1993.

Garth Brooks: One of a Kind, Workin' on a Full House. RICK MITCHELL. Simon & Schuster, 1993.

Garth Brooks. ROSEMARY WALLNER. Abdo & Daughters, 1993.

Garth Brooks: Straight from the Heart. EDWARD TALLMAN. Dillon/Macmillan, 1993.

"He's Garth Brooks. . . ." CHARLES HIRSHBERG and NUBAR ALEXANIAN. *Life*, July 1992.

"Garth Brooks. . . ." MARJIE McGRAW. *Saturday Evening Post*, July-Aug. 1992.

"Garth Brooks. . . ." MARJIE McCRAW. *Ladies Home Journal*, June 1992.

"Garth Brooks." ALANNA NASH. *Stereo Review*, Apr. 1992.

"Brooks, Garth." *Current Biography*, Mar. 1992.

"Garth power. . . ." MICHAEL McCALL. *Country Music*, Jan.-Feb. 1992.

The Garth Brooks Scrapbook. LEE RANDALL. Carol, 1992.

"Garth Brooks. . . ." *People*, Dec. 30, 1991.

"The new king of country." JIM JEROME. *People*, Oct. 7, 1991.

Brooks, Mel (Melvin Kaminsky; 1926–)

While his film comedy *Life Stinks* was finding new audiences in home video, Mel Brooks was creating the latest of his long line of comedies: *Robin Hood: Men in Tights*, a satirical look at Hollywood's latest bows-and-arrows fad, and most directly at Kevin Costner's hit appearance as the bandit of Sherwood Forest. Even the posters for the film were a takeoff on the Costner film. Brooks co-wrote (with J. David Shapiro), directed, and produced *Robin Hood*. The film starred Cary Elwes as Robin Hood, Richard Lewis as Prince John, Roger Rees as the Sheriff of Rottingham, Amy Yasbeck as the Maid Marian, Tracey Ullman as Latrine, and Brooks as Rabbi Tuckman. The film received mixed reviews, though Brooks and Ullman were very well received in their broad comic roles.

Brooklyn-born Brooks began his long career as a stand-up comic and star comedy writer on stage and in early television. He was a writer for Sid Caesar's "Your Show of Shows" (1950–54) and "Caesar's Hour" (1954–57), then co-created the television series "Get Smart," before moving into his film career as writer, director, and star of *The Producers* (1967). He became a major figure in film comedy as director, co-writer, and star of *Blazing Saddles* (1973) and *Young Frankenstein* (1974), but his career began to sag considerably with *Silent Movie* (1976) and *High Anxiety* (1977). He wrote directed, and produced *History of the World-Part I* (1981). He produced several films, among them *The Elephant Man* (1980), *My Favorite Year* (1982), and *84 Charing Cross Road* (1987). In 1991, he wrote, produced, directed, and starred in *Life Stinks*. He is married to actress Anne Bancroft.

FURTHER READING

"The cosmos according to. . . ." E. GRAYDON CARTER. *Vogue*, June 1987.

Brown, John R. (1909–93) Nebraska-born

John R. Brown joined the Houston law firm of Royston and Raynor in 1932, ultimately becoming its senior partner. He also became active in Texas Republican politics, ultimately becoming Harris County (Houston) Republican Party chairman, and was a pillar of Houston's First Presbyterian Church. Brown was appointed to the Fifth Circuit Federal Court of Appeals by President Eisenhower in 1955, as the civil rights movement began gather strength after the landmark 1954 *Brown v. the Board of Education of Topeka, Kansas* school desegregation case. The Fifth Circuit, covering most of the Deep South, immediately became the chief battleground of the fight for equal rights—and John Brown, who headed his Court of Appeals (1967–79), turned out to be a Lincoln Republican, as were his two Republican colleagues on the Court, joined by its single Democrat. Together, they wrote a major portion of a new chapter in American history, on

the whole range of civil rights issues then convulsing the South; Brown himself ordered the enrollment of James Meredith at the University of Mississippi. He was survived by his wife, Vera S. Riley, a son, a stepdaughter, two stepsons, a sister, and a brother. (d. Houston; January 22, 1993)

FURTHER READING

Obituary. *New York Times*, Jan. 27, 1993.

Brown, Ron (Ronald Harmon Brown;

1941–) Secretary of Commerce Ron Brown emerged as a powerful supporter of "managed trade" during his first year in office, taking substantial action—and threatening more action—against the discriminatory trade practices of many other countries, perhaps most notably Japan. On January 27, only a week after the Clinton inauguration, Brown sent a strong message around the world on behalf of the new administration, in the form of increased, though temporary, "anti-dumping" steel tariffs, affecting steel imports from 12 countries that heavily subsidized their steel producers, enabling them to charge very low prices for their steel in international markets, a form of unfair competition. He continued to play a major role in the year-long battle against such trade practices, perhaps most notably during his April 23–25 visit to Japan.

Late in the year, Brown weathered an accusation that he had taken a $700,000 bribe from the Vietnamese government, an accusation denied by both Brown and the Vietnamese, although Brown, who first denied any knowledge of his accuser, Nguyen Van Hao, later stated that he had blamelessly met with him on three occasions. FBI and grand jury investigations had by year's end resulted in no actions against Brown, and Republican calls for a special prosecutor gathered no great force, while President Clinton defended Brown's integrity.

Born in Washington, D.C., Brown began his career as a Washington "insider" soon after his graduation from the St. John's University School of Law in 1970. He worked in a series of increasingly responsible posts at the National Urban League (1971–79); was counsel for the Senate Judiciary Committee (1980); worked in the presidential campaign of Senator Edward Kennedy (1979–80), remaining with him in 1981; and was a partner in Patton, Boggs & Blow (1981–89). He worked with the Democratic National Committee from 1981. He was Jesse Jackson's 1988 Democratic Convention manager, a Dukakis political adviser during the 1988 presidential campaign, and in February 1989 became the trailblazing first African-American Democratic National Committee chairman.

In that position, Brown played a major role in 1992 presidential politics, for with the election of President Bill Clinton and Vice President Al Gore, he saw the climax of a political miracle he had helped create. Clinton led a revived Democratic Party into the nominating convention, a party that Brown had largely rebuilt. The convention was a unified one, a rarity for modern Democrats: Jesse Jackson, whom Ron Brown had helped convince not to run again, publicly supported Clinton, and even maverick candidate Jerry Brown, who had threatened to split the convention, did not do so, speaking to the convention without endorsing Clinton, but attacking Bush on the issues. On December 12, 1992 Clinton named Ron Brown to be his Secretary of Commerce.

Brown's 1962 B.A. was from Middlebury College, and his 1970 J.D. was from St. John's. He married Alma Arrington in 1962; they have two children.

FURTHER READING

"A talk with. . . ." FRANK McCOY. *Black Enterprise*, June 1993.
"Black clout in the Clinton administration." *Ebony*, May 1993.
"Unholy trinity. . . ." JOHN B. JUDIS. *Mother Jones*, Mar.-Apr. 1993.
"A pro tries a new course. . . ." BILL HEWITT. *People*, Jan. 18, 1993.
"Talking to the chairmen." MARY ANN FRENCH. *Essence*, July 1992.
"From two new party chairmen. . . ." *American Visions*, June 1989.
"Brown, Ronald Harmon." *Current Biography*, July 1989.

Brown, Rosellen (1939–) Novelist Rosellen Brown specializes in exploring the precariousness of daily life, in which events can suddenly throw people's whole world awry. Critical praise, which has attended her previous books, was wedded to commercial success on the publication of her latest novel, *Before and After* (1992). This stunning tale explores the effects on a New Hampshire family of the murder of a teenage girl, the main character being Carolyn Reiser, a pediatrician called to view the body, and the leading suspect her own son. On the hardcover best-seller list for six weeks in 1992, the book also sold well in paperback in 1993 and was bought for filming by TriStar Pictures, with Ted Tally doing the screenplay, Meryl Streep scheduled to star, and Barbet Schroeder to direct.

Philadelphia-born Brown received her 1960 B.A. from Barnard and 1962 M.A. from Brandeis. She has published two volumes of poetry, *Some Deaths in the Delta and Other Poems* (1970) and *Cora Fry* (1977); numerous short stories, including the collection *Street Games: A Neighborhood* (1974); and three other novels, *The Autobiography of My Mother* (1976), *Tender Mercies* (1978), and *Civil War* (1984), which won the Janet Kafka Prize for best novel by an American woman. She has also won numerous other awards, including two PEN Syndicated Fiction prizes, an American Academy and Institute of Arts and Letters Literature Award, and a Guggenheim fellowship. Brown teaches creative writing at the University of Houston. She is married to writer and high school teacher Marv Hoffman; they have two daughters.

FURTHER READING

"Rosellen Brown. . . ." JUDITH PIERCE. *Publishers Weekly*, Aug. 31, 1992.
"How far would you go?" LAUREL GRAEBER. *New York Times Book Review*, Aug. 23, 1992.
Writers on Writing. ROBERT PACK and JAY PARINI, eds. University Press of New England, 1991.

Brown, Tina (1953–) *New Yorker* editor

Tina Brown continued to kick up a storm in 1993. Brought in during 1992 to revive a highly regarded journal many felt should have remained untouched, she became a controversial celebrity within the literary world, with enthusiastic supporters and equally strong detractors. Some longtime *New Yorker* writers, including Garrison Keillor, declined to write for the magazine under her editorship. Her Valentine's Day 1993 cover, a painting of a Black woman kissing a Hasidic Jewish man, raised particular criticism, not least from the two communities portrayed; Brown explained that it simply advocated replacing conflict with love, and that she was harking back to covers under founding editor Harold Ross, which were "full of mischief . . . full of people, full of attitude." Some observers felt that, apart from somewhat earthier language and some color illustrations, the magazine had changed little in essentials, and suggested that some longtime writers seemed revived. On the other hand, some—most notably British novelist John le Carré in 1992—charged that Brown was dragging the *New Yorker* down to the British tabloid level of journalism. The *Columbia Journalism Review*'s April 1993 analysis suggested that Brown was shaping the *New Yorker* into the *Vanity Fair* "cult of personality" mold. Circulation has risen significantly, especially drawing in more younger readers. The long-term fate of Brown and the *New Yorker* remained to be seen.

Born in Maidenhead, England, Brown received her M.A. in English from Oxford University's St. Anne's College. She was a columnist at London's *Punch* magazine in 1978, and then editor-in-chief of London's *Tatler* magazine (1979–83). She moved to New York as advisor to S.I. Newhouse, owner of the then-failing *Vanity Fair*, in 1984 becoming its editor-in-chief, dramatically updating its image and reviving it commercially. In mid-1992, Newhouse brought her in to replace Robert Gottlieb as editor-in-chief of the *New Yorker*, becoming only the fourth editor of the prestigious but reportedly unprofitable magazine. Brown's own published works include the plays *Under the Bamboo Tree* (1973) and *Happy Fellow* (1977), and the books *Loose Talk* (1979) and *Life Is a Party* (1983). In 1981, Brown married editor-publisher Harold Evans, whose position at Random House makes him another major player in the Newhouse companies; they have two children.

FURTHER READING

"How Tina Brown. . . ." ELIZABETH KOLBERT. *New York Times Magazine*, Dec. 5, 1993.
"Tina's turn. . . ." MICHEAL GROSS. *New York*, July 20, 1992.
"Brown, Tina." *Current Biography*, Feb. 1990.
"The dynamic duo. . . ." LAURANCE ZUCKERMAN. *Time*, June 13, 1988.

Browner, Carol (1955–) Environmental Protection Agency (EPA) administrator

Carol Browner spent her first year in office dealing with a wide range of public health and dangerous substance matters. One of the earliest and most important issues she addressed was that of the adverse health impact of passive exposure to the smoking of others, strongly defending the January 7 EPA report on passive smoking; she pursued the issue throughout the year, despite tobacco industry lawsuits in June. In July, she urged adoption of EPA recommendations sharply attacking smoking and protecting nonsmokers, especially children, who are even more

vulnerable than adults to the respiratory ailments caused by inhaling the smoke created by others. Browner also dealt with such issues as auto emissions, radon levels in schools and homes, pesticides, lead poisoning, and the ongoing campaign against industrial pollutants and polluters.

Browner began her career as a strongly environmentalist Florida House of Representatives lawyer in 1980, soon after receiving her 1979 J.D. from the University of Florida, where she had also done her undergraduate work. Moving to Washington, she worked for Common Cause on environmental matters, and in the late 1980s as legislative director for then-Senator Al Gore, a congressional leader on environmental issues.

In January 1991, she moved back to her home state, as head of the Florida Department of Environmental Protection; in that post, she negotiated a federal-state settlement aimed at restoring ecological damage in Everglades National Park. She also developed a reputation for working with industry and ecologists to simultaneously foster development and preservation, and for speeding the pace of agency decisions, approaches criticized by some ecologists and welcomed by others. Her stated early intentions as EPA administrator ran along similar lines; she also very strongly stressed the need to restore public faith in the EPA, which she felt had sagged very greatly during the Reagan and Bush years.

Browner is married to Michael Podhorzer; they have one son.

FURTHER READING

"Twenty minutes with. . . ." WILL NIXON. *E*, Dec. 1993.
"The sinkable. . . ." FRANCIS WILKINSON. *Rolling Stone*, Oct. 28, 1993.
"Is Carol Browner. . . ." JON BOWERMASTER. *Audubon*, Sep.-Oct. 1993.
"Challenges ahead for. . . ." RICHARD MINITER. *Insight*, Feb. 8, 1993.
"No longer home alone." *Time*, Dec. 21, 1992.

Burdett, Winston (1914–93) Buffalo-born journalist Winston Burdett began his long career as a reporter for the *Brooklyn Eagle* in 1933, soon after his graduation from Harvard College. He went to Europe for CBS radio in 1939, and reported from Europe and North Africa throughout World War II. He was a correspondent for CBS after the war, in Washington, Rome, and New York, returning to Italy to stay in 1956, as chief CBS European reporter, retiring in 1978. In the mid-1950s, he told Senator Joseph McCarthy's Senate Internal Security subcommittee that he had been a communist (1937–42), and "named names" before the committee. He was survived by his wife, Giorgina Nathan, a daughter, and a son. (d. Rome; May 19, 1993)

FURTHER READING

Obituary. *Current Biography*, July 1993.
Obituary. *National Review*, June 21, 1993.
Obituary. *Variety*, June 7, 1993.
Obituary. *New York Times*, May 21, 1993.

Burgess, Anthony (John Anthony Burgess Wilson; 1917–93) A prolific writer and composer, who sometimes used the pseudonym Joseph Kell, Anthony Burgess is best known by far to worldwide audiences for his bitterly satirical novel *A Clockwork Orange* (1962), which became Stanley Kubrick's well-received 1971 film. Among his many other works are the three early novels written in the late 1950s, while he was a British education officer in Malaya, published as *The Malayan Trilogy*; the several "Enderby" book, written as Kell, beginning with *Inside Mr. Enderby* (1963); and *Earthly Powers* (1980). He was also a prolific essayist and critic. Burgess placed great stress on his interest in music, seeing himself at least as much a musician as a writer, although his work as a composer received little recognition. He also wrote several television and radio scripts and autobiographical works, including *Little Wilson and Big God: The First Part of the Confession* (1987) and *You've Had Your Time: The Second Part of the Confessions* (1991). He was survived by his second wife, Liliana Macellari, and a son. (d. London; November 22, 1993).

FURTHER READING

"A 'Clockwork' author." L. S. KLEPP. *Entertainment,* Dec. 10, 1993.
"From poetry to slang." VIVA HARDIGG. *U.S. News & World Report,* Oct. 18, 1993.
Obituary. *Variety,* Nov. 28, 1993.
Obituary. *The Times* (of London), Nov. 26, 1993.
Obituary. *New York Times,* Nov. 26, 1993.
"A thousand words before breakfast." *Economist,* Oct. 19, 1991.
"Highbrow for hire?" JAMES WOLCOTT. *Vanity Fair,* Apr. 1991.
Anthony Burgess Revisited. JOHN J. STINSON. Twayne/Macmillan, 1991.
"Burgess on life. . . ." PETER HEBBLETHWAITE. *National Catholic Reporter,* May 12, 1989.
Writers Revealed: Eight Contemporary Novelists Talk about Faith, Religion and God. ROSEMARY HARTILL. P. Bedrick, 1989.
Anthony Burgess. HAROLD BLOOM, ed. Chelsea House, 1987.
Anthony Burgess: A Study in Character. MARTINA GHOSH-SCHELLHORN. P. Lang, 1986.
Critical Essays on Anthony Burgess. GEOFFREY AGGELER, ed. G. K. Hall, 1986.

Burke, Kenneth Duva (1897–1993)
Pittsburgh-born Kenneth Burke began his long literary career in New York during the first World War, as an essayist and poet. He became a well-known literary figure during the interwar period, as a prolific reviewer, translator, essayist, poet, and music critic, also teaching part-time at several colleges. In 1931, he published the novel *Towards a Better Life.* Burke became a leading figure in the mid-1940s, as a philosopher of literature and the arts, cofounding the movement called the New Criticism. His major works were *A Grammar of Motives* (1945), *Rhetoric of Motives* (1950), and *Language as Symbolic Action* (1968). He also published volumes of short stories and criticism.

In 1981, he received the National Medal of Literature. A member of the National Institute of Arts and Letters and the American Academy of Arts and Letters, he was survived by two daughters and two sons. (d. Andover, New Jersey; November 19, 1993)

FURTHER READING

Obituary. *New York Times,* Nov. 21, 1993.
Encounters with Kenneth Burke. WILLIAM H. RUECKERT. University of Illinois Press, 1994.
Landmark Essays on Kenneth Burke. BARRY BRUMMETT, ed. Hermagoras, 1993.
Kenneth Burke: Rhetoric and Ideology. STEPHEN BYGRAVE. Routledge, 1993.
Kenneth Burke: Literature and Language as Symbolic Action. GREIG E. HENDERSON. University of Georgia Press, 1989.
The Legacy of Kenneth Burke. HERBERT SIMONS and TREVOR MELIA, eds. University of Wisconsin Press, 1988.
The Selected Correspondence of Kenneth Burke and Malcolm Cowley, 1915–1981. PAUL JAY. Viking Penguin, 1988; University of California Press, 1990.

Burnett, Carol (1936–) Versatile actress
and comedian Carol Burnett began 1993 with the television special *The Carol Burnett Show: A Reunion,* celebrating the 25th anniversary of her tremendously popular long-running show. She continued to work in television during 1993, in September appearing in the AIDS special *In a New Light,* hosted by Arsenio Hall and Paula Abdul. Forthcoming was a starring role in the television film *The Winter Garden,* opposite George Segal and Malcolm McDowell; Lee Grant directed. On stage, she starred opposite Patrick Cassidy in the Long Beach Civic Light Opera production of *Company,* and also in a revue at the Long Beach Center Theater.

San Antonio-born Burnett became a highly-regarded television comedian in the early 1960s, and was the enormously popular star of her own "The Carol Burnett Show" (1967–79). Through the early 1970s, she also appeared in several plays, including *Plaza Suite* (1970) and *I Do, I Do* (1973) on Broadway, and in such films as *Pete 'n' Tillie* (1972), *A Wedding* (1977), and *Annie* (1982), then falling into a difficult period through the 1980s. She began what became a major comeback with the Christmas 1989 television special *Julie and Carol*, shared with Julie Andrews; her "Carol & Company" (1990–91) followed. She expanded her show in the 1991–92 season into an hour-long comedy-variety series, "The Carol Burnett Show." Unfortunately, the show did not do well in the ratings and was quickly dropped by CBS. She also starred opposite Michael Caine in Peter Bogdanovich's film farce *Noises Off* (1992), based on the Michael Frayn play. In 1986, she published the autobiographical *One More Time*. Burnett attended the University of California at Los Angeles. She was formerly married to Joseph Hamilton and has three children.

FURTHER READING

"Carol Burnett...." ALAN W. PETRUCELLI. *First for Women*. Mar. 30, 1992.
"Burnett, Carol." *Current Biography*, Nov. 1990.
"Carol Burnett...." ERIC SHERMAN. *Ladies Home Journal*, Sep. 1990.
"Carol Burnett...." MARK MORRISON. *Woman's Day*, Aug. 7, 1990.
"Carol Burnett...." CHARLES BUSCH. *Interview*, Mar. 1990
Laughing Till It Hurts. J. RANDY TARABORELLI. Morrow, 1988.
Carol Burnett: The Sound of Laughter. JAMES HOWE. Viking Penguin, 1987.
Carol Burnett. CAROLINE LATHAM. New American Library-Dutton, 1986.

Burr, Raymond (1917–93) Canadian-born Raymond Burr made his Broadway debut in 1941, in the musical *Crazy with the Heat*. He began his film career in *Without Reservations* (1946), and played supporting roles, largely as "heavies," until emerging as a television star in the hugely popular "Perry Mason" series (1957–66), which is still popular in reruns throughout the world. Burr won two Emmys in the role, and continued to play Perry Mason in successor shows, including *The New Perry Mason* (1973) and *Perry Mason Returns* (1985). Burr also played in occasional Perry Mason telefilms, the last of which, "The Case of the Killer Kiss," aired in December 1993. An additional series of Perry Mason films had been planned. Burr also starred as the wheelchair-bound star of television's long-running "Ironside" series (1967–75), and in the "Kingston: Confidential" series (1975). He was

survived by a sister. (d. Healdburg, California; September 12, 1993)

FURTHER READING

Obituary. *Current Biography*, Nov. 1993.
The defense rests." J.D. PODOLSKY. *People*, Sep. 27, 1993.
Obituary. RICHARD NATALE. *Variety*, Sep. 27, 1993.
"With Raymond Burr...." MARY MURPHY. *TV Guide*, Sep. 25, 1993.
Obituary. *Variety*, Sep. 19, 1993.
Obituary. *The Times* (of London), Sep. 14, 1993.
Obituary. *New York Times*, Sep. 14, 1993.

Bush, George (George Herbert Walker Bush; 1924–) On January 20, 1993 former President George Bush and his wife, Barbara Bush, went home to Texas. The Bushes, James Baker, and other former Bush administration officials made a triumphal visit to Kuwait April 14–16, 1993; Kuwaiti security forces arrested 14 people who had allegedly planned to assassinate Bush. On June 26, a U.S. missile attack was made on Iraqi intelligence headquarters in Baghdad, in retaliation for the planned Bush assassination attempt, as explained by President Bill Clinton in a national television address soon after the attack.

At home, Bush made his first paid speech, for $80,000, before the National Restaurant Association in Chicago, and signed a publishing contract with Knopf, for a book to be co-authored with Brent Scowcroft. He also attended two significant ceremonies connected with his administration: On September 13, he and former president Jimmy Carter attended the signing of the Israel-Palestine Liberation Organization (PLO) White House peace accord; and on September 14, he and former presidents Carter and Gerald Ford attended the White House signing of the North American Free Trade Agreement (NAFTA).

President Bush's last year in office had been dominated by the presidential campaign and the state of the economy. His popularity sagged as the American economy sagged, the national debt soared, legislative "gridlock" worsened, and consumer confidence plummeted. Ultimately, even a highly negative campaign, complete with a great deal of name-calling and investigations of the private lives of his opponents and their families, failed to save him. On November 3, 1992, he won only 38 percent of the popular vote, losing his bid for re-election to Arkansas governor Bill Clinton, in a three-way race that included independent candidate Ross Perot. During the transition period following the election, Bush pardoned six Reagan administration figures allegedly implicated in the Iran-Contra affair, initiated the Somali intervention, and on January 3, 1993 signed a major arms reduction treaty in Moscow.

George Bush had defeated Michael Dukakis in the bitterly contested 1988 presidential race, becoming the 41st President of the United States in 1989, the climax of a political career that had begun in Texas in the early 1960s. He had grown up in a Republican Party family, the son of Connecticut senator Prescott Bush, and then left New England to enter the oil business in Texas in the early 1950s, co-founding the Zapata Petroleum Company in 1953 and becoming president and then board chairman of the Zapata Off Shore Company in 1956. He was an unsuccessful Republican senatorial candidate from Texas in 1964, but won a House seat in 1966, moving to Washington as a Houston congressman for two terms (1967–71). In 1970, he made another unsuccessful run for the Senate on the Republican ticket.

Bush was United States Ambassador to the United Nations during the waning days of the Vietnam War (1971–72), and then Republican National Committee chairman (1973–74). He was the chief American liaison officer in Peking (1974–76), then returning to Washington as head of the CIA (1976–77). He made an unsuccessful Republican presidential nomination run in 1980, but withdrew in favor of Ronald Reagan, and subsequently became Reagan's two-term vice president, operating in those eight years in a largely ceremonial and standby fashion, as have most vice presidents. He then succeeded Reagan as president.

The early Bush years saw a series of major international triumphs as the Cold War ended and the Soviet empire collapsed. First came the quick and easy invasion of Panama that toppled the Noriega dictatorship. Then came a series of major Soviet-American peace moves, with planned troop pullbacks and real progress on arms control and on the ending of a whole series of regional conflicts that had for decades been spurred by Soviet and American sponsorship of the combatants. With both countries acting in concert as peacemakers, and with the direct intervention of George Bush and Mikhail Gorbachev, the continuing conflicts in Nicaragua, Cambodia, Angola, Mozambique, Namibia, Ethiopia, and several other countries moved swiftly toward resolution. His last triumph was the successful prosecution of the 1991 Persian Gulf War.

George Bush's 1948 B.A. was from Yale. A navy pilot in World War II, he married Barbara Pierce in 1945. Their five surviving children are George, John, Neil, Marvin, and Dorothy; their second child, Robyn, died of leukemia at age three. During the 1988 Presidential campaign, Bush published two books, *Man of Integrity* (with Doug Wead) and *Looking Forward: The George Bush Story* (with Victor Gold).

FURTHER READING

"Revelations of Bush's diary. . . ." FRANCES FITZGERALD. *Nation*, Mar. 8, 1993.

George Bush. WILLIAM E. PEMBERTON. Rourke, 1993.

Eyes on the President: History in Essays and Cartoons—George Bush Retrospective. TOM BLANTON, et al. Chronos, 1993.

Strange Bedfellows: How Television and the Presidential Candidates Changed American Politics, 1992. TOM ROSENSTIEL. Hyperion, 1993.

"Life in Bush hell." JAMES PINKERTON. *New Republic*, Dec. 14, 1992.

"Rubbers. . . ." SIDNEY BLUMENTHAL. *New Republic*, Nov. 30, 1992.

"George Bush just didn't get it." LEE WALCZAK. *Business Week*, Nov.16, 1992.

"Bush's desperate game." JOE KLEIN. "Face to face." ANN MCDANIEL. *Newsweek*, Oct. 19, 1992.

"Bush's gamble." WILLIAM SAFIRE. *New York Times Magazine*, Oct. 18, 1992.

"War story. . . ." SIDNEY BLUMENTHAL. *New Republic*, Oct. 12, 1992.

"The final battle." GUS TYLER. *New Leader*, Oct. 5, 1992.

"Bushism, found. . . ." WALTER RUSSELL MEAD. *Harper's*, Sep. 1992.

"The case for Bush. . . ." RICHARD VIGILANTE. "The wilderness year." *New Republic*, Aug. 31, 1992.

"A conversation with. . . ." ANN MCDANIEL and TOM DEFRANK. *Newsweek*, Aug. 24, 1992.

"Finding a road. . . ." HILARY MACKENZIE. *Maclean's*, Aug. 24, 1992.

"Warrior for the status quo." MICHAEL DUFFY and DAN GOODGAME. *Time*, Aug. 24, 1992.

"Bush on the record." MICHAEL KRAMER and HENRY MULLER. *Time*, Aug. 24, 1992.

"The fight of his life." DAN GOODGAME. *Time*, Aug. 24, 1992.

"What's wrong with Bush?" *Time*, Aug. 10, 1992.

"A visit with. . . ." RICHARD BROOKHISER. *Atlantic*, Aug. 1992.

"The goofy politics of. . . ." JOHN O'SULLIVAN and WILLIAM McGURN. *National Review*, Feb. 3, 1992.

Chameleon: The Unauthorized Biography of George Bush. JONATHAN SLEVIN and STEVEN WILMSEN. Krantz, 1992.

George Bush: His World War II Years. ROBERT B. STINNETT. Macmillan, 1992.

The Renegade CIA: Inside the Cover Intelligence Operations of George Bush. JOSEPH J. TRENTO. Putnam, 1992.

George Bush's War. JEAN E. SMITH. Holt, 1992.

Buthelezi, Mangosuthu Gatsha

(1928–) During 1993, Zulu leader Gatsha Buthelezi continued to oppose the creation of a multiracial, multiparty, democratic South Africa, as envisioned by Nelson Mandela and F. W. De Klerk, but found himself in a rather isolated position, his main allies the pro-apartheid, anti-Black activists of the Conservative Party and other White splinter groups. His pursuit of the Inkatha-African National Congress war seemed to be proving unfruitful, as ANC military forces, back from exile, began to organize effective resistance and go over to the offensive against Inkatha in the townships, while his voice on the international scene all but disappeared. No longer as welcome at the White House, he seemed very much on the outside looking in, as Mandela and De Klerk shared the Nobel Peace Prize, jointly saw to the end of international sanctions against South Africa, and led their country back into the world community. Ultimately, Buthelezi was reduced to boycotting the agreement of November 18, which established multiparty democracy, a Bill of Rights for all South Africans, and national elections that would lead to majority rule. Although Buthelezi threatened to boycott the coming elections, it seemed at year's end that he might be backing away from hardline positions, with an eye toward concessions that might lead toward the establishment of a long-sought Zulu homeland.

Buthelezi became chief of the Buthelezi tribe in 1963, succeeding his father, Mathole Buthelezi. He was a Zulu administrator for two decades, becoming chief minister of the Kwa-Zulu in 1976. As the long fight for South African democracy developed during the 1970s and 1980s, he emerged as the main spokesperson and leader of the Zulus, and a third force in South African politics, for he negotiated with the White South African government on behalf of the Zulus, and often opposed the African National Congress. His followers, organized into the Inkatha movement, carried those disagreements into anti-ANC street fighting throughout the 1980s and early 1990s. Buthelezi emerged as a powerful independent force in South African politics in the early 1990s, as negotiations over the future of the country proceeded between the De Klerk government and the ANC, led by Nelson Mandela. In 1990, he published *South Africa: My Vision of the Future.*

Buthelezi attended Adams College and Fort-Hare University. He married Irene Audrey Thandekile Mzila in 1952; they have seven children.

FURTHER READING

"Buthelezi. . . ." SCOTT MACLEOD. *Time*, July 6, 1992.

"The chief steps forward. . . ." CHRISTOPHER S. WREN. *New York Times Magazine*, Feb. 17, 1991.

Gatsha Buthelezi: Chief with a Double Agenda. MZALA. Humanities, 1988.

An Appetite for Power: Buthelezi's Inkatha and South Africa. GERHARD MARE and GEORGINA HAMILTON. Indiana University Press, 1988.

Butler, Robert Olen (1945–) It was a very good year for novelist Robert Olen Butler. His *A Good Scent from a Strange Mountain* (1992), a collection of 15 dreamlike short stories told from the perspective of Vietnamese immigrants in Louisiana, won the 1993 Pulitzer Prize for fiction and was named by the American Library Association as one of the most notable books of the year. Other 1993 honors included a John Simon Guggenheim Foundation fellowship, the Richard and Hinda Rosenthal Foundation award from the American Academy of Arts and Letters, and a nomination for the PEN/Faulkner award.

His seventh novel, *They Whisper*, was scheduled for publication in January 1994, with a 75,000-copy first printing and 21-city publicity tour for the book, and renewed support for his previous novels, all reprinted in paperback. It was all quite a change for the well-reviewed, well-regarded, but—before all this—never best-selling writer.

Born in Granite City, Illinois, near St. Louis, Butler received his B.S., summa cum laude, at Northwestern University in 1967 and his M.A. in playwriting at the University of Iowa in 1969, then serving in the U.S. Army in Vietnam (1969–72). He served as editor-in-chief of *Energy User News* (1975–85), while studying at the New School for Social Research (1979–81), and continuing to write his own work. After 21 rejections, his first novel, *The Alleys of Eden*, was published to fine reviews, followed by *Sun Dogs* (1982), *Countrymen of Bones* (1983), *On Distant Ground* (1985), *Wabash* (1987), and *The Deuce* (1989). Since 1985 he has taught fiction writing at McNeese State University, Lake Charles, Louisiana, and at many summer writing conferences. Butler's first two marriages ended in divorce; he married Maureen Donlan in 1987 and has one son.

FURTHER READING

"Robert Olen Butler. . . ." Sybil S. Steinberg. *Publishers Weekly*, Jan. 3, 1994.

C

Caan, James (1939–) Two films starred veteran film star James Caan in 1993. The first was *The Program*, directed by David S. Ward, a college-set football film released in September, when interest in the game heightens. Caan starred as Coach Winters, in a cast that included real-life college football star Craig Sheffer, Halle Berry, and Omar Epps. The second was the film *Flesh and Bone*, written and directed by Steve Kloves, and co-starring Dennis Quaid and Meg Ryan, in which Caan starred as the villainous father. He was also one of the environmentally-minded stars who did readings for the film *Earth and the American Dream*, directed by Bill Couterie, and co-produced by Couterie and Janet Mercer. Still forthcoming was a starring role in *The Dark Backward*, written and directed by Adam Rifkin.

New York City-born Caan played in New York theater and television in the early 1960s, and emerged as a major player in the early 1970s, with his notable television lead in *Brian's Song* (1971), which was followed by his star-making role in *The Godfather* (1972), creating the classic "tough guy" role of Sonny Corleone. He went on to such films as *Cinderella Liberty* (1974), *Funny Lady* (1975), *Rollerball* (1975), *A Bridge Too Far* (1977), *Chapter Two* (1979), *Hide in Plain Sight* (1980; he also directed), and *Kiss Me Goodbye* (1982). He retired from filmmaking during the mid-1980s, returning with *Gardens of Stone* (1987), *Alien Nation* (1988), *Misery* (1990), *For the Boys* (1991), and *Honeymoon in Vegas* (1992). Caan attended Michigan State University, Hofstra College, and New York's

Neighborhood Playhouse. He has been married three times, since 1990 to Ingrid Hajek, and has four children, one of them adopted.

FURTHER READING

"Raising Caan." AL REINERT. *Premiere*, Dec. 1991.

Cage, Nicolas (Nicholas Coppola; 1965–) During 1993, actor Nicolas Cage starred in the film *Amos & Andrew*, a satirical comedy involving a faked hostage situation and racist attitudes. Written and directed by E. Max Frye, the

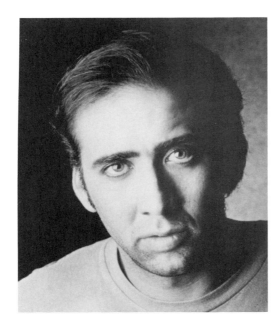

cast also included Samuel L. Jackson, Dabney Coleman, and Michael Lerner. Cage also starred opposite Dennis Hopper and Lara Flynn Boyle in the well-received television film *Red Rock West*, a comedy-thriller written and directed by John Dahl. Forthcoming were starring film roles in *Guarding Tess*, opposite Shirley MacLaine, and in *It Happened in Paradise*, written and directed by George Gallo. He was also slated to star opposite Bridget Fonda in a film directed by Andrew Bergman, tentatively titled *Cop Gives Waitress $2 Million Tip!*

California-born Cage, Francis Ford Coppola's nephew, began his career with strong supporting roles in such 1980s films as *Valley Girl* (1983), *Rumble Fish* (1983), *Racing with the Moon* (1984), *Birdy* (1984), and *The Cotton Club* (1984), and moved into leads with his role opposite Kathleen Turner in *Peggy Sue Got Married* (1986). He went on to star in *Raising Arizona* (1987); in *Moonstruck* (1988) as the one-armed baker who becomes Cher's lover; *Vampire's Kiss* (1989); *Firebirds* (1990); in the David Lynch film *Wild at Heart* (1990) as Sailor Ripley opposite Laura Dern as Lula Pace Fortune; *Zandalee* (1991); and *Honeymoon in Vegas* (1992).

FURTHER READING

"Nicolas Cage. . . ." RICHARD NATALE. *Cosmopolitan*, Dec. 1992.
"Nicolas Cage." STEVE POND. *US*, Sep. 1992.
"Nicolas Cage. . . ." MARK ROWLAND. *Cosmopolitan*, Sep. 1990.

"Rebel without. . . ." STEPHANIE MANSFIELD. *GQ—Gentlemen's Quarterly*, Aug. 1990.
"Nicolas Cage." JOHN CLARK. *Premiere*, Sep. 1990.
"The beasts within. . . ." MARK ROWLAND. *American Film*, June 1990.
"20 questions. . . ." ROBERT CRANE. *Playboy*, June 1989.

Cahn, Sammy (Samuel Cohen; 1913–93) New York City-born Sammy Cahn, a leading American lyricist, began his long career as a part-time violinist. In the early 1930s, with his first songwriting partner, Saul Chaplin, he wrote such hit songs as "Bei Mir Bist du Schön," "Shoe Shine Boy," and "Until the Real Thing Comes Along." With Jule Styne as his partner (1942–56), Cahn wrote such standards as "It's Magic," "It's Been a Long, Long Time," "Papa Won't You Dance With Me" (from their Broadway musical *High Button Shoes*), and the Oscar-winning title song for *Three Coins in the Fountain*. Cahn and Jimmy Van Heusen wrote the Oscar-winning songs "All the Way," "High Hopes," and "Call Me Irresponsible," as well as "Love and Marriage" and "Tender Trap." Active in industry affairs, Cahn was president of the National Academy of Popular Music, the "Songwriters Hall of Fame" (1973–93), and a board member of ASCAP, the American Society of Composers, Authors, and Publishers (1976–93). His autobiography was *I Should Care: The Sammy Cahn Story* (1974). He was survived by his wife, Tita, a daughter, and a son. (d. Los Angeles; January 15, 1993)

FURTHER READING

Obituary. *Current Biography*, Mar. 1993.
Obituary. *Billboard*, Jan. 30, 1993.
Obituary. *Variety*, Jan. 25, 1993.
Obituary. *The Times* (of London), Jan. 18, 1993.
Obituary. *New York Times*, Jan. 16, 1993.
"Sammy Cahn." MICHAEL FRANK. *Architectural Digest*, Apr. 1992.

Campanella, Roy (1921–93) Philadelphia-born Roy Campanella, one of the most accomplished catchers in the history of the game, began his career in 1937, in the Negro Leagues, in 1946 joining the Brooklyn Dodgers farm organization as a step toward desegregating baseball, a task accomplished by Jackie Robinson a year later. Campanella joined the Dodgers in 1948, and in the ten years that followed became a major star. His career was plagued by injuries, none of them disabling; but an automobile accident on January 28, 1956 ended it; he emerged from surgery permanently paralyzed. In the years that followed, however, his outspoken determination to continue to live a productive life made him a national figure, as he continued a long-term association with the Dodgers and acted as a spokesperson for the handicapped, through a considerable series of adversities. Campanella was elected to baseball's Hall of Fame in 1969. His autobiography was *It's Good to Be Alive* (1959). He was survived by his wife Roxie, two daughters, and three sons. (d. Woodland Hills, California; June 26, 1993)

FURTHER READING

Roy Campanella: Major-League Champion. CAROL GREENE. Childrens, 1994.
Obituary. *Current Biography,* Aug. 1993.
"Hall of Fame catcher. . . ." *Jet,* July 12, 1993.
"A hero defined. . . ." BILL MARX. *Sporting News,* July 5, 1993.
Obituary. *New York Times,* June 28, 1993.
Roy Campanella. JAMES TACKACH. Chelsea House, 1991.
"Triumph of the spirit . . ." RON FIMRITE. *Sports Illustrated,* Sep. 24, 1990.

Campbell, Kim (Avril Phaedra Campbell; 1947–) On June 13, 1993, lawyer and Canadian Defense Minister Campbell won election to the leadership of the ruling Progressive Conservative (Tory) Party, succeeding retiring party leader and Prime Minister Brian Mulroney. On June 25, she succeeded Mulroney as Prime Minister, becoming Canada's first woman prime minister. But her tenure was brief, for Mulroney's government had by its end become extraordinarily unpopular, and Campbell's rather abrasive personal style did not build rapport with Canadian voters. She was required to call a general election by November, called it for October 25, and lost by a landslide—by more than a landslide, really, for she even lost her own Vancouver seat in a debacle that took Tory membership in the House of Commons from 153 seats down to just 2, an extraordinary political disaster. She resigned on November 4, and was succeeded as Prime Minister by Liberal Party leader Jean Chrétien.

Born at Port Alberni, British Columbia, Campbell is a graduate of the University of British Columbia (UBC), with postgraduate work at the London School of Economics. She taught at Vancouver Community College before studying law at UBC. After her 1983 graduation, she practiced law and went into provincial politics. She was elected to the Canadian House of Commons as a Progressive Conservative in 1988, and swiftly rose to cabinet level, becoming Minister of State Affairs and Northern Development (1989–90), Minister of Justice and Canadian Attorney-General of Canada (1990–93), and Minister of Defense in 1993. She was formerly married.

FURTHER READING

"Challenges for a new leader." ANTHONY WILSON-SMITH. *Maclean's,* June 21, 1993.
"Kim Campbell's. . . ." PETER C. NEWMAN. *Maclean's,* June 21, 1993.
"Ms. Prime Minister." ANTHONY WILSON-SMITH. *Maclean's,* June 21, 1993.
"Canada's Mrs. Thatcher?" RUSSELL WATSON. *Newsweek,* June 14, 1993.
"The real Kim Campbell." E. KAYE FULTON and MARY JANIGAN. *Maclean's,* May 17, 1993.
"Why is this woman smiling?" ANTHONY WILSON-SMITH. *Maclean's,* Mar. 22, 1993.

Cantinflas (Mario Moreno Reyes; 1911–93) Mexico City-born Cantinflas, his country's most revered comedian and a major philanthropist, began his career touring in variety, in tent shows developing the ultimately triumphant downtrodden-common-man character that became his trademark. He began his film career in 1936, emerging as a star in *There Is the Detail* (1940); in all, he made 49 films. He was best known abroad for his role as Passepartout in Mike Todd's *Around the World in 80 Days* (1956). Cantinflas became Mexico's most popular and best paid star by far; he also became one of Mexico's most loved philanthropists, for gifts of his own money large and small, accompanied by a great many fundraising benefit appearances. He was survived by a son. (d. Mexico City; April 20, 1993)

FURTHER READING

Obituary. *Current Biography*, June 1993.
Obituary. *Variety*, Apr. 26, 1993.
Obituary. *The Times* (of London), Apr. 22, 1993.
Obituary. *New York Times*, Apr. 22, 1993.

Capriati, Jennifer (1976–) After an early exit in the first round of the 1993 U.S. Open—four years into her professional career, seeded seventh in the tournament, and ranked ninth in the world—Jennifer Capriati decided to take some time off. She had been forced to withdraw from the Evert Cup match in February, after pulling a stomach muscle. Taking a break from competition allowed Capriati to rehabilitate the right arm that had bothered her, and also to focus on school, where she was a high school senior, and on decorating her first apartment. She was originally expected to resume competitive play in February 1994, but later left her return date open.

Capriati won twice earlier in 1993, at Sydney, her first event of the season, and at the Pathmark Tennis Classic in July, defeating Mary Joe Fernandez to take her second title there. But at Wimbledon she had been knocked out in the quarterfinals by top-ranked Steffi Graf, though she had taken Graf to no fewer than 10 set points. Capriati also lost to Graf in the finals of the Canadian Open and at the Volvo International, both in August. Also in August, Capriati was one of many tennis players appearing at the Arthur Ashe Tennis Challenge to benefit the Arthur Ashe Foundation to defeat AIDS.

Capriati was trained for tennis from the age of four, first by her father Stefano Capriati, and then by Florida tennis professional Jimmy Evert, father of tennis star Chris Evert, also her mentor. She began winning junior tennis championships at the age of 12. At 13, she won junior titles at the U.S. and French Open tournaments. In 1990, then barely 14 and still an eighth-grade student at the Saddlebrook Tennis Academy, she turned professional. She won one singles tournament that year, and two singles events in 1991, plus a doubles title with Monica Seles. In 1992, she took the Olympic gold medal at the Barcelona Olympics, and also won two other tournaments.

FURTHER READING

Jennifer Capriati: Tennis Sensation. MARGARET J. GOLDSTEIN. Lerner, 1993.
Jennifer Capriati. PATRICIA LAKIN. Rourke, 1993.
Jennifer Capriati, Teenage Tennis Star. BILL GUTMAN. Millbrook, 1993.
Ladies of the Court. MICHAEL MEWSHAW. Crown, 1993.
"Net success." *Sporting News*, Sep. 7, 1992.
"Tennis menace." CINDY SCHMERLER. *Women's Sports and Fitness*, Mar. 1992.
"Learn from the game's. . . ." TIM GULLIKSON et al. *Tennis*, Dec. 1991.
"But seriously folks. . . ." CINDY SCHMERLER. *World Tennis*, June 1991.
Jennifer Capriati. MIKKI MORRISSETTE. Little, Brown, 1991.

Jennifer Capriati. JAMES R. ROTHAUS. Child's World, 1991.
Jennifer Capriati. ELLEN E. WHITE. Scholastic, 1991.

Carey, Mariah (1970–) Singer and songwriter Mariah Carey was honored by her peers again in 1993, at the 20th annual American Music Awards being named favorite female pop/rock artist. In addition, she and Michael Bolton were named songwriters of the year at the Broadcast Music Inc.'s 41st Annual Pop Awards Dinner.

In August, Carey issued "Dreamlover," the first single from her coming *Music Box* album. It was a number one pop hit, as was the second single "Hero." *Music Box* itself became a major hit, the album quickly selling more than 2 million copies, its popularity greatly helped by Carey's Thanksgiving Day television special. Carey also went on tour to plug the album; it was her first tour, and after initial uncertainty she won favorable reviews and played to very receptive audiences.

On the personal side, a lawsuit brought by her former stepfather was thrown out of court; he had claimed a share of her proceeds from the sale of Mariah Carey dolls, on the basis of an alleged oral contract. More happily, in June Carey was married to Sony Music President Tommy Mottola.

Long Island-born Carey left high school to live and work in New York City in 1987. She worked as a waitress and backup singer before signing her first recording contract, with Columbia Records. She became a star overnight in 1990, with her first album *Mariah Carey*, which sold well over 4 million copies; its ten songs included "Vision of Love," which topped the charts as the number one single for four weeks. She won two 1991 Grammy awards, the first as the best new artist of 1990 and the second for top female pop vocal for "Vision of Love." Carey won several other awards during 1991 as well, including *Billboard*'s top artist of the year award and three Soul Train awards. Her songs "Someday" and "I Don't Wanna Cry" were also 1991 number one singles. In 1992, she was named Billboard's top female pop artist of the year, and won several other awards, while her total record sales climbed over the 10 million mark.

FURTHER READING

"How sweet it is. . . ." STEVE DOUGHERTY. *People*, Nov. 22, 1993.
"Mariah Carey." CARL ARRINGTON. *TV Guide*, Nov 13, 1993.
"The lives and loves. . . ." LYNN NORMENT. *Ebony*, Nov. 1993.
"Carey, Mariah." *Current Biography*, July 1992.
"Pop meteor. . . ." CHRIS SMITH. *New York*, Sep. 23, 1991.
"Mariah Carey tells why. . . ." *Jet*, Mar. 4, 1991.
"Careerwise or couchwise. . . ." *People Weekly*, Jan. 28, 1991.
"Building the perfect diva." ROB TANNENBAUM. *Rolling Stone*, Aug. 23, 1990.
"Pop's new vision." CHRIS SMITH. *New York*, May 28, 1990.
"In person. . . ." *Seventeen*, Oct. 1990.

Carr, Philippa: See Hibbert, Eleanor.

Carter, Jimmy (James Earl Carter, Jr.; 1924–) Former President Jimmy Carter continued to play a major role in international pro-democracy and peacekeeping matters during 1993. On May 9, he headed a 200-strong international observer group monitoring Paraguay's first free, multiparty presidential election. In August, he went to the Sudan, in a largely unsuccessful attempt to mediate the long civil war

and to convince both sides to allow international relief supplies to flow into the region, to save hundreds of thousands of lives. In September, he reported continuing conversations with Somali leader Mohammed Aidid. Carter also urged President Clinton to move more strongly on the restoration of Haitian democracy, and to open negotiations with Fidel Castro.

At home, Carter's Atlanta Project continued to work on the multiple problems of his home city, with Carter initiating a crash immunization program in March. He also attended the September 13 signing of the Israel-Palestine Liberation Organization (PLO) White House peace accord, and on September 14 the White House signing of the North American Free Trade Agreement (NAFTA). He also published two new books for adults, the autobiographical *Turning Point: A Candidate, A State, and a Nation Come of Age* and *Blood of Abraham: Insights into the Middle East*, and one for young people, *Talking Peace*.

Georgia-born Carter became the 39th President of the United States in 1977, the climax of a political career that began with his four years in the Georgia Senate (1963–67). He went on to become governor of Georgia (1971–75), emerged as the surprise "outsider" winner of the Democratic presidential nomination after a long series of primary campaigns, and defeated incumbent Gerald Ford in the 1976 presidential race. His earlier career included seven years as a naval officer (1946–53), and ten years as a successful Georgia farmer and businessman at Plains, Georgia.

Jimmy Carter's very difficult presidential term was dominated by largely adverse foreign affairs matters, including the Arab oil embargo of the mid-1970s, the Iran hostage crisis that began in late 1979 and colored the rest of his presidency, and the worsening Soviet-American relations that began with the Soviet invasion of Afghanistan and resulted in the American boycott of the 1980 Moscow Olympics. His major accomplishment was the 1978 Camp David Accords, which paved the way for the 1979 Egyptian-Israeli peace treaty. After leaving the presidency, he initiated several pilot projects aimed at bringing sound low-income housing to decaying American inner cities. Carter has also been active in international mediation and human rights efforts, as in 1989 in Nicaragua, in 1990 in Ethiopia, the Sudan, and Haiti, and in 1991 in Zambia and Nicaragua. He has also been a distinguished professor at Emory University.

Carter was a key foreign policy advisor to presidential candidate and then President-elect Bill Clinton. On July 14, 1992 he addressed the Democratic National Convention in support of Clinton, his presence as the only living Democratic former President and his enthusiastic endorsement greatly helping the convention's unity theme. During 1992, Carter also developed the massive "Atlanta project," a program to help solve the problems faced by poor people in his home state's capitol city, Atlanta, Georgia.

Carter's 1947 B.S. was from the U.S. Naval Academy. He married Rosalynn Smith in 1946; they have four children. After he left office, they collaborated in writing *Everything to Gain: Making the Most of the Rest of Your Life* (1988). He has also written several other works, including *An Outdoor Journal* (1988), *America on My Mind* (1991), and *One Man, One Vote: A Candidate and a State Come of Age* (1992).

FURTHER READING

"Human rights I. . . ." DENNIS L. BRO. *JAMA*, Aug. 4, 1993.

"To grow in peace. . . ." LILLIAN N. GERHARDT and MICHAEL SADOWSKI. *School Library Journal*, Aug. 1993.

The Carter Presidency: A Re-Evaluation. JOHN DUMBRELL. St. Martin's, 1993.

The Presidency of James Earl Carter, Jr. BURTON I. KAUFMAN. University Press of Kansas, 1993.

The Carters: First Families Series. CASS A. SANDAK. Macmillan, 1993.
The Presidency and Domestic Policies of Jimmy Carter. HERBERT D. ROSENBAUM and ALEXEJ UGRINSKY, eds. Greenwood, 1993.
Jimmy Carter: Foreign Policy and Post-Presidential Years. HERBERT D. ROSENBAUM and ALEXEJ UGRINSKY, eds. Greenwood, 1993.
Jimmy Carter and the Politics of Frustration. GARLAND A. HAAS. McFarland, 1992.
The Native Son Presidential Candidate: The Carter Vote in Georgia. HANES WALTON, JR. Praeger/Greenwood, 1992.
"Jimmy Carter." ROBERT N. HOFFMAN. *Workbench,* Nov. 1991.
Jimmy Carter. ED SLAVIN. Chelsea House, 1989.
The President Builds a House: The Work of Habitat for Humanity. TOM SHACHTMAN. Simon and Schuster, 1989.

Castro Ruz, Fidel (1926–)

During 1993, Castro attempted to maintain tight political control over Cuba, while at the same time taking some steps to shore up Cuba's economy. With the United States embargo still in place, Soviet subsidies long since disappeared, his Eastern European trading partners in the process of disappearing, and Cuba's internal economy a continuing shambles, Castro's government was hard pressed to continue vital social services, or even to guarantee adequate food supplies for Cuba, with even sugar (in Cuba!) strictly rationed. So, even while behaving repressively and speaking as a hardline communist, Castro very notably in February 1993 solicited foreign oil company exploitation of Cuba's potential offshore oil resources, and welcomed foreign investment in a considerable range of other natural resources and other enterprises. In July, he announced further attempts to stimulate foreign investment, and in bids for hard currency announced that Cubans could now hold foreign currency and that five times as many Cuban exile visits were to be permitted. In September, he announced that some kinds of occupations would be allowed self-employment; farmers would be allowed to work uncultivated state land; and that hard-currency stores would be permitted, outside the existing state-run distribution system. Throughout the year, as the Cuban economy continued to fall apart, Castro's hold on the country weakened.

Alina Fernandez Revuelta, a daughter not publicly acknowledged by Castro, caused her father some embarrassment by leaving Cuba in December 1993.

After leading the successful 1959 revolution against the government of Fulgencio Batista, Castro was a leading figure in world politics until the late 1980s. He survived the U.S.-backed Bay of Pigs invasion of 1961 and also the Soviet missile withdrawal after the 1962 Cuban Missile Crisis came very close to igniting World War III, remaining in power as a Soviet ally and economic dependent through the late 1980s. Castro has played a major role in supplying and training left revolutionaries throughout Latin America, and sent tens of thousands of troops to Angola and Ethiopia in the late 1970s; withdrawal of those forces was agreed upon only in the late 1980s, under pressure from the Soviet Union. Castro attended the University of Havana, and practiced law in Havana before beginning his political career. He is married to Mirta Diaz-Bilart; they have one son. He also has several other children not publicly acknowledged.

FURTHER READING

Fidel: Castro's Political and Social Thought. SHELDON B. LISS. Westview, 1994.
Fidel Castro: Cuban Revolutionary. WARREN BROWN. Millbrook, 1994.
Fidel Castro and the Quest for a Revolutionary Culture in Cuba. JULIE M. BUNCK. Pennsylvania State University Press, 1994.
Fidel Castro. ROBERT E. QUIRK. Norton, 1993.
Guerrilla Prince: The Untold Story of Fidel Castro. GEORGIE A. GEYER. Andrews & McMeel, 1993.
Castro! DON E. BEYER. Watts, 1993.
Fidel Castro. PAUL MADDEN. Rourke, 1993.
Fidel by Fidel: A New Interview with Dr. Fidel Castro Ruz, President of the Republic of Cuba. FIDEL CASTRO et al. Borgo Press, 1993.
Cuba on the Brink: Fidel Castro, the Cuban Missile Crisis, and the Soviet Collapse. JAMES G. BLIGHT et al. Pantheon, 1993.
Castro's Final Hour. ANDRES OPPENHEIMER. Simon & Schuster, 1993.
"Is Fidel washed up?" SAUL LANDAU. *Progressive,* Aug. 1992.
"Fidel's world." PATRICK SYMMES. *American Spectator,* July 1992.
"Fidel's last resort." ANNE-MARIE O'CONNOR. *Esquire,* Mar. 1992.
The Tiger and the Children: Fidel Castro and the Judgment of History. ROBERTO L. ESCALONA. Transaction, 1992.
"Maximum leader." GEORGIE ANNE GEYER. *American Heritage,* Nov. 1991.

"The last communist." MARK FALCOFF. *Commentary*, June 1991.

"Guerrilla Prince. . . ." ARTURO CRUZ, JR. et al. *New Republic*, Apr. 22, 1991.

Guerrilla Prince: The Real Story of the Rise and Fall of Fidel Castro. GEORGIE A. GEYER. Little, Brown, 1991.

Fidel Castro. JUDITH BENTLEY. Messner, 1991

Castro's Cuba, Cuba's Fidel. LEE LOCKWOOD. Westview, 1990.

Chamorro, Violeta (Violeta Barrios de Chamorro; 1939–)

Nicaraguan President Violeta Chamorro found herself very seriously hampered by continual political infighting during 1993, as the uneasy compromise and balance between Contra and Sandinista forces that had ended the civil war proved very hard to maintain. As Sandinistas continued to hold high offices in the Nicaraguan military and government, with Chamorro even seeming to rely more and more on their support, many of her key supporters left her. Most notably, the National Opposition Union, her own 14-party coalition, went into opposition to her government in February. Armed clashes grew throughout the country, and especially in the north, where a low-level Contra-Sandinista war redeveloped. Right-wing Nicaraguan commandos seized their country's Costa Rican mission in March; a left-wing arms cache in Managua exploded in May, and such arms caches were found in many locations throughout the year. Chamorro declared a state of emergency in the north in May, while fighting continued. Three-quarters of Nicaragua's budget was provided by foreign aid, and the economy was far from viable; but in July, the U.S. Senate pressed Chamorro by suspending more than $100 million in scheduled aid payments.

Ultimately, in early September, Chamorro risked a renewed civil war, by announcing that she would fire armed forces head Humberto Ortega early in 1994; she was immediately denounced by Ortega and his brother, chief Sandinista leader Daniel Ortega. The United States and the Organization of American States supported Chamorro; the crisis continued.

Chamorro became the elected President of Nicaragua on February 25, 1990, after Sandinista leader Daniel Ortega had quite surprisingly agreed to a free election, and to honor the election results. Her election was the start of a new chapter in a story that began on January 10, 1978, when her husband, crusading newspaper editor Pedro Joaquin Chamorro Cardenal, a leading opponent of the dictator Anastasio Somoza Debayle, was murdered on a street in Managua. That murder made him a martyr, and helped trigger the series of events that led to the Sandinista revolution and the overthrow of Somoza.

Violeta Chamorro was a member of the first Sandinista government, but withdrew within a year, when she saw the Sandinistas moving toward a dictatorship of their own, and took her husband's place as the crusading editor of *La Prensa*, in opposition to Sandinista attacks on freedom. Then came ten years of civil war between Contra and Sandinista forces, with the United States helping the Contras, and Cuba and the Soviet Union helping the Sandinistas. In her first year as president of a free Nicaragua, Chamorro successfully reached agreements to disarm the former combatants, guaranteeing the freedoms that she and her husband had fought for, and trying to set her very poor and damaged country on the road to economic recovery.

Violeta Barrios and Pedro Chamorro had four children; Carlos Fernando and Claudia became highly placed Sandinistas, while Pedro Joaquin became a Contra leader and Cristiana an editor of *La Prensa*.

FURTHER READING

"The woman who. . . ." TREVOR ARMBRISTER. *Reader's Digest* (Canadian), Feb. 1991.

"Flowers for Violeta." DENNIS COVINGTON. *Vogue*, Aug. 1990.

"Chamorro, Violeta Barrios de." *Current Biography*, June 1990.

"A defiant widow. . . ." RON ARIAS. *People*, Mar. 19, 1990.

"A family affair. . . ." D'ARCY JENISH. *Maclean's*, Mar. 12, 1990.

"Chamorro. . . ." JOHN MOODY. *Time*, Mar. 12, 1990.

Life Stories of the Nicaraguan Revolution. DENIS L. HEYCK. Routledge Chapman and Hall, 1990.

Nicaragua Divided: La Prensa and the Chamorro Legacy. PATRICIA T. EDMISTEN. University Presses of Florida, 1990.

Charles, Prince of Wales (Charles Philip Arthur George; 1948–)

The Prince of Wales is the oldest son of Elizabeth II and Prince Philip, and heir to the British throne. As such,

FURTHER READING

"What's next for. . . . " INGRID SEWARD. *Good Housekeeping*, Aug. 1993.
"Scenes from a marriage." *Life*, Feb. 1993.
Behind Palace Doors: Marriage and Divorce in the House of Windsor. NIGEL DEMPSTER and PETER EVANS. Putnam, 1993.
Royal Marriages. COLIN CAMPBELL. St. Martin's, 1993.
"Royal marriage. . . ." DAME BARBARA CARTLAND. *Newsweek*, Dec. 21, 1992.
"Throne out." JERRY ADLER. *Newsweek*, Dec. 21, 1992.
"Separate lives." MICHELLE GREEN. *People*, Dec. 21, 1992.
"Royal fire storm." ANDREW PHILLIPS. *Maclean's*, Nov. 30, 1992.
"The warring Windsors." DERMOT PURGAVIE and GARTH PEARCE. *TV Guide*, Aug. 8, 1992.
"Alone together." ROBERT LACY. *Life*, Aug. 1992.
"Heartache in the palace. . . ." ANNE EDWARDS. *McCall's*, Aug. 1992.
"Royal rumpus. . . ." GEORGE RUSSELL. *Variety*, July 13, 1992.
"Love on the rocks." MICHELLE GREEN. *People*, June 29, 1992.
"Portrait of a marriage." *Newsweek*, June 22, 1992.
"What's it all about, Charlie?" ADAM PLATT. *Esquire*, June 1992.
Diana: A Princess and Her Troubled Marriage. NICHOLAS DAVIES. Birch Lane/Carol, 1992.
Charles and Diana: The Tenth Anniversary. BRIAN HOEY. Studio Books, 1991.

he is, like the other British "royals," the object of enormous worldwide media attention, directed at every aspect of his personal life. In 1993, massive media attention was once again focused on his personal life, and especially on his marital difficulties, even though he and Diana, Princess of Wales, announced their separation in December 1992. In 1993, the media focused on tapes, allegedly of 1989 telephone conversations between the Prince and Ms. Camilla Parker Bowles. They also focused on tapes allegedly containing arguments over marriage and separation matters, between the Prince and Princess. In spite of his continuing attention to environmental and social welfare matters, the media attack on the Prince of Wales mounted throughout the year, as many in Britain questioned his future and that of the monarchy itself. In November, he and Charles Clover published the book *Highgrove: An Experiment in Organic Gardening and Farming*.

Prince Charles attended Trinity College, Cambridge, and the University College of Wales. He married Lady Diana Spencer in 1981; they have two children: William Arthur Philip, born June 21, 1982; and Henry Charles Albert David, born September 15, 1984. His books include *The Old Man of Lochnagar* (1980), *A Vision of Britain* (1989), and *The Prince of Wales' Watercolours* (1991).

Charles, Ray (Robinson, Ray Charles; 1930–) In a rare treat for music lovers, Ray Charles issued a new album in 1993, *My World*. The much-acclaimed collection included songs both old and new, among them modern classics like Leon Russell's "A Song for You," issued as a single before the album's release, and Paul Simon's "Still Crazy After All These Years," as well as (unusually for Charles) several songs of social content, notably "None of Us Are Free," "One Drop of Love," and the title cut. Rounding out the album were "So Help Me God," "Let Me Take Over," "If I Could," "Love Has a Mind of its Own," and "I'll Be There." Moving into his fifth decade in music, Charles also received a National Medal of the Arts in 1993, presented by President Bill Clinton.

Born in Albany, Georgia, Charles has been blind from early childhood, and has composed and arranged in Braille. He emerged as a leading soul singer in the early 1950s, began his

recording career with Atlantic Records in 1952, and formed his own band in 1954. Charles was one of the first to join the African-American gospel and blues heritages, and to take them fully into popular music, and also became an emblematic figure during the civil rights struggles of the 1950s and 1960s, repeatedly breaking the "color line." He is best known to wide audiences for his recordings, among them "The Things I Used to Do" (1953), "I've Got a Woman" (1955), "Georgia On My Mind" (1960), and "I Can't Stop Loving You" (1962). His popularity surged again in the late 1980s and early 1990s. He has published the autobiographical *Brother Ray: Ray Charles' Own Story* (1978; revised and updated 1992), with David Ritz, and *Ray Charles: A Man and His Soul* (1986). Among his honors are ten Grammy awards, and a lifetime achievement Grammy in 1987. Formerly married, he has nine children.

FURTHER READING

"Ray Charles sings. . . ." *Jet*, May 3, 1993.
"Raw truth and joy. . . ." MICHAEL LYDON. *Atlantic*, Mar. 1991.
"Ray Charles." DAVID GROGAN. *People*, Nov. 19, 1990.
"What'd I say. . . ." JEFF LEVENSON. *Down Beat*, Jan. 1989.

Charteris, Leslie (Leslie Charles Bowyer Yin; 1907–93) Singapore-born Leslie Yin, who took Charteris as his pen name and later his legal name, was the creator of the very success-

ful Saint (Simon Templar) thriller series. He created the Saint in his third novel, *Meet the Tiger* (1928); heavily promoted by Hodder and Stoughton and further developed by the author, the series took off nationally and internationally during the 1930s. Charteris went to Hollywood in the early 1930s, worked as a screenwriter on several films, and continued to write such Saint books as *The Saint in New York* (1935), in 1939 the first of the series to be adapted into a film, with Louis Hayward in the title role. Later film versions starred George Sanders. There were three Saint television series, the best known by far being the 1960s series starring Roger Moore. Leslie Charteris was survived by his wife, Audrey Long, and a daughter. (d. London; April 15, 1993)

FURTHER READING

Obituary. *New York Times*, Apr. 18, 1993.
Obituary. *The Times* (of London), Apr. 17, 1993.

Chase, Chevy (Cornelius Crane Chase; 1943–) Film star Chase tried his hand at a late-night television talk show in 1993, with negative results. On September 7, after a great deal of publicity, his Fox network "The Chevy Chase Show" premiered, in direct competition with the Jay Leno and David Letterman shows. The Chase show never really got off the ground, receiving very adverse reviews and quickly dropping in the ratings after initial viewer curiosity had been satisfied. On October 18, less than six weeks after its premiere, it was cancelled.

His concentration all year having been on his television show, Chase appeared in little else during 1993. He did play a cameo role opposite Arnold Schwarzenegger in *The Last Action Hero*, and starred in the forthcoming film comedy *Cops and Robbers*. He was also named man of the year by Harvard's Hasty Pudding Club.

New York City-born Chase was a comedy writer and off-Broadway comedian in cabaret in the late 1960s and early 1970s, emerging in the mid-1970s as a nationally-recognized television comedian as a member of "Saturday Night Live" troupe. In the late 1970s, he also became a leading film comedian, in such movies as *Foul Play* (1978), *Oh Heavenly Dog* (1980), *Caddyshack* (1980; and the 1988 sequel), *Modern Problems* (1981), *Deal of the Century*

(1983), *Fletch* (1985; and the 1988 and 1989 sequels), *Spies Like Us* (1985), *Three Amigos* (1986), *Funny Farm* (1988), *National Lampoon's Christmas Vacation* (1989), *Nothing But Trouble* (1991), and *Memoirs of an Invisible Man* (1992). His 1967 B.S. was from Bard College and his 1970 C.C.S. from the Institute for Audio Research. Chase has been married three times and has three children.

FURTHER READING

"One down. . . ." DANA KENNEDY and FRANK SPOTNITZ. *Entertainment*, Oct. 29, 1993.
"Chevy." MARY MURPHY. *TV Guide*, Aug. 28, 1993.
"The chase is on." DINITIA SMITH. *New York*, Aug. 23, 1993.
"I'm finally growing up." DOTSON RADER. *Parade*. Apr. 19, 1992.
"Chevy Chase." MARK MORRISON. *US*, Mar. 1992.

Chavez, Cesar Estrada (1927–93)

Arizona-born Cesar Chavez, a Mexican-American, began working on his family's farm near Yuma while still a small child; at ten, after his family lost its farm in the Great Depression, he became, as did his entire family, California migrant farmworkers. He began his organizing career with Saul Alinsky's Community Service Organization in the early 1950s, and in 1958, at Delano, California, founded the National Farm Workers Association, forerunner of the United Farm Workers of America. He led the historic table grape workers strike (La Huelga; 1965–70) that won a collective bargaining contract from San Joaquin valley grape producers, in the process generating massive nationwide support for the cause (La Causa), which included a successful nationwide California table grape boycott and paved the way for the 1974 California Agricultural Labor Relations Act. Chavez emerged as one of the leading trade unionists and liberal leaders of his time. Beset by a continuing flow of nonunion migrant workers from Mexico, unfriendly federal and state administrations, and continuing employer resistance, Chavez and his union were greatly weakened during the 1980s and 1990s, as membership sharply declined and boycotts of grapes and lettuce failed. He was survived by his wife Helen and eight children. (d. San Luis, Arizona; April 23, 1993)

FURTHER READING

"Cesar's ghost. . . ." FRANK BARDACKE. *Nation*, July 26, 1993.
"A great and good man." *Commonweal*, June 4, 1993.
Obituary. *Current Biography*, June 1993.
"Viva la Causa!" EUGENE BOYLE. *America*, May 22, 1993.
"Cesar Chavez." PETER MATTHIESSEN. *New Yorker*, May 17, 1993.
"Cesar Chavez. . . ." "Threatened by fasts. . . ." VICTOR SALANDINI. "The fruits of Chavez's labor. . . ." ARCHBISHOP ROGER M. MAHONY. "Millions reaped. . . ." ARTHUR JONES. *National Catholic Reporter*, May 7, 1993.
"A secular saint. . . ." DAVID GATES. *Newsweek*, May 3, 1993.
Obituary. *The Times* (of London), Apr. 27, 1993.
Obituary. *New York Times*, Apr. 24, 1993.
Cesar Chavez: Union Leader. BRUCE W. CONORD, Chelsea House, 1993.
Cesar Chavez: Labor Leader. MARIA E. CEDENO. Millbrook, 1993.
Cesar Chavez. BURNHAM HOLMES. Raintree Steck-Vaughn, 1992.
La Causa: The Migrant Farmworkers' Story. DANA C. DE RUIZ and RICHARD LARIOS. Raintree Steck-Vaughn, 1992.
Conquering Goliath: Cesar Chavez at the Beginning, FRED ROSS. Wayne State University Press, 1992. Reprint of 1989 ed.
Cesar Chavez: Hope for the People. DAVID GOODWIN. Fawcett, 1991.
Cesar Chavez. CONSUELOS RODRIGUEZ. Chelsea House, 1991.

Chavis, Benjamin Franklin, Jr.

(1948–) On April 9, 1993, Rev. Benjamin Chavis stepped into shoes fashioned by William E. Du Bois, James Weldon Johnson, Walter White, and Roy Wilkins, as executive director of the National Association for the Advancement of Colored People (NAACP), the leading American civil rights organization of the 20th century. Rev. Chavis succeeded retiring executive director Rev. Benjamin L. Hooks, his selection coming after Rev. Jesse Jackson had withdrawn his candidacy, facing substantial opposition on the organization's board of directors.

A strongly motivated activist, Chavis immediately plunged into the work of modernizing and re-energizing the NAACP, strongly and very publicly addressing a series of major issues, as in the NAACP-mediated Denny's res-

"Ben Chavis. . . ." LYNN NORMENT. *Ebony*, July 1993.
"Getting real at the NAACP. . . ." *Newsweek*, June 14, 1993.
"Ben again. . . ." W. HAMPTON SIDES. *New Republic*, May 10, 1993.
"Chavis to lead NAACP. . . ." MATTHEW S. SCOTT. *Black Enterprise*, July 1993.

taurant chain agreement to guarantee non-discriminatory practices, the NAACP's criticism of Hughes Aircraft hiring practices, and the NAACP's increased emphasis on street crime prevention and other African-American community issues. On the personal side, a revised edition of his 1983 *Psalms from Prison* was scheduled for 1994 publication.

Born in Oxford, North Carolina, Chavis is a veteran of the southern civil rights struggles of the 1960s and 1970s. While a young minister working with the United Church of Christ in 1970, he became one of the "Wilmington 10," charged of complicity in the burning of a white-owned grocery store in Wilmington, North Carolina. He was convicted in 1976 on the basis of false evidence; his conviction was reversed in 1979, after three witnesses admitted lying at his trial. Before his NAACP appointment, Chavis was director of the United Church of Christ's Commission for Racial Justice, and active in an attempt to link environmental and racial issues.

Chavis completed his divinity degree studies at Duke University in 1979, while in the fourth year of his unjustified imprisonment; he related that he had been taken to his studies on campus in leg irons and handcuffs. He is married to Martha Chavis.

FURTHER READING

"He's no gentle Ben. . . ." JACK E. WHITE. *Time*, July 19, 1993.

Chrétien, Jean (Joseph Jacques Jean Chrétien; 1934–) On June 25, 1993, Jean Chrétien's Liberal Party won a landslide victory in the Canadian general elections, gaining 99 seats to emerge with 178 and an overwhelming majority. The incumbent Progressive Conservative party suffered an extraordinary defeat, losing 151 of its 153 seats, including the Vancouver seat of party leader and Prime Minister Kim Campbell. Chrétien succeeded Campbell as Prime Minister on November 4. The separatist Bloc Québécois gained 46 seats, to emerge dominant in Quebec.

In office, Chrétien faced the same unsolved and massive problems that had caused Brian Mulroney to resign and Kim Campbell to fail. The Canadian economy continued to fall deeper into depression, as unemployment grew and government-funded social welfare, health, and education programs were cut even further as available government revenues continued to fall. Many Canadians blamed Mulroney for the adverse effects of the 1988 Canada-U.S. free trade agreement, which they believed to be siphoning off desperately needed Canadian income at a time when the world recession was greatly hurting Canada, a trading nation. Most Canadians felt that government economic stimulus plans were wholly ineffective.

Chrétien also inherited the second great question facing Canada, the future of Quebec and the possible end of the current Canadian nation. After the 1990 failure of the 1987 Meech Lake agreements, Mulroney and other leaders, including Quebec premier Robert Bourassa, had tried again, and had developed the August 28, 1992 Charlottetown Accord, providing for recognition of a "distinct society" for Quebec within Canada, as part of a considerable range of concessions to Quebec; major federal and provincial government changes; and "aboriginal" self-government for the nation's Native Canadians. But the October 26, 1992 national referendum decisively rejected the accord, and all major questions remained unsolved when Chrétien took office. By year's end, Chrétien had expressed and then withdrew major reservations about the North American Free Trade Agreement (NAFTA), named a cabinet, and cancelled a controversial government helicopter purchase agreement. All lay ahead.

Born in Shawinigan, Quebec, Chrétien graduated from Laval University and practiced law before going into politics. He was a Liberal member of the House of Commons (1963–86). He was parliamentary secretary to the Prime Minister (1965), and then held several cabinet-level positions, his Ministries including Finance (1966), Industry, Trade and Commerce (1976–77), Finance (1977–79), Justice, Attorney-General of Canada, Social Development (1980–82), Energy, Mines and Resources (1982–84), and Secretary of State for External Affairs, Deputy Prime Minister (1984). He resigned in 1986, practiced law, and was then re-elected to Parliament from a New Brunswick constituency (1990–   ), also becoming national leader of the Liberal Party (1990–   ). His books include *Straight from the Heart* (1985) and *Finding a Common Ground* (1992). He is married to Aline Chaîné, and has three children.

FURTHER READING

"Today's man. . . ." ANTHONY WILSON-SMITH. *Maclean's*, Nov. 1, 1993.
"Tomorrow's man?" E. KAYE FULTON and MARY JANIGAN. *Maclean's*, Oct. 18, 1993.
"Questions of leadership. . . ." ROBERT LEWIS et al. *Maclean's*, Dec. 28, 1992.
"Burying the past. . . ." KEVIN DOYLE and ANTHONY WILSON-SMITH. *Maclean's*, Oct. 5, 1992.
"Jean Chrétien. . . ." ROY MACSKIMMING. *Chatelaine*, Apr. 1991.
"Chrétien looks ahead." *Maclean's*, July 2, 1990.
"Chrétien, Jean." *Current Biography*, Apr.1990.
"A cool hand at the helm. . . ." BRUCE WALLACE. *Maclean's*, Feb. 5, 1990.

Christoff, Boris (1914–93) Bulgarian-born Boris Christoff, one of the most celebrated bassos of his time, studied music in Rome from 1942, was interned as a displaced person after the war, and then returned to Rome, making his professional debut there in 1946. His long identification with the Boris Godunov title role began at Covent Garden in 1950, and in 1956 he sang it at the San Francisco Opera, in his American debut. Christoff became a leading figure in European opera, and reached far wider audiences in his many recordings, most notably in his Russian song recordings and in his recordings of *Boris Gudunov*. He was survived by his wife, Franca. (d. Rome; June 28, 1993)

FURTHER READING

Obituary. *Opera News*, Oct. 1993.
Obituary. *Billboard*, July 10, 1993.
Obituary. *The Times* (of London), June 29, 1993.
Obituary. *New York Times*, June 29, 1993.

Christopher, Warren (1925–   ) During his first year as U.S. Secretary of State, Warren Christopher spent much of his time attempting to deal with problems inherited from the previous administration, with special emphasis on the ongoing civil wars in Bosnia-Herzegovina and Somalia, and the military dictatorship in Haiti, all areas in which U.S. policies were largely unsuccessful. He did play a quietly substantial role in laying the basis for the major Middle East peace breakthrough that culminated in the historic White House Yitzhak Rabin-Yasir Arafat handshake and Palestinian autonomy agreement of September 19, 1993. Christopher acted for the United States on the whole range of foreign policy issues and relationships during 1993, from stating American support for Boris Yeltsin to warning North Korea not to develop nuclear weapons, as the United States continued to de-

velop its role as the only remaining superpower.

Pennsylvania-born Christopher began his career as a law clerk to U.S. Supreme Court Justice William O. Douglas (1949–50). Returning to California, he began his long career with the Los Angeles law firm O'Melveny and Myers, becoming a partner in 1958, and going back to the firm after periods of government service. He was a deputy U.S. Attorney General during the Johnson Administration (1967–69), and a deputy Secretary of State during the Carter years (1977–81), in 1980 becoming heavily involved in negotiations for the release of the Iran hostages, about which he wrote (with others) *American Hostages in Iran: The Conduct of a Crisis* (1985). In 1991, he chaired the Independent Commission on the Los Angeles Police Department, formed after the Rodney King beating; its report established a pervasive pattern of racism in the department and called for the resignation of police chief Daryl F. Gates.

Christopher played a substantial role in the 1992 presidential elections. During the campaign, he was a key Clinton advisor, and was part of the selection committee that recommended choosing Al Gore as the vice-presidential candidate. Immediately after the campaign, he was chosen manager of the Clinton transition team, to take day-to-day responsibility for developing recommendations for the key posts in the new administration, before himself being named Secretary of State. Christopher's 1945 B.S. was from the University of Southern California and his 1949 LL.B. from Stanford University. He is married and has four children.

FURTHER READING

"Defending his boss." DAN GOODGAME and J.F.O. MCALLISTER. *Time*, Oct. 18, 1993.
" 'A preventer of crises.' " LOUISE LIEF and TIM ZIMMERMAN. *U.S. News & World Report*, July 5, 1993.
"Clothed ambition. . . ." JACOB HEILBRUNN. *New Republic*, Feb. 1, 1993.
"The transition. . . ." BILL TURQUE. *Newsweek*, Nov. 16, 1992.

Chung, Connie (Constance Yu-hwa Chung; 1946–) A moment in social history: On June 1, 1993, Connie Chung premiered as co-host with Dan Rather on the "CBS Evening News," becoming the first Asian-American nightly news anchor on any of the big three networks and only the second woman anchor, after Barbara Walters on ABC (1976–78), and the first co-anchor ever on CBS. Commenting on the announcement of the pairing in May, which broke the three-white-male pattern that had dominated network news in recent years, Chung thanked not only CBS executives but also their wives "for raising their consciousness."

Though not the field reporter that Rather is, Chung has long been one of the most popular and recognizable television news figures, and the aim was clearly to give the nightly news something of a new look and to shore up sagging ratings. By late 1993, CBS still lagged behind ABC and sometimes NBC as well; it remained to be seen how the partnership would fare in the long run. Meanwhile Chung on her own was hosting a new CBS prime-time news magazine program "Eye to Eye With Connie Chung," which premiered in June; it was well-received, and was at times in the top dozen programs in the weekly ratings.

Born in Washington, D.C., Chung began her broadcasting career in 1969, as a Washington-area television reporter, and moved through a series of increasingly responsible and highly visible jobs in the next two decades, including seven years (1976–83) anchoring KNXT in Los Angeles and a series of anchor assignments with NBC (1983–89), before moving to CBS. There she developed a successful weekly news magazine program, but in 1990 scaled back her activities to a series of specials, under the title "Face to Face With Connie Chung," while seeking to become pregnant, in a move that reverberated with many women of her generation, who had focused on career success at the expense of some personal choices. In 1991, she reduced her work and travel schedule even further, though continuing to serve as weekend anchor of the "CBS Evening News" and filling in occasionally on CBS morning news programs. She returned to full activity in 1993. Chung received her B.S. from the University of Maryland in 1969. She is married to television talk-show host Maury Povich.

FURTHER READING

"This is her life." MARY C. HICKEY. *Ladies Home Journal*, Oct. 1993.
"Make room for Connie." RICK MARIN. *TV Guide*, June 5, 1993.
"Anchor aweigh." SHELLEY LEVITT. *People*, June 21, 1993.

"Connie Chung. . . ." ALAN EBERT. *Good Housekeeping*, June 1993.
Connie Chung: Broadcast Journalist. MARY MALONE. Enslow, 1992.
"Waking up . . ." SUSAN SCHINDEHETTE. *People*, Aug. 20, 1990.
"Chung, Connie." *Current Biography*, July 1989.
The Imperfect Mirror: Inside Stories of Television Newscasters. DANIEL PAISNER. Morrow, 1989.

Cisneros, Henry Gabriel (1947–)

During his first year in office, U.S. Secretary of Housing and Urban Development Henry Cisneros spent much time dealing with what he, in July, called "the most pressing matter in our department": the continuing and growing mass of foreclosed HUD-financed and foreclosed-on property left over from the real estate crash of the 1980s. However, no substantial progress was made toward solution of the problem, which lay with Congress, not Cisneros. Nor were any major new housing or urban development programs proposed by the Clinton administration or initiated by Congress. Cisneros and others developed some imaginative new approaches, involving such devices as higher loan limits for HUD to stimulate no-down-payment loans for home purchase, and development of plans that would encourage low-income families to buy HUD-foreclosed homes, community stimulus banks, and neighborhood reconstruction corps, but the net result of it all in 1993 was a worsening of housing situation of the poor, while private sector housing was reviving due to much lower interest rates.

Cisneros did try to focus on homelessness, on June 10 joining Washington's mayor Sharon Pratt Kelly in announcing plans to create a model D.C. program on homelessness, and later in the year delivering the plan. In early December, after a homeless woman died in the street outside his offices, he also announced the opening of some federal office buildings to the homeless and the allocation of $25 million in previously appropriated funds for homelessness. He also focused considerably on ending racism in public housing, demonstrating his concern in September, by firing the management of a Vidor, Texas housing authority that had discriminated against African-American public housing tenants. Cisneros was also editor of a new book exploring the problems of cities: *Interwoven Destinies: The Cities and the Nation* (1993).

San Antonio-born Cisneros holds a B.A. and M.A. in urban and regional planning from Texas A&M University, an M.A. in public administration from Harvard University's John F. Kennedy School, and a Ph.D. in public administration from George Washington University, after which he served a year as a White House Fellow under Secretary of Health, Education, and Welfare Elliot Richardson. His qualifications are practical, as well; he was elected to the San Antonio City Council in 1975, the year before he received his Ph.D., and in 1981, at age 33, became mayor of his home city—the first Mexican-American to hold the job in 140 years—serving until 1989. He has also served a stint as president of the National League of Cities.

In late 1988, he withdrew from politics, citing financial reasons, though probably because of media outcry over an extramarital affair with a political co-worker. In private life, he founded a successful financial firm; hosted "Texans," a quarterly television show; hosted "Adelante," a national daily Spanish-language radio show; and became deputy chairman of the Dallas Federal Reserve Bank, before leaving to join the Clinton campaign in mid-1992. Earlier, he had contributed to the book *Texas in Transition* (1986). Cisneros is married to Mary Alice Perez; they have three children.

FURTHER READING

Henry Cisneros: Mexican-American Political Leader. CHRISTOPHER HENRY. Chelsea House, 1994.
" 'They said I'd get used to it.' " ANN BLACKMAN. *Time*, Dec. 6, 1993.
"About face." JAN JARBOE. *Texas Monthly*, Mar. 1993.
Henry Cisneros: Mexican-American Leader. ELIZABETH C. MARTINEZ. Millbrook, 1993.
Henry Cisneros: A Leader for the Future, rev. ed. MAURICE ROBERTS. Childrens, 1991.
"Henry Cisneros on sabbatical." *Hispanic*, July 1989.
Henry Cisneros: Señor Alcade: A Biography of Henry Cisneros. JOHN GILLIES. Dillon/Macmillan, 1988.

Clapton, Eric (1945–)

British rock guitarist, singer, and composer Eric Clapton was greatly honored by his peers in 1993, and simultaneously scored a major commercial success. His album *Unplugged* won a Grammy as best album of the year, and brought Clapton himself a Grammy for best male rock performance. His

song "Tears In Heaven," mourning the accidental death of his young son, won a Grammy as best record of the year, and brought Clapton a Grammy for best pop male vocal performance. He and Will Jennings shared a song of the year Grammy for "Tears In Heaven," while he and Jim Gordon shared a best rock song Grammy for their new version of the old Clapton hit, "Layla." At the World Music Awards, he was named best-selling British recording artist of the year and best-selling rock artist of the year.

His work did indeed sell well: *Unplugged* was rated third for the year in Billboard's Top 200 list, and Clapton rated fourth in the Billboard 200 top album artist list. His earlier album *Time Pieces* was Billboard's top catalog album. Also in 1993, the hit single "My Back Pages," drawn from the October 1992 tribute to Bob Dylan, was released, featuring Clapton, George Harrison, David Crosby, Tom Petty, Roger McGuinn, and Neil Young. Clapton also appeared as a guitar soloist on the Ray Charles album *My World*.

Clapton played with several groups in the 1960s, including the Roosters (1963), Yardbirds (1963–65), Bluesbreakers (1965–66), Cream (1966–68), and Blind Faith (1969). He emerged as a leading solo guitarist and singer in the early 1970s, with such recordings as *Eric Clapton* (1970), *Layla* (1970), *Blind Faith* (1971), *Concert for Bangladesh* (1971), *Eric Clapton's Rainbow Concert* (1973), and *461 Ocean Boulevard* (1974). Among his later recordings were *Slowhand* (1977) *Just One Night* (1980), *Money and Cigarettes* (1983), *Journeyman* (1989), and *Un-*

plugged (1992). He appeared in the film *Tommy* (1974). He and Patti Boyd were married and divorced; he and Lori Delsanto had one son, now deceased.

FURTHER READING

The Eric Clapton Album: Thirty Years of Music and Memorabilia. MARK ROBERTY. Studio Books, 1994.
"Plugged in." STEVE FUTTERMAN. "In his own words." JANN WENNER et al. "Living on blues power." ROBERT PALMER. *Rolling Stone*, Apr. 29, 1993.
"Eric Clapton." STEVE DOUGHERTY. *People*, Mar. 1, 1993.
"Eric Clapton." ANDY WIDDERS-ELLIS. *Guitar Player*, Jan. 1992.
Eric Clapton: Lost in the Blues. HARRY SHAPIRO. Da Capo, 1992.
Musicians in Tune: Seventy-Five World-Famous Musicians Discuss the Creative Process. JENNY BOYD and HOLLY GEORGE-WARREN. Simon & Schuster, 1992.
Eric Clapton. FRED WEILER. Smithmark, 1992.
Slowhand: The Life and Music of Eric Clapton. MARC ROBERTY. Crown, 1991.
Eric Clapton: The New Visual Documentary. MARC ROBERT. Omnibus, 1990.
Rock Lives: Profiles and Interviews. TIMOTHY WHITE. Holt, 1990.
Clapton! RAY COLEMAN. Warner, 1988.
Eric Clapton. JOHN PIDGEON. Trafalgar, 1986.

Clausen, Cara: See DeBoer, Jessica.

Clayton, Richard: See Haggard, William.

Clinton, Bill (William Jefferson Blythe, IV; 1946–) U.S. President Bill Clinton's first year in office was strongly marked by his activist approach to the presidency, although on several issues he found himself facing substantial opposition within his own party. As he put it during his campaign, he intended to focus "like a laser" on the economy; but he was considerably slower than initially promised in putting an economic stimulus plan before Congress, and then suffered a major defeat in late April, withdrawing the plan on April 21, after failing to break a Republican filibuster. Clinton was also forced to compromise on his promised lifting of the ban on

gays in the military, after running into massive opposition, led in the military by General Colin Powell, and in Congress by Senator Sam Nunn. He was also unable to make much progress on the "hot spots" he had inherited from the Bush years, notably including Bosnia-Herzegovina and Somalia.

On the other hand, Clinton was able to take major pro-choice action by executive order, and did so on January 22, two days after his inauguration, sharply reversing U.S. policy on abortion at home and abroad. On domestic policy, Clinton gained much strength as the year developed, and as he learned about the possible uses of presidential power. He won the narrowest of victories in early August, his budget bill passing in the House 218–216 and in the Senator 51–50, with the deciding vote cast by Vice President Al Gore. Later in the year, he won victories in several other areas, perhaps most notably with passage of the North American Free Trade Agreement (NAFTA), and the Brady gun control bill; in the latter instance, the Republicans were forced to withdraw from a filibuster in progress, as a tremendous wave of pro-gun control public and congressional opinion rolled over the last-ditch opposition of the National Rifle Association and a few Republican senators, led by Bob Dole. President Clinton and Hillary Rodham Clinton were also able to effect an historic change in American attititudes toward acceptance of the principle of universal health insurance cover-

age, which likely would have been rejected out of hand as "socialized medicine" only a few years earlier.

As to his personal and presidential popularity, Clinton by year's end seemed to have taken the center of American politics, the sometime indecisiveness and seeming lack of believability of his early months in office behind him—probably helped by his acquisition of political professional David Gergen as White House communications director. Even his early, highly-publicized appointment problems, as with Zoë Baird and Lani Guinier, were behind him, replaced by the popularity of Attorney General Janet Reno and the extraordinarily positive impact of new Supreme Court Justice Ruth Bader Ginsburg.

Clinton had entered the Democratic presidential nomination race on October 3, 1991, running as a centrist and sounding the same themes he had been developing as chairman of the middle-of-the-road Democratic Leadership Council since 1990, with focus on the ailing American economy, universal health insurance, abortion choice, education reform, child support and welfare system reforms, and deficit reduction. He became the primary campaign frontrunner early in 1992, winning the nomination and then the presidential campaign despite direct personal attacks on such matters as his alleged extramarital affairs with Gennifer Flowers and others; his alleged "draft-dodging" during the Vietnam War; and his alleged general untrustworthiness. He was also attacked indirectly through attacks on his wife, Hillary Rodham Clinton, who was depicted by his opponents as a radical feminist. Late in the campaign, some Republicans even illegally caused his passport files to be searched for possibly derogatory information—and went so far as to seek derogatory information on his mother. Clinton's election was widely described as an extraordinary repudiation of George Bush, who had been enormously popular after the Persian Gulf War, in some job-approval polls scoring in the 90+ percent range.

On November 3, 1992, Clinton was elected 42nd President of the United States, defeating incumbent Bush and independent candidate H. Ross Perot. Clinton won in an electoral vote landslide, 370 electoral votes to Bush's 168 electoral votes; Perot won none. However, Clinton won these with only 43 percent of the popular vote (43.7 million votes), to Bush's 38 percent (38.2 million votes) and Perot's 19 percent (19.2 million votes). He and Vice President Al Gore were inaugurated on January 20, 1993.

Arkansas-born Clinton received his 1968 B.S. from Georgetown, and his 1973 J.D. from Yale; in between, he was a Rhodes Scholar at Oxford (1968–70). He taught law at the University of Arkansas Law School and was in private practice (1973–76) before entering politics as state attorney general (1977–79), then becoming governor of his home state (1979–81, and again 1983–92). Born three months after his father's death, he later took his stepfather's surname, Clinton. He and Hillary Rodham met when both were at Yale Law School; they married in 1975 and have one daughter, Chelsea. (For additional photos, see Baird, Zöe; Bentsen, Lloyd; and Reich, Robert.)

FURTHER READING

The Bill Clinton Story: Winning the Presidency. John Hohenberg. Syracuse University Press, 1994.
Bill Clinton: Eyes on the Future. Leslie Kitchen. Maryland Historical Press, 1994.
Bill Clinton: United States President. Michael D. Cole. Enslow, 1994.
Bill Clinton: As They Know Him. David Gallen. Gallen, 1994.
"Bill Clinton. . . ." Landon Y. Jones and Garry Clifford. *People,* Dec. 27, 1993.
" 'We've made real progress'. . . ." Kenneth T. Walsh and Matthew Cooper. *U.S. News & World Report,* Dec. 13, 1993.
" 'I tried to do so many things.' " Eleanor Clift. *Newsweek,* Dec. 13, 1993.
" 'That's what drives me nuts.' " Margaret Carlson and James Carney. *Time,* Dec. 13, 1993.
"Clinton on the brink. . . ." Walter Shapiro. *Esquire,* Dec. 1993.
"Bill's delivery." Viveca Novak. *Mother Jones,* Nov.-Dec. 1993.
" 'I didn't get. . . .' " Margaret Carlson et al. *Time,* Sep. 27, 1993.
" 'I want peace. . . .' " *U.S. News & World Report,* Sep. 27, 1993.
" 'I made the call. . . ." Eleanor Clift and Bob Cohn. *Newsweek,* Sep. 27, 1993.
"Clinton speaks on the economy." Marshall Loeb et al. *Fortune,* Aug. 23, 1993.
"No, Mister President, . . ." Walter Shapiro. *Esquire,* July 1993.
"That sinking feeling." Michael Duffy. *Time,* June 7, 1993.
"What's wrong? . . ." Joe Klein. *Newsweek,* June 7, 1993.
"Taken for a swim." Brit Hume. *National Review,* May 24, 1993.

"Battlin' Bill's initiation rite." Barbara Ehrenreich. *Nation,* May 24, 1993.
" 'Don't sacrifice your basic relationships' " Kenneth T. Walsh and Matthew Cooper. "America's first (working) couple." Kenneth T. Walsh. "Stress test." Matthew Cooper. *U.S. News & World Report,* May 10, 1993.
"Mr. & Mrs. President." James Deacon. *Maclean's,* Feb. 1, 1993.
"Mr. President. . . ." Kenneth T. Walsh et al. *U.S. News & World Report,* Feb. 1, 1993.
" 'My son, the president.' " William Childress. *Ladies Home Journal,* Feb. 1993.
"A talk with Clinton." Jonathan Alter et al. "Shooting the moon. . . ." Jonathan Alter. "Warm-up lessons." Tom Mathews. *Newsweek,* Jan. 25, 1993.
"Ready or not." Michael Duffy. *Time,* Jan. 25, 1993.
"High hopes. . . ." Steven V. Roberts. *U.S. News & World Report,* Jan. 25, 1993.
"The dynamic duo." Margaret Carlson. "First we have to roll up our sleeves." John F. Stacks and Henry Muller. "Moving in." Michael Kramer. "The torch is passed." Lance Morrow. *Time,* Jan. 4, 1993. "Man of the Year" issue.
Changing the Guard: How Bill Clinton Beat an Unbeatable President and a Billionaire Populist to Capture the White House. Peter Goldman. Random, 1993.
Bill Clinton: President from Arkansas. Gene L. Martin and Aaron Boyd. Tudor, 1993.
Bill Clinton: The 42nd President of the United States. Bob Italia. Abdo & Daughters, 1993.
Bill Clinton. Victoria Sherrow. Dillon/Macmillan, 1993.
Strange Bedfellows: How Television and the Presidential Candidates Changed American Politics, 1992. Tom Rosenstiel. Hyperion, 1993.
Willy Nilly: Bill Clinton Speaks Out. Edward P. Moser. Caliban/J.S. Sanders, 1993.
Our President: Bill Clinton. Bedik. Scholastic, 1993.
Bill Clinton: Our Forty-Second President. Robert Cwiklik. Millbrook, 1993.
Bill Clinton, rev. ed. Elaine Landau. Watts, 1993.
Story of Bill Clinton and Al Gore. Dell, 1993.
The Comeback Kid: The Life and Career of Bill Clinton. Charles F. Allen and Jonathan Portis. Birch Lane/Carol, 1992.
Bill Clinton: The Inside Story. Robert E. Levin. Shapolsky, 1992.
Slick Willie: Why America Cannot Trust Bill Clinton. Floyd G. Brown. Annapolis, 1992.

Clinton, Hillary Rodham (1947–)

During 1993, the first year of the Clinton administration, American First Lady Hillary Rodham Clinton began her emergence as one of the lead-

ing women of the 20th century, in the United States comparable to Eleanor Roosevelt, but perhaps better able—in this later, freer time—to exert direct impact on the course of events and the thinking of the American people. Clearly viewed by President Bill Clinton as his working partner, she influenced a great many Clinton administration initiatives. Far beyond those contributions, she directly led the fight for health care reform, as the highly visible head of the federal Task Force on National Health Care Reform spearheading that fight and playing a major role in transforming American attitudes toward universal health care, only a few years before derided as "socialized medicine." She also transformed national attitudes regarding herself; sharply attacked by Republicans as a "women's libber" during the 1992 presidential campaign, she emerged in 1993 as one of the most popular of Americans, forcing even her enemies to treat her with great respect. On the personal side, her father, Hugh Rodham, Sr., died on July 20, 1993.

In her own right, Hillary Rodham Clinton is a distinguished lawyer and law professor, children's advocate, educational reformer, and women's rights leader; indeed, she kept her own name, Hillary Rodham, until 1982, adopting Bill Clinton's name only for Arkansas political purposes, because of mounting local objections to her views on the question of keeping her own name.

Her 1969 B.A. was from Wellesley College, where she was president of college government,

and her 1973 J.D. from Yale Law School, where she served on the *Yale Review of Law and Social Action*. During and after law school, she worked at Cambridge and then in Washington with Marian Wright Edelman at the Children's Defense Fund; in later years, she was the chairman of the Fund's Board of Directors. In 1974, she was a staff member of the Impeachment Inquiry Staff of the House of Representatives Judiciary Committee, investigating the Watergate affair and the possible impeachment of President Richard M. Nixon.

She and Bill Clinton met when both were at Yale Law School. They married in 1975; she then joined him in Arkansas, where she taught law and joined the Rose Law Firm in Little Rock, there becoming a successful litigator. She also became a nationally known figure, for her work in several areas. Active in her profession, she was chair of the American Bar Association (ABA) Commission on Women in the Professions (1987–91). She also continued her nationwide work with the Children's Defense Fund and several other organizations. In Arkansas, she founded Arkansas Advocates for Children and Families (1977), and chaired the Arkansas Education Standards Committee (1983–84). She grew up in Park Ridge, Illinois. She and Bill Clinton have one daughter, Chelsea.

FURTHER READING

Meet Hillary Rodham Clinton. VALERIA SPAIN. Random, 1994.
First Lady: The Story of Hillary Rodham Clinton. AARON BOYD. M. Reynolds, 1994.
Hillary Rodham Clinton: First Lady. SUZANNE LEVERT. Millbrook, 1994.
"Bill Clinton. . . ." LANDON Y. JONES and GARRY CLIFFORD. *People*, Dec. 27, 1993.
"Clinton, Hillary Rodham." *Current Biography*, Nov. 1993.
"Who is she? . . ." NINA MARTIN. *Mother Jones*, Nov.-Dec. 1993.
"Scenes from a marriage. . . ." JOE KLEIN. *Newsweek*, Oct. 4, 1993.
"Hillary Rodham Clinton. . . ." JANE CHESNUTT. *Woman's Day*, Sep. 21, 1993.
"What's love. . . ." CHRISTOPHER HITCHENS. *Vanity Fair*, Sep. 1993.
"Whose Hillary is she, anyway?" WALTER SHAPIRO. *Esquire*, Aug. 1993.
"A hundred days of Hillary." MARGARET CARLSON. *Vanity Fair*, June 1993.
"Saint Hillary." MICHAEL KELLY. *New York Times Magazine*, May 23, 1993.

"Mother, daughter. . . ." MARIAN BURROS. *Family Circle*, May 18, 1993.

"The male media's. . . ." KATHA POLLITT. *Nation*, May 17, 1993.

"Her own woman." MICHELLE GREEN. *People*, May 10, 1993.

" 'We've had some good times.' " "At the center of power." Both by MARGARET CARLSON. *Time*, May 10, 1993.

" 'Don't sacrifice your basic relationships'. . . ." KENNETH T. WALSH and MATTHEW COOPER. "America's first (working) couple." KENNETH T. WALSH. *U.S. News & World Report*, May 10, 1993.

" 'There's a lot more coming.' " KENNETH T. WALSH and MATTHEW COOPER. *U.S. News & World Report*, May 3, 1993.

"Is it worth it?" " 'First Ladies I admire.' " " 'We are all responsible.' " All by DOTSON RADER. *Parade*, Apr. 11, 1993.

"The age of the smart woman." GAIL COLLINS. *Ladies Home Journal*, Apr. 1993.

"Hillary Clinton gets personal." ROXANNE ROBERTS. *Redbook*, Mar. 1993.

"Look out, it's superwoman!" SALLY QUINN. " 'We are all in this together.' " JOE KLEIN. "Hillary's role." HOWARD FINEMAN and MARK MILLER. *Newsweek*, Feb. 15, 1993.

"Mr. & Mrs. President." JAMES DEACON. *Maclean's*, Feb. 1, 1993.

"Can she deliver?" DAVID RUBEN. *Parenting*, Feb. 1993.

"Power mom." HOWARD G. CHUA-EOAN. *People*, Jan. 25, 1993.

"Now, the first chief advocate. . . ." KENNETH T. WALSH. *U.S. News & World Report*, Jan. 25, 1993.

"The dynamic duo." MARGARET CARLSON. " 'First we have to roll up our sleeves.' " JOHN F. STACKS and HENRY MULLER. *Time*, Jan. 4, 1993.

"Hillary Clinton. . . ." CARL SFERRAZZA ANTHONY. *Good Housekeeping*, Jan. 1993.

Hillary Rodham Clinton: A First Lady for Our Time. DONNIE RADCLIFFE. Warner, 1993.

Hillary Clinton: Inside Story. JUDITH WARNER. NAL-Dutton, 1993.

Hillary Clinton. JULIE BACH. Abdo & Daughters, 1993.

Hillary Rodham Clinton, a New Kind of First Lady. JoANN B. GUERNSEY. Lerner, 1993.

Hillary Rodham Clinton. VICTORIA SHERROW. Dillon/Macmillan, 1993.

Close, Glenn (1947–) Veteran stage and screen star Close, having won a Tony for her 1992 Broadway role in *Death and the Maiden*, returned to the stage again in 1993, starring as aging film star Norma Desmond opposite Alan Campbell as Joe Gillis in Andrew Lloyd Webber's musical version of Billy Wilder's 1950 classic film *Sunset Boulevard*. Directed by Trevor Nunn, the play opened in Los Angeles in December, to mixed reviews, although Close drew generally strong praise; it was scheduled to open in New York in 1994. Close also co-produced and starred in the television film *Skylark*, a sequel to their 1991 *Sarah, Plain and Tall*, as mail order bride Sarah Wittig opposite Christopher Walken as Jacob Witting; she won an Emmy nomination for the role.

Forthcoming was a starring role in the film *The Paper*, in a cast that included Robert Duvall, Marisa Tomei, and Randy Quaid; Ron Howard directed. Also forthcoming was a starring role as Col. Margarethe Cammermeyer, who was dismissed from the armed forces after making her lesbian sexual preferences known; Close and Barbara Streisand were co-producing the fact-based film.

Connecticut-born Close, on stage from the early 1970s, emerged as a stage and screen star in the 1980s, winning a Tony for her Broadway role in *The Real Thing* (1984) and playing leads in such films as *The World According to Garp* (1982), *The Big Chill* (1983), *The Natural* (1984), *Fatal Attraction* (1987), *Dangerous Liaisons* (1988), *Reversal of Fortune* (1990), *Hamlet* (1990), and *Meeting Venus* (1991). Her 1974 B.A. was from the College of William and Mary. She was previously married, to Cabot Wade and then to James Marlas, and has one child.

FURTHER READING

"Close to her heart." MELANIE BERGER. *Ladies Home Journal*, Jan. 1993.

"Glenn Close." FRANK SPOTNITZ. *American Film*, Nov.-Dec. 1991.

"Getting Close. . . ." STEPHEN FARBER. *Connoisseur*, Aug. 1991.

Cole, Natalie (1950–) The year 1993 brought a new album from Natalie Cole, her first since the 1991 smash hit *Unforgettable*. In *Take a Look*, she again sang a group of old standards, many of them from her father's time and all of them appealing to her audiences, beginning with the title track "Take a Look," a song with an equal rights message, written by Clyde Otis, that was identified with Aretha Franklin in the 1960s. She also sang such classics as "I Wish

You Love" and "As Time Goes By," and added some calypso songs popular in an earlier day, such as "Fiesta in Blue." The album was a solid success, though not the commercial smash hit that some had expected. On the other hand, neither was *Unforgettable*—until it won its Grammys early in the year following its release. *Take a Look* was Billboard's fourth-rated jazz album for 1993, while Cole was seventh-rated top jazz artist. Cole also appeared as an actress in a guest spot in the television series "I'll Fly Away."

Los Angeles-born Cole emerged as a star with her first recording, the album *Inseparable*, which included "This Will Be," which won her a 1975 Grammy award as best new artist, and a 1976 Grammy as best rhythm and blues female vocalist. Always popular, but not until the early 1990s a superstar, her albums included *Natalie* (1976), *Unpredictable* (1977), *I Love You So* (1979), *Don't Look Back* (1980), *I'm Ready* (1983), and *Unforgettable* (1991), the last a homage to her father, jazz musician Nat "King" Cole (d. 1965), in which she sang many of his old songs—electronically adding her voice to his in one song. At the 34th annual Grammy Awards ceremonies, in 1992, she and the album won an unexpected six Grammy Awards, and she quite suddenly emerged as a new superstar. Cole has also won a wide range of other awards, including two National Association for the Advancement of Colored People (NAACP) Image awards and an American Music Award. Her 1972 B.A. was from the University of Massachusetts. She is married to Marvin J. Yancy.

FURTHER READING

" 'I learned about forgiveness.' " Ovid Demaris. *Parade*, Nov. 7, 1993.
"At home with. . . ." Alan Carter. *Redbook*, Oct. 1993.
"Architectural Digest visits. . . ." Michael Frank. *Architectural Digest*, Sep. 1993.
"Natalie Cole says. . . ." *Jet*, July 5, 1993.
"Cole, Natalie." *Current Biography*, Nov. 1991.
"The untold story. . . ." Laura B. Randolph. *Ebony*, Oct. 1991.
"Natalie Cole's. . . ." David Wild. *Rolling Stone*, Sep. 19, 1991.

Collins, Albert

Collins, Albert (1932–93) Texas-born blues and jazz guitarist Albert Collins grew up in Houston, and began his career in the 1950s, playing in cabaret. His debut recording was the single "The Freeze" (1958). He continued to record in Texas into the 1960s, his best-known works of that period being the single "Frosty" and the album *Truckin' With Albert Collins* (1965). Encouraged by the rock group Canned Heat, he moved to California in 1968, and though successful on the nightclub circuit did not find an audience for his recordings. In 1978, Chicago's Alligator Records began to issue the series of records that were to make him a major figure, among them the Grammy-nominated albums *Ice Pickin* (1978), *Frostbite* (1980), *Frozen Alive* (1981), and *Cold Snap* (1986). He won several W.C. Handy Awards for his work with the blues, including a 1983 best blues album of the year for *Don't Lose Your Cool*. Collins also shared a Grammy with Robert Cray and Johnny Copeland for the album *Showdown* (1985). He was survived by his wife, songwriter Gwendolyn Collins. (d. Las Vegas; November 24, 1993)

FURTHER READING

Obituary. *Billboard*, Dec. 11, 1993.
"The lone star of blues guitar." David Gates. *Newsweek*, Dec. 6, 1993.
Obituary. *Variety*, Nov. 29, 1993.
Obituary. *The Times* (of London), Nov. 26, 1993.
Obituary. *New York Times*, Nov. 26, 1993.
"Bone-chilling blues. . . ." Andy Widders-Ellis. "Albert Collins. . . ." Jas Obrecht. *Guitar Player*, July 1993.
"Albert Collins." Dan Erlewine. *Guitar Player*, Aug. 1992.
"Albert Collins. . . ." David Whiteis. *Down Beat*, May 1991.

Collins, Phil

Collins, Phil (1951–) Singer, songwriter, drummer, and actor Phil Collins exercised all of his multiple talents in 1993. In his well-received new album *Both Sides*, Collins wrote, produced, and sang all the songs, and played all the instruments. Some of the songs were "Both Sides Of The Story" (also issued as a hit single), "We Wait And Wonder," "Everyday," and "Survivors." On December 8, Collins hosted the fourth annual Billboard Music Awards, at Universal City, California.

Collins also starred as an insurance investigator in the comedy-thriller film *Frauds*, directed by Stephan Elliott, in a cast that included Hugo Weaving and Josephine Byrnes. He also appeared in the fact-based television fiction film

Phil Collins. TOBY GOLDSTEIN. Ballantine, 1987.
The Phil Collins Story. JOHNNY WALLER. H. Leonard, 1986.

Conn, Billy (1918–93) Light-heavyweight and heavyweight boxer Billy Conn grew up in Pittsburgh, where he began his boxing career as a teenager in 1935. He quickly emerged as a leading light-heavyweight, and in 1939 became light-heavyweight champion, defeating Melio Bettina. Two years later, he became a heavyweight in order to fight champion Joe Louis, the world's leading boxer, for that title, and came very close to defeating Louis in their 15-round match. So far ahead on points after 10 rounds that he would have won the title if he had stayed the course, Conn tried and failed to knock out Louis, who instead knocked out Conn in the 13th round to retain his title. A projected rematch was interrupted by the World War II service of both fighters, and Louis knocked out Conn again during a 1946 rematch. Conn retired from the ring after the second Louis fight, returned, lost to Louis again, this time by decision in a 1948 six-round exhibition match, and permanently retired. He was survived by his wife Mary Louise, three sons, two sisters, and a brother. (d. Pittsburgh; May 29, 1993)

FURTHER READING

Obituary. *Current Biography*, Aug. 1993.
Obituary. *The Times* (of London), June 3, 1993.
Obituary. *New York Times*, May 30, 1993.

And The Band Played On, on the AIDS epidemic, based on the Randy Shilts book, and directed by Roger Spottiswoode, in a cast that included Matthew Modine, Alan Alda, Nathalie Baye, David Dukes, Richard Gere, Glenne Headly, Anjelica Huston, Swoosie Kurtz, Steve Martin, Ian McKellen, and Lily Tomlin.

London-born Collins joined the rock band Genesis in 1971, as the group's drummer, and became lead singer in 1975, recording such albums as *And Then There Were Three* (1978), *Abacab* (1981), and *Genesis* (1983). He emerged as a major rock soloist in the 1980s, starting with the album *Face Value* (1981), followed by his Grammy-winning, Oscar-nominated song "Against All Odds (Take a Look at Me Now)," the title song of the 1984 film, and the Grammy-winning album *No Jacket Required* (1985), with its number one singles "One More Night" and "Sussudio." In 1991, his "Another Day in Paradise," a song about homelessness, won the Grammy for best record of the year. In 1992, he issued the album *The Shorts*, the first of a projected two-album set titled "Genesis Live: The Way We Walk." He also starred in the film *Buster* (1988), co-writing the Grammy-winning "Two Hearts." He has been married twice, last to Jill Collins in 1984, and has three children.

FURTHER READING

Genesis of Phil Collins. SCOTT NANCE. Movie Publications Services, 1991.

Connally, John Bowden, Jr. (1917–93) Texas-born John Connally practiced law in Houston and Fort Worth after his World War II military sevice as a naval officer, beginning his political career by working in the congressional campaigns of Lyndon Johnson and managing Johnson's 1948 Senatorial campaign. He also became a lawyer and then a business manager for Texas oil billionaire Sid W. Richardson. Connally managed Johnson's 1960 vice-presidential campaign, and was appointed federal Navy Secretary by President John F. Kennedy in 1961. He resigned to make a successful Texas gubernatorial run, and was state governor (1963–69). He was seriously wounded while sitting in the front seat of President Kennedy's automobile during the 1963 Kennedy assassination. He became Treasury Secretary (1971–72) under Republican president Richard Nixon, bolting the Democratic Party to campaign for Nixon in 1972; leaving the Nixon administration shortly after the election, he survived Watergate, being acquitted on all counts in 1975. He then went into oil and real estate in Texas; when the overheated real estate market collapsed in the early 1980s, he was thrown into bankruptcy. With Mickey Herskowitz, he wrote the autobiographical *In History's Shadow: An American Odyssey* (1993). He was survived by his wife, Idanell, a daugher, and two sons. (d. Floresville, Texas, February 27, 1993)

FURTHER READING

Obituary. *Current Biography*, Aug. 1993.
"More than myth." PAUL BURKA. *Texas Monthly*, Aug. 1993.
"The shadow of Dallas." *New Yorker*, July 5, 1993.
Obituary. *The Times* (of London), June 17, 1993.
Obituary. *New York Times*, June 16, 1993.
Texas Big Rich: Exploits, Eccentricities, and Fabulous Fortunes Won and Lost. SANDY SHEEHY. Morrow, 1990.
The Lone Star: The Life of John Connally. JAMES RESTON, JR. HarperCollins, 1989.

Connery, Sean (Thomas Connery; 1930–)

In his 60s still one of the world's top film actors, Sean Connery in 1993 starred in yet another powerful character lead (one written with him in mind) in the film *Rising Sun*. Connery played Los Angeles Police Department detective John Connor whose supposedly expert knowledge of at least some Japanese is called upon by LAPD detective lieutenant Web Smith (Wesley Snipes), when they investigate the suspicious death of a young woman at a party in a Japanese corporate headquarters. The film, based on Michael Crichton's novel, was directed by Philip Kaufman, and written by Kaufman and Crichton. Co-starring were Harvey Keitel, Hiryuki Tagawa, and Tatjana Patitz, whose murder during a sex scene provided the event from which the plot unfolded. The film generated substantial protests from Asian-American groups angered by its allegedly anti-Asian bias. Forthcoming was a starring role in the film *Just Cause*, directed by Arnold Glincher.

On the personal side, Connery verified that he had contracted throat cancer, and that he had been successfully treated by radiation therapy in London during July and August.

Edinburgh-born Connery was on stage and screen in small roles during the 1950s and early 1960s; he became an instant star as sex-symbol James Bond in *Dr. No* (1962), and went on to become a worldwide celebrity in six more James Bond films: *From Russia With Love* (1963), *Goldfinger* (1964), *Thunderball* (1965), *You Only Live Twice* (1967), *Diamonds are Forever* (1971), and *Never Say Never Again* (1982). But he soon became far more than a sex symbol, showing himself to be a strong and flexible actor, in such films as *A Fine Madness* (1966), *The Molly Maguires* (1970), *The Wind and the Lion* (1975), *The Man Who Would Be King* (1975), *Robin and Marian* (1976), *Cuba* (1979), *The Untouchables* (1986; winning a best supporting actor Oscar), *The Name of the Rose* (1987), *Indiana Jones and the Last Crusade* (1989), *Family Business* (1989), *The Hunt for Red October* (1990), *The Russia House* (1990), and *Medicine Man* (1992). Connery has been married twice and has one child, the actor Jason Connery.

FURTHER READING

"Great Scot." ZOE HELLER. *Vanity Fair*, June 1993.
Sean Connery. JOHN PARKER. Contemporary, 1993.
The Films of Sean Connery. LEE PFEIFFER and PHILIP LISA. Carol, 1993.
" 'It's the books. . . .' " PETER SWET. *Parade*, May 10, 1992.
"Finely aged Scot." STEVEN GOLDMAN. *US*, Mar. 1992.
"Straight talk." JOHN H. RICHARDSON. *Premiere*, Feb. 1992.
Sean Connery: From 007 to Hollywood Icon. ANDREW YULE. Fine, 1992.
The Films of Sean Connery. ROBERT SELLERS. St. Martin's, 1991.
"A man called Connery." SUSAN SCHINDEHETTE. *People*, Dec. 18, 1989.
"Sean Connery. . . ." JOHN CULHANE. *Reader's Digest*, Aug. 1989.
"Connery. . . ." BEN FONG-TORRES. *American Film*, May 1989.

Connick, Harry, Jr. (1967–)

In creative terms, it was a relatively quiet year for Connick, although his November 1992 release, *25*, issued in celebration of his own 25th birthday, was played and sold largely in 1993, and was Billboards's fifth-rated top jazz album for the year; Connick himself was the fifth-ranked top jazz artist. In November 1993, he issued the well-received holiday album *When My Heart Finds Christmas*, singing some original compositions as well as a wide range of seasonal standards, from the title song to "Ave Maria" and "Sleigh Ride," backed by choir and orchestra. He also issued the video *New York Big Band Concert*, based on his appearances at New York's Paramount Theater during his 1991–92 world tour. In February, New Orleans native Connick had the notable honor of reigning as Bacchus at the Krewe of Bacchus's 25th anniversary parade, two days before Mardi Gras.

New Orleans-born jazz and pop singer, songwriter, and pianist Connick studied with James Booker, 3rd, and Ellis Marsalis (head of the Marsalis jazz clan) in his hometown while still in high school, and at the same time received much of his practical training playing the piano in French Quarter jazz clubs. Arriving in New York City at age 18, he attended the Manhattan School of Music, and, with door-opening help from Wynton Marsalis, cut his first jazz record, *Harry Connick, Jr.* (1987). A year later, at age 20, he cut his second record, *20* (1988). Then came his breakthrough soundtrack contributions to the film *When Harry Met Sally . . .* (1989), followed by the albums *Lofty's Roach Souffle* (1990), *We Are in Love* (1990), *Blue Light, Red Light* (1991), and *Eleven*, recorded when he was 11 years old. He made his film debut in *Memphis Belle* (1990) and also appeared in *Little Man Tate* (1991).

FURTHER READING

"Harry Connick, Jr. . . ." JOHN McDONOUGH. *Down Beat*, Jan. 1993.
"Connick, Harry, Jr." *Current Biography*, Nov. 1990.
"Harry's double take." BECCA PULLIAM. *Down Beat*, Oct. 1990.
"The entertainer. . . ." ROB TANNENBAUM. *Rolling Stone*, Mar. 23, 1989.

Constantine, Eddie (Edward Constantinowsky; 1917–93) Los Angeles-born Eddie Constantine, an actor, singer, and dancer, studied music at the Vienna Conservatory and trained in Europe and America as a singer, but began his career as a chorus dancer on Broadway and

in Hollywood. In France from 1949, he sang in Parisian cabaret, became a protégé of Edith Piaf, and suddenly emerged as a major European action film star in the 1950s, as American FBI agent Lemmy Caution in the French film series of that name. In the early 1960s, he also starred in several French "New Wave" films, among them Jean-Luc Godard's *Alphaville*. Constantine became a major star in Germany later in his career, making many German theatrical films and starring in German television. He became a French citizen. He was survived by his wife, Maja Faber-Janssen, and a daughter. (d. Weisbaden, Germany; February 25, 1993)

FURTHER READING

Obituary. *The Times* (of London), Mar. 15, 1993.
Obituary. *New York Times*, Mar. 2, 1993.

Coppola, Francis Ford (1939–) During 1993, Coppola planned and ultimately in late autumn began filming his next major film, *Mary Shelley's Frankenstein*, produced by Coppola's American Zoetrope, directed by Kenneth Branagh, and starring Branagh as Victor Frankenstein and Robert DeNiro as the monster, in a cast that includes Helena Bonham-Carter, Tom Hulce, Aidan Quinn, John Cleese, and Ian Holm. Coppola also issued a laser-disc expanded version of his 1992 film hit *Bram Stoker's Dracula*, with his audio-track comments throughout, and the book *Coppola and Eiko on Dracula*.

Still forthcoming was an American Zoetrope-produced film version of Frances Hodgson Burnett's children's story *The Secret Garden*, starring Kate Maberly as Mary Lennox and Maggie Smith as the housekeeper. Also forthcoming was a series of longform videos, to be co-produced by American Zoetrope.

Detroit-born Coppola is best known by far for two films: *The Godfather* (1972; he directed and co-wrote the screenplay), which won Oscars for best film and best screenplay, and *The Godfather Part II* (1974; he directed, produced and wrote the screenplay), which won Oscars for best film, best director, and best screenplay, among others. Together, these Sicilian-American Mafia stories are one of the greatest achievements of the American cinema; Coppola also combined them, with additional material, into a "novel for television" that some observers thought even better than the individual films. Although he created many other films, including the notable *Apocalypse Now* (1979), *Peggy Sue Got Married* (1986), *Tucker: The Man and His Dream* (1988), and *Bram Stoker's Dracula* (1992), nothing else even came close to duplicating the achievement of his massive Godfather films. His 1991 *The Godfather Part III* was generally received as a pale imitation of his two great films.

Coppola's 1958 B.A. was from Hofstra University, and his 1968 M.A. in cinema from UCLA. He married Eleanor Neil, and has had three children, one of whom died in a boating accident in 1986. Eleanor Coppola directed *Hearts of Darkness: A Filmmaker's Apocalypse* (1991), about the filming of *Apocalypse Now*, with contemporary footage. Actress Talia Shire is Coppola's sister; actor Nicolas Cage is his nephew; the late Carmine Coppola, who scored *The Godfather Part II*, was his father.

FURTHER READING

"Godfather country: in the lush hills. . . ." HAMISH BOWLES. *Vogue*, June 1993.
"One from the art." DAVID EHRENSTEIN. *Film Comment*, Jan.-Feb. 1993.
"Coppola, Francis Ford." *Current Biography*, July 1991.
"Francis Ford Coppola." DAVID BRESKIN. *Rolling Stone*, Feb. 7, 1991.
Coppola. PETER COWIE. Macmillan, 1990.
On the Edge: The Life and Times of Francis Coppola. MICHAEL GOODWIN and NAOMI WISE. Morrow, 1989.
Hollywood Auteur: Francis Coppola. JEFFERY CHOWN. Praeger/Greenwood, 1988.

Cosby, Bill (1937–)

Back at NBC, under the multiyear, multiproject development agreement concluded in 1992, Cosby developed a major new television show: the "Bill Cosby Mystery Movie" series, in which he plays a scene-of-crime forensic scientist. Early plans were to star Cosby in four two-hour "light mystery" movies, which in turn would be spun off into a weekly hourlong mystery series the following season. But that was not Cosby's only reported NBC involvement; throughout 1993, persistent rumors circulated that Cosby was going to again try to buy control of NBC from the General Electric Company, though nothing concrete had eventuated by year's end. Meanwhile, although "The Cosby Show" had ended its long run, Cosby continued to be a very familiar face in many countries, as his television shows continued their decades of reruns. "I Spy" had another kind of life in store, as well, in the form of a forthcoming series based on the original series.

Cosby also continued to spend a good deal of his time in public service work of many kinds. He also briefly entered Los Angeles politics, strongly backing the unsuccessful mayoral candidacy of his old friend Stan Sanders.

Philadelphia-born Cosby became a television star and pioneering African-American performing artist in the thriller "I Spy" (1965–68), and went on to star in his own "The Bill Cosby Show" (1969–71), which later had a second life (1972–73). He also became a leading solo comedy performer and recording artist, as well as starring in several films, including *Uptown Saturday Night* (1974), *Let's Do It Again* (1975), *Mother, Jugs and Speed* (1976), and *Ghost Dad* (1989). With "The Cosby Show" (1984–92), he became one of the leading performers in American television, and with that also a leading celebrity. During 1992, he also starred in a remake of "You Bet Your Life," the old Groucho Marx television series. Cosby's books include *The Wit and Wisdom of Fat Albert* (1973), *Fatherhood* (1986), *Time Flies* (1987), *Love and Marriage* (1989), and *Childhood* (1991). Cosby attended Temple University; his 1972 M.A. and 1977 Ed.D. were from the University of Massachusetts. He married Camille Hanks in 1964; they have five children.

FURTHER READING

" 'Someone at the top. . . .' " *Newsweek*, Dec. 6, 1993.
Bill Cosby, Entertainer. MARIANNE RUUTH. Holloway, 1993.
Bill Cosby. BRUCE W. CONORD. Chelsea House, 1993.
"The Cosby Show's. . . ." LISA SCHWARZBAUM. *Entertainment*, May 1, 1992.
Bill Cosby. SOLOMON HERBERT and GEORGE HILL. Chelsea House, 1992.
"Bill Cosby. . . ." MICHAEL BOURNE. *Down Beat*, Sep. 1991.
"Cosby talks." BOB THOMAS. *Good Housekeeping*, Feb. 1991.
Bill Cosby: The Changing Black Image. ROBERT ROSENBERG. Millbrook, 1991.
Cosby. RONALD L. SMITH. St. Martin's, 1987.
Bill Cosby: Family Funny Man. LARRY KETTELKAMP. Messner, 1987.
Bill Cosby: Superstar. PATRICIA S. MARTIN. Rourke, 1987.

Cosby. RONALD L. SMITH. St. Martin's, 1986.
The Picture Life of Bill Cosby. BARBARA JOHNSTON ADAMS. Watts, 1986.

Costner, Kevin (1955–) Now one of the world's superstars, Kevin Costner in 1993 was still seen throughout the world in *The Bodyguard* (1992), opposite Whitney Houston, whose song "I Will Always Love You," became a worldwide hit. Costner's major film of 1993 was the well-received *A Perfect World*, in which he starred as escaped killer Butch Haynes, opposite Clint Eastwood as Texas Ranger Red Garnett, and T. J. Lowther as the child Costner kidnaps, who becomes more son than hostage to him; Laura Dern also starred as a criminologist; Eastwood directed.

During the spring and summer of 1993, Costner filmed the forthcoming *Wyatt Earp*, written and directed by Lawrence Kasdan. Also forthcoming were the films *Waterworld*, directed by Kevin Reynolds; and *The War*, directed and produced by Jon Avnet.

California-born Costner emerged as a film star from the mid-1980s, in *Silverado* (1985), *The Untouchables* (1987), *No Way Out* (1987), *Bull Durham* (1988), *Field of Dreams* (1989), *Dances With Wolves* (1990), *Robin Hood: Prince of Thieves* (1991), and *JFK* (1992). Costner had made his directorial debut with the enormously successful *Dances With Wolves*, which won seven Oscars out of twelve nominations, including best

picture, best director, and best adaptation; he also won the Directors Guild of America's best director award and Golden Globe awards for best picture and director, and published *Dances with Wolves: The Illustrated Story of the Epic Film* (1990). Costner attended California State University. He is married to Cindy Silva; they have three children.

FURTHER READING

"Whitney Houston and. . . ." *Jet*, Dec. 14, 1992.
"You asked for him!" *Teen*, Jan. 1992.
"Costner in control." EDWARD KLEIN. *Vanity Fair*, Jan. 1992.
"Into the woods. . . ." STEPHANIE MANSFIELD. *GQ—Gentlemen's Quarterly*, July 1991.
"Safe sex symbol. . . ." BARBARA LIPPERT. *M Inc.*, June 1991.
"Kevin Costner. . . ." SALLY OGLE DAVIS. *Ladies Home Journal*, Apr. 1991.
"Kevin Costner." FRED SCHRUERS. *Rolling Stone*, Nov. 29, 1990.
"Pack leader. . . ." MARJORIE ROSEN. *People*, Nov. 19, 1990.
"Dancing with the wolves." FRED SCHRUERS. *Premiere*, Oct. 1990.
"Costner, Kevin." *Current Biography*, June 1990.

Couric, Katie (Katherine Couric; 1957–) Katie Couric's star continued to rise in 1993. She was still highly successful as co-host with Bryant Gumbel of NBC's morning "Today" show and, seeking to shore up its primetime ratings, NBC brought in Couric for "Now with Tom Brokaw and Katie Couric," a primetime weekly news magazine pairing her with the evening news anchor. That, too, showed strength; its premiere edition, in August, took the sixth spot in the weekly Nielsen ratings.

"Today" itself was in some turmoil, since Jeff Zucker, the producer who had been given much credit for the show's revival, left to produce "Now"; Steve Friedman, "Today" producer from 1980 to 1987, returned to that spot. The program has led the ratings only occasionally since the badly handled 1989 replacement of Jane Pauley with Deborah Norville, and then *her* 1991 replacement with Couric. NBC was reportedly building a new multimillion-dollar street-level studio, with plate-glass windows, facing Rockefeller Plaza, from which "Today" would air starting in mid-1994—as the original show did

(1952–58). On her own, Couric in June conducted an hour-long special, *Hillary: America's First Lady*, the first nationally broadcast in-depth interview with Hillary Rodham Clinton since President Clinton's inauguration.

Virginia-born Couric began her career in broadcast journalism after her 1979 graduation from the University of Virginia with a degree in American studies. That year, she worked as an assistant in ABC's Washington, D.C. television news department. She joined the Cable News Network (CNN) as a Washington-based editor in 1980, and moved to Atlanta for CNN, working as an assignment editor and newscaster with "Take Two." She moved to Miami's WTJI as a reporter in 1984, and back to Washington in 1986 as a reporter for WRC, an NBC affiliate. In 1989, she moved to an NBC network job, as a Pentagon correspondent, soon working as a weekend anchor and in 1990 joining "Today" as a national correspondent. Couric became co-host temporarily in February 1991 and then permanently in April 1991. She is married to attorney Jay Monahan, originally based in Washington, D.C., but from 1993 in New York; they have a daughter.

FURTHER READING

"Live wire." Karen Schneider. *People*, Aug. 9, 1993.

"Couric, Katie." *Current Biography*, Mar. 1993.

"Katie Couric today." Joanne Kaufman. *TV Guide*, Feb. 6, 1993.

"Katie Couric." *People*, Dec. 28, 1992.

"Catching up with. . . ." Judy Flander. *Saturday Evening Post*, Sep.-Oct. 1992.

"Katie and Chris. . . ." Joanne Kaufman. *Ladies Home Journal*, Aug. 1992.

" 'Don't call me perky.' " Jennet Conant. *Redbook*, June 1992.

"Katie Couric. . . ." Chris Chase. *Cosmopolitan*, May 1992.

"The Today Show's. . . ." Charla Krupp. *Glamour*, July 1991.

Courier, Jim (James Spencer Courier; 1970–) Early in 1993, Jim Courier was at the top of the tennis rankings, although he had not won a tournament since the French Open in July 1992. That drought ended in February, when he took his second straight Australian Open, both times defeating Stefan Edberg, for his fourth Grand Slam singles title. He also won his second straight Italian Open in May over Goran Ivanisevic, and the U.S. Hardcourts title at Indianapolis in August, defeating Boris Becker for the first time in seven tries. That latter win briefly put him back at number one, a ranking he and Pete Sampras were trading back and forth through 1993.

But the rest of the year, in particular the other Grand slam events, did not go as planned. At the U.S. Open in September, Courier suffered a stunning upset at the hands of virtually unknown 14th-ranked French player Cédric Pioline. At the French Open, where he was two-time defending champion, he lost in the finals in five hard-fought sets to another relative unknown, 10th-seeded Spaniard Sergi Bruguera. Courier also reached the final at Wimbledon, where he lost the match and his number-one ranking to Sampras. By year's end he had lost the number-two ranking, also, to Michael Stich.

In August, Courier was one of numerous tennis luminaries to play in the Arthur Ashe Tennis Challenge to benefit the Arthur Ashe Foundation for the Defeat of AIDS. In December, Courier, who had helped the United States win its second straight Davis Cup in 1992, was again selected to the team.

Born in Dade City, Florida, Courier began his tennis training at the Harry Hopman tennis academy at Bardmoor, Florida, then moving to the Nick Bollettieri academy. He won his first tournament, at Florida's Orange Bowl, when only 16 in 1986, and won there again a year later. He joined the professional tennis tour in 1988, but was far from being a shooting star, winning his first singles tournament at Basel, Switzerland in 1989. Courier began working with coach José Higueras in 1990, and in 1991 emerged as a world-class tennis star, as men's singles winner at the French Open, as well as at four other tournaments, and as a finalist at the U.S. Open. In that year, he jumped in the men's singles world rankings from 25th to second. In 1992, he was at times ranked number one, winning five tournaments, including two majors: the Australian Open and his second straight French Open.

FURTHER READING

"Jim Dandy. . . ." DAVID HIGDON. *Tennis*, June 1993.
"An American in Paris." RICHARD FINN. *Sporting News*, June 8, 1992.
"Top hat." FRANZ LIDZ. *Sports Illustrated*, Feb. 24, 1992.
"Pardon his dust. . . ." WILLIAM PLUMMER. *People*, July 1, 1991.
"Jim Courier. . . ." MARK WINTERS. *World Tennis*, Feb. 1989.

Crichton, Michael (John Michael Crichton; 1942–) Michael Crichton's already-popular novels gained a big boost in June 1993 from the enormous success of Steven Spielberg's summer blockbuster film of his novel *Jurassic Park*, starring Jeff Goldblum, Laura Dern, Sam Neill, Richard Attenborough, and a host of engineered dinosaurs. Simultaneously, Crichton published *Jurassic Park: The Movie Storybook*. Another Crichton novel, *Rising Sun*, a controversial murder-mystery involving Japanese-American rivalry, also appeared as a major film, starring Sean Connery (written with him in mind), Wesley Snipes, and Harvey Keitel. Crichton is listed as co-writer of both screenplays, and co-producer for *Jurassic Park*, though he left *Rising Sun* seven weeks into the project, reportedly because director Philip Kaufman changed the identity and ethnicity of the villain.

Both books quickly went back onto the best-seller lists, as did some of Crichton's earlier works; by July he had a total of five books among the top ten best-sellers in their categories, including *Congo*, *Sphere*, and his first novel, *A Case of Need*. A new book, *Disclosure: A Novel*, focusing on sexual harassment in an electronics company, was scheduled for release in 1994; shortly after *Jurassic Park*'s release, Warner Brothers bought film rights to the novel for a record-tying $2.5 million (broken later in the year by the $3.75 million paid for John Grisham's new, as-yet-untitled novel), with a reported $250,000 bonus if the book becomes a best-seller. *Congo*, bought several years ago, was also headed for production; it would be his seventh book filmed. Crichton also published two children's books, *Dinosaurs of Jurassic Park: An All Aboard Reading Book* and *Raptor Attack: A Three-D Storybook*, and produced a revised edition of his 1977 art book *Jasper Johns*, scheduled for 1994 publication. Crichton was also among those courageous enough to supply juvenile writing for *First Words: Earliest Writings from 42 Favorite American Authors*, edited by Paul Mandelbaum.

Chicago-born, Long Island-raised Crichton received his A.B., summa cum laude in anthropology, and M.D. from Harvard University, in 1964 and 1969, then working as a postdoctoral fellow at La Jolla, California's Salk Institute (1969–70), training he was later to use in his medical, scientific, often futuristic thrillers. After a first novel, *A Case of Need*, under the pseudonym Jeffery Hudson, which won an Edgar (Mystery Writers of America's Edgar Allan Poe Award) as the best mystery novel and was filmed as *The Carey Treatment* (1972), Crichton quickly established himself as a popular novelist under his own name with books such as *The Andromeda Strain* (1969), *The Terminal Man* (1972), *Five Patients* (1970), *The Great Train Robbery* (1975), *Eaters of the Dead* (1976), *Congo* (1980), *Electronic Life* (1983), *Sphere* (1987), *Travels* (1988), *Jurassic Park* (1990), and *Rising Sun* (1992). Crichton has also developed a second career as a film director; he wrote and directed the films *Westworld* (1973), *Coma* (1977), *The Great Train Robbery* (1978), from his own novel, *Looker* (1981), and *Runaway* (1984), and also directed *Physical Evidence* (1989). Crichton's fourth wife is Anne-Marie Crichton; he has a daughter.

FURTHER READING

"Crichton, Michael." *Current Biography*, Nov. 1993.
"Michael Crichton. . . ." KEN GROSS. *People*, Nov. 19, 1990.

Crichton, Robert (1925–93) Albuquerque-born Robert Crichton tried farming in the late 1940s, after frontline army service in World War II and subsequent graduation from Harvard University. After going broke, he turned to writing, beginning with short stories for *Argosy* and other magazines. His first book was the bestselling *The Great Impostor* (1959), the story of chameleon-like Ferdinand Demara, Jr., who was played by Tony Curtis in Robert Mulligan's 1961 film version of the book. Crichton's first novel was the bestseller *The Secret of Santa Vittoria* (1966); Anthony Quinn and Anna Magnani starred in Stanley Kramer's 1969 film version. Crichton was survived by his wife, Judith Feiner, a son, a sister, and a brother. (d. New Rochelle, New York; March 23, 1993)

FURTHER READING

Obituary. *The Times* (of London), Mar. 27, 1993.
Obituary. *New York Times*, Mar. 24, 1993.

Cronyn, Hume (Hume Blake; 1911–) American television audiences had the rare privilege of seeing Hume Cronyn and Jessica Tandy, both now in their mid-80s, create yet another joined set of roles in 1993. Hailed as America's leading theatrical couple, the Canadian actor and British actress, partners on stage and screen for more than four decades, starred in the acclaimed television film *To Dance with the White Dog*, she on screen briefly as his wife, who dies, he on screen throughout the film as her survivor, attempting to deal with loss and pain by conjuring up an imaginary white dog, whom nobody else can see, which he insists is a reincarnation of his dead wife.

Cronyn also played a strong supporting role as assassinated Supreme Court Justice Abraham Rosenberg in the film *The Pelican Brief*, written and directed by Alan Pakula, based on John Grisham's best-selling novel about assassination and intrigue in high places. The cast included Julia Roberts, Denzel Washington, Sam Shepard, John Heard, Robert Culp, and John Lithgow. Cronyn was nominated for a Golden Globe award as best supporting actor in a television miniseries or film for his performance in *Broadway Bound*.

Ontario-born Cronyn has been on stage professionally for 60 years, in character roles from the 1930s, and in leading roles from the 1950s. His long, celebrated partnership with Jessica Tandy has included co-starring roles in *The Fourposter* (1951), *A Delicate Balance* (1966), *The Gin Game* (1977), and *Foxfire* (1982). He won a Tony for his Polonius in *Hamlet* (1964). He made his screen debut in *Shadow of a Doubt* (1943), and went on to play strong character roles in such films as *The Seventh Cross* (1944), *Lifeboat* (1944), *Sunrise at Campobello* (1960), *The World According to Garp* (1982), *Cocoon* (1985), *Age-Old Friends* (1989), and *Christmas on Division Street* (1991). His autobiography is *A Terrible Liar* (1991). Cronyn attended Ridley University, McGill University, and the New York School of Drama. He and Jessica Tandy have been married since 1942, and have three children.

FURTHER READING

The Magic of Theater. DAVID BLACK. Macmillan, 1993.
"He drives Miss Daisy . . ." Eve Drobot. *Saturday Night*, Oct. 1991.
"Doyen of theater . . ." Helle Bering-Jensen. *Insight*, Oct. 21, 1991.
"Two lives, one ambition . . ." Gerald Clarke. *Time*, Apr. 2, 1990.
"Happily ever after." Jeanne Marie Laskas. *Life*, Apr. 1990.

Cruise, Tom (Thomas Cruise Mapother, IV; 1962–) After the great box office success of *A Few Good Men* (1992), for which he also won a best actor Golden Globe nomination, Cruise starred in yet another commercial blockbuster in 1993. The film was *The Firm*, directed by Sydney Pollack and based on the best-selling John Grisham novel. Cruise starred as honest lawyer Mitch McDeere, who found himself in a corrupt law firm and decided to straighten things out, opposite Gene Hackman as a crooked senior lawyer in his firm, in a cast that included Jeanne Tripplehorn as Cruise's wife, Hal Holbrook, Terry Kinney, Wilford Brimley, Ed Harris, Holly Hunter, David Strathairn, and Gary Busey.

Forthcoming was a starring role in *Interview with a Vampire*, directed by Neil Jordan, with a cast that included Brad Pitt, Antonio Banderas,

Tom Cruise. MARIE CAHILL. Smithmark, 1992.
"From here to maturity. . . ." *Seventeen,* July 1991.
"A Cruise in outer space. . . ." JAN GOLAB. *California,* June 1991.
"Burn a little rubber. . . ." JEANNIE PARK. *People,* July 23, 1990.
"What's driving. . . ." JEANNE MARIE LASKAS. *Life,* June 1990.
"Cruise at the crossroads." TRIP GABRIEL. *Rolling Stone,* Jan. 11, 1990.
"Playboy interview. . . ." ROBERT SCHEER. *Playboy,* Jan. 1990.
Top Gun: The Films of Tom Cruise. ED GROSS. Pioneer, 1990.
Tom Cruise. JOLENE ANTHONY. St. Martin's, 1988.

and Stephen Rea—though many people, including Anne Rice, author of the "Vampire Chronicles" books, believed that Cruise would be miscast as the worldly vampire Lestat.

Born in Syracuse, New York, Cruise has been a very popular star since the early 1980s, in such films as *Risky Business* (1983), *All the Right Moves* (1983), *Legend* (1984), *Top Gun* (1986), *The Color of Money* (1986), *Rain Man* (1988), *Born on the Fourth of July* (1989; he won a best actor Oscar nomination for his portrayal of disabled Vietnam War veteran Ron Kovic), *Days of Thunder* (1990), *A Few Good Men* (1992), and *Far and Away* (1992). He was previously married to Mimi Rogers (1987–90); he married Nicole Kidman in 1990.

FURTHER READING

"No more Mr. Nice Guy." ROD LURIE. *Los Angeles Magazine,* Oct. 1993.
"Tom Cruise has it covered." TOM O'NEILL. *Us,* Jan. 1993.
Tom Cruise. JULIE BACH. Abdo & Daughters, 1993.
"Tom Cruise." TRISH DEITCH ROHRER and TY BURR. *Entertainment,* Dec. 11, 1992.
"Crazy for each other." ELIZABETH SPORKIN. *People,* June 8, 1992.
"Too live Cruise." DAVID RENSIN. *Movies USA,* June 1992.
"Tom Cruise." PATRICK GOLDSTEIN. *Rolling Stone,* May 28, 1992.
"Irish risky." MELINA GEROSA. *Entertainment,* May 22, 1992.

Crystal, Billy (1947–) As host of the 64th annual Academy Awards show, his fourth Academy Awards broadcast in a row, Crystal on March 29, 1993 was again one of the world's most highly visible comedians, reaching an estimated billion or more viewers in that single show-beginning with his arrival on stage riding a horse. He has won his own awards, as well; these included two American Comedy Awards, one for his hosting of the 1992 Academy Awards show (which also won him an Emmy nomination for best performance in a variety or music program; he had earlier won it for his 1991 hosting job), the other for lifetime achievement. He also shared a Cable Ace Award from the National Academy of Cable Programming with Whoopi Goldberg and Robin Williams, for their television special "Comic Relief V"; a sixth "Comic

Relief" program was scheduled for January 1994. Also forthcoming was the sequel *City Slickers II: The Legend of Curly's Gold*, produced and co-written by Crystal, and co-starring Daniel Stern, Jon Lovitz, and Jack Palance.

New York-born Crystal worked as a comedian in cabaret in the mid-1970s, and moved into television in the long-running "Soap" (1977–81), which was followed by the short-lived "The Billy Crystal Hour" (1982). He was well-received as a continuing character on "Saturday Night Live" (1984–85) and has also appeared in several telefilms. He began playing film leads in the late 1980s, in *Running Scared* (1986), *Throw Momma From the Train* (1987), *Memories of Me* (1988), and *When Harry Met Sally . . .* (1989), for which he and co-star Meg Ryan won American Comedy Awards. He also shared a 1990 Emmy for best variety or musical show. With Dick Schaap, he wrote *Absolutely Mahvelous* (1986). Crystal attended Nassau Community College and New York University. He is married to Janice Crystal; they have two children.

FURTHER READING

"Billy's big night." MARGARET CARLSON. *TV Guide*, Mar. 27, 1993.
"Billy the kid rides high." MARGARET CARLSON. *Time*, Oct. 19, 1992.
"Mahvelous Billy Crystal." DAVE STONE. *Cosmopolitan*, Oct. 1992.
" 'Scary is good'." DICK SCHAAP. *Parade*, Sep. 13, 1992.
"Billy Crystal." KENT BLACK. *Los Angeles*, Sep. 1992.
"Cover Q&A." FRANK SANELLO. *Los Angeles*, Sep. 1991.
"Billy Crystal. . . ." BARBARA GERBASI. *McCall's*, July 1991.

Culkin, Macaulay (1980–) Although
Home Alone 2 was scarcely a critical success, it was a box office smash, as had been *Home Alone*, and child star Culkin continued to be a worldwide box office draw in 1993. His major 1993 film was *The Good Son*, directed and co-produced by Joseph Ruben, and co-starring Elijah Wood, Wendy Crewson, and David Morse, in which Culkin played the role of an evil little boy. He also appeared in the title role of the film *George Balanchine's The Nutcracker*, directed by Emile Ardolino and performed by the New York City Ballet. Forthcoming was a starring role opposite

Ted Danson, who plays Culkin's father in the film *Getting Even with Dad*, directed by Howard Deutch, about a child who coerces his ex-convict father into going straight. Also forthcoming was a lead in the film *Richie Rich*, directed by Donald Petrie.

Culkin began his career at age four, acting in Off-Broadway plays and later appearing as a featured dancer in the New York City Ballet's annual *The Nutcracker* at Lincoln Center. His films include *Rocket Gibraltar* (1988) as Burt Lancaster's grandson, *See You in the Morning* (1989), *Uncle Buck* (1989) as John Candy's nephew, *Jacob's Ladder* (1990), *Home Alone* (1990), *Only the Lonely* (1991), *My Girl* (1991), and *Home Alone 2* (1992). Culkin comes from a theatrical family, brought onto the stage (along with his four brothers and two sisters) by his father, actor Christopher (Kit) Culkin, now his children's theatrical manager; actress Bonnie Bedelia is his aunt.

FURTHER READING

Macaulay Culkin. ROSEMARY WALLNER. Abdo & Daughters, 1993.
"The American man at age ten." SUSAN ORLEAN. *Esquire*, Dec. 1992.
Macaulay Culkin. MIRIAM TAGER. Dell, 1992.
"Baby, it's you." ZOE F. CARTER. *Premiere*, Nov. 1991.
"Macaulay Culkin." KAREN JAEHNE and KAREN KUEHN. *Interview*, July 1991.
"Macaulay Culkin. . . ." ERIC SHERMAN. *Ladies Home Journal*, May 1991.

"The kid who. . . ." MAYNARD GOOD STODDARD. *Saturday Evening Post*, Apr. 1991.
"Running away. . . ." TOM GLIATTO. *People*, Dec. 17, 1990.

Cuomo, Mario Matthew (1932–) Often mentioned as a possible first Clinton Supreme Court nomination, New York governor Cuomo in April 1993 publicly took himself out of consideration, choosing instead to remain in New York. Many thought that he would seek a fourth gubernatorial term, and he did nothing to discourage such speculation. Nor was it considered terribly unlikely that Cuomo, perhaps the country's leading liberal Democrat, still might make a run for the presidency in 1996 or 2000. In Albany, Cuomo and legislative leaders on April 1, the first day of the state's fiscal year, finally hammered out a state budget, effective three days later. On the personal side, Cuomo issued a new book, *More Than Words: The Speeches of Mario Cuomo*.

New York-born Cuomo moved into politics after two decades as a practicing lawyer and law teacher. He was New York Secretary of State (1975–79), lieutenant governor (1979–82), and became his party's candidate and then governor in 1983, after defeating then-New York City mayor Ed Koch in a hotly contested primary campaign. He wrote of the gubernatorial contest in his *Diaries of Mario M. Cuomo: The Campaign for Governor* (1984).

As governor, he became a powerful Democratic Party leader. Since his keynote address to the 1984 Democratic national convention, he has been thought to be a leading contender for the American Presidency, even though he is a much-attacked Catholic liberal who has refused to modify his pro-choice views, in spite of one Catholic cleric's statement that he was "in serious risk of going to hell" because of his pro-choice stand, and in spite of Cardinal O'Connor's later-denied threat of excommunication. Cuomo has also declined to reverse his long-standing opposition to the death penalty. After a long public debate with himself, Cuomo decided not to seek the 1992 Democratic Presidential nomination, but did not endorse Clinton until the nomination fight was over, and Clinton was clearly going to be the winner. Ultimately, though, he endorsed Clinton, on July 15, 1992 delivering a powerful nominating speech at the Democratic National Convention, and then backing Clinton without reservation during the campaign that followed.

Cuomo's B.A. was from St. John's College, in 1953, his LL.B. from St. John's University. He is married to the former Mathilda Raffa; they have five children.

FURTHER READING

"Cuomo vadis:. . . ." JEFFREY ROSEN. *New Republic*, Apr. 26, 1993.
"No justice, no peace. . . ." DAVID A. KAPLAN. *Newsweek*, Apr. 19, 1993.
"Court test. . . ." Jeff Rosen. *New Republic*, Sep. 28, 1992.
"Message from a kibitzer." GLORIA BORGER; DAVID GERGEN. *U.S. News & World Report*, July 20, 1992.
"The man who would not run." BARBARA GRIZZUTI HARRISON. *Playboy*, July 1992.
"The coward." SIDNEY BLUMENTHAL. *New Republic*, Mar. 16, 1992.
"Why Cuomo said no." GARRY WILLS. *New York Review of Books*, Jan. 30, 1992.
"Mario's calling." JACOB WEISBERG. *New Republic*, Dec. 2, 1991.
"Cuomo's hologram. . . ." JOE KLEIN. *New York*, Oct. 7, 1991.
"The state of the governor. . . ." ELIZABETH KOLBERT. *New York Times Magazine*, Feb. 10, 1991.

Mario Cuomo: A Biography. Robert S. McElvaine. Macmillan, 1988.

Cusack, Cyril James (1910–93)

Born in Durban, South Africa, Cyril Cusack and his mother, actress Alice Cole, went to Ireland when he was six; his childhood was spent touring in repertory with his mother and her companion, Irish actor Brefni O'Rourke, and his film debut came at the age of seven. Cusack joined Dublin's Abbey Theatre in 1932, in the following 13 years appearing in at least 65 plays and becoming a leading figure in the Irish theatre, while also appearing in major roles in the English theatre. He formed his own company in 1945, and managed Dublin's Gaiety Theatre. In 1963, he joined the Royal Shakespeare Company, and in 1964 the Old Vic. Very much a person of the theatre, Cusack also appeared in many films, including *Odd Man Out* (1947), *The Spy Who Came In From the Cold* (1965), *The Day of the Jackal* (1973), and *My Left Foot* (1989). Cusack wrote *Between the Acts and Other Poems* (1990). He was survived by his wife Mary, four daughters—all actresses: Sinead, Sorchia, Niamh, and Catherine—and two sons. (d. London; October 7, 1993)

FURTHER READING

Obituary. *Variety*, Oct. 8, 1993.
Obituary. *The Times* (of London), Oct. 8, 1993.
Obituary. *New York Times*, Oct. 8, 1993.

Cyrus, Billy Ray (1962–)

With his second album, *It Won't Be The Last*, Cyrus proved that his extraordinary success of 1992 was not just a fluke; the well-received album included such songs as "When I'm Gone," "Ain't Your Dog No More," and "Somebody New." He also issued the hit single "She's Not Cryin' Anymore," and starred on television in ABC music's *The Billy Ray Cyrus Special—Dreams Come True.*

Cyrus won several honors during 1993. At the 20th annual American Music Awards, he was voted favorite new artist, and his "Achy Breaky Heart" was voted favorite single. At the World Music Awards, he was voted best international new artist of the year. "Achy Breaky Heart" was the voted the most performed country song of the year at the 41st annual BMI Country Awards presentation in Nashville. Beyond honors, *Some Gave All* sold nine million copies, and was rated by Billboard as the top country album of 1993.

Cyrus's hometown is Flatlands, Kentucky. He attended Kentucky's Georgetown College, dropping out when he was 20 to pursue a singing career. He began singing in local bands, and spent five years trying to break into the Nashville country music industry, making his first breakthrough in 1991. In 1992, he enjoyed a sudden, massive success, with his enormously popular single and video "Achy Breaky Heart," followed quickly by the album of which it was part, *Some Gave All*, which headed right for the top of the charts. He was formerly married, to Cindy Smith.

FURTHER READING

"Hey, Billy Ray. . . ." Bob Millard. *Country Music*, Nov.-Dec. 1993.
"On the road with. . . . ." Terri Mauro. *First for Women*, Aug. 9, 1993.
"Billy Ray's biggest fans." Jeff Rovin. *Ladies Home Journal*, May 1993.
"The voices of. . . ." Joe Rhodes. *TV Guide*, Feb. 13, 1993.
"Billy Ray Cyrus. . . ." Michael Segell. *Cosmopolitan*, Jan. 1993.
Billy Ray Cyrus: A Photographic Scrapbook. Rick Baumgartner. Blue Acorn, 1993.
My Billy Ray Cyrus Story: Some Gave Too Much. Kari Reeves et al, eds. Eggman, 1993.
"Billy Ray Cyrus." Marjie McGraw. *Country Music*, Nov.-Dec. 1992.
"Country hunks." Marjie McGraw. *Ladies Home Journal*, Oct. 1992.
"One from the heart." Bob Cannon. *Entertainment*, July 17, 1992.

D

Dafoe, Willem (1955–) In 1993, actor Willem Dafoe starred as defense attorney Frank Dulaney opposite Madonna, Joe Mantegna, and Anne Archer in the courtroom thriller *Body of Evidence*, directed by Uli Edel. The story line of the not very well-received film featured Madonna accused of literally murdering a man by overstraining him with too much in the way of sexual encounter; her body was therefore alleged to have been the weapon used. Forthcoming was a starring role in the far more substantial, though not necessarily any more plausible, thriller *Clear and Present Danger*, directed by Philip Noyce and co-starring Harrison Ford, James Earl Jones, and Anne Archer. Also forthcoming was a starring role opposite Miranda Richardson in the film *Tom and Viv*, directed by Brian Gilbert.

Wisconsin-born Dafoe began his career in the theater, joining the off-Broadway Wooster Group theater company in 1975. He appeared in several films during the early 1980s, among them *The Loveless* (1983) and *To Live and Die in L.A.* (1985). His breakthrough role came in *Platoon* (1986), for which he received an Oscar nomination, which was followed by *The Last Temptation of Christ* (1988), *Off Limits* (1988), *Mississippi Burning* (1988), *Triumph of the Spirit* (1989), *Born on the Fourth of July* (1989), *Cry-Baby* (1990), *Flight of the Intruder* (1990), *Wild at Heart* (1990), *White Sands* (1992), and *Light Sleeper* (1992). He attended the University of Wisconsin. He has one child.

FURTHER READING

"Willem Dafoe." RUSSELL BANKS. *Interview*, Jan. 1993.
"Willem Dafoe. . . ." MICHAEL LASSELL. *Advocate*, Aug. 13, 1992.
"The wild one." RICHARD B. WOODWARD. *New York*, Aug. 27, 1990.
"Willem Dafoe. . . ." *Interview*, May 1990.
"Dafoe, Willem." *Current Biography*, Apr. 1990.
"Willem Dafoe. . . ." EVELYN RENOLD. *Cosmopolitan*, Jan. 1989.
"Ladies and gentlemen. . . ." MARK KRAM. *Esquire*, Jan. 1989.

The New Breed: Actors Coming of Age. KAREN HARDY and KEVIN J. KOFFLER. Holt, 1988.

Daly, John (1966–)

John Daly had one notable achievement in 1993. At the U.S. Open at Baltusrol, in Springfield, New Jersey, he did what no other golfer had ever done: at the 17th hole, the longest hole in U.S. Open history, previously thought unreachable in two shots. He hit a 630-yard uphill green with, first, a 325-yard drive, and then a 305-yard shot that went 45 feet beyond the cup. "Long John," as he is known, had been responding to challenges to "hit 17 in two," and the crowd responded with what is known as a "Daly roar" at his power. Not surprisingly, at year's end, Daly led the Professional Golfers Association (PGA) tour in driving distance, averaging 288.9 yards; he won over $225,000 in 24 events. Daly also participated in the Chrysler American Great 18 Championship, a designed-for-television special, in which he and other selected golfers played 18 holes at 18 different golf courses around the world.

Otherwise, it was not a good year for Daly. He won no tournaments, and in November was suspended indefinitely from the PGA Tour for various infractions. He had twice during the year broken off without completing a round, once hitting a ball over the heads of a large hillside crowd. A recovering alcoholic, Daly had been forced to withdraw from the tour in late 1992, missing the opening of the 1993 season; in December, he was undergoing Tour-mandated rehabilitation counseling to shorten the suspension. Daly would be eligible to play again starting in late March 1994, though he could play on the PGA European Tour.

Arkansas-born Daly is a self-taught golfer, who modeled himself after golf great Jack Nicklaus. He began his professional career playing on the Ben Hogan circuit, a "minor league" developmental tour, where his biggest victory was the Utah Open. He made a notable entry onto the PGA Tour by winning the PGA championship in 1991, and was named rookie of the year. In 1992, he published *Grip It and Rip It! John Daly's Guide to Hitting the Ball Farther Than You Ever Have Before*, written with John Andrisani. Daly attended the University of Arkansas. Previously divorced, Daly married Bettye Fulford in 1992; they have one daughter.

FURTHER READING

"Full blast." DAVE KINDRED. *Golf*, Nov. 1991.
"A real long shot." MIKE PURKEY. *Golf*, Oct. 1991.

Danson, Ted (1947–)

Television and film star Ted Danson went through several major professional and personal changes in 1993. Having decided that he did not want to go on in the long-running top-rated television comedy "Cheers," he announced in 1992 that he was leaving the show in 1993, effectively closing it down. The series ended its 11-year run on NBC in May, with top ratings for its final episodes, and Danson won an Emmy as best actor in a comedy series, He then turned his attention to a variety of film and television projects, some of them through his own production company. In his first major post-"Cheers" role, he starred opposite Whoopi Goldberg in the hit comedy "Made in America," directed by Richard Benjamin. Forthcoming was a starring role opposite Macaulay Culkin in *Getting Even with Dad*, as Culkin's ex-convict father, whom Culkin coerces into going straight, directed by Howard Deutch. Also forthcoming was a starring role opposite Mary Steenburgen in the film *Pontiac Moon* directed by Peter Medak.

On the personal side, Danson and his wife, Casey (Cassandra), divorced. Goldberg and Danson became companions while making *Made in America*, and stayed together for most of the year, until separating. Danson also figured in a highly publicized incident, in which he appeared in blackface and told racially oriented jokes at the Friars Club roast of Goldberg. Although Goldberg pointed out that she had fully participated in preparing his role, many African-Americans and others were offended.

Danson worked in the New York theater and in television in the early 1970s, beginning his film career with *The Onion Field* (1979), followed by such films as *Body Heat* (1981), *Creepshow* (1983), *Just Between Friends* (1986), *Three Men and a Baby* (1987), *Cousins* (1989), *Dad* (1990), and *Three Men and a Little Lady* (1990). In 1982, he became a star of "Cheers," and won a 1990 Emmy as best actor in a comedy series. His large body of television work also includes the Emmy-winning *Something About Amelia* (1984) and the telefilm *When the Bough Breaks* (1986). Danson attended Stanford University and Carnegie-Mellon University. He has been married twice and has two children. (For additional photo, see Goldberg, Whoopi.)

FURTHER READING

"Blacks fail to see humor . . ." *Jet*, Nov. 1, 1993.
"Danson in the dark." LUCY KAYLIN.
   GQ—Gentleman's Quarterly, July 1993.
"Whoopi Goldberg and Ted Danson . . ." *Jet*, June 14, 1993.
"Heat on the set." SHELLEY LEVITT. *People*, June 7, 1993.
"Three men and. . . ." JEFF ROVIN. *Ladies Home Journal*, Dec. 1990.
"Danson, Ted." *Current Biography*, Oct. 1990.

Davis, Ossie (1917–   ) Television claimed most of Ossie Davis's attention during 1993. As Ponder Blue, he once again starred opposite Burt Reynolds in the primetime series "Evening Shade," playing in ensemble with Elizabeth Ashley, Charles Durning, Marilu Henner, and Hal Holbrook. He also appeared in the three-part television miniseries *Alex Haley's "Queen,"* in a cast that included Danny Glover, Ann-Margret, Martin Sheen, Jasmine Guy, Tim Daly, Halle Berry, Madge Sinclair, and Paul Winfield.

On film, Davis appeared in *Grumpy Old Men*, starring Jack Lemmon and Walter Matthau, in a cast that included Ann-Margret, Burgess Meredith, Daryl Hannah, Kevin Pollak, Buck Henry, and Christopher McDonald. Forthcoming was a role as a reading voice in Ken Burns's

Baseball, in a reading cast that includes Amy Madigan, Paul Newman, John Turturro, Gregory Peck, and Paul Winfield. Davis also published *Purlie Victorious: A Commemorative.*

Georgia-born Davis has been on stage for over 50 years, as actor, writer, director, and producer, and is one of the leading African-American theater figures of his time. He is best known for his creation of the Walter Lee Younger role in *A Raisin in the Sun* (1959; and the 1961 film version), opposite his wife, Ruby Dee, as Ruth Younger; and for his play *Purlie Victorious* (1961; and the 1963 film version, titled *Gone Are the Days*), in which he created the title role. He has also directed such films as *Cotton Comes to Harlem* (1970) and *Black Girl* (1972), and has acted in scores of films and telefilms, including his notable *The Emperor Jones* (1955), *Harry and Son* (1983), *Do the Right Thing* (1989), and *Jungle Fever* (1991). He appeared in continuing roles in the television series "B.L. Stryker" (1989–90). He and Dee also had a radio series, the "Ossie Davis and Ruby Dee Story Hour" (1974–78). His other written works include *Langston: A Play* (1982) and *Escape to Freedom: A Play about Young Frederick Douglass* (1989), and the novel *Just Like Martin* (1993).

Davis attended Howard University (1935–38). He and Dee married in 1948 and have worked together in the theater and as social activists ever since; they have three children, one of whom is actor-playwright Guy Davis.

FURTHER READING

"One miracle at a time." W. CALVIN ANDERSON. *American Visions*, Apr.-May 1992.

Day-Lewis, Daniel (1957–) In another acclaimed performance, celebrated young actor Daniel Day-Lewis starred in 1993 as unjustly imprisoned Belfast Irish Catholic Gerry Conlon in the film *In the Name of the Father*, opposite Peter Postlethwaite as his father and Emma Thompson as his lawyer. Terry George and Jim Sheridan adapted the fact-based film from Conlon's book *Proved Innocent*; it was directed by Sheridan.

Day-Lewis scored a second 1993 triumph as rich young New York lawyer Newland in the film *The Age of Innocence*, a faithful screen adaptation of the Edith Wharton novel, set in 1870s New York high society. The film co-starred Winona Ryder as his fiancée, and Michelle Pfeiffer as sophisticated Elena Olenska, who has just returned to New York from her marriage to a Polish Count; it was written by Jay Cocks and Martin Scorsese, and directed by Scorsese. Others in the cast included Alec McCowen, Alexis Smith, Geraldine Chaplin, Michael Gough, and Jonathan Pryce; Joanne Woodward narrated.

Day-Lewis emerged as a leading dramatic actor in several late 1980s films, including *My Beautiful Laundrette* (1985), *A Room With a View* (1985) and *The Unbearable Lightness of Being* (1988). In 1990, he won a best actor Oscar and best actor awards from the British Academy, the National Society of Film Critics, and the New York and Los Angeles critics' circles for his performance in *My Left Foot*, as the late Christy Brown, a gifted Irish writer and painter so severely afflicted by cerebral palsy that he had sure control over only his left foot. In 1989, Day-Lewis starred in Richard Eyre's production of *Hamlet* at Britain's National Theatre. In 1992, he created a new interpretation of the Hawkeye role in film *The Last of the Mohicans*. The son of writer Cecil Day Lewis and actress Jill Bolcom, he attended the Old Vic Theatre School.

FURTHER READING

"Actor from the shadows. . . ." JOAN JULIET BUCK. *New Yorker*, Oct. 12, 1992.
"The intensely imagined life. . . ." RICHARD B. WOODWARD. *New York Times Magazine*, July 5, 1992.
"Day-Lewis, Daniel." *Current Biography*, July 1990.
"Risk taker supreme. . . ." MATTHEW GUREWITSCH. *Connoisseur*, Dec. 1989.

DeBoer, Jessica (Anna Lee Schmidt; 1991–) On August 2, 1993, 2-year-old Jessica DeBoer was taken from the Ann Arbor, Michigan home of her adoptive parents, **Jan** and **Roberta DeBoer**, and pursuant to court order was delivered into the hands of her natural parents, **Cara** and **Daniel Schmidt**, who then took her to their home in Iowa. The battle for the child's custody, which drew increasing media attention as it developed, began in 1991, when her natural mother, then Cara Clausen, sought to regain her a few weeks after giving her up for adoption. Ultimately, in the autumn of 1992, the Iowa Supreme Court upheld a lower court decision awarding custody to Cara Schmidt, by invalidating the DeBoers's adoption because Ms. Schmidt had falsified the adoption forms. The Michigan Supreme Court and the U.S. Supreme Court refused to upset the Iowa ruling, and the child was forcibly returned to her natural parents. As had by then become "normal," commercial screen and publication companies rushed to cash in on the child's tragedy, one result being the September 1993 television film *Whose Child Is This? The War for Baby Jessica*.

FURTHER READING

"This is what you thought . . ." *Glamour*, Jan. 1994.
"Baby Jessica." *People*, Dec. 27, 1993.
"The lessons of Jessica." SALLIE TISDALE. *Parenting*, Nov. 1993.
"Biology and destiny." *National Review*, Sep. 6, 1993.
"In whose best interest?" NANCY GIBBS et al. *Time*, July 19, 1993.

Deighton, Len (1929–) The normally rather private Len Deighton made an unusual five-city publicity tour from New York to Los Angeles in August, his first in a decade, after the publication of his latest novel, *Violent Ward*. The well-known author of British thrillers departed from the norm in another way, setting his new novel in Los Angeles and focusing on a new central character, abrasive criminal lawyer Mickey Murphy. Some reviewers saw the work as in the Dashiell Hammett style, and his central character as worthy of supporting a series on his own. Wearing a different hat, Deighton in November published a well-received new non-fiction work, *Blood, Tears, and Folly: An Objective Look at World War II*, his history of the conflict's early days, through early 1942. During 1993, he was working on a new trilogy, tentatively titled *Faith*, *Hope*, and *Charity*, as well as a cookbook.

London-born Deighton served in Britain's Royal Air Force (RAF), as a photographer, be-fore attending the St. Martin's School of Arts and graduating from the Royal College of Art, then working as a magazine illustrator in New York. He has been a leading writer of thrillers since publication of his first novel *The Ipcress File* (1961), which was adapted into the 1965 Sidney Furie film, starring Michael Caine as Harry Palmer. Deighton followed up with *Funeral in Berlin* (1964) and *Billion Dollar Brain* (1966); the film versions of both novels also starred Caine. Deighton's other most famous characters are Bernard Samson and Fiona Samson, spies married to each other, who appeared in two trilogies: *Berlin Game* (1984), *Mexico Set* (1985), and *London Match* (1986); and *Spy Hook* (1988), *Spy Line* (1989), and *Spy Sinker* (1990), as well as *Winter* (1987). Among Deighton's other novels are *An Expensive Place to Die* (1967), *Spy Story* (1974), *SS-GB* (1979), *MAMista* (1991), and *City of Gold* (1992). He has also written several books on French cooking and numerous non-fiction books, generally on military history. Deighton is married and has two sons.

FURTHER READING

"Len Deighton. . . ." LISA SEE. *Publishers Weekly*, July 12, 1993.
Len Deighton: An Annotated Bibliography 1954–1985. EDWARD MILWARD-OLIVER. Santa Teresa Press, 1988.

De Klerk, Frederik Willem (1936–) During 1993, South African President F.W. De Klerk surmounted a wide range of obstacles to bring multiparty democracy and lasting peace closer in his country. On November 18, the African National Congress (ANC), De Klerk's National Party, and 19 other political parties agreed on a historic new constitution that would establish multiparty democracy and would, through the adoption of a Bill of Rights, guarantee "fundamental rights" for all South Africans, with a resulting transition to majority, or Black, rule in South Africa. National elections were scheduled for April 27, 1994, as had been announced by De Klerk and Mandela in Washington on July 2; these would establish a coalition government to rule for five years following the election. South Africa's 10 Black "homelands" would be dissolved and reintegrated into

South African society. The ANC and other formerly antigovernment military forces would become part of an integrated South African military. Although the Zulu Inkatha Party, the pro-apartheid Conservative Party, and several smaller parties opposed and boycotted the agreement, momentum and majority sentiment were clearly on the side of the government and the ANC in the months that followed.

De Klerk and Nelson Mandela led South Africa back into the world community in 1993, as South African participation in international sports competitions resumed, foreign companies once again began to freely trade with and locate in South Africa, and the country returned to international financing and monetary systems. On July 2, they each met with President Clinton in the White House, and on July 4 they were jointly awarded Liberty Medals in Philadelphia by We the People 2000. At their joint request, remaining American and Canadian sanctions against South Africa were lifted in September. Clearly, the two men were far from being friends, or even publicly amicable; but they were able to seize the opportunity to change the future of their country without the long, bloody war that had for so long seemed the inevitable outcome of apartheid. For this, De Klerk and Mandela shared the 1993 Nobel Peace Prize.

De Klerk practiced law in the 1960s and early 1970s, and was elected to the national assembly in 1972. He became Transvaal leader of the ruling National Party in 1982. He held several cabinet posts from the mid-1970s, was education minister in the government of Pieter Willem Botha, and succeeded Botha as head of the National Party in February 1989. Botha resigned as president in August 1989; De Klerk became acting president, and was named to a full five-year presidential term in September, bringing with him a new spirit of reconciliation between the races. In October 1989, De Klerk released eight long-term political prisoners, including Walter Sisulu and six other ANC leaders, and Jafta Masemola of the Pan Africanist Congress. On February 2, 1990, he legalized the ANC and several other outlawed organizations, and on February 11 freed ANC leader Nelson Mandela, opening a new chapter in South African history. On August 7, 1990 the ANC agreed to a full ceasefire, bringing 30 years of guerrilla war to an end. The government in turn agreed to free many more political prisoners, allow many exiles to freely return home, and relax several re-

pressive laws, and lived up to its promises, beginning the long negotiation process that would in 1993 bring a new constitution and a new day to South Africa.

De Klerk attended Potchefstroom University. He married Marike Willemse in 1959; they have three children.

FURTHER READING

"Mandela and De Klerk speak out." *Time*, June 14, 1993.
"De Klerk's Gorbachev problem." BILL KELLER. *New York Times Magazine*, Jan. 31, 1993.
" 'The road of conflict. . . .' " LALLY WEYMOUTH. *Newsweek*, Sep. 28, 1992.
" 'Our struggle is. . . .' " BARRY SHELBY. *World Press Review*, May 1992.
" 'No racism in the New South Africa.' " *Newsweek*, Mar. 2, 1992.
"Great black hope." *Economist*, Feb. 29, 1992.
Politics in South Africa: From Vorster to de Klerk. IAN DERBYSHIRE. CKG Publications, 1992.
"The mandate for. . . ." ARNAUD DE BORCHGRAVE. *Insight*, July 2, 1990.
"After apartheid. . . ." COLIN VALE and R.W. JOHNSON. *National Review*, Oct. 15, 1990.
"The authoritarian center. . . ." SANFORD J. UNGAR. *New Republic*, Oct. 1, 1990.
"de Klerk, Frederick Willem." *Current Biography*, Feb. 1990.

Del Rey, Lester (Ramon Felipe Alvarez del Rey; 1915–93) Minnesota-born Lester Del Rey, a science fiction writer and leading science fiction editor and publisher, began his writing career in 1938, with publication of his story "The Faithful" in John W. Campbell's *Astounding Science Fiction* magazine. He continued to publish with Campbell through the late 1940s, then branching out, largely into young adult science fiction. He also edited several science fiction magazines and the anthology *Science Fiction Stories of the Year* (1972–76). In 1976, he and his wife, editor Judy-Lyn Benjamin (who died in 1986), founded the science fiction house Del Rey Books. There were no survivors. (d. New York City; May 10, 1993)

FURTHER READING

Obituary. *Analog Science Fiction and Fact*, Nov. 1993.
Obituary. *The Times* (of London), May 21, 1993.

de Mille, Agnes (1905–93) New York-born Agnes de Mille was a choreographer whose work transformed the Broadway musical theater. She began her career as a dancer, in London and New York in the early 1920s, made her choreographic debut in 1928 with "Stage Fright," and in 1933 choreographed the dances for Cole Porter's *Nymph Errant*, starring Gertrude Lawrence. Her first substantial breakthrough came in 1942, with her choreography of Aaron Copland's *Rodeo*, and her major breakthrough in 1943, with *Oklahoma!*, which for the first time fully integrated classical and modern forms into the American musical theater. She went on to choreograph scores of works for the theater and ballet, including such classic musicals as *One Touch Venus* (1943), *Bloomer Girl* (1944), *Carousel* (1945), *Allegro* (1947; and directed); *Brigadoon* (1947), *Gentlemen Prefer Blondes* (1949), and *Paint Your Wagon* (1951), and created such ballets as *Fall River Legend* (1948) and *Texas Fourth* (1976), continuing her career despite a severe stroke in 1975. She wrote several books on the dance and several autobiographical works, including *Dance to the Piper* (1987); her most recent works were *Portrait Gallery: Artists, Impresarios, Intimates* (1990) and *Martha: The Life and Work of Martha Graham* (1991). De Mille was the daughter of playwright William de Mille, granddaughter of playwright Henry de Mille, and niece of producer-director Cecil B. De Mille. She was survived by a son. (d. New York City; October 7, 1993)

FURTHER READING

"Native dancer." CRAIG BROMBERG. *People*, Oct. 25, 1993.
Obituary. *The Times* (of London), Oct. 9, 1993.
Obituary. *New York Times*, Oct. 8, 1993.
Obituary. *Variety*, Oct. 8, 1993.
"Agnes de Mille. . . ." MOLLY McQUADE. *Publishers Weekly*, Aug. 23, 1991.
Agnes de Mille: Dancing off the Earth. BEVERLY GHERMAN. Atheneum/Macmillan, 1990.
Agnes De Mille. MARGARET SPEAKER-YUAN. Chelsea House, 1990.

Deming, W(illiam) Edwards

(1900–93) Iowa-born W. Edwards Deming, a leading production processes analyst and advocate of quality control in manufacturing, emerged as a major figure in 1950, when invited to advise Japanese industry on quality control. One of his major prescriptions, the development of an enduring workplace partnership between managers and workers to guarantee product quality, was well-suited to Japanese working relationships, and his workplace approach, coupled with some of his statistical methods, became pervasive in Japanese industry. Deming was therefore widely credited with having made a major contribution to postwar Japanese competitive success in international markets. He was later hired by many American companies with similar ends in mind, but the need to change American corporate cultures to accommodate his views produced at best mixed results. Among his published works was *Out of the Crisis* (1986). He was survived by two sisters. (d. Washington, D.C.; December 20, 1993)

FURTHER READING

Obituary. *The Times* (of London), Dec. 24, 1993.
Obituary. *New York Times*, Dec. 21, 1993.
"Deming, W. Edwards." *Current Biography*, Sep. 1993.
"A day in the life of Ed Deming." RICK TETZELI. *Fortune*, Jan. 11, 1993.
The World of W. Edwards Deming, 2nd ed. CECELIA S. KILIAN. SPC Press, 1992.
"25 who help the U.S. win . . . ." LOUIS KRAAR. *Fortune*, Spring-Summer 1991.
"Ed Deming wants big changes . . . ." LLOYD DOBYNS. *Smithsonian*, Aug. 1990.
"The gurus of TQM . . . ." ELLIS PINES. *Aviation Week & Space Technology*, May 21, 1990.
The Man Who Discovered Quality: How W. Edwards Deming Brought the Quality Revolution to America—The Stories of Ford, Xerox, and GM. ANDREA GABOR. Random, 1990; Viking Penguin, 1992.
Dr. Deming: The American Who Taught the Japanese about Quality. RAFAEL AGUAYO. Carol, 1990; Simon & Schuster, 1991.

Demme, Jonathan (1944–) In 1993, film director Jonathan Demme followed up his hugely successful *The Silence of the Lambs* (1991) with a complete change of pace, directing and co-producing the very well received AIDS-discrimination film *Philadelphia*. Tom Hanks starred as the rising young attorney fired for alleged incompetence but in fact for having AIDS, opposite Denzel Washington as Hanks's own lawyer in the discrimination case brought by Hanks against his old law firm; the cast included Jason Robards as a leading member of the old firm, Mary Steenburgen as Robards's assistant, Antonio Banderas as Hanks's companion, and Joanne Woodward and Julius "Dr. J." Erving in cameos. Bruce Springsteen wrote the song "Streets of Philadelphia," played behind the credits; it was his first written directly for a film.

Demme also produced two films: *Household Saints*, directed by Nancy Savoca, and starring Tracey Ullman and Vincent D'Onofrio; and *Amos and Andrew*, written and directed by E. Max Frye and starring Nicolas Cage. Forthcoming was the sequel to *The Silence of the Lambs*.

Long Island-born Demme began his film career in the late 1960s, as a writer in the publicity departments of several film companies and *Film Daily*, and as a producer of television commercials. He co-wrote and co-produced several Roger Corman films in the early 1970s, and made his feature film directorial debut with *Caged Heat* (1974). He went on to direct such films as *Crazy Mama* (1975), *Melvin and Howard* (1980), *Swing Shift* (1984), *Something Wild* (1986), *Swimming to Cambodia* (1987), *Married to the Mob* (1988), *Miami Blues* (1990), *The Silence of the Lambs* (1991)—which swept the top Oscars, including best picture, director, actor, actress, and screenplay—and *Cousin Bobby* (1992). Demme attended the University of Florida. He is married to Joanne Howard; they have one child.

FURTHER READING

"The players." ANDREW CORSELLO and AMY DONOHUE. *Philadelphia*, Dec. 1993.

"Only lambs are silent." ELIZABETH GLEICK. *People*, June 22, 1992.

"Heavy estrogen." GARY INDIANA. *Interview*, Feb. 1991.

"Identity check." GAVIN SMITH. *Film Comment*, Jan.-Feb. 1991.

Deng Xiaoping (T'eng Hsiao-ping; 1904–)

Though ill and rarely making public appearances, Deng Xiaoping at 89 still ruled China—and still endorsed the combination of market economy development and political repression he had so strongly directed in early 1992, the economic portion of this described as a "socialist market economy." His program was explicitly endorsed again by the National People's Congress (parliament) at its March meeting, and by the Communist Party Central Committee in November, although it became increasingly clear throughout the year that China's economy was seriously overheating with escalating inflation, rising corruption, massive population shifts, and the emergence of an affluent commercial class threatening the stability prized above all by China's communist leadership. Deng continued to push forward his protégé, Communist Party general secretary and military chairman Jiang Zemin, who also became president in March. But hardline premier Li Peng was also re-elected, though with some opposition, signaling the continuance of the Chinese communist conservative-liberal power struggle that will emerge when Deng no longer rules, whether or not Li Peng, reportedly ill, is the leader of the conservative cause.

Deng joined the Communist Party of China in the 1920s, while a student in France. He fought through the whole length of the Chinese Civil War (1927–49) and is a survivor of the 1934 Long March. During communist ascendency, he became a major moderate leader, was purged twice (1973 and 1976), and survived to become the primary leader of Chinese communism. Deng attended the French School in Chongqing, studied in France during the 1920s, and attended Moscow's Far Eastern University. He married Cho Lin; the couple had five children. During 1993, Deng issued what was generally regarded as his final volume of speeches. His youngest daughter, Deng Rung, published an authorized biography of Deng.

FURTHER READING

Deng Xiaoping: And the Making of Modern China. RICHARD EVANS. Viking Penguin, 1994.

"Deng's new hope: China." *Economist*, Oct. 24, 1992.

"Can Deng square the circle?" BRIAN CROZIER. *National Review*, July 6, 1992.

The New Emperors: China in the Era of Mao and Deng. HARRISON E. SALISBURY. Little, Brown, 1992; Avon, 1993.

"Rise of a perfect apparatchik. . . ." WILLIAM R. DOERNER. *Time*, July 10, 1989.

"An unlikely 'emperor.'" MARY NEMETH and LOUISE DODER. *Maclean's*, May 29, 1989.

Deng Xiaoping. ULI FRANZ. Harcourt Brace, 1988.

De Niro, Robert (1945–) In a long-sought career expansion, Robert De Niro moved into film directing in 1993, directing, co-producing, and starring in *A Bronx Tale*, co-starring Chazz Palminteri and Joe Pesci. The well-received film, set in a Bronx Italian-American community, was adapted for screen from his own play by Palminteri. Also in 1993, De Niro starred as Chicago police crime scene photographer "Mad Dog" Dobie, opposite Una Thurman as Glory, the woman made his "present" for a week by mobster Frank Milo (Bill Murray), whose life he had saved, in the film *Mad Dog and Glory*, directed by Bill McNaughton. De Niro also starred opposite Ellen Barkin in the film *This Boy's Life*, directed by Michael Caton-Jones, as the stepfather of a teenager, Leonardo DeCaprio, their conflict being at the center of the work.

Forthcoming was a starring role as the monster in *Mary Shelley's Frankenstein*, opposite Kenneth Branagh as Victor Frankenstein, the film being directed by Branagh and produced by Francis Ford Coppola. Also forthcoming was a role as artist Jackson Pollock, opposite Barbra Streisand as artist Lee Krasner, Pollock's wife.

New York-born De Niro became one of the leading actors of the American cinema in the mid-1970s, beginning with his strong supporting roles in *Bang the Drum Slowly* (1973), *Mean Streets* (1973), and as the young Vito Corleone in *The Godfather, Part II* (1974), for which he won a best supporting actor Oscar. He went on to star in *Taxi Driver* (1976), *The Deer Hunter* (1978), and *Raging Bull* (1980), for which he won a best actor Oscar. In the 1980s, he starred in such films as *Once Upon a Time in America* (1984), *Brazil* (1985), *Midnight Run* (1988), *We're No Angels* (1989), and *Stanley and Iris* (1989). In the 1990s, he has starred in *Goodfellas* (1990), *Awakenings* (1990), *Cape Fear* (1991), *Guilty by Suspicion* (1991), *Backdraft* (1991), and *Night and the City* (1992). He was previously married and has two children.

FURTHER READING

"A walk and a talk. . . ." PETER BRANT and INGRID SISCHYM. *Interview*, Nov. 1993.
"De Niro direct." JULIA REED. *Vogue*, Sep. 1993.
"De Niro, Robert." *Current Biography*, May 1993.
"Tribeca tries harder." CHRISTIAN MOERK and MICHAEL FLEMING. *Variety*, Feb. 1, 1993.
The Films of Robert DeNiro. DOUGLAS BRODE. Carol, 1993.
"Awake and sing." FRED SCHRUERS. *Premiere*, Jan. 1991.
"De Niro. . . ." *Video Review*, Mar. 1989.
Robert De Niro: The Hero Behind the Mask. KEITH McKAY. St. Martin's, 1986.

Dennehy, Brian (1939–) Stage and screen star Brian Dennehy appeared in several television films during 1993. Outstanding among them was his starring role opposite Joanne Woodward in *Foreign Affairs*, she as an English literature professor in Britain researching a forthcoming book, he as a retired Oklahoma engineer, the film based on Alison Lurie's novel. Dennehy also starred in the fact-based story of a 1970s cult leader who turned mass murderer in *The Ervil LeBaron Story*. Another fact-based television film was the miniseries *Murder in the Heartland: Parts I & II*, the story of 1950s mass murderer Charlie Starkweather and his 14-year-old girlfriend Caril Ann Fugate; Tim Roth starred; Dennehy was nominated for a best supporting actor Emmy. Other television films included *Jack Reed: Badge of Honor*, with Dennehy as a police officer, opposite Susan Ruttan and Alice Krige, and *Final Appeal*, with Dennehy playing a disbarred alcoholic lawyer who defended his sister (JoBeth Williams), after she shot her husband and his mistress. Meanwhile Dennehy began shooting a new primetime television series, "Birdland," a possible mid-season replacement in early 1994.

Connecticut-born Dennehy saw service with the Marine Corps in Vietnam. In the mid-1970s, he emerged as a strong supporting player in a wide range of character roles on stage and screen, with a notable role off-Broadway in *Streamers* (1976) and his film debut in *Semi-Tough* (1977). He became best known for such films as *F.I.S.T.* (1978), *First Blood* (1982), *Gorky Park* (1983), *Never Cry Wolf* (1983), *Finders Keepers* (1984), *Cocoon* (1985), *Silverado* (1985), *F/X* (1986), *Legal Eagles* (1986), *Return to Snowy River* (1988), *Miles from Home* (1988), *Cocoon: The Return* (1988), *The Last of the Finest* (1989), and *Presumed Innocent* (1990). He has also appeared in the television series "Big Shamus, Little Shamus" (1979) and "Star of the Family" (1982–83), as well as in many television films. Notable stage appearances were in *The Cherry Orchard* (1988) and *The Iceman Cometh* (1990). Dennehy graduated from Columbia University and did postgraduate work at Yale University. He is married and has three children.

FURTHER READING

"Brian Dennehy." *Playboy*, Nov. 1993.
"Brian Dennehy...." Bob Daly. *Chicago*, Sep. 1990.
"Heavy duty." Jean Nathan. *Interview*, Mar. 1990.
"They call him...." Marion Long. *GQ—Gentlemen's Quarterly*, May 1989.

De Rita, Joe (1909–93) American comedian Joe De Rita began working as a child in vaudeville, as part of the family act, the Dancing De Ritas, and made his career as a standup comic in cabaret. He joined the Three Stooges as Curly in 1959, replacing Joe Besser. The slapstick act in that period made a hugely successful comeback with the release of its old short theatrical films to television. The Three Stooges became a worldwide television success, and its principals major stars—Moe Howard, Larry Fine, and De Rita—went on to make such new "Stooges" films as *Snow White and the Three Stooges* (1961) and *The Three Stooges in Orbit*, the act ending in 1971. De Rita was survived by his wife Jean, and by two stepsons. (d. Los Angeles, July 3, 1993)

FURTHER READING

Obituary. *The Times* (of London), July 6, 1993.
Obituary. *New York Times*, July 5, 1993.

Dern, Laura Elizabeth (1967–)
Emerging young star Laura Dern appeared in two major films during 1993. The first, opening in June, was Steven Spielberg's *Jurassic Park*, the archetypal dinosaur special-effects science-fiction film that became a worldwide commercial hit and the highest grossing film ever. Directed by Spielberg, with screenplay by Michael Crichton and David Koepp, based on Crichton's novel, the film also starred Sam Neill, Jeff Goldblum, and Richard Attenborough. Dern also starred as a criminologist in *A Perfect World*, opposite Kevin Costner as escaped killer Butch Haynes, Clint Eastwood as Texas Ranger Red Garnett, and T.J. Lowther as the child Costner kidnaps, who becomes more son than hostage to him; Eastwood directed.

Santa Monica-born Dern, the daughter of actors Bruce Dern and Diane Ladd, began her professional career as a teenager, in such films as *Foxes* (1980) and *Ladies and Gentlemen, the Fabulous Stains* (1982). She became a juvenile lead in *Mask* (1985), *Smooth Talk* (1985), and in David Lynch's exploration of the seamy side of American smalltown life, *Blue Velvet* (1986). She emerged a star as Lula Pace Fortune opposite Nicolas Cage as Sailor Ripley in Lynch's *Wild at Heart* (1990), and won an Oscar nomination for her role in *Rambling Rose* (1991). She attended the Lee Strasberg Institute in Los Angeles and London's Royal Academy of Dramatic Art.

FURTHER READING

"Jurassic spark...." David Wild. *Rolling Stone*, June 24, 1993.
"Laura Dern." *Playboy*, Mar. 1993.
"Laura Dern." Bart Bull. *Harper's Bazaar*, June 1992.
"Wild innocent." Mark Rowland. *American Film*, July 1991.
"Screen veteran Bruce Dern and...." Marjorie Rosen. *People*, Oct. 8, 1990.
"Childhood's end." Phoebe Hoban. *Premiere*, Sep. 1990.
"Laura Dern." Gary Indiana; Kurt Markus. *Interview*, Sep. 1990.
"Behind her blue eyes." Laurie Ochoa. *American Film*, Oct. 1989.

DeVito, Danny (Daniel Michael DeVito; 1944–) In 1993, actor, director, and producer Danny DeVito starred in *Jack the Bear*, playing the newly widowed father of two young boys,

Danny DeVito (left) and Miko Hughes

who moves to California and becomes a late-night television horror-film host. DeVito was critically applauded for his portrait of a difficult, loving father, as was Robert J. Steinmiller for his portrait of one of De Vito's sons, in a cast that also included Jack Leary, Dylan Leary, and Miko Hughes. Marshall Herskovitz made his theater film directorial debut with the film; in television, he had been one of the creators of the series "Thirtysomething." DeVito also appeared as the voice of the dog Rocks in the film *Look Who's Talking Now*, the third in the "Look Who's Talking" series. Forthcoming was a starring role in the film *Renaissance Man*, directed and produced by Penny Marshall, in a cast that included Marky Mark and Stacey Dash.

New Jersey-born DeVito was a New York stage actor before making his main career in Hollywood. He appeared in such off-Broadway productions as *The Man With a Flower in His Mouth* (1969) and *One Flew Over the Cuckoo's Nest* (1971), recreating his role in the 1975 film version, and went on to such films as *Car Wash* (1976), and *Goin' South* (1978). Then came his role as Louie DePalma in the long-running television series "Taxi" (1978–83), for which he won a 1981 Emmy, and roles in such films as *Terms of Endearment* (1983), *Romancing the Stone* (1984), *Jewel of the Nile* (1985), *Ruthless People* (1986), and starring roles in *Tin Men* (1987), *Throw Momma from the Train* (1987; he also directed), *Twins* (1988), *The War of the Roses*

(1989; he also directed), *Other People's Money* (1991), *Batman Returns* (1992), and *Hoffa* (1992; he also directed). DeVito is married to actress Rhea Perlman, and has three children.

FURTHER READING

"Danny DeVito." *Playboy*, Feb. 1993.
"Danny DeVito. . . ." MICHAEL J. BANDLER. *Ladies Home Journal*, Jan. 1990.
"Funny as hell." ROBERT SEIDENBERG. *American Film*, Sep. 1989.
The Taxi Book: The Complete Guide to TV's Most Lovable Hacks. JEFF SORENSEN. St. Martin's, 1987.

De Vries, Peter (1910–93) Chicago-born Peter De Vries began his writing career in the late 1930s, while an editor of Chicago's *Poetry* magazine. His well-received first novel was *Who Wakes the Bugler?* (1940). He began his long association with *The New Yorker* in the early 1940s, as a poetry editor and story writer. His first major success came with the best-selling *Tunnel of Love* (1954), which he adapted into the long-running 1957 play, basis of the 1958 film. His novels, many of them satirizing suburban life and concerns, included *Comfort Me with Apples* (1956), *The Mackerel Plaza* (1958), *The Tents of Wickedness* (1959), *Through the Fields of Clover* (1961), and *Reuben, Reuben* (1964), the last the basis of the 1983 Robert Ellis film, starring Tom Conti. Several of his other works also spawned movies, including *How Do I Love Thee?* (1970) and *Pete 'n Tillie* (1972). He was survived by a daughter and two sons. (d. Westport, Connecticut, Sep. 28, 1993).

FURTHER READING

"A jolly old elf. . . ." PAUL THEROUX. *New York Times Book Review*, Dec. 5, 1993.
"Of many things." GEORGE W. HUNT. *America*, Oct. 23, 1993.
"Community of laughter . . ." RALPH C. WOOD. *Christian Century*, Oct. 20, 1993.
Obituary. *The Times* (of London), Oct. 4, 1993.
Obituary. *New York Times*, Sep. 29, 1993.

Diana, Princess of Wales (Diana Frances Spencer; 1961–) Although she and Charles, Prince of Wales, had formally separated in December 1992, the personal life of Princess

Diana continued to be a focus of worldwide media attention throughout the year. Much publicity surrounded the publication of excerpts from taped telephone conversations, allegedly between prince and princess and allegedly concerning marital disputes. London's *Daily Mirror* and *Sunday Mirror* even sold newspapers by printing photos of her exercising in a leotard at a gym; injunctions forced them to stop publishing the photos, as an intrusion on privacy. On December 3, as attacks on the British royal family and on the monarchy itself mounted, she announced that she was sharply cutting her public appearances, and substantially withdrawing from public life.

Diana Spencer, Princess of Wales, worked as a kindergarten teacher in London before her marriage. She married Charles, Prince of Wales, heir to the British throne, in July 1981, in a ceremony watched worldwide by hundreds of millions of viewers. During the twelve years that followed, they remained great celebrities, every step and misstep chronicled and photographed in great detail by the media. In the later years of their marriage, media attention has focused on reported marital strains, and in 1992 it became apparent that strains did indeed exist. On December 9, 1992, the Prince and Princess of Wales announced their separation. They have two children: William Arthur Philip, born June 21, 1982; and Henry Charles Albert David, born September 15, 1984.

FURTHER READING

"The outsider. . . ." MICHELLE GREEN. *People*, Dec. 6, 1993.

"The tarnished crown." ANTHONY HOLDEN. *Cosmopolitan*, Sep. 1993.

"What's next. . . . " INGRID SEWARD. *Good Housekeeping*, Aug. 1993.

"Princess Diana. . . ." GEORGINA HOWELL. *Vogue*, May 1993.

"Di goes it alone." MICHELLE GREEN. *People*, Apr. 12, 1993.

"Diana's revenge." ANTHONY HOLDEN. *Vanity Fair*, Feb. 1993.

"Princess Diana. . . ." TIM COPELAND. *New Woman*, Feb. 1993.

"Scenes from a marriage. " *Life*, Feb. 1993.

"Dishing Di." *Ladies Home Journal*, Jan. 1993.

The Tarnished Crown: Princess Diana and the House of Windsor. ANTHONY HOLDEN. Random, 1993.

Diana, Princess of Wales. JULIA DELANO. Smithmark, 1993.

Princess Diana: Glitter, Glamour, and a Lot of Hard Work. NANCY E. KRULIK. Scholastic, 1993.

Princess Diana: Royal Ambassador. RENORA LICATA. Blackbirch, 1993.

Diana: Her True Story. ANDREW MORTON. Simon & Schuster, 1992.

Diana in Private: The Princess Nobody Knows. COLIN CAMPBELL. St. Martin's, 1992.

Diana: A Princess and Her Troubled Marriage. NICHOLAS DAVIES. Birch Lane/Carol, 1992; Bantam, 1993.

Crown Princess: A Biography of Diana. JOSEPHINE FAIRLEY. Thomas Dunne/St. Martin's, 1992.

Diebenkorn, Richard (1922–93) Portland-born Richard Diebenkorn, a leading American painter and teacher for more than four decades, began his career in the late 1940s, his work then much influenced by the abstract impressionists of the then-emerging New York School, though with strong affinities for the work of Edward Hopper and such earlier painters as Matisse and Bonnard. His debut exhibition came in San Francisco in 1948, at the California Palace of the Legion of Honor, and began the process of recognition that was by the mid-1950s to establish him as a leading West Coast abstract expressionist. But in 1955 he sharply changed direction, focusing on figurative work. He moved back to abstract work in 1967, after moving from Stanford University to the University of California at Los Angeles, and from Palo Alto to Santa Monica, where he painted his "Ocean Park" series (1967–88). He was survived by his wife, Phyllis, and two children. (d. Berkeley, California; March 30, 1993)

FURTHER READING

"Diebenkorn redux." ADAM GOPNIK. *New Yorker*, May 24, 1993.

Obituary. *Current Biography*, May 1993.

Obituary. *The Times* (of London), Apr. 1, 1993.

Obituary. *New York Times*, Mar. 31, 1993.

"A life outside." MICHAEL KIMMELMAN. *New York Times Magazine*, Sep. 13, 1992.

Temperaments: Artists Facing Their Work. DAN HOFSTADTER. Knopf, 1992.

Richard Diebenkorn. GERALD NORDLAND. Rizzoli, 1988.

Matt Dillon (right) and Mary Louise Parker

Dillon, Matt (1964–   ) In 1993, Matt Dillon starred opposite Danny Glover in *The Saint of Fort Washington*, Dillon as a quiet, unworldly young man forced out of his home onto the streets of New York, Glover as a streetwise Vietnam War veteran who tries to help the homeless Dillon, the two becoming close friends; directed by Tim Hunter. The cast also includes Rick Aviles and Nina Siemaszko. Dillon also starred in the well-received comedy *Mr. Wonderful*, as Gus, a blue collar worker who tries to find a new husband for his ex-wife, played by Annabella Sciorra, largely to end his alimony payments; but in the process they are once again drawn to each other. Co-starring are Mary Louise Parker, William Hurt, and Vincent D'Onofrio; Anthony Minghella directed. Forthcoming were starring roles in the films *Golden Gate*, written by David Henry Hwang and directed by John Madden; and *The Boxer and the Blonde*, directed by Andy Volk.

Born in New Rochelle, New York, Dillon began his movie career as a teenager, in *Over the Edge* (1979), quickly followed by *Little Darlings* (1980), which established him as a leading teenage Hollywood star. During the 1980s, he starred in such films as *My Bodyguard* (1980), *Liar's Moon* (1982), *Tex* (1982), *The Outsiders* (1983), *Rumblefish* (1983), *The Flamingo Kid* (1984), *Native Son* (1986), *Kansas* (1988), *Drugstore Cowboy* (1989), *Bloodhounds of Broadway* (1989), *A Kiss Before Dying* (1991), and *Singles*

(1992). His younger brother is the actor Kevin Dillon.

FURTHER READING

"From here to maturity. . . ." *Seventeen*, July 1991.
"Matt Dillon." BRENDON LEMON. *Interview*, Apr. 1991.
"The Dillon papers." BRET EASTON ELLIS. *American Film*, Feb. 1991.
"Mighty Matt." CARL WAYNE ARRINGTON. *Rolling Stone*, Nov. 30, 1989.

Dinkins, David Norman (1927–   ) On November 2, 1993, Democrat David Dinkins, New York City's first African-American mayor, was defeated after a single term by challenger Rudolph W. Giuliani, who ran on the Republican and Liberal lines. Giuliani's campaign had played mainly on racial themes in a deeply divided city, and although Giuliani denied a play to racism, the vote was strikingly along racial lines, with Giuliani winning 75 percent of the White vote in a city with five registered Democrats to every Republican, and Dinkins winning 95 percent of the African-American vote. Equally strikingly, the other citywide Democratic candidates won by landslides.

Although New York City had suffered no major racial clashes in 1993, Dinkins continued to face deepening and unresolved ethnic and racial tensions. He was badly hurt by the July 20, 1993 New York City criminal justice division report on the 1991 Crown Heights riots, which sharply criticized Dinkins for tardy and inadequate action to control the riots. Dinkins was also very badly hurt by the discovery that asbestos inspections of the city's public schools had been badly done, forcing a massive emergency re-inspection that postponed scheduled school openings in September, on the eve of the mayoral election. In late November, Columbia University announced that Dinkins would join the faculty of its School of International and Public Affairs after leaving office.

New Jersey-born Dinkins practiced law and politics in New York City from the mid-1950s. He was elected to the State Assembly in 1965 and served in several appointive posts, withdrawing from a deputy's mayor's position in 1973, at least partly because he had failed to file tax returns for several years. He was City Clerk (1975–85), and then was the elected borough president of Manhattan (1985–88). He became the historic first African-American mayor of

New York City in 1989, after defeating incumbent mayor Edward Koch in the 1989 Democratic mayoral primary, and defeating Republican Rudolph Giuliani in the general election. Dinkins attended Howard University and Brooklyn Law School. He married Joyce Burrows in 1953; they have two children.

FURTHER READING

"Buttoned up." TODD S. PURDUM. *New York Times Magazine*, Sep. 12, 1993.
"Change partners." ANDY LOGAN. *New Yorker*, June 14, 1993.
"On the Offensive." RICHARD BROOKHISER. *National Review*, Feb. 1, 1993.
"Mayor Dinkins. . . ." SAM ROBERTS. *New York Times Magazine*, Apr. 7, 1991.
"Being there." MARIE BRENNER. *Vanity Fair*, Jan. 1991.
Changing New York City Politics. ASHER ARIAN et al. Routledge, 1991.
"Dinkins, David Norman." *Current Biography*, Mar. 1990.

Dixon, Sharon Pratt: See Kelly, Sharon Pratt Dixon.

Doctorow, E.L. (Edgar Lawrence Doctorow, 1931–)

It was a non-fiction year for E.L. Doctorow, though he has been quoted as saying there is no fiction or non-fiction, only narrative. His literary offering for 1993 was *Jack London, Hemingway and the Constitution: Selected Essays, 1977–1992*, a collection of writings previously presented in journals such as the *Nation*, *New York Times Book Review*, and *Harpers*. They range from biographical-critical commentaries on writers such as London, Hemingway, Thoreau, Orwell, Dreiser, and James Wright to political-historical essays on popular songs, the Constitution, 19th-century New York, and the writer's position in society. On another front, Doctorow was a prime mover in organizing a new round-the-clock, book-oriented cable television channel called Booknet, including an interactive purchasing service, the Cable Bookstore; a launch was planned for 1994.

New York-born Doctorow worked in publishing in the 1960s, during the early stages of his writing career, and later held several university teaching positions. He became recognized as a major author in the 1970s, with his novels *The*

Book of Daniel (1971) and *Ragtime* (1975). In the 1980s, he published *Loon Lake* (1980), *Lives of the Poets* (1984), the American Book Award-winning *World's Fair* (1985), and *Billy Bathgate* (1989), his Prohibition-era tale focusing on Dutch Schultz, which won the National Book Critics' Circle Award and the PEN/Faulkner Award (both 1990) and was made into the 1991 Robert Benton film. Doctorow's B.A. was from Kenyon College, in 1952. He married Helen Setzer in 1954; they have three children.

FURTHER READING

Understanding E.L. Doctorow. DOUGLAS FOWLER. University of South Carolina Press, 1992.
"The audacious lure . . ." ALVIN SANOFF. *U.S. News & World Report*, Mar. 6, 1989.
Writers at Work: The Paris Review Interviews. GEORGE PLIMPTON, ed. Viking Penguin, 1988.

Dole, Bob (Robert Joseph Dole; 1923–)

Republican Senate minority leader Bob Dole began his single-minded opposition to incoming President Bill Clinton even before Clinton's inauguration, allowing no time for the traditional "honeymoon" period enjoyed by most incoming presidents, and carrying through the themes of the hard-fought 1992 election campaign. Dole successfully attacked the Clinton economic stimulus plan in February, and led the Republican filibuster that killed the plan. But at a cost, for

Clinton was then able to characterize Dole and the Republicans as seekers of unproductive "gridlock," and with increased concentration and developing skills won a substantial series of legislative battles. On one issue, the North American Free Trade Agreement (NAFTA), Republicans joined centrist and conservative Democrats to pass the bill. But soon afterward, Dole once again attempted to lead a Republican filibuster, this one to block passage of the Brady gun control bill; that failed most damagingly, ending the 1993 congressional session on a losing and self-isolating note. More personally, Dole's campaign organization paid a $120,000 fine for election law violations during his 1988 presidential primary campaign. Dole was widely regarded as a major possible contender for the Republican Presidential nomination in 1996.

Kansas-born Dole has spent three decades in Washington, starting with his four congressional terms (1961–69). A leading Republican, he has served in the Senate since 1969, and as Senate Republican leader since 1985. He was chairman of the Republican National Committee (1971–73), and his party's unsuccessful Vice-Presidential candidate in 1976. He made unsuccessful runs for the Republican presidential nomination in 1980 and 1988. A staunch Republican Party supporter, he campaigned hard for the Bush-Quayle ticket in 1992, as he had in 1988, even after his primary defeat by Bush. He was elected to a fifth Senate term in 1992, by a huge majority, with 64 percent of the vote. On the personal side, Dole "went public" in 1992 when he found that he had prostate cancer, in an attempt to help others understand and deal with the problem. His treatment was reportedly entirely successful.

Dole's B.A. and LL.B were from Topeka's Washburn Municipal University. In 1975, he married Elizabeth Hanford Dole, with whom he published *Doles: Unlimited Partners* (1988); American Red Cross president, she was formerly Secretary of Labor.

FURTHER READING

"Robert Dole. . . ." J. D. PODOLSKY. *People*, Dec. 13, 1993.
"King Robert. . . ." FRED BARNES. *New Republic*, Apr. 5, 1993.
"Kemp vs. Dole." FRED BARNES. *New Republic*, Dec. 14, 1992.
"Bob Dole speaks. . . ." CORY SERVAAS. *Saturday Evening Post*, July-Aug. 1992.
"The two Bobs." WILLIAM MCGURN. *National Review*, Dec. 2, 1991.
Bob Dole: American Political Phoenix. STANLEY G. HILTON. Contemporary, 1988.

Donald, James (1917–93) Aberdeen-born James Donald studied at the London Theatre Studio, and made his London stage debut in *The White Guard* (1938). His breakthrough role came in 1943, when he created the role of Roland Maule in Noël Coward's *Present Laughter*. During World War II, he appeared in several war films, including Coward's and David Lean's *In Which We Serve* (1942). He played strong supporting roles on the London stage during the postwar period, also appearing in several British films. His first breakthrough film role was as Theo Van Gogh, Vincent Van Gogh's brother, opposite Kirk Douglas in *Lust For Life* (1956); his second at Major Clipton, the camp doctor in Lean's *The Bridge On the River Kwai* (1957). He continued to appear in many stage and screen roles on both sides of the Atlantic until his retirement due to ill health in the early 1970s, then turning to grapegrowing and winemaking in Wiltshire. He was survived by his wife, Ann, and a stepson. (d. Wiltshire, England; August 3, 1993)

FURTHER READING

Obituary. *New York Times*, Aug. 16, 1993.
Obituary. *The Times* (of London), Aug. 11, 1993.

Doolittle, James Harold (1896–1993) Air general Jimmy Doolittle began his flying career in the Army Signal Corps during World War I, and was a flying instructor for the army during and after the war, completing his education in aeronautical engineering in the early 1920s. He was also a stunt and long-distance flyer and test pilot from the early 1920s, and in 1929 made the first all-instrument takeoff and landing. He was in private industry (1930–40), but with the onset of World War II, returned to active duty as a test pilot. In early 1942, then-Lieutenant Colonel Doolittle organized and on April 18, 1942 led the historic carrier-based B-25

first bombing raid on Tokyo and other Japanese cities, causing little physical damage, but providing an enormous morale boost to hard-pressed Allied forces in the Pacific. He was awarded a Congressional Medal of Honor and promoted to brigadier general. Later, he commanded the 12th Air Force in Britain and North Africa (1942), the 15th Air Force in Italy (1943), the 8th Air Force in England (1944), and ended the war in the Pacific, by then a Lieutenant-General. Doolittle returned to private industry after the war. With Carroll V. Glines, he wrote *I Could Never Be So Lucky Again: The Memoirs of General James H."Jimmy" Doolittle* (1991). He was survived by a son. (d. Pebble Beach, California; September 27, 1993)

FURTHER READING

"General Jimmy . . ." *Air Progress*, Dec. 1993.
"Gen. Doolittle. . . ." *Aviation Week & Space Technology*, Oct. 4, 1993.
"Lieutenant-General James Doolittle." *Times*, Sep. 29, 1993.
Obituary. *The Times* (of London), Sep. 29, 1993.
Obituary. *New York Times*, Sep. 29, 1993.
" 'Tokyo bombed! Doolittle do'od it.' " JAMES A. COX. *Smithsonian*, June 1992.
"Against all odds." EDWARD OXFORD. *American History Illustrated*, Mar.-Apr. 1992.

Dorsey, Thomas A. ("Georgia Tom" Dorsey; 1899–1993)

Georgia-born Tom Dorsey, a prolific blues and gospel music composer and a celebrated blues and jazz pianist and guitarist, began his career in cabaret at 12. Several of his blues songs became recording hits in the late 1920s, most notably "It's Tight Like That" (1928). During the 1930s, Dorsey emerged as the leading African-American figure in gospel music, a term he probably coined, during his long career writing more than a thousand gospel songs. He organized Chicago's Pilgrim Baptist Church gospel choir in 1932, also becoming a leading gospel song publisher. Among his best known gospel songs were "If You See My Saviour," "Peace in the Valley," and "Take My Hand, Precious Lord," the last a Mahalia Jackson standard and a favorite of Rev. Martin Luther King, Jr.; it was played at his funeral, in 1968. Dorsey, often described as the "father" of

gospel music, was survived by his wife, Kathryn, a daughter, and a son. (d. Chicago; January 23, 1993)

FURTHER READING

The Rise of the Gospel Blues: The Music of Thomas Andrew Dorsey in the Urban Church. MICHAEL W. HARRIS. Oxford University Press, 1994.
Obituary. *Jet*, Feb. 8, 1993.
"Their amazing grace." JERRY ADLER. *Newsweek*, Feb. 8, 1993.
Obituary. *The Times* (of London), Feb. 1, 1993.
Obituary. *New York Times*, Jan. 25, 1993.
We'll Understand It Better By and By: Pioneering African American Gospel Composers. BERNICE J. REAGON, ed. Smithsonian, 1993.
Thomas A. Dorsey and the Rise of Gospel Music. MICHAEL W. HARRIS. Oxford University Press, 1992.

Dos Santos, José Eduardo (1942–   )

The peace treaty of May 1991, between José Eduardo Dos Santos as leader of the Popular Movement for the Liberation of Angola (MPLA) and Jonas Savimbi as leader of the National Union for the Total Independence of Angola (UNITA) did not hold. The long Angolan civil war resumed on October 30, 1992, after Savimbi refused to accept the electoral victory of Dos Santos, charging massive fraud. A UN-sponsored truce in early November 1992 also failed to hold, as fighting intensified throughout the country. In January, government forces successfully attacked UNITA forces in many cities, but UNITA soon retook much of the territory it had held during the civil war, in March capturing Huambo, Angola's second largest city, while the fighting claimed tens of thousands of lives. On May 19, the United States recognized the Dos Santos government, ending its long support for UNITA, but the fighting continued. By mid-September, when the UN voted to impose sanctions on UNITA, Savimbi's forces held an estimated two thirds of the country. In October, both sides stated their willingness to resume peace talks, while the war continued, by then having claimed an estimated 50,000–100,000 lives in 1993 alone.

For Dos Santos, the signing of the May 1991 peace treaty had seemed the end of two consecutive wars that had occupied his entire adult life. He has been an activist in the MPLA since he joined it in 1961. He went into exile that year and became president of the MPLA youth organization. He was educated in the Soviet Union (1963–70), as a petroleum engineer and telecommunications specialist, the latter skills being used when he returned to the Angolan war of independence in 1970. He became a member of the MPLA central committee in 1974, was foreign minister of the new Soviet-backed MPLA Angolan government in 1975, and held several cabinet-level posts during the next four years, as the civil war continued. After the death of President Augustinho Neto, Dos Santos became Angolan president, commander in chief, and head of the MPLA.

FURTHER READING

"Fact sheet. . . ." *U.S. Department of State Dispatch*, Sep. 23, 1991.
" 'We have taken. . . .' " BRUCE W. NELAN. *Time*, July 3, 1989.

Douglas, Michael (Michael Kirk Douglas; 1944–) In a highly controversial role, actor-producer Michael Douglas in 1993 starred in *Falling Down*, as a newly jobless Los Angeles defense worker who on his way home finds himself in a traffic jam, abandons his car, and sets off for home on foot across the city, his rage and frustration mounting incident by incident, and

soon erupting into repeated violence, complete with the language of hate and bigotry, as when he berates a Korean shopowner. Douglas is clearly meant by the makers of the film to be a kind of "everyman," goaded beyond endurance by the repeated abrasions of contemporary city life. Robert Duvall and Barbara Hershey co-starred; Joel Schumacher directed. The film drew protests from Korean and other ethnic and minority groups. In September, Douglas received the 1993 American Cinematheque Award.

Son of actor Kirk Douglas, Michael Douglas first became a star in the television series "The Streets of San Francisco" (1972–75), paired with Karl Malden. Moving into films, he produced the Oscar-winning *One Flew Over the Cuckoo's Nest* (1975) and the notable nuclear-accident film *The China Syndrome* (1979), and produced and starred in such films as *Romancing the Stone* (1984), *Jewel of the Nile* (1985), and *The War of the Roses* (1989), all three with Kathleen Turner, also starring in such films as *A Chorus Line* (1985), *Fatal Attraction* (1987), and *Wall Street* (1987; he won a best actor Oscar and a Golden Globe Award), *Black Rain* (1989), *Shining Through* (1992), and *Basic Instinct* (1992). Douglas's 1967 B.A. was from the University of California. He married Diandra Mornell Luker in 1977; they have one son.

FURTHER READING

"Do we love him when he's angry?" *Independent*, June 12, 1993.
"Michael and Diandra Douglas. . . ." DEBORAH NORVILLE. *McCall's*, Nov. 1992.
"Just your basic. . . ." T. KLEIN. *Cosmopolitan*, May 1992.
"Adventures in the skin trade. . . ." TRISH DEITCH ROHRER et al. *Entertainment*, Apr. 3, 1992.
"Michael Douglas." JUDITH THURMAN. *Architectural Digest*, Apr. 1992.
"Steaming up the screen." BRIAN D. JOHNSON. *Maclean's*, Mar. 30, 1992.
"Business as usual." DAVID THOMSON. *Film Comment*, Jan.-Feb., 1990.
Michael Douglas and the Douglas Clan. ANNENE KAYE and JIM SCLAVUNOS. Knightsbridge, 1990.
"A prince. . . ." LINDA BLANDFORD. *New York Times Magazine*, Dec. 3, 1989.

Dove, Rita Frances (1952–) On May 18, 1993, Rita Dove was named U.S. Poet Laureate by James H. Billington, the Librarian of Congress. She was the first African-American woman and the youngest person to hold the post. Born in Akron, Ohio, Dove emerged as a leading American poet in the 1980s, with the collections *The Yellow House on the Corner* (1980), *Museum* (1983), *Thomas and Beulah* (1986; awarded a 1987 Pulitzer prize), and *Grace Notes* (1989). A new volume, *Selected Poems*, was issued in 1993. She also has written the short story collection *Fifth Sunday* (1985) and the novel *Through the Ivory Gate* (1992). She taught English at Arizona State University (1981–89), then moving to the University of Virginia. Her B.A. was from Miami University, in Oxford, Ohio, and her M.F.A. from the University of Iowa. She is married to German novelist Fred Viebahn, and has one child.

FURTHER READING

Life Notes: Personal Writings by Contemporary Black Women. PATRICIA SCOTT-BELL, ed. Norton, 1994.
"Bold type. . . ." DONNA M. WILLIAMS. *Ms.*, Nov.-Dec. 1993.
"Rooms of their own." TONI MORRISON and JACK E. WHITE. *Time*, Oct. 18, 1993.
Writer on Her Work. JANET STERNBURG. Norton, 1991.

Downey, Robert, Jr. (1965–) For his title role in *Chaplin* (1992), Downey won the best actor award of the British Academy of Film and Television Arts (BAFTA), and was nominated for a best actor Academy Award and

Golden Globe award. In 1993, he starred as a banker in the comedy-fantasy ghost story *Heart and Soul*, directed by Ron Underwood. He also starred in the film *Short Cuts*, directed by Robert Altman, in a cast that included Tim Robbins, Fred Ward, Anne Archer, Jennifer Jason Leigh, Jack Lemmon, Andie MacDowell, Matthew Modine, Lily Tomlin, and Tom Waits. In another medium, he recorded the single "Smile," a song by Charlie Chaplin.

Forthcoming were starring roles in the satirical film *Natural Born Killers*, directed by Oliver Stone, in a cast that also includes Woody Harrelson, Juliette Lewis,. Tommy Lee Jones, Tom Sizemore, and Rodney Dangerfield; and in *Him*, directed and produced by Norman Jewison, in a cast that includes Marisa Tomei and Bonnie Hunt.

New York City-born Downey, the son of filmmaker Robert Downey, made his screen debut at the age of five, in his father's film *Pound* (1970), and played in several other children's roles. He emerged as a star in his late teens, in such films as *Baby, It's You* (1983), *Firstborn* (1984), *Tuff Turf* (1985), *Back To School* (1986), *Less Than Zero* (1987), *Johnny Be Good* (1988), *Chances Are* (1989), *True Believer* (1989), *Air America* (1990), and *Too Much Sun* (1991). He also narrated the documentary *The Last Party*, about the 1992 presidential election campaign. He is married to actress Deborah Falconer.

FURTHER READING

"Ladies and the tramp." BOB SPITZ. *US*, Jan. 1993.
"20 questions. . . ." *Playboy*, Aug. 1991.
"Cinema Scion." KENNETH TURAN and KAREN KUEHN. *Interview*, Apr. 1989.
"Hollywood's newest golden boy." PHOEBE HOBAN. *Premiere*, Apr. 1989.
"Arresting appeal. . . ." BETSY BORNS. *Harper's Bazaar*, Feb. 1989.

Dreyfuss, Richard (Richard Stephan Dreyfuss; 1947–) For Richard Dreyfuss, 1992 had brought a hit Broadway play, *Death and the Maiden*. In 1993, he starred in the adaptation of a hit Broadway play into film, this one *Lost in Yonkers*, the screen version of Neil Simon's 1991 Pulitzer Prize-winning play, adapted by Simon and directed by Martha Coolidge. Dreyfuss played Uncle Louie, a small-time gangster in hiding at the house of Grandma Kurnitz (Irene

Richard Dreyfuss (right) and Mike Damus

Worth). Mercedes Ruehl recreated her stage role, as Aunt Bella. Dreyfuss also starred as a detective in the Seattle-set comedy-thriller film *Another Stakeout*, opposite Emilio Estevez as his detective partner; John Badham directed. Forthcoming was a starring role in a so-far-untitled Bruce Beresford-directed film, co-starring Linda Hamilton and John Lithgow.

New York-born Dreyfuss became a leading film star of the 1970s, with his roles in *American Graffiti* (1973), *The Apprenticeship of Duddy Kravitz,* (1974), *Jaws* (1975), *Close Encounters of the Third Kind* (1977), and *The Goodbye Girl* (1977), for which he won a best actor Oscar. He went on the star in such films as *Whose Life Is It Anyway?* (1981), *Down and Out in Beverly Hills* (1986), *Tin Men* (1987), *Always* (1989), *Rosencrantz and Guildenstern Are Dead* (1991), *Once Around* (1991), and *What About Bob?* (1991). On television he co-produced and starred in the HBO telefilm *Prisoner of Honor*, on France's Dreyfus affair, and was the voice of general William T. Sherman in the PBS documentary *Lincoln* (1992). Dreyfuss attended San Fernando Valley State College (1965–67). In 1992, he filed for divorce from Jeramie Rain; they have three children.

FURTHER READING

"Richard Dreyfuss." CLAUDIA DREIFUS. *Progressive*, May 1993.

"Against all odds." SUSAN SCHINDEHETTE. *People*, Mar. 4, 1991.
"Richard Dreyfuss, . . ." DIGBY DIEHL. *Cosmopolitan*, Nov. 1990.

Drysdale, Don (1937–93) California-born Don Drysdale attracted notice as a high school pitcher, and joined the Brooklyn Dodger organization in 1954, while still in his teens. He quickly emerged as a leading major league pitcher and was a mainstay of many pennant-winning Brooklyn and Los Angeles Dodger teams, winning more than 200 games over 14 years (1956–69). He was on 10 National League All Star teams, won the Cy Young award in 1962, played on three world championship Dodger teams and five pennant-winners, and in his day held several pitching records. He entered the baseball Hall of Fame in 1984. After retiring, he became a highly regarded network baseball broadcaster, and was on tour with the Dodgers at the time of his death. With Bob Verdi, Drysdale wrote *Once a Bum, Always a Dodger: My Life in Baseball* (1990). He was survived by his wife, basketball star and broadcaster Ann Meyers Drysdale, two daughters, and two sons. (d. Montreal, July 3, 1993)

FURTHER READING

Obituary. *Current Biography*, Sep. 1993.
"This Dodger was a giant . . ." LYLE SPENCER. *Sporting News*, July 12, 1993.
Obituary. *New York Times*, July 5, 1993.

Duke, Doris (1912–93) New York City-born Doris Duke, the only child and heir of American industrialist James Buchanan Duke, inherited an estimated $50 million in assets on his death in 1925, and became the focus of enormous and apparently entirely unwanted media attention as "the world's richest woman." Media attention intensified around her two marriages, to James Cromwell (1935–43) and Porfirio Rubirosa (1947–48), and to highly publicized subsequent liaisons. Duke actively managed her assets, and as a philanthropist exhibited a wide range of interests, giving substantial amounts of money to such causes as historic preservations, AIDS research, and animal rights protection. She was survived by an adopted daughter, Charlene Heffner. (d. Beverly Hills; October 28, 1993)

FURTHER READING

"The death and delirious life. . . ." DINITIA SMITH. *New York*, Dec. 6, 1993.
"The burden of riches . . ." MARK GOODMAN. *People*, Nov. 15, 1993.
Obituary. *The Times* (of London), Oct. 30, 1993.
Obituary. *New York Times*, Oct. 29, 1993.
The Richest Girl in the World: The Extravagant Life and Fast Times of Doris Duke. STEPHANIE MANSFIELD. Putnam, 1992.
Daddy's Duchess: An Unauthorized Biography of Doris Duke. TOM VALENTINE and PATRICK MAHN. Carol, 1987.

Dunaway, Faye (Dorothy Faye Dunaway; 1941–)

Veteran film and television star struck out in a new direction in 1993, finally agreeing to try a primetime television comedy series. It was "It Had to Be You;" she played a moneyed Boston publisher, opposite Robert Urich, who played a carpenter; their love affair was to have been the motor force of the show. Unfortunately, the show did not quickly find a large enough audience, and was quickly cancelled. Also on television, she guest-starred opposite Peter Falk in the television film *Columbo: It's All in the Game.*

On film, Dunaway also starred in *Arizona Dream*, directed by Emir Kusturica, with Johnny Depp, Jerry Lewis, and Lili Taylor co-starring; the film, which had opened in Paris in 1992, opened in the U.S. in 1993. Another starring film role was in the Portland-set film thriller *The Temp*, directed by Tom Holland, opposite Timothy Hutton and Lara Flynn Boyle.

Florida-born Dunaway became a film star in 1967, with her portrayal of 1930s midwestern outlaw Bonnie Parker in *Bonnie and Clyde*. She went on to become a leading Hollywood star, in such films as *The Thomas Crown Affair* (1968), *Chinatown* (1974), *Network* (1976; she won a best actress Oscar), as Joan Crawford in *Mommie Dearest* (1981; she decribed the role as "career suicide"), *Barfly* (1987), *The Handmaid's Tale* (1990), and *Double Edge* (1992). On television, she appeared as revivalist preacher Aimee Semple McPherson in *The Disappearance of Aimee* (1976) and in the title role of *Evita Peron* (1982), going on to roles in *Cold Sassy Tree* (1990), *Silhouette* (1990), and as the disembodied voice of Gaia, the mother goddess of the Earth, in the five-part, ten-hour epic miniseries "Voice of the Planet" (1991). Dunaway attended Boston University. She was formerly married to Peter Wolf, is married to Terrence O'Neill, and has one child.

FURTHER READING

"Dorothy Faye Dunaway." GRAHAM FULLER. *Interview*, Feb. 1993.
"Faye Dunaway." TINA JOHNSON. *Harper's Bazaar*, Sep. 1989.
Faye Dunaway. ALLAN HUNTER. St. Martin's, 1986.

Durning, Charles (1923–)

Now late in his career, veteran stage, screen, and television star Charles Durning devoted much of 1993 to work in television, in a strong continuing supporting role in the comedy series "Evening Shade," playing in ensemble with Burt Reynolds, Elizabeth Ashley, Ossie Davis, Jay R. Ferguson, Marilu Henner, and Hal Holbrook. He also starred in the television drama *The Music of Chance*, an American Playhouse presentation, directed by Philip Haas and co-starring James Spader, Mandy Patinkin, Joel Grey, and M. Emmet Walsh.

Durning has been a strong character actor for over 30 years, creating a wide range of notable roles on stage, screen, and television. In the theater he memorably played the governor in *Best Little Whorehouse in Texas*, and won a Tony as best featured actor in a play for his role as Big Daddy in the 1990 Broadway revival Tennessee Williams's *Cat on a Hot Tin Roof*. On film, he was especially notable as Jessica Lange's father and Dustin Hoffman's would-be suitor in *Tootsie* (1982). Among his other films are *The Sting* (1973), *Mass Appeal* (1984), *The Rosary Murders* (1987), *Far North* (1988), *Dick Tracy* (1990), and *V.I. Warshawski* (1991). He has also appeared in many television films, including *Queen of the Stardust Ballroom* (1975). Durning married Mary Ann Amelio in 1974. He was born in Highland Falls, New York, and attended New York University and Columbia University.

FURTHER READING

"An actor deals with his dark side." DOTSON RADER. *Parade*, Oct. 10, 1993.
"Playing a fiery big daddy. . . ." TOBY KAHN. *People*, June 4, 1990.

Duvall, Robert (1931–) For his title role
in the 1992 television film *Stalin*, veteran screen
star Robert Duvall was nominated for an Emmy
as best lead actor in miniseries or special, and a
Golden Globe award as best actor in a television
miniseries or telefilm. In 1993, Duvall starred
opposite Richard Harris, Shirley MacLaine,
Piper Laurie, and Sandra Bullock in the film
Wrestling Ernest Hemingway, directed by Randa
Haines, about the friendship of two old men, one
of them former sea captain Harris, the other Cuban bachelor and ex-barber Duvall. He also
starred as Indian scout Al Sieber in the film *Geronimo*, opposite Wes Studi in the title role and
Gene Hackman; Walter Hill directed. A third
major film role was as a police officer, opposite
Michael Douglas in *Falling Down*; Joel Schumacher directed. Forthcoming was a starring
role in the film *The Paper*, directed by Ron Howard, and co-starring Michael Keaton, Glenn
Close, Marisa Tomei, and Randy Quaid.

San Diego-born Duvall was recognized as a
powerful supporting actor in such films as *To
Kill a Mockingbird* (1963), *True Grit* (1969),
M*A*S*H (1970), the first two *Godfather* films
(1972; 1974), *Network* (1976), and *Apocalypse
Now* (1979). He went on to win a best actor Oscar for his lead in *Tender Mercies* (1983), while
continuing to play strong supporting roles and
sometimes leads in such films as *Colors* (1988),
Days of Thunder (1990), *The Handmaid's Tale*
(1990), *Rambling Rose* (1991), and *Convicts*
(1991). On television, he played a notable
Dwight D. Eisenhower in the miniseries *Ike*
(1979). A graduate of Principia College, Duvall
is married to Gail Youngs.

FURTHER READING

"Robert Duvall." LAURA DERN. *Interview*, Oct. 1991.

Dylan, Bob (Robert Alan Zimmerman;
1941–) Legendary singer and songwriter Bob
Dylan issued another folk and blues album in
1993: *World Gone Wrong*, a collection of classics
sung and played solo by Dylan, as he had done in
his 1992 album *Good As I Been to You*. Singles
releases and videos based on the album were in
preparation. He also issued the single "Step it
Up and Go," from *Good as I Been to You*. Another single was "My Back Pages," a live recording from his October 1992 30th-anniversary

Madison Square Garden concert, featuring
George Harrison, David Crosby, Tom Petty,
Roger McGuinn, Eric Clapton, and Neil Young.
Most of the concert was reproduced on the music
video *Bob Dylan: The 30th Anniversary Concert
Celebration*, including the episode in which Sin-
ead O'Connor was unfortunately booed off the
stage for having torn up a picture of Pope John
Paul II two weeks earlier on "Saturday Night
Live." Scheduled for 1994 publication was Dy-
lan's *Tarantula: Poems*.

Duluth-born Dylan was one of the leading
countercultural figures of the early 1960s, an
enormously popular folk-rock singer and composer known to millions for many of his own
songs, such as "The Times They are A-Changin"
(1963) and "Blowin' in the Wind" (1963). Later
in the 1960s, and through the 1970s and 1980s,
he was much more a rock than a folk-rock musician. Although he continued to be a very popular figure in concert and on records, his impact
was greatest in the early years, when he burst
upon the scene as a 1960s emblem of protest.
Dylan made a substantial comeback on records
and in performance, starting in 1989, with his
album *Oh Mercy* and a world tour. In 1990, his
new album *Under the Red Sky*, was very well
received, as were two *Traveling Wilburys* albums (1988; 1990), made with George Harrison,
Tom Petty, and Jeff Lynne, and (on the first album, made before his late 1988 death) Roy Or-
bison. In 1991, he released *The Bootleg Series,
Volumes 1–3 (Rare and Unreleased) 1961–91*, a

three-CD boxed set carrying 58 Dylan tracks, approximately a quarter of which had never before been released on records. Dylan attended the University of Minnesota, in 1960.

FURTHER READING

"Knockin' on heaven's door. . . ." BOB CANNON. Entertainment, July 30, 1993.

Bob Dylan: A Bio-Bibliography. WILLIAM McKEEN. Greenwood, 1993.

"Bringing folk back home. . . ." JAY COCKS. Time, Oct. 26, 1992.

Alias Bob Dylan. STEPHEN SCOBIE. Empire Publication Services, 1992.

Bob Dylan: A Man Called Alias. RICHARD WILLIAMS. Holt, 1992.

Hard Rain: A Dylan Commentary. TIM RILEY. Knopf, 1992; Random, 1993.

"Dylan, Bob." Current Biography, Oct. 1991.

"Forever young. . . ." MARC ELIOT. California, June 1991.

"Bob Dylan. . . ." TOM PIAZZA. New York Times Book Review, May 26, 1991.

"Subterranean half-century blues." Economist, May 25, 1991.

Bob Dylan Behind the Shades. CLINTON HEYLIN. Summit, 1991.

Wanted Man: In Search of Bob Dylan. JOHN BAULDIE, ed. Carol, 1991.

Dylan Companion: A Collection of Essential Writing about Bob Dylan. ELIZABETH THOMSON. Delacorte, 1991.

Bob Dylan: Portraits from the Singer's Early Years. DANIEL KRAMER. Carol, 1991.

Bob Dylan, Performing Artist: The Early Years 1960–1973. PAUL WILLIAMS. Underwood-Miller, 1991.

Positively Bob Dylan: A Thirty-Year Discography, Concert and Recording Session Guide, 1960–1989. MICHAEL KROGSGAARD. Popular Culture, 1991.

Bob Dylan: American Poet and Singer: An Annotated Bibliography and Study Guide of Sources and Background Materials, 1961–1991. RICHARD D. WISSOLIK et al, eds. Eadmer, 1991.

Dylan: A Biography. BOB SPITZ. McGraw-Hill, 1989.

Death of a Rebel. MARC ELIOT. Watts, 1989.

E

Eastwood, Clint (1930–) Always a major box office draw, actor, director, and producer Clint Eastwood emerged clearly as a major figure in the art of film during 1993, as his peers clearly recognized the worth of his unique body of work. His 1992 film *Unforgiven* won the best picture Oscar, and brought him personally the best director Oscar. He also won best director awards from the Directors Guild of America Golden Globes and National Society of Film Critics, which also named the film best picture.

In 1993, Eastwood directed and starred in the film *A Perfect World*, as Texas Ranger Red Garnett, opposite Kevin Costner as escaped killer Butch Haynes, T. J. Lowther as the child Costner kidnaps, who becomes more son than hostage to him; Laura Dern also starred as a criminologist. Eastwood the actor was also much praised for his role as a career Secret Service agent trying to prevent the assassination of a President, in the film *In the Line of Fire*, directed by Wolfgang Petersen, opposite John Malkovich as the assassin and Rene Russo as another agent.

On the personal side, actress Frances Fisher and Eastwood had a daughter, Francesca Ruth, her first and his third child.

San Francisco-born Eastwood was a star in television as the lead in the western series "Rawhide" (1958–65). He pursued the same western themes in the Italian-made Sergio Leone "spaghetti westerns" that made him a worldwide star, beginning with *A Fistful of Dollars* (1967). He then went on to become one of the most durable of all international action film stars. Beginning with *Play Misty For Me* (1971), he directed, produced, and starred in many of his films, such as *Honkytonk Man* (1982), *Bird* (1988; about jazz great Charlie Parker), *White Hunter, Black Heart* (1990), and *The Rookie* (1990). Eastwood attended Los Angeles City College. Previously divorced, Eastwood has three children; his son, Kyle, appeared in *Honkytonk Man*. (For additional photo, see Hackman, Gene.)

FURTHER READING

Clint Eastwood: The Man and His Films. EDWARD GALLAFENT. Continuum, 1994.

"Eastwood's world." ANNE THOMPSON. *Entertainment*, Dec. 10, 1993.

"Clint Eastwood. . . ." GIL GIBSON. *Ladies Home Journal*, Aug. 1993.

"Architectural Digest visits . . ." SUSAN CHEEVER. *Architectural Digest*, July 1993.

"Go ahead, make my career." PAUL A. WITTEMAN. *Time*, Apr. 5, 1993.

"Clint Eastwood. . . ." STUART FISCHOFF. *Psychology Today*, Jan.-Feb. 1993.

Clint Eastwood: Riding High. DOUGLAS THOMPSON. Contemporary, 1993.

Clint Eastwood: Hollywood's Loner. MICHAEL MUNN. Parkwest, 1993.

The Films of Clint Eastwood. BORIS ZMIJEWSKY and LEE PFEIFFER. Carol, 1993.

Clint Eastwood: A Cultural Production. PAUL SMITH. University of Minnesota Press, 1993.

"Clint Eastwood. . . ." DAVID BRESKIN. *Rolling Stone*, Sep. 17, 1992.

"Shooting to kill. . . ." SEAN FRENCH. *Times*, Sep. 10, 1992.

"Scraps of hope. . . . ." HENRY SHEEHAN. *Film Comment*, Sep.-Oct. 1992.

"Play mayor for me. . . ." BENJAMIN SVETKEY. *Entertainment*, Apr. 3, 1992.

Clint Eastwood: Malpaso. FUENSANTA PLAZA. Ex Libris (CA), 1991.

"Eastwood, Clint." *Current Biography*, Mar. 1989.

The Films of Clint Eastwood. BORIS ZMIJEWSKY and LEE PFEIFFER. Carol, 1988.

Clint Eastwood. JEFFREY RYDER. Dell, 1987.

Clint Eastwood. FRANCOIS GUERIF. St. Martin's, 1986.

FURTHER READING

Obituary. *Down Beat*, June 1993.
Obituary. *Current Biography*, Apr. 1993.
"Billy. . . ." *Jet*, Mar. 22, 1993.
Obituary. *Billboard*, Mar. 20, 1993.
Obituary. *Variety*, Mar. 15, 1993.
Obituary. *The Times* (of London), Mar. 10, 1993.
Obituary. *New York Times*, Mar. 9, 1993.

Eckstine, Billy (William Clarence Eckstein; 1914–93) Pittsburgh-born singer and bandleader Billy Eckstine began his professional career in the early 1930s, as a singer in cabaret. His first major break came in 1939, when he became a singer with the band of Earl "Fatha" Hines. He began his recording career with Hines in 1940. Eckstine led his own big band (1944–47), and with it played a major role in the emergence of bebop; his vocalist was Sarah Vaughan and his band members such luminaries as Dizzy Gillespie, Charlie Parker, Art Blakey, and Miles Davis. Eckstine, who had recorded as a singer with his band, emerged in the late 1940s and 1950s as a leading popular singer, with such songs as "Fools Rush In," "Everything I Have Is Yours," "My Foolish Heart," "Body and Soul," and "Passing Strangers." Though musical styles changed, he continued to tour and work in cabaret into his seventies. He was survived by seven children. (d. Pittsburgh; March 8, 1993)

Elders, Joycelyn (1933–) On September 7, 1993, after more than nine months of determined but ultimately failed opposition by conservatives, Dr. Elders was confirmed as U.S. Surgeon General. She had been nominated by incoming President Bill Clinton on December 24, 1992, but her nomination had not been pursued by the administration early in 1993 because of fears of a losing nomination fight. In July, the Congressional Black Caucus strongly pushed her nomination forward, and in hearings before the Senate Labor and Human Resources Committee, she successfully defended her pro-abortion, pro-sex education, pro-teenage condoms views, and refuted charges of financial irregularities. Her nomination moved through the committee on July 30, but opponents were able to delay Senate approval of her nomination until September 7. Partly drawing on her confirmation fight experiences, Elders in November published the book *Dancing with the Bears*, with a foreword by the Rev. Jesse Jackson.

Dr. Elders is a leading Arkansas pediatrician, who became a resident in pediatrics at Little Rock's University of Arkansas Medical Center in 1961 and was chief pediatric resident at the center (1963–64). She continued to research, teach, and pursue her career as a clinical pediatrician in association with the center until 1987, and was an assistant professor of pediatrics (1967–71), associate professor (1971–76), and full professor (1976–87). She was appointed director of the Arkansas Department of Public Health in 1987 by governor Bill Clinton, leaving that post to become Surgeon General.

As chief public health official in Arkansas, Dr. Elders was a powerful advocate of preventive health care, and especially of care aimed at preventing unwanted teenage pregnancies. She strongly supported the development of sex education clinics in the schools, including the distribution of contraceptives to teenagers, on this and several other issues colliding head-on with anti-abortion and religious fundamentalist groups in her state; but she was fully supported by then-Governor Clinton, and her position prevailed.

Arkansas-born Elders's 1952 B.A. was from Philander Smith University, her 1960 M.D. from the University of Arkansas Medical Center, and her 1967 M.S. in biochemistry from the University of Arkansas Medical Center. Her publications include more than 100 professional articles. She is married to high school basketball coach Oliver B. Elders; they have two children.

FURTHER READING

"The prescriptions of Dr. Yes." LYNN ROSELLILNI. *U.S. News & World Report*, July 26, 1993.
"Life and death. . . ." FLOYD G. BROWN. *National Review*, Apr. 26, 1993.
"The crusade of. . . ." STEVE BARNES. *New York Times Magazine*, Oct. 15, 1989.

Elizabeth II (Elizabeth Alexandra Mary; 1926–   ) In 1993, Queen Elizabeth made a considerable attempt to restore the tarnished image of the British royal family, greatly damaged by the events of 1992, which she had called her "annus horribilis," with its enormous and very unflattering media attention to "Fergie" (Sarah Ferguson, Duchess of York), marital separations involving two of her sons and their wives, the

destructive fire at Windsor Castle, and growing criticism of the royal family and of the monarchy as an institution in a democratic society. One major move was an agreement to once again begin paying taxes on the huge royal income, though the royal family would be exempt from inheritance taxes and the royal art and jewel collections would be tax exempt. A major public relations gesture was the opening of some portions of Buckingham Palace to the public.

Although nothing like the 1992 disasters occurred in 1993, media attention and public pressure on the monarchy did not lessen. By year's end, however, "Fergie" was largely out of public view, Princess Diana had largely withdrawn from public life, and the Prince of Wales had refocused on environmental and social welfare matters, while royal family rehabilitation attempts continued.

Elizabeth II is the daughter of George VI and Elizabeth Angela Marguerite, the Queen Mother. She succeeded her father to the throne in 1952, becoming Queen of the United Kingdom of Great Britain and Northern Ireland. She married Philip Mountbatten, the Duke of Edinburgh, in 1947, and is the mother of Prince Charles (1948–   ), Princess Anne (1950–   ), Prince Andrew (1960–   ), and Prince Edward (1964–   ).

FURTHER READING

The BBC Book of Royal Memories, 1947–1990. CAROLINE ELLIOTT, ed. Parkwest, 1994.

Queen Elizabeth II. SUSAN AUERBACH. Rourke, 1993.
The Queen: The New Biography. JOHN PARKER.
   Trafalgar, 1993.
Elizabeth R: The Role of the Monarchy Today.
   ANTONY JAY. Parkwest, 1993.
Elizabeth and Philip. CHARLES HIGHAM and ROY
   MOSELEY. Berkley, 1993.
The Rise and Fall of the House of Windsor. A.N.
   WILSON. Norton, 1993.
Royal Marriages. COLIN CAMPBELL. St. Martin's, 1993.
*Long to Reign over Us: Memories of Coronation Day
   and Life in the 1950s.* KENNETH MCLEISH and
   VALERIE MCLEISH. Trafalgar, 1993.
"The rest of the mess." *First for Women,* Oct. 19,
   1992.
"A royal mess." *First for Women,* Oct. 19, 1992.
"God save the Queen!" ROBERT K. MASSIE. *Vanity
   Fair,* Oct. 1992.
"The monarchy will prevail." HUGO YOUNG.
   Newsweek, June 22, 1992.
"The fall of. . . ." STUART REID. *American Spectator,*
   May 1992.
*Queen Elizabeth II: 1952–1992: A Pictorial
   Celebration of Her Reign.* PENNY JUNOR.
   Longmeadow, 1992.
*The Queen: A Revealing Look at the Private Life of
   Elizabeth II.* DOUGLAS KEAY. St. Martin's, 1992.
"Windsor knot. . . ." CHRISTOPHER HITCHENS. *New York
   Times Magazine,* May 12, 1991.
Sovereign: Elizabeth II and the Windsor Dynasty.
   ROLAND FLAMINI. Delacorte, 1991.
Royal Sisters. ANNE EDWARDS. Morrow, 1990.

Escobar Gaviria, Pablo (1949–93) Co-
lombian drug smuggler Pablo Escobar Gaviria
and one bodyguard were killed by Colombian
police and military forces in an exchange of gun-
fire, after being found in their Medellín hideout.
He had been in hiding since his July 1992 escape
while being moved from one jail to another, or,
as some reports indicated, while being moved
from jail in Colombia to captivity in the United
States; what actually happened was unclear. Escobar began his career as a young criminal in his
hometown of Medellín in the mid-1960s, and by
the mid-1970s headed an international drug
smuggling cartel, which during the 1980s waged
terrorist war on the Colombian government, as-
sassinating hundreds, including three presidential candidates and scores of judges and law
enforcement officials. By the late 1980s, he and
his associates dominated the Colombian drug
trade and sources of supply in Colombia and
neighboring countries, while moving large
quantities of cocaine across U.S. borders virtu-

ally at will. Intense American and Colombian
efforts ultimately forced his 1991 negotiated
"surrender," but only to a custom-built fortress
from which he continued to operate his drug cartel. He was survived by his wife, Victoria, a
daughter, and a son. (d. Medellín, Colombia; December 2, 1993)

FURTHER READING

"Escobar's dead end." KEVIN FEDARKO. *Time,* Dec. 13,
   1993.
"Death on the spot. . . ." RUSSELL WATSON. *Newsweek,*
   Dec. 13, 1993.
"Death of a drug lord. . . ." D'ARCY JENISH. *Maclean's,*
   Dec. 13, 1993.
Obituary. *New York Times,* Dec. 3, 1993.

Esposito, John: See Beers, Katie.

Esposito, Meade (1908–93) Brooklyn-
born Meade Esposito began his rise to power in
the Brooklyn Democratic organization by winning a leadership contest in Canarsie in 1960.
He rose to power in the 1960s, and in 1969 became head of the powerful Brooklyn Democratic
organization, a behind-the-scenes fixer and
power broker who held his leadership uninterruptedly until 1983. During that period, Esposito became a major figure in city, state, and
national Democratic politics, though never holding elective office, holding that power long after
the New York City Tammany machine had lost
much of its power to reformers and party inde-
pendents. He lost some of his power during the
early 1980s, giving up his post as Brooklyn Democratic leader in 1983, though continuing to informally exert great influence until corruption
scandals caught up with him and many of his
associates. In 1987, he was convicted, received a
two-year suspended term, and was fined
$500,000. Although other charges were later
dropped, his career was over. He was survived
by a daughter. (d. New York City; September 3,
1993)

FURTHER READING

Obituary. *The Times* (of London), Sep. 8, 1993.
Obituary. *New York Times,* Sep. 5, 1993.

Espy, Mike (Alphonso Michael Espy; 1953–) His nomination as U.S. Secretary of Agriculture confirmed by the Senate on January 21, Mike Espy faced a crisis immediately upon taking office. On January 13, hundreds of people in the Northwest had begun to become ill because of contaminated hamburgers, most of them eaten at the Jack in the Box restaurant chain. By late February, three children had died, and the media and nation had fully focused on the antiquated inspection methods and inadequate meat inspection staff of the Department of Agriculture, long sharply criticized by consumer groups for being far too lenient and deeply associated with the meat industry. President Clinton ordered the hiring of a small number of new meat inspectors as protests grew, and Espy began the job of overhauling food inspection standards and procedures. On February 5, he presented a set of recommendations to a House agriculture subcommittee, and on March 15 proposed a major set of changes that would bring American meat inspection into the latter part of the 20th century. On August 11, he announced proposed new meat and poultry labeling rules. Still to be addressed were the very wide range of major problems confronting American agriculture, and especially American family farmers.

Espy, an attorney, worked with Central Mississippi Legal Services (1978–80), moving into state government as a Mississippi assistant Secretary of State (1980–84) and as state Director of Consumer Protection (1984–85). He made a successful run for Congress in 1986, winning by a slim margin to become the first African-American since Reconstruction to represent Mississippi's Delta region. In office, he served on the House Agriculture Committee and several other committees central to the interests of his district, especially focusing on the needs of its agricultural poor. He helped pass the Lower Mississippi River Valley Development Act, which set up the Delta Commission.

Mississippi-born Espy's 1975 B.A. was from Howard University, and his 1978 J.D. from the University of Santa Clara. He was formerly married to Sheila Bell, and has two children.

FURTHER READING

"Espy, Mike." *Current Biography*, Oct. 1993.
"Black clout in the Clinton administration." *Ebony*, May 1993.

"Mike Espy. . . ." LARKIN WARREN. *Esquire*, Dec. 1989.

Estefan, Gloria Maria (1957–) Singer and songwriter Gloria Estefan issued the Spanish-language hit album *Mi Tierra* in 1993, reaching more for her Cuban roots than for the Latino motifs that had made her a popular star. The album was acclaimed, for itself and as a major step forward in her career. She also issued several singles drawn from the album, very notably including the title song. "Con Los Anos Que Me Quedan" and "Tradicion" also became hits, as did the single "Go Away," drawn from her *Greatest Hits*. Her single "I See Your Smile" was Billboard's fourth-ranked hot contemporary single, and she was the sixth-ranked adult contemporary artist.

Estefan was very active in Florida hurricane relief, organizing several benefit concerts, as well as contributing heavily. For her work, she was named 1994 MusicCares Person of the Year by the National Academy of Recording Arts & Sciences.

Havana-born Estefan emigrated to the United States with her family at the age of two, and grew up in the Miami area. She emerged as a very popular composer, singer, and recording star in the late 1980s, with such songs as "Anything for You" (1987), "Rhythm Is Gonna Get You" (1987), "Don't Wanna Lose You" (1989), and "Coming Out of the Dark" (1991), winning several Grammy nominations. Her albums include *Primitive Love* (1985), *Let It Loose* (1987), *Cuts Both Ways* (1989), *Into the Light* (1991), and *Greatest Hits* (1992). In 1987, she sang at the Seoul Olympics and the St. Louis World Series, and in 1992 at the Superbowl. In March 1990, while touring, she was very seriously injured in a vehicular collision, but made an extraordinary recovery, returning to her career only a year later. Estefan has been very active in philanthropic activities, as in campaigns against AIDS and leukemia, and for flood relief, and has received several humanitarian awards. Her B.A. was from the University of Miami. She is married to Emilio Estefan, Jr., and has one child.

FURTHER READING

"Miami's patron saint." LEONARD PITTS, JR. *Entertainment*, July 30, 1993.

"Spanish is the loving tongue." DAVID TOOP. *Times*, July 9, 1993.

Gloria Estefan: International Pop Star. SHELLY NIELSEN. Abdo and Daughters, 1993.

Gloria Estefan: Entertainer. DAVID SHIRLEY. Chelsea House, 1993.

Gloria Estefan, Cuban-American Singing Star. FERNANDO GONZALEZ. Millbrook, 1993.

" 'My toughest moment.' " GLENN PLASKIN. *Ladies Home Journal*, Nov. 1992.

"Love and money." ANNA MARIA ARIAS. *Hispanic*, May 1991.

Gloria Estefan. GRACE CATALANO. St. Martin's, 1991.

Gloria Estefan. REBECCA STEFOFF. Chelsea House, 1991.

"My miracle." GLORIA ESTEFAN and KATHRYN CASEY. *Ladies Home Journal*, Aug. 1990.

"The power and the Gloria." DAISANN MCLANE. *Rolling Stone*, June 14, 1990.

"Singer Gloria Estefan. . . ." STEVE DOUGHERTY. *People*, Apr. 9, 1990.

"Gloria Estefan:. . . ." JOHN MILWARD. *TV Guide*, Jan. 20, 1990.

Ewing, Patrick Aloysius (1962–) Has

Patrick Ewing had his chance at a National Basketball Association (NBA) championship and lost it, or would 1993–94 be his season of destiny? That was the question vexing New York Knick fans. Ewing certainly had a strong year in 1993. He was named to the Eastern Conference All-Star team for the sixth year in a row, though

this time on the second team, behind newcomer Shaquille O'Neal, and was fourth in the most valuable player voting. He led the Knicks to the second-best record in the conference, giving the top team, the Chicago Bulls, a strong run in the playoffs, finally losing, as the Bulls then won a third straight NBA championship.

When Michael Jordan suddenly retired from basketball before the 1993–94 season, voices all around the league were saying this was the Knicks'—and Ewing's—chance to win it all. Ewing himself broke Walt Frazier's record of 14,617 career points to become the Knicks' all-time leading scorer. But the same night he broke that record, the Knicks lost their key point guard, Doc Rivers, to a season-ending knee injury; the team had already lost another starter, forward Charles Smith. Ewing himself had a strained neck and was out or sub-par for several games in November. Suddenly the Knicks were struggling; while Ewing's hope for a title remained, but was somewhat dimmed. Late in 1993, Ewing released a new video, *Patrick Ewing: Standing Tall.*

Jamaica-born Ewing is one of the leading centers in modern basketball, which became apparent while he was still a college player at Georgetown University, where he took his team to three National Collegiate Athletic Association (NCAA) finals, winning the championship in 1984, when he was named Most Valuable Player of the Final Four. In his senior year, he won a host of "player of the year" awards, including the Kodak Award, Rupp Trophy, and Naismith Trophy. After his 1985 graduation, Ewing joined the New York Knicks, beginning a career that would take him to seven All-Star games (1986; 1988–93, as starting center 1990–92) and international celebrity, even without a longed-for national championship. Ewing has also been on two Olympic gold-medal-winning teams, in 1984 and the "Dream Team" at Barcelona in 1992. Ewing married Rita Williams in 1990; they have one daughter; Ewing also has a son.

FURTHER READING

"Michael Jordan vs. . . . ." GEORGE CASTLE and GARY BINFORD. *Sport*, May 1993.

Sports Great Patrick Ewing. JACK KAVANAGH. Enslow, 1992.

"Ewing, Patrick." *Current Biography*, May 1991.

"Patrick Ewing." SPIKE LEE. *Interview*, May 1990.

Patrick Ewing. MATTHEW NEWMAN. Macmillan, 1986.

Falco, Louis (1943–93) A leading dancer and choreographer, New York City-born Louis Falco attended New York's High School of Performing Arts, and began his professional career while still at school, dancing with the Charles Weidman company. He joined the Jose Limón company in 1960, quickly gaining leading roles. In 1967, he founded his own Louis Falco Dance Company, presentng his own works, and was very soon recognized as a major modern choreographer, for such works as "Argot," "Huescape," and "Sleepers." During the 1970s and 1980s, Falco also choreographed works for many of the world's major dance companies, also often appearing as a guest star. He also moved into films and television in the 1980s, beginning with his choreography of Alan Parker's dance film *Fame*, and went on to choreograph portions of several films. Falco, who died of AIDS-related illness, was survived by two sisters and a brother. (d. New York City, March 26, 1993)

FURTHER READING

Obituary. *The Times* (of London), Mar. 29, 1993.
Obituary. *New York Times*, Mar. 27, 1993.

Faldo, Nick (1957–) At the British Open, in Sandwich, England, in July 1993, British golfer Nick Faldo had the chance to win the championship for the fourth time, the third in four years. In the second round, with a dramatic 18th-hole birdie, he broke the tournament course record at the Royal St. George's course with a 63, which also tied him with five other players for the lowest round ever in a British Open. But in the final round, he lost to Greg Norman, whom he had defeated in a playoff at the 1990 British Open. It was also the first year in Faldo's professional career that he did not win a major tournament, though at the time of the Open he still topped the Sony Rankings.

Faldo became a leading junior British golfer in the mid-1970s, and turned professional in 1976. He was voted best new British golfer of the year in 1977, and went on to build a solid, unspectacular career, emerging as a major figure only a decade later, after rebuilding his entire game in 1985. His major wins include the 1987 British Open; the 1988 French Open; the 1989 and 1990 Masters; the French Open again in 1989; a second British Open in 1990, a stunning win by five strokes, with a record-setting 18 strokes under par; the Irish Open in 1991; and a third British Open in 1992, a year he had four other tournament wins. Faldo also published a book, *Golf: The Winning Formula* (1992). Faldo attended the University of Houston. He is married to Gill Faldo, and has two children.

FURTHER READING

"Faldo, Nick." *Current Biography*, Sep. 1992.
"Nick Faldo." *Sporting News*, Apr. 15, 1991.
"Do you know me? . . . ." RICK REILLY. *Sports Illustrated*, Apr. 8, 1991.
"What's next for Nick?" MICHAEL MCDONNELL. *Golf*, Feb. 1991.

Farr, Heather (1965–93)

Farr, Heather (1965–93) Phoenix-born Farr began taking golf lessons at the age of 7, and was a rising amateur golfer in her early teens, although her height (she was 5' 1" at maturity) made it difficult for her drive the ball as far as many of her competitors. She was Arizona state amateur champion at the age of 13, and at 15 was American Junior Golf Association player of the year. She was twice an all-American golfer while at Arizona State University, and played on the 1984 Curtis Cup and World Amateur teams. She became a professional at the age of 20, beginning a very promising career. In 1989, she was found to have breast cancer, and began a four-and-a-half year struggle to survive, with repeated chemotherapy and radiation treatments, and a total of 15 operations. She also struggled to continue her career in golf, winning the admiration of her peers and public; but after returning on a limited basis late in 1990 was unable to play professionally again, although there seemed some hope early in 1992. She was survived by her husband, Goran Lingmerth, her father, mother, and sister. (d. Scottsdale, Arizona; November 20, 1993)

FURTHER READING

"A battler to the end." RICHARD HOFFER. *Sports Illustrated*, Nov. 29, 1993.
Obituary. *New York Times*, Nov. 22, 1993.

Farrow, Mia Villiers (1945–)

Farrow, Mia Villiers (1945–) The highly publicized Mia Farrow-Woody Allen personal and professional breakup and subsequent bitter custody fight over their three children ended in June 1993. Farrow won custody of the children, with only limited visitation rights won by Allen. In September, a Connecticut states attorney announced that he would not press charges against Allen for alleged sexual molestation of his daughter.

The Allen-Farrow relationship had started in 1980; they never married, but had three children, two of them adopted. Farrow has six other children as well, five of them adopted Vietnamese. The situation opened publicly when Allen sued for custody of their three children; Farrow opposed his suit. Soon afterward, Allen and Soon-Yi Farrow Previn, Farrow's 21-year-old adopted daughter, announced that they were in love. Though they were not related, the media implied that the relationship was incestuous. Farrow also caused the filing in Connecticut of child molestation charges involving one of the Farrow-Allen children. As the publicity grew immense, and after enormous damage had been done to all concerned, the judge in the case had in 1993 issued a "gag" order, forbidding the parties to discuss the case further anywhere but in court.

Farrow resumed her professional life in 1993. After dropping out of the Mike Nichols film *Wolf* because of the pressures created by the custody case, she filmed the forthcoming Ireland-set comedy *Widow's Peak*, directed by John Irvin, and co-starring Joan Plowright and Natasha Richardson, which began shooting in Ireland in June. Also forthcoming was a role in David Frankel's film *Miami*, in a cast that includes Sarah Jessica Parker, Anthony Banderas, Kevin Pollack, and Paul Mazursky. Farrow's autobiography was scheduled for 1994 publication.

Los Angeles-born Farrow became a star in television as Alison Mackenzie in "Peyton Place" (1964–66). In movies, she became a star in *Rosemary's Baby* (1968), going on to such films as *John and Mary* (1969), *The Great Gatsby* (1973), *Death on the Nile* (1978), *Zelig* (1983), *Broadway Danny Rose* (1984), *Hannah and Her Sisters* (1986), *Radio Days* (1987), *Crimes and Misdemeanors* (1989), *Alice* (1990), *Shadows and Fog* (1992), and *Husbands and Wives* (1992). She also appeared in several leading stage roles in Britain during the mid-1970s, as a member of the Royal Shakespeare Company. The daughter of actress Maureen O'Sullivan and director John Farrow, she has been married twice, to Frank Sinatra and Andre Previn; Woody Allen was her longtime companion.

FURTHER READING

"Mia's story." MAUREEN ORTH. *Vanity Fair*, Nov. 1992.
"Everything you always. . . ." PHOEBE HOBAN. *New York*, Sep. 21, 1992.
"A family affair." TOM GLIATTO. *People*, Aug. 31, 1992.
"Woody and Mia. . . ." ERIC LAX. *New York Times Magazine*, Feb. 24, 1991.
Mia: The Life of Mia Farrow. EDWARD Z. EPSTEIN. Delacorte, 1991.
Mia Farrow: Flower Child, Madonna, Muse. SAM RUBIN and RICHARD TAYLOR. St. Martin's, 1989.

Feld, Bernard (1919–93) For much of his life a leading advocate of nuclear disarmament, Bernard Feld was a physicist, who during World War II worked with Enrico Fermi and Leo Szilard at the University of Chicago and Los Alamos to develop the atomic bomb. Shaken by remorse after the August 1945 atom bombings of Hiroshima and Nagasaki, he left government in 1946, taught physics at the Massachusetts Institute of Technology, and became a mainstay of the developing anti-nuclear weapons movement. He was a founder of the the Federation of American Scientists, and of the Pugwash movement, president of the Albert Einstein Peace Foundation, and editor of the *Bulletin of Atomic Scientists*. He published a book of essays, *A Voice Crying in the Wilderness: Essays on the Problem of Science and World Affairs* (1979), and several works on disarmament, including *New Directions in Disarmament* (1981), edited with William Epstein. He was survived by his wife, painter Ellen Banks Feld, two daughters, and three brothers. (d. New York City; February 19, 1993)

FURTHER READING

"Remembering Bernie . . ." ALBERT WATTENBERG et al. *Bulletin of the Atomic Scientists*, May 1993.
Obituary. *New York Times*, Feb. 20, 1993.

Fellini, Federico (1920–93) One of the greatest directors in film history, Federico Fellini first emerged as co-screenwriter of Roberto Rossellini's two post-World War II classics, *Open City* (1945) and *Paisan* (1946). He moved into directing, continuing to write all his screenplays, with *Variety Lights* (1950), which starred his wife Giulietta Masina (they married in 1943); she also starred in his Oscar-winning classics *La Strada* (1954) and *The Nights of Cabiria* (1957), and the equally classic *Juliet of the Spirits* (1965). His major works also included *The White Sheik* (1952), *La Dolce Vita* (1960), *8 1/2* (1963), *Fellini Satyricon* (1969), *The Clowns* (1970), *Amarcord* (1974), *Casanova* (1976), *City of Women* (1979), *Orchestra Rehearsal* (1979), *And the Ship Sails On* (1984), *Ginger and Fred* (1986), *The Voice of the Moon* (1990), and *Intervista* (1992). Fellini was awarded a special Oscar for lifetime achievement in 1993; it was his fifth Academy Award. He was survived by Giulietta Masina. (d. Rome; Oct. 31, 1993)

FURTHER READING

"Arrivederci, Fellini." RICHARD A. BLAKE. *America*, Dec. 4, 1993.
"Addio, maestro . . . ." KAREN S. SCHNEIDER. *People*, Nov. 15, 1993.
Obituary. *Variety*, Nov. 15, 1993.
"Federico Fellini. . . ." LAWRENCE O'TOOLE. *Entertainment*, Nov. 12, 1993.
"The magic of Fellini." PATRICIA HLUCHY. *Maclean's*, Nov. 8, 1993.
"The maestro of the movies." JACK KROLL. *Newsweek*, Nov. 8, 1993.
"Ringmaster and clown . . . ." RICHARD CORLISS. *Time*, Nov. 8, 1993.
"Il maestro." *Economist*, Nov. 6, 1993.
"La Dolce Vita's last act." DEBORAH YOUNG. *Variety*. Nov. 1, 1993.
Obituary. *The Times* (of London), Nov. 1, 1993.
Obituary. *New York Times*, Nov. 1, 1993.
"Federico Fellini." KAREN S. SCHNEIDER. *People*, Jan. 18, 1993.
Critical Essays on Federico Fellini. PETER BONDANELLA and CRISTINA DEGLI-ESPOSTI, eds. G.K. Hall, 1993.
The Cinema of Federico Fellini. PETER BONDANELLA. Princeton University Press, 1992.
Comments on Film. Federico Fellini. CSU Press, Fresno, 1988.
The Films of Federico Fellini. CLAUDIO G. FAVA and ALDO VIGANO. Carol, 1988.
Fellini: A Life. HOLLIS ALPERT. Paragon House, 1987.

Sally Field (right) and Robin Williams

Field, Sally (1946–) Sally Field starred opposite Robin Williams in one of the smash hits of 1993, the film *Mrs. Doubtfire*, directed by Chris Columbus and co-starring Pierce Brosnan and Harvey Fierstein. Field plays Williams's wife, who has just ejected him from their home;

disguising himself as a woman, he returns to live in their home as a nanny. Large audiences chose to disregard the patent absurdity of her failure to recognize him, treating the cross-dressing fantasy as appealing light comedy. Field also starred opposite Don Ameche and Michael J. Fox in *Homeward Bound: The Incredible Journey*, based on the Sheila Burnford novel and directed by Duwayne Dunham; all three played dog and cat voices.

Pasadena-born Field became a star in two television series, "Gidget" (1965–66) and "The Flying Nun (1967–1970), and also appeared in the series "The Girl With Something Extra" (1973). She later emerged as a major dramatic actress, winning best actress Oscars for *Norma Rae* (1979) and *Places in the Heart* (1984), and appearing in such films and telefilms as *The Way West* (1967), *Sybil* (1976; she won an Emmy), *Smokey and the Bandit* (1977), *Hooper* (1978), *The End* (1978), *Absence of Malice* (1981), *Murphy's Romance* (1985; she was also executive producer), *Steel Magnolias* (1989), *Soapdish* (1991), and *Not Without My Daughter* (1991). Field attended the Actor's Studio. Producer Alan Griesman is her second husband, and she has three children.

FURTHER READING

"Queen for a decade." MARC ELIOT. *California*, Sept. 1991.
"She likes herself! . . ." ELIZABETH SPORKIN. *People*, July 8, 1991.
"The perils of being perky." MAUREEN DOWD. *McCall's*, July 1991.
"Sally Field . . . ." MICHAEL J. BANDLER. *Ladies Home Journal*, Feb. 1990.
Sweethearts of Sixties TV. RONALD L. SMITH. St. Martin, 1989.
Sally Field. JASON BONDEROFF. St. Martin's, 1987.

Fine, Reuben (1914–93)

Chess master, psychologist, and author Reuben Fine began playing chess as a gifted 8-year-old, and achieved his first major recognition at 18, when he played to a draw against chess master Alexander Alekshine. He turned professional in 1932, and during the next 16 years emerged as an internationally recognized chess player and a strong contender for the world championship. He won 8 of the 13 international tournaments in which he competed, and retired from international competition for lack of money in 1938, while at the top of his game. He later became a Freudian psychologist, writing several books in his field. He also became a widely distributed chess author, achieving wide acceptance of such books as *Basic Chess Endings* (1941) and *The Middle Game in Chess* (1952). He was survived by his wife Marcia, one daughter, and one son. (d. New York City; March 26, 1993)

FURTHER READING

Obituary. *The Times* (of London), Mar. 30, 1993.
Obituary. *New York Times*, Mar. 27, 1993.

Finney, Albert (1936–)

After a brief 1992 London run in Ronald Harwood's play *Reflected Glory*, cut short when the money and Finney's pay packet ran out, Finney went back to films in 1993. He starred as Warren Odom in the film *Rich in Love*, opposite Jill Clayburgh as his wife, who has just left him, in a cast that included Kathryn Erbe, Kyle MacLachlan, and Piper Laurie; Bruce Beresford directed. Forthcoming was a starring role in a filmed remake of the classic *The Browning Version*, in a cast that includes Greta Scacchi, Matthew Modine, and Ben Silverstone; Mike Figgis directed.

Born in Lancashire, Finney has been a major figure in the British theater for thirty years, from his appearance as *Billy Liar* (1960). He went on to star in such plays as *Luther* (1961), *A Day in the Death of Joe Egg* (1967), *Krapp's Last Tape* (1973), and in a wide range of classic works, including his National Theatre *Macbeth* (1978). At the same time, he became a film star, as *Tom Jones* (1963), as Hercule Poirot in *Murder on the Orient Express* (1974), and in such films as *Gumshoe* (1972), *Annie* (1982), *Under the Volcano* (1984), *Orphans* (1987), *Miller's Crossing* (1990), and *The Playboys* (1992). In 1990, he made a highly acclaimed appearance on the London stage in Ronald Harwood's *Another Time*. Finney attended the Royal Academy of Dramatic Art. He has been married to Jane Wenham and Anouk Aimée, and has one child.

FURTHER READING

Albert Finney: In Character. QUENTIN FALK. Parkwest, 1993.

Foley, Thomas Stephen (1929–)

Speaker of the House Thomas Foley found himself in a sharply changed political situation in 1993, with a Democratic administration and Congress beginning a historic new day, although many in both parties proved very resistant to the kinds of major changes proposed by the activist administration led by President Bill Clinton. Early in the year, the new administration faltered, unable to move its economic stimulus past a successful Republican filibuster, encountering embarrassing appointment problems, and suffering foreign policy reverses. But Clinton gained strength as the year developed, and Foley was able to participate in a far-from-Zdeadlocked Congress, which ultimately passed Clinton's budget plan, the North American Free Trade Agreement (NAFTA), the Brady gun-control bill, and significant though not entirely completed campaign finance reform and crime control bills. On the personal side, Foley in July closed a highly profitable and controversial stock trading account which had been criticized by Republicans, while strongly denying any wrongdoing.

Spokane-born Foley practiced law and was Washington state assistant attorney-general before going to Washington, D.C. as a lawyer in 1961. A liberal Democrat, he entered the House in 1965, and in 25 uninterrupted years rose to become chairman of the House Democratic Caucus in 1976, majority whip in 1981, and majority leader in 1987. He was elected 49th Speaker of the House on June 6, 1989, replacing James C. Wright, who had resigned while facing charges of ethics violations. Foley weathered the "gridlocked" final years of the Bush administration, the House bank overdraft and post office scandals, and the "anti-incumbent" 1992 election well, winning re-election to a 15th House term from his eastern Washington State district with 55 percent of the vote. Foley's 1951 B.A. and 1957 LL.B. were from the University of Washington. He married Heather Strachan in 1968; she is one of his key congressional aides.

FURTHER READING

"Foley flexes." Richard Blow. *Mother Jones*, July-Aug. 1993.
"Mr. Nice Guy. . . ." Bill Whalen. *Insight*, Aug. 19, 1991.
"Hill potatoes. . . ." Fred Barnes. *New Republic*, May 20, 1991.
"Foley's law." Michael Oreskes. *New York Times Magazine*, Nov. 11, 1990.
"Foley, Thomas Stephen." *Current Biography*, Sep. 1989.

Ford, Gerald Rudolph, Jr. (Leslie King, Jr.; 1913–)

Former President Gerald Ford, who had in 1992 addressed the Republican National Convention on behalf of President George Bush, and then unsuccessfully campaigned with Bush in Michigan, went on the campaign trail again in 1993, for the unsuccessful Wisconsin congressional candidacy of Republican Martin Neumann, defeated by Democrat Peter Barca in the May 4 special election for the seat of Secretary of Defense Les Aspin. Beyond that, he largely limited his appearances to ceremonial ones, as in representing the United States at the crowning of Belgian king Albert II, who on August 9 succeeded his brother Baudouin I. He also appeared, with former presidents Carter and Bush, at the September 14 White House signing of the North American Free Trade Agreement (NAFTA).

Omaha-born Ford, then Vice President, became the 38th President of the United States in August 1974, with the resignation of Richard Nixon, who faced impeachment because of his complicity in the Watergate affair. A month later, Ford pardoned Nixon. A year earlier, Ford had been appointed by Nixon to replace Vice President Spiro Agnew, who had resigned under fire.

The Ford presidency was relatively uneventful, seeming especially so after the turbulence of the 1960s, the Vietnam War, and the shock of Watergate. That shock did enable him to curb the excesses of the CIA and other national security organizations; beyond that, he began little new legislation, attempted with little success to mediate continuing Middle East crises, and furthered American relations with China. Ford defeated Ronald Reagan's bid for the Republican presidential nomination, but was himself defeated by Jimmy Carter in the 1976 presidential election. He wrote of his life and experiences in *A Time to Heal: The Autobiography of Gerald R. Ford* (1979).

Earlier, Ford had been an All-American college football player, a naval officer in World War II, and a lawyer in Grand Rapids (1941–49). He went to Washington as a Congressman in 1949, and became minority leader of the House (1965–73). His 1935 B.A. was from the University of Michigan, his LL.B from Yale in 1941. Ford married Elizabeth "Betty" Bloomer in 1948; they have four children.

FURTHER READING

Time and Chance: Gerald Ford's Appointment with History: 1913–1974. JAMES CANNON. HarperCollins, 1993.
Gerald R. Ford and the Politics of Post-Watergate America. BERNARD FIRESTONE and ALEXEJ UGRINSKY, eds. Greenwood, 1992.
The Limits of Power: The Nixon and Ford Administrations. JOHN R. GREENE. Indiana University Press, 1992.
"Kissinger's web." WALTER ISAACSON. *Vanity Fair*, Sep. 1992.
Farewell to the Chief: Former Presidents in American Public Life. RICHARD N. SMITH and TIMOTHY WALCH, eds. High Plains, 1990.
Gerald R. Ford's Date with Destiny: A Political Biography. EDWARD L. SCHAPSMEIER and FREDERICK H. SCHAPSMEIER. P. Lang, 1989
Gerald R. Ford: President. SALLIE RANDOLPH. Walker, 1987.

Ford, Harrison (1942–) Action film star Harrison Ford scored another commercial hit in 1993, starring as escaped death row convict Dr. Richard Kimble in the title role of the film *The Fugitive*, based on the 1960s television series.

Tommy Lee Jones co-starred as pursuing U.S. Marshal Samuel Gerard, and Sela Ward as the wife Kimble has been unjustly convicted of murdering. Andrew Davis directed the critically acclaimed classic chase thriller, a heavy box office draw. Ford also was one of many celebrities who read for Bill Coururie's environmental film *Earth and the American Dream*, and one of the celebrities interviewed for the television special *George Lucas: Heroes, Myths and Magic*. He revisited earlier triumphs in another way, as well, making a guest appearance in the series opener of television's "The Young Indiana Jones." Forthcoming was a starring role in *Clear and Present Danger*, directed by Philip Noyce and co-starring James Earl Jones, Anne Archer, and Willem Dafoe.

Chicago-born Ford played largely in supporting roles, working part-time as a carpenter, for a decade before breaking through to become a leading movie actor as Han Solo in *Star Wars* (1977). He completed the Star Wars trilogy with *The Empire Strikes Back* (1980) and *Return of the Jedi* (1983), meanwhile doing the blockbuster Indiana Jones trilogy: *Raiders of the Lost Ark* (1981), *Indiana Jones and the Temple of Doom* (1984), and *Indiana Jones and the Last Crusade* (1989). Among his other films are *Witness* (1985), *The Mosquito Coast* (1986), *Working Girl* (1988), *Presumed Innocent* (1990), *Regarding Henry* (1991), and *Patriot Games* (1992). Ford attended Ripon College. He has been married twice and has two children.

FURTHER READING

"Off camera." LAWRENCE GROBEL. *Playboy*, Sep. 1993.
"The fugitive star." DAVID HALBERSTAM. *Vanity Fair*, July 1993.
"Harrison Ford. . . ." MARTHA FRANKEL. *Movies USA*, May 1992.
"Harrison Ford. . . ." NATALIE GITTELSON. *McCall's*, June 1991.
The Films of Harrison Ford. ED GROSS. Pioneer Books, 1990.
Harrison Ford. MINTY CLINCH. Trafalgar Square, 1988.
Harrison Ford. TOLEDO VARE. St. Martin's, 1988.

Foster, Jodie (Alicia Christian Foster; 1962–) Oscar-winning actress Jodie Foster starred in another smash hit in 1993. In *Sommersby*, a remake of *The Return of Martin*

Guerre, she starred as Laurel, the wife of American Civil War soldier Jack (Richard Gere), who was missing in action and has been presumed dead. He returns—perhaps not the same man—two years after the war, and tries to restart his life with his wife and son. Jon Amiel directed; the cast included James Earl Jones, Lanny Flaherty, and Wendell Wellman.

Forthcoming was a starring role opposite Mel Gibson and James Garner in *Maverick*, directed by Richard Donner. Another major forthcoming film was the sequel to *The Silence of the Lambs*, with Foster once again slated to star opposite Anthony Hopkins as psychopathic killer Dr. Hannibal "the Cannibal" Lecter. Also forthcoming was *The Dinosaur Man*, based on Dr. Susan Baur's work with schizophrenics; Foster will direct and star in the film, and will also direct and star in the forthcoming *Jean Seberg*, based on the life of the American actress. She continued to work on several other projects as well, some of them through her own Egg Pictures production company.

Los Angeles-born Foster was a leading child actor in television, beginning with "Mayberry, R.F.D." in 1969. In her early teens, she played major roles in such films as *Alice Doesn't Live Here Any More* (1975) and *Taxi Driver* (1976). She then made the often extremely difficult transition to adult roles, in such films as *The Hotel New Hampshire* (1984), *Five Corners* (1986), *The Accused* (1988), for which she won a best actress Oscar, *Shadows and Fog* (1992), and *Little Man Tate* (1992; she also directed). Her B.A. was from Yale, in 1985.

FURTHER READING

"Jodie Foster. . . ." MARK HARRIS et al. *Entertainment Weekly*, Apr. 2, 1993.
"Foster, Jodie." *Current Biography*, Aug. 1992.
"Foster child. . . ." TOM GLIATTO et al. *People*, Nov. 18, 1991.
"What's driving Miss Jodie?" MICHAEL SEGELL. *Redbook*, Nov. 1991.
"Wunderkind." ARION BERGER. *Harper's Bazaar*, Nov. 1991.
"Burden of the gift." JULIE CAMERON. *American Film*, Nov.-Dec. 1991.
"A screen gem turns director." RICHARD CORLISS. *Time*, Oct. 14, 1991.
"Jodie Foster." INGRID SISCHY. *Interview*, Oct. 1991.
"Jodie Foster." PHILLIP ZONKEL. *Seventeen*, Oct. 1991.
"Jodie Foster. . . ." BRIAN D. JOHNSON. *Maclean's*, Sep. 16, 1991.
"Jodie Foster." GEARI HIRSHEY. *Rolling Stone*, Mar. 21, 1991.
"Yet again. . . ." TRACY YOUNG. *Vogue*, Feb. 1991.
"Child of the movies." JONATHAN VAN METER. *New York Times Magazine*, Jan. 6, 1991.

Foster, Vincent W. Jr. (1945–93) On July 20, 1993, White House deputy counsel Vincent Foster apparently committed suicide, at Fort Marcy Park, on the Virginia side of the Potomac River, opposite Washington, D.C. A lifelong friend of President Bill Clinton, and a colleague of Hillary Rodham Clinton in Little Rock's Rose law firm, Foster was a highly regarded lawyer of impeccable reputation before going to Washington to serve in the Clinton administration. He was said to have become despondent over his negligible involvement in a small-scale political flareup over the May-June handling of the firing of the White House travel office staff, which was followed by several Wall Street Journal editorials attacking Foster and several of his colleagues, but his apparent suicide was seemed to occasion great surprise on the part of most of those who knew him. He was survived by his wife, Lisa Foster.

FURTHER READING

"The troubled view. . . ." BOB COHN. *Newsweek*, Aug. 23, 1993.
"The hidden anger of. . . ." ELEANOR CLIFT and BOB COHN. *Newsweek*, Aug. 9, 1993.
"The mystery of. . . ." HOWARD FINEMAN and BOB COHN. *Newsweek*, Aug. 2, 1993.
"The suicide." SIDNEY BLUMENTHAL. *New Yorker*, Aug. 9, 1993.
"Where hope ends." MARGARET CARLSON. *Time*, Aug. 2, 1993.
"The crucible of high office." KENNETH T. WALSH. *U.S. News & World Report*, Aug. 2, 1993.

Fox, Michael J. (1961–) In the romantic film comedy *For Love or Money*, set largely in an expensive Manhattan hotel, Fox starred as concierge Doug Ireland, opposite Gabrielle Anwar, in a cast that included Anthony Higgins and Michael Tucker; Barry Sonnenfeld directed and co-produced. Fox also starred in the film *Life with Mikey*, directed by James Lapine. Fox plays a former child star who operates a children's the-

atrical agency, discovers a major new talent, and solves many of his own lingering problems. A third starring role was in the film *Homeward Bound: The Incredible Journey*, based on the Sheila Burnford novel about two pet dogs and a cat find themselves in far places, and head for home; Fox, Don Ameche, and Sally Field star as the voices of the animals; Duwayne Dunham directed. Forthcoming was a starring role in the film *Greed*, directed by Jonathan Lynn and costarring Kirk Douglas, Nancy Travis, Olivia d'Abo, Bob Balaban, and Ed Begley Jr.

Vancouver-born Fox became a popular television player as the conservative young son in the series "Family Ties" (1982–89), and a film star in the teenage fantasy-comedies *Back to the Future* (1985), *Back to the Future II* (1989), and *Back to the Future Part III* (1990). He also starred in the highly regarded *Casualties of War* (1989), *The Hard Way* (1991), and *Doc Hollywood* (1991). He married Tracy Pollan in 1988; they have one child.

FURTHER READING

"Michael J. Fox." JEFF GILES. *US*, July 1993.
"The return of. . . ." MELANIE BERGER. *Ladies Home Journal*, July 1993.
"Walking tall with. . . ." CHRIS CHASE. *Cosmopolitan*, Apr. 1991.
"The new age of. . . ." PAUL DOUGHERTY. *California*, Mar. 1991.
Secret of Michael J. Fox's Success. EDWARD GROSS. Movie Publications Services, 1990.
"Getting back to his future." MICHAEL ALEXANDER. *People*, Dec. 4, 1989.
Michael J. Fox Scrapbook. MIMI KASBAH. Ballantine, 1987.
Michael J. Fox. KEITH E. GREENBERG. Lerner, 1986.

Freeh, Louis Joseph (1950–) On July 20, President Bill Clinton announced the nomination of federal District Court Judge Louis Freeh to be Director of the Federal Bureau of Investigation (FBI), replacing William S. Sessions. Freeh was confirmed by the Senate on August 6.

Jersey City-born Freeh was an FBI agent (1975–81), then becoming a federal prosecutor in the southern district of New York, whose reputation was greatly enhanced by his role in the successful Mafia prosecutions of the mid-1980s. In 1989, he headed the southern district's organized crime strike force. He was appointed a federal district judge in 1991 by President George Bush. Freeh's J.D. was from Rutgers University. He is married to Marilyn Freeh, and has four children.

FURTHER READING

"The squeaky-clean G-man." JAMES CARNEY. *Time*, Aug. 2, 1993.
"The new G-man at the top." BRIAN DUFFY. *U.S. News & World Report*, Aug. 2, 1993.
"Making a difference . . ." *U.S. News & World Report*, Aug. 26, 1991.

Freeman, Morgan (1938–) Taking on an entirely new kind of role, stage and screen star Morgan Freeman turned film director in 1993, releasing the well-received *Bopha*, the film he began to shoot in Harare, Zimbabwe in late 1992. Based on a play by South African Percy Mtwa, the work was set in South Africa soon after the 1976 Soweto protests. Danny Glover starred as a Black master sergeant in the South African police; his tragedy is the center of the story. The cast also included Maynard Eziashi, Malcolm McDowell, Alfre Woodard, and Marius Weyers. Freeman also narrated the "National Geographic Explorer" series program *Volga, the Soul of Russia*. Forthcoming was a starring role opposite Tim Robbins in the film *Rita Hayworth*

and the Shawshank Redemption, written and directed by Frank Darabont.

Freeman has spent most of his long career in the theater, winning a 1978 Tony nomination for his role in *The Mighty Gents*, and appearing in a considerable range of Shakespearean and other classical roles. He emerged as a leading screen and stage player late in his career, beginning with his lead off-Broadway as Hoke Colburn, the Black chauffeur in *Driving Miss Daisy* (1987), and in strong supporting roles in such films as *Street Smart* (1987) and *Clean and Sober* (1988). His major breakthrough came in 1989, with his film re-creation of the *Driving Miss Daisy* role, for which he won a 1990 Oscar nomination. In the same year, he appeared in *Glory*, and was Joe Clark role in *Lean On Me*. In 1990, he appeared as Petruchio opposite Tracey Ullman in the New York production of *The Taming of the Shrew*. In 1991, he played Azeem in *Robin Hood: Prince of Thieves*, and in 1992 played in *The Power of One* and *Unforgiven*. He has also appeared as a regular on two television series: public television's children's show "The Electric Company" (1971–76) and for a time in the early 1980s on "Another World," a daytime soap opera.

FURTHER READING

"Alternate roots." MEREDITH BERKMAN. *Entertainment*, Oct. 22, 1993.
"Freeman, Morgan." *Current Biography*, Feb. 1991.

"In the driver's seat. . . ." JANICE C. SIMPSON. *Time*, Jan. 8, 1990.
"Two for the road." HENRY ALFORD and PAULA BULLWINKEL. *Interview*, Nov. 1989.
"Johnny Handsome. . . ." ROBERT SEIDENBERG. *American Film*, Oct. 1989.

Friedan, Betty Goldstein (1921–   ) The woman who helped spark the 1960s feminist movement, who first wrote of the "problem that had no name . . . that American woman are kept from growing to their full human capacities," in the 1990s hoped to do the same for the question of aging, a question affecting both men and women, though women live disproportionately longer than men. In *The Fountain of Age* (1993), Betty Friedan produced a heavily researched but still deeply personal work, exploring freshly the questions of youth and age, and the possibilities of new roles for older people, rejecting their ghettoization in modern society. Through the years, Friedan has remained active in women's affairs, speaking widely, as in April at a symposium titled "Women and Power: New Images and Realities," and as an honored guest a year earlier at a "Women in Film" gathering.

Born in Peoria, Illinois, Betty Goldstein received her A.B., summa cum laude, from Smith College in 1942 and became a research fellow at the University of California at Berkeley in 1943. After marrying Carl Friedan in 1947, she had three children; they divorced in 1969. Friedan came to prominence in 1963 with publication of her book, *The Feminine Mystique*, which called on women to reject stereotypical roles as wives and mothers for wider independent status in the community, as equal professionals and wage-earners, and was especially directed to those who, like herself, had not up to that time seriously used their college educations. The work became a best-seller, and in the new feminist movement it generated, Friedan became a leader, as founder and first president of the National Organization of Women (NOW) (1966). A reformer, rather than a revolutionary, Friedan resigned that post in 1970, remaining as chair of its advisory committee (1970–72) and serving on the board of NOW's Legal Defense and Education Fund. Seeking a wider popular base, she continued active on women's issues, notably the Equal Rights Amendment (ERA); served as vice-president of the National Association to Repeal

Abortion Laws (1970–73); and helped develop organizations such as National Women's Political Caucus (1971) and the First Women's Bank (1973). In her book *The Second Stage* (1981; rev. ed., 1986), she explored what she felt were negative tendences in the women's movement, especially rejection of family relationships and values, calling instead for equality between women and men, in the home and in society. Other works included *It Changed My Life: Writings on the Women's Movement* (1976) and a wide range of magazine and newspaper articles. Friedan has held numerous posts on commissions and at universities, including Yale, Harvard, and Columbia, from 1987 as distinguished visiting professor in the schools of journalism and of social work at the University of Southern California.

FURTHER READING

"Old is not a dirty word." CHARLIE ROSE. *Ladies Home Journal*, Nov. 1993.
"The good news about women and aging." JUDITH STONE. *Glamour*, Nov. 1993.
"Images of age." *Psychology Today*, Nov.-Dec. 1993.
"An evolving feminist. . . ." STEPHEN GOODE. *Insight*, Oct. 25, 1993.
"New age fighter." JOAN SMITH. *Guardian*, Oct. 18, 1993.
"Betty Friedan." *Playboy*, Sep. 1992.
Breaking Barriers: The Feminist Movement. JAMES ARCHER. Viking, 1991.
"Betty Friedan: the housewife who. . . ." *Life*, Fall 1990.
Betty Friedan: Fighter for Women's Rights. SONDRA HENRY and EMILY TAITZ. Enslow, 1990.
Betty Friedan. SUSAN TAYLOR-BOYD. Gareth Stevens, 1990; abr. ed. *Betty Friedan: Speaking Out for Women's Rights*, by BARBARA BEHM and TAYLOR-BOYD, 1992.
Betty Friedan. JUSTINE BLAU. Chelsea House, 1990.
"Friedan, Betty." *Current Biography*, Mar. 1989.
Betty Friedan: A Voice for Women's Rights. MILTON MELTZER. Puffin, 1986.

Frohnmayer, John Edward (1921–)

In 1993, former National Endowment for the Arts (NEA) chairman John Frohnmayer put a coda to his controversial career in the Washington hot seat with publication of his book, *Leaving Town Alive: Confessions of an Arts Warrior*. Though some critics found the work ingenuous and evasive, especially those who thought

Frohnmayer's NEA tenure a failure, others found the book laudable for its scathing account of the cynicism and cowardice of Washington political life, and the personal price paid by those who come to the capital, supposedly in public service.

Also in 1993, some 1990 correspondence between Frohnmayer and then-president George Bush, urging Frohnmayer to find solutions for "excessive cases," was released by attorneys for four artists, after an out-of-court settlement of $252,000 was reached in the case of *Finley* v. *NEA*. Approximately $50,000 of that amount was to be divided among the four artists—Karen Finley, Holly Hughes, John Fleck, and Tim Miller, known as the NEA Four—with over $200,000 earmarked for legal fees. After the settlement, Frohnmayer said he thought the case should have gone to a judge and jury, rather than "leaving it up for each side to say they had been vindicated."

Frohnmayer was appointed NEA head by President Bush in 1989. After several controversies in which he upheld free speech, he in August 1990 canceled grants to the four artists, all accused of "obscenity." He went on to deny several more grants, and to institute an "anti-obscenity oath," a pledge by those receiving federal grants through the NEA that they would not use the money to create "obscene" art. Some artists refused to take offered NEA grants as long as the oath was in effect. Although the federal government denied that any political considerations were involved, government documents revealed that Frohnmayer had, indeed, cited political considerations in refusing the grants. He began to change his position in late 1990, and during 1991 emerged as a defender of several controversial NEA grants, supporting what he called freedom of expression, and what such groups as the Reverend Pat Robertson's Christian Coalition and Reverend Donald Wildman's American Family Association called pornography. On February 21, 1992, Frohnmayer resigned, under continued pressure from right-wing Republicans, notably then-presidential candidate Pat Buchanan, who had attacked Bush for his support of Frohnmayer and the NEA, which Buchanan called part of "the arts and crafts auxiliary of the Eastern liberal establishment."

Oregon-born Frohnmayer practiced law in Oregon (1972–89). He was also a member of the Oregon Arts Commission (1978–85), and a singer, active in the development of regional musical groups. His 1964 B.A. was from Stanford University, his 1969 M.A. from the University of Chicago, and his 1972 J.D. from the University of Oregon. He married Leah Thorpe in 1967; they have two children.

FURTHER READING

" 'The nature of the beast'. . . ." DANIEL GLICK. *Newsweek*, Mar. 16, 1992.
"Frohnmayer, John Edward." *Current Biography*, Apr. 1990.

Fujimori, Alberto (1938–) Peruvian

president Alberto Fujimori, dictator since his seizure of power in 1992, continued to fight the far-from-over Peruvian Civil War during 1993. Despite the capture of Shining Path leader Abimeal Guzmán Reynoso and many of his associates, left-wing guerrillas still operated throughout the country, committing a series of bombing attacks even as Fujimori spoke to the nation on June 5, the anniversary of his dissolution of Congress, the closing of the courts, and the institution of the reign of terror that followed. Fujimori was also threatened by dissidents within his own army and other Peruvian elites; although only the army seemed able to oust him, its support was throughout the year quite uncertain, with Fujimori having whatever support the popular polls seemed to show. Those polls, showing him to be a very popular ruler, were somewhat at variance with other data: Fujimori's new constitution, consolidating and extending his rule, was favored by only 53 percent of those voting on October 31.

On the economic side, Fujimori was complimented by the International Money Fund for his success in checking Peru's runaway inflation, and foreign investment money began to flow into Peru; on the other hand, Peru's austerity programs created massive numbers of new poor, forcing even Fujimori to call for expansion of social services at some time in the future.

Peruvian-born Fujimori, the son of Japanese-Peruvian immigrants, attended La Molina, the National Agrarian University, graduating in 1961, and then taught at the university. His 1969 master's degree was in mathematics, from the University of Wisconsin. He became dean of the science faculty at La Molina in 1984, was

principal of the university (1984–89), and was president of the Peruvian National Council of Principals (1987–89). He scored an upset victory over novelist Mario Vargas Llosa in the 1990 presidential election. On April 5, 1992, with the support of the military, he seized dictatorial power, dissolving the federal Congress, the regional assemblies, and the courts, and ruling by decree. On September 12, 1992, he scored a major Civil War victory, with the capture of Shining Path leader Abimeal Guzmán Reynoso; but the civil war continued. Fujimori married civil engineer Susana Higuchi in 1974; they have four children.

FURTHER READING

"Saving the state in Peru." NATHAN GARDELS and ABRAHAM LOWENTHAL. *New Perspectives Quarterly*, Fall 1993.
"The unshining path. . . ." GUSTAVO GORRITI. *New Republic*, Feb. 8, 1993.
"Casting stones." MIKE MOORE. "Can Fujimori save Peru?" MICHAEL RADU. *Bulletin of the Atomic Scientists*, July-Aug. 1992.
"Fujimori defends. . . . " MARIELLA BALBI et al. *World Press Review*, July 1992.
"Fujimori's plot . . . ." SARAH KERR. *New York Review of Books*, June 25, 1992.
"The 'Karate Kid'. . . ." TOM VOGEL, JR. *Commonweal*, Jan. 11, 1991.
"Fujimori, Alberto." *Current Biography*, Nov. 1990.
"Fujimori. . . ." JEFFREY KLAIBER. *America*, Sep. 8, 1990.
"Who is. . . . " LINDA ROBINSON. *U.S. News & World Report*, Apr. 23, 1990.
"Engulfed by 'the Tsunami'. . . ." FREDERICK UNGEHEUER. *Time*, Apr. 23, 1990.
"The man from nowhere." *Economist*, Apr. 14, 1990.

Fulghum, Robert L. (1937–) In 1993,

best-selling author and Unitarian minister Robert Fulghum published his fourth volume of inspirational musings, this one titled *Maybe (Maybe Not): Second Thoughts on a Secret Life*, notably what you are thinking while you seem to doing something else. His third book, *Uh Oh* (1991) also appeared in paperback. Rather than do a traditional publicity tour, Fulghum organized a "Twenty-Two Cities, Twenty-Two Causes, One Good Reason Tour," which eventually expanded to over 40 cities, with Fulghum criss-crossing the country from Washington State and back again between August and No-

vember, speaking at philanthropic events in communities large and small, the aim being to raise money for charities, including Literacy Volunteers, Amnesty International, Special Olympics, and Habitat for Humanity. In May, Fulghum went on an eight-city Massachusetts-to-Miami bus tour with an all-author rock band called the Rock Bottom Remainders, including Amy Tan, Stephen King, Barbara Kingsolver, Dave Barry, and Fulghum on mandocello. The group is publishing a book about themselves, *Mid-Life Confidential*, due in 1994.

Texas-born Fulghum studied for the ministry and was a part-time minister in Bellingham, Washington and then in Seattle (1961–85), and an art instructor at Seattle's Lakeside School (1971–88). He became a best-selling author with his book *All I Really Need to Know I Learned in Kindergarten: Uncommon Thoughts on Common Things* (1988), which he stresses did not mean that kindergarteners understand everything, but rather that young children there learn many of the fundamental issues of existence. Fulghum followed this with the books *It Was on Fire When I Lay Down on it* (1989) and *Uh Oh: Reflections from Both Sides of the Refrigerator Door* (1991). He also hosted an hour-long television special *Fulghum and Family* (1992). His degrees are from Baylor Baptist University and Starr King School for the Ministry. He is married to Lynn Edwards, and has two children.

FURTHER READING

"Talking with. . . ." JILL RACHLIN. *People*, Aug. 30, 1993.
"Sermons from Rev. Feelgood." *Time*, July 2, 1990.
"The golden rule in two volumes." DIANA WEST. *Insight*, Mar. 19, 1990.
"Lessons from the sandbox." PATRICIA LEIGH BROWN. *New York Times Magazine*, July 23, 1989.
"Robert Fulghum. . . ." *People*, Feb. 27, 1989.

Gallo, Julio (1910–93) Oakland-born Gallo, with his older brother Ernest, developed the E. & J. Gallo Winery of Modesto, California into one of the world's largest winemakers and distributors, producing low-priced wines of an even consistency that found very large markets after World War II. Julio, in charge of wine production, made innovative use of new winemaking technology to make such wines as Thunderbird and Ripple, wines much favored by those who wanted large quantities of inexpensive wine. The firm also produced several other very popular table wines. In 1981, their company also began to produce middle-price-range "premium" wines, though Julio Gallo reportedly did not reverse his longstanding refusal to produce vintage—that is, yearly—wines. He was survived by his wife, Aileen, who was injured in the automobile accident that took his life, a daughter, and a son. (d. Modesto, California; May 2, 1993)

FURTHER READING

"Gallo's big gamble." JAMES LAUBE. *Wine Spectator*, June 30, 1993.
"Julio Gallo dies in auto wreck." JAMES LAUBE. *Wine Spectator*, June 15, 1993.
Obituary. *The Times* (of London), May 5, 1993.
Obituary. *New York Times*, May 3, 1993.
Blood and Wine: The Unauthorized Story of the Gallo Wine Empire and the Family Scandal That Threatened to Destroy It. ELLEN HAWKES. Simon & Schuster, 1993.

Gallo, Robert Charles (1937–) The bitter French-American dispute over who discovered HIV, the virus that causes AIDS, and over the alleged misconduct of Dr. Robert Gallo, took yet another 180-degree turn in 1993.

Gallo, head of the U.S. National Cancer Institute's laboratory of tumor cell biology and a leading AIDS researcher at the U.S. National Institutes of Health, and French AIDS researcher Luc Montagnier had been jointly credited with discovery of the virus, both deriving enormous worldwide prestige and the prospect of Nobel Prizes from the discovery. But Montagnier had long claimed that Gallo did not really discover the virus, instead using samples that Montagnier had sent to him. Both claimed credit for the discovery in 1984, beginning a long controversy that ultimately generated a French lawsuit and a 1987 court settlement, though Montagnier and other French researchers continued to charge Gallo with misappropriation of the French specimens. In 1991, Montagnier suggested that Gallo had been sent a contaminated specimen which then grew to replace the different specimens both had been working on, a theory that Gallo seemed to generally accept. But several investigations continued.

In the spring of 1992, a National Institutes of Health (NIH) Office of Scientific Integrity report cleared Gallo of any wrongdoing. The report was immediately attacked by a National Academy of Sciences panel of experts asked to review it, and by the U.S. House of Representatives Subcommittee on Oversight and Investigations. On December 30, 1992, after a three-year-long investigation, the Federal Office of Research Integrity found that Gallo had been guilty of scientific misconduct, in "falsely reporting" a key research fact. Gallo continued to deny all wrongdoing. But on Nov. 12, 1993, all U.S. government charges against Gallo were unconditionally dropped, a few days before his final appeal was scheduled to be heard before an appeals board of the Department of Health and Human Services. In dropping all charges, the Office of Scientific Integrity claimed once again that Gallo was guilty of misconduct, but that it could not prove its charges because the appeals board was insisting on a standard of evidence that could not be provided. Gallo, who had steadfastly denied all wrongdoing for four years, felt that he had been completely cleared, which on the face of the matter was so, for the government had stated that it could not prove its longstanding charges before that body legally set up to evaluate those charges. France's Pasteur Institute continued to press its accusations against Gallo. The controversy also figured in the 1993 television version of Randy Shilts's 1986 book, *And the Band Played On*, in which Gallo was played by Alan Alda.

Connecticut-born Gallo is one of the world's leading tumor cell biologists. He has been associated with the National Cancer Institute of the National Institutes of Health since 1965, in a series of increasingly responsible positions, and has been head of its tumor cell biology laboratory since 1972. He has also taught courses at Cornell and George Washington University, published numerous scientific works, and received many honors and awards for his work. A recent book is *Virus Hunting: Cancer, AIDS, and the Human Retrovirus: A Story of Scientific Discovery* (1991).

FURTHER READING

"AIDS' relentless adversary. . . ." SHANNON BROWNLEE. *U.S. News & World Report*, June 3, 1991.
"Taking credit for AIDS." JUDITH COLP. *Insight*, May 13, 1991.
"Profile: AIDS dispute. . . ." TIM BEARDSLEY. *Scientific American*, Jan. 1991.

Garcia Marquez, Gabriel (1928–) Colombian Nobel Laureate Gabriel Garcia Marquez shifted the venue and length of his literary fiction in 1993. Where his previous major works have been novels set in Latin America, his new work was a collection of shorter pieces set in Europe, *Strange Pilgrims: Twelve Stories*, translated by Edith Grossman. The main characters are Latin Americans making literal or figurative pilgrimages of some sort, as travelers or exiles abroad, their tales generally told from the perspective of aging. Garcia Marquez noted, in the book's prologue, that the stories were written over some 18 years, but rewritten and revised after a 1992 tour of Europe. On the personal side, he had surgery for lung cancer in May 1992, a localized tumor reportedly being removed.

A leading Latin American novelist, Garcia Marquez won the Nobel Prize for literature in 1982, in recognition of a body of novels and short stories that by then had made him a world figure, and included the novels *One Hundred Years of Solitude* (1967), *Death of a Patriarch* (1975), and *Love in the Time of Cholera* (1984). His most recent major work is the novel *The General in His Labyrinth* (1989), published in the United States in September 1990. Politically an independent, critical of both socialism and capitalism, Garcia Marquez was influenced by Marxism in the early 1960s and became a close personal friend of Cuban leader Fidel Castro; as a result he was for 33 years, until 1991, officially barred by immigration laws from entering the United States. He attended the National University at Bogota. He is married to Mercedes Garcia Marquez; they have two children.

FURTHER READING

Gabriel Garcia Marquez: Solitude and Solidarity. MICHAEL BELL. St. Martin's, 1993.
The First Garcia Marquez: A Study of His Journalistic Writing from 1948–1955. ROBERT L. SIMS. University Press of America, 1992.
"Gabriel Garcia Marquez." MANUEL OSORIO. *UNESCO Courier*, Oct. 1991.
Garcia Marquez: The Man and His Work. GENE H. BELL-VILLADA. University of North Carolina Press, 1990.
"Love and. . . ." TIM MCCARTHY. *National Catholic Reporter*, May 12, 1989.

Garner, James (James Baumgarner; 1928–) Veteran stage and screen star James Garner starred in 1993 as ultimately defeated Nabisco head F. Ross Johnson, in the fact-based, well-received television film *Barbarians at the Gate*, the story of the 1980s Nabisco takeover, directed by Glen Jordan and written by Larry Gelbart. Jonathan Pryce played corporate raider Henry Kravis, and Peter Riegert was Shearman Lehman investment banker Peter Cohen, in a cast that also included Joanna Cassiday, Fred Dalton Thompson, Leilani Ferrer, Matt Clark, Jeffrey DeMunn, David Rasche, and Tom Aldredge. Garner won an Emmy nomination for the role.

Garner also starred in the "alien invader" film, *Fire in the Sky*, directed by Robert Lieberman and co-starring D. B. Sweeney. Forthcoming was a supporting role in the film *Maverick*, based on Garner's 1960s television series, still in worldwide reruns. Mel Gibson was starring in the title role, opposite Jodie Foster; Richard Donner directed.

Oklahoma-born Garner began his long career in the mid-1950s, in a small, non-speaking role in *The Caine Mutiny Court Martial* (1954), and in bit parts in television. He quickly emerged as a major television series star, in the title role of the western "Maverick" (1957–61), and later as private investigator Jim Rockford in "The Rockford Files" (1974–80). His wide range of films included *Sayonara* (1957), *The Great Escape* (1963), *The Americanization of Emily* (1964), *Marlowe* (1969), *They Only Kill Their Masters* (1972), *Victor/Victoria* (1982), *Murphy's Romance* (1985), and *Sunset* (1987). He also starred in such telefilms as *Promise* (1986), which won five Emmys, including best drama; and *My Name Is Bill W* (1989), in the title role as the founder of Alcoholics Anonymous. Garner attended the University of Oklahoma. He married Lois Clarke in 1956; they have three children.

FURTHER READING

"James Garner." MICHELE WILLENS. *TV Guide*, Mar. 20, 1993.

Gaston, Cito (1944–) Some said winning the World Series in 1992 was a fluke. But when the Toronto Blue Jays won again in 1993, it was clear that their championship was no accident.

And since a substantial portion of the team had changed during that year, it was equally clear that the architect of their success was manager Cito Gaston. One key to his achievement was that he convinced the players to work together as a team, and to make or accept choices that would be good for the team, even if disappointing to them individually. This was most clearly indicated in Game 3 of the World Series in his controversial decision to bench the league's leading hitter, lefthand-batter John Olerud—though admittedly the man behind him was second in the league, righthand-hitting Paul Molitor. Though the decision was much criticized, Olerud and other team members accepted the change, and Gaston had the best answer to his critics: a win, with Molitor driving in three runs and scoring three, one on a solo homer, and at first base helping in a seventh-inning double play to end a Phillies' rally. In another instance, earlier in the year, when Rickey Henderson joined the team, he had the players in the starting lineup draw up their "ideal" batting order, all therefore having a say in the final order, determined by Gaston. In the end, the Blue Jays knocked out the Chicago White Sox for the American League pennant, and then defeated the Philadelphia Phillies 4 games to 2 to take the World Series.

In July, as manager for the American League in the All-Star game, Gaston took some heat for selecting four of his own players to the three elected by the fans, for a total of seven Jays, especially because at that point his team was in a ten-straight-loss slump; Gaston's response was: "I took six world champions and a Hall of Famer. I apologize for nothing."

Born in San Antonio, Texas, Gaston graduated from high school in Corpus Christi, Texas in 1962. He began his major league career as a player with the Atlanta Braves (1967), moved to the San Diego Padres (1969–74), being named to the All-Star team in 1970, then back to Atlanta (1975–78) and on to the Pittsburgh Pirates (1978). After a year as minor league coach with the Atlanta Braves (1981), Gaston moved to the Toronto Blue Jays as hitting instructor (1982–89) and then manager (1989–   ). He is married to Denise Gaston and has two children.

FURTHER READING

"Despite critics. . . ." JOHN RAWLINGS. *Sporting News*, Nov. 1, 1993.
"Baseball's minority managers." WALTER LEAVY. *Ebony*, May 1993.
"Gaston, Cito." *Current Biography*, Apr. 1993.

Gephardt, Richard Andrew (1941–   )
House Majority Leader Richard Gephardt backed many Clinton administration proposals during 1993, and continued to be a key Democratic Party spokesperson on some aspects of foreign affairs, especially in the area of trade imbalances resulting from the protective policies of many countries, most notably Japan. Focusing on these areas, and with considerable labor support, he had during the presidential campaign sharply attacked the North American Free Trade Agreement (NAFTA), one of the few specific agreements to emerge from the final year of the Bush administration. He maintained his opposition to the agreement as Clinton adminstration support for it grew, in mid-August sharply criticizing the supplemental environmental and labor agreements as inadequate, and on September 21 announcing his formal opposition to NAFTA. But his opposition was on the single issue, signaling no break with President Clinton; in the same period, for example, he strongly supported the Clinton health plan, with its proposal for universal health insurance. Gephardt continued to look forward, with a possible run for the presidency still in view.

St. Louis-born Gephardt began his political career as a St. Louis alderman (1971–76); his con-gressional career began in 1979. He was a strong contender for the Democratic presidential nomination in 1988. In July 1991, he took himself out of the 1992 presidential race, though nearly returned to the race in February 1992, as President George Bush began to look far less invulnerable. He endorsed Bill Clinton on April 12, and addressed the Democratic National Convention in Clinton's favor on July 16. On the personal side, Gephardt had encountered some bad publicity because of his 28 overdrafts on the House bank, when that scandal became news, but was in no way seriously damaged, as attested by his landslide re-election victory in November 1992, with 66 percent of the vote to his opponent's 34 percent.

Gephardt's 1962 B.S. was from Northwestern University, and his 1965 J.D. from the University of Michigan. He married Jane Ann Byrnes in 1966; the couple have three children.

FURTHER READING

"Wanted. . . ." DOUGLAS HARBRECHT. *Business Week*, Nov. 19, 1990.
"Gephardt speaks for the majority." BILL WHALEN. *Insight*, July 3, 1989.
"Man for all seasons. . . ." MORTON M. KONDRACKE. *New Republic*, July 3, 1989.

Gere, Richard (1949–   )
In the film *Sommersby*, a remake of *The Return of Martin Guerre*, Gere starred as Jack, an American Civil War soldier, who was missing in action and has been presumed dead. He returns—perhaps not the same man—two years after the war, and tries to restart his life with his wife and son. Jodie Foster starred as his wife Laurel, in a cast that included James Earl Jones, Lanny Flaherty, and Wendell Wellman; Jon Amiel directed.

Gere also starred as a manic-depressive in the film *Mr. Jones*, opposite Lena Olin as his psychiatrist, who becomes his lover, with Anne Bancroft as a second therapist; Mike Figgis directed and Gere co-produced. He also played a cameo role in the television film *And The Band Played On*, based on the Randy Shilts book about the early days of the AIDS crisis; Roger Spottiswoode directed. Forthcoming were the films *Intersection*, directed by Mark Rydell and co-starring Sharon Stone, Lolita Davidovich, and Martin Landau; and *Higgins Beach*, directed by

Jon Amiel, starring opposite Michelle Pfeiffer. Gere, who is active in Tibet-related affairs, used his presenter's role at the 1993 Academy Awards show to ask his worldwide audience to speak for the freedom of Tibet from Chinese domination.

Philadelphia-born Gere began his theater career in the early 1970s, and became a star in such films as *Report to the Commissioner* (1975), *Looking for Mr. Goodbar* (1977), *Yanks* (1979), *An Officer and a Gentleman* (1982), and *Internal Affairs* (1989). After several years in the doldrums, Gere's career received an enormous boost from the unexpected popularity of *Pretty Woman* (1990), the Pygmalion-like romantic comedy in which he co-starred with Julia Roberts. Long interested in Buddhism and Eastern philosophy, Gere is the founder and chairman of Tibet House. In October 1991, he met the Dalai Lama at Kennedy Airport, to begin 62 Tibet-related events organized into the International Year of Tibet. He attended the University of Massachusetts. He and model Cindy Crawford married in 1991.

FURTHER READING

"True romance." KAREN S. SCHNEIDER. *People*, Oct. 18, 1993.
"The model and. . . ." HERB RITTS and JULIA REED. *Vogue*, Nov. 1992.

Gergen, David Richmond (1942–)
On May 29, 1993, in a move that surprised many, President Bill Clinton named longtime Washington insider and communications professional David Gergen, who had served three Republican presidents, to be his new White House communications director. Gergen replaced George Stephanopolous, who remained a key figure in Clinton's White House staff. Clinton explained his move as an attempt to rebuild public perception of his administration as centrist and bipartisan, themes he stressed repeatedly in the months that followed, perhaps most notably in his campaign for the North American Free Trade Agreement (NAFTA), which drew at least as much Republican as Democratic support. Gergen played his developing role very much behind the scenes in the White House, and seemingly to considerable effect, as Clinton's popularity ratings climbed in late 1993.

Durham, North Carolina-born Gergen began his career in and around government in 1971, as a Nixon administration staffer, joining the White House writing group as a special assistant to the president (1973–74). He stayed on after Nixon's resignation, as head of White House communications for President Ford (1975–77). With the change to a Democratic adminstration, Gergen joined the American Enterprise Institute, editing its magazine (1977–81). He rejoined the White House staff as President Reagan's assistant for communications (1981–83). He became a fellow at the John F. Kennedy School of Government (1983–85), and then went back to Washington as editor of the magazine *U.S. News & World Report* (1985–93), also becoming a well-known news analyst in television, notably on the *Macneil/Lehrer News Hour*. Gergen's B.A. was from Yale University, and his J.D. from Harvard University. He is married to Anne Gergen, and has two children.

FURTHER READING

"David Gergen. . . ." MICHAEL KELLY. *New York Times*, Oct. 31, 1993.
"All the presidents' man. . . ." FRANCIS WILKINSON. *Rolling Stone*, Sep. 2, 1993.
"Presidency by vignette. . . ." BILL TURQUE. *Newsweek*, July 12, 1993.
"Dave." SIDNEY BLUMENTHAL. *New Yorker*, June 28, 1993.
"Press gang." FRED BARNES. *New Republic*, June 21, 1993.
"The staff shuffle. . . ." BILL TURQUE. *Newsweek*, June 7, 1993.

Gerstner, Louis Vincent, Jr. (1942–)
On March 26, 1993, greatly troubled IBM named RJR Nabisco Holdings chairman Louis Gerstner its new chairman and chief executive officer, for the first time reaching outside the computer industry for leadership. Faced by the rapid obsolescence of its hugely expensive mainframe computer business, coupled with failure to keep up with smaller computer companies in a wide range of areas, IBM had cut its worldwide workforce from 400,000 to 300,000 from 1986 to 1992, and even more in early 1993, but still found itself failing, with losses of almost $5 billion in 1992. In late July, Gerstner announced a major restructuring of the company, accompanied by many plant closings, further massive early re-

tirements and layoffs that would take employment down to 225,000 by the end of 1994, and a further $8.9 billion charge for carrying through the program. At year's end, the results of Gerstner's strategy remained to be seen.

New York City-born Gerstner was a leading management consultant before going into direct management. He was a director of McKinsey & Co. (1965–78) before joining the American Express Company as an executive vice-president in 1981. He held a succession of high positions in that company, and was its president (1985–89), before becoming chairman and chief executive officer of RJR Nabisco (1989–93). Gerstner also sits on the boards of several corporations and institutions. His B.A. was from Harvard College, and his M.B.A. from Harvard University. He is married to Elizabeth Robins Link, and has two children.

FURTHER READING

"Rethinking IBM . . . ." JUDITH H. DOBRZYNSKI. *Business Week*, Oct. 4, 1993.
"Abort, retry, fail?" GEOFFREY BREWER. *Sales & Marketing Management*, Oct. 1993.
"Lou Gerstner's 'vision'. . . ." HANK GILMAN. *Newsweek*, Aug. 9, 1993.
"Lou Gerstner's first 30 days." *Fortune*, May 31, 1993.
"Faith in a stranger." CATHERINE ARNST. *Business Week*, Apr. 5, 1993.
"The RJR Nabisco. . . ." LAURA ZINN. *Business Week*, Apr. 5, 1993.

"Gerstner, Louis Vincent Jr." *Current Biography*, June 1991.
"Louis Gerstner's script. . . ." *U.S. News & World Report*, May 20, 1991.
"Completing a circle." WILTON WOODS. *Fortune*, Apr. 10, 1989.

Gesell, Gerhard (1910–93) Los Angeles-born Gerhard Gesell, who as a federal District Court judge in Washington presided over several key aspects of the Watergate cases, began his career as a lawyer with the Securities and Exchange Commission (1935–41), and then went into private practice in Washington, while taking on several advisory assignments for the federal government. He was appointed to the federal judiciary by President Lyndon B. Johnson in 1967. In 1971, he ruled that the *Washington Post* could continue to publish the Pentagon Papers. He also ruled against the Nixon administration on a number of other matters as the Watergate scandal unfolded, and ultimately brought the whole matter to a close by ruling against the illegal dismissal of special prosecutor Archibald Cox and forcing disclosure of the Nixon tapes. In 1974, he sentenced Nixon aide John Ehrlichman to a five-year prison term. Fifteen years later, Gesell also presided over the Iran-Contra trial of Oliver North. He was survived by his wife, Marion Pike, a daughter, a son, and a sister. (d. Washington, D.C.; February 19, 1993)

FURTHER READING

Obituary. *The Times* (of London), Feb. 23, 1993.
Obituary. *New York Times*, Feb. 21, 1993.

Gibson, Mel (1956–) In 1993, actor Mel Gibson further expanded his career, making his well-received directorial debut with the film *The Man without a Face*, starring Gibson and and Nick Stahl, based on the 1972 Isabelle Holland novel. Gibson also was one of several celebrities who did readings in Bill Couturie's environmentalist film *Earth and the American Dream*, among them Jeremy Irons, Alec Baldwin, Anthony Hopkins, Gene Hackman, Jack Lemmon, Mary Steenburgen, Harrison Ford, James Caan, Ed Asner, Sam Waterston, Christopher Reeve, Bette Midler, Dustin Hoffman, and Michael Keaton.

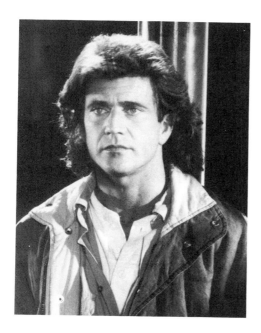

Lethal Hero: Mel Gibson Biography. ROLAND PERRY. Oliver, 1993.

"Mel Gibson. . . ." JEANNE MARIE LASKAS. *Redbook*, Nov. 1992.

Mel Gibson. NEIL SINYARD. Outlet, 1992.

"Mel-o-drama. . . ." ROY SEKOFF . *Seventeen*, Jan. 1991.

"Mel Gibson. . . ." JOHN LAHR. *Cosmopolitan*, Dec. 1990.

"Road worrier. . . ." *Harper's Magazine*, Aug. 1990.

"Talking with. . . ." CARSON JONES. *Redbook*, Aug. 1990.

Mel Gibson: Australia's Restless Superstar. KEITH McKAY. Doubleday, 1986.

Forthcoming was a starring title role in the film *Maverick*, a remake of the 1960s James Garner television series, opposite Jodie Foster and Garner, now in a supporting role; Richard Donner directed. Also forthcoming was a considerable change of pace; Gibson will host "Rabbit Ears Radio," a new American Public Radio weekly children's show, which will present classic children's stories narrated by leading players.

Born in Peekskill, New York, Gibson emigrated to Australia with his family in 1968. He appeared on stage and screen in Australia from 1977, in South Australian regional theatre in the classics, in several television series, and most notably in the film *Tim* (1979). He soon became a popular worldwide film star, in such action films as *Mad Max* (1979), and its two sequels: *The Road Warrior* (1982) and *Mad Max Beyond Thunderdome* (1985); the dramas *Gallipoli* (1981) and *The Year of Living Dangerously* (1983); the *Lethal Weapon* films (1987; 1989; 1992); *Bird on a Wire* (1990); and *Air America* (1990). Gibson attended the Australian National Institute of Dramatic Arts. He married Robyn Moore in 1979; they have six children.

FURTHER READING

"Mad Mel." RACHEL ABRAMOWITZ. *Premiere*, Sep. 1993.

"Mel Gibson." TRISH DEITCH ROHRER. *Us*, Sep. 1993.

"To Mel and back." ALLEN BARRA. *Entertainment*, Aug. 20, 1993.

Gielgud, John (Arthur John Gielgud; 1904–) At 89, the great actor John Gielgud remained active in film, television, and radio, though no longer taking on the stage roles that for more than seven decades placed him at the forefront of the English-language theater. He appeared in a Disney film, *Stick With Me, Kid*, in an episode of the television series "Lovejoy," lived in his country home near Aylesbury, Buckinghamshire, and was receptive to new projects, which certainly came. On his 90th birthday, on April 14, 1994, BBC radio will broadcast his fifth *King Lear*. Also forthcoming was a role in the CBS television miniseries *Scarlett*, based on Alexandra Ripley's best-selling novel, a "sequel" to *Gone With the Wind*, in a cast that includes Timothy Dalton as Rhett Butler opposite Joanne Whalley-Kilmer as Scarlett O'Hara.

One of the leading actors of the English-speaking theater for more than seven decades, and the grandnephew of the celebrated actress Ellen Terry, London-born Gielgud made his stage debut in 1921, and by 1929 had become a highly regarded Shakespearean actor at the Old Vic, going on to play major roles in Shakespeare for the next half century, perhaps most notably as *Hamlet*. He directed a legendary 1935 *Romeo and Juliet* in London, alternating with Laurence Olivier in the Mercutio and Romeo roles. Late in his career, he created several modern roles, among others in *Nude With Violin* (1956), *Tiny Alice* (1964), *Home* (1970), and *No Man's Land* (1970). Although Gielgud made his film debut in 1921 and played leads in the films *Secret Agent* (1936) and *Julius Caesar* (1970), he has for most of his career been primarily a theater actor. In recent years, however, he has played numerous strong supporting roles in such films as *Murder* on the Orient Express (1974), Arthur (1981; he won a best supporting actor Oscar), Chariots of Fire (1981), and Shining Through (1992), and in such television productions as Brideshead Revisited (1981) and War and Remembrance (1988). Among his writings are Early Stages: A Theatrical Reminiscence (1939), Stage Directions (1963), An Actor in His Time (1981), Backward Glances: Times for Reflection and Distinguished Company (1990), and Acting Shakespeare (1992).

FURTHER READING

"A man for all seasons. . . ." GERALD C. LUBENOW. Newsweek, Mar. 21, 1988.

Gill, Vince (1957–) Country singer, songwriter, and instrumentalist Vince Gill emerged in 1993 as one of the top figures in country music, winning a wide range of awards. He won three Grammys, as top male country vocalist for his performance of the song "I Still Believe In You;" for the song itself, written with John Barlow Jarvis; and for best country vocal performance in the album I Still Believe In You (1992). He was nominated in eight categories at the Country Music Association awards, winning in five: entertainer of the year, male vocalist of the year, song of the year for "I Still Believe In You," songwriter of the year with Jarvis for the same song, and album of the year for I Still Believe In You. At the Broadcast Music Inc. Awards, he

was one of three songwriters cited for creating three songs that were cited as BMI's most played.

During 1993, Gill released the hit Christmas album Let There Be Peace on Earth. On two hit singles he was both performer and co-writer: "No Future In The Past," written with C. Jackson, and "One More Last Chance," with G. Nicholson. A third hit single was his duet with Reba McEntire "The Heart Won't Lie." Gill was also one of several country artists who appeared in the album Common Threads: The Songs of the Eagles; he sang "I Can't Tell You Why." At year's end, he was ranked fourth on Billboard's hot country singles and track artist list and eighth on the top country music artist list.

Oklahoma-born Gill emerged as a country music star in the late 1980s, on tour and with the solo albums The Way Back Home (1987), When I Call Your Name (1990), Pocket Full of Gold (1991), and I Never Knew Lonely (1992). He won his first Grammy in 1990, for best male country performance, and won two Country Music Association awards in 1991. He is married to Janis Gill; they have one child.

FURTHER READING

"Vince Gill's blue Christmas." PATRICK CARR. Country Music, Sep.-Oct. 1993.
"Vince Gill. . . ." JON SIEVERT. Guitar Player, Mar. 1992.
"Vince Gill. . . ." Country Music, Mar.-Apr. 1992.
"Vince and Janis Gill." CYNTHIA SANZ. People, June 10, 1991.

Gillespie, Dizzy (John Birks Gillespie; 1917–93) South Carolina-born Dizzy Gillespie began his long professional career as a jazz trumpeter in Philadelphia, in 1935. Moving to New York, he played during the late 1930s with Teddy Hill, Cab Calloway, Benny Carter, Duke Ellington, and Billy Eckstine, while he, Charlie Parker, Thelonius Monk, and others developed bebop. Gillespie formed his own big band (1946–50), in that period fully developing his merger of Afro-Cuban elements into jazz, and in the decades that followed toured widely, latterly with his United Nations Band. His works included the signature "A Night In Tunisia" (1942), "Salt Peanuts" (1945), and "Manteca" (1947). Gillespie appeared in several films, including A Night in Havana (1990) and The Winter in Lisbon

(1992). In 1990, he received the first Duke Ellington Award, and the National Medal of the
Arts. His autobiography, covering the early
years, was *To Be or Not to Bop: Memoirs of Dizzy
Gillespie* (1955), written with Al Fraser. He was
survived by his wife, Lorraine. (d. Englewood,
New Jersey; January 6, 1993)

FURTHER READING

Dizzy Gillespie: Musician. TONY GENTRY. Chelsea
House, 1994.
Dizzy Gillespie and the Birth of Bebop. LESLIE
GOURSE. Atheneum/Macmillan, 1994.
"Dizzy Gillespie." "John Birks Gillespie, 1917-'93."
ZAN STEWART. "Remembering Dizzy." JOHN
MCDONOUGH. "Setting diamonds." HOWARD MANDEL.
"All Dizzy's children." HOWARD MANDEL. "The
memorial service." MICHAEL BOURNE.
"Tilt-o-trumpet." ED ENRIGHT. "Blindfold Test. . . ."
LEONARD FEATHER. *Down Beat,* Apr. 1993.
"Dizzy Gillespie, 1917–1993." DAVE HELLAND. *Down
Beat,* March 1993.
"Dizzy Gillespie." STEVE FUTTERMAN. *Rolling Stone,*
Feb. 18, 1993.
Obituary. *Current Biography,* Feb. 1993.
"Bop till you drop." DAVID STANDISH and NEIL TESSER.
Playboy, Feb. 1993.
Obituary. *New Yorker,* Jan. 25, 1993.
"Dizzy Gillespie. . . ." DAVID HAJDU. *Entertainment,*
Jan. 22, 1993.
"Jazz's last hero trumpeter. . . ." DAVID GATES.
Newsweek, Jan. 18, 1993.
"Dizzy Gillespie 1917–1993." JAY COCKS. *Time,* Jan.
18, 1993.
"King of the horn. . . ." DIANE TURBIDE. *Maclean's,*
Jan. 18, 1993.
Obituary. *Variety,* Jan. 11, 1993.
Obituary. *The Times* (of London), Jan. 8, 1993.
Obituary. *New York Times,* Jan. 7, 1993.
"Gillespie, Dizzy." *Current Biography,* Jan. 1993.
Dizzy Gillespie. TONY GENTRY, Holloway, 1993.
Jazz Stars. RICHARD RENNERT, ed. Chelsea House,
1993.
*Dizzy: John Birks Gillespie in His Seventy-Fifth
Year.* LEE TANNER, ed. Pomegranate, 1993.
Waiting for Dizzy. GENE LEES. Oxford University
Press, 1991.
Dizzy Gillespie. TONY GENTRY. Chelsea House, 1991.
Dizzy Gillespie. BARRY MCRAE. Phaidon Universe,
1989.

Gilliatt, Penelope Connor (1932–93)

London-born Penelope Gilliatt briefly attended
Bennington College and worked for New York's
Institute For Pacific Relations before returning

to London as staff writer for *Vogue.* She was a
highly influential film critic for *The Observer*
(1961–67), then returning to New York as a film
critic, features writer, and short story writer for
The New Yorker (1968–79), later continuing to
write for that magazine. Gilliatt wrote the
Oscar-nominated screenplay for John Schlesinger's film *Sunday, Bloody Sunday* (1971). She
also wrote five novels, beginning with *One By
One* (1965) and including *The Cutting Edge*
(1979) and *A Woman of Singular Occupation*
(1989). Among her other works were the short
story collections *Come Back If It Doesn't Get Better* (1969), *Nobody's Business* (1972), *They Sleep
Without Dreaming* (1985), and *Twenty-Two Stories* (1986); the nonfiction work *To Wit: A Lifetime of Comedy* (1990); and a wide range of
articles and essays, many of them reflecting her
peace movement and populist-oriented political
views. She was survived by a daughter and a
sister. (d. May 9, 1993)

FURTHER READING

Obituary. *Variety,* May 17, 1993.
Obituary. *The Times* (of London), May 12, 1993.
Obituary. *New York Times,* May 11, 1993.

Gingrich, Newt (Newton Leroy Gingrich;

1943–) In some respects, notably abrasive
Georgia Republican and House Minority Whip
Newt Gingrich attempted to create a less stri-
dent and divisive image during 1993. That was
certainly so during the North American Free
Trade Agreement (NAFTA) debate, in which he
and many other Republicans supported the pact
and the Clinton position, although even then
Gingrich found a way to attack Clinton, by publicly doubting the strength of Clinton's commitment. Some thought that Gingrich wanted to
appear more moderate in order to advance his
campaign for the House Republican leadership,
to be vacated in 1994 by the retirement of Minority Leader Robert H. Michel. As of mid-
October 1993, Gingrich was the sole contender
for the job, reportedly with more than 100 of 175
House Republicans pledged to him.

In most other visible respects, Gingrich was
unchanged, attacking every possible Democratic
target; for example, he directly attacked the ethics of House Speaker Thomas S. Foley, after
news reports that Foley had profited from in-

vestments in new stock issues, opportunities allegedly opened to him because of his position; and Gingrich directly attacked Secretary of Defense Les Aspin for allegedly refusing field command pleas for more armored units in Somalia.

Pennsylvania-born Gingrich taught at West Georgia College before his election to the House of Representatives in 1979. He drew national attention (1987–88) as chief accuser of Democratic House Speaker Jim Wright, who ultimately resigned from the House. In August 1989, he urged ethics probes of seventeen other congressional Democrats, as well. Gingrich himself was accused of earlier ethics violations in April 1989, soon after his March 1989 selection as House Republican Whip, and faced further ethics charges in October; but all charges against him were dropped in March 1990. During 1992, Gingrich himself was heavily criticized for his 22 overdrawn checks in the House of Representatives banking scandal, and for his expensive government-supplied limousine and driver, which he gave up during the primary campaign. But he survived, won a close primary fight in July, and went on to again win a congressional seat. He played a notably abrasive attack role during the 1992 presidential campaign, at a late-August Bush campaign rally in Georgia even going so far as to compare Governor Bill Clinton to Woody Allen, calling Allen "a perfect model of Bill Clinton's Democratic values," and implying that the Democratic platform encouraged incest.

Gingrich attended Emory and Tulane universities. With David Drake and Marianne Gingrich, he published *Window of Opportunity: A Blueprint for the Future* (1984). He has been married twice, and has two children.

FURTHER READING

"Housebreaker." WILLIAM STERNBERG. *Atlantic*, June 1993.
"House revolutionary." ADAM CLYMER. *New York Times Magazine*, Aug. 23, 1992.
"A party's Newt testament. . . ." DANIEL WATTENBERG. *Insight*, Nov. 12, 1990.
"Having read George Bush's lips. . . ." BILL HEWITT. *People*, Nov. 12, 1990.
"New Newt news." DAVID BEERS. *Mother Jones*, Feb.-Mar. 1990.
"Master of disaster. . . ." DAVID BEERS. *Mother Jones*, Oct. 1989.
"Gingrich, Newton Leroy." *Current Biography*, July 1989.

Giniger, Henry (1922–93) Brooklyn-born Henry Giniger, a journalism graduate of Columbia University, began his career as a frontline Marine correspondent for *Stars and Stripes*. He joined the *New York Times* Paris bureau in 1946, and spent his entire career with the *Times*. His post-World War II reporting from France chronicled the rebuilding and re-emergence of that country during the postwar period, and he supplied notable reportage on major events throughout the continent, as in his reporting from Budapest during the 1956 Hungarian Revolution, and his coverage of the long Algerian War of Independence and its multiple impacts on France. Giniger operated out of the *Times* Mexico City bureau (1965–72), then returning to Europe to head the Madrid bureau. He later headed the Montreal and Ottawa bureaus, and was an editor with the Week in Review section, retiring in 1987. He then returned to France. He was survived by his wife, Janine, a stepdaughter, and a sister. (d. Paris; March 7, 1993)

FURTHER READING

Obituary. *The Times* (of London), Mar. 10, 1993.
Obituary. *New York Times*, Mar. 8, 1993.

Ginsburg, Ruth Bader (1933–) On June 14, 1993, President Bill Clinton nominated Judge Ruth Bader Ginsburg to the Supreme Court, replacing retiring Justice Byron R. White. She was confirmed by the Senate August

3, by a vote of 96–3, after unanimous endorsement by the Senate's Judiciary Committee. A long-term civil liberties and women's rights advocate and lawyer, though a moderate in stance and a consensus-builder in practice, Ginsburg quickly and quite actively participated in the work of the Court early in the 1993–94 term. In her first decision, she joined Justices Harry Blackmun and John Paul Stevens in their minority vote to grant a stay of execution to convicted Texas murderer Johnny James, who was then executed. In the landmark *Harris v. Forklift Systems* case, she joined the unanimous Court in ruling that workers need not prove that they had suffered psychological damage or were unable to perform their tasks to successfully charge sexual harassment, instead applying the rule of "workplace equity;" but her concurring opinion seemed to go further than that of most of her colleagues in the sexual harassment area. That seemed quite appropriate, as during the late 1960s and early 1970s, while director of the American Civil Liberties Union Women's Rights Project, Ginsburg fought and won several of the most important women's rights cases of the modern period, winning 5 of the 6 cases she argued before the Supreme Court.

New York City-born Ginsburg's B.A. was from Cornell University. She attended Harvard Law School and then Columbia Law School, receiving her LL.B. and J.D from the latter. She clerked with U.S. District Court Judge Edmund Palmieri (1959–61), and then taught law at Rutgers Law School (1963–72) and Columbia Law School (1972–80), becoming the first woman named a tenured law professor at Columbia. She was appointed to the federal Court of Appeals for the District of Columbia by President Jimmy Carter in 1980. She is married to lawyer Martin D. Ginsburg and has two children, a son and a daughter, who is also a lawyer.

FURTHER READING

"Meet our new. . . ." ANGELA HUNT. *Glamour*, Oct. 1993.
"Justice for women." ELAINE SHANNON. *Vogue*, Oct. 1993.
"The book of Ruth. . . ." JEFFREY ROSEN. *New Republic*, Aug. 2, 1993.
"Two lives of. . . ." STEVEN V. ROBERTS. *U.S. News & World Report*, June 28, 1993.
"The list." JEFFREY ROSEN. *New Republic*, May 10, 1993.

Gish, Lillian

Gish, Lillian (1893–1993) The celebrated actress Lillian Gish was on stage at the age of five, sometimes with her younger sister, Dorothy Gish, who was on stage at four. In 1912, introduced by Mary Pickford, the sisters began their long association with D.W. Griffith, appearing in *An Unseen Enemy*. Lillian Gish became one of the leading film players of her time, starring in such classic silent films as *Birth of a Nation* (1914), *Hearts of the World* (1918), *Way Down East* (1920), *Orphans of the Storm* (1922), *Romola* (1924), and *The Scarlet Letter* (1926). Her popularity sagged in the late 1920s, and waned even more with the advent of sound and new filmmaking styles. She made her career largely on the stage after the silent film era, later returning to the movies in supporting roles in such films as *Duel In the Sun* (1946) and *Night of the Hunter* (1957), also appearing in many television films. Her last film was *Whales In August* (1987). With Ann Pinchot, she wrote *The Movies, Mr. Griffith, and Me* (1969). There were no survivors. (d. New York City; February 27, 1993)

FURTHER READING

Obituary. *Current Biography*, Apr. 1993.
"Lillian Gish. . . ." RICHARD A. BLAKE. *America*, Mar. 20, 1993.
"A passing of legends . . . ." *People*, Mar. 15, 1993.
"Lillian Gish. . . ." LILLIAN BURR. *Entertainment*, Mar. 12, 1993.
Obituary. *Variety*, Mar. 8, 1993.
Obituary. *The Times* (of London), Mar. 1, 1993.
Obituary. *New York Times*, Mar. 1, 1993.

Giuliani, Rudolph W.

Giuliani, Rudolph W. (1944–   ) On November 2, 1993, Republican-Liberal candidate Rudolph Giuliani won the New York City mayoralty race, defeating incumbent Democratic mayor David Dinkins by a 51 percent to 48 percent majority in a city with five Democrats registered to every Republican. Dinkins had been New York's first African-American mayor, and this was his first re-election campaign. The winning Giuliani campaign played heavily on racial themes in a highly polarized city, although strongly denying any play to racist sentiments. In the end, Giuliani won more than three-quarters of the White vote (meaning that he won more Democratic than Republican votes) and Dinkins won 95 percent of the African-American

Rudolph Giuliani and family on Inauguration Day

vote. In other key city races, other Democrats won by wide margins.

New York City-born Giuliani began his long career as a government prosecutor in the early 1970s, as an assistant U.S. attorney for the Southern District of New York, then moving up to become an associate deputy U.S. attorney in the Justice Department (1975–77). He was in private practice during the Carter years, in the New York City law firm of Patterson, Belknap, Webb and Tyler, moving back into government with Ronald Reagan as U.S. attorney for New York's Southern District (1983–89), there achieving prominence as an aggressive and successful prosecutor in a wide range of cases. He left government to make an unsuccessful New York City mayoral run in 1989, and practiced with White & Case (1989–90) and Anderson Kill Olick & Oshinsky (1990–93). His B.A. was from Manhattan College, and his J.D. from New York University.

FURTHER READING

"A city divided. . . ." Eric Pooley. New York, Nov. 15, 1993.
"Radicals at work." Economist, Nov. 6, 1993.
"Rudy's shot. . . ." John Taylor. New York, Oct. 11, 1993.
"Rudy's reversals. . . ." James Traub. New Republic, Sep. 9, 1991.
"Rudolph Giuliani. . . ." Todd S. Purdum. New York Times Magazine, July 25, 1993.
"Change partners." Andy Logan. New Yorker, June 14, 1993.
"From Milken to the Mafia. . . ." Barron's, Nov. 26, 1990.
"Rudy's fall from grace." New York, Aug. 21, 1989.
Courtroom Crusades. Mark Litwak. Morrow, 1989.
The Prosecutors. James B. Stewart. Simon & Schuster, 1987.

Glass, Philip (1937–   ) One of the major new musical events of the year was the premiere of Philip Glass's new two-act chamber opera *Orphée*, adapted by Glass from the Jean Cocteau film, edited by Robert Brustein; directed by Francesca Zambello, and conducted by Martin Goldray. The cast included Eugene Perry as Orphée, Elizabeth Futral as Eurydice, and Richard Fracker as Heurtebise, and Paul Kirby as Cégeste.

In 1993, Glass recorded his "Low" Symphony, which had made its American premiere with the Brooklyn Philharmonic Orchestra in 1992. The work, based on the instrumental music in David Bowie's 1977 album *Low*, proved very popular, becoming the top-selling classical album of the year. Glass also signed a 5-year contract with Nonesuch to record many of his older works, and to issue first recordings of several works, including *Orphée* and the music for Robert Wilson's "Civil Wars."

Forthcoming was another major opera, *The White Raven*, with libretto by Robert Wilson, scheduled to premiere in 1994. The opera was commissioned by the Portuguese government to commemorate the voyages of Portuguese explorer Vasco da Gama, who opened the East to Europeans by sailing around Cape Horn into the Indian Ocean.

In his developing body of work, Baltimore-born Glass has wiped out any "line" that might still be said to exist between modern classical and popular music. He emerged as a leading modern composer in the late 1960s, after a Paris period in which he worked with Ravi Shankar and studied with Nadia Boulanger, then weaving modernist and Indian themes and techniques into his music. He founded the Philip Glass Ensemble in 1968, and became a well-known figure on tour and a popular recording artist in the early 1970s, with such works as *Music in 12 Parts* (1971–74) and *Glassworks* (1982). He also began a major career as a classical composer in the 1970s, with *Einstein On the Beach*, still his best known classical work, and the other two parts of his celebrated "portrait opera" trilogy: *Akhnaten* (1980) and *Satyagraha* (1985). Among his other operas are *The Civil Wars* (1982–84), *The Making of the Representative for Planet 8* (1988), *One Thousand Airplanes on the Roof* (1988), *Mattogrosso* (1989), and *The Hydrogen Jukebox* (1990), produced in collaboration with poet Allen Ginsberg and visual artist Jerome Sirlin, starting from a cantata based on Ginsberg's anti-war poem, "Wichita Vortex Sutra." In 1987, he published the memoir *Music by Philip Glass*. Glass attended the University of Chicago and the Julliard School of Music. He was formerly married, and has two children.

FURTHER READING

"A persistent voyager. . . ." JAMES R. OESTREICH. *New York Times Magazine*, Oct. 11, 1992.
"Glass plus." K. ROBERT SCHWARZ. *Opera News*, Oct. 1992.
"Philip Glass. . . ." *Connoisseur*, Feb. 1991.
American Music Makers. JANET NICHOLS. Walker, 1990.

Glover, Danny (1947–) As South Africa moved toward establishment of a multiracial society, Glover starred as a black master sergeant in the South African police soon after the 1976 Soweto protests; his personal tragedy is the center of the film *Bopha*, based on a play by South African Percy Mtwa, and directed by Morgan Freeman, in his directorial debut.

Glover also starred opposite Matt Dillon in *The Saint of Fort Washington*, directed by Tim Hunter, with Glover as a streetwise Vietnam War veteran who tries to help the homeless Dillon, the two becoming close friends. Glover also played Alex Haley in the television miniseries "Alex Haley's 'Queen,'" set in the 19th century in slavery days and freedom; the cast included Halle Berry as Queen, Jasmine Guy, Tim Daly, Ann-Margret, Martin Sheen, and Ossie Davis. Forthcoming was a starring role in the baseball comedy-fantasy *Angels in the Outfield*, in a cast that included Brenda Fricker, Jay O. Sanders, Joseph Gordon Levitt, and Milton Davis; William Dear directed.

San Francisco-born Glover, a civil rights activist during his late 1960s college years, entered the theater through appearances as an amateur in the works of such playwrights as Amiri Baraka and Athol Fugard, and worked as a professional in supporting roles on stage throughout the 1970s. He appeared in a Yale Repertory Theater production of Fugard's *Master Harold and the Boys* (1982). On screen, he played in such films as *Escape from Alcatraz* (1979), *Chu Chu and the Philly Flash* (1981), *Out* (1982), and *Iceman* (1984), before his breakthrough starring role as Moze opposite Sally Field in *Places in the Heart* (1984). In 1985, he starred opposite Whoopi Goldberg in *The Color Purple*, and also in *Witness* and *Silverado*. He then reached huge audiences in the thrillers *Lethal Weapon* (1985), *Lethal Weapon II* (1987), *Predator II* (1990), and *Lethal Weapon III* (1992), also starring in such films as *To Sleep With Anger* (1990), *Flight of the Intruder* (1991), *Grand Canyon* (1991), and *A Rage in Harlem* (1991). Glover's B.S. was from San Francisco State University. He is married to the former Asake Bomani, and has one child.

FURTHER READING

"Glover's leap." LISA SCHWARZBAUM. *Entertainment*, June 12, 1992.
"Danny Glover." MARJORIE ROSEN and LOIS ARMSTRONG. *People*, Feb. 10, 1992.
"An everyman. . . ." KITTY BOWE HEARTY. *Premiere*, Feb. 1992.
"Danny Glover." *Playboy*, Sep. 1991.
"Danny Glover. . . ." *GQ—Gentleman's Quarterly*, July 1989.

Whoopi Goldberg (right) and Ted Danson

Goldberg, Whoopi (Caryn Johnson; 1950–) For stage, screen, and television star Whoopi Goldberg, 1993 was another extremely active year. She starred opposite Ted Danson in the hit film comedy *Made in America*, directed by Richard Benjamin. Then she starred again as Deloris in *Sister Act II*, the sequel to her hit comedy *Sister Act* (1992), this time returning to the convent to straighten out its school; the cast included Maggie Smith, Kathy Najimy, Barnard Hughes, Mary Wickes, and James Coburn; Bill Duke directed.

Goldberg also filmed the forthcoming film *Corrina, Corrina*, written and directed by Jessie Nelson, and co-starring Ray Liotta. Other forthcoming films were *Boys on the Side*, directed by Herbert Ross, and co-starring Mary Louise Parker and Drew Barrymore; and *T. Rex*, which she agreed to do after its producer sued to force her to fulfill the commitment; in it, she was slated to play a police officer partnered with a dinosaur. Her late night television talk show did not survive its 1992–93 first season; it was cancelled because of its low ratings.

On the personal side, she and Ted Danson became companions while making *Made in America*, and stayed together for most of the year, until separating. After a highly publicized incident, in which he appeared in blackface and told racially oriented jokes at a Friars Club roast of Goldberg, she defended Danson, pointing out that she had fully participated in preparing his appearance.

New York City-born Goldberg, who had previously worked as a popular cabaret and stage entertainer, emerged as a film star in *The Color Purple* (1985; she received an Oscar nomination), and went on to such films as *Jumpin' Jack Flash* (1986), *Fatal Beauty* (1987), *Burglar* (1988), *The Long Walk Home* (1990), and *Sarafina* (1992). In 1990, she scored a major success—including a best supporting actress Oscar—as the Harlem-based psychic in the year's surprise top-grossing film, *Ghost*, opposite Patrick Swayze and Demi Moore. She also starred opposite Jean Stapleton in the short-lived television series "Bagdad Cafe" (1990). She had a one-woman show on Broadway in 1984, and toured in a second one-woman show in 1988. Goldberg was previously married, and has one child.

FURTHER READING

Whoopi Goldberg: Entertainer. ROSE BLUE. Chelsea House, 1994.
"Whoopi Goldberg returns. . . ." *Jet*, Dec. 13, 1993.
"Blacks fail to see humor. . . ." *Jet*, Nov. 1, 1993.
"Whoopi Goldberg and Ted Danson. . . ." *Jet*, June 14, 1993.
"Heat on the set." SHELLEY LEVITT. *People*, June 7, 1993.
"Girl talk with. . . ." DEBORAH NORVILLE. *McCall's*, June 1993.
"Whoopi Goldberg." ROD LURIE. *Los Angeles*, May 1993.
Whoopi Goldberg: From Street to Stardom. MARY A. ADAMS. Dillon/Macmillan, 1993.
"Whoopi Goldberg." *People*, Dec. 28, 1992.
" 'I knew what I wanted to be.' " DOTSON RADER. *Parade*, Nov. 1, 1992.
"Witty, gritty. . . ." JAMIE DIAMOND. *Cosmopolitan*, Nov. 1992.
"Funny lady." MELANIE BERGER. *Ladies Home Journal*, Oct. 1992.
"Whoopi Goldberg." DAVID RENSIN. *US*, Oct. 1992.
"The joy of being Whoopi." JOHN SKOW. *Time*, Sep. 21, 1992.
"Whoopi Goldberg." MATTHEW MODINE. *Interview*, June 1992.
"The prayer. . . ." JESS CAGLE. *Entertainment*, May 29, 1992.

Goldblum, Jeff (1952–) Stage and screen star Jeff Goldblum in 1993 played to massive worldwide audiences, starring in Steven Spielberg's blockbuster film *Jurassic Park*, about modern genetically engineered dinosaurs that break free from a theme park and become a danger to humanity. The film, which exploited humanity's deepest fears about science gone mad, while at the same time a very appealing special effects triumph, became not only the commercial picture of the year, but the highest grossing film ever released. Directed by Spielberg, with screenplay by Michael Crichton and David Koepp, based on Crichton's novel, the film also starred Sam Neill, Laura Dern, and Richard Attenborough.

Pittsburgh-born Goldblum played in the New York theater in the early 1970s, most notably in *Two Gentlemen of Verona* (1971). His wide range of films includes *Invasion of the Body Snatchers* (1978), *The Big Chill* (1983), *The Right Stuff* (1983), *Silverado* (1985), *The Fly* (1986), *Beyond Therapy* (1987), *Earth Girls Are Easy* (1989; opposite Geena Davis, then his wife), *Twisted Obsession* (1990), *The Tall Guy* (1990), *Mr. Frost* (1990), *Fathers and Sons* (1992), and *Deep Cover* (1992). He also appeared in the television series "Tenspeed and Brownshoe" (1980), and in the telefilms *The Race for the Double Helix* (1987) as scientist James Watson, *Framed* (1990), and *The Favor, the Watch and the Very Big Fish* (1991). Goldblum attended the Neighborhood Playhouse. He was previously married to actress Geena Davis (1987–91).

FURTHER READING

"Jeff Goldblum. . . ." SABINE DURRANT. *Independent*, July 22, 1993.
"Married . . . with chicken." JOHANNA SCHNELLER. *GQ—Gentlemen's Quarterly*, June 1989.

Golding, William Gerald (1911–93)

Cornwall-born William Golding published his first work, a poetry collection, while still at Oxford, in 1934. In the two decades that followed, he pursued several occupations, following World War II naval service with teaching, acting, and directing. His first, and by far his best known, novel was *Lord of the Flies* (1954), an enduring best-seller that also became a cult classic, especially for high school and college students, and which was adapted twice for film, in 1963 by Peter Brook, and in 1990 by Henry Hook. Golding's others works included the novels *The Inheritors* (1955), *Pincher Martin* (1956), *The Spire* (1964), *Darkness Visible* (1978), *The Papermen* (1984), and the maritime trilogy set during the Napoleonic Wars: the Booker Prize-winning *Rites of Passage* (1980), *Close Quarters* (1987), and *Fire Down Below* (1989). Some of his many essays were collected in *The Hot Gates*

and Other Occasional Pieces (1966). Golding was awarded the 1983 Nobel Prize for literature. He was survived by his wife, Ann Brookfield, a daughter, and a son. (d. Truro, Cornwall; June 19, 1993)

FURTHER READING

Obituary. *Current Biography*, Aug. 1993.
Obituary. *America*, July 31, 1993.
Obituary. *Variety*, June 22, 1993.
Obituary. *The Times* (of London), June 21, 1993.
"William Golding. . . ." JOHN CAREY. *Sunday Times* (of London), June 20, 1993.
Obituary. *New York Times*, June 20, 1993.
William Golding. LAWRENCE S. FRIEDMAN. Continuum, 1993.
William Golding. KEVIN MCCARRON. State Mutual, 1990.
The Novels of William Golding. STEPHEN J. BOYD. St. Martin's, 1988.
Critical Essays on William Golding. JAMES R. BAKER, ed. G.K. Hall, 1988.
William Golding. JAMES GINDIN. St. Martin's, 1988.
William Golding, rev. ed. BERNARD F. DICK. Twayne/Macmillan, 1987.
William Golding: The Man and His Books. JOHN CAREY, ed. Farrar, Straus & Giroux, 1987.
William Golding: A Critical Study. V.V. SUBBARAO. Apt, 1987.

Gonzalez Márquez, Felipe (1942–)

Spanish Prime Minister Felipe Gonzalez Márquez, secretary general of the Spanish Socialist Workers Party (PSOE), won a fourth term in the June 6 elections for the lower house of parliament (Cortes), though his party did lose 16 seats and its majority. On July 14, he took office again, this time at the head a coalition government that included two small nationalist Catalan and Basque parties. Before the elections, Gonzalez Márquez faced corruption scandals that had damaged his party and forced him to call the elections five months earlier than planned. But before and after the elections, he and his country faced enormous economic problems that did not respond to interest rate declines and other government initiatives, as the unemployment rate continued to top 20 percent during the year. The European Community Maastricht Treaty, on which Gonzalez Márquez pinned much hope, did finally achieve ratification, after more than 18 months of debate involving several countries; but its implementation was to be slow, because of economic problems throughout the European Community. At year's end, Gonzalez Márquez still led Spain, but with a minority party and in a weak economic and therefore weak political position.

Gonzalez Márquez became a member of the then-illegal Spanish Socialist Workers Party in 1964, having been a socialist youth group member since 1962. He rose to become his party's leader, and succeeded Adolfo Suarez González as prime minister with his party's victory in the 1982 elections. He was the first socialist prime minister of Spain since the Spanish Civil War; his election signaled the full emergence of a new Spain after the long night of the Franco period. In 1986, he took Spain into the European Common Market. He won a third term in the October 1989 elections, though only by one parliamentary seat; and on review that seat was lost by his party, leaving him without a clear parliamentary majority. Gonzalez Márquez attended the Catholic University of Louvaine. He is married to Carmen Romero; they have three children.

FURTHER READING

"Gonzalez vows. . . ." RICHARD OWEN. *Times*, Feb. 11, 1992.

Goodman, John (1952–) Still a fixture on American television screens, John Goodman in 1993 continued to star opposite Roseanne Arnold in "Roseanne," winning a Golden Globe award as best actor in a television musical or comedy for the role. He also pursued his film career, starring in two films. In *Born Yesterday*, based on the Garson Kanin play and a remake of the 1950 George Cukor classic film comedy, he starred as Harry Brock, in the Broderick Crawford role, opposie Melanie Griffith in the Judy Holliday role and Don Johnson in the William Holden role; Luis Mandoki directed. Goodman also starred in the film *Matinee*, directed by Joe Dante, in a cast that included Cathy Moriarty, Simon Fenton, and Omri Katz. Goodman was also the voice of Rex in the animated film *We're Back! A Dinosaur's Story*.

Forthcoming was a starring role in a live-actor version of the animated series "The Flintstones," directed by Brian Levant, and co-starring Elizabeth Perkins, Rick Moranis, Rosie O'Donnell and Elizabeth Taylor. Also forthcoming was a starring role in the title role of the television film *Huey Long*.

Before his "Roseanne" role catapulted him to stardom, Missouri-born Goodman had played in strong character roles in the theater and in films, on Broadway in such plays as *Loose Ends* (1979) and *Big River* (1985), and in such films as *Eddie Macon's Run* (1983), *True Stories* (1986), and *Raising Arizona* (1987). His other films include *Sea of Love* (1989), *Always* (1989), *Stella* (1990), *King Ralph* (1991), *Barton Fink* (1991), and *The Babe* (1992), as baseball star Babe Ruth. Goodman attended Southwest Missouri State College. He married Anna Elizabeth (Annabeth) Hartzog in 1989; they have one daughter.

FURTHER READING

"Bat man." ALLEN BARRA. *Entertainment*, May 1, 1992.
" 'The Babe' comes alive." ANDREA ZANI. *Sporting News*, Apr. 20, 1992.
"John Goodman." JAMES GREENBERG. *Us*, Apr. 1992.
"The Babe." VIC ZIEGEL. *Life*, Apr. 1992.
"John Goodman is. . . . " PETE RICHMOND. *GQ—Gentleman's Quarterly*, Apr. 1992.
"Being the big guy. . . ." PETER DE JONGE. *New York Times Magazine*, Feb. 10, 1991.
"John Goodman." TOM GREEN. *Los Angeles*, Mar. 1991.
"John Goodman. . . ." ERIC SHERMAN. *Ladies Home Journal*, Feb. 1991.
"John Goodman. . . ." FRED ROBBINS. *Woman's Day*, May 1, 1990.
"Everybody's all American. . . ." RICHARD ZOGLIN. *Time*, Feb. 19, 1990.

Gorbachev, Mikhail Sergeyevich

(1931–) His political career in eclipse in his own country, Mikhail Gorbachev remained a world figure in 1993, who very actively worked to support democracy in the countries of the former Soviet Union, and who published and spoke throughout the world. His Moscow foundation remained the center of his work, and his criticism of the Yeltsin government was undiminished, extending to its armored suppression of the Oct. 3–4 Moscow insurrection. As president of the International Green Cross/Green Crescent, Gorbachev intensified his environmental commitment, forming a Board of Directors that included such luminaries as Javier Pérez de Cuéllar, Carl Sagan, Toshiki Kaifu, and Thor Heyerdahl, and developing projects for the new organization.

On the personal side, Raisa Gorbachev continued to recover from the stroke she suffered during the failed 1991 rightwing coup, though she suffered something a setback in 1993 due to a broken arm.

Mikhail Gorbachev's early career proceeded in orthodox Soviet fashion: he joined the Communist Party of the Soviet Union in 1952, and for the next 33 years moved up through the party and government. He became a member of his party's central committee in 1971 and later minister of agriculture (1978–85). In 1985, he became General Secretary of the Soviet Communist Party Central Committee and effectively leader of the Soviet Union. In power, he immediately began the processes of internal change. His two main slogans were *perestroika*, meaning a massive restructuring of the Soviet economy, away from central planning, bureaucracy, and full state ownership and toward a market economy, private enterprise, and even private ownership of land; and *glasnost*, or "openness," meaning a move toward basic democratic freedoms.

Abroad, Gorbachev also moved very quickly once in power. In a series of meetings with presidents Reagan and Bush, he initiated what became the end of the 45-year-long Cold War, beginning with the 1987 intermediate nuclear forces (INF) treaty, the first of a series of major Soviet-American peace moves, with planned troop pullbacks and, for the first time in decades, real progress on arms control. In the process, he and the American presidents also helped to negotiate the end of conflicts in Nicaragua, Cambodia, Angola, Mozambique, Namibia, Ethiopia, and several other countries, with both superpow-

ers ending their long sponsorship of opposing parties in many regional conflicts. At the same time, he normalized relations with China, bringing that 30-year-old conflict to an end. And, during the late 1980s, he essentially agreed to set the peoples of Eastern Europe free, encouraging the development of what became independent, non-communist governments in Poland, Czechoslovakia, Hungary, Bulgaria, Romania, and East Germany. The developments in East Germany led directly to the tearing down of the Berlin Wall and the 1990 unification of Germany.

On August 19, 1991 Gorbachev was placed under house arrest while vacationing in the Crimea, as part of an abortive right-wing coup that failed when he refused to sign away power, and when Boris Yeltsin led the massive resistance that developed in Moscow and several other cities. The coup collapsed on August 21st, after having generated a second Russian Revolution that swept away the remnants of Soviet communism—and ultimately swept away the Soviet state itself. As it turned out, Gorbachev's day was done; he failed to hold the Soviet state together, and Yeltsin and other leaders gained control of what became a set of successor countries. Gorbachev resigned; he is seen by many throughout the world as still by far the greatest Soviet leader of the 20th century.

In 1990, Gorbachev was awarded the Nobel Peace Prize. Among his written works are *Toward a Better World* and *Perestroika: New Thinking for Our Country and the World* (both 1987), *At the Summit: A New Start in U.S.-Soviet Relations* (1988), and *Perestroika and Soviet-American Relations* (1990). Gorbachev attended Moscow State University and the Stavropol Agricultural Institute. He and Raisa Maximova Titorenko married in 1956; they have one child.

FURTHER READING

"Gorbachev. . . ." BRIAN CROZIER. *National Review*, July 19, 1993.
"History's man. . . ." ANTHONY WILSON-SMITH. *Maclean's*, Apr. 5, 1993.
The Gorbachev Encyclopedia: Mikhail Gorbachev: the Man and His Times, March 11, 1985-December 25, 1991. JOSEPH L. WIECZYNSKI, ed. C. Schlacks, 1993.
Mikhail Gorbachev and the End of Soviet Power. JOHN MILLER. St. Martin's, 1993.
"What's it all about, Gorby?" DAVID REMNICK. *Vanity Fair*, Aug. 1992.

" 'Yeltsin. . . .' " PAUL KLEBNIKOV. *Forbes*, June 8, 1992.

"Mikhail Gorbachev's. . . ." MASSIMO CALABRESI. *National Review*, Jan. 20, 1992.

Gorbachev, Yeltsin and the Last Days of the Soviet Empire. NEIL FELSHMAN. Thomas Dunne/St. Martin's, 1992.

The Sons of Sergei: Khrushchev and Gorbachev as Reformers. DONALD R. KELLY and SHANNON G. DAVIS, eds. Praeger/Greenwood, 1992.

Mikhail Gorbachev. ANNA SPROULE. Gareth Stevens, 1992.

The Gorbachev Version. RICHARD HUGO. Zebra, 1992.

Gorbachev: The Story of a Survivor. NEIL FELSHMAN. St. Martin's, 1991.

Gorbachev and After. STEPHEN WHITE. Cambridge University Press, 1991.

Gorbachev and His Reforms. RICHARD SAKWA. Prentice-Hall, 1991.

Mikhail Gorbachev. MICHEL TATU. Columbia University Press, 1991.

The Impact of Gorbachev. DEREK SPRING, ed. Columbia University Press, 1991.

Mikhail Gorbachev. JEROME MOGA. Bantam, 1991.

The Gorbachev Phenomenon: A Historical Interpretation, rev. ed. MOSHE LEWIN. University of California Press, 1991.

Mikhail Gorbachev. JOHN W. SELFRIDGE. Chelsea House, 1991.

Why Gorbachev Happened: His Triumphs and His Failure. ROBERT G. KAISER. Simon & Schuster, 1991.

Mikhail Gorbachev: Revolutionary for Democracy. ANNA SPROYLE. Gareth Stevens, 1991.

Gordon, Michael

Gordon, Michael (1909–93) Baltimore-born Michael Gordon began his acting and directing career shortly after graduating from Yale Drama School in 1932, working with New York's Theater Union and with the Group Theatre (1935–40). He moved to Hollywood in 1940, and began directing low-budget films in 1942, going back to Broadway to direct *Home of the Brave* (1945). Back in Hollywood in the late 1940s, he directed the screen adaptation of Lillian Hellman's *Another Part of the Forest* (1948) and *Cyrano de Bergerac* (1950). In 1951, he was blacklisted after refusing to "name names" before the House Un-American Activities Committee, and returned to the theater. He later reportedly did inform on others to that committee; in any event, he was removed from the blacklist, his first Hollywood film thereafter being *Pillow Talk* (1959), followed by such films as *Boys' Night Out* (1962), *Move Over Darling* (1963), and *The Impossible Years* (1970). He was survived by two daughters and a son. (d. Los Angeles; Apr. 29, 1993)

FURTHER READING

Obituary. *Variety*, May 10, 1993.
Obituary. *The Times* (of London), May 6, 1993.

Gore, Al (Albert Gore, Jr.; 1948–) As promised by President Bill Clinton, Vice-President Al Gore played a substantial role during the Clinton administration's first year, considerably beyond the "stand-by" role traditionally built into the vice-presidency. On January 22, two days after the inauguration, he announced abolition of the Bush administration's pro-business, anti-environmental Council on Competitiveness, and then went on to become chief administration spokesperson on environmental matters. He also took up the always-difficult question of governmental waste, on March 3 beginning a six-month-long "national performance review," and on September 7 introduced the Clinton-Gore "reinventing government" reorganization plan, the next night appearing on the David Letterman show as part of the administration's campaign for passage. Gore was highly visible throughout the year in support of adminstration policies, and June 25 was even able to play a very direct role, breaking the tie to pass the president's budget proposal in the Senate. In November, on the televised "Larry King Live," Gore supported the government position on the North American Free Trade Agreement (NAFTA) against political critic Ross Perot; he was widely regarded as having won the debate, possibly tipping the balance in favor of passage.

Gore is the son of longtime Tennessee Congressman and then Senator Albert Gore, and grew up in Washington, D.C. Like his father, he opposed the Vietnam War, and thought of leaving the country to avoid the draft, but in the end volunteered, seeing Army service in Vietnam (1969–71). He returned home to a job as an investigative reporter for Nashville's *The Tennessean* (1971–76). Turning to politics, he served four terms in the House of Representatives (1977–85), and was elected to the Senate in 1984. He made an unsuccessful presidential primary run in 1988, and in 1989 was positioning himself for a 1992 run when his youngest child, Albert Gore III, was seriously injured in an automobile accident. Gore spent much of his discretionary time after that focusing on his son's recovery and related family matters, and in 1991 declared himself out of the presidential race— only to find himself running with Bill Clinton in 1992.

Gore played a moderate's role during his congressional career, voting for arms control, for only some defense cuts, for civil rights, and for education, child support, and welfare reform. While focusing on his son's recovery, Gore developed a very special interest in the environment, which resulted in the book *Earth in the Balance: Ecology and the Human Spirit*, a 1992 bestseller. Also published under the names of Clinton and Gore was the campaign book *Putting People First*. Gore also spoke very strongly on environmental matters at the 1991 Rio de Janiero Earth Summit. His environmental commitment was unsuccessfully attacked by Republican leaders during the election campaign; their attempt to depict him as a "radical environmentalist," labeling him "ozone man," seemed to have little adverse effect on the Clinton-Gore campaign.

Gore attended Washington, D.C.'s St. Albans preparatory school. His 1969 B.A. was from Harvard University. He also attended the Vanderbilt University School of Religion (1971–72). He and Mary Elizabeth (Tipper) Aitcheson married in 1970; their four children are Karenna, Kristin, Sarah, and Albert III.

FURTHER READING

Al Gore: Vice President. REBECCA STEFOFF. Millbrook, 1994.

"Where are you Al?" L.J. DAVIS. *Mother Jones,* Nov.-Dec. 1993.

"The big vision. . . ." KATHERINE BARRETT and RICHARD GREENE. *Financial World,* Oct. 26, 1993.

"Al Gore. . . ." HOWARD GLECKMAN and SUSAN B. GARLAND. *Business Week,* Sep. 13, 1993.

"Has anyone seen this man?" WALTER SHAPIRO. *Esquire,* Sep. 1993.

"Ask Al Gore." *Newsweek,* Mar. 29, 1993.

"Gore. . . ." ELEANOR CLIFT. *Newsweek,* Jan. 25, 1993.

Al Gore: Vice President of the United States. BOB ITALIA. Abdo & Daughters, 1993.

Story of Bill Clinton and Al Gore. Dell, 1993.

" 'The revenge of. . . .' " HILARY MACKENZIE. *Maclean's,* Nov. 16, 1992.

"Tennessee waltz." BILL HEWITT. *People,* Nov. 16, 1992.

"How to stay in the loop." BILL TURQUE. *Newsweek,* Oct. 26, 1992.

"Al Gore's double life." ALEX S. JONES. *New York Times Magazine,* Oct. 25, 1992.

"Quayle vs. Gore." STANLEY W. CLOUD. " 'We're not measuring the drapes.' " S.C. GWYNNE and ELIZABETH TAYLOR. *Time,* Oct. 19, 1992.

"Green giant." PHILIP SHABECOFF. "What it takes. . . ." FRED BARNES. "The other Al. . . ." MARTIN PERETZ. *New Republic,* Oct. 19, 1992.

"Captain Planet for veep." RONALD BAILEY et al. *National Review,* Sep. 14, 1992.

"The wonks. . . ." SIDNEY BLUMENTHAL. *New Republic,* Aug. 3, 1992.

"Gore. . . ." WALTER SHAPIRO. *Time,* July 20, 1992.

"Baby boom ticket. . . ." ANDREW BILSKI. *Maclean's,* July 20, 1992.

"Albert Arnold Gore, Jr." *Facts on File,* July 16, 1992.

Al Gore, Jr.: His Life and Career. HANK HILLIN. Birch Lane/Carol, 1992.

Gore, Tipper

Gore, Tipper (Mary Elizabeth Aitcheson Gore; 1948–) During 1993, Tipper Gore worked as an advisor on mental health questions with the White House's Task Force on National Health Care Reform, chaired by Hillary Rodham Clinton. In doing so, she worked closely with Clinton, the two women traveling widely, both together and separately during the early, research and study period, and then working together to explain and "sell" the entire health care plan to Congress and the American people.

Gore focused strongly on including mental health care in the universal health care plan she had helped develop, in this carrying through longtime interests and commitments, especially toward children in need of mental health services. She had earlier co-chaired a National Mental Health Association children's matters group and chaired Tennessee Voices for Children, which campaigned for community-based mental health services for children, and had also worked in children's mental health advocacy groups in Washington, D.C.

Tipper Gore grew up in Virginia and attended a girl's school in Washington, D.C. She met Al Gore at his high school prom, and that meeting was to color her entire future, for they soon decided to make their lives together. He went to Harvard, and she followed him to Boston, attending Garland Junior College and graduating with a major in psychology from Boston College in 1970. They married a month after her graduation. She also gained an M.A. in clinical psychology from Nashville's George Peabody College, but did not pursue a career in psychology. She did become a photographer with Nashville's *The Tennessean* in the mid-1970s, but gave up professional photography when Al Gore was elected to Congress in 1976.

In 1985, Tipper Gore became a national figure when, with a group of other congressional wives, she led what became a national campaign to label what she felt were morally objectionable records, because their lyrics were thought to promote sex, drugs, and violence. Her highly publicized campaign included testimony before one of her husband's Senate committees. The record industry soon responded to the pressure, and agreed to label some records, an action intensely distasteful to those in the entertainment industries and to civil libertarians. Tipper Gore, who was also in favor of banning such record sales to minors—if such a ban were indeed constitutional—found herself hailed by many conservatives, who wanted to go much further, and actively disliked by many who saw her campaign as censorship. Although she went on to write *Raising PG Kids in an X-Rated Society* (1987), she ultimately pulled back from her crusade when it became clear that it was hurting her husband's 1988 presidential campaign bid. During the 1992 campaign, Democratic strategists portrayed her as misunderstood on the matter, and she went to considerable lengths to point out that she had really loved rock music ever since her teenage years. The strategy seemed to work very successfully. Tipper and Al Gore have four children: Karenna, Kristin, Sarah, and Albert III.

FURTHER READING

"The liberal in the inner circle." MATTHEW COOPER. *U.S. News & World Report*, July 19, 1993.
"Her life. . . ." SANDRA MCELWAINE. *Good Housekeeping*, Mar. 1993.
Tipper Gore. JULIE BACH. Abdo & Daughters, 1993.
Tipper Gore. JOANN B. GUERNSEY. Lerner, 1993.
"Tennessee waltz." BILL HEWITT. *People*, Nov. 16, 1992.
"First friends. . . ." HOWARD G. CHUA-EOAN. *People*, Nov. 16, 1992.
"The other partner. . . ." RICHARD LACAYO. July 20, 1992.
Running Mates. ANN GRIMES. Morrow, 1990.
"A new breed of Democratic wives. . . ." *People*, Feb. 22, 1988.
"Unfair labeling." GERALDINE A. FERRARO. *New Republic*, Jan. 18, 1988.

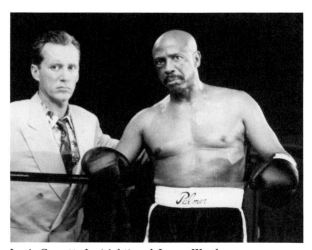

Louis Gossett, Jr. (right) and James Woods

Gossett, Louis, Jr. (1936–) Stage, screen, and television star Lou Gossett in 1993 conceived, co-produced, and starred opposite Blair Underwood in the acclaimed television film *Father and Son: Dangerous Relations*, about an African-American father who abandons his wife and 5-year-old son, only to meet his son 20 years later, when they are both in prison; Gossett's message about love and responsibility was clearly and very forcefully stated.

Gossett also starred in the television miniseries *Return to Lonesome Dove*, the sequel to the popular 1989 western miniseries; in a cast that included Jon Voight, Barbara Hershey, Rick

Schroeder, William Petersen, and Oliver Reed. Forthcoming were starring roles in the films *Curse of the Starving Class*, directed by Michael J. McClary and co-starring Kathy Bates, and James Woods; and *Flashfire*, directed by Elliot Silverstein and co-starring Billy Zane, Kristen Minter, Tom Mason, and Louis Giambalvo.

After over two decades as a highly regarded character actor in theater, films, and television, Brooklyn-born Gossett won an Emmy for his role as Fiddler in television's *Roots* (1977). He then went on to win a best supporting actor Oscar in *An Officer and a Gentleman* (1982), and to appear in such films as *Iron Eagle* (1985; and two sequels), *The Principal* (1987), *Toy Soldiers* (1991), and *Diggstown* (1992). On television, he had the title role in the miniseries "Sadat" (1983); his other telefilms include *A Gathering of Old Men* (1987), *Zora Is My Name!* (1990), *El Diablo* (1990), *Sudie and Simpson* (1990), *Carolina Skeletons* (1991), *The Josephine Baker Story* (1991), *Keeper of the City* (1992), *Liberators: Fighting on Two Fronts in World War II* (1992), and *Abraham Lincoln: A New Birth of Freedom* (1992). Gossett's B.A. was from New York University, in 1959.

FURTHER READING

"Family business. . . ." MARK GOODMAN. *People*, May 6, 1991.
"Gossett, Louis, Jr." *Current Biography*, Nov. 1990.

Gould, Jack (John Ludlow Gould; 1914–93) A leading television and radio critic, Gould began his long career in journalism right out of high school, as a copy boy for the *New York Herald Tribune*. He joined the drama department of the *New York Times* in 1937, and spent his entire career with the *Times*, retiring in 1972. From 1944, he was the newspaper's chief radio and television critic, and became a major figure as the television industry was introduced and grew enormously in the late 1940s and during the 1950s. His major contributions were in the areas of responsible programming and ethics, as television news departments fought for their place in the world of commercial television, and as that world spawned a succession of scandals. He was survived by three sons. (d. Concord, California; May 24, 1993)

FURTHER READING

Obituary. *The Times* (of London), May 28, 1993.

Gow, Ronald (1897–1993) British writer and producer Ronald Gow was a teacher before turning fully to the stage in the early 1930s. His first major success came in 1934, with his stage adaptation of Walter Greenwood's Depression-era novel *Love On the Dole*; the play featured Wendy Hiller as Sally Hardcastle in her first starring role. Hiller and Gow married in 1937; she also later starred in his stage adaptations of *Tess of the D'Urbervilles* (1946) and *Ann Veronica* (1949). Gow's many other plays included *A Full Treatment* (1959) and *A Boston Story* (1966), though none of his works enjoyed the impact and success of *Love On the Dole*. He was survived by Wendy Hiller, and their daughter and son. (d. April 27, 1993)

FURTHER READING

Obituary. *The Times* (of London), May 4, 1993.

Graf, Steffi (Stephanie Maria Graf; 1969–) The violence of an obsessed fan cast a shadow over all of tennis in 1993 and over Steffi Graf in particular. In April, at the WTA Citizen Cup in Hamburg, a German man obsessed with Graf reached over the spectator's fence during a changeover and stabbed Monica Seles in the back, his avowed intention to keep her from playing and so to allow Graf to regain her number-one ranking in the world. Clearly shaken, Graf lost in the finals at the match.

The two had dominated women's tennis in the previous two years, with Seles somewhat stronger, but Graf close behind. With Seles out, as she was through the end of 1993, Graf seemed, as one observer put it, sad and solitary. Graf was one of the first to visit Seles in the hospital, expressing shock and support from herself and other players, but she had no power to change the event.

During the rest of the year, Graf racked up victories over almost all of the opponents that came her way, winning eight out of the nine events she entered, including the French Open (her first since 1988), Wimbledon (her fifth, despite a painful foot ailment), the German Open (her seventh), the Canadian Open, the U.S. Open (her third), and after October foot surgery, the Virginia Slims (her third), bringing her total Grand Slam titles to 14 and in the process breaking Seles's 1992 record for single-year earnings with a total of over $2.8 million. Graf was also one of the many tennis stars who played in the Arthur Ashe Tennis Challenge to benefit the Arthur Ashe Foundation to Defeat AIDS in August.

Steffi Graf emerged as a leading under-14 tennis player in the early 1980s, turning professional at age 13. She won the German Open in 1986 and from 1987 was the world's dominant tennis player, with a string of 66 consecutive victories. She took the French Open in 1987, and became World Champion in 1988, the year she won the U.S., Wimbledon, Australian, and French Opens, along with the Olympic championship. Among her succeeding major victories were the U.S., Wimbledon, and German Opens again in 1989; the Australian Open in 1990; and Wimbledon in 1991 and 1992. During that period, she held the number one world ranking for a record 186 consecutive weeks, before losing it to Monica Seles in 1991, and regaining it only temporarily later that year. Graf was coached from her earliest years by her father, Peter, and then by Pavel Slozil (1987–91).

FURTHER READING

"Dark star." HARM CLUEVER and PETER RIEBSCHLAEGER. *Tennis*, Nov. 1992.
"The spirit of '88." ANDREA LEAND. *World Tennis*, Feb. 1991.
Steffi Graf. JAMES R. ROTHAUS. Child's World, 1991.
Steffi Graf. Little, Brown, 1990.
"Serving her country." CURRY KIRKPATRICK. *Sports Illustrated*, June 26, 1989.
"Graf, Steffi." *Current Biography*, Feb. 1989.
Steffi Graf. JUDY MONROE. Crestwood House/Macmillan, 1988.

Granger, Stewart (James Lablache Stewart; 1913–93) A romantic action film star of the 1940s and 1950s, Stewart Granger began his career on stage in repertory in the mid-1930s, making his London stage debut in *The Sun Never Sets* (1938). After wartime military service, he emerged as a star in *The Man In Grey* (1943), following up with such films as *Fanny By Gaslight* (1943), *Waterloo Road* (1944), *Caesar and Cleopatra* (1945), *Captain Boycott* (1947), and *Saraband For Dead Lovers* (1948). The Hollywood portion of his career began with *King Solomon's Mines* (1950), and included such films as *Scaramouche* (1952), *The Prisoner of Zenda*

(1952), *Beau Brummel* (1954), *Moonfleet* (1955), and *Bhowani Junction* (1956). His career waned from the 1960s, though he did such films as *Sodom and Gomorrah* (1962) and *The Wild Geese* (1978), and appeared in television. Granger's Broadway debut came more than half a century after his London stage debut, in Somerset Maugham's *The Circle*, opposite Glynis Johns and Rex Harrison. In 1981, he published *Sparks Fly Upward*. Granger's first and second wives were the actresses Elspeth March and Jean Simmons, his third Viviane Lecerf. He was survived by three daughters and a son. (d. Los Angeles; August 16, 1993)

FURTHER READING

Obituary. *Variety*, Aug. 30, 1993.
Obituary. "The Briton picked. . . ." DAVID ROBINSON. *The Times* (of London), Aug. 18, 1993.
Obituary. *New York Times*, Aug. 18, 1993.

Greenspan, Alan (1926–) Federal Reserve System head Alan Greenspan, long a conservative mainstay in American government, decisively threw his support toward economic stimulation and the economic initiatives of the incoming Clinton administration during 1993. On Wednesday, February 17, he emphasized that support, sitting beside Hillary Rodham Clinton during President Clinton's televised speech before Congress and the nation, and on February 19 he specifically endorsed Clinton's deficit reduction package and financial stimulus plans before the Senate Banking Committee, even suggesting that the Federal Reserve might be willing to cut interest rates further to stimulate the economy, should the Clinton plan prove to be a temporary depressant. Although the economic stimulus package was defeated by a Republican filibuster, Greenspan continued to restimulate the economy throughout the year, lifting restrictions that made it difficult for banks to lend to small businesses, keeping interest rates low, and consistently acting to create conditions in which economic growth could occur. Given the deflationary impact of much of the Clinton program, it became clear that Greenspan and the Federal Reserve were the chief source of economic stimulus in the United States, and that Greenspan had reversed the role he had played during the Republican years. He remained cautious in his public utterances, however, continuing to warn that interest rates must inevitably go up again in the future, and that their upturn would come quickly if warranted by an inflationary surge.

Greenspan, a leading free-market economic conservative, was a key economic consultant to presidents Nixon and Ford, and was chairman of the National Council of Economic Advisors (1974–76). He moved into the center of national economic activity when he was appointed head of the Federal Reserve System by President Ronald Reagan. He was reappointed to a second term by President Bush in July 1991. During 1992, as the deep recession worsened and unemployment grew, Greenspan began to revise his long-held optimistic view of the economy; by early September 1992, the Federal Reserve had lowered its discount rate and federal funds rate to 3 percent—and to little immediate avail, much to the discomfort of President George Bush, who lost the White House in November largely on economic issues. A New Yorker, Greenspan received his B.S. in 1948, his M.A. in 1950, and his Ph.D. in 1977, all from New York University.

FURTHER READING

"Look who's talking, too." ALAN GREENBLATT. "Why Alan Greenspan. . . ." WILLIAM GREIDER. *Washington Monthly*, Dec. 1993.
Lost Prophets: An Insider's View of the Modern Economists. ALFRED L. MALABRE. Harvard Business, 1993.
"The politician-economist. . . ." GLORIA BORGER. *U.S. News & World Report*, July 1, 1991.
"Alan Greenspan's. . . . " ROB NORTON. *Fortune*, Apr. 8, 1991.
"Is Alan Greenspan impotent?" ROBIN WRIGHT. *New Republic*, Apr. 9, 1990.
"Greenspan, Alan." *Current Biography*, Jan. 1989.

Gretzky, Wayne (1961–) Hockey great

Wayne Gretzky was sidelined for eight months with a back injury that threatened his career. Troubled by the cumulative effects of blindside hits over his hockey-playing years, more proximately he received an accidental blow during pre-season training camp in 1992, which placed him in a hospital, where doctors feared paralysis. His wife, Janet Jones, was already in the hospital, about to give birth to their third child. Months of rehabilitation followed for the painful

condition. Not until December 1992 was Gretzky able to once again take to the ice, and then only under the careful direction of his doctors. By January 1993 he joined his teammates for squad practice and then resumed play. Even so, on June 1993, after his Los Angeles Kings were defeated by the Montreal Canadiens in the Stanley Cup finals, he suggested that he might retire.

But by September 1993, he had signed a new three-year contract for $25.5 million, and in October kicked off the new season with a remarkable 7 goals and 17 assists in the opening game, and seemed ready to resume his expert play. Whether he would once again be dominant in a game that included younger stars such as Mario Lemieux and Eric Lindros remained to be seen.

After early play with the Peterborough Petes and Sault Ste. Marie Greyhounds (both 1978–79) and the Indianapolis Racers (1978–79), Ontario-born Gretzky became the leading player of the National Hockey League (NHL) during the 1980s, as high-scoring center for the Edmonton Oilers (1979–88), then the Los Angeles Kings (1988–). He was rookie of the year (1979), the NHL's Most Valuable Player nine times in ten years (1980–87, 1989), and seven times the league's leading point scorer (1981–87), in October 1990 reaching a landmark 2000 points in regular season, a record building since then. He has also received the Lady Byng Memorial trophy (1980; 1991–92); the Art Ross Memorial trophy (1981–87; 1991–92), and the Conn Smythe trophy as MVP in the playoffs (1985; 1988), and was named Sportsman of the Year (1982) by *Sports Illustrated*. His publications include *Gretzky: From the Backyard Rink to the Stanley Rink* (1985), written with Jim Taylor, and *Gretzky: An Autobiography* (1990), written with Rick Reilly. He married Janet Jones in 1988; they have three children.

FURTHER READING

"Wayne's world." WALTER ROESSING. *Boys' Life*, Mar. 1993.
Wayne Gretzky: A Biography. GERRY REDMOND. InBook, 1993.
Wayne Gretzky. ALEKSANDRS ROZENS. Rourke, 1993.
"Say it ain't so. . . ." JAMES DEACON and NORA UNDERWOOD. *Maclean's*, Oct. 5, 1992.
Wayne Gretzky. J. ROMAINE. Outlet, 1992.
Wayne Gretzky. Scholastic, 1992.
"Ten living legends. . . ." STEVE WULF. *Sports Illustrated*, Dec. 23, 1991.

"A great 30th. . . ." JAY GREENBERG. *Sports Illustrated*, Jan. 28, 1991.
Wayne Gretzky: Hockey Great. Tom Raber. Lerner, 1991.
"The charmed life of Wayne and Janet." *Chatelaine*, Nov, 1990.
Wayne Gretzky. Steve Hanks. St. Martin's, 1990.

Griffith, Melanie (1957–)

In yet another major film role, Melanie Griffith in 1993 starred in *Born Yesterday*, based on the Garson Kanin play and a remake of the 1950 George Cukor classic film comedy. She was the not-at-all-stupid former showgirl Billie Dawn, in the role originated by Judy Holliday, opposite John Goodman as Harry Brock, in the Broderick Crawford role—now a wheeler-dealer real estate operator, but in 1950 a scrap metal king. Griffith's husband, Don Johnson, starred in the William Holden role. Luis Mandoki directed the film, which received mixed reviews, though Griffith was well received in the role. Forthcoming were starring roles in the films *Nobody's Fool*, written and directed by Robert Benton and co-starring Paul Newman, Jessica Tandy, and Bruce Willis; and *Milk Money*, directed by Richard Benjamin.

New York City-born Griffith got off to a quick start, playing strong young supporting roles in three 1975 films: *Night Moves*, *The Drowning Pool*, and *Smile*, but then encountered personal and professional problems. She re-emerged as a leading dramatic actress in the mid-1980s, in such films as *Something Wild* (1986), *The Milagro Beanfield War* (1988), and *Stormy Monday* (1988), scored a major hit opposite Harrison Ford in *Working Girl* (1988; she won an Oscar nomination), and followed up with starring roles in *Pacific Heights* (1990), *The Bonfire of the Vanities* (1990), *Paradise* (1991), *Shining Through* (1992), and *A Stranger Among Us* (1992). She is married to actor Don Johnson; they have one child.

FURTHER READING

"The hottest romance. . . ." STEVE DITLEA and NANCY STEDMAN. *Redbook*, Mar. 1993.
"In the bedroom. . . ." MERYL GORDON. *Redbook*, Jan. 1992.
"Melanie Griffith. . . ." LAURIE WERNER. *Woman's Day*, Nov. 26, 1991.
"Melanie Griffith." BILL HIGGINS. *Los Angeles Magazine*, Oct. 1991.
"Griffith, Melanie." *Current Biography*, Oct. 1990.
"Melanie mellows out." BONNIE SIEGLER. *Ladies Home Journal*, Oct. 1990.
The New Breed: Actors Coming of Age. KAREN HARDY and KEVIN J. KOFFLER. Holt, 1988.

Grimond, Joseph (1913–93)

Scottish-born Grimond, a leading British Liberal politician of the 1950s and 1960s, entered politics after military service during World War II, in 1945, losing his first bid for a parliamentary seat. After working for the the United Nations Relief and Rehabilitation Adminstration and as the director of the Scottish National Trust, he won a parliamentary seat in the 1950 elections, becoming one of nine Liberals in the House of Commons. He was leader of the Liberal Party (1956–67), a period in which his party at first substantially increased its popular vote and then fell back sharply. He continued to be a leading figure in his party until his move to the House of Lords (1983). Grimond wrote many essays and newspaper articles and several books, among them his *Memoirs* (1979). He was survived by his wife, Laura, a daughter, and two sons. (d. Orkney, Scotland; October 24, 1993)

FURTHER READING

"Marching to the sound. . . ." IAN AITKEN. *New Statesman & Society*, Nov. 12, 1993.
Obituary. *Economist*, Oct. 30, 1993.
Obituary. *The Times* (of London), Oct. 26, 1993.
Obituary. *New York Times*, Oct. 26, 1993.

Grisham, John (c. 1955–)

It was a record-setting year for John Grisham. In March 1993, he published *The Client*, focusing on a children's advocate and her 11-year-old client, who has inadvertently learned some dangerous secrets; the novel immediately shot to the top of the best-seller list. That same month, Grisham's previous three legal thrillers held the top three spots on the mass market paperback best-seller list, the combination being an all-time first. Cassette versions of all of his novels also held four of the top 10 spots on the audiobook best-seller list.

Three of Grisham's books were also in film production at the same time, believed to be another first. *The Firm*, filmed by Sydney Pollack and starring Tom Cruise, Wilford Brimley, and

Gene Hackman, became a major hit when released in July, sparking even greater sales of the book, which by that time had over 10 million copies in print. *The Pelican Brief*, directed by Alan Pakula and starring Denzel Washington and Julia Roberts as the law student who figures out who planned the assassination of two Supreme Court justices, opened late in 1993. Meanwhile Joel Schumacher was filming *The Client*. In addition, Universal Pictures agreed to pay a record-breaking $3.75 million for the film rights to Grisham's next, still-untitled novel.

In 1993, Grisham and his wife also announced formation of the Renee and John Grisham Fund at the University of Mississippi in Oxford, wholly funding a new Emerging Southern Writers in Residence program and reviving the Visiting Writers series formerly run (1979–1991) by previous writer-in-residence Willie Morris.

Grisham began his writing career with a courtroom drama involving paternal revenge, *A Time to Kill* (1989). Only a modest success on its initial publication, its sales took off with the success of his next two books, *The Firm* (1991) and *The Pelican Brief* (1992), both runaway bestsellers. Grisham's J.D. was from the University of Mississippi. He practiced law in Southhaven, Mississippi, and was elected to the Mississippi House of Representatives in 1984, resigning before the conclusion of his second term, when his books began to be lucrative. He is married to Renee Grisham; they have two children.

FURTHER READING

"Grisham, John." *Current Biography*, Sep. 1993.
"The Grisham brief." ROBIN STREET. *Writer's Digest*, July 1993.
"John Grisham. . . ." MICHELLE BEARDEN. *Publishers Weekly*, Feb. 22, 1993.
"Tales out of court." KIM HUBBARD. *People*, Mar. 16, 1992.

Guinier, Lani (Carol Lani Guinier; 1949–) Law professor Lani Guinier found herself in the midst of a firestorm in 1993, after President Bill Clinton nominated her on April 29th to head the Justice Department's Civil Rights Division. Conservatives immediately mounted an attack on her record, labeling her the "quota queen," and focusing on recent articles on the Voting Rights Act proposing "weighted voting" to give minorities more rep-

resentation where discrimination is widespread. Such ideas are not new, and are used in some local communities with the approval of the Justice Department, but the Clinton administration—occupied with other matters—failed to defend Guinier, and reportedly asked her to wait until confirmation hearings before defending herself. That time never came. As chances of confirmation diminished, the administration withdrew the nomination on June 3rd, provoking another storm, this time from many African-Americans. Clinton, a law school classmate, later said he had not previously read the controversial articles and could not support them. Guinier herself took the high road, in a June 4th news conference defending her own record and refusing to criticize Clinton personally. In July, Guinier was given the Torch of Courage award by the NAACP.

New York-born Guinier, daughter of noted lawyer and academic Ewart Guinier, received her B.A. cum laude from Radcliffe College (Harvard University) in 1971, and her J.D. in 1974 from Yale Law School, where she met Bill Clinton and Hillary Rodham. After serving as a law clerk (1974–76) and juvenile court referee (1976–77) in Michigan, she became a special assistant in the Civil Rights Division of the Department of Justics (1981–88) in the Carter administration. She was later assistant counsel at the NAACP Legal Defense & Educational Fund (1981–88), before becoming a professor at the University of Pennsylvania Law School (1988–). She is married to Nolan Bowie and has one child, Nikolas.

FURTHER READING

"Lani Guinier. . . ." DAVID J. GARROW. *Progressive*, Sep. 1993.
"Guinier. . . ." ELLIS COSE. *Newsweek*, Aug. 23, 1993.
"Idea woman." *New Yorker*, June 14, 1993.
"Guinier miss. . . ." ABIGAIL THERNSTROM. *New Republic*, June 14, 1993.

Gunn, Moses (1929–93) St. Louis-born Moses Gunn taught speech and drama at Grambling College before moving to New York City in the early 1960s to pursue a professional career in the theater. He made his 1962 New York stage debut in *The Blacks*, and went on to play in a wide range of works, among them *In White America*, *Titus Andronicus*, *Twelfth Night*,

Othello, The Poison Tree (he received a Tony nomination), *The First Breeze of Summer, Daddy Goodness,* and *Blood Knot,* and won several Obie Awards, as well as a distinguished performer award for his 1967–68 appearances with the Negro Ensemble Company. He also played in several feature films, including *Nothing But a Man, The Great White Hope, Shaft, The Iceman Cometh,* and *Ragtime* (he won an Image Award). His many television roles included that of Kintango in "Roots" (1977; he received an Emmy nomination). He was survived by his wife, Gwendolyn Gunn, a daughter, a son, three sisters, and a brother. (d. Guilford, Connecticut; December 17, 1993)

FURTHER READING

Obituary. *Variety,* Dec. 26, 1993.
Obituary. *New York Times,* Dec. 20, 1993.

Gwynne, Fred (Frederick Hubbard Gwynne; 1926–93) New York City-born Fred Gwynne, a versatile stage and screen actor best known for his comic television roles, made his Broadway stage debut in *Mrs. McThing* (1952), also appearing in *Irma La Douce* (1954). He emerged as a television star as a police officer in the series "Car 54, Where Are You?" (1961–63), and became a household name and worldwide celebrity as Herman Munster in the series "The Munsters" (1964–66). He also played strong supporting roles in many theatrical and television films, while also starring and playing strong supporting roles in a wide range of plays, winning an off-Broadway Obie award for his role in *Grand Magic* (1979). His plays included *Cat on a Hot Tin Roof* (1974) and the *Texas Trilogy* (1976), while his films included *The Cotton Club* (1984), *Fatal Attraction* (1987), and *My Cousin Vinny* (1992). He was also the author of several children's books, from *Best In Show* (1958) to *Easy to See Why* (1993). He was survived by his wife, Deborah Flater, two daughters, and two sons. (d. Taneytown, Maryland; July 2, 1993)

FURTHER READING

Obituary. *Publishers Weekly,* July 26, 1993.
Obituary. *Variety,* July 6, 1993.
Obituary. *The Times* (of London), July 5, 1993.
Obituary. *New York Times,* July 3, 1993.

Gene Hackman (left) and Clint Eastwood

Hackman, Gene (1930–) Veteran film star Gene Hackman was much honored in 1993 for his role as the brutal sheriff in Clint Eastwood's 1992 western *Unforgiven*; Hackman was named best supporting actor with an Academy Award, as well as the British Academy of Film and Television Arts, Golden Globes, and the National Society of Film Critics. In 1993, Hackman starred as a corrupt lawyer, opposite Tom Cruise as his honest protégé, in the blockbuster commercial success *The Firm*, directed by Sydney Pollack and based on the best-selling John Grisham novel. Hackman also starred as General George Crook in the film *Geronimo*, about the Apache guerrilla fighter, opposite Wes Studi in the title role, and Robert Duvall as Indian scout Al Sieber; Walter Hill directed. Hackman was also one of many celebrities who did read-

ings for Bill Couturie's ecological conservation film *Earth and the American Dream*. Forthcoming was the western film *The Quick and the Dead*, co-starring Sharon Stone.

California-born Hackman became a star in his best actor Oscar-winning role as Popeye Doyle in *The French Connection* (1971), a role he repeated in *The French Connection II* (1975). Among his other films are *The Poseidon Adventure* (1972), *The Conversation* (1974), *Night Moves* (1975), the notable *Mississippi Burning* (1988), *The Package* (1989), *Postcards from the Edge* (1990), *Narrow Margin* (1990), *Loose Cannons* (1990), *Class Action* (1991), and *Company Business* (1991). In 1992, he starred on Broadway opposite Glenn Close and Richard Dreyfuss in Ariel Dorfman's play *Death and the Maiden*. He was previously married to Faye Maltese, and has three children.

FURTHER READING

"Gene Hackman's winning wave." JOHN CULHANE. *Reader's Digest*, Sep. 1993.
"Hollywood's uncommon man." MICHAEL NORMAN. *New York Times Magazine*, Mar. 19, 1989.
"Fire this time. . . ." ELIZABETH L. BLAND et al. *Time*, Jan. 9, 1989.
Gene Hackman. ALLAN HUNTER. St. Martin's, 1988.

Haggard, William (Richard Henry Clayton; 1907–93) Richard Clayton pursued two careers, as a civil service administrator and as best-selling spy novelist William Haggard. As Clayton, he joined the Indian Civil Service in

1931, and became a judge in India during the 1930s. He spent World War II in Special Operations in India and Burma, and after the war returned to Britain, and was administrator in the Board of Trade from 1946 until his retirement in 1969. He began his writing career in 1958, with the novel *Slow Burner*, in which he created the continuing character who appeared in all of his books: Colonel Charles Russell of the Security Service, who survived through more than a score of novels, ending with *The Vendetta* (1990). He also published *The Little Rug Book* (1972), about oriental carpet collecting. He was survived by a daughter and a son. (d. October 7, 1993)

FURTHER READING

Obituary. *The Times* (of London), Nov. 5, 1993.

Haldeman, H.R. "Bob" (Harry Robbins Haldeman; 1926–93) Los Angeles-born H.R. Haldeman was an advertising executive before working in Richard M. Nixon's 1956 vice-presidential campaign. He was Nixon's chief advance man during the 1960 presidential campaign and Nixon's 1968 presidential campaign manager. As Nixon's White House Chief of Staff (1969–73), he became a major figure, who used his ability to control access to the president to develop considerable personal political power, which he wielded very abrasively. As the Watergate scandal developed, it became clear that he had been a central figure, and on April 30, 1973 he was forced to resign. He was convicted of Watergate-related charges in 1975, and served 18 months in prison, then spending the rest of his life in business in California. Haldeman published the book *The Ends of Power* (1978), written with Joseph DiMona. He was survived by his wife, Joanne Horton, two daughters, and two sons. (d. Santa Barbara, California; November 12, 1993)

FURTHER READING

"President Nixon's alter ego." TOM MORGANTHAU. *Newsweek*, Nov. 22, 1993.
Obituary. *The Times* (of London), Nov. 15, 1993.
Obituary. *New York Times*, Nov. 13, 1993.

Hall, Adelaide (1901–93) New York City-born Adelaide Hall made her Broadway debut in the chorus of the historic Eubie Blake-Noble Sissle African-American musical *Shuffle Along* (1921) and was featured in the musical *Runnin' Wild* (1923). She gained recognition as a major jazz singer with her improvised melody opposite Duke Ellington on their recording of "Creole Love Call" (1927). She starred on Broadway in *Blackbirds of 1928*, introducing the classic "I Can't Give You Anything But Love" and dancing opposite Bill "Bojangles" Robinson in the hit show. She toured Europe with the show, and stayed in Paris in 1929, liking what she saw and having no desire to return to American racism. Although she spent the early 1930s back in the United States in vaudeville and cabaret, she and her husband, Bert Hicks, returned to Europe in 1934, ran several nightclubs in Paris and London, and settled in London. She became a popular radio and recording star, appeared in London in *Kiss Me Kate* (1951) and and several other shows, and appeared on Broadway in *Jamaica* (1957). Her career sagged after Hicks's death in 1963, but she made a comeback in concert in the 1970s and 1980s. There were no survivors. (d. London; Nov. 7, 1993)

FURTHER READING

Obituary. *Billboard*, Nov. 20, 1993.
Obituary. *New York Times*, Nov. 10, 1993.
Obituary. *The Times* (of London), Nov. 8, 1993.

Hall, Arsenio (1955–) In the 1993 late-night talk show wars, David Letterman's move to CBS opposite Jay Leno on the "Tonight" show, and the addition of Chevy Chase with his own offering, caused many to predict the demise of Arsenio Hall's talk show. Certainly Hall's ratings dropped, but by year's end, Chase had dropped out of the running and Hall was still holding his own. In January, on Hall's 4th anniversary show, President Bill Clinton appeared via video. On May 13, 1993, Hall held a celebratory 1,000th program at the Hollywood Bowl; airing May 14th, and benefiting the Magic Johnson Foundation, the program featured Naughty By Nature (with Heavy D) and Duran Duran, and climaxed with guest star Madonna doing torrid versions of "Fever" and "The Lady Is a Tramp." Earlier in March and then again in May, Hall broke industry taboos by having as a guest lesbian comedian Lea DeLaria, the first comic to do openly gay material on a major late-night television show.

Also in 1993, Hall made his debut as executive producer of the film *Bopha!*, directed by Morgan Freeman and starring Danny Glover and Alfre Woodard, about South Africa's 1976 Soweto uprisings, shot in Zimbabwe; he consulted with Nelson Mandela on the film's authenticity. In September, Hall and Paula Abdul again hosted a two-hour television special, *In a New Light*, with numerous celebrities providing music, comedy, and commentary to change views about AIDS.

Cleveland-born Hall began his career as a standup comedian in the late 1970s, and moved to Los Angeles in the early 1980s. His first sustained talk show exposure was on the late-night "Thicke of the Night" (1983); he was also host of "Solid Gold," a pop music series. He was a guest host on Fox's "The Late Show" in 1987, and appeared in the film *Coming to America* (1988), before breaking through with "The Arsenio Hall Show" (1989-). His B.A. was from Kent State University.

FURTHER READING

"Arsenio gets serious." DEBORAH GREGORY. *Essence*, Nov. 1993.
"Arsenio Hall." LAWRENCE GROBEL. *TV Guide*, May 8, 1993.
Arsenio Hall. NORMAN KING. Morrow, 1993.
"The big dis." ROD LURIE. *Los Angeles*, Nov. 1992.
"Claiming the late-night crown." LYNN NORMENT. *Ebony*, June, 1992.
"Arsenio Hall. . . ." MARK HARRIS. *Entertainment*, Apr. 17, 1992.
"Arsenio Hall talks. . . ." LAURA B. RANDOLPH. *Ebony*, Dec. 1990.
"The rise and rise. . . ." DIGBY DIEHL. *Cosmopolitan*, Mar. 1990.
" 'Let's get busy!'. . . ." RICHARD ZOGLIN. *Time*, Nov. 13, 1989.
"Alone at the top." PATRICK GOLDSTEIN. *Rolling Stone*, Nov. 2, 1989.
"Late-night cool." MICHAEL NORMAN. *New York Times Magazine*, Oct. 1, 1989.
"Hall, Arsenio." *Current Biography*, Sep. 1989.

Hani, Chris (Martin Thembisile Hani; 1942–93)

On April 10, 1993, Chris Hani, the General Secretary of the South African Communist Party, was assassinated by right-wing White gunmen outside his home in Boksburg, in the Transvaal, east of Johannesburg. In response, rioting broke out in several townships and cities, most notably in Cape Town, with many injuries and at least 15 South African dead of all ethnic and racial groups. But repeated pleas by African National Congress (ANC) leader Nelson Mandela, President F.W. De Klerk, Archbishop Desmond Tutu, and other leaders to keep the peace and not disrupt the negotiations toward multiracial democracy then in process were ultimately successful, the murder seeming to draw South Africans together rather than split them and destroy the peace process.

On Oct. 14, 1993, Janusz Walus, a member of the fascist Africaner Resistance Movement, and Clive Derby-Lewis, a leading Conservative Party activist, were convicted of the murder and sentenced to death. The latter's wife, Gaye Derby-Lewis, was acquitted.

Chris Hani became an African National Congress activist while still in high school in Transkei. His college degree was in classics, from largely White Rhodes University in Grahamstown. In 1962, he joined the ANC military wing, the Unkonto we Size (Spear of the Nation). Arrested and convicted soon after, he jumped bail and fled abroad after his appeal was denied, thereafter fighting in Zimbabwe (Rhodesia) until arrested in neighboring Botswana, where he was imprisoned for two years. He ran substantial guerrilla operations out of Lesotho into South Africa during the later 1970s and early 1980s, becoming army chief of staff (1987), and then general secretary of the South African Communist Party (1991). He returned to South Africa in 1990, and while at first skeptical of the power-sharing negotiations that characterized the beginning of a new day for his country had in 1993 become a leading figure in the move toward peaceful reconciliation in South Africa. He was survived by his wife, Limpho, and three daughters.

FURTHER READING

"Death of a black militant. . . ." RUSSELL WATSON and MARK WHITAKER. *Newsweek*, Apr. 19, 1993.
"A martyr for the young lions." SCOTT MACLEOD. *Time*, Apr. 19, 1993.
Obituary. *The Times* (of London), Apr. 12, 1993.

Hanks, Tom (1956–)

In 1993, Tom Hanks starred with substantial success in two very different films. He and Meg Ryan co-starred as lovers who meet only near the end of the film in

FURTHER READING

"A Philadelphia Story." BRAD GOOCH. *Advocate*, Dec. 14, 1993.
"Tom Hanks. . . ." JENNET CONANT. *Esquire*, Dec. 1993.
"The players." ANDREW CORSELLO and AMY DONOHUE. "Tom, Denzel and me." DAVID BERTUGLI. *Philadelphia*, Dec. 1993.
"The nice man. . . ." LISA SCHWARZBAUM et al. *Entertainment*, July 9, 1993.
"Big again." BRUCE WEBER and DAVID WILD. *Vogue*, July 1993.
" 'It's a cool gig' . . . ." CAROL TROY. *American Film*, Apr. 1990.
"Tom Hanks." NANCY ANDERSON. *Good Housekeeping*, May 1989.
"Tom Hanks, seriously." CHRISTOPHER CONNELLY. *Premiere*, Apr. 1989.
"Hanks, Tom." *Current Biography*, Apr. 1989.
"Hanks to you." BEVERLY WALKER. *Film Comment*, Mar.-Apr. 1989.
"Playboy interview. . . ." DAVID SHEFF. *Playboy*, Mar. 1989.
Tom Hanks. TRAKIN. St. Martin's, 1987.

Sleepless In Seattle, a light romantic comedy that was a great success during the summer season. The film was directed by Nora Ephron, shot by Sven Nykvist, and co-written by Ephron, David S. Ward, and Jeff Arch, based on a story by Arch.

In December, Hanks starred in a very heavyweight film, indeed, the well-received AIDS-discrimination story, *Philadelphia*, directed and produced by Jonathan Demme. Hanks played a rising young attorney fired for alleged incompetence but in fact for having AIDS, opposite Denzel Washington as Hanks's own lawyer in the discrimination case brought by Hanks against his old law firm; the cast included Jason Robards as a leading member of the old firm, Mary Steenburgen as Robards's assistant, Antonio Banderas as Hanks's companion, and Joanne Woodward and Julius "Dr. J." Erving in cameos.

California-born Hanks appeared in the television series "Bosom Buddies" (1980–82), then emerged as a film star in the mid-1980s, with *Splash* (1984), and went on to star in such films as *Bachelor Party* (1984), *Volunteers* (1985), *The Man with One Red Shoe*, (1985), *The Money Pit* (1986), *Every Time We Say Goodbye* (1986), *Big* (1988), *Punchline* (1988), *Turner and Hooch* (1989), *Joe Versus the Volcano* (1990), and *The Bonfire of the Vanities* (1990). Hanks attended California State University at Sacramento. He is married to Rita Wilson; they have two children.

Havel, Vaclav (1936–) Playwright, symbol of dissent, and first president of free Czechoslovakia, Vaclav Havel is a major figure in recent European history. On July 17, 1992, after the Slovak National Council had passed a declaration of sovereignty, Havel resigned his presidency, saying that he could no longer function as president because he opposed the breakup of his country. On Febuary 2, 1993, he became the first President of the new Czech Republic, separated from independent Slovakia. During the balance of the year, substantial problems developed between the two new countries as they went their separate ways. Czech-Slovak trade dropped sharply, an abortive currency union was quickly scrapped, and disputes over such matters as former shared property and border matters proved hard to resolve, as was the question of the flow of refugees through both countries into Germany, after Germany sharply limited asylum under internal Nazi pressure.

On Aug. 26, Havel and Russian President Boris Yeltsin signed a Czech-Russian friendship treaty, officially proclaiming a new era of amity between the two countries; but by year's end new Czech fears had arisen, as fascism and nationalism rose in Russia, signaled by the strong electoral showing of Russian fascist Vladimir

Zhirinovsky; and as Nazi strength once again grew in neighboring Germany.

Havel has been a leading Czech playwright since the early 1960s; such plays as *The Garden Party* (1963) and *The Memorandum* (1967) helped bring about the "Prague Spring" of 1968, and were repressed after the Soviet invasion that destroyed the new Czech government. Havel's plays were banned from the Czech stage for two decades while he continued to be a leading dissenter. A leader of the Charter 77 organization in 1977, he was under house arrest (1977–79), in prison (1979–1983), and again in prison (early 1989).

On December 29, 1989, he became interim President, the first non-communist president of his country since 1948. On July 5, 1990 he was re-elected to the presidency for a full two-year term. In power, he dealt with the aftermath of the Communist decades, and began to move Czechoslovakia into the European and world economies. On June 21, 1991 the last Soviet troops left Czechoslovakia. On June 28, 1991 a Budapest meeting of Eastern European leaders disbanded the multinational Council for Mutual Economic Assistance (Comecon), a Soviet economic control instrument. On July 1, 1991 Havel hosted a Prague meeting of Eastern European leaders, which disbanded the Warsaw Pact, the last remaining instrument of Soviet military control.

In 1964, Havel married Olga Splíchalová, to whom he wrote *Letters to Olga* (1989) from prison. Among his other non-dramatic works were *Vaclav Havel; Or, Living in Truth* (1987), *Open Letters; Selected Writings 1965–1990* (1990), and *Summer Meditations: On Politics, Morality and Civility In a Time of Transition* (1992).

FURTHER READING

" 'There is a kind of absurdity.' " ANDREW NAGORSKI. *Newsweek*, Feb. 1, 1993.

"The short, happy exile. . . ." GUY MARTIN. *Esquire*, Feb. 1993.

"Public enemies." VLADIMIR TISMANEANU. *Society*, Jan.-Feb. 1993.

" 'I cherish a certain hope.' " LANCE MORROW. *Time*, Aug. 3, 1992.

"Crushed velvet." HENRIK BERING-JENSEN. *Insight*, June 1, 1992.

"A conversation with. . . ." ADAM MICHNIK. *World Press Review*, Mar. 1992.

"Scenes from 'Absurdistan.' " ROBERT ELIAS. *Humanist*, Jan.-Feb. 1992.

" 'Uncertain Strength'. . . ." DANA EMINGEROVA et al. *New York Review of Books*, Aug. 15, 1991.

"Havel's choice." STEPHEN SCHIFF. *Vanity Fair*. Aug. 1991.

" 'Parallels with a prison'. . . ." ANDREW NAGORSKI. *Newsweek*, July 22, 1991.

"Vaclav Havel." LINA WERTMULLER et al. *Interview*, May 1991.

Vaclav Havel: The Authorized Biography. EDA KRISEOVA. Atlantic Monthly, 1991; St. Martin's, 1993.

After the Velvet Revolution: Vaclav Havel and the New Leaders of Czechoslovakia Speak Out. TIM D. WHIPPLE, ED. Freedom House, 1991.

Hawking, Stephen William (1942–)

British physicist Stephen Hawking's new 1993 book was actually a compilation of the new and the not-so-new. In *Black Holes and Baby Universes: And Other Essays*, Hawking gathered various articles, including his first for a general audience, from a 1977 issue of *Scientific American*, and more recent thinking on the possibility of a unified physical theory and on "baby universes" that may exist in black holes. The book also included transcribed interviews; lectures, including audience questions and his answers; and autobiographical writings, focusing notably on his youth and on how he deals with ALS (amyotrophic lateral sclerosis or Lou Gehrig's disease). The book also appeared in an audio version, read by Simon Prebble. A fan of *Star Trek*, Hawking made a June guest appearance with a holographic image of Albert Einstein on television's *Star Trek: The Next Generation*. That same month saw the home video release of Errol Morris's award-winning documentary film *A Brief History of Time* (1992), based on Hawking's book, much of it narrated by Hawking using his personal computer synthesizer, that being his only way of "speaking."

Oxford-born Hawking has made key contributions to modern scientific theory, most notably as to the nature of black holes, gravitational theory, and the "big bang" theory of the origin of the universe. He was educated at University College, Oxford and Trinity Hall, Cambridge, and has been associated with Cambridge in a series of research and teaching positions since 1965. He created a surprise best-seller with his *A Brief History of Time: From the Big Bang to Black Holes* (1988), a clearly written work on the nature of reality and the origins of the universe. Hawking also published a reader's companion to the film of the book (1992). A worldwide symbol of human ability to triumph over terribly adverse personal problems, Hawking has been progressively disabled by ALS from the age of 20; by the early 1990s, he was left the use of only some facial muscles and one finger of his left hand, which he used to successfully run a computer and a motorized wheelchair, while he continued to teach and write. In 1990, Hawking ended his long marriage to Jane Wilde; he has three children.

FURTHER READING

Stephen Hawking: Physicist. MELISSA MCDANIEL. Chelsea House, 1994.
Stephen Hawking: A Life in Science. MICHAEL WHITE and JOHN GRIBBIN. NAL-Dutton, 1993.
"Heart and mind." ARTHUR LUBOW. *Vanity Fair*, June 1992.
Unlocking the Universe: A Biography of Stephen Hawking. SHERIDAN SIMON. Dillon, 1991.
"Stephen Hawking and. . . ." CHET RAYMO. *Commonweal*, Apr. 6, 1990.
"Playboy interview. . . ." MORGAN STRONG. *Playboy*, Apr. 1990.

Hawkins, Erskine (1914–93) Birmingham-born Erskine Hawkins, a bandleader, trumpeter, and composer, began his bandleading career while still at Alabama State Teachers College, leading the 'Bama State Collegians band. After a move to New York in 1934, the band was renamed the Erskine Hawkins Orchestra and became one of the leading big bands of the 1930s and 1940s, playing at the Savoy Ballroom and recording for Bluebird and Victor, with such members as Avery Parrish, Bill Johnson, Sam Lowe, Haywood Henry, Dud Bascomb, Julian Bascomb, and Julian Dash. Hawkins, Dash, and Johnson wrote and introduced the classic "Tuxedo Junction" (1939), later Glenn Miller's signature song, and several other classics of the swing era. Later in his career, with a smaller band, Hawkins was a fixture at the Concord Hotel, in the Catskills. He was survived by a sister. (d. Willingboro, New Jersey; November 11, 1993)

FURTHER READING

Obituary. *New York Times*, Nov. 13, 1993.

Hayes, Helen (Helen Hayes Brown; 1900–93) On stage from the age of five, Helen Hayes made her Broadway debut at age nine in Lew Fields' production of *Old Dutch*, going on to play several juvenile leads. She was a star on Broadway from the mid-1920s, in such plays as *Caesar and Cleopatra* (1925), *What Every Woman Knows* (1926), *Coquette* (1927), *Mary of Scotland* (1933), and *Victoria Regina* (1935), her most notable role, later starring in many other plays, including *Harriet* (1943), *Happy Birthday* (1946; she won a Tony), *Mrs. Mcthing* (1952), *Time Remembered* (1957; she won a second Tony), and *A Touch of the Poet* (1958). Her film appearances were infrequent, but included her Oscar-winning starring role in *The Sin of Madelon Claudet* (1931), *Arrowsmith* (1931), *A Farewell to Arms* (1932), and later *Anastasia* (1956) and her best supporting actress Oscar-winning role in *Airport* (1970). She also appeared in many television films. She won a third Tony for lifetime achievement in 1980. Among her published works were *On Reflection: An Autobiography* (1968), written with Sandford Dody; *Twice over Lightly* (1972), with Anita Loos; the inspirational *A Gathering of Hope* (1983); *Our Best Years* (1984), with Marion Gladney; *Helen Hayes: My Life in Three Acts* (1990), with Katherine Hatch; and a mystery, *Where the Truth Lies* (1988), with Thomas Chastain. Her husband was playwright Charles MacArthur, who died in 1956. She was survived by her son, actor James MacArthur, and three grandchildren. (d. Nyack, New York; March 17, 1993)

FURTHER READING

"End of the Helenic age." LAWRENCE O'TOOLE. *Entertainment Weekly*, Apr. 2, 1993.
Obituary. *Current Biography*, May 1993.
"A child of the century." *People*, Mar. 29, 1993.
Obituary. *Variety*, Mar. 22, 1993.
Obituary. *The Times* (of London), Mar. 19, 1993.
Obituary. *New York Times*, Mar. 18, 1993.
Helen Hayes: A Bio-Bibliography. DONN B. MURPHY and STEPHEN MOORE. Greenwood, 1993.
Helen Hayes. MARY KITTREDGE. Chelsea House, 1990.

Hearst, William Randolph, Jr.
(1908–93) New York City-born William Randolph Hearst, Jr., was the second of the five sons of newspaper publisher William Randolph Hearst, the thinly veiled model for Charles Fos-

ter Kane in Orson Welles's *Citizen Kane*. The younger Hearst began his long publishing career in the early 1930s, as a reporter for a Hearst newspaper, the *New York American*, and soon became its publisher until he became editor-in-chief of the Hearst newspapers in 1955, breaking his tenure to work as a war correspondent (1943–45). In January 1955, he led a Hearst reporting team to the Soviet Union, where they interviewed premier Nikita Khrushchev and other leaders, generating a series of eight articles that won the 1956 international reporting Pulitzer Prize. Hearst was the uncle of Patricia "Patty" Hearst, kidnapped in 1974 and later imprisoned after her participation in a Symbionese Liberation Army bank robbery; his 1978 campaign for her release was successful. He published *The Hearsts: Father and Son* (1991), written with Jack Casserly. He was survived by two sons. (d. New York City; May 14, 1993)

FURTHER READING

Obituary. *Current Biography*, July 1993.
Obituary. *Variety*, May 24, 1993.
Obituary. *The Times* (of London), May 17, 1993.
Obituary. *New York Times*, May 16, 1993.

Hepburn, Audrey (Edda Hepburn-Ruston; 1929–93)

Brussels-born Audrey Hepburn grew up in London, but was caught in occupied Holland during World War II, then returning to London, where she was a dancer and had small parts in several plays and films. Her breakthrough came with her starring role on Broadway in the hit *Gigi* (1951), and her film breakthrough with her starring role opposite Gregory Peck in William Wyler's *Roman Holiday* (1953), for which she won a best actress Oscar. She won a best actress Tony for *Ondine* (1954), and then went on to star in a score of films, among them *Sabrina* (1954), *War and Peace* (1956), *Funny Face* (1957), *Love in the Afternoon* (1957), *The Nun's Story* (1959), *Breakfast at Tiffany's* (1961), *Charade* (1963), *My Fair Lady* (1964), *Wait Until Dark* (1967), and *Robin and Marian* (1976). She became a world figure in a quite different way during the 1980s, as a goodwill ambassador for UNICEF, the United Nations Children's Fund. She was survived by her companion, Dutch actor Robert Wolders, and two sons. (d. Tolochenaz, Switzerland; January 20, 1993)

FURTHER READING

Audrey Hepburn: A Celebration. SHERIDAN MORLEY. Trafalgar, 1994.
"Audrey Hepburn." DIANA MAYCHICK. *Cosmopolitan*, Nov 1993.
"Ode to Audrey." PAMELA FIORI. *Town & Country*, Oct. 1993.
"Unforgettable Audrey." MEG COHEN. *Harper's Bazaar*, Apr. 1993.
"Serene majesty." RICHARD CORLISS. *Film Comment*, Mar.-Apr. 1993.
Obituary. *Current Biography*, Mar. 1993.
"Farewell, fair lady." LAWRENCE O'TOOLE. *Entertainment*, Feb. 5, 1993.
"Farewell, angel. . . ." BRIAN D. JOHNSON. *Maclean's*, Feb. 1, 1993.
"Film's fairest lady. . . ." JAY COCKS. *Time*, Feb. 1, 1993.
"A princess in disguise." DAVID ANSEN. *Newsweek*, Feb. 1, 1993.
"Our fair lady." SUSAN SCHINDEHETTE. *People*, Feb. 1, 1993.
"Goodbye, fair lady." *U.S. News & World Report*, Feb. 1, 1993.
Obituary. *Variety*, Jan. 25, 1993.
Obituary. *The Times* (of London), Jan. 22, 1993.
Obituary. *New York Times*, Jan. 21, 1993.
Audrey Hepburn: An Intimate Portrait. DIANA MAYCHICK. Carol, 1993.
"Hepburn heart." DOMINICK DUNNE. *Vanity Fair*, May 1991.
"Audrey Hepburn." FRANK THOMPSON. *American Film*, May 1990.

Hepburn, Katharine (1907–   )

In her mid-80s, and halfway through her seventh decade as one of the most celebrated stage and screen stars of the century, Katharine Hepburn continued to work, and to be very much in the public eye. Her best-selling autobiography, *Me: Stories of My Life*, published in 1991, continued to sell very well in its paperback and audio editions, and to it she added another autobiographical work: *All About Me*, a 90-minute documentary film, co-written and co-produced by Hepburn, Joan Kramer, and David Heeley; Heeley directed the work, which was shown on the TNT television network in January. The film was not all about Hepburn, but to a large extent about Hepburn and Spencer Tracy, whose 27-year-long personal and professional partnership ended with his death 25 years ago, but is still entirely alive to worldwide audiences.

Hepburn was hospitalized for a few days in

Connecticut early in the year, as it turned out for exhaustion, rather than because of illness. That in no way stopped her from continuing on: in November, she was in Vancouver, shooting *This Can't Be Love*, a CBS television fiction film, in which she and Anthony Quinn starred as old lovers.

Hepburn's career began on stage, in 1928, but it is her work as a leading film actress that has made her a world figure. She has won four best actress Oscars—more than any other performer—and starred opposite Spencer Tracy in nine classic films. Her first film role was a lead opposite John Barrymore in *Bill of Divorcement* (1934). She went on to win Oscars for *Morning Glory* (1936); opposite Tracy in their last film together, *Guess Who's Coming to Dinner* (1967); *The Lion in Winter* (1968); and *On Golden Pond* (1981). Some of her other most notable films were *Little Women* (1933), *Stage Door* (1937), *Holiday* (1938), *The Philadelphia Story* (1940; also the 1939 Broadway play), *Woman of the Year* (1942), *Keeper of the Flame* (1942), *The Sea of Grass* (1947), *State of the Union* (1948), *Adam's Rib* (1949), *The African Queen* (1951), *Pat and Mike* (1952), *Summertime* (1955), *Desk Set* (1957), *Suddenly Last Summer* (1959), *Long Day's Journey Into Night* (1962), *A Delicate Balance* (1973), and *Rooster Cogburn* (1976). She was honored for her lifetime achievement at the Kennedy Center in 1990. On Broadway, she also played the lead in *Coco* (1969).

Hepburn attended Bryn Mawr College. A previous book was *The Making of "The African Queen": Or How I Went to Africa with Bogart, Bacall and Huston and Almost Lost My Mind* (1987). She was formerly married, to Ludlow Ogden Smith.

FURTHER READING

" 'I'm 85, but I'm tough.' " LAWRENCE EISENBERG. *New Choices for Retirement Living*, June 1993.

"Katharine Hepburn. . . ." JAMES BRADY. *Parade*, Jan. 17, 1993.

Katharine Hepburn: A Hollywood Portrait. SARAH P. DANIELSON. Smithmark, 1993.

Kate: The Katharine Hepburn Album. LAUREN TARSHIS. Putnam, 1993.

"Katharine Hepburn. . . ." CHRISTINE REINHARDT. *McCall's*, Dec. 1992.

" 'My toughest moment.' " GLENN PLASKIN. *Ladies Home Journal*, Nov. 1992.

"A bad case of Hepburn." MARGARET CARLSON. *Time*, June 29, 1992.

"Kate on Kate." JOCELYN McCLURG. *Saturday Evening Post*, Jan.-Feb. 1992.

Hollywood Royalty: Hepburn, Davis, Stewart and Friends Recall the Screen's Golden Years. GREGORY SPECK. Birch Lane/Carol, 1992.

Katharine Hepburn: Hollywood Legends. Outlet, 1992.

"Kate talks straight." MYRNA BLYTH. *Ladies Home Journal*, Oct. 1991.

"Kate the great." LIZ SMITH. *Vogue*, Sep. 1991.

"Katharine Hepburn." POPE BROCK. *People*, Nov. 5, 1990.

"Katharine Hepburn. . . ." SUSAN WARE. *History Today*, Apr. 1990.

"Katharine Hepburn. . . ." A. SCOTT BERG and JOHN BRYSON. *Architectural Digest*, Apr. 1990.

The Private World of Katharine Hepburn. JOHN BRYSON, Photographer. Little, Brown, 1990.

The Films of Katharine Hepburn, rev. ed. HOMER DICKENS. Carol, 1990.

Katharine Hepburn. CAROLINE LATHAM. Chelsea House, 1989.

Young Kate: The Remarkable Hepburns and the Childhood That Shaped an American Legend. CHRISTOPHER ANDERSEN. Holt, 1988.

Tracy and Hepburn. GARSON KANIN. Fine, 1988.

Herlihy, James Leo

Herlihy, James Leo (1927–93) Detroit-born James Leo Herlihy studied acting at the Pasadena Playhouse theater school (1948–50), appearing in approximately 50 plays in the western regional theater (1948–52). He also became a playwright; his first play, *Streetlight Sonata*, premiered at the Pasadena Playhouse in 1950, and was followed by many other plays and television scripts. His play *Moon Over Capricorn* opened off Broadway in 1953, and *Blue Denim* opened on Broadway in 1958. His well-received first novel, *All Fall Down*, appeared in 1960, and was adapted into the 1962 film. He was best known by far for the novel *Midnight Cowboy* (1965) and its film version (1969), which starred Dustin Hoffman and Jon Voight. His final novel was *Season of the Witch* (1971). He also published two collections of short stories. He was survived by a brother. (d. Los Angeles; October 21, 1993)

FURTHER READING

Obituary. *New York Times*, Nov. 22, 1993.

Obituary. *The Times* (of London), Nov. 20, 1993.

Hersey, John Richard (1914–93)

Born in Tientsin, China, child of a missionary and social service family, John Hersey was educated in Britain and America, began his association with writers and their world as Sinclair Lewis's secretary in 1937, and that year joined *Time* magazine as a reporter, going to the Far East for *Time* in 1939 and working as a war correspondent from 1942. His first book was *Men on Bataan* (1942), followed by *Into the Valley* (1943), and then by his Pulitzer Prize-winning novel *A Bell For Adano* (1944), about the post-battle American occupation of an Italian village. He followed it with *Hiroshima* (1946), a factual treatment of the atomic bombing of that city. In 1950 came his Warsaw Ghetto novel *The Wall*, the third of his major works. His later works included the novels *A Single Pebble* (1956), *The Child Buyer* (1959), and *The Algiers Motel Incident* (1968), about civil rights abuses in Detroit. Hersey was an anti-Vietnam War activist during the 1960s and early 1970s. He was survived by his wife, Barbara Day Kaufman, two daughters, and three sons. (d. Key West, Florida; March 24, 1993)

FURTHER READING

Obituary. *Current Biography*, May 1993.
"An all-American foreigner." DAVID GATES. *Newsweek*, Apr. 5, 1993.
Obituary. *Variety*, Mar. 29, 1993.
Obituary. *The Times* (of London), Mar. 26, 1993.
Obituary. *New York Times*, Mar. 25, 1993.
John Hersey Revisited. DAVID SANDERS. Twayne/Macmillan, 1990.

Hershey, Barbara (Barbara Herzstein; 1948–)

Veteran film star Barbara Hershey appeared in several movies in 1993. In the highly controversial film *Falling Down*, directed by Joel Schumacher, she starred opposite Michael Douglas and Robert Duvall in the story of a laid-off Los Angeles defense worker (Douglas), who abandons his car in a traffic jam and sets off for home, his mounting frustration and rage quickly leading to violence and overt bigotry. Hershey also starred opposite Debra Winger and Gabriel Byrne in the film *A Dangerous Woman*, directed by Stephen Gyllenhaal, as a wealthy, widowed California ranch owner, aunt of the deceptively straightforward central character (Winger). A third film role was in the British comedy-farce

Splitting Heirs, directed by Robert Young and co-starring Rick Moranis and Eric Idle; and a fourth in *Swing Kids*, directed by Thomas Carter and set in Nazi Germany, in a cast that included Robert Sean Leonard, Christian Bale, and Frank Whaley. In television, Hershey appeared in "Return to Lonesome Dove," the sequel to the 1989 western miniseries; Jon Voight, Rick Schroder, Louis Gossett, Jr., William Petersen, and Oliver Reed co-starred.

Hollywood-born Hershey began her career in television, in the mid-1960s appearing in the series "The Monroes" (1967–68) and in several series guest roles and television films. She continued to appear in television throughout her career, and won an Emmy for her role in *Killing in a Small Town* (1990). She made her film debut in *With Six You Get Egg Roll* (1968), then appearing in a long series of supporting roles, gaining reognition in the 1980s, in such films as *The Stunt Man* (1980), *The Right Stuff* (1983), *The Natural* (1984), *Hannah and Her Sisters* (1986), *Tin Men* (1987), *Shy People* (1987; she won the Golden Palm award as best actress at the Cannes Film Festival), *A World Apart* (1988; winning a second Golden Palm at Cannes), *The Last Temptation of Christ* (1988), *Tune in Tomorrow* (1989), *Paris Trout* (1991), and *Defenseless* (1991). She has one son.

FURTHER READING

"Hershey, Barbara." *Current Biography*, Aug. 1989.
"A woman apart." ROBERT GOLDBERG. *Savvy Woman*, Feb. 1989.

"Barbara Hershey. . . ." DAVID DENICOLO. *Glamour*, Feb. 1989.

Hibbert, Eleanor Burford (Jean Plaidy, Victoria Holt, Philippa Carr, Elbur Ford, et al; 1910–93)

London-born Eleanor Hibbert was a prolific writer, using several pen names. She began her career under her given name, Eleanor Burford, and began publishing in 1941, with the novel *Passionate Witness*. In 1947, she adopted the pseudonym Jean Plaidy for *Beyond the Blue Mountains*, the first of her 90 Plaidy historical romances. In 1961, she introduced Victoria Holt, with the very successful *Mistress of Mellyn*, the first of the 31 Holt novels. And in 1972 she introduced Philippa Carr, her vehicle for yet another group of novels. Hibbert's work was an extraordinary commercial success, and hardly a matter of critical comment. There were no survivors. (d. on a cruise ship in the Mediterranean; January 18, 1993)

FURTHER READING

Obituary. *The Times* (of London), Jan. 21, 1993.
Obituary. *New York Times*, Jan. 21, 1993.

ANGELO TITTONI

Hijuelos, Oscar (1951–)

With his new novel, Cuban-American novelist Oscar Hijuelos laid aside a masculine perspective for a personal world totally dominated by the feminine, as suggested by the title, *The Fourteen Sisters of Emilio Montez O'Brien*, the youngest child and only boy in a 15-child Pennsylvania family with a Cuban mother and Irish father. The multigenerational saga, following nearly a century of family history, was well-received, with some lauding it as a prose poem; bidding for paperback rights was brisk, as was speculation about film possibilities. Hijeulos himself was widely interviewed in connection with publicity for the book.

Born in Manhattan of Cuban immigrant parents, Hijuelos received his B.A. and M.A. from City College of New York. While working on inventory control in an advertising agency, he wrote his first novel, *Our House in the Last World* (1984), a semi-autobiographical work set among Cuban emigrés in Spanish Harlem; it won him a National Endowment of the Arts (NEA) grant and the American Academy of Arts and Letters Rome Prize, including a year in Italy. He did not gain wide public attention until his second novel, *The Mambo Kings Play Songs of Love* (1989), about two Cuban musicians, brothers, seeking to make it big in 1950s New York, who find love along the way. It won the 1990 Pulitzer Prize (he was the first Hispanic writer to do so), was nominated for the National Book Award and the National Book Critics Circle Award, was translated into ten languages, and was the basis of Arnold Glimcher's 1992 film, scripted by Cynthia Cidre and starring Armand Assante and Antonio Banderas as the brothers, Cesar and Nestor. Hijuelos is divorced.

FURTHER READING

" 'A house filled with women.' " SUSANNAH HUNNEWELL. *New York Times Book Review*, Mar. 7, 1993.
" 'Sisters' act." DINITIA SMITH. *New York*, Mar. 1, 1993.
Growing up Latino: Memoirs and Stories. HAROLD AUGENBRAUM and ILAN STAVANS, eds. Houghton Mifflin, 1993.
"Wandering around 1952." JOSEPH A. CINCOTTI. *New York Times Book Review*, Aug. 27, 1989.
"Oscar Hijuelos. . . ." SYBIL STEINBERG. *Publishers Weekly*, July 21, 1989.

Hill, Anita Faye (1956–)

Two years after the extraordinary confrontation between Professor Anita Faye Hill and Judge and then-Supreme Court nominee Clarence Thomas, which shocked the watching world and revitalized the American women's movement, Hill remained a very quiet figure, who shunned the spotlight and had not sought to capitalize financially or politically on her worldwide celebrity. In spite of that, she remained a highly controversial figure, lauded and even revered by many, and attacked and even hated by others. In June 1993, David Brock's extremely controversial book, *The Real Anita Hill,* which attacked Hill in every possible way, became a bestseller; it was hailed by some as sound investigative journalism and sharply condemned by others as a calculated, baseless set of smears, and continued to fuel the ongoing national argument about whether to believe Hill or Thomas. At the time of the confrontation, most Americans, as reported by several surveys, believed Thomas, but by 1993, sentiment had decisively swung toward belief of Hill.

Controversy pursued her at home in Oklahoma, as well, where conservatives attempted to block the creation of an endowed chair at the University of Oklahoma Law School, the Anita Faye Hill Professorship. Fundraising had begun, and the chair was intended to foster the study of the rights of women in the workplace, a major professional interest for Hill.

Hill was born in Morris, Oklahoma, the youngest of 13 children. She attended Lone Tree Baptist Church and was valedictorian of her class at Morris High School, having been a straight-A student, secretary of the student council, member of the National Honor Society, and member of the Future Homemakers of America and the Pep Club. She attended Oklahoma State University, and graduated with honors (1977). She attended Yale Law School (1977–80), interned at the Washington, D.C. law firm of Ward, Harkrader, and Ross while in law school, and joined the firm after graduation. She became personal assistant to Thomas at the Office of Civil Rights of the U.S. Education Department in 1981, and moved with him to the U.S. Equal Employment Opportunity Commission. She left Washington to teach law at Oral Roberts University (1983).

Hill became a worldwide figure in the struggle for women's rights in 1991, when she charged then-Supreme Court nominee Thomas with sexual harassment during the years she worked for him. Her confrontation with Thomas and the Senate Judiciary Committee came before a worldwide television audience. She has taught law at the University of Oklahoma since 1986, and became a tenured full professor in 1990.

FURTHER READING

"Her word against his." David Brock. *National Review,* May 10, 1993.
Anita Hill. Bob Italia. Abdo & Daughters, 1993.
The Real Anita Hill: The Untold Story. David Brock. Free Press, 1993.
"One year later. . . ." Ronald M. Dworkin. *New York Times Book Review,* Oct. 25, 1992.
"The untold story." Gloria Borger and Ted Gest. *U.S. News & World Report,* Oct. 12, 1992.
"The real Anita Hill." David Brock. *American Spectator,* Mar. 1992.
"Anita Hill: no regrets." Jill Nelson. *Essence,* Mar. 1992.
"Why Anita Hill lost." Suzanne Garment. *Commentary,* Jan. 1992.
"Anita Hill: law professor." Lauren Hutton. *Interview,* Jan. 1992.
Capitol Games: Clarence Thomas, Anita Hill, and the Behind-the-Scenes Story of a Supreme Court Nomination. Timothy M. Phelps and Helen Winternitz. Disney, 1992; HarperCollins, 1993.
"She could not keep silent." Bill Hewitt and Beth Austin. *People,* Oct. 28, 1991.
"A question of character." Richard Lacayo. "An ugly circus." Nancy Gibbs. *Time,* Oct. 21, 1991.
"Thomas and Hill. . . ." Eloise Salholz. "Anatomy of a debacle." David A. Kaplan. "A moment of truth." *Newsweek,* Oct. 21, 1991.
"Judging Thomas." Gloria Borger. *U.S. News & World Report,* Oct. 21, 1991.

Hodes, Art (1904–93) The family of Art Hodes emigrated from Russia to the United States when he was six months old; he grew up in Chicago, took piano lessons at Hull House, became immersed in the jazz that had by then moved up the Mississippi from New Orleans, and became one of the young White musicians who adopted the jazz idiom as their own. Hodes became a classic jazz pianist, playing in Chicago in cabaret in the late 1920s and moving to New York in the early 1930s. He played in several groups before forming his own group in the early 1940s. In 1946, he founded his own recording company, published a jazz magazine, and hosted a jazz radio program on WNYC. His career waned, and he moved back to Chicago in 1950, touring widely in the four decades that followed, and regained his earlier popularity with the jazz revival of the 1980s. His autobiography was *Hot Man: The Life of Arts Hodes* (1991), written with Chadwick Hansen; the two had co-edited *Selections from the Gutter: Portraits from the Jazz*

Record (1977). He was survived by his wife, Jan, three daughters, and two sons. (d. Chicago; March 4, 1993)

FURTHER READING

"Art Hodes. . . ." JOHN LITWEILER. *Down Beat*, June 1993.
Obituary. *The Times* (of London), Mar. 8, 1993.
Obituary. *New York Times*, Mar. 6, 1993.

Holley, Robert (1922–93) Nobel Prize-winning biologist Robert Holley graduated from the University of Illinois in 1942 and earned his 1947 doctorate in organic chemistry from Cornell University, where he was a member of the five-person team that first synthesized penicillin. He taught organic chemistry at Cornell (1948–58), then moving to the Cornell-based U. S. Department of Agriculture's Plant, Soil, and Nutrition Laboratory, where he and his team worked for three years to successfully produce one-30th of an ounce of alanine transfer RNA (ribonucleic acid) from 200 pounds of yeast, and four years more to completely describe the genetic code of the RNA molecule. His seminal achievement brought him a shared 1968 Nobel Prize for medicine and physiology, and many other honors and positions. He taught at Cornell again (1962–66), chairing the biochemistry department (1965–66), and then moved to the Salk Institute for Biological Studies. He was survived by his wife, Ann Dworkin, a son, and three brothers. (d. Los Gatos, California; February 11, 1993)

FURTHER READING

Obituary. *Current Biography*, Apr. 1993.
Obituary. *The Times* (of London), Feb. 16, 1993.
Obituary. *New York Times*, Feb. 14, 1993.

Holt, Victoria: See Hibbert, Eleanor.

Holyfield, Evander (1962–) On November 13, 1992, in what was named "Fight of the Year," Evander Holyfield had lost the heavyweight title of the world to Riddick Bowe, while

gaining the respect of the boxing comunity, which until then had eluded him. After that fight, Holyfield announced his retirement; but in January 1993 was persuaded to return by his friend, rap performer Hammer, who became his advisor. In June, though not in top condition and the heaviest of his career, a lackluster Holyfield won a unanimous 12-round decision against Alex Stewart at Atlantic City. But that was just a prelude to his November 7 championship rematch with Bowe. That memorable Las Vegas contest, held in an outdoor stadium at Caesar's Palace, had both boxers in aggressive form, often fighting beyond the bell, with more than 600 punches landed, though no knockdowns. In the end, Holyfield regained his heavyweight crown.

In one of the more bizarre events to occur in boxing, the fight was interrupted for 20 minutes in Round 7 after a man in a motorized paraglider appeared from the air, his ropes tangled in a bank of lights; fearing an assassination attempt on one of the notable spectators, including Louis Farrakhan and Jesse Jackson, some people battered the man until he was removed and the fight resumed. Bowe's pregnant wife, Judy, fainted and his 82-year-old trainer, Eddie Futch, had heart palpitations; both were removed for medical attention.

The crown won by Holyfield was divided; Bowe had declined to fight Lennox Lewis when and where specified and had literally thrown away the World Boxing Council belt, which then went to Lewis. In the Las Vegas fight, Holyfield won back the International Boxing Federation and the World Boxing Association crowns. A fight with Lewis for a unified title was under discussion at year's end.

Earlier in 1993, Holyfield had acted as chair umpire at an exhibition to benefit the Arthur Ashe Foundation for the Defeat of AIDS. He had also played a doubles match, paired with Magdalena Maleeva, losing to New York Mayor David Dinkins and Gigi Fernandez, in a match umpired by Bowe.

Born in Alabama and raised in Atlanta, Holyfield won a bronze medal in the 1984 Olympics and turned professional in 1986. For most of his career, he has been a light-heavyweight, rather than a heavyweight, and became World Boxing Association Junior Heavyweight world champion by defeating Dwight Qawi in 1986. He took the heavyweight championship from James "Buster" Douglas in October 1990, and defended it successfully three times, being undefeated until the loss to Bowe, with a record to that point of 28–0, with 22 knockouts and estimated career earnings of $80 million. Holyfield was divorced in 1991, and has four children.

FURTHER READING

Champions of the Ring: The Lives and Times of Boxing's Heavyweight Heroes. GERALD SUSTER. Parkwest, 1993.
"Wild night." PAT PUTNAM. *Sports Illustrated,* Nov. 15, 1993.
"Holyfield, Evander." *Current Biography,* Aug. 1993.
"Three minutes to history. . . ." KATHERINE DUNN. *Esquire,* Feb. 1993.
"The real deal. . . ." GARY CARTWRIGHT. *Texas,* June 1991.
"No joke. . . ." PAT PUTNAM. *Sports Illustrated,* Apr. 29, 1991.
"Evander Holyfield. . . ." DOUGLAS C. LYONS. *Ebony,* Jan. 1991.
"Evander Holyfield. . . ." *Jet,* Nov. 19, 1990.
"At last!" David Miller. *Sport,* Nov. 1990.

Hopkins, Anthony (1937–) Now recognized as one of the world's leading stage and screen stars, and in the peak years of his career, Anthony Hopkins appeared in several major films opening in 1993. *The Remains of the Day,* directed by James Ivory, and written by Ruth Prawer Jhabvala, based on the novel by Kazuo

Ishiguro, starred Hopkins as the quintessential butler opposite Emma Thompson, in a cast that included James Fox, Christopher Reeve, Peter Vaughan, Hugh Grant, Michael Lonsdale, and Tim Pigott-Smith. *The Trial,* directed by David Jones, and written by Harold Pinter, from Franz Kafka's novel, starred Hopkins, Kyle MacLachlan, Jason Robards, Jean Stapleton, and Juliet Stevenson. *Shadowlands,* William Nicolson's film adaptation of his own play, directed by Richard Attenborough, starred Hopkins as C. S. Lewis and Debra Winger as Joy Gresham. *The Innocent,* directed by John Schlesinger, starred Hopkins opposite Isabella Rossellini, in a cast that included Campbell Scott and Ronald Nitschke. On television, Hopkins starred in *Selected Exits,* based on the recollections of Gwyn Thomas.

Forthcoming were the films *The Road to Wellville,* based on the novel by T. Coraghessan Boyle, directed by Alan Parker, and co-starring Bridget Fonda and Matthew Broderick; and *Legends of the Fall,* directed by Ed Zwick and co-starring Brad Pitt.

Hopkins played in repertory during the early 1960s; he joined the National Theatre in 1967, the same year that he made his film debut in *The Lion in Winter.* A few of his most notable theater roles were in the title role of *Macbeth* (1972; National Theatre), *Equus* (1974–75; on Broadway); *Pravda* (1985; National Theatre), *King Lear* (1986; National Theatre), and *Anthony and Cleopatra* (1987; title role, National Theatre). He has appeared in such films as *The Looking Glass War* (1967), *A Bridge Too Far* (1976), *Magic* (1978), *The Elephant Man* (1978), *The Bounty* (1984; as Captain Bligh), *84 Charing Cross Road* (1987), *Desperate Hours* (1989), *The Silence of the Lambs* (1991; he won a best actor Oscar), *Spotswood* (1991), *Howard's End* (1992), and *Bram Stoker's Dracula* (1992), and in a wide range of television roles, winning Emmys in *The Lindbergh Kidnapping Case* (1975) and *The Bunker* (1980), and playing such title roles as *Kean* (1980) and *Othello* (1981). Hopkins attended the Welsh College of Music and Drama and the Royal Academy of Dramatic Art. His second wife is the former Jennifer Lynton; he has one daughter.

FURTHER READING

Anthony Hopkins: A Biography. MICHAEL F. CALLAN. Scribner/Macmillan, 1994.

Anthony Hopkins: The Authorized Biography.
QUENTIN FALK. Interlink, 1993.
"In step with. . . ." JAMES BRADY. *Parade*, Apr. 26,
1992.
"Nicholson? Brando? . . ." LISA LIEBMANN. *Interview.*
Apr. 1992.
" 'Call me Tony.' " RITA GAM. *World Monitor*, Apr.
1992.
"Anthony Hopkins'. . . ." MARTHA FRANKEL. *Movies
USA*, Mar.-Apr. 1992.
"Anthony Hopkins." DAVID GRITTEN. *M Inc.*, Aug.
1991.
"Anthony Hopkins. . . ." JIM JEROME. *People*, Mar. 4,
1991.
Anthony Hopkins: Too Good to Waste. QUENTIN FALK.
Isis (NY), 1990.

Horszowski, Mieczyslaw (1892–1993)

Born in Lvov, Poland, now part of Ukraine, Mieczyslaw Horszowski was a child prodigy, who began playing the piano at three, was composing and playing the classics at five, and began his 92-year-long performing career at seven. He began his studies with Theodor Leschetizky in Vienna in 1899, and made his Warsaw debut at the age of nine, in 1901, playing a Beethoven concerto, and his New York debut in 1906, after having toured widely in Europe and South America. After limiting his public performances for some years in favor of academic studies, he fully returned to the concert stage, and for seven decades was one of the world's leading pianists, in concert and on records. He survived such great contemporaries as Artur Rubinstein and Pablo Casals, at whose French and Puerto Rico festivals he appeared for decades. He was also a leading teacher at Philadelphia's Curtis Institute from 1940. There were no survivors. (d. Philadelphia; May 22, 1993)

FURTHER READING

Obituary. *Billboard*, June 5, 1993.
Obituary. *The Times* (of London), May 25, 1993.
Obituary. *New York Times*, May 24, 1993.

Hosokawa, Morihiro (1938–)

On August 8, 1993, Japan New Party head Morihiro Hosokawa was elected Prime Minister by the lower house of the Japanese parliament, replacing Liberal Democratic Party (LDP) leader Kiichi Miyazawa and ending, at least for a time, the LDP's long dominance of Japanese political life. Beset by long-term, widespread corruption scandals involving its top leadership, and by recession and greatly depressed stock markets, the LDP lost its parliamentary majority, though remaining the largest single party in parliament, with 223 of 511 seats. Hosokawa's New Party won only 35 seats, and he ruled uneasily at the head of a seven-party coalition.

Hosokawa named a coaliton cabinet that included three women and only one holdover, both great departures from previous practice in Japan, and then set about initiating the very difficult processes of political and economic reform. Among his early moves were the first official Japanese statement that World War II was an act of Japanese aggression; intensification of trade talks with the U.S., leading to some further opening of Japanese domestic markets; negotiations with Russian president Boris Yeltsin on the disputed Kurile Islands; and considerable economic stimulus attempts. Hokosawa also strongly resisted renewed attempts to remilitarize Japan.

Born in Kumamoto province, Hosokawa is the grandson of former Japanese Prime Minister Fumimaro Konoe (1937–39; 1940–41), who committed suicide in 1945, while awaiting trial as a war criminal. Hosokawa attended Tokyo's Sophia University, began his career as a journalist in 1963, and entered the upper house of parliament as a Liberal Democrat in 1971, leaving in

1983 to become governor of Kumamoto, which his family had long ruled as a feudal domain, or *daimyo* (1632–1868). During his tenure as governor (1983–90), Hosokawa sharply opposed central government policies, and in 1992 left the ruling Liberal Democratic Party to form the Japan New Party. He is married to Kayoko Hosokawa.

FURTHER READING

"Japanese parliament elects. . . ." *Facts on File*, Aug. 12, 1993.

Houphouët-Boigny, Felix (1905–93)

Felix Houphouët-Boigny, a graduate of the French West African medical school at Dakar, practiced medicine in the Ivory Coast (1925–40), then managing his family's lands. He organized the Ivory Coast Democratic Party (1945), and represented the Ivory Coast in the French National Assembly (1946–59), in the same period leading the campaign for Ivory Coast independence. He served in the French cabinet (1950–53), became an advisor to several French prime ministers and to Charles De Gaulle, and then became the first Prime Minister (1959) and first President of the Ivory Coast (1960–93), a position he held until his death. He also became a major figure in Africa, as head of a Western-oriented state often going against the tide, as when he, in the early 1970s, called for dialogue with racist South Africa. Late in his career, as the Ivory Coast encountered massive economic problems, his hold weakened somewhat; that was also caused by the erection of what was widely regarded as his folly, the $200 million Catholic Basilica of Our Lady of Peace at his home town, Yamoussoukro. He was survived by several children. (d. Ivory Coast; December 7, 1993)

FURTHER READING

Obituary. *The Times* (of London), Dec. 8, 1993.
Obituary. *New York Times*, Dec. 8, 1993.
Political Leaders of Contemporary Africa South of the Sahara: A Biographical Dictionary. HARVEY GLICKMAN, ed. Greenwood, 1992.
"Houphouët-Boigny, Felix." *Current Biography*, July 1991.
"Ivory Coast's 'old man'. . . ." APRIL OLIVER. *National Catholic Reporter*, Nov. 16, 1990.

Houston, Whitney (1963–)

Throughout 1993, Whitney Houston continued to build on the tremendous popularity of the soundtrack from the film *The Bodyguard* (1992), in which she played opposite Kevin Costner. In *Billboard's* year-end ratings, Houston was ranked the top pop singles artist, the top adult contemporary singles artist, and the top r & b singles artist. "I Will Always Love You" spent 14 weeks at the top of the Billboard Hot 100 list, and was rated the top single of the year and the top r & b single of the year. *The Bodyguard* soundtrack was the top pop and the top r & b album of the year. "I Will Always Love You" received the Soul Train best r & b single, female, award.

Houston issued several more popular singles from *The Bodyguard* during the year, including "I'm Every Woman," "Queen of the Night," "I Have Nothing," and "Run To You." She and her husband, singer Bobby Brown, issued the single "Something in Common," from Brown's album *Bobby*. On the personal side, Houston and Brown became parents of a baby girl.

New Jersey-born Houston suddenly emerged as a leading popular singer in the mid-1980s, with her first album, the Grammy-winning *Whitney Houston* (1985), followed by *Whitney* (1986), and with such songs as "Didn't We Almost Have it All," "The Greatest Love of All," and "How Will I Know." In 1990, her single "I'm Your Baby Tonight," from the album of the same name, also hit number one, as did her 1991 "All the Man That I Need." Houston is the daughter of singer Cissy Houston, and the cousin of singer Dionne Warwick.

FURTHER READING

"WH: down and dirty." ANTHONY DeCURTIS. *Rolling Stone*, June 10, 1993.
"Pregnant pause." MEREDITH BERKMAN and KATE MEYERS. *Entertainment*, Feb. 5, 1993.
"Whitney Houston. . . ." LYNN NORMENT. *Ebony*, Jan. 1993.
"Thoroughly modern Whitney." LYNN HIRSCHBERG. *Vanity Fair*, Nov. 1992.
"20 questions. . . ." *Playboy*, May 1991.
"Whitney Houston." DAVID VAN BIEMA. *Life*, Oct. 1990.
"Whitney Houston." *Harper's Bazaar*, Sep. 1989.
The Picture Life of Whitney Houston. GENE BUSNAR. Watts, 1988.
Whitney Houston. KEITH E. GREENBERG. Lerner, 1988.

Howard, Ron (1954–) As Ron Howard's 1992 film *Far and Away* was completing its 1993 journey through video rentals and foreign distribution, and beginning its long life in cable television, Howard was working on new projects. One of them was a highly visible film that was to be based on a book not yet written: In July, Universal Pictures announced that it had paid a recordbreaking $3.75 million for the film rights to the next legal thriller by John Grisham, among whose works are *The Firm* and *The Client*; Howard was set to direct. Also forthcoming was the film *The Paper*, directed by Howard and starring Michael Keaton, Glenn Close, Robert Duvall, Marisa Tomei, and Randy Quaid. Howard himself also appeared in the television special *George Lucas: Heroes, Myths and Magic*, narrated by James Earl Jones.

Oklahoma-born Howard was a child star in television, as Opie in "The Andy Griffith Show" (1960–68), and later in "The Smith Family" (1971–72) and "Happy Days" (1974–80). He also appeared in such films as *The Music Man* (1962), *American Graffiti* (1973), and *The Shootist* (1976). As an adult, he directed, and in several instances co-wrote and co-produced such films as *Splash* (1984), *Cocoon* (1985), *No Man's Land* (1987), *Clean and Sober* (1988), *Willow* (1988), *Parenthood* (1989), and *Backdraft* (1991). Howard was also, with long-time associate Brian Glazer, executive producer and writer of the television series spun off from *Parenthood*. He at-tended the University of Southern California. He married Cheryl Alley in 1975; they have five children.

FURTHER READING

"Ron Howard." JOHN CLARK. *Premiere*, Apr. 1991.

Howe, Irving (1920–93) New York City-born Irving Howe began his writing and teaching career after his armed forces service in World War II. He worked as a free-lance writer in New York City during the late 1940s and early 1950s, for such publications as *Partisan Review*, *The New York Times*, and *Commentary*, emerging as a leading Cold War anti-communist intellectual and at the same time advocating democratic socialism. In 1954, he was a founder of the magazine *Dissent*, which carried forward these views. He later very sharply opposed the main organizations and leaders of the New Left during the 1960s and 1970s. Howe began his teaching career at Brandeis University in 1953, and later taught at Stanford University, Hunter College, and New York's City University. A prolific essayist, his best known work was the book *World of Our Fathers*, about the turn-of-the-century Eastern European Jewish migration to the United States, which won a 1976 National Book Award. He was survived by his wife, Llana, a daughter, and a son. (d. New York City; May 5, 1993)

FURTHER READING

"Irving Howe " TODD GITLIN. *Tikkun*, July-Aug. 1993.
Obituary. *Current Biography*, July 1993.
"Remembering Irving Howe." LEON WIESELTIER. *New York Times Book Review*, May 23, 1993.
Obituary. *New Yorker*, May 17, 1993.
Obituary. *The Times* (of London), May 8, 1993.
Obituary. *New York Times*, May 6, 1993.

Hughes, Dorothy (Dorothy Belle Flanagan, 1904–93) Kansas City-born Dorothy Hughes, a poet and novelist, began her career as a journalist in Albuquerque and Los Angeles during the 1920s. In 1931, she publilshed her single poetry collection *Dark Certainty*. Her novels meeting little success, she focused on the mystery genre, in 1940 publishing her first, well-received mystery *The So Blue Marble*, and then emerged as a writer of dark psychological mystery novels in the 1940s, while continuing to free-lance in Hollywood. Hughes was blacklisted after publicly opposing the House Un-American Activities Committee in the late 1940s, continuing to work as a mystery writer and anthologist, probably with more recognition abroad than in her home country. She was survived by two daughters and a son. (d. Ashland, Oregon; May 6, 1993)

FURTHER READING

Obituary. *The Times* (of London), June 2, 1993.

Hunter, Holly (1958–)

Holly Hunter emerged as a leading actress in 1993, for her starring role as Ada McGrath opposite Harvey Keitel and Sam Neill in Jane Campion's acclaimed film *The Piano*, for which she won a best actress award at the Cannes Film Festival. The film itself won the festival's first prize, the Palme d'Or. She and the movie were equally acclaimed when the film opened in the United States late in the year; she won the best actress award of the Los Angeles Film Critics Association.

Also in 1993, Hunter won an Emmy award as best actress in a mniseries or special for role for her starring role in the television film *The Positively True Adventures of the Alleged Texas Cheerleader-Murdering Mom*. She also won praise for a strong supporting role in the film *The Firm*, directed by Sidney Pollack.

Georgia-born Hunter appeared in several regional theater productions and in New York in the Beth Henley plays *Crimes of the Heart* (1981) and *The Wake of Jamey Foster* (1982) before entering her film career. She made her film debut in *Raising Arizona* (1987), and scored an early breakthrough in a starring role in *Broadcast News* (1987), for which she won an Oscar nomination and best actress awards from the New York Film Critics Circle, the National Board of Review, and the Berlin Film Festival. She went on to several less-well-received films, including *Always* (1990), *Miss Firecracker* (1989), and *Once Around* (1991). In television, she won a 1990 best actress Emmy for her role in *Roe v. Wade*, and starred in several other television films. Her 1980 B.F.A. was from Carnegie-Mellon University.

FURTHER READING

"The return of Holly's comet." JACK KROLL. *Newsweek*, Nov. 15, 1993.
"Hunter season." JEANNINE STEIN. *Advocate*, July 27, 1993.
"No Southern comfort." JACK MATHEWS. *American Film*, Dec. 1989.

Hurley, Bobby, Jr. (1971–)

In 1993, young Bobby Hurley ended a remarkable college basketball career, which included three trips to the NCAA Finals, and two successive national championships. Although Duke University's Blue Devils did not make it into the 1993 NCAA finals, many thought Hurley was playing his best, averaging 17 points and 8 assists a game. Overall, he set a new all-time NCAA record for total career assists, and a Duke record for three-point shots. His jersey, No. 11, was retired by the school in an emotional celebration.

In the National Basketball Association (NBA) college draft, Hurley was the first pick of the Sacramento Kings, seventh pick overall, signing a six-year, $16.5 million contract with the Kings. Though some had questioned how the short-of-six-foot Hurley would fare in the NBA, he was having a more-than-respectable rookie year, by November averaging over 8 points and nearly 7 assists per game. He also was spokesman for a new line of "In the Zone" sneakers put out by Foot Locker, had a diary in a Sacramento newspaper, and played a part in a movie, *Blue Chips*, scheduled for release in 1994.

But all that suddenly paled when, on December 12, he almost died after an auto accident. When his pickup was hit by another car, Hurley was thrown 20 feet into a drainage ditch. His injuries were many and devastating, including two collapsed lungs and a severed trachea, which required eight hours of emergency surgery to re-attach. Hurley was placed on an artificial respirator and in intensive care for some days while his recovery was in doubt. But on December 24, he was released from the hospital to spend Christmas with his family in Sacramento, and interviewed on television during at half-time of the holiday basketball game. Once the life-and-death questions were past, primary concern focused on Hurley's other injuries, notably a badly damaged knee and shoulder, which would require months of rehabilitation, and possibly surgery, before any future return to play.

Hurley's first coach was his father, Bob, Sr., both informally and at St. Anthony High School in his hometown of Jersey City, New Jersey. In his senior year, Hurley led the school to a 32–0 record and to a state and national championship. He then moved on to become point guard of Duke University's Blue Devils, taking them to the NCAA final three times (1990–1992) for two national championships (1991; 1992). His brother, Danny, is also a college basketball player, at Seton Hall.

FURTHER READING

"When Hurley comes marching in." MIKE LUPICA. *Esquire*, Mar. 1993.

Hussein, Saddam (1937–) Two years after the end of the Persian Gulf War, Saddam Hussein ruled unopposed in Iraq, his armies largely resupplied. The continuing sanctions imposed by the United Nations after the war continued to affect the quality of Iraqi material life, but had no perceptible impact on Hussein's ability to rule and to make war against his internal enemies. The "no-fly" zones imposed by the UN served to protect Kurdish minorities in the north from bombing attacks, but while they protected Shiites in the south from bombing attacks, they did nothing to protect them from Iraqi armored attacks, which by year's end had forced 200,000–300,000 Iraqi Shiites to leave their homes, most of them fleeing into exile over the Iranian bor-

der. During their continuing, unimpeded attack on the Shiites, Iraqi forces diverted waterways, draining swamp areas that had provided refuge for Shiite refugees.

Hussein's forces challenged Allied commitment in Iraq continually during the year, ground batteries attacking patrolling warplanes and drawing return fire on many occasions, most notably in January, when Allied aircraft and missiles massively responded to Iraqi attacks on planes patrolling Kurdish and Shiite areas. On June 26, an American missile attack on Iraqi intelligence headquarters in Baghdad was launched, in retaliation for an alleged Iraqi-originated plot to assassinate former President George Bush during a visit to Kuwait. UN arms inspectors were blocked by Iraqis on several occasions during the year, the Iraqis backing away from further confrontation for the time being, under threat of Allied military action. Iraqi forces also on several occasions fired on Kuwaiti patrols on the Iraq-Kuwait border. At year's end, the long, low-level war between Saddam Hussein's Iraq and much of the rest of the world continued.

Born in Takrit, Iraq, Hussein joined the Ba'ath socialist party in 1957, and went into Egyptian exile in 1958, after taking part in the failed attempt to assassinate General Karim Kassem, premier of the Iraqi republic. He returned to Iraq in 1963, after the army coup in which Kassem was killed. Hussein was a leader of the Ba'ath coup of 1968, and took full power in 1971, then surrounding himself with followers from his home village, instituting a reign of terror in his country, and becoming the dictator of Iraq. He also then began to develop a massive "cult of personality" around himself.

In 1980, Hussein's forces attacked Iran, beginning the Iran-Iraq war (1980–88); his forces used large amounts of poison gas against the Iranians, although such chemical warfare had been outlawed throughout the world. In the late 1980s, after the 1988 ceasefire with Iran, his forces continued to use poison gas, this time against Iraq's own rebellious Kurdish population, killing thousands of civilians, and forcing hundreds of thousands to flee into exile. With the end of the Iran-Iraq war, Hussein emerged as a Middle Eastern strongman. On August 2, 1990, his armies invaded and took oil-rich Kuwait. He then turned toward far richer Saudi Arabia, whether to invade or intimidate, and was met by the American-led multinational response, coupled with UN action, that resulted in sanctions, blockade, and ultimately the Persian Gulf War.

Hussein attended Cairo University and Baghdad's al-Mujstanseriya University. He married Sajidal Khairalla in 1963, and has four children.

FURTHER READING

"High time." Albert Wohlstetter. *National Review*, Feb. 15, 1993.

"At his request." *Economist*, Jan. 16, 1993.

Saddam Hussein. Jane Claypool. Rourke, 1993.

Saddam Hussein. Nita Renfrew. Chelsea House, 1993.

"Saddam's best ally." Leslie Cockburn and Andrew Cockburn. *Vanity Fair*, Aug. 1992.

" 'Back from the living dead'. . . ." Ray Wilkinson. "The stalking of Saddam." Charles Lane. *Newsweek*, Jan. 20, 1992.

Saddam Hussein. Nita Renfrew. Chelsea House, 1992.

Saddam Speaks on the Gulf Crisis: A Collection of Documents. Ofra Bengio, ed. Syracuse University Press, 1992.

Rogues' Gallery: America's Foes from George III to Saddam Hussein. Larry Hedrick. Brasseys, 1992.

"How Saddam survived. . . ." Gail Sheehy. *Vanity Fair*, Aug. 1991.

"His war, his peace. . . ." *Economist*, Feb. 23, 1991.

"Saddam. . . ." Lisa Beyer. *Time*, Jan. 7, 1991.

Saddam Hussein: A Political Biography. Efraim Karsh and Inari Rautsi. Pergamon, 1991.

Outlaw State: Saddam Hussein's Quest for Power and the Gulf Crisis. Elaine Sciolino. Wiley, 1991.

Saddam Hussein: A Political Biography. Efraim Karsh. Free Press, 1991.

Instant Empire: Saddam Hussein's Ambition for Iraq. Simon Henderson. Mercury House, 1991.

Saddam Hussein and the Crisis in the Gulf. Judith Miller and Laurie Mylorie. Random, 1990.

Huston, Anjelica (1952–) Reprising one of her most popular roles, Anjelica Huston in 1993 again starred as Morticia in *Addams Family Values*, the sequel to *The Addams Family*, opposite Raul Julia as Gomez, in a cast that included Christopher Lloyd, Joan Cusack, Carol Kane, Christina Ricci, Carel Struvcken, Jimmy Workman, and Christopher Hart; Barry Sonnenfeld directed. The film was well received, though less of a box office smash than its predecessor. She also starred in Woody Allen's light comedy *Manhattan Murder Mystery*, written and di-

rected by Allen, and co-starring Allen, Diane Keaton, and Alan Alda. In Roger Spottiswoode's pioneering AIDS film *And The Band Played On*, based on Randy Shilts's book, Huston played a cameo role as a pediatrician. Huston starred in television, as well, opposite Sam Neill in the two-part four-hour television film *Family Pictures*, directed by Philip Saville, as a mother who focuses a great deal of her life on the plight of an autistic child.

Born in Los Angeles but raised in Ireland, Huston took a critical pounding when her father, actor-director John Huston, cast the 15-year-old in his film, *A Walk With Love and Death* (1967). She retreated from film to the stage, emerging as a leading dramatic film actress in the mid-1980s, winning a best supporting actress Oscar as Maerose Prizzi in John Huston's *Prizzi's Honor* (1985); and starring in *Gardens of Stone* (1987), *The Dead* (1987; screenplay by brother Tony Huston); *A Handful of Dust* (1988), John Huston's last film; *Enemies, A Love Story* (1989); *Crimes and Misdeameanors* (1989); *The Grifters* (1990); *The Witches* (1990); and *The Addams Family* (1991). The granddaughter of actor Walter Huston, she worked with acting coach Peggy Feury. In 1990, she ended a 17-year relationship with Jack Nicholson. She married sculptor Robert Graham in 1993.

FURTHER READING

"Anjelica Huston. . . ." Jeff Silverman. *Cosmopolitan*, Mar. 1993.

"Anjelica Huston." Nancy Griffin. *Harper's Bazaar*, June 1992.

"Anjelica Huston. . . ." *People*, Dec. 30, 1991.

"Anjelica Huston." Susan Morgan. *Interview*, Dec. 1991.

"Huston Addams." Susan Morgan. *Interview*, July 1991.

"A bit of a coyote. . . ." David Thomson. *American Film*, Nov. 1990.

"Anjelica Huston. . . ." Vicki Woods. *Vogue*, Nov. 1990.

"Huston, Anjelica." *Current Biography*, July 1990.

Anjelica Huston: The Lady and the Legacy. Martha Harris. St. Martin's, 1989.

The Hustons. Lawrence Grobel. Macmillan, 1989.

Hutchison, Kay Bailey (1943–) On June 5, 1993, Republican Texas state treasurer Kay Bailey Hutchison defeated interim Democratic senatorial appointee Bob Krueger by a

her on five felony counts in connection with her senatorial campaign. She called all charges politically motivated and without any merit, as the situation continued to develop. In October, all charges were dropped, on a technicality; in December, they were reinstated.

Galveston-born Hutchison began her career in broadcast journalism (1969–71), covering the Texas legislature for Houston's KPRC-TV. In 1972, as Kay Bailey, she became the first woman Republican to be elected to that body, serving until her 1976 appointment by President Gerald Ford as vice-chairperson of the National Transportation Safety Board (1976–78). She was general counsel and a senior vice president of the Republic of Texas Corporation (1979–81), and then made an unsuccessful Congressional run. She was in private practice with Hutchison, Boyle, Brooks & Fisher in Dallas until her election as Texas State Treasurer (1990). Her LL.B. was from the University of Texas. She is married to Texas politician and lawyer Ray Hutchison.

landslide 2–1 vote, in a runoff election for the U.S. Senate seat vacated by U.S. Treasury Secretary Lloyd Bentsen. Hutchison, the first woman Senator from Texas, who had campaigned as a very conservative anti-Clinton candidate, vowed to go to Washington to fight hard against tax increases and social programs. She was sworn in on June 14, four days after investigators in her home state announced that they were probing possible campaign irregularities. On September 27, a Texas grand jury indicted

FURTHER READING

"The trials of Senator Sweet." PAUL BURKA. *Texas Monthly*, Nov. 1993.
"Kay Bailey Forehead. . . ." JACOB WEISBERG. *New Republic*, Oct. 18, 1993.
Kay Bailey Hutchison: Lone Star Girl. ARTHUR F. IDE. Monument Press, 1993.

I

Ibuse, Masuji (1898–1993) Born near Hiroshima, Masuji Ibuse was early in his career considerably influenced by his studies of French literature and readings in Russian literature. In the mid-1920s, his short stories in western modes were replaced by short stories and novels in more traditional Japanese modes, in such works as *Life at Mr. Tange's* (1931), *A War Diary* (1938), and *Tajinko Village* (1939). He was a war correspondent during World War II, then resuming his long career. He emerged as a major figure and is best known, by far, abroad for his novel *Black Rain* (1966), a massive work on the city and people of Hiroshima before and after the American atom bombing of August 6, 1945. He was also an essayist and poet. No information was available on survivors. (d. July 10, 1993)

FURTHER READING

Obituary. *The Times* (of London), July 14, 1993.
Obituary. *New York Times*, July 1, 1993.
Pools of Water, Pillars of Fire: The Literature of Ibuse Masuji. JOHN W. TREAT. University of Washington Press, 1988.

Ice-T (Tracy Marrow; c. 1955-60–   ) The nationwide controversy over rap musician Ice-T's 1992 song "Cop Killer" followed him throughout 1993. The song, which drew massive protests for such lyrics as "I've got my 12-gauge sawed off . . . I'm 'bout to dust some cops off . . . die, pig, die;" and "I'm 'bout to kill me somethin . . . a pig stopped me for nuthin;" and "What do you want to be when you grow up? . . . Cop killer!" was withdrawn by Ice-T and Time Warner in July 1992, but the immediate damage to his burgeoning career was done. He and Time Warner parted company in January 1993, cancelling recording, cable television, and book publishing plans; and Home Box Office withdrew his planned entertainment and talk show. He did release his next album, *Home Invasion*, through his own company in the spring of 1993; it enjoyed early sales, but suffered greatly from lack of national promotion and distribution. Ice-T continued to defend his position, supported by his young, African-American core audience.

Forthcoming was a starring role opposite Rutger Hauer and Charles S. Dutton in the film *Surviving the Game*, directed by Ernest Dickerson; Ice-T plays a homeless man being hunted by the Hauer character. Also forthcoming were a role in the film *Johnny Mnemonic*, directed by Robert Longo, and an as-told-to book, *The Ice Opinion*, written with Heidi Seigmund, scheduled for 1994 publication.

Newark-born Ice-T grew up in South Central Los Angeles, in the street gang culture that provides the setting for his music. His first recording was *The Coldest Rap* (1982), which led to work as a disc jockey and to a role in the film *Breakin'* (1984). He emerged as a popular rap musician in the late 1980s, with the appearance of his album *Rhyme Pays* (1987). Even more popular was his album *The Iceberg Freedom of Speech* (1989). He also scored a major success as an undercover police officer in the film *New Jack City* (1991), and in 1992 starred in the action-thriller film *Trespass*. His companion is Darlene Ortiz; they have one child.

FURTHER READING

"Words from. . . ." ALAN LIGHT. *Rolling Stone*, May 27, 1993.
"Ice capades." MEREDITH BERKMAN. *Entertainment*, Dec. 18, 1992.
"Ice T. . . ." ALAN LIGHT. *Rolling Stone*, Aug. 20, 1992.

Irons, Jeremy (1948–)

As his 1992 film *Damage* moved onto home screens, Jeremy Irons starred in 1993 in another major art film, David Henry Hwang's screen adaptation of his own hit play *M. Butterfly*. Irons played diplomat René Gallimard, in love with a Chinese opera star, transvestite Song Liling (John Lone), who he thinks is a woman, in a cast that included Barbara Sukova and Ian Richardson; David Cronenberg directed. Irons also starred on television in *The Dream*, Murray Watts's hour-long adaptation of a Dostoevsky short story. He was also one of the celebrity performers who did readings in Bill Couturie's environmentalist film *Earth and the American Dream*. Still forthcoming was a starring role in the film *House of the Spirits*, based on the Isabel Allende novel, set in Chile;

Jeremy Irons (above) and John Lone

co-starring were Meryl Streep, Winona Ryder, Glenn Close, and Antonio Banderas.

Irons emerged as a screen and stage star in the early 1980s. In 1981, he created the Charles Ryder role in the television miniseries "Brideshead Revisited," the celebrated adaptation of the Evelyn Waugh novel. In the same year, he played opposite Meryl Streep in *The French Lieutenant's Woman*. He went on to star in such films as *Moonlighting* (1982), *Betrayal* (1983), *The Wild Duck* (1983), *Swann in Love* (1984), *The Mission* (1986), *Dead Ringers* (1989), *Frankenstein Unbound* (1989), *A Chorus of Disapproval* (1989), *Reversal of Fortune* (1990), winning a best actor Oscar for his portrayal of Claus von Bulow, and *Kafka* (1991). He won a Tony as best leading actor in a drama for *The Real Thing* (1984). He and Sinead Cusack have two children.

FURTHER READING

"A question of character." GEORGINA HOWELL. *Vogue*, Jan. 1993.
"Metamorphosis." HARLAN KENNEDY. *American Film*, Nov.-Dec. 1991.
"Claus encounters." ELLEN STERN. *GQ—Gentlemen's Quarterly*, Nov. 1990.
"Irons." DAVID DENICOLO. *Interview*, June 1990.
Actors: A Celebration. RITA GAM. St. Martin's, 1988.

Ivory, James Francis (1928–)

In 1993, celebrated film director James Ivory added another major art film to his long list of triumphs, as his peers were still recognizing his 1992

Howard's End, which won nine Oscar nominations, including a best director nomination for Ivory, as well as best director nominations from the Directors Guild of America and Golden Globes Awards.

Ivory's new film was *The Remains of the Day*, written by Ruth Prawer Jhabvala, based on the 1989 novel by Kazuo Ishiguro, and produced by Ismail Merchant, Mike Nichols, and John Calley. Anthony Hopkins starred as the quintessentially loyal and dedicated 1930s English butler Stevens, opposite Emma Thompson as Miss Kenton, another employee of Lord Darlington, played by James Fox. The cast also included Christopher Reeve, Peter Vaughan, Hugh Grant, Michael Lonsdale, and Tim Pigott-Smith. It opened to critical acclaim, and was generally seen as a strong contender many 1994 honors.

Forthcoming was the film *Jefferson in Paris*, with screenplay by Jhabvala, and starring Nick Nolte and Greta Scacchi, slated to be the first Merchant-Ivory film produced under the long-term financing agreement with Disney signed in 1992.

California-born Ivory began his long, fruitful collaboration with Merchant and Jhabvala in the early 1960s, with such films as *Shakespeare Wallah* (1965), *Bombay Talkie* (1970), and *Autobiography of a Princess* (1975), all of them largely set in India. His later films included *The Europeans* (1979), *Heat and Dust* (1983), *A Room with a View* (1986), *Maurice* (1987), *Slaves of New York* (1989), and *Mr. and Mrs. Bridge* (1990). Ivory's 1951 B.F.A. was from the University of Oregon, his M.A. from the University of Southern California.

FURTHER READING

"Doing it right the hard way. . . ." RICHARD CORLISS. *Time*, Mar. 16, 1992.

Films of Merchant Ivory. ROBERT E. LONG. Abrams, 1991.

"Mr. and Mrs. Bridge." GRAHAM FULLER. *Interview*, Nov. 1990.

J

Jackson, Bo (Vincent Edwards Jackson; 1962–) Bo Jackson is used to confounding naysayers. One of only a few two-sport professional athletes, he is the only one ever to have been an All-Star in two sports, baseball and football. Then, in January 1991, playing as a running back for the Los Angeles Raiders football team in a playoff game against the Cincinnati Bengals, Jackson's hip was injured in a tackle; a condition called avascular necrosis developed, in which the bone dies for lack of blood circulation. His athletic career, it was assumed, was over. But that was not Jackson's idea. He may, indeed, have left football for good, but baseball was still open to him. He lost the rest of 1991

and all of 1992, during which time he had hip replacement surgery and set about his rehabilitation program.

Early in 1993, Jackson joined the Chicago White Sox, becoming the first professional athlete ever to play with an artificial hip. It is typical of the man that in the first swing of his first at-bat of the season, this "bionic man" hit a 400-foot home run into the rightfield seats. Before a hand injury early in the season, Jackson played in the outfield surprisingly well, considering not just his recovery but also that he had not played there since October 1990. For the overall season he was used on a part-time basis, sometimes in the outfield, often as a designated hitter, batting .232, hitting 16 home runs with 45 RBI's, and helping his team to their first division championship since 1983, though they lost the pennant to the Toronto Blue Jays who went on to win the World Series. Earlier, in May, Jackson singled in the eighth inning to foil a no-hit bid by the New York Yankees' one-handed pitcher, Jim Abbott (who later did pitch a no-hitter); from first base, Jackson saluted Abbott, as one observer put it, "One miracle man honoring another." In December 1993, Jackson became a free agent, having rejected a new-season offer from the White Sox.

Born in Bessemer, Alabama, Jackson attended Auburn University, where he excelled at baseball, track, and football, winning the Heisman trophy for the latter in 1985, when he averaged 162.4 yards per game, becoming Auburn's all-time leading rusher. In baseball, he was a pitcher in high school, hitting a national record 20 home runs in 25 games in his final year. He joined the Kansas City Royals baseball team (1986–91), the following year also beginning play with the Los Angeles Raiders football team (1987–91). In 1989, he led the American League All-Star voting, then became one of only five players to lead-off the All-Star Game with a home run, and one of only two (with Willie Mays) to homer and steal a base in the same game; he was named most valuable player. In football, he was unanimously named to the National Football League's All-Rookie Team, in 1987, and went to the Pro Bowl in 1990. After his hip-destroying injury, in 1991, he was released by Kansas City, then signed an option with the Chicago White Sox. He published *Bo Knows Bo: The Autobiography of a Ballplayer* (1990), written with Dick Schaap. Jackson is married to Linda Garrett and has two sons and a daughter.

FURTHER READING

"Bo knows. . . ." MAURICE WEAVER. *Ebony*, Aug. 1993.
Bo Jackson: A Star for All Seasons. JOHN DEVANEY. Walker, 1992.
"Bo Jackson." DICK SCHAAP. *Sport*, Oct. 1991.
"Bo Jackson." *Sporting News*, Aug. 12, 1991.
"Jackson, Bo." *Current Biography*, June 1991.
"Don't tell Bo. . . ." WILLIAM PLUMMER. *People*, May 20, 1991.
Bo Jackson. JAMES R. ROTHAUS. Child's World, 1991.
Bo Jackson. Scholastic, 1991.
Bo Jackson. JOHN ROLFE. Lerner, 1991.
Bo Jackson: Baseball-Football Superstar. RICK L. JOHNSON. Dillon/Macmillan, 1991.
Bo Jackson. JOHN ROLFE. Little, Brown, 1991.
Bo Jackson. BILL GUTMAN. Pocketbooks, 1991.
Bo Jackson: Pro Sports Superstar. ROM RABER. Lerner, 1991.
Bo Jackson: Playing the Games. ELLEN E. WHITE. Scholastic, 1990.
Bo Jackson. STEPHEN HANKS. St. Martin's, 1990.
Sports Great Bo Jackson. RON KNAPP. Enslow, 1990.
Bo Jackson: A Star for All Seasons. JOHN DEVANEY. Walker, 1988.

Jackson, Janet (1966–　) Janet Jackson issued a new album in 1993, the first of three albums covered by her March 1991, $40 million agreement with Virgin Records, which had made her one of the world's most highly paid perform-

ers. It was *Janet*, a potpourri of songs that did well commercially, though many reviewers thought it rather unfocused and self-consciously sexual in content. Its lead single, "That's The Way Love Goes," was a hit, as were, to a lesser extent, several of the singles from the album issued throughout the year. Jackson also began her screen career in 1993, starring in *Poetic Justice*, written and directed by John Singleton, in a cast that included Tupac Shakur and Maya Angelou. The film, about African-American life in California, was set in south central Los Angeles and Oakland. The song "Again," written for the film, became a popular single Jackson recording.

On the personal side, Jackson could not help becoming enmeshed in the huge media outcry accompanying the child abuse allegations against her brother, Michael Jackson, though there was no hint of personal involvement.

As a child, Jackson appeared with her brothers, as the Jackson Five. She made three albums in the early 1980s: *Janet Jackson* (1982), *Dream Street* (1984), and *Control* (1986); the latter introduced several hit singles, and suggested the major career that would blossom a few years later. She scored a major success in 1989, with the hit album *Rhythm Nation: 1814*. Singer and dancer Jackson began her first concert tour on March 1, 1990 in Miami, and from there went on to tour the United States, Japan, and Europe. In January 1991, her "Love Will Never Do (Without You)" became a number one pop single. She was formerly married.

FURTHER READING

"Sexual healing. . . ." DAVID RITZ. *Rolling Stone*, Sep. 16, 1993.
"Grown-up Janet Jackson talks. . . ." LYNN NORMANT. *Ebony*, Sep. 1993.
"Planet Janet." STEVE POND. *Us*, Aug. 1993.
"Janet's Passions." DAVID RITZ. *Essence*, May 1993.
"Jackson, Janet." *Current Biography*, June 1991.
La Toya: Growing up in the Jackson Family. LA TOYA JACKSON and PATRICIA ROMANOWSKI. NAL-Dutton, 1991.
"Janet Jackson. . . ." ROBERT E. JOHNSON. *Ebony*, Feb. 1990.
"Free at last." ANTHONY DECURTIS. *Rolling Stone*, Feb. 22, 1990.
My Family, The Jacksons. KATHERINE JACKSON. St. Martin's, 1990.
Janet Jackson. D.L. MABERY. Lerner, 1988.
Janet Jackson: In Control. NANCY ROBISON. Dillon, 1987.

Jackson, Jesse Louis (1941–) Jesse Jackson, who only a few years before was the leading African-American politician in the country, found himself in many respects far out in the political cold in 1993. He continued to be highly visible, visiting Haiti in January and South Africa in May, for Oliver Tambo's funeral, and still received media coverage in such situations as the New Jersey gubernatorial election aftermath and the New York City mayoral election. But without a substantial political base of his own or in the Democratic Party, Jackson had lost much of his political strength. He suffered a major personal defeat in April, when he was forced to withdraw as a candidate for the job of executive director of the National Association for the Advancement of Colored People (NAACP) because of lack of support. Late in the year, Jackson became highly visible in the campaign against violence in African-American communities. Still a "shadow Senator" from the District of Columbia, Jackson also campaigned for D.C. statehood during 1993, and on August 26 was arrested, with D.C. mayor Sharon Pratt Kelly and others, for blocking Pennsylvania Avenue during a D.C. statehood demonstration.

Long active in the civil rights movement, Jackson directed the Southern Christian Leadership Operation Breadbasket (1967–71), and in 1971 founded Operation PUSH (People United to Save Humanity), and later the Rainbow Coalition. He made an unsuccessful bid for the Democratic presidential nomination in 1984 and again in 1988, but emerged as a major figure, especially after his electrifying address to the 1988 convention. Jackson did not run for the Presidency in 1992, was denied the vice presidential nomination by Bill Clinton, seemed responsive to Jerry Brown and Ross Perot, and ultimately spoke to the July Democratic National Convention in support of Clinton, and then campaigned for Clinton all over the country.

South Carolina-born Jackson received his 1964 B.A. from North Carolina Agricultural and Technical University. After postgraduate work at the Chicago Theological Seminary, he became a Baptist minister in 1968. In 1988, he published *A Time to Speak: The Autobiography of the Reverend Jesse Jackson.* He married Jacqueline Brown in 1964; they have five children.

FURTHER READING

Jesse Jackson and Black People. AMIRI BARAKA. Third World, 1994.
Civil Rights Leaders. RICHARD RENNERT, ed. Chelsea House, 1993.
Race, Politics and the White Media: The Jesse Jackson Campaigns. ARNOLD GIBBONS. University Press of America, 1993.
Black American Politics: From the Washington Marches to Jesse Jackson, 2nd ed. MANNING MARABLE. Routledge Chapman & Hall, 1993.
"America's great black hope." ALEXANDER COCKBURN and ANDREW KOPKIND. *New Statesman & Society*, July 10, 1992.
"The gift." Feb. 3, 1992. "History is upon us." Feb. 10, 1992. "Without portfolio." Feb. 17, 1992. MARSHALL FRADY. *New Yorker*. (Parts I-III of *Outsider* series.)
I Am Somebody!: A Biography of Jesse Jackson. JAMES HASKINS. Enslow, 1992.
Keep Hope Alive: Super Tuesday and Jesse Jackson's 1988 Campaign for the Presidency. PENN KIMBALL. Joint Center for Political Studies, 1992.
"From Jim Crow. . . ." MARILYN BERLIN SNELL. *New Perspectives*, Summer 1991.
Jesse Jackson and Political Power. TERESA CELSI. Millbrook, 1991.
Jesse Jackson. ROBERT JAKOUBEK. Chelsea House, 1991.
Jesse Jackson: A Biography. PATRICIA C. MCKISSACK. Scholastic, 1991.
Jesse Jackson: Still Fighting for the Dream. BRENDA WILKINSON. Silver Burdett, 1990.
The Jackson Phenomenon: The Man, the Power, and the Message. ELIZABETH O. COULTON. Doubleday, 1989.
Jesse Jackson: A Voice for Change. STEVE OFFINOSKI. Fawcett, 1989.

Jackson, Michael Joseph (1958–) In

March 1993, world-famous singer Michael Jackson was awarded a Grammy Legend Award at the 35th Annual Grammy Awards. Earlier, in February, he had given his first live interview ever, with Oprah Winfrey, airing as a 90-minute prime-time special, the greatest controversy being whether he had chemically lightened his skin; he said not, though he used makeup because of a skin condition.

But then 1993 became a nightmare year for Michael Jackson. His musical career and humanitarian record had made him a worldwide figure, but his career and reputation were overwhelmed by highly publicized charges of child sex abuse. Whether the charges were true or not, Jackson was indicted, tried, and convicted in the media without having appeared in any legal proceeding. The storm broke in late August, when Los Angeles police confirmed a story that investigation of child sex abuse allegations against Jackson had been underway for a week. A 13-year-old boy filed a civil lawsuit against him in early September. Jackson, then on tour in Asia, denied all charges, claiming that they were part of an extortion plan. As pressure grew, Jackson canceled several scheduled appearances, and on November 14 canceled his world tour and went into hiding, stating that pain from an earlier operation and current pressures had addicted him to painkillers, and that he was seeking treatment. The pressure increased, as the singer's estranged sister, La Toya Jackson, publicly

accused him of a history of child molestation. At year's end, Jackson had reappeared in the United States, ready to face any civil and possible criminal charges, as the media continued its relentless attack. Meanwhile, the contract for Jackson's Nation Films, which had produced no films for Columbia Pictures since its 1991 inception, was set to expire in January 1994.

Indiana-born Jackson began his extraordinary career in 1969, as the 11-year-old lead singer of his family's singing group, The Jackson Five. He became a leading popular soloist in the late 1970s, with such albums as *Off the Wall* (1979), *Thriller* (1982), which sold over four million copies, *Bad* (1987), and such singles as "I Can't Stop Loving You," along with many popular videos. His 1991 album *Dangerous* generated the 1991 single "Black or White," his hit 1992 video "Remember the Time," and such 1992 hit singles as "In the Closet," "Jam," and "Heal the World." Jackson starred opposite Diana Ross in the film version of *The Wiz* (1978) and in *Moonwalker* (1988).

FURTHER READING

Michael Jackson: Entertainer. LOIS NICHOLSON. Chelsea House, 1994.
"Time to face the music." DANA KENNEDY. *Entertainment*, Dec. 17, 1993.
"The vanishing." ELIZABETH GLEICK. *People*, Nov. 29, 1993.
"Family and fans support. . . ." *Jet*, Sep. 13, 1993.
"Is this the end? . . ." DANA KENNEDY and NISID HAJARI. *Entertainment*, Sep. 10, 1993.
"Michael's world." CATHLEEN McGUIGAN. *Newsweek*, Sep. 6, 1993.
"Beyond the pale." KEN TUCKER et al. *Entertainment*, Feb. 26, 1993.
Michael Jackson. Andrews & McMeel, 1993.
Michael Jackson: King of Pop. LISA CAMPBELL. Branden, 1993.
"Ebony/Jet interview with. . . ." ROBERT E. JOHNSON. *Ebony*, Nov. 1992.
"Michael Jackson. . . ." MICHAEL GOLDBERG. *Rolling Stone*, Jan. 9, 1992.
The Michael Jackson Scrapbook. LES LEE. Citadel Press/Carol, 1992.
Michael Jackson: The Magic and the Madness. J. RANDY TARABORRELLI. Carol, 1991.
La Toya: Growing up in the Jackson Family. LA TOYA JACKSON and PATRICIA ROMANOWSKI. NAL-Dutton, 1991.
Michael Jackson: A Life in Music. HAL SCHUSTER. Movie Publications, 1990.
My Family, The Jacksons. KATHERINE JACKSON. St. Martin's, 1990.

Sequins and Shades: The Michael Jackson Reference Guide. CAROL TERRY. Popular Culture, 1989.

Moonwalk. MICHAEL JACKSON. Doubleday, 1988; Writers Digest, 1989.

Michael Jackson Electrifying. GREG QUILL. Barron's, 1988.

Jackson, Phil (Philip Douglas Jackson; 1946–) No team had done it since the Boston Celtics in the 1960's; but the Chicago Bulls, under coach Phil Jackson, won their third straight National Basketball Association (NBA) championship in June 1993. To do so, they first fought off the New York Knicks' powerful and physical challenge in the Eastern Conference finals, after losing the first two games, then defeated the Western Conference champions, the Phoenix Suns. The Bull's four-year playoff record of 55 wins to 19 losses under Jackson also gives him the highest percentage of playoff wins of any coach in NBA history, at .743. With the Bulls having best record in the Eastern Conference at mid-season, Jackson would normally have been coach of the January 1993 All-Star game, but was barred by league rules from repeating in that position, and so was replaced by second-place Knicks' coach Pat Riley.

In the autumn of 1993, Jackson found he would be tested as never before. Just before the season opened, Bulls' superstar Michael Jordan suddenly announced his retirement from basketball, leaving a gaping hole in the team, as in the sport as a whole, and causing Jackson and his staff to recast their coaching approaches and game plans, a problem further complicated by injuries to several other key players early in the season. By the beginning of 1994, the Bulls had a respectable but not earth-shaking 18–9 record, which was seventh in the league. But no one was counting them out.

Montana-born Jackson was twice an All-American basketball player at the University of North Dakota in the mid-1960s. A strong defensive forward, he was drafted by the New York Knicks in 1967, and spent 11 years with the Knicks, missing the 1970 championship season because of an injury, but playing on the 1973 championship team. He ended his career with the New York Nets, and stayed on as an assistant coach and then television analyst. He compiled a winning record as coach of the Albany Patroons of the Continental Basketball Association (1982–87), capturing the CBA championship (1984) and being named coach of the year (1985), and then joined the Bulls as an assistant coach. He succeeded Doug Collins as head coach in 1989, and immediately emerged as a major figure in basketball, coaching the Bulls to the Eastern Division finals. By having Jordan score less and distribute the ball more to others, Jackson guided his team to three straight NBA championships (1991–1993); he was the only person ever to have coached championship teams in both the NBA and CBA. He wrote an early autobiography of himself and his Knick days, *Maverick* (1975). Jackson is married, and has five children.

FURTHER READING

"Jackson, Phil." *Current Biography*, July 1992.

"The age of Jackson." JEFF COPLON. *New York Times Magazine*, May 17, 1992.

"Phil Jackson's courtly attitude." *GQ—Gentleman's Quarterly*, Feb. 1992.

"For whom the Bulls toll." JACK MCCALLUM. *Sports Illustrated*, Nov. 11, 1991.

Jackson, Reggie (Reginald Martinez Jackson; 1946–) For Mr. October it was Mr. Cooperstown, as Reggie Jackson was the sole player elected to baseball's Hall of Fame in 1993, only the 29th player ever to be elected in his first year of eligibility (after five years' retirement) and the 216th overall. Jackson gathered 93.6 percent of the votes cast by members of the Baseball Writers Association, the 10th-highest percentage ever. Two weeks later, Jackson's number, 44, was retired by the Yankees, only the 14th in that organization's history. Earlier in the year, Jackson had joined the Yankees, brought in by one-time boss and some-time nemesis, George Steinbrenner, as a special advisor to "evaluate talent."

Pennsylvania-born Jackson attended Arizona State University, breaking into the major leagues with the Kansas City, then Oakland, Athletics (1967–75), briefly visited the Baltimore Orioles (1976), moved on to the Yankees (1977–81), then played out his career as a designated hitter for the California Angels (1982–86) and finally Oakland again (1987). His nickname "Mr. October" indicated his value in the season stretch, as he played for 11 division champion teams: Athletics (1971–75), Yankees (1977–78, 1980–81), and Angels (1982–86); his most notable performance was in Game 6 of the 1977 World Series, hitting a record-tying three home runs, for a record-breaking five homers in the series, won by the Yankees, and the highest slugging percentage at 1.250. Though setting records for strikeouts, he hit a total of 563 home runs, 11 of them grand slams; had 1551 runs and 1702 runs batted in; and ended with a career World Series batting percentage of .357 and slugging percentage of .755. Jackson was American League Most Valuable Player and *Sporting News* Major League Player of the Year (1973) and a member of the AL All-Star Team (1969, 1971–75, 1977–82, 1984). Among his books are *Reggie* (1975), with Bill Libby; *Inside Hitting* (1975), with Joel Cohen; *Reggie Jackson Scrapbook* (1978); and *Reggie* (1984), with Mike Lupica. An adviser to the Upper Deck sports card manufacturing company, Jackson is divorced and has a daughter. His father, Martinez Jackson, played in baseball's segregated Negro Leagues.

FURTHER READING

"Reggie Jackson. . . ." Patrick S. Washburn. *Boys' Life*, Sep. 1993.
"The gall of fame." Michael Angeli. *Sports Illustrated*, Aug. 2, 1993.
"I, Reggie. . . ." Mike Lupica. *Esquire*, June 1993.
"The first to be free. . . ." Leigh Montville. *Sports Illustrated*, Apr. 16, 1990.

Jagger, Mick (Michael Philip Jagger; 1941–) Still fronting the Rolling Stones, as he has done for three decades, Jagger also issued a well-received new solo album in February 1993: *Wandering Spirit*, co-produced with highly successful record producer and promoter Rick Rubin. Among the songs on the album were "Wandering Spirit," "Wired All Night," "Sweet Thing," "Put Me in the Trash," the traditional air "Handsome Molly," Bill Withers's "Use Me," Frederick Knight's "I've Been Lonely for So Long," "Evening Gown," "Hang on to Me Tonight," "Angel in My Heart," the traditional "Lady Jane," and "Don't Tear Me Up." Later in the year, Jagger also released single recordings of "Don't Tear Me Up" and "Out Of Focus."

Jagger was, in 1962, the chief organizer of the Rolling Stones; he and Keith Richards were the group's main songwriters, and Jagger was its leading performer, playing the role of an angry, deeply alienated, uncontrollably violent, mythic sexual figure, a model for the scores of other such rock and popular music figures who would follow. Such albums as *The Rolling Stones* (1964; and two 1965 sequels), *Aftermath* (1966) and *Their Satanic Majesties Request* (1967), coupled with their worldwide tours, established them as one of the leading popular musical groups of the century. In 1969, after a murder by their Hell's Angels security guards at an Altamont, California Stones concert, the group toned down their image somewhat. Although they continued to tour and record throughout the 1980s, their popularity lessened after the mid-1970s. Yet their very successful 1989–90 world tour showed that the 28-year-old rock group still had enormous vitality and drawing power. Jagger appeared in the film *Ned Kelly* (1969), and in the film of the Altamont concert, *Gimme Shelter* (1972). He has also done several solo recordings.

Jagger attended the London School of Economics. He was formerly married to Bianca Jagger (Bianca Pérez Morena de Macîas) (1971–79), and married his longtime companion, model Jerry Hall, in 1990. Jagger has five children, the three youngest with Hall.

FURTHER READING

Mick Jagger: Primitive Cool. CHRISTOPHER SANDFORD. St. Martin's, 1994.
"Mick Jagger." KURT LODER. *Esquire*, Apr. 1993.
"The Stones at 50." BRIAN D. JOHNSON. *Maclean's*, Feb. 15, 1993.
"Adulation guaranteed " GILES SMITH. *Independent*, Jan. 25, 1993.
Mick Jagger: The Story Behind the Rolling Stone. DAVIN SEAY. Birch Lane/Carol, 1993.
Jagger Unauthorized. CHRISTOPHER ANDERSEN. Delacorte, 1993.
The Rolling Stones Album: Thirty Years of Music and Memorabilia. GEOFFREY GIULIANO. Viking/Studio Books, 1993.
"Mick's moves." STEPHEN SCHIFF. *Vanity Fair*, Feb. 1992.
Rolling Stones. DAVID CARTER. Outlet, 1992.
Time Is on My Side: The Rolling Stones Day-By-Day, 1962–1984. ALAN STEWART and CATHY SANFORD. Popular Culture, 1992.
The Rolling Stones' Rock and Roll Circus. MIKE RANDOLPH. Chronicle Books, 1991.
Rolling Stones Images. DAVID FRICKE. Simon & Schuster, 1991.
Blown Away: The Rolling Stones and the Death of the Sixties. A.E. HOTCHNER. Simon & Schuster, 1990.
Rolling Stones Complete Recording Sessions. MARTIN ELLIOTT. Borgo Press/Sterling 1990.
The Rolling Stones Chronicle. MASSIMO BONANNO. Holt, 1990.
The Rolling Stones. TIM DOWLEY. Seven Hills, 1989.
It's Only Rock 'n' Roll: My On-the-Road Adventures with the Rolling Stones. CHET FLIPPO. St. Martin's, 1989.
The Rolling Stone Interviews: The 1980s. St. Martin's, 1989.

Janeway, Eliot (1913–93) New York City-born Eliot Janeway, an economist, stock market advisory service publisher, and writer, began to emerge on the national scene with his 1937 articles for *The Nation*, predicting the 1937–38 economic downturn. He edited a newsletter for Henry Luce (1944–48), and in 1955 began the group of widely circulated advisory newsletters that would grow into the Janeway Publishing and Research Corporation. The first of his several books was *Struggle For Survival* (1951), on the World War II American wartime economic mobilization, his last *The Economics of Chaos* (1989). Janeway was also a widely read syndicated columnist. Throughout his career, Janeway was a notable and sometimes correct pessimist, predicting impending economic and political disaster. Closely associated with Lyndon B. Johnson during the 1950s and 1960s, he broke with President Johnson in 1965, over the expansion of the Vietnam War. He was survived by his wife, the writer Elizabeth Hall Janeway, and two sons. (d. New York City; February 8, 1993)

FURTHER READING

Obituary. *Current Biography*, Apr. 1993.
Obituary. *The Times* (of London), Feb. 13, 1993.
Obituary. *New York Times*, Feb. 9, 1993.

Janzen, Lee MacLeod (1964–   ) American golfer Lee Janzen won his first major tournament, and his third on the Professional Golfers Association (PGA) Tour, in June 1993, when he took the 93rd U.S. Open at Baltusrol, in Springfield, New Jersey. On a suffocatingly hot day, he fell into a tie with Payne Stewart in the final round, but hit three birdies in the last five holes, including an extraordinary chip shot from the rough on the 16th hole, for a two-stroke victory. He also entered the record books, tying the U.S. open scoring record of 272 set by Jack Nicklaus in 1980, and becoming only the second person (after Lee Trevino in 1968) to break 70 on all four rounds of the Open, with 67–67–69–69. Earlier in the year, Janzen had won the Phoenix Open, a pro-am tournament in which he was partnered with Charles Barkley; Janzen was also a member of the successful 1993 Ryder Cup team.

Born in Austin, Minnesota, Janzen graduated

in 1986 with a degree in marketing from Florida Southern College, there winning the 1986 Division II National Championship and being selected to the All-American first team in 1985 and 1986. Turning professional that year, he played on the U.S. Gold (mini) Tour, and was its leading money winner in 1989, the year he joined the PGA Tour. Janzen joined the winner's circle for the first time in 1991, winning the Northern Telecom Open, rising to 9th spot on the PGA Tour. He is married to Beverly Janzen and has one stepdaughter; in late 1993, they were expecting a baby.

FURTHER READING

"Perfect-Lee." DAVID BARRETT. *Golf*, Aug. 1993.
"Sweet sixteen. " RICK REILLY. *Sports Illustrated*, June 28, 1993.
"For openers. . . ." BOB VERDI. *Sporting News*, June 28, 1993.

Jennings, Peter Charles (1938–)

News anchor Peter Jennings started 1993 by signing a new multi-year contract with ABC-though reportedly only after receiving an offer to become a Paris-based correspondent for CBS's top-rated news magazine "60 Minutes." During the year, Jennings widened his lead over the nightly news competition, a lead he has held almost uninterruptedly since 1989. Seeking to close the gap, CBS in June added Connie Chung as co-host with Dan Rather; long-term results were not yet in, but by year's end they had fallen further behind ABC and even behind NBC's Tom Brokaw.

In April, "World News Tonight" was given a new executive producer, Emily Rooney; both she and Jennings were later quoted as saying that they wanted to pay more attention to what conservatives were saying; when this sparked concern, both stressed that they were attempting to make their news reporting more "inclusive." Rooney, however, lasted only eight months on the job; she was reportedly replaced after abrasion developed between her and other staff members.

Jennings also hosted two more of his 90-minute Saturday-morning television specials for young people. In February, in an extraordinary coup, he had President Bill Clinton answering questions from children in an audience at the White House and from callers in other studio audiences and in homes around the country. In November, in *Kids in the Crossfire: Violence in America*, Jennings moderated discussions among teenagers about violence in their lives, with no less a guest than Attorney General Janet Reno.

In March, Jennings personally went to report from the former Yugoslavia, despite ABC management's concern for his safety, since nine journalists had been killed there in 1992; to minimize the danger, Jennings kept a low profile, not announcing the trip. On his return he hosted a special on the region, *The Land of the Demons*.

On the personal side, Jennings and his wife, writer Kati Marton, separated in 1993 after 14 years of marriage.

Toronto-born Jennings worked in Canadian broadcasting before joining ABC News in 1964. During the next two decades, much of that time spent abroad, he rose to become chief London correspondent for ABC, and in 1983 became the anchor of "World News Tonight," one of the three chief American reporters and interpreters of the news. Jennings attended Carleton University, and his LL.D. is from Rider College. He has been married three times and he has two children.

FURTHER READING

"Covering the 'holocaust.' " PETER ROSS RANGE. *TV Guide*, May 15, 1993.

"How 'Stanley Stunning'. . . ." ALAN EBERT. *Good Housekeeping*, Apr. 1991.

Anchors: Brokaw, Jennings, Rather and the Evening News. ROBERT GOLDBERG and GERALD J. GOLDBERG. Birch Lane/Carol, 1990.

"The kiss of the anchor man." E. JEAN CARROLL. *Playboy*, Dec. 1990.

"Peter Jennings gets no self-respect." ELIZABETH KAYE. *Esquire*, Sep. 1989.

"The A-B-Cs of Peter Jennings." NORMAN ATKINS. *Rolling Stone*, May 4, 1989.

Jhabvala, Ruth Prawer

Jhabvala, Ruth Prawer (1927–) Honored by her film industry peers, Ruth Prawer Jhabvala in 1993 won an Academy Award for best adapted screenplay, for *Howard's End*. She also was also nominated for a Golden Globe best screenplay award for the film.

Her major 1993 screenplay was for the film *The Remains of the Day*, adapted from the Kazuo Ishiguro novel, directed by James Ivory, and produced by Mike Nichols, John Calley, and Ismail Merchant. Anthony Hopkins starred as the 1930s butler who devotes his life to his far-from-worthy fascist-sympathizer employer, as he would to any employer, as a matter of honorable dedication, in the process destroying an possibility of living a life of his own. Emma Thompson co-starred, as another employee in the same household, whose attempts at bulding a relationship with the butler are ultimately fruitless.

As a novelist, Jhabvala also produced a new book, *Poet and Dancer*, set in New York. Like so much of her other work, it is about distancing and the intersection of two cultures. Forthcoming were the film *Jefferson in Paris*, directed by Ivory, produced by Merchant, and starring Nick Nolte; a film biography of Pablo Picasso; and a film adaptation of the Henry James novel *The Wings of the Dove*.

German-born Jhabvala lived in India (1951–75), where much of her work is set, and in the United States thereafter. A distinguished novelist and short story writer, she has also written several classic screenplays, many of them directed by James Ivory. Some of her best known novels are *The Nature of Passion* (1956), *The Householder* (1960), *Heat and Dust* (1975), *In Search of Love and Beauty* (1983), and *Three Continents* (1987). Her filmscripts include *The Householder* (1963) *Shakespeare Wallah* (1965), *The Guru* (1969), *Bombay Talkie* (1971), *Autobiography of a Princess* (1975), *Roseland* (1977), *Hullabaloo over Georgie and Bonnie's Pictures* (1978), *Jane Austen in Manhattan* (1980), *Quartet* (1981), *Heat and Dust* (1983), *The Bostonians* (1984), *Room With A View* (1986; she won a best screenplay Oscar), and *Mr. and Mrs. Bridge* (1990). Her M.A. is from the University of London. She is married to Indian architect Cyrus S.H. Jhabvala, and has three children.

FURTHER READING

"A cinematic sensibility." JAMES ATLAS. *Vogue*, Mar. 1993.

"The book of Ruth." JOSEPHINE HART. *Vanity Fair*, Mar. 1993.

Silence, Exile and Cunning: The Fiction of Ruth Prawer Jhabvala, 2nd ed. YASMINE GOONERATNE. Apt, 1993.

"Doing it right the hard way. . . ." RICHARD CORLISS. *Time*, Mar. 16, 1992.

Ruth Prawer Jhabvala: Fiction and Film. JAYANTI BAILUR. Arnold/South Asia, 1992.

Ruth Prawer Jhabvala. RALPH J. CRANE. Twayne/Macmillan, 1992.

" 'Mr. and Mrs. Bridge.' " GRAHAM FULLER. *Interview*, Nov. 1990.

The Fiction of Ruth Prawer Jhabvala. LAURIE SUCHER. St. Martin's, 1989.

Joel, Billy

Joel, Billy (William Martin Joel; 1949–) Four years after issuing his last album, Billy Joel in 1993 issued the hit album *River of Dreams*, which quickly went to the top of the record sales charts, and by year's end had spent 20 weeks on the Billboard top 200 chart, selling more than 2 million copies. It was preceded by release of the title cut as a hit single. Joel's songs "Shades of Grey" and "All About Soul," both drawn from the album, were also hit singles.

During 1993, Joel continued to press his multiple court cases. In 1990, he became involved in a long, expensive lawsuit against his former brother-in-law and manager, Frank Weber, ultimately winning $2 million in damages, and in the years that followed mounted legal actions against his former accounting firm and his former law firm.

New York City-born Joel became a leading popular recording artist in the mid-1970s, with such albums as *Piano Man* (1974), *Streetlight Serenade* (1974), *The Stranger* (1976), *52nd Street* (1978), *Glass Houses* (1980), *An Innocent Man* (1983), *The Bridge* (1986), *Live in the U.S.S.R.* (1987), *A Matter of Trust* (1988), and *Storm Front* (1990). His voice was featured in the animated film *Oliver and Company* (1988). Previously divorced, Joel married model Christie Brinkley in 1985, and has one child.

FURTHER READING

"Backstage with. . . ." JIM JEROME. *People Weekly*, Dec. 13, 1993.
"Little Billy. . . ." LINDA SANDERS. *Entertainment*, Sep. 10, 1993.
"Billy Joel. . . ." DAVID WILD. *Rolling Stone*, Jan 25, 1990.

John Paul II, Pope (Karol Wojtyla; 1920–)

In 1993, Pope John Paul II continued to travel widely, and to pursue a set of major conservative themes, most notably, regarding abortion, sexual activity, and dissent within Catholicism. In February, he visited Benin, Uganda, and Sudan. In Uganda, a country desperately afflicted with an AIDS epidemic that had so far infected an estimated 1.5 million, the Pope urged chastity for young Ugandans, rather than the use of condoms to combat the spread of the disease. In Muslim-ruled Sudan, itself engaged in a bitter civil war with its Christian and animist south, the Pope attempted to play a peacemaker's role, also trying to soften the impact of Muslim fundamentalist attacks on Christians.

In August, he visited Jamaica, Mexico, and the United States; at the Catholic World Youth Day rally in Denver, he spoke again on the main issues that continued to animate his papacy, although his comments on abortion were somewhat less sharp than those in his prepared speech. In Denver, Pope John Paul also condemned the sexual abuse of children by some American Catholic priests, a matter that was in the process of convulsing American Catholicism. He had in June also issued a letter in which he condemned child sex abuse by some in the Catholic clergy. In September, he visited Latvia, Lithuania, and Estonia; it was his first visit to any of the countries of the former Soviet Union.

Still absolutely opposed to the ordination of women, the Pope also sharply criticized feminists on other grounds, in particular condemning those American Catholic women's groups that worshipped any form of an "earth goddess." In 1993, the Pope issued his tenth encyclical: *Veritatis Splendor (The Splendor of Truth)*.

On the personal side, Pope John Paul tripped on his robe and broke his shoulder in November, at the Vatican.

John Paul II is the first Pope of Polish origin, and the first non-Italian Pope of the past four centuries. He was ordained as a Catholic priest in 1946, and then moved steadily upward in the Polish Catholic Church, becoming a professor of theology in the 1950s, and ultimately archbishop of Crakow (1963–78). He became a Cardinal in 1967, and then Pope in 1978. He has been largely a very conservative Pope, strongly opposing abortion and strongly discouraging liberal social action on the part of the priesthood. He attended Cracow's Jagellonian University and Rome's Angelicum.

FURTHER READING

At the Center of the Human Drama: The Philosophical Anthropology of Karol Wojtyla-Pope John Paul II. KENNETH L. SCHMITZ. Catholic University Press, 1994.
"States of savagery. . . ." JAS GAWRONSKI. *Guardian*, Nov. 2, 1993.
"Veritatis Splendor." LAWRENCE S. CUNNINGHAM, et al. *Commonweal*, Oct. 22, 1993.
"Pope soldiers on. . . ." PETER HEBBLETHWAITE. *National Catholic Reporter*, Oct. 22, 1993.
"The prophetic humanism. . . ." AVERY DULLES. *America*, Oct. 23, 1993.
"Encyclical nails. . . ." PETER HEBBLETHWAITE. *National Catholic Reporter*, Oct. 8, 1993.
"The Pope takes on. . . ." BRIAN ROBERTSON. *Insight*, Sep. 13, 1993.

"Seen from far out. . . ." *National Catholic Reporter*, Aug. 27, 1993.

"Profiles." Robin Edwards. *National Catholic Reporter*, Aug. 27, 1993.

"Mixed blessings." Kenneth L. Woodward. *Newsweek*, Aug. 16, 1993.

John Paul II Speaks to Youth! World Youth Day. Catholic News Service Staff, ed. Ignatius, 1993.

God's Politician: Pope John Paul II, the Catholic Church, and the New World Order. David Willey. Thomas Dunne/St. Martin's, 1993.

Pope John Paul Two. Jay Wilson. Chelsea House, 1992.

Portrait of John Paul II. Andre Frossard. Ignatius, 1990.

Pope John Paul II: Pilgrim of Peace. Crown, 1987.

Johnson, Earvin "Magic," Jr.

(1959–) Earvin Johnson, Jr., plays basketball with such skill and style that he was long ago nicknamed "Magic." He also loves the game, and ever since his retirement in November 1991, because he has HIV, the virus that causes AIDS, he has looked back longingly at the high level of competition that he so enjoyed. After playing in the National Basketball Association All-Star Game in early 1992, where he was MVP, and winning the Olympic gold medal with the "Dream Team" in Barcelona's Summer Olympics, he joined his Los Angeles Lakers for the preseason in 1992, intending to play a limited schedule, but then retired again before the 1992–93 season formally began. Not that he has given up playing basketball. During 1993, Johnson traveled around the world with his own team of All-Stars, all former NBA players, playing challenge games with basketball clubs abroad and generally acting as an international NBA ambassador.

Nor has he given up the idea of playing again in the NBA. Though clearly his wife, his doctors, and his own sense of "reality," as he put it, are against the notion, as late as August 1993, while preparing for his eighth annual Mid-Summer Night Magic all-star game for charity, held at Los Angeles's Forum, he raised the possibility of returning to the Lakers. He even suggested that, if he were not welcome there, he might play for the New York Knicks, now under his old coach Pat Riley. Nor has Johnson given up the idea of owning a team. He had hoped to become owner of an expansion team in Toronto, but that franchise was given to others.

Meanwhile, Johnson continued his campaign to educate young people about the danger of HIV and AIDS. The audio version of Johnson's book *What You Can Do to Avoid AIDS*, prepared by Robert O'Keefe, won a 1993 Grammy Award in the spoken word category; profits from the book go to the Magic Johnson Foundation for prevention, education, research and care in the battle against AIDS. Also getting wide exposure was *Time Out: The Truth About HIV, AIDS, and You* (1992), produced by Arsenio Hall, anchored by Johnson and Hall. On a personal level, Johnson was still the target of a $2 million suit by a Michigan woman who claims Johnson infected her with HIV.

Michigan-born Johnson attended Michigan State University, leading his team to the 1979 NCAA championship. In his 12 professional seasons, he led the Los Angeles Lakers to the NBA finals nine times for five NBA titles (1980; 1982; 1985; 1987; 1988); was picked most valuable player in the playoffs three times (1980; 1982; 1987); and was named the league's MVP three times (1987; 1989; 1990). Twelve times an NBA All-Star, he was selected MVP for the first time in the 1990 All-Star Game, and again in the game played after his retirement, in 1992. Overall, Johnson amassed 17,239 points in 874 games, for an average of 19.7 a game; took down 6,376 rebounds; had 1,698 steals, second only to Maurice Cheeks's 2,197; and had 9,921 assists, in the 1990–91 season breaking the previous NBA record of 9,888. With his friend and rival, Larry Bird, and later with Michael Jordan, Johnson dominated basketball in the 1980s. He also revolutionized the way the game was played, being the first large player—at 6' 9"—to dominate as a point guard. With his versatility, skill, and magnetic personality, he helped to make basketball popular worldwide. Johnson has also been a leader in establishing summer all-star games and other fund-raising events to benefit inner-city and minority youth. A member of the National Commission on AIDS, he resigned in September 1992 over the Bush administration's lack of support for AIDS research and services. In retirement, Johnson was a sometime basketball commentator on NBC (1992–). Among his autobiographical works are *Magic* (1983), with Richard Levin; *Magic's Touch* (1989), with Roy S. Johnson; and *Magic Johnson: My Life* (1992), with William Novak. He is married to retailer Earletha (Cookie) Kelly; they have one child. He also has a son from a previous relationship.

FURTHER READING

"The Magic act." CHARLES P. PIERCE.
   GQ—Gentleman's Quarterly, Feb. 1993.
Magic Johnson: Basketball Wizard. MARTIN
   SCHWABACHER. Chelsea House, 1993.
"The two and only." BOB RYAN. Sports Illustrated,
   Dec. 14, 1992.
"In the shadow of AIDS. . . ." TODD GOLD. People,
   Oct. 19, 1992.
"My Life." MAGIC JOHNSON. People, Oct. 19,
   1992.
" 'I'm still strong.' " JACK MCCALLUM. Sports
   Illustrated, Aug. 17, 1992.
"A reason to believe." JEFF WEINSTOCK. Sport, June
   1992.
"The importance of being Earvin." ROGER BRIGHAM.
   Advocate, Apr. 21, 1992.
"Magic and Cookie Johnson. . . ." LAURA B.
   RANDOLPH. Ebony, Apr. 1992.
"Magic Johnson: athlete." PAUL MONETTE. Interview,
   Jan. 1992.
Sports Great Magic Johnson, rev. ed., JAMES
   HASKINS. Enslow, 1992.
Magic Johnson, Basketball Great. SEAN DOLAN.
   Chelsea House, 1992.
Magic Johnson. BOB ITALIA. Abdo and Daughters,
   1992.
Magic Johnson: Hero On and Off Court. BILL
   GUTMAN. Millbrook Press, 1992.
Magic Johnson: Backcourt Wizard. KEITH E.
   GREENBERG. Lerner, 1992.
Magic Johnson: Basketball's Smiling Superstar.
   RICK L. JOHNSON. Dillon/Macmillan, 1992.
Magic Johnson. Scholastic, 1991.
Magic Johnson. MICHAEL E. GOODMAN. Crestwood,
   1988.

Johnson, Jimmy

Johnson, Jimmy (James William Johnson; 1943–) Football coach Jimmy Johnson reached the top early in 1992 when his Dallas Cowboys defeated the Buffalo Bills in Super Bowl XXVII, making him the only football coach in history to win both a Super Bowl title and a national college championship. Johnson had been rebuilding the team to just that end, but few thought he would succeed quite so soon. Observers credited the team's rise to Johnson's experience with and commitment to success, and to his passion for playing intelligently, without foolish errors. He published a book about the experience in *Turning the Thing Around: Pulling America's Team Out of the Dumps—and Myself Out of the Doghouse* (1993), written with Ed Hinton.

The 1993 season was not easy, however, with a holdout by star running back Emmitt Smith and injury to also-stellar quarterback Troy Aikman. Yet despite being the "team to beat," the Cowboys posted a strong record of 13–4 and at year's end were in the running for a second Super Bowl.

Texas-born and raised, Johnson was a notable defensive lineman in high school and at the University of Arkansas, where his team won the 1964 national championship, and where he met Jerry Jones, now owner of the Cowboys. After 14 years as a coaching assistant, especially on defense, at Louisiana Tech, Florida State, Wichita State, Iowa State, Oklahoma State, his alma mater Arkansas, and Pittsburgh, Johnson returned to Oklahoma for his first head coaching job (1979–83), rebuilding what had been a losing program; he was named Big Eight Coach of the Year after his first season. Then, at the University of Miami (1984–88), he coached the Hurricanes to a 52–9 record, twice winning the Orange Bowl (1987–88), and taking the national championship (1987), a year flanked by number-two finishes (1986; 1988). When Jerry Jones bought the Cowboys, he brought in his old friend to rebuild the team; the first year (1989) brought a miserable 1–15 record, which gradually built to 13–3 in 1992. Johnson is divorced and has two sons.

FURTHER READING

"Jimmy Johnson. . . ." JOHN ED BRADLEY. *Esquire*, Sep. 1993.
"The happiest man in America?" STEVE BUCKLEY. *Sport*, July 1993.
"Tom who?" GARY CARTWRIGHT. *Texas Monthly*, Mar. 1993.
"The hungriest coach. . . ." GARY CARTWRIGHT. *Texas Monthly*, Sep. 1992.
"Jimmy Johnson." *Sporting News*, Oct. 8, 1990.

Jones, James Earl (1931–) Veteran stage, screen, and television star James Earl Jones appeared in several films during 1993. He starred opposite Thomas Ian Griffith in the thriller *Excessive Force*, directed by Jon Hess, and also starred opposite Karen Allen in the baseball story *The Sandlot*, set in 1962. In *Sommersby*, a remake of *The Return of Martin Guerre*, a post-Civil War drama directed by Jon Amiel, he played a strong supporting role in a cast that included Jodie Foster, Richard Gere, Lanny Flaherty, and Wendell Wellman Jones. He also appeared in the film *The Meteor Man*, written and directed by Robert Townsend and set in Washington, D.C., in a cast that included Marla Gibbs, Eddie Griffin, Robert Guillaume, and Luther Vandross.

On television, Jones starred as manager-trainer Percy Banks opposite Courtney B. Vance as his fighter in the film, *Percy and Thunder*, directed by Ivan Dizon. Jones also narrated the television special *George Lucas: Heroes, Myths and Magic* and a one-hour documentary, *Outcry L.A.: Riots, Trials, Recovery*, exploring the causes of the April 1992 Los Angeles uprising through footage shot by former L.A. gang members and other amateurs. Continuing to work in a variety of media, Jones did an acclaimed narration of Aaron Copland's *Lincoln Portrait*, as part of a recording done by the Seattle Symphony and Chorale. The year 1993 also saw publication of his memoirs, *James Earl Jones: Voices and Silences*, co-authored with Penelope Niven. Jones also participated in the inauguration celebration in January, introducing the Clintons and the Gores.

Forthcoming were starring roles in the film *Clean Slate*, produced by Richard D. Zanuck and Lili Fini Zanuck for MGM, and co-starring Kevin Pollak, Dana Carvey, and Valeria Golino; the American Playhouse public television film *Hallelujah*, opposite Dennis Haysbert, Phylicia Rashad and Tracy Douglas; the film *Clear and Present Danger*, directed by Philip Noyce and co-starring Jones, Anne Archer, and Willem Dafoe; and *The Vernon Johns Story*, with Jones as the civil rights leader, in a Kareem Abdul-Jabbar production.

Mississippi-born Jones has been a leading figure in the American theater since his starring role as African-American heavyweight champion Jack Jefferson (inspired by the real-life Jack Johnson) in *The Great White Hope* (1968; on film 1970). A classical actor of enormous range, Jones is highly regarded for such roles as *Macbeth* (1962), *King Lear* (1973), Hickey in *The Iceman Cometh* (1973), *Othello* (1982), and his starring role in *Fences* (1988), for which he won a Tony. He was the voice of Darth Vader in *Star Wars* (1977), played Alex Haley in television's miniseries "Roots II" (1979), and played major roles in such films as *Gardens of Stone* (1987), *Field of Dreams* (1989), *The Hunt for Red October* (1990), and *Convicts* (1991). Jones's 1957 B.A. was from the University of Michigan. He married Cecilia Hart in 1982. He is the son of actor Robert Earl Jones.

FURTHER READING

"James Earl Jones." JOHN CLARK. *Premiere*, June 1992.

Jones, Quincy (Quincy Delight Jones, Jr.; 1933–) A central figure in American popular music, Quincy Jones began 1993 by introducing the new American president; on January 17, he produced *An American Reunion: The People's Inaugural Celebration*, the first major event of the Clinton-Gore inaugural, and their first inaugural appearance, before an audience of 300,000 at the Lincoln Memorial.

A few weeks later, on February 9, Jones and his wife, actress Nastassja Kinski, became the parents of a baby girl, Kenya Julia Miambi Sarah Jones. In August, Jones was involved in another kind of birth-the launch of his *Vibe* magazine, dedicated to rap music, a Quincy Jones-Time Warner co-venture. The first issue carried a cover picture of Snoop Doggy Dogg. Warner Reprise Video also released the documentary *Miles Davis and Quincy Jones: Live at Montreux,*

Chicago-born Jones has had a long and varied career, which in four decades has included arranging and working as a trumpeter with Lionel Hampton and Dizzy Gillespie in the mid-1950s; as an arranger for many of the leading singers of the 1950s and 1960s; in the 1960s as music director and producer for Mercury Records; and as composer and conductor of many film scores. From 1969, he was a prolific recording artist, with such albums as *Walking in Space* (1969), *Smackwater Jack* (1971), and *Mellow Madness* (1975). He was most notably producer of the Michael Jackson records *Off the Wall* (1980) *Thriller* (1982) and *Bad* (1987). His 1989 album *Back on the Block*, sold over a million copies and in 1991 brought him six Grammy awards, making him the most honored pop artist in the history of the awards, with a total of 25 Grammys during his long career. His documentary *Listen Up: The Lives of Quincy Jones* was widely distributed in 1990. Jones attended the Berkeley College of Music and the Boston Conservatory.

FURTHER READING

"The piano next door. . . ." *Economist*, July 20, 1991.
"On Q." DIANE K. SHAH. *New York Times Magazine*, Nov. 18, 1990.
"Quincy Jones." STEVE DOUGHERTY. *People*, Oct. 15, 1990.
"Story of Q." BRENDAN LEMON. *Interview*, Sep. 1990.
"Playboy interview. . . ." ALEX HALEY. *Playboy*, July 1990.
"Quincy Jones." ELIOT TIEGEL. *Stereo Review*, June 1990.

"After 40 years. . . ." ALDORE COLLIER. *Ebony*, Apr. 1990.
"Back on the block. . . ." ROBERT L. DOERSCHUK. *Interview*, Jan. 1990.
"Herbie & Quincy. . . ." JOSEF WOODARD. *Down Beat*, Jan. 1990.
Quincy Jones. RAYMOND HORRICKS. Hippocrene, 1986.

Tommy Lee Jones (right), Hiep Thi Le, and children, Phuong Huu Le and Don Ho, Jr.

Jones, Tommy Lee (1946–) In what was very much a breakthrough year, Tommy Lee Jones starred in three varied and interesting roles. In *Heaven and Earth*, Oliver Stone's third Vietnam War film, Jones starred as an American soldier in Vietnam, opposite Hiep Thi Le as Le Ly Hayslip; they marry and then live in the United States. The story, covering three decades of Hayslip's life, was based on two autobiographical works by Hayslip: *When Heaven and Earth Changed Places*, written with Jay Wurts, and *Child of War, Woman of Peace*, with James Hayslip.

Jones also starred as U.S. Marshal Samuel Gerard, who pursues Dr. Richard Kimble (Harrison Ford), an escaped prisoner unjustly convicted of murder, in the very popular chase thriller *The Fugitive*, based on the 1960s television series; Andrew Davis directed. Jones also starred opposite Kathleen Turner in the film *House of Cards*, written and directed by Michael Lessac.

Forthcoming were starring roles in *Natural Born Killers*, directed by Oliver Stone and co-starring Woody Harrelson, Robert Downey, Jr., and Juliette Lewis; *Blown Away*, directed by Stephen Hopkins and co-starring Jeff Bridges; *The Client*, directed by Joel Schumacher and co-starring Susan Sarandon; and *The Ty Cobb Story*, written and directed by Ron Shelton.

Texas-born Jones made his Broadway debut in *A Patriot for Me* (1969) and his film debut in *Love Story* (1970). He also appeared in several other New York stage productions, including *Ulysses in Nighttown* and *True West*. Among his films are *Jackson County Jail* (1976), *Rolling Thunder* (1977), *Coal Miner's Daughter* (1980), *Back Roads* (1981), *Nate and Hayes* (1983), *The River Rat* (1984), *Black Moon Rising* (1986), *The Big Town* (1987), *Stormy Monday* (1988), *The Package* (1989), *Fire Birds* (1990), *Blue Sky* (1991), and *JFK* (1992; he received an Oscar nomination). He won an Emmy in the television film *The Executioner's Song* (1982), his many television appearances also include *Lonesome Dove* (1989). His B.A. was from Harvard University. He is married to Kimberlea Cloughley, and has two children.

FURTHER READING

"The fugitive. . . ." MIMI SWARTZ. *Texas Monthly*, Oct. 1993.
"Hot damn, he's good." RICHARD CORLISS. *Time*, Sep. 6, 1993.

Jordan, Michael (1963–) On October 6, 1993, basketball superstar Michael Jordan stunned the world by announcing his retirement from the sport. As the shock wore off, however,

many could understand how Jordan could come to make that decision. He said it was primarily because he had nothing left to prove on the court and he wanted to leave at the peak of his game. He had, after all, just won his third straight National Basketball Association (NBA) championship, an achievement denied even the great Larry Bird and Earvin "Magic" Johnson, and had (as usual) been named most valuable player of the playoffs, posting records for average of 41 points per game, total number of points (246) and number of field goals (101).

But there were other reasons as well. Prime among them, Jordan's father, James, had been murdered in July, apparently killed in a North Carolina highway rest area; his body was unrecognized and unclaimed until mid-August when his car was found in a remote South Carolina creek. The two Jordans had always been close, and the loss had a powerful impact. In early September, Jordan's Celebrity Challenge on Hilton Head Island, off South Carolina, went ahead without the star, who said he was not mentally ready to face the public so soon afterward.

Earlier, in June, San Diego sports executive Richard Esquinas had published a book called *Michael and Me: Our Gambling Addiction . . . My Cry for Help!*, in which he charged that he had won $1.25 million from Jordan in private golf bets in 1991. After some days of silence, Jordan said that amount was "substantially less" than the "preposterous" amounts reported, and stressed that he was not a compulsive gambler. In May, he had been widely criticized for making a late-night trip to Atlantic City between the first and second playoff games in New York against the Knicks; Jordan, whose father accompanied him, said he was simply seeking some time off for relaxation.

Not that Jordan's retirement took him completely out of the spotlight. Just three weeks after his announcement, he appeared in a one-on-one televised interview with Oprah Winfrey and a week later on "Larry King Live." These and other such appearances were partly to publicize his new book, *Rare Air: Michael on Michael*, a combination memoir by Jordan and photographic essay by Walter Iooss, Jr., which by year's end was sitting on the best-seller charts. He was also widely seen in many advertisements, as he has been one of the most successful players ever commercially, with an estimated commercial income of $32 million in 1992 alone. The night before his retirement announcement, Jordan had thrown the first pitch to open the American League playoffs in Chicago, while rumors of his decision swirled through the crowd.

There was some speculation that Jordan would later return to basketball, rumors fueled by Jordan practicing with the Bulls on occasion. Under NBA rules, Jordan would need unanimous approval by the NBA board to return during the 1993–94 season, but could be reinstated at will later. Jordan also seemed to be considering trying for a career in baseball.

Jordan was one the leading basketball players of the late 1980s and early 1990s. He starred at the University of North Carolina, winning the NCAA national championship in 1982. He was on the team that won the Olympic gold medal in 1984, and again with the "Dream Team" in 1992. Astonishingly selected third in the NBA college draft (after Hakeem Olajuwon and Sam Bowie), Jordan joined the Bulls, becoming NBA rookie of the year (1985). In the career that built from there, he was named the NBA's most valuable player three times (1988; 1991; 1992); a member of the All-Star starting team for seven straight years (1987–93), and most valuable player in the All-Star game (1988); defensive player of the year (1988); and member of the NBA All-Defense first team six straight times (1988–93). He led the Bulls to three straight championships (1991–93), was named MVP in all three playoffs, and himself won seven straight scoring titles (1987–93), only the second player ever (along with Wilt Chamberlain) to do so. At his retirement, he was the 15th leading scorer all time, with 21,541 points, and held records for career scoring averages for the regular season (32.3 points per game), the playoffs (34.6), and the All-Star game (21.0). He scored 50 or more points 33 times, with a playoff record of 63 points in a 1986 game, and a record 23 consecutive points in a 1987 game. Jordan and his wife, Juanita, have three children.

FURTHER READING

Michael Jordan: Star Guard. RON KNAPP. Enslow, 1994.
Michael Jordan, Basketball Great. SEAN DOLAN. Chelsea House, 1994.
"The untouchable." GEORGE CASTLE. "The golf course." STEVE GORDON. "Giving back." TERRY MULGANNON. "The price of fame." LACY J. BANKS. "Courting greatness." BOB RYAN. "The Jordan years." WILLIAM LADSON. *Sport*, Dec. 1993.

"A truly death-defying. . . ." RICHARD LAPCHICK. "Europe loses. . . ." IAN THOMSEN and TED RODGERS. "Retired or just tired?" PAUL ATTNER. "One loss. . . ." WILLIAM C. RHODEN. " 'The desire isn't there.' " JACK MCCALLUM. *Sports Illustrated*, Oct. 18, 1993.
" 'Pouring salt. . . .' " SHARON BEGLEY. *Newsweek*, Aug. 30, 1993.
"The mysterious death of 'Pops.' " MARK STARR. *Newsweek*, Aug. 23, 1993.
"Michael Jordan vs. . . ." GEORGE CASTLE and GARY BINFORD. *Sport*, May 1993.
Michael Jordan. CHIP LOVITT. Scholastic, 1993.
"Michael Jordan." *Playboy*, May 1992.
Hang Time: Days and Dreams with Michael Jordan. BOB GREENE. St. Martin's, 1992.
The Jordan Rules: The Inside Story of a Turbulent Season with Michael Jordan and the Chicago Bulls. SAM SMITH. Simon & Schuster, 1992.
Taking to the Air: The Rise of Michael Jordan. JIM NAUGHTON. Warner, 1992.
Michael Jordan. BOB ITALIA. Abdo and Daughters, 1992.
Michael Jordan: Basketball Camp. BILL GUTMAN. Millbrook Press, 1992.
Michael Jordan: Basketball Skywalker. THOMAS R. RABER. Lerner, 1992.
Sports Great Michael Jordan. NATHAN AASENG. Enslow, 1992.
Michael Jordan. JACK CLARY. Smithmark, 1992.

Jordan, Richard (Robert Anson Jordan; 1937–93) New York City-born Jordan, an actor, director, producer, and writer, was best known for his television and film roles. He spent much of his career in the theatre, including eight seasons with the New York Shakespeare Festival, and major involvement during the 1970s with the Los Angeles Actor's Theater. He won an acting Obie for his role in Vaclav Havel's *Protest* (1983). Jordan received a Golden Globe award for his central role as Joseph Armagh in the 10-hour television miniseries *Captains and Kings* (1976). He made his film debut in *Lawman* (1970), and played in such films as *The Friends of Eddie Coyle* (1973), *Interiors* (1978), *The Hunt for Red October* (1990), and *Posse*. He also starred in and co-wrote *Gettysburg* (1993). Formerly married to the actress Blair Brown, he was survived by a son, his mother, three sisters, and a brother. (d. Los Angeles; August 30, 1993)

FURTHER READING

Obituary. *Variety*, Sep. 1, 1993.
Obituary. *New York Times*, Sep. 1, 1993.

Joyner-Kersee, Jackie

(Jacqueline Joyner-Kersee; 1962–) It may not have been the prettiest, but it was probably Jackie Joyner-Kersee's gutsiest performance. That was the consensus after the 1993 world outdoor track and field championships, where Joyner-Kersee took the gold medal in the grueling two-day, seven-event heptathlon-including the 100-meter hurdles, the high jump, the shotput, the 200 meters, the long jump, the javelin, and the 800 meters-at which she has so long excelled. Joyner-Kersee was ill with a fever and struggled with asthma during the two days of the heptathlon, but in the final event, the 800-meter run, trailing defending world champion, Sabine Braun of Germany, and needing to surpass Braun by 6/10ths of a second, she came from behind to win by a full three seconds. After the stirring win, her 18th in the heptathlon, she was so exhausted that she was unable to take a victory lap; but ten minutes later she returned to acknowledge the crowd's cheers and honor her rivals. Her final total of 6,837 points was far below her world record 7,291 points set in 1988. But the nature of the win certainly gave support to the commonly expressed view that Joyner-Kersee may be the world's great woman athlete-perhaps the greatest athlete in the world, woman or man. Meanwhile she was preparing for the Atlanta Olympics in 1996, and possibly "ending her career on American soil." Also in 1993, she wrote with Lindsey Johnson *A Woman's Place Is Everywhere: Inspirational Profiles of Female Leaders Who Are Shaping and Expanding the Role of Women in American Society Today*, scheduled for 1994 publication.

Born in East St. Louis, Joyner early built up a long string of wins, with her four successive national junior pentathlon championships, starting at the age of 14, and including a silver heptathlon medal at the 1984 Olympics, a 1987 world heptathlon championship, a 1988 Olympic gold medal in the long jump, and a record-breaking two consecutive Olympic gold medals in the heptathlon, in 1988, with a record-setting 7,291 points, and again in 1992. Also in 1992, she won an Olympic bronze medal in the long jump, after earlier breaking her own women's indoor record in that event. With six of the only seven over-7,000 point heptathlon performances in history, she will long be recognized as a preeminent athlete. Her 1985 B.A. was from the University of California at Los Angeles. She is married to UCLA track and field coach—and her own coach—Bobby Kersee.

FURTHER READING

Jackie Joyner-Kersee. CARL R. GREEN. Crestwood/Macmillan, 1994.
"In step with. . . . ." JAMES BRADY. *Parade*, June 13, 1993.
"Wonder woman." NEIL CHEN. *Money*, Spring 1993.
"First lady." SUSANNA LEVIN. *Women's Sports and Fitness*, Jan.-Feb. 1993.
Jackie Joyner-Kersee: Super Woman. MARGARET J. GOLDSTEIN and JENNIFER LARSON. Lerner, 1993.
Jackie Joyner-Kersee: Track-and-Field Star. CAROL FUCHS. Rourke, 1993.
"Bound for glory." NEIL LEIFER. *Newsweek*, July 6, 1992.
"Defending her reign." RICHARD FINN. *Sporting News*, June 29, 1992.
"Cosmo talks to:. . . ." RALPH GARDNER, JR. *Cosmopolitan*, June 1989.
"Jackie Joyner-Kersee. . . ." DAN CHU. *People*, Jan. 30, 1989.
"Woman of the Year. . . ." DAVE NIGHTINGALE. *Sporting News*, Jan. 2, 1989.

Judd, Wynonna

(1964–) In her second full year on her own, after the 1992 retirement of her partner and mother, Naomi Judd, Wynonna (as she has chosen to be called profes-

recording career with the album *The Judds-Wynonna and Naomi*. They very quickly emerged as country music stars, with a series of top-of-the-charts singles, and such number one albums as *Why Not Me* (1984), *Rockin' With the Rhythm* (1985), and *Heartland* (1987). Their many honors included four Grammys (1985; 1986; 1987; 1989), four Academy of Country Music Awards (1984; 1985; 1986; 1989), two Country Music Association Awards (1988; 1989), and a wide range of other awards. The Judds had a cross-country farewell tour in 1991 before Naomi retired, because she had contracted as-yet uncurable chronic hepatitis. They won their final shared Grammy in 1992 for their hit single "Love Can Build a Bridge" (1991), also the title of Naomi's 1993 autobiography, written by Bud Schaetzle. On her own, Wynonna won Billboard's 1992 award for best country single for "I Saw the Light," and was nominated as best country female artist. Her sister is actress Ashley Judd.

FURTHER READING

" 'My toughest moment.' . . ." GLENN PLASKIN. *Ladies Home Journal*, Nov. 1992.

"Here comes the Judd." JAMES HUNTER. *US*, Oct. 1992.

"One for the road." STEVE DOUGHERTY and JANE SANDERSON. *People*, Dec. 9, 1991.

"The Judds." MARY MURPHY. *TV Guide*, Nov. 30, 1991.

"The Judds. . . ." BOB ALLEN. *Country Music*, Nov.-Dec. 1991.

"The Judds' farewell song." KATHRYN CASEY. *Ladies Home Journal*, Nov. 1991.

Wynonna Judd. ROSEMARY WALLNER. Abdo & Daughters, 1991.

"Making Music City listen." BOB MILLARD. *Country Music*, Sep.-Oct. 1989.

Behind Closed Doors: Talking with the Legends of Country Music. ALANNA NASH. Knopf, 1988.

sionally) continued to emerge as a long-term country music star. Her 1992 hit album *Wynonna* spent a total of 66 weeks on the Billboard top 200 list, and she was ranked Billboard's No. 2 hot country singles and track artist for 1993. Her second album, *Tell Me Why*, was not as much a smash hit as the first, but the album's title song "Tell Me Why," was one of the hit singles of the year, as was another single from the album, "Only Love." Wynonna spent much of the year touring in support of her records; in April, she and singer Clint Black began a joint seven-month North American tour of 90 cities. She was nominated as best female vocalist at the 27th Annual Country Music Association Awards.

Born when her mother, Naomi, was still in high school, the two formed a singing partnership in 1984, after several moves that included her mother's divorce, the two began their joint

K

Kanin, Michael (1910–93) Rochester-born Michael Kanin began his career as a visual artist, turning to writing after an eye injury while working in New York in the 1930s. He and his wife, Fay Mitchell Kanin, were collaborators from the late 1930s, as sometimes were he and his brother, Garson Kanin. Michael Kanin shared a screenwriting Oscar with Ring Lardner, Jr. for the Tracy-Hepburn film *Woman of the Year* (1942); co-wrote such films as *The Cross of Lorraine* (1944), *Centennial Summer* (1946), and *Rhapsody* (1954); and received an Oscar nomination for *Teacher's Pet* (1956). He and Fay Mitchell Kanin also wrote several plays, including *Rashomon and The Gay Life* (1961). He also produced *A Double Life* (1947) and directed *When I Grow Up* (1951). He was a charter member of Writers Guild of America West. He was survived by Fay Mitchell Kanin and a son. (d. Los Angeles; March 12, 1993)

FURTHER READING

Obituary. *Variety*, Mar. 22, 1993.
Obituary. *New York Times*, Mar. 16, 1993.
Obituary. *The Times* (of London), Mar. 8, 1993.

Kantor, Mickey (1939–   ) President Bill Clinton's United States Trade Representative, Mickey Kantor, a tough and sometimes abrasive negotiator, wasted no time in making his presence felt on the international scene. On February 1, 1993, he threatened to prohibit telecom-munications and power generation contracts with European Community (EC) countries, beginning his campaign to use American pressure to bring the stalled GATT (General Agreement on Tariffs and Trade) talks to a successful conclusion. During the year, he strongly and publicly attacked discriminatory EC and Japanese trade practices, and repeatedly threatened to impose sanctions on the EC, Japan, Brazil, India, and many other countries. At the same time, he strongly pushed forward the North American Free Trade Agreement (NAFTA), negotiating the Mexican-American supplementary environmental and labor agreements that made it palatable enough for a majority of Congress.

Early in his legal career, Kantor was committed to representing those on the underside of American society. In 1967, he and Valerie Kantor, then his wife, founded the federally funded South Florida Migrant Labor Services organization, and during the Carter years he served on the board of directors of the Legal Services Corporation, there meeting and becoming a friend of Hillary Rodham Clinton.

In 1975, Kantor became a partner in the Los Angeles law firm of Manatt, Phelps, Phillips, and Kantor, and in the years that followed became a leading California lawyer, with a strong corporate practice, also becoming active in California Democratic politics. He was a key aide to California Governor Jerry Brown in several campaigns, breaking with Brown during the 1992 presidential campaign, when he was chairman of the successful Clinton/Gore run.

Kantor's 1961 B.A. was from Vanderbilt University, and his 1967 LL.B. from Georgetown University. He was a U.S. Navy officer (1961–65). Previously divorced, he is married to Heidi Schulman; they have three children.

FURTHER READING

"Trade warrior." DAN GOODGAME. *Time*, Mar. 15, 1993.
"FOB story." MICKEY KAUS. *New Republic*, Dec. 28, 1992.

Keating, Charles Humphrey, Jr.

(1923–   ) On January 6, 1993, a Los Angeles federal jury found Charles Keating guilty on 73 of 77 criminal counts in the Lincoln Savings and Loan Association case. His son, Charles H. Keating, 3rd, was found guilty on 64 counts. On July 8, the elder Keating was sentenced to a 12 years and seven months term of imprisonment, to run concurrently with his ten-year California state sentence. U.S. District Court Judge Mariana Pfaeizer also set $122.4 million in restitution, the latter probably an empty gesture due to previous state levies and legal costs.

On September 16, 1993, Arizona Democratic Senator Dennis DeConcini, one of the "Keating Five," announced that he would not seek a fourth term in the Senate. Although the Senate Ethics Committee had in 1991 dropped all charges against him with only a mild rebuke concerning his appearance of misconduct, his long involvement in the Lincoln Savings and Loan case had seriously hurt him in his home state, and was widely thought to have been a major factor in his decision.

Charles Keating emerged as a corporate takeover figure in the late 1970s, as executive vice president of the Cincinnati-based American Financial Corporation. He bought control of the Lincoln Savings Bank, in Irvine, California in 1984 for $51 million and began the process of building it into a high-flying $6 billion bank, heavily invested in junk bonds and heavily committed to what turned out to be very weak real estate loans, many of them to American Continental Corporation. Faced with opposition from the Federal Home Loan Bank Board, Keating engaged in a long-running battle with regulators, which included substantial contributions to many key Washington and state politicians, and set the stage for the investigations of Senators DeConcini, John Glenn, Alan Cranston, John McCain, and Donald W. Riegle, Jr., who came to known in the media as the "Keating Five." Lincoln was taken over by federal bank regulators on April 14, 1990, as the national savings and loan crisis developed; the cost of the government bailout was estimated to be well over $2 billion.

Convicted of 17 state charges of securities fraud by a California jury on December 3, 1991, Keating was sentenced to a maximum ten-year prison term in April 1992. In July, a Tucson, Arizona federal jury awarded $3.3 billion in damage claims against Keating and $5 billion more against three co-defendants. A federal judge later substantially reduced the judgments, to approximately $1.9 billion against Keating and his co-defendants.

Keating was, from the early 1970s, also a substantial Cincinnati-based antipornography contributor; he founded an antipornography organization in the 1950s, and was a member of the Presidential Commission on Obscenity and Pornography (1969–70).

Keating attended the University of Cincinnati and was a star swimmer, becoming 1946 national collegiate breast stroke champion. He married Mary Elaine Fette in 1941; they have six children.

FURTHER READING

Trust Me: The Extraordinary Adventures of Charles Keating. CHARLES BOWDEN and MICHAEL BINSTEIN. Random, 1993.
"Profit without honor." JOE MORGENSTERN. *Playboy*, Apr. 1992.
"Mr. S & L. . . ." KATHLEEN KERWIN. *Business Week*, Nov. 25, 1991.
"The great banks robbery. . . ." JAMES K. GLASSMAN. *New Republic*, Oct. 8, 1990.
"Money talks. . . ." MARGARET CARLSON. *Time*, Apr. 9, 1990.
"Dirty bookkeeping. . . ." DAVID CORN. *New Republic*, Apr. 2, 1990.
"The man who shot. . . ." PHIL GARLINGTON. *California*, Mar. 1990.
"Seven sorry senators. . . . " MARGARET CARLSON. *Time*, Jan. 8, 1990.
The Greatest-Ever Bank Robbery: The Collapse of the Savings and Loan Industry. MARTIN MAYER. Macmillan, 1990.

Keaton, Diane

(1946–   ) Fourteen years after her last Woody Allen film, Keaton in 1993 starred opposite Allen in the very well received light comedy *Manhattan Murder Mystery*, written and directed by Allen, and co-starring Anjelica Huston, Alan Alda, Jerry Adler, and Lynn Cohen. Keaton was a late casting decision; the role had originally been set for Mia Farrow, whose personal and professional relationship with Allen ended abruptly and very publicly in 1992. Keaton starred in quite another kind of comedy, as well, as the voice of Daphne the Poodle in *Look Who's Talking Now*, the third in the "Look Who's Talking" series. She also was nominated for a Cable Ace award as best actress in a movie or miniseries for her starring role in *Running Mates* (1992), her television debut.

Forthcoming was a remake of the sequel to *Father of the Bride, Father's Little Dividend*. Keaton will again star in the Joan Bennett role, opposite Steve Martin as the father in the Spencer Tracy role, with Kimberly Williams again in the Elizabeth Taylor role as the bride. Also forthcoming was the title role in the television film *Amelia Earhart*.

California-born Keaton made the transition from the New York theater to Hollywood in Woody Allen's *Play It Again Sam*, starring opposite Allen on Broadway in 1971 and again in the 1972 film version. She was Michael Corleone's wife in the classic *Godfather* films (1972; 1974), won a best actress Oscar for Allen's *Annie Hall* (1977), and also starred in his *Interiors* (1978) and *Manhattan* (1979). She went on to star in such films as *Reds* (1981), *The Little Drummer Girl* (1984), *Crimes of the Heart* (1986), *Radio Days* (1987), *The Godfather Part III* (1990) reprising her Kay Corleone role, *The Lemon Sisters* (1990), and *Father of the Bride* (1991). In 1991, she directed *Wildflower*, her first full-length television film, and in 1992 starred in the television film *Running Mates*. She was a student at New York's Neighborhood Playhouse in 1968.

FURTHER READING

"Keaton's comeback." SEAN ELDER. *Vogue*, Sep. 1993.
"Diane in La-La Land." PATRICK PACHECO. *Connoisseur*, Jan. 1992.
Diane Keaton: The Story of the Real Annie Hall. JONATHAN MOOR. St. Martin's, 1989.

Keaton, Michael (Michael Douglas; 1951–)

After his worldwide 1992 hit in *Batman Returns*, Keaton undertook a very difference kind of role in 1993, starring as Dogberry a well-received film version of Shakespeare's *Much Ado About Nothing*, adapted, directed, and co-produced by Kenneth Branagh. Branagh played Benedick, in a cast that co-starred Emma Thompson as Beatrice, Denzel Washington as Don Pedro, Robert Sean Leonard as Claudio, and Keanu Reeves as Don John. Keaton also starred as a young husband stricken with terminal cancer, opposite Nicole Kidman as his wife, in *My Life*, written and directed by Bruce Beresford. He was also one of the many celebrity performers who did readings in Bill Couterie's environmentalist film *Earth and the American Dream*. Forthcoming was a starring role in the film *The Paper*, directed by Ron Howard and co-starring Glenn Close, Robert Duvall, Marisa Tomei, and Randy Quaid.

Pittsburgh-born Keaton began his career as a comedian with the Los Angeles Second City group, appeared in television from the mid-1970s, and played in such films as *Night Shift* (1982), *Mr. Mom* (1983), and *Touch and Go* (1987). He emerged as a star in the film drama *Clean and Sober* (1988), and in the title role of *Batman* (1989), followed by *The Dream Team* (1989) *One Good Cop* (1991), and *Batman Returns* (1992). Keaton attended Kent State University. He married Caroline McWilliams in 1982; they have one child.

FURTHER READING

"Michael Keaton." *Playboy*, July 1992.
"Masked man. . . ." TRIP GABRIEL. *Entertainment*, June 19, 1992.
"Michael Keaton. . . ." DIGBY DIEHL . *Cosmopolitan*, Nov. 1991.
"Batman and the new world order." CAROL CALDWELL. *Esquire*, June 1991.
"Batguy." TERRI MINSKY. *Premiere*, July 1989.

Keeler, Ruby (1910–93)

Halifax-born Ruby Keeler moved to New York City at the age of four. She made her debut at 13, in the chorus of George M. Cohan's *The Rise of Rose O'Reilly*, and then worked in cabaret, moved into small theater roles, and was about to begin rehearsals for *Whoopee* when she met and married Al Jolson in 1928, then interrupting her career for five years. In 1933, Keeler made her film debut, starring as Peggy Sawyer in Lloyd Bacon's classic musical *42nd Street*, opposite Warner Baxter and Dick Powell, choreographed by Busby Berkeley; one of her songs was "Shuffle Off to Buffalo." She went on to star opposite Powell in *Gold Diggers of 1933* and *Footlight Parade*, with Jolson in *Go Into Your Dance*, and also starred in several other films during the 1930s. Her marriage to Jolson ended in 1940, and she retired after her remarriage in 1941. Her last film was *Sweetheart of the Campus* (1941). In 1971, Keeler made a startling and quite unexpected comeback on Broadway as the star of a hit revival of *No, No, Nanette*, recommended into the job by Busby Berkeley, at 74 the production supervisor of the work. She was survived by three daughters and two sons. (d. Los Angeles; February 28, 1993)

FURTHER READING

Obituary. *Current Biography*, Apr. 1993.
"A passing of legends. . . ." *People*, Mar. 15, 1993.
Obituary. RICHARD NATALE. *Variety*, Mar. 8, 1993.
Obituary. *The Times* (of London), Mar. 2, 1993.
Obituary. *New York Times*, Mar. 1, 1993.
Tap!: The Greatest Tap Dance Stars and Their Stories 1900–1955. RUSTY M. FRANK. Morrow, 1990.

Keillor, Garrison (1942–) America's reigning folk humorist, and expert on the gently ridiculous, the incongruous, and the ludicrous, was in good form again in 1993; this time Garrison Keillor's main new literary offering was *The Book of Guys*, a series of humorous and sometimes laugh-out-loud stories about guys from Lonesome Shorty, Omoo the Wolf Boy, and Norman Conquest, to Keillor himself, detailing his debut in a high-school talent show. On the book's publication in November, Keillor made a 20-city "Show of Guys" tour, accompanied by some members of his "Prairie Home Companion" crew, with a companion theatre piece to the book, singing and reading from *The Book of Guys* to appreciative audiences across the country, and briefly touring in Britain as well. In 1993, Keillor also had a 10-minute-a-day early-morning radio show called *The Writer's Almanac*. He ended the year with a Christmas show in New York City. Word was that his radio show would resume its original "Prairie Home Companion" name in 1994.

Minnesota-born Keillor was creator, writer, and announcer of the enormously popular radio show "A Prairie Home Companion," which he hosted for 13 years (1974–87). After moving briefly to Denmark, Keillor settled in New York City, where he began a new show, "American Radio Company" (1991–), which he then moved with him back to St. Paul, Minnesota in late 1992. His written works include *Happy to Be Here* (1982); *Lake Wobegon Days* (1985), which in its audio form received a 1987 Grammy for best non-musical recording; *Leaving Home* (1987); *We Are Still Married* (1989); and his first novel, *WLT: A Radio Romance* (1991), also released on audiotape. He has also published numerous audiotapes, including *Local Man Moves to City* (1991), about his love-hate relationship with New York; *Stories*, readings of his own short fiction (1992); and the musical record *Garrison Keillor and the Hopeful Gospel Quartet* (1992). For television he has also done several specials, including *Garrison Keillor's Home* (1991). Keillor's B.A. was from the University of Minnesota in 1966. He married Ulla Skaeverd in 1985; he has one son and three stepchildren.

FURTHER READING

"How guys. . . ." VIC SUSSMAN. *U.S. News & World Report*. Nov. 15, 1993.
Garrison Keillor. PETER SCHOLL. Twayne/Macmillan, 1993.
"The Hicksville boy. . . ." LESLEY WHITE. *Sunday Times*. Oct. 4, 1992.
"Garrison Keillor. . . ." PAUL ALEXANDER. *M Inc.*, Oct. 1991.
"Still mad." CHUCK BENDA. *MPLS-St. Paul*, Jan. 1991.
Garrison Keillor: A Voice of America. JUDITH Y. LEE. University Press of Mississippi, 1991.

Keitel, Harvey (1941–) In 1993, Harvey Keitel starred as George Baines opposite Holly Hunter as Ada McGrath and Sam Neill as Stewart in *The Piano*, written and directed by Jane Campion. The acclaimed film won the Palme d'Or at the Cannes Film Festival, and was very well received upon opening in New York later in the year.

Keitel also starred in the film *Rising Sun*, about the murder of a young woman during a sexual encounter at a party in a Japanese corporation's headquarters, and the Los Angeles Police Department investigation that followed. The film, based on Michael Crichton's novel, was directed by Philip Kaufman, and written by Kaufman and Crichton; Sean Connery, Wesley

Snipes, Hiryuki Tagawa, and Tatjana Patitz co-starred.

A third starring role was in the film *Snake Eyes*, directed by Abel Ferrara, with Keitel as a film director opposite Madonna and James Russo as her husband and co-star in a film Keitel is directing; she is sleeping with both men. Forthcoming was a starring role in the film *Imaginary Crimes*, directed by Anthony Drazen.

Brooklyn-born Keitel spent the early part of his career in supporting roles in the theater. He made his film debut in *Who's That Knocking at My Door?* (1968), and broke through into strong supporting film roles in Martin Scorsese's *Mean Streets* (1973), followed by such films as *Alice Doesn't Live Here Anymore* (1975), *Taxi Driver* (1976), *Mother Jugs and Speed* (1976), *Buffalo Bill and the Indians* (1976), *The Border* (1981), *Nemo* (1983), *Wise Guys* (1986), *The Last Temptation of Christ* (1988), *The Two Jakes* (1990), *Bugsy* (1991; he received an Oscar nomination), *Thelma and Louise* (1991), *Sister Act* (1992), and *Reservoir Dogs* (1992). He has also appeared in many television films.

FURTHER READING

"Heaven, hell, Harvey Keitel." NICK TOSCHES. *Esquire*, Sep. 1993.
"Harvey Keitel. . . ." JULIAN SCHNABEL. *Interview*, Dec. 1992.
"Harvey Keitel." JOHN CLARK. *Premiere*, Sep. 1990.
"Jake. . . ." JULIAN SCHNABEL. *Interview*, Aug. 1990.

Kelly, Sharon Pratt Dixon (1944–)

Facing a continuing and so far uncontrollable drug epidemic and an almost equally uncontrollable rise in street killings, and having cut the police force considerably during 1992 for budgetary reasons, Washington, D.C. mayor Sharon Pratt Kelly made a dramatic call for federal help in 1993. In late October, she asked President Bill Clinton to delegate to her his authority to call out the National Guard in the District of Columbia, matching the powers held by state governors. She also advocated a series of other crimefighting moves, among them gun control measures, the trial of some 14-year-olds as adults, building a maximum security prison, federal aid for police training, and paying substantially increased police overtime while recruiting additional police. President Clinton responded that he could not by law delegate to her his power to call out the National Guard in the District, but instructed Attorney-General Janet Reno to set up a multi-agency task force to develop some additional help for the District. During 1993, very few beneficial effects were seen in the District, as crime, killings, and drugs continued to make life very nearly intolerable for large numbers of its residents, many of them federal government employees. In June, Mayor Kelly and Housing and Urban Development Secretary Henry Cisneros announced plans to create a model D.C. program on homelessness, and later in the year delivered the plan, which Mayor Kelly was trying to fund at year's end.

Mayor Kelly, Eleanor Holmes Norton, and Jesse Jackson continued to lead the fight for D.C. statehood, and President Clinton continued to support their position, but no progress was reported on that front.

A third-generation Washingtonian, Sharon Pratt graduated from Howard University Law School in 1968. Three years later, married and having borne two children, she joined her father's general practice law firm. In 1972 she began teaching public interest law at the innovative Antioch Law School in Washington. From 1976, she worked at the Potomac Electric Power company as a corporate lawyer, becoming vice president for consumer affairs. While still at PEPCO, she was elected D.C.'s delegate to the Democratic National Committee in 1977, and in 1984 became the first African-American and first woman to be treasurer of the Democratic National Committee. In 1991, she became the first elected African-American woman mayor of a major city, succeeding Marion Barry, who had not run for re-election after his 1990 conviction on cocaine-possession charges; she won by a landslide 86 percent of the vote. She had been elected in 1990 as Sharon Pratt Dixon, and changed her name to Kelly after her December 1990 marriage to James R. Kelly, 3rd. Her first two years in office yielded mixed results. She was formerly married to Arrington L. Dixon, chairman of the D.C. Council under ex-mayor Marion Barry. They had two daughters.

FURTHER READING

"Prattfall. . . ." KEN CUMMINS. *New Republic*, Feb. 8, 1993.
"Trust me." HARRY JAFFE et al. *Washingtonian*, May 1991.
"Sharon Dixon. . . ." GLORIA BORGER. *U.S. News & World Report*, Dec. 31, 1990.

Kennedy, Anthony McLeod (1936–)

Justice Anthony Kennedy, in 1992 viewed by many as an emerging centrist on the Supreme Court, voted with the conservative majority on most major issues during 1993. Speaking for a unanimous Court, he wrote the opinion in *Church of the Lukumi Babalu Aye v. City of Hialeah*, ruling unconstitutional three city ordinances banning ritual animal sacrifice. He also joined the majority in several other key cases, including *Harris v. Forklift Systems*, in which the Court ruled unanimously that workers need not prove that they had suffered psychological damage or were unable to perform their tasks to successfully charge sexual harassment, instead applying the rule of "workplace equity"; *Herrera v. Collins*, which sharply limited the ability of those on death row to gain stays of execution on the basis of alleged later discovery of new evidence; *Sale v. Haitian Centers Council*, which ruled that Haitian refugees could be intercepted in international waters and forcibly returned to Haiti without violating American and international law; *Zobrest v. Catalina Foothills School District*, ruling that local governments could pay for special services to the disabled in parochial schools, as compliance with federal equal educational opportunities for the disabled laws; *Bray v. Alexandria Women's Health Clinic*, which allowed abortion protestors to legally block abortion clinics; *Shaw v. Reno*, which made it possible to challenge "bizarrely" shaped voting districts formed to provide minority representation as unconstitutional; *St. Mary's Honor Center v. Hicks*, ruling that workers must provide proof of specific discrimination against them to claim protection of civil rights laws; *Lamb's Chapel v Center Moriches Union Free School District*, in which the Court ruled unanimously that religious groups had equal access to school facilities as other organizations in the community; and a unanimous *Wisconsin v. Mitchell*, ruling that states could proscribe increased sentences for hate-motivated crimes. He wrote a dissenting opinion in *Alexander v. Reno*, which ruled that the First Amendment did not protect $25 million of books and movies destroyed, many of them not obscene, after a seller had been convicted as a pornographer.

California-born Kennedy was appointed to the Sacramento-based Ninth Circuit U.S. Court of Appeals in 1975; he had been recommended for the post by then-California governor Ronald Reagan. Thirteen years later, in 1988, President Reagan appointed him to the Supreme Court, after the earlier nomination of Robert Bork was rejected by the Senate. Kennedy's 1958 B.A. was from Stanford, his 1961 LL.B. from Harvard. He is married to Mary Davis; they have three children.

FURTHER READING

Anthony Kennedy. BOB ITALIA. Abdo and Daughters, 1992.
Turning Right: The Making of the Rehnquist Supreme Court. DAVID G. SAVAGE. Wiley, 1992.
"A new day in court." LAUREN TARSHIS and JAMES EARL HARDY. *Scholastic Update*, Nov. 1, 1991.
Reshaping the Supreme Court: New Justices, New Directions. ANNE B. RIERDEN. Watts, 1988.
Packing the Courts: The Conservatives' Campaign to Rewrite the Constitution. HERMAN SCHWARTZ. Macmillan, 1988.

Kennedy, Ted (Edward Moore Kennedy; 1932–)

With his personal problems of earlier years behind him, and with Democrat Bill Clinton in the White House, Senator Ted Kennedy fully emerged as a leading Senate liberal, as chairperson of the Senate Labor and Human Resources Committee and a member of the Judiciary Committee positioned to press for passage of many of the main features of the Clinton agenda. During 1993, Kennedy initiated and saw through to fruition legislation making blockage of access to abortion clinics a federal offense; fought unsuccessfully to lift the existing ban on the immigration of those with AIDs or the HIV virus; led the successful fights for the confirmation of Surgeon General Joycelyn Elders and National Endowment for the Humanities chairperson Sheldon Hackney; and took the lead in supporting the Clinton healthcare plan. In November, he and Senator Daniel Patrick Moynihan clashed over which Senate committee would take up the Clinton plan, Moynihan's more conservative Finance Committee, or Kennedy's far more liberal Labor and Human Resources Committee; the quite important issue was unresolved at year's end.

In late July, Kennedy was the target of a biography by Joe McGinniss, titled *The Last Brother*, which featured fictional thoughts and dialogue attributed to him by the author. The book received mostly poor notices from the vast majority of its reviewers, for its facts, its fiction, and its writing. Author William Manchester, author of *The Death of the President* (1967) later accused McGinniss of plagiarizing 187 passages from his work, charges McGiniss denied.

Boston-born Kennedy is the fourth son of Joseph and Rose Fitzgerald Kennedy, and the brother of President John Fitzgerald Kennedy, assassinated in 1963, and Senator Robert Francis Kennedy, assassinated while a presidential candidate in 1968. He has represented Massachusetts in the Senate since 1963. He probably would have been his party's presidential candidate in 1972 or later elections, but for the 1969 Chappaquiddick incident, in which he left the scene of a fatal accident.

Kennedy's B.A. was from Harvard, in 1956, his LL.B. from the University of Virginia, in 1959. He married Washington lawyer Victoria Reggie in 1992. He was formerly married to Virginia Joan Bennett, and has a daughter and two sons; Ms. Reggie has a daughter and a son.

FURTHER READING

"The end of Camelot." JOE MCGINNISS. *Vanity Fair*, Sep. 1993.

"Inside Ted's head. . . ." J.D. PODOLSKY. *People*, Aug. 9, 1993.

"Biography or soap opera?" PAUL GRAY. *Time*, July 12, 1993.

The Last Brother. JOE MCGINNISS. Simon & Schuster, 1993.

Senator: My Ten Years with Ted Kennedy. RICHARD E. BURKE. St. Martin's, 1993.

Chappaquiddick: The Real Story. JAMES LANGE and KATHERINE DEWITT, JR. Thomas Dunne/St. Martin's, 1993.

Good Ted, Bad Ted: The Two Faces of Edward M. Kennedy. LESTER DAVID. Birch Lane/Carol, 1993.

"Tales of Ted." SHARON ISAAK. *Entertainment*, Oct. 30, 1992.

"Time to marry?" TOM GLIATTO. *People*, Mar. 30, 1992.

"The K-list. . . ." DEBRA WISE. *Mademoiselle*, Feb. 1992.

"Sobering times." EVAN THOMAS and MARK STARR. *Newsweek*, Dec. 9, 1991.

Chappaquiddick Revealed. KENNETH R. KAPPEL and JOHN H. DAVIS. Shapolsky, 1989.

Senatorial Privilege: The Chappaquiddick Coverup. LEO DAMORE. Regnery, 1988.

Kerry, John Forbes (1943–) As chairman of the Senate Select Committee on POW-MIA Affairs, Senator John Kerry, the junior Democratic Senator from Massachusetts, continued to focus on the fate of the American prisoners of war thought by many to have been left in Vietnam after American withdrawal. On January 13, after a 15-month investigation, his committee issued its final report, which concluded that no American prisoners of war (POWs) were now being held in Vietnam or elsewhere in former Indochina, despite repeated, inadequately documented claims to the contrary. Kerry's committee did feel that there were still open questions, and that some prisoners may have been left behind, but flatly disbelieved that there had been any American government cover-up in the matter, although the committee did criticize the Nixon administration and the military for its secretive behavior at the time. The committee report was unanimous, though some Senators expressed reservations on some matters of detail; but the committee did not go along with Kerry's call for the lifting of the trade embargo on Vietnam and an accelerated pace of normalization of relations. Kerry continued to work on the issue during the balance of the year, and visited Vietnam May 31-June 1, at the head of a Congressional delegation.

Denver-born Kerry served as a young, front-line naval lieutenant in Vietnam (1966–69), winning a Silver Star and a Bronze Star with an Oak Leaf Cluster, and was wounded three times. In 1969, he became a founder and national coordinator of Vietnam Veterans Against the War. He was an assistant county district attorney (1976–79), practiced law in Boston (1979–82), and was state Lieutenant Governor (1983–85).

Kerry won election to the Senate in 1985. In 1987, while investigating international drug trading, as chairman of Senate Foreign Relations Subcommittee on Terrorism, Narcotics, and International Operations, he discovered the secret $20 million Bank of Credit and Commerce International (BCCI) account of Panamanian general Manuel Noriega, starting the trail of events that led to exposure of the massive BCCI-First American Bankshares scandal. He is the author of *The New Soldier* (1971). Kerry's B.A. was from Yale University, and his J.D. from Boston College. He is married to the former Julia Stimson Thorne; they have two children.

FURTHER READING

"Kerry, John Forbes." *Current Biography*, June 1988.

Kessler, David Aaron (1952–) Asked

to stay on as head of the Food and Drug Administration (FDA) by incoming President Bill Clinton in 1993, Dr. David Kessler continued and expanded a multitude of health protection activities. Full and truthful food labeling continued to be a major focus, with comprehensive contents labeling and new restaurant menu disclosures mandated. On June 14, the FDA introduced a major new initiative, proposing new labeling rules for vitamins and other dietary supplements. During 1993, Kessler strongly defended FDA restriction on the use of silicon gels in breast implants, and added new studies of saline implants. He also met with the manufacturers of RU-486, and on April 20 licensed Population Council-sponsored clinical trials of that so-called abortion pill. Among his agency's many approvals were new drugs for leukemia and epilepsy, and many new medical devices, including the first FDA-approved female condom, Reality.

A magna cum laude graduate of Amherst College, Kessler's 1978 LL.B. was from the University of Chicago and his 1979 medical degree from Harvard University Medical School. He also took courses at the New York University Graduate School of Business Administration. His residency was in pediatrics at Johns Hopkins, while in the same period he was a consultant to the Senate Labor and Human Resources Committee (1981–84). He was attached to New York's Montefiore Medical Center (1984–91), the last six

years as director of the Jack D. Weiler Hospital, part of the Montefiore-Albert Einstein Hospital complex. He also taught food and drug law at Columbia Law School (1986–90), and served on a Health and Human Services commission set up to review the operation of the FDA, before taking over as its chairman in 1991. Kessler reorganized and revitalized the FDA, quickly and effectively moving against false and misleading food labeling, speeding up evaluation and approval procedures, greatly limiting the use of silicon gel breast implants, and turning the agency into a strongly activist health protector. Kessler is married to lawyer Paulette Steinberg: they have two children.

FURTHER READING

"FDA, drugs & you." *American Legion*, Jan. 1993.
"Under a microscope. . . ." MAGGIE MAHAR. *Barron's*, Mar. 2, 1992.
"An apple a day." MARLENE CIMONS. *Runner's World*, Feb. 1992.
"The best public service." *Business Week*, Jan. 13, 1992.
"Kessler, David Aaron." *Current Biography*, Sep. 1991.
"A shot in the arm. . . ." HERBERT BURKHOLZ. *New York Times Magazine*, June 30, 1991.
"Food fight! . . . ." DAVID GROGAN. *People*, June 24, 1991.
"The enforcer. . . ." *Newsweek*, May 27, 1991.

Kevorkian, Jack (1928–) During 1993,

Dr. Jack Kevorkian continued to press his campaign for physician-assisted suicide, which he calls *medicide*, and for which he has invented suicide devices. By December, "Dr. Death," as he is known in the media, had been present at 20 suicides. Under a new Michigan law making it a felony to assist in suicides, Kevorkian was indicted three times in 1993, and was, at year's end, mounting a challenge to the constitutionality of that law while continuing his work. On November 30, he refused to post bond after his third indictment, which alleged that he had assisted in a suicide while out of jail on bail after his second indictment. In jail, he resumed the hunger strike that he had been conducting while in jail on the previous charge. On December 14, a Michigan judge ruled unconstitutional the law Kevorkian was accused of breaking. On December 15, the judge released Kevorkian, who promised not to assist in any more suicides while the remaining charges against him proceeded through the courts. He remained under surveillance.

Kevorkian first came to public attention in April 1990, when he appeared on the *Donahue* show, describing his suicide machine. In June 1990, Janet Adkins, a 54-year-old English professor who had seen the show and was suffering from the early stages of Alzheimer's disease, used his machine to kill herself. First degree murder charges were brought against Kevorkian, but then dropped.

Born and educated in Michigan, Kevorkian was licensed as a physician in 1953, interned in Michigan hospitals, and then worked as a pathologist at the Pacific Hospital in Long Beach, California, until 1982. An advocate of euthanasia throughout his medical career, Kevorkian has published various books and articles on the subject. His 1991 book, *Prescription: Medicine: The Goodness of Planned Death*, received considerable public attention in the United States, as part of the continuing "right-to-die" debate. Kevorkian has been unemployed since 1982; he believes that is because of his upsetting ideas.

FURTHER READING

"The real Jack Kevorkian." MARK HOSENBALL. *Newsweek*, Dec. 6, 1993.

"Kevorkian speaks his mind." "Rx for death." NANCY GIBBS. *Time*, May 31, 1993,

"A conversation with. . . ." FRANK WASHINGTON and TODD BARRETT. *Newsweek*, Mar. 8, 1993.

Dr. Death: Murder or Mercy? Jack Kevorkian's Rx: Death: The Trials of Jack Kevorkian. THOMAS OEHMKE. Lifetime, 1993.

"Mercy's friend or foe?" NANCY GIBBS. *Time*, Dec. 28, 1992.

"The paradoxes of 'rational' death." ROBERT BARRY. "Masks of autonomy." JOHN J. CONLEY. "The suicide machine." NORMAN K. DENZIN. "Assisted suicide and professional responsibilities." WILLIAM J. WINSLADE and KYRIAKOS S. MARKIDES. *Society*, July-Aug. 1992. (Special *Medicide: New Humanism or Old Euthanasia?* issue.)

"The odd odyssey of. . . ." GLORIA BORGER. *U.S. News & World Report*, Aug. 27, 1990.

"The right to die. . . ." D'ARCY JENISH. *Maclean's*, June 25, 1990.

"A vital woman. . . ." BONNIE JOHNSON et al. *People*, June 25, 1990.

"The doctor's suicide van. . . ." MELINDA BECK. *Newsweek*, June 18, 1990.

Khasbulatov, Ruslan Imranovich

(1942–) During the first several months of 1993, Russian parliamentary Speaker Ruslan Khasbulatov headed the hardening opposition to Boris Yeltsin, blocking many of Yeltsin's proposed reforms and challenging the legitimacy of the Yeltsin government. But Khasbulatov, perhaps because of the weakness of popular and armed forces support for the conservative position, was somewhat equivocal; for example, he declared himself opposed to Yeltsin's impeachment shortly before the failed March 28 attempt to impeach Yeltsin. Yet after Yeltsin's April 25 referendum victory, Khasbulatov, now joined by vice president Alexandr Rutskoi, charged electoral fraud, and hardened his opposition to Yeltsin. Ultimately, Khasbulatov and Rutskoi led the unsuccessful armed insurrection of October 3–4, surrendering after the armored attack on the White House that ended the brief revolt. He, Rutskoi, and several other leaders of the insurrection were charged on October 15 with organizing mass disturbances against the government. During the year, his book *The Struggle for Russia: Power and Change in the Democratic Revolution* was published.

Born in Grozny, politician and economist Khasbulatov, like so many other Russian leaders, grew up and advanced in the Communist system. He attended Kazan State University and Moscow University, taught for the Consomnol Central Committee (1970–72), worked at the Soviet Academy of Sciences library (1972–74) and at the Research Institute of Higher Education (1974–79), and taught economics at the Plekhanov Institute of National Economy (1979–90) before going into politics in the new Russia. He became a Russian People's Deputy in 1990, and quickly rose, becoming first vice-chair and then acting chair of the Supreme Soviet in 1991.

FURTHER READING

" 'The president is. . . .' " JOHN KOHAN and YURI ZARAKHOVICH. *Time*, Apr. 26, 1993.

"Boris the bunny:. . ." *Economist*, Feb. 13, 1993.

Kidman, Nicole

(1967–) Australian film star Nicole Kidman starred in 1993 in the mystery-thriller film *Malice*, as Tracy, a student who is nearly killed in an attack by an unknown

"Kidman cruises to the top." *Mademoiselle*, Nov. 1993.
"Nicole Kidman." *Playboy*, July 1992.
"Crazy for each other." ELIZABETH SPORKIN. *People*, June 8, 1992.
"No kidding." WILLIAM NORWICH. *Vogue*, June 1992.

assailant; Alec Baldwin co-starred as Jed, a brain surgeon who may or may have been implicated in the attack. Harold Becker directed a cast that also included Bill Pullman, Peter Gallagher, Bebe Neuwirth, George C. Scott, and Anne Bancroft.

Kidman also starred opposite Michael Keaton in the film *My Life*, he as as a young husband stricken with terminal cancer, she as his pregnant wife; Bruce Beresford wrote and directed. The cast included Bradley Whitford, Queen Latifah, Michael Constantine, Rebecca Schull, and Haing S. Ngor.

Kidman made her film debut at age 14, in the film *Bush Christmas* (1980), and in the same year appeared in *BMX Bandits*, then starred in the Disney miniseries *Five Mile Creek* (1983), and in the film *Windrider* (1984). Her breakthrough role came in the Australian television miniseries *Vietnam* (1986). She also starred in the television miniseries *Bangkok Hilton*. Her American theatrical film debut came in *Dead Calm* (1987); she went on to such films as *Days of Thunder* (1990), *Flirting* (1991), *Billy Bathgate* (1991), and *Far and Away* (1992). She and Tom Cruise met while making *Days of Thunder*, and married in 1990.

FURTHER READING

"The US interview. . . ." MARGY ROCHLIN. *Us*, Dec. 1993.
"Don't call her Mrs. Cruise." JENNET CONANT. *Redbook*, Nov. 1993.

King, Larry (1933–) Talk show host Larry King continued to play a highly visible role in "media politics," most notably in November, when his "Larry King Live" television show was the forum agreed upon for the debate between Vice President Al Gore and political critic Ross Perot on the North American Free Trade Agreement (NAFTA), then before the Congress. NAFTA's fate had been in some doubt, but after the debate, and what many regarded as a clear win for Gore, it passed with votes to spare—and an enhanced reputation for Larry King. The 90-minute Cable News Network (CNN) program drew King's highest ratings ever, with over 11 million households watching, despite running opposite the highly rated "Roseanne."

In July, President Bill Clinton himself appeared on the call-in show, his first appearance since taking office. And earlier, in March, King's program assessed Clinton's first 100 days with four White House correspondents: ABC's Brit Hume, CBS's Susan Spencer, NBC's Andrea Mitchell, and CNN's Wolf Blitzer. In April, Janet Reno appeared in her first nationally televised in-depth interview since becoming Attorney

General. In May, when Clinton's friends Harry Thomason and Linda Bloodworth-Thomason were being criticized as "Hollywood types" bad for the Clintons, King's show was one of the places where they appeared to defend themselves. Indeed, King has become so well-known in American life that he was even the subject of jokes in Mel Brooks's 1993 comedy film *Robin Hood: Men in Tights*. During 1993, King signed a new six-year contract with CNN, which will have him on the air for six nights, not just five. In November he published a new book about his presidential campaign experiences, *On the Line: The New Road to the White House*, written with Mark Stencel.

Brooklyn-born King spent his early career as a broadcaster in Miami, working as a disc jockey for various radio stations (1957–71). Then, at first still in the Miami area, developing a wider broadcasting career, while also working as a writer, as for the *Miami Herald*, *USA Today*, and *Sporting News*. He began "The Larry King Show" on radio in 1978, and began "Larry King Live" on the Cable News Network (CNN) in 1985, there winning various cable industry awards beginning in 1987. The International Radio and TV Society named him Broadcaster of the Year in 1989. King took a quantum leap forward in visibility during the 1992 presidential campaign when Ross Perot announced, on King's February 20, 1992 program, that he would run for president if drafted; soon all the candidates were making pilgrimages to the show. King has also appeared in the movies *Ghostbusters* (1984) and *Lost in America* (1985); acted as host for the Goodwill Games (1990); and written several books, including *Larry King* (1982) with Emily Yoffe; *Tell It to the King* (1988) with Peter Occhiogrosso; *Mr. King, You're Having a Heart Attack* (1989) with B.D. Colen; and *When You're from Brooklyn, Everything Else Is Tokyo*, with Marty Appel. He has been married six times to five women, and has two children.

FURTHER READING

Strange Bedfellows: How Television and the Presidential Candidates Changed American Politics, 1992. TOM ROSENSTIEL. Hyperion, 1993.
"Larry King." *People*, Dec. 28, 1992.
"A King who can listen." STANLEY CLOUD. *Time*, Oct. 5, 1992.
"Larry King." DAVID RENSIN. *TV Guide*, July 25, 1992.
"The maestro of. . . ." THOMAS MEYER. *New York Times Magazine*, May 26, 1991.
"King vs. King. . . ." LISA DEPAULO. *Philadelphia*, May 1991.
"Playboy interview: . . . ." DAVID RENSIN. *Playboy*, Aug. 1990.
"All alone. . . ." LYNN ROSELLINI. *U.S. News & World Report*, Jan. 15, 1990.

King, Rodney Glenn (1966–) The March 1991 beating of African-American Rodney King set in motion a chain of events that grew into the massive April 30–May 2, 1992 Los Angeles riots. On the night of March 3, 1991, King was dragged from his car and subjected to a brutal beating by White Los Angeles police officers. Unbeknownst to them, the beating was being videotaped by a nearby resident, and was then broadcast on television, night after night, to the whole world. Ultimately, charges were filed against four police officers—**Sgt. Stacey C. Koon**, and officers **Laurence M. Powell, Theodore J. Briseno**, and **Timothy E. Wind**—who were tried in March and April 1992 in neighboring Ventura County, by a jury that included no African-Americans. On April 30, 1992, all four officers were acquitted on all but one count against one officer, on which the jury could not make a decision. That night, the Los Angeles riots began. Rodney King, who had seen his assailants acquitted, pleaded for calm and an end to the riots, at one point asking poignantly, "Can't we all get along?" King was arrested twice more in 1991 and 1992; in both instances, no prosecutions resulted.

On August 3, 1992, a Los Angeles grand jury indicted the same four police officers on federal charges of violating King's civil rights. On April 17, 1993, officers Koon and Powell were convicted on some of the charges by a federal jury in Los Angeles; officers Briseno and Wind were acquitted. On August 4, 1993, Koon and Powell were sentenced to very light terms of imprisonment by Judge John G. Davies, who openly expressed sympathy for them. Koon published his version of these events in *Presumed Guilty: The Tragedy of the Rodney King Affair* (1992), written with Robert Deitz.

FURTHER READING

"The untold story. . . ." DAVID WHITMAN. *U.S. News & World Report*, May 31, 1993.

"Larger than life. . . ." ELLIS COSE. "Looking past the verdict." TOM MATHEWS and DAVID A. KAPLAN. *Newsweek*, Apr. 26, 1993.

"Putting justice in the dock." WILLIAM A. HENRY, III. "Unhealed wounds." RICHARD LACAYO. *Time*, Apr. 19, 1993.

Lying Eyes: The Shocking Truth Behind the Corruption and Brutality of the LAPD and the Beating of Rodney King. TIM OWENS and ROD BROWNING. Thunder's Mouth, 1993.

No Justice No Peace: From Emmett Till—Rodney King. TERRY MORRIS. Africentric, 1993.

Reading Rodney King—Reading Urban Uprising. ROBERT GOODING-WILLIAMS, ed. Routledge, 1993.

"The selling of Rodney King." PETER BOYER. *Vanity Fair*, July 1992.

"Following orders." BARRY SCHECK. *New Republic*, May 25, 1992.

"How the defense. . . ." BOB COHN and DAVID KAPLAN. *Newsweek*, May 11, 1992.

"Anatomy of an acquittal." RICHARD LACAYO. *Time*, May 11, 1992.

Understanding the Riots: Los Angeles and the Aftermath of the Rodney King Verdict. LOS ANGELES TIMES STAFF. Los Angeles Times, 1992.

Rodney King and the L.A. Rebellion: Analysis and Commentary by 13 Independent Black Writers. RAS M. COLLIER et al. United Brothers, 1992.

" 'Damn! They gonna lynch us!' " MIKE SAGER. *GQ—Gentleman's Quarterly*, Oct. 1991.

King, Stephen (1947–)

Horror-meister Stephen King's major new work in 1993 was not a novel but a collection of short fiction, *Nightmares and Dreamscapes*; not surprisingly, given his track record, the well-reviewed book was a main selection of the Book-of-the-Month Club and quickly jumped onto the bestsellers lists. King was also one of several authors courageous enough to supply some juvenile writings for a collection called *First Words: Earliest Writings from 42 Favorite American Authors*, edited by Paul Mandelbaum.

The year also saw the release of two new films based on previous King novels: April brought *The Dark Half*, directed by George Romero and starring Timothy Hutton and Amy Madigan in a Jekyll-and-Hyde tale; then in August, *Needful Things*, directed by Fraser Heston and starring Max von Sydow as satanic giftshop-owner Leland Gaunt, who seduces local villagers, including Ed Harris, Bonnie Bedelia, Amanda Plummer, and J.T. Walsh. February also saw the release of *Children of the Corn II: The Final*

Sacrifice, a sequel to the 1984 film based on the King novel. In May, King's *The Tommyknockers*, starring Marg Helgenberger, Jimmy Smits and Joanna Cassidy, was a two-part made-for-television movie. Meanwhile, *The Stand* was in production as a forthcoming eight-hour television miniseries, with King as co-producer. King also found time in May for an eight-city Massachusetts-to-Miami bus tour with an all-author rock band called the Rock Bottom Remainders, including Amy Tan, Dave Barry, Barbara Kingsolver, Robert Fulghum, and King on rhythm guitar. The group was publishing a book about themselves, *Mid-Life Confidential*, during 1994.

Maine-born King received his 1970 B.S. from the University of Maine, then taught English at the Hampden Academy (1971–73), before embarking on his writing career. Among his many novels are *Carrie* (1974), *Salem's Lot* (1975), *The Shining* (1976), *The Stand* (1978; republished uncut, 1990), *Firestarter* (1980), *Danse Macabre* (1981), *Cujo* (1981), *Pet Sematary* (1983), *The Talisman, Cycle of the Werewolf* (1985), *Skeleton Crew* (1986), *The Eyes of the Dragon* (1987), *Misery* (1987), *The Tommyknockers* (1987), *The Dark Half* (1989), *Four Past Midnight* (1990), *Needful Things* (1991), *Gerald's Game* (1992), *Doris Claiborne* (1992), and the *Dark Tower* series: *The Gunslinger* (1982), *The Drawing of the Three* (1987), and *The Waste Lands* (1991). He has also published many short stories and short screenplays, as well as novels under the name of Richard Bachman, including *Rage* (1977), *The Long Walk* (1979), *Roadwork* (1981), *The Running Man* (1982), and *Thinner* (1984). Many of King's works have been adapted for the screen, among them *Carrie* (1976), *The Shining* (1980), *Christine* (1983), *The Dead Zone* (1983), *Stand By Me* (1986; based on *The Body*), *The Running Man* (1987), *Pet Sematary* (1989), and *Misery* (1990); King himself directed from his own scripts *Children of the Corn* (1984) and *Maximum Overdrive* (1986). He also wrote an original screenplay for *Stephen King's Sleepwalkers* (1992). King married Tabitha Jane Spruce in 1971; they have three children.

FURTHER READING

The Complete Stephen King Encyclopedia: The Definitive Guide to the Works of America's Master of Horror. STEVEN J. SPIGNESI. Contemporary, 1993.

The Work of Stephen King: An Annotated

Bibliography and Guide. MICHAEL R. COLLINGS. Borgo Press, 1993.

Writers Dreaming—Dreamers Writing: 25 Writers Discuss Dreams and the Creative Process. NAOMI EPEL. Crown, 1993.

Stephen King: Master of Horror. ANNE SAIDMAN. Lerner, 1992.

Stephen King's America. JONATHAN DAVIS. Starmont House, 1992.

In the Darkest Night: The Student's Guide to Stephen King. TIM MURPHY. Starmont House, 1992; Borgo Press, 1992.

The Stephen King Short Story Concordance. CHRIS THOMSON. Starmont House, 1992.

More Stephen King and Clive Barker: The Illustrated Guide to the Masters of the Macabre. JAMES VAN HISE. Movie Pubs Services, 1992.

Stephen King A to Z: A Dictionary of People, Places and Things in the Works of the King of Horror. STEPHEN SPIGNESI. Popular Culture, 1992.

Stephen King: The Second Decade: Danse Macabre to the Dark Half. TONY MAGISTRALE. Twayne/Macmillan, 1992.

The Work of Stephen King: An Annotated Bibliography and Guide. MICHAEL R. COLLINGS. Borgo Press, 1992.

The Dark Descent: Essays Defining Stephen King's Horrorscape. TONY S. MAGISTRALE, ed. Greenwood, 1992.

"Stephen King." MARK MARVEL. *Interview*, Oct. 1991.

Stephen King: Man and Artist, rev. ed. CARROL F. TERRELL. North Lights, 1991.

The Stephen King Story. GEORGE BEAHM. Andrews & McMeel, 1991.

Kingsolver, Barbara Ellen (1955–)

American novelist Barbara Kingsolver created some widely popular characters in her first novel, *The Bean Trees*, notably the narrator, Marietta "Taylor" Greer, and the abandoned young Cherokee girl, Turtle, whom she informally adopts en route cross-country to Arizona. In 1993, Kingsolver fans were delighted with the appearance of a sequel, *Pigs in Heaven*, following the same characters. Drawing very much on current life, the novel hinges on the appearance of Turtle on an Oprah Winfrey show about "Children Who Have Saved Lives," which triggers attempts to wrest Turtle from Taylor. The sequel was as popular as the first novel, and jumped onto the bestseller lists even before its official publication date of June 30, largely because of support from independent booksellers, who have three times nominated Kingsolver novels for their ABBY award of the book they most enjoy selling. The novel also won the Los Angeles Times Book Prize for fiction.

A featured speaker at the American Booksellers Association convention in Miami in May and the American Library Association convention in June, Kingsolver then went on a 21-city publicity tour. She also made an eight-city Massachusetts-to-Miami bus tour in May with an all-author rock band called the Rock Bottom Remainders, including Amy Tan, Stephen King, Dave Barry, Robert Fulghum, and Kingsolver on keyboards. The authors are publishing a book about the group, *Mid-Life Confidential*, due in 1994.

Born in Annapolis, Maryland, Kingsolver received a 1977 B.A. magna cum laude from De-Pauw University and a 1981 M.S. from the University of Arizona, where she studied population biology, and worked as a technical writer in the office of arid lands studies (1981–85). She became a free-lance journalist in 1985, then a full-time writer in 1987, gaining wide attention with her first novel, *The Bean Trees* (1988) and *Homeland and Other Stories* (1989), both honored by the American Library Association. Her other works include *Holding the Line: Women in the Great Arizona Mine Strike of 1983* (1989); the novel *Animal Dreams* (1990), which won the PEN fiction prize and the Edward Abbey Ecofiction Award; and the poetry collection *Another America* (1992). Kingsolver married chemist Joseph Hoffman in 1985; they have a daughter.

FURTHER READING

"La pasionaria. . . ." MICHAEL NEILL. *People*, Oct. 11, 1993.

"In life, art. . . ." MICHAEL J. FARRELL. *National Catholic Reporter*, May 22, 1992.

"Intimate revelations." JOSEPH A. CINCOTTI. *New York Times Book Review*, Sep. 2, 1990.

"Barbara Kingsolver. . . ." LISA SEE. *Publishers Weekly*, Aug. 31, 1990.

Kite, Tom (1949–)

American golfer Tom Kite continued his winning ways in 1993. In February, he put on a spectacular display at the Bob Hope Chrysler Classic in La Quinta, California, posting the lowest under-par figure ever for a PGA Tour event, with a 10-under-par 62 on the final round. His total also broke the previous 90-hole-event record by four shots and the tournament record by six, with five under-60 rounds:

67–67–64–65–62. Then in March, at the Nissan Los Angeles Open, Kite won again, with birdies on four of the last five holes. With his 1993 winnings to that point, Kite became the first player ever on the PGA Tour to win over $8 million, with Tom Watson way back in second place with $6 million. Back trouble later slowed him, though he lost the Kemper Open in May by just one stroke. Kite was also a member of the successful 1993 Ryder Cup team, and participated in the Chrysler American Great 18 Championship, a designed-for-television special, in which he and other selected golfers played 18 holes at 18 different golf courses around the world.

Kite joined the Professional Golfers Association (PGA) Tour in 1972, but did not make a major impact until 1980 when he won the European Open. In 1981 he was named Golfer of the Year by two organizations, won the Vardon Trophy (again in 1982), and headed the PGA Tour money list. He was a member of the World Cup Team (1984; 1985) and the Ryder Cup Team (1981; 1983; 1985; 1987; 1989), and was PGA Player of the Year and leading money winner in 1989, when he won the Players Championship. He won his first major tournament in 1992, the U.S. Open at California's Pebble Beach, also winning the BellSouth Classic; by year's end, his career total of 17 wins made him the all-time leading PGA money winner, with over $7.5 million, $1 million in 1992 alone. Kite attended the University of Texas. He and his wife, Christy, have a daughter and twin sons.

FURTHER READING

"Major accomplishment." DAVID BARRETT. *Golf*, Aug. 1992.
"Different kinds of dreamers." DAVD KINDRED. *Sporting News*, June 29, 1992.
"Tom Kite. . . . " MIKE BRYAN. *Golf*, Nov. 1989.

Kline, Kevin Delaney (1947–) As his 1992 films, *Consenting Adults* and *Death Becomes Her*, moved strongly into video rental in 1993, Kevin Kline starred in another contemporary film. In *Dave*, directed by Ivan Reitman, Kline played two roles, that of the President of the United States, Bill Mitchell, and that of the President's lookalike stand-in, Dave Kovic, compelled to replace the President, who had become very ill. Sigourney Weaver co-stars, as First

Lady Ellen Mitchell, whom Kovic seems to fool; Frank Langella also stars. The light comedy was quite well received. Forthcoming was the film *Princess Caraboo*, directed by Michael Austin and starring Kline, Phoebe Cates, Wendy Hughes, and Stephen Rea.

Kline also starred as the Duke in the New York Shakespeare Festival Central Park Delacorte Theater production of *Measure for Measure*, directed by Michael Rudman He also took on a much more active role in the affairs of the Public Theater and Shakespeare Festival, becoming an artistic associate, after artistic director JoAnne Akalaitis was replaced by playwright and director George C. Wolfe.

St. Louis-born Kline became a star on Broadway in the late 1970s, winning a Tony for *On the Twentieth Century* (1978), starring in *Loose Ends* (1979), and winning a second Tony for *Pirates of Penzance* (1980), a role he repeated in the 1983 film version. He also appeared off-Broadway in the early 1970s, and played the title role in *Richard III* (1983), *Henry V* (1984), and *Hamlet* (1986). On screen, he also played in such films as *Sophie's Choice* (1982), *The Big Chill* (1983), *Silverado* (1985), *A Fish Called Wanda* (1988; he won a best supporting actor Oscar), *I Love You to Death* (1990), *Soapdish* (1991), *Grand Canyon* (1991), and *Chaplin* (1992). In 1990, he also starred in and directed *Hamlet* for PBS's "Great Performances" series. Kline's B.A. was from Indiana University; he also attended the Julliard School. He married Phoebe Cates in 1989; they have one child.

FURTHER READING

"Kevin can wait." ROSS WETZSEON. *New York*, May 10, 1993.
"Kevin Kline. . . ." SHARI ROMAN. *Video*, Dec. 1991.
"Kevin's choice." JOE MORGENSTERN. *Connoisseur*, July 1991.

Klos, Elmar (1910–93) Czech film director Elmar Klos was a leading figure in the Czech New Wave film movement of the 1960s, as was his collaborator Jan Kadar (1918–79). By far, their best-known film was *The Shop on Main Street*, a trailblazing work that dealt openly with Nazi and Slovakian attacks on Jews in Slovakia during World War II. The movie won the 1965 best foreign film Oscar. They began their collab-

oration with *The Hijacking* (1952), and went on to make several other films together; one of them, *The Third Wish*, was deemed politically incorrect by the state, and cost them five years of their careers, though they were not jailed. Their last film together was *Adrift*, in process in 1968 when the Russian invasion of Czechoslavakia came, and completed by Kadar in Hollywood in 1971. Klos, who did not flee, was banned from films, returning as a teacher of film studies and essayist only after his country became free. No information was available on survivors. (d. Prague, Czech Republic; July 19, 1993)

FURTHER READING

Obituary. *New York Times*, Aug. 2, 1993.
Obituary. *The Times* (of London), July 27, 1993.

Knebel, Fletcher (1911–93) Ohio-born

Fletcher Knebel, a journalist and author, began his long newspaper career with brief stays on the Coatesville *Daily Record*, Chattanooga *News*, and Toledo *News Bee* before settling down at the Cleveland *Plain Dealer* (1936–50); he was their Washington corrspondent (1937–50), then moving to the Washington bureau of Cowles Communications (1950–64). He wrote the widely syndicated column "Potomac Fever" (1951–63). He and Charles W. Bailey II co-authored the bestselling Cold War novel *Seven Days in May* (1962), about a nearly-successful coup plot by a group of high-ranking military officers against an American president who tried to seriously negotiate with the Soviet Union. It was adapted into the 1964 John Frankenheimer film, starring Burt Lancaster and Kirk Douglas. Knebel's other novels also included *Night of Camp David* (1965), *Trespass* (1969), *The Dark Horse* (1972), and *The Bottom Line* (1974). He was survived by his wife, Constance Wood, and a son. (d. Honolulu; February 26, 1993)

FURTHER READING

Obituary. *New York Times*, Feb. 28, 1993.

Kohl, Helmut (1930–) The very difficult

economic and political integration of East Germany into a united Germany and the rise of a new Naziism continued to plague German Chancellor and Christian Democratic Party leader Helmut Kohl during 1993. In addition, economic growth in Germany was adversely affected by a worldwide recession, and unemployment remained high, feeding dissatisfaction. For Kohl, that meant major losses of public esteem; his job performance rating hovered in the 25–35 percent range for much of the year, while that of his probable 1994 opponent, Rudolf Scharping of the Social Democratic Party (SPD), climbed into the 50–55 percent range. His party's support fell, as well, with right-wing parties making substantial gains even as massive anti-Nazi demonstrations forced government prosecutions of small numbers of Nazis and the number of overt Nazi attacks slightly lessened. But new German restrictions on the granting of asylum to refugees were widely regarded at least as a partial victory for the Nazis, who continued to be highly visible in German life-even as the world's media turned to other matters.

Kohl did score something of a victory when the European Community's Maastricht Treaty was ratified, though implementation of the treaty was to be slow because of economic conditions. But his victories were few during 1993, his right-of-center views and party were being successfully attacked from both the right and left. How he—or his successor—would handle the renewed rise of Naziism continued to be one of the world's central questions.

Kohl began his political career in the Rhineland, becoming Christian Democratic Party chairman in the Rhineland (1966–73) and deputy national chairman of his party in 1969; he has been national chairman since 1973. He was opposition leader in the West German parliament (1976–82), and then succeeded chancellor Helmut Schmidt. Throughout his career he has been a rather careful centrist, much concerned with the development of the European Community and pursuing a Western-oriented, but also independent course. Kohl attended the University of Frankfurt and the University of Heidelberg. He married Hannelore Renner in 1960; the couple has two children.

FURTHER READING

"Kohl. . . ." ROBERT J. DOWLING et al. *Business Week*, May 18, 1992.
"King Kohl. " T.S. ALLMAN. *Reader's Digest* (Canadian), May 1991.
"Who's sitting pretty. . . ." *Business Week*, Mar. 11, 1991.

"Helmut Kohl. . . ." Bruce W. Nelan. *Time*, Jan. 7, 1991.

"Herr Klutz. . . ." Anne McElvoy. *New Republic*, Dec. 10, 1990.

"Driving toward. . . ." Henry Muller and Karsten Prager. *Time*, June 25, 1990.

"Kohl power." Edward M. Steen. *Inc.*, Nov. 1990.

"Helmut Kohl. . . ." David Gow. *World Press Review*, Oct. 1990.

Koon, Stacey C.: See King, Rodney.

Koppel, Ted (1940–)

Veteran broadcast journalist Ted Koppel announced his intention to become a permanent free agent in 1993. Though his contract was up in late 1993, and though he might be foregoing additional salary and security, he chose not to sign a new one, stating that he had no intention of leaving ABC but wanted to maintain the ability to do so in the future. Reportedly Koppel's stance was sparked by his desire to maintain his focus on his late-night news program "Nightline," and be free to turn down such ABC requests as joining Peter Jennings and Barbara Walters as rotating anchors on a projected new prime-time news magazine tentatively titled *Turning Point.*

In the meantime, while David Letterman, Jay Leno, and Arsenio Hall were fighting each other in the late-night talk show wars, Koppel held his own with "Nightline," sometimes leading in the ratings, though carried by only about two-thirds of the ABC stations. He also expanded the show's scope to include more investigative reports, such as an analysis of the financial and administrative structure of Ross Perot's organization United We Stand, and other special coverage, such as the notable two-part interview he and Nina Totenberg conducted with Harry Blackmun, something rarely granted by a sitting Supreme Court Justice. Even with "Nightline"'s standard interview-discussion format, the program is more often making news, as with interviews of Attorney General Janet Reno after the Waco raid. Another especially notable program, in April, featured the forepersons of the two Rodney King beating trials, as part of an exploration of how the juries reached differing verdicts.

British-born Koppel emigrated to the United States with his German refugee family in 1953. He began his broadcasting career at New York's WMCA Radio in 1963, in that year moving to ABC News, where he has spent his entire career. He went to Vietnam as an ABC correspondent, worked in Hong Kong and Miami as an ABC bureau chief, was ABC's chief diplomatic correspondent (1971–80), and anchored the "ABC Saturday Night News" (1975–1977). In March 1980, he emerged as a leading figure in American broadcast journalism, as ABC turned its nightly reports on the Iran hostage crisis into the Koppel-anchored Monday-to-Friday "Nightline," identified with him ever since. In 1992, he was inducted into the Academy of Television Arts and Sciences' Hall of Fame. With Marvin Kalb, he wrote *In the National Interest* (1977). Koppel's B.A. in journalism was from Syracuse University, his M.A. in journalism from Stanford. He is married to Grace Anne Dorney; they have four children.

FURTHER READING

"Anchor monster. . . ." John Katz. *Rolling Stone*, Jan. 10, 1991.

Koresh, David (Vernon Howell, c. 1960–93)

On February 28, 1993, four U.S. federal agents of the U.S. Bureau of Alcohol, Tobacco, and Firearms (ATF) were killed during a "surprise" armed attack on "Mount Carmel," the compound of the Branch Davidian cult, near Waco, Texas. The cult, which had originated in the mid-1930s as a split-off from the Seventh Day Adventist Church, was led by self-styled Messiah David Koresh (born Vernon Howell), who took over its leadership in the mid-1980s. Koresh and his followers were ready for the attack; heavily armed, they succeeded in driving off the attackers and their helicopter support.

Federal agents, now led by the Federal Bureau of Investigation, began a siege and unsuccessful set of negotiations with Koresh, who did release 35 cult members during the course of the siege, with two others escaping. On April 19, after 51 days, federal armored forces attacked the compound, with no fire or other emergency vehicles present. In the brief gun battle and massive fire that resulted, a reported 86 Branch Davidians died, including Koresh; 17 of them were children. Government forces stated that most of the deaths had been a mass suicide. Government reports on the disaster, on September 30 and October 8, sharply criticized the ATF for its handling of the February 28 attack, while finding no fault with U.S. Attorney-General Janet Reno and the FBI for the April 19 armored attack. ATF director Stephen Higgins subsequently resigned, and other ATF officials were disciplined.

FURTHER READING

Prophets of the Apocalypse: David Koresh and Other American Messiahs. KENNETH R. SAMPLES, et al. Baker, 1994.

"The last revelation. . . . IVAN SOLOTAROFF. *Esquire,* July 1993.

"The enemy within: . . ." GARY CARTWRIGHT. "David Koresh. . . ." JAN JARBOE. *Texas Monthly,* June 1993.

"In the grip of a psychopath." RICHARD LACAYO. " 'Oh my God, they're killing themselves!' " NANCY GIBBS. *Time,* May 3, 1993.

"The final days of David Koresh." HARRISON RAINIE. *U.S. News & World Report,* May 3, 1993.

"The Messiah of Waco." BARBARA KANTROWITZ. *Newsweek,* Mar. 15, 1993.

"Cult of death." RICHARD LACAYO. *Time,* Mar. 15, 1993.

"Zealot of God." JOE TREEN. *People,* Mar. 15, 1993.

Inside the Cult: A Member's Exclusive Chilling Account of Madness and Depravity in David Koresh. MARC BREAULT. NAL-Dutton, 1993.

See No Evil: Blind Devotion and Bloodshed in David Koresh's Holy War. TIM MADIGAN. Summit (TX), 1993.

Massacre at Waco: The Shocking True Story of Cult Leader David Koresh and the Branch Davidians. CLIFFORD L. LINEDECKER. St. Martin's, 1993.

Kravchuk, Leonid Makarovich

(1934–) Ukrainian president Leonid Kravchuk spent 1993 dealing with intractable economic problems. Ukraine continued to slide into an economic crisis, as inflation soared, production fell, and even basic necessities became scarce. Nor could the country's politicans and economists agree on solutions, Kravchuk leading the way in two contradictory directions by calling for "liberalization" side by side with intensified central planning. Premier Leonid Kuchma, at odds on economic policy with Krav-

chuk and the parliament for much of the year, ultimately resigned in early September. Kravchuk took direct control of the government from acting premier Yefim Zvyalgilsky in late September. To avoid the kind of power struggle and deadlock that had led to the October 3–4 Russian insurrection, Kravchuk and the parliament set early local, parliamentary and presidential elections.

On the vitally important question of nuclear disarmament, some progress was made, with U.S. agreement to supply $175 million for the dismantling of Ukrainian missiles and other nuclear matters. But a Ukrainian-Russian agreement to send all nuclear warheads to Russia for dismantling fell through, as did the the July Ukrainian-Russian agreement on the future of the Black Sea fleet. The extent of Kravchuk's commitment to nuclear disarmament remained an open question.

Kravchuk began his career as a political economy teacher in the city of Chernovtsy, then moving on to work for the Communist Party, which he joined in 1958. Most of his career was spent as a party ideology secretary in a series of minor posts. But with the rise of Mikhail Gorbachev, and the wholly new situation Gorbachev created in the Soviet Union, Kravchuk in the late 1980s became a reform leader, and in due course a leader of the powerful movement to secede from the Soviet Union. He was elected President of Ukraine by its parliament on July 23, 1990, and elected directly by popular vote on December 2, 1991. In power, Kravchuk moved very cautiously on the economic side, the pace of privatization moving hardly at all, while Ukraine's economy remained largely centrally planned, but from Kiev, rather than Moscow. Prices, however, were allowed to rise, the net result being a high rate of inflation coupled with all the old ills of central planning—and without some of Ukraine's old markets in the countries of the former Soviet Union and in Eastern Europe. Kravchuk attended Kiev University. He is married to political economist Antonina Kravchuk; they have one son.

FURTHER READING

"Kravchuk, Leonid M." *Current Biography,* Jan. 1993.

"The end of the U.S.S.R." GEORGE J. CHURCH. *Time,* Dec. 23, 1991.

"Divided they fall. . . ." DOUGLAS STANGLIN. *U.S. News & World Report,* Dec. 30, 1991.

"A house of cards." MALCOLM GRAY. *Maclean's*, Dec. 16, 1991.
"Europe's new state: Ukraine." *Economist*, Dec. 7, 1991.
"Your pace or mine?" *Economist*, June 22, 1991.

Kristofferson, Kris (1936–)

Actor and country music figure Kris Kristofferson starred in 1993 in the well received film *Paper Hearts*, about the dissolution of a failed marriage. The film was written and directed by Rod McCall, who also co-produced with Catherine Wanek, and the cast also included Sally Kirkland, James Brolin, and Pamela Gidley. Kristofferson also starred in the action-adventure television film *Trouble Shooters: Trapped Beneath the Earth*, in a cast that included David Newsom and Leigh J. McCloskey, about a series of disasters from which his character ultimately emerged. He was also one of the celebrity performers involved in the four-hour music video *Bob Dylan: The 30th Anniversary Concert Celebration*. Still forthcoming was a starring role opposite Lance Henriksen in the film *Knights*, a fantasy set in the wake of a cataclysm.

Texas-born Kristofferson has appeared in such films as *Cisco Pike* (1972), *Blume in Love* (1973), *Alice Doesn't Live Here Anymore* (1974), *The Sailor Who Fell From Grace With The Sea* (1976), *Heaven's Gate*, (1981), *Rollover* (1981), *Welcome Home* (1990), and *Christmas in Connecticut* (1992). He has also appeared in such telefilms as *Stagecoach* (1986), *Amerika* (1987), *Pair of Aces*. (1990; and the 1991 sequel), and *Miracle in the Wilderness* (1991). He is also a well-known country singer and songwriter, with numerous songs and albums, starting with *Kristofferson* (1970); in 1992, he issued a two-CD set, each containing 17 of his songs, on one sung by him, on the other sung by others. He also often sings with Willie Nelson, Johnny Cash, and Waylon Jennings as The Highwaymen. Kristofferson attended Pomona College and was a Rhodes Scholar at Oxford University. He has been married three times, and has three children.

FURTHER READING

"Kristofferson." ROSA JORDAN. *Progressive*, Sep. 1991.
Written in My Soul: Rock's Great Songwriters . . . Talk about Creating Their Music. BILL FLANAGAN. Contemporary, 1986.

Kurtzman, Harvey (1924–93)

A leading 20th-century cartoonist, and a social historian, Harvey Kurtzmann began his long cartoon career soon after his graduation from New York City's High School of Music and Art. His cartoons were first published in *Magno Comics* in 1943, and in several other comic books during the 1940s. He joined William Gaines's EC Comics in 1950, and there in 1952 originated the seminal *MAD* magazine. With its mix of wholly relevant, very dark satire and slapstick comedy, the magazine became a cult object for the young, generating a new kind of American humor and a host of similar publications, and was an integral part of the developing counterculture of the 1960s. Kurtzman later created several other humor magazines, including *Trump*, *Humbug*, and *Help*. He also wrote children's books, *My Life As a Cartoonist* (1988), and *From Aargh! to Zap!: Harvey Kurtzman's Visual History of the Comics* (1991). He was survived by his wife, Adele, three daughters, a son, and two brothers (d. Mount Vernon, New York; February 21, 1993)

FURTHER READING

"Kurtzman's Mad world." ADAM GOPNIK and ART SPIEGELMAN. *New Yorker*, Mar. 29, 1993.
"Harvey Kurtzman. . . ." TY BURR. *Entertainment*, Mar. 5, 1993.
Obituary. *The Times* (of London), Mar. 4, 1993.
Obituary. *New York Times*, Feb. 23, 1993.

Kutner, Luis (1908–93)

One of the world's leading human rights advocates, Luis Kutner clerked for Clarence Darrow while a student at the University of Chicago law school, and began his long, unsuccessful campaign for World Habeas Corpus in 1931. In the early 1930s, he also began an almost as long, but far more successful advocacy of the Living Will concept; he is generally credited with being the originator of the concept, now law in many American states. In 1961, Kutner was a co-founder of Amnesty International. He practiced law in Chicago for six decades, fighting many individual human rights and civil rights cases in the United States and abroad, representing a wide range of clients. He was survived by his wife, Rose, a son, and a sister. (d. Chicago; March 1, 1993)

FURTHER READING

Obituary. *The Times* (of London), Mar. 5, 1993.
Obituary. *New York Times*, Mar. 4, 1993.

L

Lamborghini, Ferruccio (1916–93)

Italian industrialist Ferruccio Lamborghini began his career as a mechanic, using skills acquired while serving in the Italian army during World War II. From 1948 to 1958, often using scrap parts, he built his Lamborghini Trattori into a successful tractor manufacturer, then diversifying into heating sytems, in 1960 founding Lamborghini Buciatori to carry the heating system portion of his business. A fast sports car enthusiast, he produced his first sports car model in 1963, and during the decade that followed produced the fast, powerful Miura and Countach models for which he became a household name. Overextended, he sold his controlling interest in his company in the early 1970s, then retired. He was survived by a son. (d. Perugia, Italy; February 20, 1993)

FURTHER READING

Obituary. *Motor Trend*, June 1993.
"An iron fist in a velvet glove." LUCA CIFFERI. *Autocar & Motor*, Mar. 17, 1993.
Obituary. *The Times* (of London), Feb. 23, 1993.
Obituary. *New York Times*, Feb. 22, 1993.
Great Auto Makers and Their Cars. ROBERT ITALIA. Oliver (MN), 1993.
"Lamborghini illustrated." PETE LYONS. *Consumer Guide*, Jan. 15, 1989.

lang, k.d. (Kathy Dawn Lang; 1962–)

Canadian popular and country music artist k.d. lang won major recognition from her peers in 1993. At the 35th Annual Grammy Awards, she received three nominations, and was awarded her second Grammy, this one for best female pop vocal performance, for "Constant Craving." Her video version of "Constant Craving" won an MTV Video award as best female video. At the 20th annual American Music Awards, she was voted favorite new adult contemporary artist.

In 1993, she issued the album *Music From the Motion Picture Soundtrack: Even Cowgirls Get The Blues*. The album contained seven vocal and nine instrumental pieces, and was probably not intended to be a full-scale lang effort; but it was very well received as an album, with several of her songs, including "Hush Sweet Lover" and "Just Keep Me Moving" becoming hits.

Lang continued to be active in a considerable number of social causes, perhaps most notably on environmental and animal rights issues. On the personal side, she attempted to discourage an unauthorized biography in preparation, by refusing to cooperate and asking her friends to join her refusal, although the author disclaimed any intent to injure her.

Born in the small town of Consort, Alberta, Canada, lang began her career as a performance artist singing country music while still at Alberta's Red Deer College. She made her professional singing debut in cabaret in Edmonton, Alberta, and in 1984 formed her first group, the Reclines. Moving to Toronto and gaining in popularity as she toured, she also cut her first country music album, *A Truly Western Experience* (1984). She made her U.S. debut in New York City in 1985, and from that appearance came her association with Sire Records, which issued her albums *An-*

gel With a Lariat (1986) and *Shadowland* (1988), neither of them a great commercial hit, but both critically acclaimed. Lang won a 1990 best female country vocalist Grammy award for her fourth album *Absolute Torch and Twang*. She then took a two-year break from recording, returning as a popular, rather than country artist with the hit album *Ingenue*, with such singles as "Constant Craving," "The Mind of Love," and "Miss Chatelaine."

During her two-year break, lang starred in Percy Adlon's film *Salmonberries*, in large part a lesbian love story. In June 1992, for the first time, she publicly declared herself to be a lesbian; although she had previously made her sexual orientation clear, and had attracted a devoted lesbian audience in addition to her much larger country and crossover popular music audiences. An activist in many social causes, including animal rights, lang has sparked considerable controversy, most notably with her anti-meat ads.

FURTHER READING

"lang, k.d." MIM UDOVITCH. *Rolling Stone*, Aug. 5, 1993.
"k.d. lang cuts it close." LESLIE BENNETTS. *Vanity Fair*, Aug. 1993.
K.D. Lang: Carrying the Torch. WILLIAM ROBERTSON. InBook, 1993.
"K.D. gets real." PETER GODDARD. *Chatelaine*, Sep. 1992.
"Lang, K.D." *Current Biography*, Sep. 1992.
"Virgin territory. . . ." BRENDAN LEMON. *Advocate*, June 16, 1992.
"Midnight cowgirl." KRISTINE MCKENNA. *US*, May 1992.
"Torch and twang. . . ." DON GILLMOR. *Reader's Digest (Canadian)*, Oct. 1990.
"Lesley Gore on. . . . " LESLEY GORE. *Ms.*, July-Aug. 1990.
"The amazing k.d. lang." CHARLA KRUPP. *Glamour*, Feb. 1990.
"Another country." HOLLY GLEASON. *Harper's Bazaar*, Oct. 1989.

Langmuir, Alexander Duncan

(1910–93) California-born Alexander Langmuir, a leading public health doctor, began his career in the 1930s, with the New York State and then Westchester County health departments. After World War II service, he taught at Johns Hopkins University, where he had re-ceived his public health degree, leaving in 1948 to join the federal health service in Atlanta. There, he created the Epidemic Intelligence Corps, and from 1949 until his retirement in 1970 he was chief epidemiologist of the national health service. Langmuir was largely responsible for creating the tremendously valuable concept of disease monitoring, detecting and tracking growing new outbreaks of disease and taking steps to confine the growth of disease into local areas and prevent their spread into epidemics, as in the case of Legionnaire's disease. He was also responsible for the early field training of much of the federal public health corps, and a major figure in American public health. After his retirement, he taught at Harvard Medical School and Johns Hopkins. He was survived by three daughters and a son. (d. Baltimore; November 22, 1993)

FURTHER READING

Obituary. *New York Times*, Nov. 24, 1993.

Lansbury, Angela Brigid (1925–)

Once again, Angela Lansbury was a major television star as Cabot Cove mystery writer and detective Jessica Fletcher in "Murder, She Wrote," which continued to show strongly in its 8 P.M. Sunday night slot into the 1993–94 season. Reruns of earlier shows on other channels also drew substantial audiences. As she had done in the 1992–93 season, she broadened the show somewhat, choosing a New York setting that again allowed her much greater plot and ethnic variety. In December, Lansbury committed to another year of the show, through the 1994–95 season. Her son and business associate, David Shaw, also announced that Lansbury was developing plans to play Emily Pollifax in a series of films based on the Dorothy Gilman detective novels.

In 1993, Lansbury hosted the *45th Annual Primetime Emmy Awards* show. She herself received nominations for an Emmy as best lead actress in a drama series, and for a Golden Globe as best actress on a television drama.

British-born Lansbury began her long film and theater career with a supporting role in *Gaslight* (1944), and played competently in over a score of substantial film roles during the following 25 years. But it was on Broadway and in television, both much later, that she became a major star. She won four Tony Awards on Broadway, for *Mame* (1966), *Dear World* (1969), *Gypsy* (1973), and *Sweeney Todd* (1979). Then, quite late in her career, she became a major television star with "Murder, She Wrote" (1984–), also starring in such television films as *The Shell Seekers* (1989), *The Love She Sought* (1989), and *Mrs. 'Arris Goes to Paris* (1992). She also starred as the teapot Mrs. Potts in the hit animated film *Beauty and the Beast* (1991). She has published *Angela Lansbury's Positive Moves* (1991). Lansbury married Peter Shaw in 1949; they have two children.

FURTHER READING

"Auntie Angela." KEVIN ALLMAN. *Advocate*, Sep. 22, 1992.
"Gardens, she wrote." SUSAN SWIMMER. *Ladies Home Journal*, July 1992.
"She's conquered movies. . . ." RICHARD ALLEMAN. *Vogue*, Dec. 1991.
Angela Lansbury: A Biography. MARGARET W. BONNANO. Thomas Dunne/St. Martin's, 1987.

Lazar, Irving Paul "Swifty" (1905–93)

Nicknamed "Swifty" by Humphrey Bogart, for whom he secured five acting jobs in a single day, Irving Lazar was a leadng film, theatrical, and literary agent, with a massive celebrity client list. He began his career as a lawyer in New York City, and soon began representing literary and show business clients, and in the 1930s was with the Music Corporation of America. After World War II service, Lazar emerged as one of the leading agents of the postwar period, operating on both coasts though focusing on Hollywood. His clients were a "Who's Who" of literature and show business, among them Lillian Hellman, Cole Porter, Richard Rogers, Richard M. Nixon, and Neil Simon. Largely a lone operator, rather than one who built a substantial agency organization, Lazar was personally a rather flamboyant figure, whose parties, deals, and feuds were for several decades part of the show business news. There were no survivors. (d. Beverly Hills, December 29, 1993)

FURTHER READING

Obituary. *New York Times*, Jan. 1, 1994.
"The king of the deal." MICHAEL KORDA. *New Yorker*, Mar. 29, 1993.

Leakey, Frida (Henrietta Wilfrida Avern; 1902–93)

Frida Avern, traveling in Africa in the late 1920s, met archaeologist and paleontologist Louis Leakey in Kenya; he was then in the early stages of the major East African work that would ultimately transform humanity's understanding of its origins. She and Leakey married in 1928; they then worked together in East Africa and periodically lived in England until their divorce in 1936, shortly before his second marriage, to Mary Leakey. Frida Leakey's illustrations are found in some of Louis Leakey's earliest books. After their divorce, she worked as a broadcaster on Africa for the BBC through the late 1930s. After World War II, she was active in local affairs at Girton, near Cambridge. She was survived by a daughter and a son. (d. August 19, 1993)

FURTHER READING

Obituary. *The Times* (of London), Sep. 1, 1993.

le Carré, John (David John Moore Cornwell; 1931–)

As the Cold War ended at the turn of the 1990's, many people tut-tutted that the great days of the spy novel, and of spy novelist extraordinaire John le Carré, were past. That they had misjudged both the situation and their man was made evident with the 1993 publication of his latest novel: *The Night Manager*. In this, as in the best of le Carré's novels, at least since *The Spy Who Came in From the Cold* (1963), anger is never far from the surface, though controlled and harnessed in the service of action. It is anger that motivates the character of the title, Jonathan Pine, to tilt against corrupt and corrupting arms dealer Dicky Roper, stand-in for a host of more obscurely seen enemies in a world dominated by drugs, arm dealers, and money-laundering. Not by accident, the hotel at the center of the action is in Zurich; as le Carré commented in an interview, "Switzerland itself is the metaphor for the sanitizing of some of these disgusting industries." Many critics lauded le Carré's successful move beyond the Cold War, and audiences apparently did as well, landing the book on the bestseller lists. Le Carré himself displayed a good deal of anger and passion as he appeared in interviews on a publicity tour for the book, and was outspoken about the state of the world, including the public unveiling of Stella Rimington, head of Britain's Secret Service, a position in the past referred to only as MI5. *The Night Manager* also appeared in an audio verson, read by le Carré himself. Also in 1993, le Carré brought a lawsuit in Britain to halt Graham Lord's proposed biography about him, on grounds of defamation; it was settled out of court, the book then being abandoned.

Born in Poole, Dorset, England, le Carré studied at Switzerland's Bern University (1948–49), then took a B.A. in modern languages at Oxford University's Lincoln College (1956). After teaching at Eton College (1956–58), he joined the British Foreign Service (1959–64), stationed in Germany from 1961. His first novel, *Call for the Dead* (1960), basis for the film *The Deadly Affair* (1967), starring James Mason and Simone Signoret, introduced the spymaster who would be his most famous character: George Smiley. This was followed by *A Murder of Quality* (1962); *The Spy Who Came in From the Cold* (1963), basis for the 1965 film, which won both the Mystery Writers of America and British Crime Writers novel-of-the-year awards; *The Looking-Glass War* (1965); *A Small Town in Germany* (1968); and *The Naive and Sentimental Lover* (1971). He is best-known for his Karla trilogy, the first and third parts of which were made into television miniseries (1977 and 1982), starring Alec Guinness as George Smiley: *Tinker Tailor Soldier Spy* (1973); *The Honorable Schoolboy* (1977), which won the James Tait Black Memorial prize and the Crime Writers Association gold dagger; and *Smiley's People* (1980). His other novels include *The Little Drummer Girl* (1983); *A Perfect Spy* (1986); *The Russia House* (1989), basis for the 1990 film; and *The Secret Pilgrim* (1991), the final tales of George Smiley. Among his honors are the Grand master award of the Mystery Writers of America (1986), the Malparte prize (1987), and the Crime Writers Association's diamond dagger award (1988). Le Carré's 1954 marriage to Alison Ann Sharp ended in divorce in 1972; they had three sons. He married Valerie Jane Eustace in 1972; they have one son.

FURTHER READING

John le Carré. LynnDianne Beene. Twayne/Macmillan, 1992.
" 'We distorted. . . .' " Walter Isaacson and James Kelly. *Time*, July 5, 1993.
" 'I was heartily sick of it'." Craig R. Whitney. *New York Times Book Review*, Jan. 6, 1991.
"Spies who come in. . . ." Viktor Orlik. *World Press Review*, Oct. 1989.
"The thawing of. . . ." Alvin P. Sanoff. *U.S. News & World Report*, June 19, 1989.
"In from the cold." Tom Mathews. *Newsweek*, June 5, 1989.
The Quest for le Carré. Alan Bold, ed. St. Martin's, 1988.
Corridors of Deceit: The World of John le Carré. Peter Wolfe. Bowling Green University Press, 1987.
John Le Carré. Harold Bloom, ed. Chelsea House, 1987.

Ledoux, Fernand (1897–1993) Belgian-born French actor Fernand Ledoux pursued simultaneous stage and screen careers that spanned more than six decades. After World War I military service, he studied at the Academy of Dramatic Art, and made his stage debut at the Comédie Française in 1923, in the first of more than 800 stage roles, among them a very notable creation of Molière's *Tartuffe*. Ledoux made his silent screen debut in 1918, and in the 1930s played in several substantial film roles, as in Jean Renoir's *The Human Beast* (1938), opposite Jean Gabin and Simone Simon. Late in his career, he played strong supporting roles in several English-language films, for which he is best known abroad, as in *The Longest Day* and *Freud*. His final flm was Henry Verneuil's satire *A Trillion Dollars* (1982). He was survived by four children. (d. Calvados, Normandy, France; September 21, 1993)

FURTHER READING

Obituary. *The Times* (of London), Oct. 22, 1993.
Obituary. *New York Times*, Sep. 23, 1993.

Lee, Brandon (1965–93) On March 31, 1993, while filming his own death scene in the forthcoming action film *The Crow* on location in Wilmington, North Carolina, Brandon Lee was accidentally shot and killed. Another actor did the shooting, using a .44 calibre pistol that was thought to have been loaded with blanks; instead, a live round was fired, seriously wounding Lee, who died at a regional hospital after unsuccessful emergency surgery. No charges were filed, as local prosecutors concluded that criminal negligence was not involved in the accident. The son of kung fu action film star Bruce Lee, who died in 1973, Brandon Lee's career had so far mirrored that of his father. He had appeared in several kung fu action films, played opposite David Carradine in television's *Kung Fu: The Movie* (1986), and starred in the kung fu film *Rapid Fire* (1992). He was survived by his mother, Linda, and a sister.

FURTHER READING

"Lethal weapon." MICHAEL A. LIPTON. *People*, Apr. 19, 1993.
"The brief life. . . ." MARK HARRIS et al. *Entertainment*, Apr. 16, 1993.
"Safety first–again. . . ." ANDY MARX and KATHLEEN O'STEEN. *Variety*, Apr. 5, 1993.
"Son of Bruce breaks loose." MICHAEL A. LIPTON. *People*, Sep. 7, 1992.
Obituary. *The Times* (of London), Apr. 5, 1993.

Lee, Pinky (Pincus Leff; 1908–93) St. Paul-born Pinky Leff, whose trademark was his lisp, began his career as a comic in burlesque in the 1930s, and played in variety through the 1940s, also appearing in such 1940s films as *Lady of Burlesque* and *Earl Carroll's Vanities*. He made his television debut in variety in 1950, and co-hosted the musical variety show "Those Two" (from 1951–53). He emerged as a star of early children's television in the very popular "The Pinky Lee Show" (1954–56). He hosted a second children's program, "The Gumby Show" (1957), but left after a few months, in a dispute with NBC, effectively ending his television career. Lee continued to work in variety for the rest of his career. He was survived by his wife, Bebe, a daughter, and a son. (d. Misson Viejo, California; April 3, 1993)

FURTHER READING

Obituary. *Variety*, Apr. 12, 1993.
Obituary. *New York Times*, Apr. 7, 1993.

Lee, Spike (Shelton Jackson Lee; 1957–) Filmmaker Spike Lee's 1992 film *Malcolm X* completed its theatrical run, and moved successfully into home video rental in 1993; apparently, some who had been daunted by its 3 hour and 19 minute length were far more willing to view it at home. Lee spent 1993 largely in developing new projects, among them several films and the comic book series "Comics from Spike," announced as a series of comic books on matters of African-American interest, and also a vehicle for the adaptation of some Lee films into comic books.

Forthcoming was the film *Clockers*, directed by Lee and produced by Martin Scorsese. Lee was also slated to write, direct, and produce the film *Crooklyn, N.Y.*, and to appear as an actor in the film *The D.R.O.P. Squad*, directed by David Johnson. On the personal side, lawyer Tonya Linette Lewis and Lee announced their engagement.

Atlanta-born Lee has made several films, including *She's Gotta Have It* (1986) and *School Daze* (1988); with Lisa Jones, he wrote books about the making of both films. He became a notable and very controversial filmmaker in 1989, with release of his film *Do the Right Thing*, a fictional story that sharply explored racial tensions in his home area of Bedford-Stuyvesant, in Brooklyn. Denzel Washington starred in Lee's equally controversial 1990 film *Mo' Better Blues*, attacked by many as anti-Semitic for its story of the exploitation of African-American artists, in this instance by two Jewish club owners. His 1991 film was *Jungle Fever*, an interracial love story. Lee's 1979 B.A. was from Morehouse College, and his 1983 M.A. in filmmaking from New York University.

FURTHER READING

Spike Lee: Filmmaker. BOB BERNOTAS. Enslow, 1993.
Spike Lee. G. DINERO. Dell, 1993.
" 'I'm for truth. . . .' " ANNE THOMPSON. *Entertainment*, Nov. 27, 1992.
"Words with Spike." JANICE C. SIMPSON. *Time*, Nov. 23, 1992.
"X, lies and videotapes?" PLAYTHELL BENJAMIN. *Guardian*, Nov. 18, 1992.
"Great Xpectations." RALPH WILEY. *Premiere*, Nov. 1992.
"Spike goes the extra mile. . . ." *Scholastic Update*, Oct. 23, 1992.
"Spike Lee hates. . . ." BARBARA GRIZZUTI HARRISON. *Esquire*, Oct. 1992.
"Movies. . . ." DAVID DENBY. *New York*, Sep. 14, 1992.
"Black and white movies." RICHARD BROOKS. *Observer*, May 17, 1992.
"The battle to film. . . . " JANICE C. SIMPSON. *Time*, Mar. 16, 1992.
Spike Lee. ALEX PATTERSON. Avon, 1992.

"Spike Lee. . . ." DAVID BRESKIN. *Rolling Stone*, July 11, 1991.

"Spike Lee. . . ." ELVIS MITCHELL. *Playboy*, July 1991.

"Spiking a fever. . . ." JACK KROLL. *Newsweek*, June 10, 1991.

"Spike's peak. . . ." GERRI HIRSHEY. *Vanity Fair*, June 1991.

Five for Five: The Films of Spike Lee. TERRY McMILLAN. Stewart Tabori & Chang, 1991.

Lehrer, Jim (James Charles Lehrer; 1934–) Best-known as co-anchor with Robert MacNeil of the "MacNeil/Lehrer NewsHour," Jim Lehrer put his knowledge of inside Washington to good use in a new novel, *Blue Hearts*, a political thriller, a departure for Lehrer. A chance meeting with a former Secretary of State (and fellow ex-CIA agent) draws the main character, retired CIA agent Charlie Henderson, back into action, in a tale that involves what one reviewer called an "original and extremely plausible theory about the Kennedy assassination." Reviewers pointed out that Lehrer's inside view of Beltway folks and their actions was much of the fun of the book. Lehrer's wife, Kate Staples Lehrer, had published her own novel in 1993, *When They Took Away the Man in the Moon*; the pair conducted a joint authors' tour. Another novel, *Fine Lines*, was scheduled for 1994 publication.

Meanwhile, the nightly PBS "The MacNeil/Lehrer NewsHour" continued to be as one of tele-vision's most successful and longest-running partnerships. While backup anchor Judy Woodruff left for CNN, Roger Mudd returned from a year at Princeton University to provide solid support to the team, with Margaret Warner later added.

Kansas-born Lehrer was a reporter for the *Dallas Morning News* (1959–61), then moving to the *Dallas Times Herald* as reporter and later city editor (1961–70). He moved into broadcast journalism as a correspondent and producer for KERA-TV, Dallas (1970–72). He joined the Public Broadcasting System in 1972, and in 1973 began his long association with Robert MacNeil; they won an Emmy for their live coverage of the Senate Watergate hearings. The "Robert MacNeil Report," with Lehrer as Washington correspondent, began in 1975, and became their award-winning "MacNeil/Lehrer Report" in 1976 and "The MacNeil/Lehrer NewsHour" in 1983. Lehrer's many awards include several Emmys, a George Polk Award, and a Peabody award. Lehrer has also hosted several PBS specials. His novels include *Viva Max* (1966), *We Were Dreamers* (1975), *Kick the Can* (1988), *Crown Oklahoma* (1989), *The Sooner Spy* (1990), and *Short List* (1992). He has also written the plays *Chili Queen* (1986) and *Church Key Charlie Blue* (1987) and the memoirs *A Bus of My Own* (1992). His 1956 journalism degree was from the University of Missouri. He is married to author Kate Staples Lehrer, and has three children. (For additional photo, see MacNeil, Robert.)

FURTHER READING

"MacNeil/Lehrer. . . ." MORGAN STRONG. *Playboy*, June 1991.

Leinsdorf, Erich (1912–93) Vienna-born Erich Leinsdorf completed his musical education at the University of Vienna and the Vienna Music Academy. He made his professional debut as a pianist, but his long career was as a conductor, beginning as an assistant to Arturo Toscanini at the Salzburg Festival. He emigrated to the United States in 1937, made his American conducting debut at the Metropolitan Opera in 1938, and joined the Met in 1939, staying until 1943, his tenure marked by the kinds of disputes over discipline, rehearsal requirements, and textual accuracy that were to characterize much of his career and shorten some of his associations. His longest tenures were a nine-year stay at the Rochester Philharmonic in the 1940s and early 1950s and six-year stay as musical director of the Boston Symphony (1962–69), a period in which he introduced many new works at Tanglewood. While at Rochester, he made a highly regarded series of recordings. Later in his career, he toured widely as a guest conductor. Leinsdorf published *Cadenza: A Musical Career* (1976) and *The Composer's Advocate: A Radical Orthodoxy for Musicians* (1981). He was survived by his wife, Vera Graf, and five children. (d. Zurich, Switzerland; September 11, 1993)

FURTHER READING

Obituary. *Opera News*, Dec.11, 1993.
Obituary. *Current Biography*, Nov. 1993.
Obituary. *Billboard*, Sep. 25 1993.
Obituary. *The Times* (of London), Sep. 13, 1993.
Obituary. *New York Times*, Sep. 12, 1993.
"Erich Leinsdorf . . . ." WILLIAM WEAVER. *Architectural Digest*, Oct. 1993.

Lemieux, Mario (1965–)

For many hockey fans, the analogy is simple: Mario Lemieux is to hockey as Michael Jordan is (or was) to basketball. Lemieux has been league scoring leader four times, including 1993, and led his team, the Pittsburgh Penguins, to two successive Stanley Cups, and almost to a third in 1993. In the middle of the 1992–93 season, after signing a record $42 million seven-year contract in October 1992, he was poised to challenge Wayne Gretzky's single-season scoring record, reaching 100 points by the turn of the year.

But that is only half the story. For Lemieux has also faced enormous personal problems. Not just the bad back, which afflicts so many professional athletes, and which required Lemieux to have off-season surgery in 1990 and again in 1993. Not just the injuries, like the broken bone in his left hand suffered in a slashing attack by New York Ranger Adam Graves that caused him to miss five playoff games in 1992, though he returned for the finals to lead the Penguins to their second straight title. But for Lemieux there was also a life-threatening bout with Hodgkins' disease, a type of cancer affecting the lymphatic system. He was diagnosed in January 1993, had a cancerous lump removed from his neck, and underwent 22 sessions of radiation treatment in 30 days.

With all this, Lemieux's love of hockey is so great that in mid-February 1993, still in the midst of the radiation treatments and only six weeks after neck surgery, he began skating again. On the last day of his treatment, March 2nd, he jetted to Philadelphia to join his teammates in an actual game, where he was cheered by the rival Flyers' crowd and, despite fatigue from the radiation, scored a goal and an assist. At season's end, although he had missed 24 games, he was once again the league's scoring leader; on the way, between March 5 and April 9, he scored at least one point in each of 16 games, helping his team to a league record of 17 consecutive wins, on April 9th alone getting five goals, in a display so remarkable that even the fans in his rival team's home stadium, New York's Madison Square Garden, gave Lemieux a standing ovation. Whether the cancer has been fully cured will not be known for five years. After July back surgery, Lemieux briefly returned to his team in late October and early November, but was obliged to leave again for further rehabilitation. He was honored in 1993 with hockey's Bill Masterton trophy for dedication to the sport.

On the personal side, Lemieux married Nathalie Asselin in June 1993; they had had their first child in April.

Montreal-born Lemieux has spent his whole professional career with the Pittsburgh Penguins, since 1984, winning two Stanley Cups (1991; 1992). Four-time league scoring leader, he also won the Hart Memorial trophy for most valuable player (1988; 1989), and the Conn Smythe trophy for most valuable player in the playoffs (1991; 1992). He reached a milestone 400 career goals in March 1992.

FURTHER READING

"More than magnificent." D'ARCY JENISH. *Maclean's*, Apr. 26, 1993.
"The legend grows." JON SCHER. *Sports Illustrated*, Apr. 19, 1993.
Mario Lemieux (Super Mario). TED COX. Childrens, 1993.
Mario Lemieux: Wizard with a Puck. BILL GUTMAN. Houghton Mifflin, 1992.
Mario Lemieux. BOB ITALIA. Abdo & Daughters, 1992.
Mario Lemieux: Wizard with a Puck. BILL GUTMAN. Millbrook, 1992.
"Guts and glory. . . ." J. DAVID MILLER et al. *Sport*, July 1991.

"20 questions. . . ." PAUL ENGLEMAN. *Playboy*, Apr. 1989.
"Make room for Lemieux." AUSTIN MURPHY. *Sports Illustrated*, Feb. 6, 1989.

Lemmon, Jack (John Lemmon III; 1925–) In 1993, veteran actor Jack Lemmon's major work was a starring role in the film *Grumpy Old Men*, directed by Donald Petrie, in which he and Walter Matthau play two Minnesota neighbors and friends who become competitors for the attention of a new woman in town, played by Ann-Margret; Ossie Davis, Burgess Meredith, and Daryl Hannah co-starred. Lemmon also played an acclaimed featured role in Robert Altman's film *Shorts Cuts*, and was one of the celebrity actors who did readings for Bill Couturie's environmentalist film *Earth and the American Dream*. On television, Lemmon starred opposite Matthew Broderick in David Mamet's adaptation of his own play *A Life in the Theatre*, directed by Gregory Mosher.

Boston-born Lemmon played in early television, and began his long film career by winning a best supporting actor Oscar for his portrayal of Ensign Pulver in *Mister Roberts* (1954). Nineteen years later, he won a best actor Oscar for *Save the Tiger* (1973). Among his other films, some of the most notable were *Bell Book and Candle* (1958), *Some Like It Hot* (1959), *The Apartment* (1960), *Days of Wine and Roses* (1962), *Irma La Douce* (1963), *The Odd Couple* (1968), *The Prisoner of Second Avenue* (1975),

The China Syndrome (1978), *Missing* (1981), *Mass Appeal* (1984), *Dad* (1989), and *Glengarry Glen Ross* (1992). Lemmon's B.A. and B.S. were from Harvard. Formerly married to Cynthia Boyd Stone, he married Felicia Farr in 1962, and has two children.

FURTHER READING

"Saint Jack." MICHAEL WILMINGTON. *Film Comment*, Mar.-Apr. 1993.
"Jack Lemmon." JOHN CLARK. *Premiere*, Nov. 1992.
"An everyman. . . ." PHILIP FRENCH. *Observer*, Oct. 25, 1992.
"Laughing on the outside." TOM JUNOD and MICHAEL O'NEILL. *Life*, Oct. 1992.
Actors: A Celebration. RITA GAM. St. Martin's, 1988.
The Films of Jack Lemmon. JOE BALTAKE. State Mutual, 1987.

Leno, Jay (James Douglas Muir Leno; 1950–) In the 1993 late-night talk show television wars, this time sparked by David Letterman's move from a slot on NBC following Jay Leno's "Tonight Show" to a CBS slot opposite "Tonight," most observers expected Leno to come out ahead, largely because the show had been a fixture for 30 years. It did not quite work out that way. Letterman showed up strongly from the start and at year's end remained well ahead in the ratings. Indeed, though Leno maintained respectable ratings, he did not come in first until September, when his guest was Burt Reynolds, and many viewers were tuning in to see the premiere of "Late Night with Conan O'Brien," slotted to follow Leno.

It had been a difficult year for Leno. In January, less than a year into his new job, NBC had refused to guarantee his position, publicly leaving him dangling, while they debated whether or not to offer the "Tonight" spot to Letterman. Even so, when Letterman was finally released to go to CBS, Leno was gracious to an old friend, whom he had helped get started in the business, and on whose show he himself had often appeared. In January, when Letterman's move was announced, Leno graciously wished Letterman well at his new network.

Born in New York's suburbs and raised in Massachusetts, Leno began his career as a stand-up comic at Boston nightclubs while studying for a speech degree at Emerson College. He later worked New York clubs and wrote for television's "Good Times." He has toured widely, hosted two of his own NBC Specials, made numerous guest appearances, and published four books of odd or absurd newspaper cuttings, many sent by fans. He was a frequent guest on both the "Tonight Show Starring Johnny Carson" and the then-following "Late Night with David Letterman" from 1977, and was a guest host on the "Tonight Show" from 1986, the exclusive guest host from 1987, then taking over from Carson in May 1992. Leno married scriptwriter Mavis Nicholson in 1980.

FURTHER READING

"The joke's on us." VICTOR GOLD. *Washingtonian*, Nov. 1993.

"Jay." FRANK SWERTLOW. *TV Guide*, Aug. 28, 1993.

"Who gets the last laugh?" DOTSON RADER. *Parade*, July 18, 1993.

"Why is everybody. . . . " MARK HARRIS. *Entertainment*, Aug. 14, 1992.

"Jay Leno: the early years." STEVE BUCKLEY. *Boston*, May 1992.

"Hosts of trouble." FRANK SWERTLOW. *Entertainment*, Apr. 10, 1992.

"Midnight's mayor. . . ." RICHARD STENGEL. *Time*, Mar. 16, 1992.

The World of Jay Leno: His Humor and His Life. BILL ADLER and BRUCE CASSIDAY. Birch Lane/Carol, 1992.

"Wipe that smirk. . . ." PETER W. KAPLAN AND PETER STEVENSON. *Esquire*, Sep. 1991.

"The funniest man. . . ." SEAN PICCOLI. *Insight*, July 22, 1991.

"Playboy interview. . . ." DICK LOCHTE. *Playboy*, Dec. 1990.

"He-e-ere's Jay Leno." GRAYDON CARTER. *Reader's Digest*, Feb. 1990.

"The joker." GRAYDON CARTER. *Rolling Stone*, Nov. 2, 1989.

"He-e-e-e-e-r-e's Jay Leno!" STU SCHREIBERG. *Cosmopolitan*, Sep. 1989.

"Jay Leno." MERRILL SHINDLER. *Los Angeles*, Aug. 1989.

"Jawing with Jay Leno." MARY BILLARD. *GQ—Gentleman's Quarterly*, Aug. 1989.

"Jay Leno. . . ." PETER TAUBER. *New York Times Magazine*, Feb. 26, 1989.

Comic Lives: Inside the World of American Stand-Up Comedy. BETSY BORNS. Simon & Schuster, 1987.

Leontovich, Eugenie (1900–93) Moscow-born Eugenie Leontovich studied at the Moscow Art Theatre before the Bolshevik Revolution of 1917. Her father and brothers, who fought with the White armies, were killed during the Russian Civil War; she escaped to Paris and then emigrated to the United States in 1922. Her major work during her long career in the American theater was as a highly regarded teacher, but she also appeared in several plays, and worked as a director and writer. As an actress, she was favorably received in such plays as *Grand Hotel* (1930), *Twentieth Century* (1932), *Tovarich* (1935), and *Anastasia* (1954). She co-wrote *Dark Eyes* (1943) and directed and starred off-Broadway in *Anna K* (1972), which she adapted from *Anna Karenina*. She appeared in several films, including *The Rains of Ranchipur* (1955). There were no survivors. (d. New York City; April 2, 1993)

FURTHER READING

Obituary. *New York Times*, Apr. 3, 1993.

Letterman, David (1947–   ) In a move accompanied by a great deal of publicity, CBS hired NBC late-late-night show host David Letterman to compete directly with Jay Leno, who had succeeded Johnny Carson on NBC's venerable "Tonight" show. NBC replaced Letterman with comedian Conan O'Brien. Operating out of Broadway's refurbished Ed Sullivan Theater, Letterman and his new CBS show debuted on August 30, to generally favorable reviews, and quickly moved into a leading position among the several competing late shows. Letterman emerged as a major celebrity in the process, gaining and generally maintaining a ratings lead over the Leno "Tonight" show in the early months of their contest for viewers. He was aided by such guests as Vice President Gore and many highly visible entertainers.

Letterman began his career as announcer in his home town of Indianapolis. Moving to Los Angeles in the mid-1970s, he worked as a comedy writer for many television performers, performed as a comedian with The Comedy Store, appeared in many guest roles, and was a frequent guest on the "Tonight" show. He emerged as a substantial television personality in 1980, in his own NBC morning show, the David Letterman Show. He began writing and starring in his long-running NBC "Late Night With David Letterman" show in 1982; two collections of his "Top Ten" lists were published in book form

(1990; 1991). A highly respected figure in television, Letterman has won six Emmys. His B.A. was from Ball State University.

FURTHER READING

"The politics of irony. . . ." ALEX ROSS. *New Republic*, Nov. 8, 1993.
"New Dave dawning." RICHARD ZOGLIN and RICHARD CORLISS. *Time*, Aug. 30, 1993.
"Dave." BRUCE FEIRSTEIN. *TV Guide*, Aug. 28, 1993.
"David Letterman. . . ." *Cosmopolitan*, Apr. 1993.
"David Letterman. . . ." BILL ZEHME. *Rolling Stone*, Feb. 18, 1993.
The David Letterman Story. CAROLINE LATHAM. Watts, 1987.
Comic Lives: Inside the World of American Stand-Up Comedy. BETSY BORNS. Simon & Schuster, 1987.

Levinson, Barry L. (1932–) In a sharp departure from his recent big-budget Hollywood films, director Barry Levinson in 1993 returned to Baltimore, his home town, as the developer and producer of the unusual television series "Homicide: Life on the Street," about a Baltimore homicide squad. The series, shot in semi-documentary style, was much in the tradition of the classic "Hill Street Blues" series, with many continuing stories, and a large cast playing in ensemble. It was acclaimed by most critics, praised by the National Association for the Advancement of Colored People (NAACP) for its treatment of African-American life-and did not find much of an audience, lasting only nine episodes before being cancelled for low ratings. Levinson won an Emmy nomination for best directing in a drama series. In 1993, he also published the book *Levinson on Levinson*. Forthcoming was a film comedy-satire on Hollywood life, written and directed by Levinson and starring Christian Slater and Joe Pesci.

Baltimore-born Levinson worked as a writer and comedian in television, and as a screenplay writer, before turning to directing feature films. His early screenplays include *Silent Movie* (1976) and *High Anxiety* (1977) (both co-written with Mel Brooks), *And Justice for All* (1979), *Inside Moves* (1980), and *Best Friends* (1982). He made his directorial debut with the well-received *Diner* (1982), and went on to direct and in some instances co-write such films as *The Natural* (1984), *Good Morning Vietnam* (1987), *Tin Men* (1987), *Rain Man* (1988; he won a best director Oscar), *Avalon* (1990), and *Toys* (1992). He has published *Diner Guys* (1989) and *Avalon, Tin Men, and Diner: Three Screenplays* (1990). Levinson attended American University.

FURTHER READING

"Storyteller." GAVIN SMITH. *Film Comment*, Nov.-Dec. 1990.
"Baltimore. . . ." BEN YAGODA. *American Film*, Nov. 1990.
"Levinson, Barry." *Current Biography*, July 1990.
"Barry in Baltimore." ALEX WARD. *New York Times Magazine*, Mar. 11, 1990.
"Good morning, Barry Levinson." DAN GREENBURG. *Playboy*, Mar. 1989.

Lewis, Reggie (1965–93) Baltimore-born Reggie Lewis was a basketball star, whose Dunbar High School team had a 50–0 season. At Northeastern University, he was named ECAC North Atlantic Conference Rookie of the Year, then Player of the Year a record three times running (1985–87). He joined the Boston Celtics in 1987, playing behind Larry Bird and being named the Sixth Man of the Year for the 1988–89 season. Then, as Bird's back gave out, Lewis gradually took over, becoming the team's leading scorer in the 1991 playoffs and an All-Star in 1992; he averaged 20.8 points a game in the 1992–93 season and was the team's captain. On April 29, 1993, during a playoff game, Lewis briefly collapsed. A heart condition was diagnosed and Lewis was warned not to resume playing basketball. Lewis sought a second opinion indicating otherwise and was undergoing further testing and monitoring when, while shooting casual baskets at the Celtics training center at Brandeis University, he collapsed and could not be revived. He was survived by his wife, Donna Harris, and a son, Reginald. (d. Waltham, Massachusetts; July 27, 1993)

FURTHER READING

"A city in mourning." E.M. SWIFT. *Sports Illustrated*, Aug. 9, 1993.
"A star dies on the court." DAVID A. KAPLAN. *Newsweek*, Aug. 9, 1993.
"Did Reggie Lewis have to die?" CHRISTINE GORMAN. *Time*, Aug. 9, 1993.
"The green light. . . ." STEVE BUCKLEY. *Sport*, Nov. 1992.

Lewis, Reginald F. (1943–93) A leading
African-American lawyer, corporate manager, and financier, Baltimore-born Reginald Lewis graduated from Harvard Law School in 1968, went into practice with Paul Weiss Rifkin Wharton and Garrison, and then formed Lewis and Clarkson, a law firm focusing on venture capital matters. In 1983, he led his own venture capital group in the acquisition of the failing McCall Pattern Company, and four years later sold the then-healthy company, making tens of millions of dollars in the process. In 1987, he acquired the diversified international operations of the Beatrice Companies for $985 million, and in the years that followed built them into his own highly successful TLC International, developing estimated personal assets in the $400 million range. Lewis also became a major philanthropist and art collector. He was survived by his wife, Loida Nicolas, two daughters, his mother, stepfather, two half-brothers, and two half-sisters. (d. New York City; January 19, 1993)

FURTHER READING

"Late business magnate. . . ." *Jet*, Apr. 26, 1993.
"Black business. . . ." MATTHEW S. SCOTT. *Black Enterprise*, Mar. 1993.
Obituary. *Jet*, Feb. 8, 1993.
Obituary. *New York Times*, Jan. 20, 1993.
"Beatrice International's IPO." THOMAS N. COCHRAN. *Barron's*, Dec. 4, 1989.

Li Peng (1928–) Chinese Premier Li Peng
was re-elected to a second five-year term at the March meeting of the National People's Congress (parliament), though with some opposition, unusual in China. During 1993, he continued to support Deng Xiaoping's development of a "socialist market economy," coupled with continued political repression, although it was clear that Li, as leader of China's hardline sentiment, had major reservations regarding Deng's policies. Li was silent as to the possible shortcomings of the new economic policy in 1993, even as it became increasingly clear throughout the year that China's economy was seriously overheating, with escalating inflation, rising corruption, massive population shifts, and the emergence of an affluent commercial class threatening the stability viewed as absolutely indispensable by the hardliners in the communist leadership—and especially so since the 1989

Tienanmen Square massacre and the dissolution of the Soviet Union. Li reflected his mixed policy concerns throughout the year, sharply resisting international pressures on the question of political repression while at the same time pressing with great success for expansion of China's export trade. During 1993, there were continuing unconfirmed reports that he was in ill health, and might therefore not be a major factor in the conservative-liberal power struggle that would follow Deng's era; what was clear was that such a struggle was inevitable.

Li Peng began his long, steady rise in the Chinese Communist bureaucracy as a young protégé of premier Zhou En-lai. He emerged as a major figure in the 1980s, serving as minister of power in 1981 and as a Politburo member in 1985. In the late 1980s, as great tension developed between the liberal and conservative wings of the Chinese leadership, he became a conservative faction leader. Throughout the world, he is viewed as the chief architect of the 1989 Tiananmen Square massacre. Li attended the Moscow Power Institute. He married Zhu Lin in 1958; the couple has three children.

FURTHER READING

Tiananmen Square. SCOTT SIMMIE and BOB NIXON. University of Washington Press, 1989.
"Li Peng." *Current Biography*, Nov. 1988.

Limbaugh, Rush (Rush Hudson Limbaugh, III; 1951–) Broadcasting celebrity
Rush Limbaugh continued to deliver his strong, many would say offensive, opinions on radio and on television during 1993. A conservative pundit, Limbaugh plays heavily on mistrust of government, jabbing widely at "feminazis," "environmental wackos," "the arts and croissant crowd," the old chestnut "commie libs," and the Eastern establishment in general, though his own show now originates from New York. Limbaugh's radio audience is estimated at 20 million, of which his producer, Roger Ailes, estimates two-thirds agree with Limbaugh's brand of ideological conservatism; these are the fans Limbaugh calls "dittoheads," many of whom gather daily in "Rush rooms," restaurants that have Limbaugh's showed piped in. Limbaugh's style can make enemies of all sides; only after the December 1993 resolution of a long-

standing argument did the Pentagon agree to allow Limbaugh's show to be broadcast to military stations, and even then only one hour of the three-hour show.

Building on his celebrity, Limbaugh delivered a one-two punch to the nation's bestseller lists, following his bestselling *The Way It Ought To Be* (1992), which sold over 3 million copies in hardcover—making it possibly the bestselling hardcover nonfiction book ever—with a new book, *See, I Told You So*, which had the largest initial printing in American publishing history, at 2 million copies, and immediately jumped to the top of the bestseller lists. Limbaugh also publishes a 12-page monthly newsletter, with approximately 370,000 subscribers. December saw rumors that Limbaugh was engaged to his book editor, Judith Regan.

Born in Cape Girardeau, Missouri, Limbaugh attended Southeast Missouri State for a year, then worked as a disc jockey at various stations and in public relations until 1988 when he began hosting "The Rush Limbaugh Show," which came to be broadcast on nearly 500 radio stations around the county. In 1992 he developed a late-night television version of "The Rush Limbaugh Show." He has been divorced twice.

FURTHER READING

"Playboy interview. . . ." *Playboy*, Dec. 1993.

"The politics of irony. . . ." ALEX ROSS. *New Republic*, Nov. 8, 1993.

"Big mouths." KURT ANDERSEN. *Time*, Nov. 1, 1993.

"The leader of the opposition." JAMES BOWMAN. *National Review*, Sep. 6, 1993.

"Show time in the Rush Room. . . ." AMY BERNSTEIN. *U.S. News & World Report*, Aug. 16, 1993.

"What a Rush!" STEVEN ROBERTS. *U.S. News & World Report*, Aug. 16, 1993.

"The Rush is on." JOHN McCOLLISTER. *Saturday Evening Post*, May-June 1993.

"Limbaugh, Rush." *Current Biography*, Mar. 1993.

The Rush Limbaugh Story: Talent on Loan from God. PAUL D. COLFORD. Thomas Dunne/St. Martin's, 1993.

Rush Hour: The Politics, Persona and Timing of the Rush Limbaugh Phenomenon. MIKE TOWLE. Summit (TX), 1993.

Rush Limbaugh and the Bible. DANIEL J. EVEARITT. Horizon House, 1993.

"An interview with. . . ." MARGARET CARLSON. "Conservative provocateur. . . ." RICHARD CORLISS. *Time*, Oct. 26, 1992.

"Rush Limbaugh." MARK GOODMAN. *People*, Oct. 19, 1992.

"Bull Rush." PETER J. BOYER. *Vanity Fair*, May 1992.

"The Rush hours." LEWIS GROSSBERGER. *New York Times Magazine*, Dec. 16, 1990.

Lithgow, John Arthur (1945–) Stage, screen, and television star John Lithgow once again appeared in a wide range of works in 1993. In late spring, he opened as the villain Qualen opposite Sylvester Stallone in the mountain-hopping action film *Cliffhanger*. For the Christmas season, he appeared as newspaper editor Smith Keen in the blockbuster film *The Pelican Brief*, written and directed by Alan Pakula, based on John Grisham's bestselling novel, and starring Julia Roberts and Denzel Washington. He also starred in the Mexico-set western *The Wrong Man*, directed by Jim McBride, in a cast that included Rosanna Arquette, Kevin Anderson, and Jorge Cervera, Jr.

His television appearances included a starring role in the television film *Love, Cheat, and Steal*, as investment banker Paul Harrington, caught in triangle with his wife and her ex-con former husband; it was written and directed by William Curran. In a change of pace, he also starred in the HBO animated film *The Country Mouse and the City Mouse: A Christmas Tale*, as the voice of city mouse Alexander, opposite Crystal Gayle, as the voice of country mouse Emily. Forthcoming was a starring role in a film directed by Bruce Beresford, co-starring Richard Dreyfuss and Linda Hamilton.

LLOYD WEBBER, ANDREW

Rochester-born Lithgow began playing substantial roles on the New York stage in the early 1970s, in such plays as *The Changing Room* (1972), *Beyond Therapy* (1982), *Requiem for a Heavyweight* (1985), and *M. Butterfly* (1988). His most notable films include *The World According to Garp* (1982; he received an Oscar nomination), *Terms of Endearment* (1983; and a second Oscar nomination), *The Manhattan Project* (1986), *Memphis Belle* (1990), *At Play in the Fields of the Lord* (1991), and *Raising Cain* (1992). He has also appeared in several television films, including *The Day After* (1983), *Amazing Stories* (1987; he won an Emmy) and *The Boys* (1991). Lithgow is a 1967 Harvard University graduate, and also attended the London Academy of Music and Dramatic Art (LAMDA). He has been married twice, last to Mary Yeager in 1981, and has two children.

FURTHER READING

"Ready to go over the edge." DEVON JACKSON. *People*, July 5, 1993.

Lloyd Webber, Andrew (1948–) One of the major theatrical events of 1993 was the American opening of the stage musical *Sunset Boulevard*, with music by Andrew Lloyd Webber, and book and lyrics by Don Black and Christopher Hampton; based on the classic 1950 Billy Wilder film, it was directed by Trevor Nunn. Glenn Close starred as aging silent film star Norma Desmond, played in the film by Gloria Swanson, opposite Alan Campbell as Joe Gillis (originally William Holden) and George Hearn as Max von Mayerling (originally Erich von Stroheim). The play opened in Los Angeles in December to mixed reviews, although Close won generally strong reviews; the play had premiered at Lloyd Webber's Sydmonton Festival in 1992, then moved to the London stage earlier in 1993, with Patti LuPone in the central role. The play was set to open in New York in 1994. Forthcoming was a film version of the Lloyd Webber-Tim Rice musical *Evita*, with Oliver Stone slated to write the screenplay and and direct.

On the personal side, Lloyd Webber's wife, Madeleine Gordon, gave birth to their second child, Richard William.

Lloyd Webber emerged as a leading musical theater composer in 1968 with *Joseph and the Amazing Technicolor Dreamcoat*, lyrics by Tim Rice; he then wrote the trailblazing rock opera *Jesus Christ Superstar* (1970), with lyrics again by Rice. He won Tonys for the musicals *Evita* (1978) and *Cats* (1981). Among his other musical hits are *Starlight Express* (1984), *The Phantom of the Opera* (1988), and *Aspects of Love* (1989). His compositions also include the *Requiem Mass* (1975) and *Variations on a Theme by Paganini* (1977), as well as the film scores for *Gumshoe* (1971), *Jesus Christ Superstar* (1973), and *The Odessa File* (1974). Lloyd Webber attended Oxford University and the Royal Academy of Music. He married fashion entrepreneur Madeleine Gordon in 1991; he has been married twice before, until 1990 to singer-actress Sarah Brightman, and has four children. He is the brother of cellist Julian Lloyd Webber.

FURTHER READING

"Hit man meets. . . ." MATT WOLF. "West End wizard. . . ." *Variety*, July 19, 1993.
"Andrew Lloyd Webber. . . ." TOM GLIATTO. *People*, July 23, 1990.
Andrew Lloyd Webber: His Life and Works. MICHAEL WALSH. Abrams, 1989.

Loy, Myrna (Myrna Adele Williams; 1905–93) Montana-born Myrna Loy, who grew up in cabaret, began her career as a dancer in cabaret, and made her film debut in *What Price Glory?* (1925). She became a featured film player in the late 1920s, made the transition to sound, and emerged as a major Hollywood star as Nora Charles opposite William Powell as Nick Charles in the classic film comedy-murder mystery *The Thin Man* (1934). She and Powell made 5 more "Thin Man" films in the next 13 years. Among her many other films were *The Great Ziegfeld* (1936), *The Rains Came* (1939); the classic *The Best of Our Lives* (1946); and *Mr. Blandings Builds His Dream House* (1948). A lifelong activist in humanitarian and social causes, Loy broke off her film career to work with the Red Cross during World War II, and during the early postwar period was a film advisor with the U.S. delegation to UNESCO (United Nations Educational, Scientific and Cultural Organzation). A liberal and Democrat, she strongly opposed McCarthyism during the 1940s and 1950s, and worked with Eleanor Roosevelt and other liberal Democrats in several presidential campaigns and on several social issues. She published the autobiographical *Myrna Loy: On Being and Becoming* (1987), written with James Kotsilibas-Davis. There were no survivors. (d. New York City; December 14, 1993)

FURTHER READING

Obituary. *The Times* (of London), Dec. 16, 1993.
Obituary. *New York Times*, Dec. 15, 1993.
"Myrna Loy." GARY GIDDENS. *American Film*, Aug. 1991.
"Arthur Hornblow, Jr. and. . . ." A. SCOTT BERG. *Architectural Digest*, Apr. 1990.

Lucas, John Harding, Jr. (1953–) The *New York Times* described John Lucas as "back from the dead"—an apt phrase, because John Lucas had nearly destroyed his career as a premier point guard in the National Basketball Association (NBA) through drug use. But in 1986, after undergoing NBA-mandated treatment, he recognized the need for an after-care program for players like himself and made that idea a reality, establishing a series of counseling and fitness programs in NBA cities, and then in 1992 opening a facility in Houston, aimed precisely at helping athletes not only overcome drugs but also resume their temptation-laden professional lives. In 1991, he also bought and himself coached the Miami Tropics, a team in the United States Basketball League, as a transition league for recovering players.

His work gained nationwide attention when, in the middle of the 1992–93 season, Lucas was appointed the new coach of the San Antonio Spurs, coincidentally the team's first Black coach. His unconventional coaching methods, which some have described as "empowering" players, led to a turnaround for the team, which went 40–22 under Lucas, after having been 9–11 under his predecessor. Finishing second in their division, the Spurs made it to the Western Conference semifinals, but were knocked off by the Phoenix Suns. As the new 1993–94 season started, Lucas was there again, at year's end having guided the Spurs to a 19–11 record, while continuing his work with troubled athletes throughout the basketball league and other sports.

North Carolina-born Lucas received his B.A. from the University of Maryland in 1976 and was the first pick in the 1976 NBA draft, starting his professional career with the Houston Rockets (1976–78), and being named the NBA's All-Rookie Team (1977) and the NBA All-Star Team (1977; 1978). He then began to move around the league, his career punctuated by suspensions due to drug use, to the Golden State Warriors (1978–81), the Washington Bullets (1981–83), the San Antonio Spurs (1983–84), the Rockets again (1984–86), the Milwaukee Bucks (1986–88), and finally the Seattle Supersonics (1988–89), ending his career as number 10 all-time assist leader. Lucas married Debbie Fozard in 1978 and has three children.

FURTHER READING

"John Lucas. . . ." DOUGLAS C. LYONS. *Ebony*, June 1993.
" 'If I can come back. . . .' " HANK WHITTEMORE. *Parade*, May 16, 1993.
"The 12-step coach." HARVEY ARATON. *New York Times Magazine*, Apr. 11, 1993.
"A second chance." GLENN ROGERS. *Sporting News*, Jan. 18, 1993.

M

McCarthy, Cormac (1933–) American novelist Cormac McCarthy was a double winner in 1993, his novel *All the Pretty Horses* winning both the National Book Award and the National Book Critics Circle Award as the best work of fiction published in 1992. McCarthy's earlier novels had been set in eastern Tennessee, sparking comparisons with southern writers such as William Faulkner or Carson McCullers, but this new novel, the first of an ambitious projected trilogy, focuses on the growing to manhood of a young Texan in post-World War II Mexico, where the Old West survives in an Hispanic setting. Many critics favorably reviewed the book, some praising its lush language, though some found it occasionally a bit too fulsome. Scheduled for 1994 publication were *Crossing* and a play, *The Stonemason*. Another novel was in progress.

Born in Providence, Rhode Island, McCarthy attended the University of Tennessee, then served in the U.S. Air Force (1953–56). The recipient of various creative writing grants and honors, including the Ingram-Merrill Foundation grant (1960), the American Academy of Arts and Letters traveling fellowship to Europe (1965–66), a Rockefeller Foundation grant (1966), and a Guggenheim fellowship (1976), McCarthy has published several previous novels, including *The Orchard Keeper* (1965), which won the William Faulkner Foundation award, *Outer Dark* (1968), *Child of God* (1974), *Suttree* (1979), and *Blood Meridian or the Evening Redness in the West* (1985), as well as the teleplay *The Gardener's Son* (1977), and numerous other shorter writings. He is married to Anne de Lisle.

FURTHER READING

Perspectives on Cormac McCarthy. EDWIN T. ARNOLD and DIANNE C. LUCE, eds. University Press of Mississippi, 1993.
"The invisible man." ROBERT DRAPER. *Texas Monthly*, July 1992.
"Cormac McCarthy's. . . ." RICHARD B. WOODWARD. *New York Times Magazine*, Apr. 19, 1992.
The Achievement of Cormac McCarthy. VEREEN BELL. Louisiana State University Press, 1988.

McCartney, Paul (1942–) Now both a legendary and very live figure in popular music, Paul McCartney had an extremely active and fruitful year. In February, he released the well-received album *Off the Ground*, co-produced with Julian Mendelsohn, preceded by a release of its leadoff song "Hope of Deliverance," which became a hit single, as did later the singles "Off the Ground" and "C'Mon People."

McCartney toured during much of 1993: two very notable concerts were his appearance headlining the national Earth Day concert on April 16 at the Hollywood Bowl, all proceeds going to Concerts for the Environment; and his first live television concert, performed at Charlotte, North Carolina in mid-June. While touring, he recorded a second album, *Paul Is Live*. Forthcoming was the documentary *The Long and Winding Road*, with former Beatles Ringo Starr and George Harrison.

Liverpool native McCartney is a major figure in popular music. With John Lennon, George Harrison and Ringo Starr, he was a member of the Beatles (1960–70), as rhythm guitarist and then bass guitarist. He and Lennon wrote a great many of the Beatles' songs, such as "Yesterday," "Strawberry Fields Forever," and "Sgt. Pepper's Lonely Hearts Club Band," and he was often the group's lead singer. In 1970, he went on his own, and in 1971 formed Wings, continuing to compose, perform, and record for worldwide audiences during the next two decades. In 1989, he went on the road for the first time in 13 years, with a highly successful world tour, which also produced a live album, *Tripping the Live Fantastic*, released in November 1990. *The Liverpool Oratorio*, his first classical work, premiered in 1991. In 1984, McCartney published *Give My Regards to Broad Street*. He married Linda Eastman in 1969; they have four children.

FURTHER READING

Paul McCartney: Behind the Myth. Ross Benson. Trafalgar, 1993.
Illustrated Paul McCartney. Geoffrey Giuliano. Book Sales, 1993.
Turn Me on, Dead Man: The Complete Story of the Paul McCartney Death Hoax. Andru J. Reeve. Popular Culture, 1993.
"Winged Beatle. . . ." *Economist*, June 13, 1992.
"Rock meets classical." Dennis Polkow. *Musical America*, Jan.-Feb. 1992.
Blackbird: The Life and Times of Paul McCartney. Geoffrey Giuliano. NAL-Dutton, 1991.
Strange Days: The Music of John, Paul, George and Ringo Twenty Years On. Walter Podrazik. Popular Culture, 1991.
"Paul McCartney." Tom Mulhern. *Guitar Player*, July 1990.
Yesterday: The Biography of a Beatle. Chet Flippo. Doubleday, 1988.
It Was Twenty Years Ago Today. Derek Taylor. Simon & Schuster, 1987.

MacDowell, Andie (Rose Anderson MacDowell; 1958–)

In 1993, actress Andie MacDowell starred opposite Liam Neeson in the film thriller *Deception*, directed by Graeme Clifford, as a woman who travels abroad to investigate the suspicious death of her husband in an airplane crash. She also starred in Robert Altman's film *Short Cuts*, based on eight stories and a poem by Raymond Carver, as adapted for film by Altman and Frank Barhydt. The large cast also included Tim Robbins, Fred Ward, Anne Archer, Robert Downey, Jr., Jennifer Jason Leigh, Jack Lemmon, Matthew Modine, Lily Tomlin, and Tom Waits.

MacDowell also starred opposite Bill Murray in the film *Groundhog Day*, about a television weatherman who covers the annual event at Punxsutawney, Pa., only to find himself literally trapped in an eternal repeat of the day. Forthcoming was a starring role in the film *Bad Girls*, directed by Tamara Davis and co-starring Mary Stuart Masterson, Madeleine Stowe, Drew Barrymore, and Dermot Mulroney.

South Carolina-born MacDowell was a model before making her film debut in *Greystoke: the Legend of Tarzan, Lord of the Apes* (1984). Her breakthrough role came in *sex, lies, and videotape* (1989); she then went on to star in *Green Card* (1990), *Hudson Hawk* (1991), and *The Object of Beauty* (1991). MacDowell attended Winthrop College. She is married to Paul Qualley, and has two children.

FURTHER READING

"Southern comfort." Kevin Sessums. *Vanity Fair*, Mar. 1993.
Andie MacDowell. Bob Italia. Abdo & Daughters, 1992.
"Andie gets real." Dawn Cotter and Christina Ferrari. *McCall's*, Aug. 1991.
"Andie swings into stardom." David Denicolo. *Glamour*, Nov. 1990.
"Fine and Andie." *Interview*, Sep. 1989.
"Why is Andie. . . ." Ann Elliot. *Mademoiselle*, Aug. 1989.
"Sex, lies, and. . . ." Eric Pooley. *New York*, July 17, 1989.

McEntire, Reba (1955–)

For country singer Reba McEntire, 1993 was another strong year. Her 1992 album *It's Your Call* continued to sell well, its title song also becoming a hit single. Her 1991 album *For My Broken Heart* was voted favorite country album at the 20th annual American Music Awards, and she was voted favorite country female artist. Her album of *Greatest Hits, Volume 2* was a hit during the 1993 Christmas season. She and Vince Gill also

FURTHER READING

"Heaven on Earth. . . ." MARTHA FRANKEL. *McCall's*, Dec. 1993.
"Reba rising." SUSAN ELLIOTT. *Woman's Day*, Nov. 3, 1992.
"Educating Reba." JESS CAGLE. *Entertainment*, Oct. 29, 1993.
" 'I'm a survivor.' " KATHRYN CASEY. *Ladies Home Journal*, Mar. 1993.
"Reba McEntire. . . ." MARJIE McGRAW. *Country Music*, Jan.-Feb. 1993.
Reba: Country Music's Queen. DON CUSIC. St. Martin's, 1991.
"Reba McEntire. . . ." BOB ALLEN. *Country Music*, Nov.-Dec. 1990.
"Talking with. . . ." LAURA FISSINGER. *Redbook*, Jan. 1990.
"Reba McEntire. . . ." TIM ALLIS. *People*, Sep. 18, 1989.

scored a hit with the *The Heart Won't Lie*. Billboard rated her No. 3 country artist for the year.

McEntire also starred opposite Burt Reynolds in the television film *The Man From Left Field*, about a Little League team and their coach; Reynolds directed and co-produced. In July, Bantam Books announced that McEntire had signed a contract to publish her memoirs, for a reported advance of $1 million or more.

Oklahoma-born McEntire began her career as a recording artist in 1978 with the debut album *Reba McEntire*, and emerged in 1984 as one of the leading country music singers of her time with the album *My Kind of Country*, a hit that brought the first of her many major awards, as Country Music Association female vocalist of the year, an award repeated in 1985, which saw the release of her album *Have I Got a Deal for You*. Her albums include *Whoever's In New England* and *What Am I Gonna Do About You*, both released in 1986; *The Last One to Know* and *Reba McEntire's Greatest Hits*, both in 1987; *Reba* (1988); *Reba Live!* and *Sweet 16*, both in 1989; *Rumor Has It* (1990); *For My Broken Heart* (1991), honoring the death of her tour manager and seven band members in a March 1991 airplane accident; and *It's Your Call* (1992). She has also appeared in the film *Tremors* (1990), and opposite Kenny Rogers in the television miniseries "The Gambler IV." Previously married, McEntire is now married to her manager, Narvel Blackstock, with whom she runs Starstruck Enterprises; she has one child.

McFARLAND, "SPANKY" (George Emmett McFarland 1928–93) Dallas-born Spanky McFarland was one of the greatest child stars of Hollywood's Golden Age. He began his career at age three, modeling baby clothes in his home town, did a Wonder Bread commercial, was "discovered" by director Hal Roach, and hired to play fat boy Joe Cobb in Roach's "Our Gang" ("Little Rascals") comedies. His "Our Gang" debut was *Free Eats* (1932); it was the first of scores of appearances in the series, from which he retired in 1942. He also appeared in 14 feature-length films, among them *The Trail of the Lonesome Pine* (1936) and *The Woman in the Window* (1944), his last film. He later worked in a variety of non-entertainment jobs, entering a new period of celebrity when the old series became a long-running worldwide television hit. He was survived by his wife, Doris, and three children. (d. Grapevine, Texas; June 30, 1993)

FURTHER READING

Obituary. *The Times* (of London), July 2, 1993.
Obituary. *New York Times*, July 1, 1993.

McKELLEN, Ian (1939–) Celebrated British actor Ian McKellen appeared in several American films during 1993, perhaps most notably starring opposite Stockard Channing, Don-

He has also appeared often on television. In 1991, he was Cameron Mackintosh professor of contemporary theatre at Oxford University.

In 1991, McKellen accepted a knighthood, becoming Sir Ian. The honor was especially notable because he had been openly working on behalf of gay rights in Britain since announcing his own homosexuality on a BBC program three years earlier. Some fellow gay activists criticized him for accepting the honor from a Conservative government they felt was anti-gay. But he was publicly defended by many other gay artists, who felt that the honor was "a significant landmark in the history of the British gay movement."

FURTHER READING

"Out and about with Sir Ian." BEN BRANTLEY. *Vanity Fair*, June 1992.
"Sympathy for the devil." LAWRENCE O'TOOLE. *New York Times Magazine*, Apr. 5, 1992.
"McKellen. . . ." JACK PITMAN. *Variety*, Jan. 7, 1991.

ald Sutherland, Will Smith, and Mary Beth Hurt in John Guare's film version of his hit play *Six Degrees of Separation*, directed by Fred Schepisi. He also starred in *The Ballad of Little Jo*, written and directed by Maggie Greenwald, and co-starring Suzy Amis and Bo Hopkins. McKellen also appeared as Death in Arnold Schwarzenegger's *The Last Action Hero*, and in a searing and central role as AIDS-struck Bill Kraus in Roger Spottiswoode's *And The Band Played On*, the HBO film based on the Randy Shilts book.

Forthcoming was a much-awaited film version of Shakespeare's *Richard III*, starring McKellen in the title role. He won his fifth Olivier for his acclaimed 1991 stage portrayal of Richard, and did an American tour in the role in 1992.

A leading British actor since the early 1960s, McKellen has played on stage in a wide range of leading roles. He made his stage debut in 1961, joined the National Theatre Company in 1965, made his Broadway debut in 1966 in *The Promise*, and was a founder of the Actor's Company in 1972. His debut with the Royal Shakespeare Company came in 1974, with his role in *Dr. Faustus*. He further developed his international reputation with *Bent* (1979) and *Amadeus* (1980), for which he won a Tony on Broadway. He toured in his one-man show *Acting Shakespeare* in 1984, played in a series of major roles with the National Theatre during the 1980s, and was an associate director of the National Theatre (1984–86). His films include *Alfred the Great* (1965), *Plenty* (1985), and *Scandal* (1988).

Mackendrick, Alexander (1912–93)

Boston-born Alexander Mackendrick grew up in Glasgow. He began his career as an artist, worked in advertising, and moved into scriptwriting and documentary filmmaking during the 1930s. After World war II service, he joined Ealing Studios in 1946, working in the art department and scriptwriting before he moved into directing. His directorial debut came with the classic comedy *Whisky Galore* (*Tight Little Island*) (1948). He then directed the classic Alec Guinness comedy *The Man in the White Suit* (1951), followed by his drama about a deaf girl, *Mandy* (1952). His third Ealing film was the dark comedy *The Maggie* (1953), and his fourth and last the classic Guinness comedy *The Ladykillers* (1955). He then moved to Hollywood, where his single major success was *Sweet Smell of Success* (1957), though he made several other Hollywood films. His later work was as a teacher; he was dean of the California Institute of the Arts film department (1969–78). He was survived by his wife, Hilary, and three sons. (d. Los Angeles; December 21, 1993)

FURTHER READING

Obituary. *The Times* (of London), Dec. 27, 1993.
Obituary. *New York Times*, Dec. 24, 1993.

Lethal Innocence: The Cinema of Alexander Mackendrick. PHILLIP KEMP. Heinemann, 1991.

MacLaine, Shirley (Shirley MacLean Beaty; 1934–)

Film star, entertainer, and author Shirley MacLaine appeared in 1993 in the film *Wrestling Ernest Hemingway*, directed by Randa Haines; about the friendship of two old men, one of them a former sea captain Harris (played by Richard Harris), the other a Cuban bachelor and ex-barber (played by Robert Duvall). MacLaine played Harris's landlady and love interest, in a cast that included Piper Laurie and Sandra Bullock.

Forthcoming was a starring role opposite Nicolas Cage in the film *Guarding Tess*, written by Hugh Wilson and Peter Torkovei, and directed by Wilson. Also still forthcoming was a reprise of her Oscar-winning role as Aurora Greenway in *Terms of Endearment* in a 15-years-later sequel, *The Evening Star*, based on the Larry McMurtry novel; the project had been announced in 1992.

On the personal side, MacLaine bought a ranch in New Mexico, which she planned to make her main home.

Virginia-born MacLaine, the sister of actor Warren Beatty, became a Hollywood star in the 1960s in such light films as *The Apartment* (1960), *Two for the Seesaw* (1962), *Irma La Douce* (1963), and *Sweet Charity* (1969). Later in her career, she became a leading dramatic actress, in such films as *The Turning Point* (1977), *Being There* (1979), *Terms of Endearment* (1983; she won a best actress Oscar), *Madame Souszatska* (1988), *Steel Magnolias* (1989), *Waiting for the Light* (1990), *Postcards from the Edge* (1990), and *Used People* (1992). She also produced, co-directed, and appeared in the documentary film *The Other Half of the Sky: A China Memoir* (1975), and has written several very popular books, including *Many Happy Returns* (1984), *Dancing in the Light* (1985), *Don't Fall Off the Mountain* (1987), and *Dance While You Can* (1991). She was previously married, and has one child.

FURTHER READING

"Still kicking over the traces." VALERIE GROVE. *Times*, Jan. 31, 1992.
"Write while you can. . . ." BILL GOLDSTEIN. *Publishers Weekly*, Aug. 8, 1991.

"The real MacLaine." NANCY COLLINS and ANNIE LEIBOVITZ. *Vanity Fair*, Mar. 1991.
Shirley MacLaine and the New Age Movement. JAMES W. SIRE. Inter-Varsity, 1988.

McLarty, Thomas "Mack" (1946–)

New White House Chief of Staff Mack McLarty was, as expected, far less a "power broker" than some recent occupants of the job, and more a quiet, trusted aide. He found himself in a big, complicated job, though, and encountered some highly publicized problems during the first year of the Clinton administration. Most embarrassing was the White House travel office fiasco, in which all seven staff members of the White House travel service were dismissed on May 19 for alleged financial irregularities, with five of them reinstated on May 25, when it turned out that a distant Clinton cousin and a Clinton friend had allegedly been involved in seeking jobs and business, and that the FBI had been brought into the matter improperly. On July 2, McLarty issued a statement in which he took blame for the unjustified firings and FBI involvement, and reprimanded four key members of the White House staff. Another flood of unfavorable publicity followed the suicide of deputy White House counsel Vincent W. Foster on July 20, with McLarty forced to defend himself for withholding the contents of Foster's suicide note for 24 hours after Foster's death.

McLarty is one of Clinton's oldest friends. He was born in Hope, Arkansas, went to kindergarten with Clinton, and attended Boys State with Clinton. McLarty went into his family's automobile dealership business in Hope after his 1968 graduation from the University of Arkansas. In 1984, he became chairman and chief executive officer of Arkla, Inc. (Arkansas Louisiana Gas Company), a natural gas distribution firm. He has also long been a Little Rock civic leader. McLarty became a key figure in the organization of Clinton's presidential campaign, and was a member of his transition team before becoming White House Chief of Staff. He is married to Donna McLarty; they have two children.

FURTHER READING

"The Mack factor." ELIZABETH GLEICK. *People*, Mar. 22, 1993.
"They call him Mack. . . ." MICHAEL DUFFY. *Time*, Dec. 28, 1992.

"Bill and Mack. . . ." DAVID DODSON. *Business Week*, Nov. 23, 1992.

McMillan, Terry (1951–) Self-help is Terry McMillan's middle name. When her first novel, *Mama*, was published in 1987, with minimal support from its publisher, McMillan mounted a letter-writing campaign to booksellers and scheduled her own promotional reading tour, creating a modest but unusual success for the first novel. When that same publisher wanted extensive revisions in her second book, *Disappearing Acts*, she went to another publisher, who supported her vision of the novel. In her third book, *Waiting to Exhale*, she wrote about four 30-something women who, like herself, were on their own and taking charge of their own lives, for better or for worse. On its publication in March 1992, the novel became a surprise massive bestseller; by the end of 1992 nearly 700,000 copies were in print, and the book's popularity was still building into 1993, when paperback and large print versions of the book appeared.

During 1993 McMillan was writing a screenplay for *Disappearing Acts*, and was also scheduled to write the script for *Waiting to Exhale*, sold in 1993 for later filming. She also won the New York Women in Communications' Matrix Award honoring career achievement by women in books, presented to her in April 1993 by director Spike Lee at a Waldorf-Astoria event.

Born and raised in Port Huron, Michigan, McMillan attended Los Angeles City College, then the University of California at Berkeley, receiving a B.A. in journalism. Her first short story, "The End," was published in 1976. Moving to New York, she briefly studied at Columbia University, then becoming a word processor in a law firm. Encouraged by fellow members of the Harlem Writers Guild, and aided by a stay at the MacDowell Colony, she produced her first novel, *Mama* (1987). This was followed by *Disappearing Acts* (1989) and *Waiting to Exhale* (1992). She also edited *Breaking Ice: An Anthology of Contemporary Black Writers* (1990) and *Five for Five: The Films of Spike Lee* (1991). She has one son.

FURTHER READING

"Terry McMillan exhales. . . ." LAURA B. RANDOLPH. *Ebony*, May 1993.
"McMillan, Terry." *Current Biography*, Feb. 1993.
"Terry McMillan. . . ." AUDREY EDWARDS. *Essence*, Oct. 1992.
"Oh brother. . . ." KATE MUIR. *Observer*, Aug. 30, 1992.
"McMillan's millions." DANIEL MAX. *New York Times Magazine*, Aug. 9, 1992.

McMurtry, Larry (1936–) Fans of *Lonesome Dove* took heart in 1993 when they learned that Larry McMurtry had written a sequel to his notable 1985 novel, basis for the 1989 television miniseries, the most popular in five years and responsible for a resurgence of interest in Westerns. Perhaps not coincidentally, that miniseries was replayed in 1993, again to large audiences, and was also released for home video. McMurtry's new novel, *Streets of Laredo*, takes place two decades after the death of Gus McCrae (played on screen by Robert Duvall), as the Old West is settling down to become the New West, and focuses on his old partner, Captain Woodrow Call (Tommy Lee Jones on screen), also including the ex-whore Lorena and awkward cowboy Pea Eye Parker.

In what will undoubtedly be confusing to viewers, a new television miniseries, *Return to Lonesome Dove*, aired in 1993, was also a sequel, but was neither based on *Streets* nor by McMurtry (instead by John Wilder); though McMurtry was a consultant early in the planning, he stressed that the "two stories have nothing to do with each other" and are inconsistent. Nor did it have Jones or most others in the original cast, starring instead Jon Voight and Louis Gossett, Jr., playing a new character. Meanwhile, the film version of McMurtry's *The Evening Star*, another sequel, was in production, with Shirley MacLaine reprising her Oscar-winning role as Aurora Greenway from the 1983 movie *Terms of Endearment*, again opposite Jack Nicholson.

Texas-born McMurtry received his B.A. from North Texas State College in 1958 and his M.S. from Rice University in 1960. After teaching at Texas Christian University, in Fort Worth (1961–62), he returned to Rice to teach English and creative writing (1963–69), and was later a visiting professor at George Mason College (1970) and American University (1970–71); he was also a Wallace Stegner fellow (1960) and Guggenheim fellow (1964). He is by far best known for his fiction, including *Horseman, Pass By* (1961), *Leaving Cheyenne* (1963), *The Last Picture Show* (1966), *Moving On* (1970), *All My Friends Are Going to be Strangers* (1972) and its sequel *Some Can Whistle* (1989), *Terms of Endearment* (1975; basis of the Oscar-winning 1983 film) and its sequel *The Evening Star* (1992), *Somebody's Darling* (1978), *Cadillac Jack* (1982), *The Desert Rose* (1983), the Pulitzer Prize-winning *Lonesome Dove* (1985), *Anything for Billy* (1988), and *Buffalo Girls* (1990). As a screenwriter, he also wrote the script for *The Last Picture Show* (1971), sharing the Academy Award's best adaptation award with director and co-writer Peter Bogdanovich, and its sequel *Texasville* (1987); other screenplays include *Montana* (1989), *Memphis* (with Cybil Shepard; 1991), and *Falling From Grace* (1992). McMurtry has also written numerous articles, essays, and book reviews, some of them collected in *In a Narrow Grave: Essays on Texas* (1968) and *Film Flam: Essays on Hollywood* (1988). McMurtry is co-owner of the Booked Up Book Store, Washington, Texas (1970–). He was formerly married to Josephine Ballard (1959–66); he has one son.

FURTHER READING

"Return of the native son." JAN REID. *Texas Monthly*, Feb. 1993.
"Lonesome dude." CEIL CLEVELAND. *M Inc.*, Dec. 1990.
Taking Stock: A Larry McMurtry Casebook. CLAY REYNOLDS et al, eds. SMU Press, 1989.
Larry McMurtry's Texas: Evolution of a Myth. LERA T. LICH. Eakin-Sunbelt, 1988.

McNeil, Claudia (1916–93) Baltimore-born Claudia McNeil, a notable dramatic actress, began her career as a singer in cabaret, vaudeville, and radio. She made her New York stage debut in *The Crucible* (1953), and appeared as a singer in Langston Hughes's *Simply Heavenly* (1957). She emerged as a powerful dramatic actress on Broadway in Lorraine Hansberry's *Raisin in the Sun*, as the mother of the poor Chicago African-American family at the center of the play. She recreated the role in the 1961 film version, directed by Daniel Petrie and co-starring Signey Poitier, Ruby Dee, Diana Sands, and Steven Perry; and also in the 1977 revival and the 1981 musical version of the play, *Raisin*. McNeil also played in many stage and televison roles, and made a singing comeback in cabaret in the late 1970s. There were no survivors. (d. Englewood, New Jersey; November 25, 1993)

FURTHER READING

Obituary. *New York Times*. Nov. 29, 1993.

Robert MacNeil (right) and Jim Lehrer

MacNeil, Robert Breckenridge

(1931–) As the senior member of American television's longest-lasting and highly successful television nightly news duo, paired with Jim Lehrer on PBS's "The MacNeil/Lehrer NewsHour," Robert MacNeil continued to provide solid news and analysis of the major stories, day in and day out. Long-time backup anchor Judy Woodruff left the show for CNN, but Roger Mudd rejoined it after a year away as a professor of journalism at Princeton University; Margaret Warner was later added to provide additional backup.

During 1993, MacNeil along with Liz Smith and Shari Belafonte hosted a pilot for a projected new PBS series, "First Edition," which would feature interviews with current authors, previews of new books or films based on books, and more general book news and history. In December, MacNeil also hosted a PBS special *Dance in America: Balanchine Celebration* on "Great Performances." A revised edition of *The Story of English* was also published; the book, written with Robert McCrum and William Cran, accompanied the notable 1986 PBS series of the same name.

Montreal-born MacNeil began his broadcasting career as an actor in radio and a radio and television announcer in Halifax, Nova Scotia (1951–55). He moved into journalism as a Reuters editor in London (1955–60), and was an NBC news correspondent (1960–67), successively based in London, Washington, and New York. He was a London-based BBC correspondent with the "Panorama" series (1967–71), also in that period working in U.S. public television, which became a full-time affiliation in 1971. Originally sole anchor on the show, largely shaping the format, MacNeil began his long association with Jim Lehrer in 1973 with their Emmy-winning daily live coverage of the Senate Watergate hearings on PBS. Their award-winning "MacNeil/Lehrer Report," originally named the "Robert MacNeil Report," began in 1975, and became "The MacNeil/Lehrer News-Hour" in 1983. MacNeil was co-author and host of the Emmy and Peabody-winning nine-part series "The Story of English" (1986), and co-author of the accompanying book. He has also hosted several PBS specials. His other published works include *The People Machine, The Influence of Television on American Politics* (1968), *The Right Place at the Right Time* (1982), *The Way We Were: 1963, the Year Kennedy Was Shot* (1988), *Wordstruck* (1989), and the novel *The Burden of Desire* (1992). A graduate of Ottawa's Carleton University, MacNeil is married and has four children.

FURTHER READING

"Stranger to fiction." BRUCE HEADLAM. *Saturday Night*, Mar. 1992.

"MacNeil/Lehrer. . . ." MORGAN STRONG. *Playboy*, June 1991.

Madonna (Madonna Louise Ciccone; 1958–   ) During 1993, public interest in Madonna seemed to fade considerably. After having lived at the top of the charts for years, she was only No. 43 on the 1993 Billboard 200 list, and she had no major hit single recordings or videos during the year, though she did issue the singles "Bad Girl" and "Rain," both drawn from her 1992 album *Erotica*. She began a new world tour in London in September, which she called "Girlie Show."

Madonna also continued to pursue her film career, though with mixed results, starring in the film *Body of Evidence*, directed by Uli Edel and co-starring Willem Dafoe, Joe Mantegna, and Anne Archer; in the absurdist courtroom drama, she is is charged with having used her body to to literally kill a man with sex. She also starred in the film *Dangerous Game*, directed by Abel Ferrara, and co-starring Harvey Keitel and James Russo. Forthcoming was a 4-hour autobiographical television miniseries *Madonna: The Early Years*.

Michigan-born Madonna has been one of the best-known celebrities of her time, both for concert performances and for such albums as *Madonna* (1983), *Like a Virgin* (1983), *True Blue* (1986), *You Can Dance* (1987), *Like a Prayer* (1989), *The Immaculate Collection* (1990), and *Erotica* (1992), the latter preceded by a single and accompanied by a music video, both also named "Erotica." These were accompanied by simultaneous publication of her picture book *Sex*. Madonna is also a competent actress, as demonstrated in such films as *Desperately Seeking Susan* (1985) and *Who's That Girl?* (1987), and in her Broadway stage debut in *Speed-the-Plow* (1988). In 1990, she played Breathless Mahoney in Warren Beatty's *Dick Tracy*, which sparked her "Blond Ambition" international concert tour, the album *I'm Breathless* (1990), and the documentary film *Truth or Dare: In Bed With Madonna*. She also appeared in the films *A League of Their Own* (1992) and *The Player* (1992). Her videos included "Justify My Love." Madonna was formerly married to actor Sean Penn (1985–89). She attended the University of Michigan (1976–78).

FURTHER READING

The I Hate Madonna Handbook. ILENE ROSENZWEIG. Thomas Dunne/St. Martin's, 1994.

"Chameleon in motion." MIKE MYERS and HERB RITTS. *Interview*, June 1993.

Madonna: Portrait of a Material Girl. REBECCA GULICK. Courage, 1993.

Desperately Seeking Madonna: In Search of the Meaning of the World's Most Famous Woman. ADAM SEXTON. Delacorte, 1993.

Madonna: The Early Days. MICHAEL McKENZIE. Worldwide Televid, 1993.

Madonna. Andrews & McMeel, 1993.

Madonna Speaks. BRUCE NASH et al. Tribune (FL), 1993.

"Madonna." *People*, Dec. 28, 1992.

"Madonna. . . ." JAMIE MALANOWSKI. *Esquire*, Dec. 1992.

"Madonna revealed." JOANNE KAUFMAN and PAMELA GUTHRIE O'BRIEN. *Ladies Home Journal*, Nov. 1992.

"Sex and money." GISELLE BENATAR et al. *Entertainment*, Nov. 6, 1992.

"Talking with Madonna. . . ." DAVID ANSEN. *Newsweek*, Nov. 2, 1992.

" 'Sex' is the latest lode. . . ." D.T. MAX. *Variety*, Oct. 26, 1992.

"Madonna in wonderland." MAUREEN ORTH and STEVEN MEISEL. *Vanity Fair*, Oct. 1992.

"Weekend in the material world." NEAL RUBIN. *Entertainment*, Aug. 28, 1992.

Material Girl: Madonna in the 90s. TIM RILEY. Disney, 1992.

Madonna: The Book. NORMAN KING. Morrow, 1992.

Madonna Revealed: The Unauthorized Biography. DOUGLAS THOMPSON. Dorchester, 1992.

Madonna: Blonde Ambition. MARK BEGO. Harmony/Crown, 1992.

The Madonna Scrapbook. LEE RANDALL. Citadel Press/Carol, 1992.

Madonna Revealed. DOUGLAS THOMPSON. Carol, 1991.

Madonna, Unauthorized. CHRISTOPHER ANDERSEN. Simon & Schuster, 1991.

Madonna: Her Complete Story. NAL-Dutton, 1991.

Madonna. WILLIAM RUHLMANN. Smithmark, 1991.

Major, John (John Major Ball; 1943–   ) Although he had won a surprising victory over Labour in the 1992 general elections, British Prime Minister John Major experienced serious difficulty throughout 1993. The British economy continued to sag, despite some summer manufacturing gains, as unemployment continued to top ten percent, massive deficits grew, and social services were cut further. The Liberal Democrats and Labour continued to gain strength, and the Conservative Party lost strength; in May, Conservative candidates suffered crushing defeats in many local elections. Major's own popularity fell, as well: In June, national polls showed approval ratings of only 16–21 percent for Major, by far the lowest for any prime minister since the beginning of World War II.

Major did score a victory in July, with House of Commons ratification of the European Community Maastricht Treaty, but implementation of the treaty was to be very slow because of European economic conditions. He also won something of a victory late in the year, on December 15 with Irish Prime Minister Albert Reynolds issuing a joint declaration on Northern Ireland aimed at creating a framework for peace, though the Provisional wing of the Irish Republican Army responded with an at least temporary increase in armed violence. On the personal side, he scored a victory in a libel suit against the magazine *New Statesman and Society*, which had printed a story accusing him of an extramarital affair.

Within his own party, Major continued to be attacked, signaling his political weakness; most notably, he was attacked in former Prime Minister Margaret Thatcher's autobiography *The Downing Street Years*. As the year closed, he and his party faced a very uncertain future.

London-born Major's first career was with the Standard Chartered Bank (1965–79). He joined the Conservative Party in 1960, was a Lambeth Borough Councillor (1968–71), and became a member of Parliament in 1979, after two unsuccessful tries. His rise in the Thatcher government was very rapid; by 1985, he was a junior minister at the department of health, and by 1986 social security minister. He became Treasury chief secretary in 1987, foreign secretary in July 1989, Chancellor of the Exchequer in October 1989, and then at 47 the youngest British Prime Minister of the 20th century, succeeding Margaret Thatcher on November 27, 1990. In office, he quickly canceled the enormously unpopular poll tax, and developed a more moderate Conservative government than that of Thatcher. He supported the Persian Gulf War without reservation, sending British heavy armor into the ground offensive when it came, to join the air and sea forces already in place. He led the Conservative Party to electoral victory in the April 1992 general elections. Major married Norma Johnson in 1970; they have two children.

FURTHER READING

"Thatcherism today." STUART HALL and IAN AITKEN. *New Statesman & Society*, Nov. 26, 1993.

"The curious case of John Major's 'mistress.'" STEVE PLATT and NYTA MANN. *New Statesman & Society*, Jan. 29, 1993.

"When niceness. . . ." JULIA LANGDON. *New Statesman & Society*, Nov. 6, 1992.

"Major says. . . ." MICHAEL JONES. *Sunday Times*, July 12, 1992.

"Major's hour." *Economist*, Apr. 11, 1992.

"John Major at bat." CRAIG WHITNEY. *New York Times Magazine*, Mar. 29, 1992.

"Major. . . ." DANIEL PEDERSEN. *Newsweek*, Mar. 23, 1992.

"Major looks. . . ." MICHAEL WHITE. *Guardian*, Jan. 2, 1992.

John Major: The Making of the Prime Minister. BRUCE ANDERSON. Trafalgar Square, 1992.

"Major player. . . ." EDWARD PEARCE. *New Republic*, Jan. 21, 1991.

John Major: Prime Minister. PRESS ASSOCIATION STAFF AND JOHN JENKINS. Trafalgar Square, 1991.

"A quiet dropout. . . ." BILL HEWITT. *People*, Dec. 10, 1990.

"Thatcher's favorite." ANDREW BILSKI. *Maclean's*, Dec. 3, 1990.

"John Major." *Economist*, Nov. 24, 1990.

"Major, John." *Current Biography*, Oct. 1990.

Malkovich, John (1953–) Stage and screen star John Malkovich's main 1993 film was *In the Line of Fire*, directed and co-produced by Wolfgang Petersen. Malkovich starred as assassin Mitch Leary, engaged in attempting to kill an American president, opposite Clint Eastwood as Secret Service agent Frank Horrigan, assigned to protect the President, and Rene Russo, as a second Secret Service agent.

Malkovich was also the narrator in the film *Alive*, based on the Pier Pauls Read book about the ordeal of a group of plane crash survivors in the Andes; it was adapted by John Patrick Shanley and directed by Frank Marshall. Forthcoming were a starring role as Kurtz in a television film adaptation of Joseph Conrad's novel *Heart of Darkness*; and Malkovich's own stage adaptation of Don DeLillo's novel *Libra*, which he was to direct at Chicago's Steppenwold Theater Company.

Before becoming a New York stage player, Illinois-born Malkovich was from 1976 a leading member of Chicago's Steppenwolf Theater Company. He won an Obie off-Broadway for his role in *True West* (1982), appeared as Biff opposite Dustin Hoffman's Willy Loman in the 1984 Broadway revival of *Death of Salesman*, and took his highly praised stage performance in Lanford Wilson's *Burn This* from New York to London late in 1990, making his British stage debut. He began his film career in 1984 with *Places in the Heart*, and went on to strong dramatic roles in such films as *The Killing Fields* (1984), *Eleni* (1985), *The Glass Menagerie* (1987), *Empire of the Sun* (1987), *Dangerous Liaisons* (1988), *The Sheltering Sky* (1990), *The Object of Beauty* (1991), *Of Mice and Men* (1992), *Shadows and Fog* (1992), and *Jennifer Eight* (1992). Malkovich has also acted and directed in regional theater, and appeared on television. He is married to actress Glenne Headly.

FURTHER READING

"No Method in his madness." SIMON HATTENSTONE. *Guardian*, Aug. 26, 1993.
"The touch of evil. " JESS CAGLE. *Entertainment*, Aug. 6, 1993.
"What is. . . ." DAVID GRITTEN. *Cosmopolitan*, Nov. 1992.
"Life, art and Malkovich." JOE MORGENSTERN. *Playboy*, May 1990.
"Wild card." BECKY JOHNSTON and BRIGITTE LACOMBE. *Interview*, Mar. 1989.

Mamet, David Alan (1947–) Writer and director David Mamet adapted his own 1976 play *A Life in the Theatre* for television in 1993. The television film, starring Jack Lemmon and Matthew Broderick, and directed by Gregory Mosher, was one of the high points of the 1993–94 season, and especially so for Lemmon's performance. Mamet's highly controversial 1992 play *Oleanna*, about an allegedly very sweet, decent, blameless male professor and an allegedly vicious, man-hating woman student, who files false charges of sexual harassment against him, opened in London, where the argument over the play continued, with many calling the play bitterly sexist and others defending it as truthtelling. Mamet received an American Academy

of Arts and Letters 1993 Award of Merit for Drama. Forthcoming were a film version of *Oleanna*, three short plays set in Chicago, and collectively titled *The Old Neighborhood*, and a novel.

Chicago-born Mamet emerged as a substantial playwright in the 1970s with such works as *Sexual Perversity in Chicago* (1973), *American Buffalo* (1976), *A Life in the Theater* (1976), *The Woods* (1977), *Edmond* (1983), *Glengarry Glen Ross*, (1984; he won the Pulitzer Prize for drama), and *Speed-The-Plow* (1987). His screenplays include *The Postman Always Rings Twice* (1981), *The Verdict* (1982), *The Untouchables* (1987), *We're No Angels* (1989), and *Homicide* (1991). He co-wrote and directed the film *House of Games* (1987), and wrote and directed *Things Change* (1988). Among his nonfiction works are *Writing in Restaurants: Essays and Prose* (1986), *On Directing Film* (1990), and the autobiographical *The Cabin: Reminiscence and Diversions* (1992). Mamet's B.A. was from Goddard College. Previously married to actress Lindsay Crouse, Mamet is married to actress-singer-songwriter Rebecca Pidgeon.

FURTHER READING

David Mamet and Film: Illusion-Disillusion in a Wounded Land. GAY BREWER. McFarland, 1993.
"Theater. . . ." RICHARD DAVID STORY. *New York*, Sep. 14, 1992.
David Mamet: Language As Dramatic Action. ANNE DEAN. Fairleigh Dickinson, 1990.
American Voices: Five Contemporary Playwrights in Essays and Interviews. ESTHER HARRIOTT. McFarland, 1988.
David Mamet. DENNIS CARROLL. St. Martin's, 1987.

Mandela, Nelson Rolihiahia (1918–) During 1993, African National Congress (ANC) President Nelson Mandela successfully pursued what had for so long seemed only a dream-the creation of a multiracial South African democracy. But it was not without difficulty: violence continued throughout the country, as right-wing White and Inkatha forces tried to derail the peace process by means of repeated mass murders, and the ANC-Inkatha war continued. A crucial test came after the April 10 assassination of communist and ANC leader Chris Hani, when rioting broke out in many locations, including Capetown; but Mandela and other Black

leaders were able to stop the development of full-scale civil war.

On November 18, the ANC, F.W. De Klerk's National Party, and 19 other political parties agreed on a historic new constitution that would establish multi-party democracy and through the adoption of a Bill of Rights guarantee "fundamental rights" for all South Africans, with a resulting transition to majority, or Black, rule in South Africa. National elections were scheduled for April 27, 1994 (as had been announced by Mandela and De Klerk in Washington on July 2), which would establish a coalition government to rule for five years following the election. South Africa's 10 Black "homelands" would be dissolved and reintegrated into South African society. ANC and other formerly anti-government military forces would become part of an integrated South African military. Although the Zulu Inkatha Party, the pro-apartheid Conservative Party, and several smaller parties opposed and boycotted the agreement, momentum and majority sentiment were clearly on the side of the government and the ANC in the months that followed. Mandela helped blunt the force of the right-wing opposition by declaring ANC willingness to discuss the question of later creating a White homeland in southern Africa.

Mandela and De Klerk led South Africa back into the world community in 1993, as South African participation in international sports competitions resumed, foreign companies once again began to freely trade with and locate in South Africa, and the country returned to international financing and monetary systems. On July 2, they each met with President Clinton in the White House, and on July 4 they were jointly awarded Liberty Medals in Philadelphia by We the People 2000. At their joint request, remaining American and Canadian sanctions against South Africa were lifted in September. Clearly, the two men were far from being friends, or even publicly amicable; but they were able to seize the opportunity to change the future of their country without the long, bloody war that had for so long seemed the inevitable outcome of apartheid. De Klerk and Mandela shared the 1993 Nobel Peace Prize. Mandela also published *Nelson Mandela Speaks: Forging a Democratic, Nonracial South Africa* (1993).

Early in his career, Mandela was a leading advocate of non-violence (1944–60), but both he and the previously nonviolent ANC turned to violence after the Sharpeville Massacre of 1960. He was imprisoned in 1962, sentenced to life imprisonment for sabotage. During his 28-year-long imprisonment, he became a worldwide symbol of the long fight against South African racism. On February 11, 1990, his release by De Klerk's new South African government ushered in a new period in South African history, leading to a full ceasefire after 30 years of guerrilla warfare. Mandela was elected President of the ANC in 1991.

Mandela attended the University College of Fort Hare and the University of the Witwatersrand, and practiced law in Johannesburg in the early 1950s. He married Winnie Mandela, his second wife, in 1958; they separated in 1992; they have two daughters. Among his autobiographical writings are *No Easy Walk to Freedom* (1986) and *Nelson Mandela: The Struggle Is My Life* (rev. ed., 1986). With Fidel Castro, he also wrote *How Far We Slaves Have Come!* (1991). A further autobiography is in preparation.

FURTHER READING

"Manners maketh Mandela." PHILIP VAN NIEKERK. *Observer*, Oct. 17, 1993.
"Building a new South Africa...." ALLISTER SPARKS. *World Press Review*, Aug. 1993.
"Mandela reaches out to business." MARSHALL LOEB. *Fortune*, July 12, 1993.
"Mandela and De Klerk speak out." *Time*, June 14, 1993.
Chained Together: Mandela, De Klerk, and the Struggle to Remake South Africa. DAVID B. OTTAWAY. Random, 1993.
" 'We understand white's fears.' " *Newsweek*, Mar. 2, 1992.
Nelson Mandela: The Fight Against Apartheid. STEVEN OTFINOSKI. Millbrook Press, 1992.
Nelson Mandela: Voice of Freedom. LIBBY HUGHES. Macmillan, 1992.
Nelson Mandela: The Man, the Struggle, the Triumph. DOROTHY HOOBLER and THOMAS HOOBLER. Watts, 1992.
"Mandela...." SCOTT MACLEOD. *Time*, Jan. 7, 1991.
Nelson Mandela: Strength and Spirit of a Free South Africa. BENJAMIN PROUND. Gareth Stevens, 1991.
Nelson Mandela: Symbol of Resistance and Hope for a Free South Africa. E.S. REDDY, ed. Apt Books, 1991.
Nelson Mandela. BRIAN FEINBERG. Chelsea House, 1991.
Nelson Mandela. RICHARD TAMES. Watts, 1991.
Mandela, Tambo, and the African National Congress: The Struggle Against Apartheid, a

Documentary Study, 1948–1990. SHERIDAN JOHNS and R. HUNT DAVIS, JR., eds. Oxford University Press, 1991.

Mankiewicz, Joseph Leo (1909–93)

Wilkes-Barre-born Joseph Mankiewicz began his long film career in 1929, starting as a writer. He won the first of his many Oscar nominations as the co-writer of *Skippy* (1931), and became a Metro-Goldwyn-Mayer producer in 1935; among his produced films were *Fury* (1936), *The Philadelphia Story* (1940), and *Woman of the Year* (1942). In 1946, he began a notable directing career; among his films were *Dragonwyck* (1946), which he also wrote; *The Ghost and Mrs. Muir* (1947); *A Letter to Three Wives* (1948), which won him best directing and best screenplay Oscars; and *All About Eve* (1950), which also won him directing and screenplay Oscars. His films also included the *Five Fingers* (1952), *Julius Caesar* (1953; direction and screenplay), *Cleopatra* (1963), and *Sleuth* (1972). He was the brother of screenwriter Herman Mankiewicz. He was survived by his wife, Rosemary Matthews, a daughter, and three sons. (d. Mount Kisco, New York; February 5, 1993)

FURTHER READING

Obituary. *Current Biography*, Apr. 1993.
Obituary. *Variety*, Feb. 15, 1993.
Obituary. *The Times* (of London), Feb. 8, 1993.
Obituary. *New York Times*, Feb. 6, 1993.
"Hollywood legend. . . ." PETER STONE and BRIGITTE LACOMBE. *Interview*, Aug. 1989.

Maradona, Diego Armando (1961–)

In February 1993, amid cries of "Olé, Diego," Argentine fans welcomed back the man they believe to be the greatest soccer player in the world, as well as a national hero. He was making his return playing for the Argentine national team, for which he was named captain, and many hoped that he would lead his country to the next World Cup, as he had in 1986. More impartial observers thought Maradona would have a long way to go to regain the dominance he had shown in the years before his 15-month suspension from international play for cocaine use and possession in 1991.

Maradona had begun to work himself back into competitive condition playing for Seville in the Spanish League, from September 1992 until his release in June 1993, but even so he was far from what he had been. Some observers suggested that, although his ability to score may be limited, he could still have enormous value as a playmaker. In September 1993, Maradona signed with the Argentine professional team Newell's Old Boys. In December, he pulled a muscle in his left leg, which would keep him out of action for several weeks. Meanwhile, he and his team-along with soccer teams and fans around the world-were pointing toward the 1994 World Cup, to be held in the United States.

A child soccer prodigy, Maradona turned professional in 1976, with the Buenos Aires Argentinos Juniors team, later switching to the Boca Juniors, and appearing on the national team. To his great disappointment, he did not make the 1978 World Cup national team, though he did play in 1982, a year his team did not make the finals. His contract was sold to Barcelona in 1982, and in 1984 to Naples, where he led the Napoli club to Italian league titles (1987; 1990), and to a European Soccer Cup win (1989). In an extraordinary triumph, he led the Argentine national team to victory in the World Cup in 1986. In 1991, he tested positive for cocaine use and was suspected from international play through June 1992; he was later arrested for cocaine possession. He married longtime companion Claudia Villafanes in a strikingly lavish ceremony in 1989; they have two daughters.

FURTHER READING

"Maradona, Diego." *Current Biography*, Nov. 1990.
"The biggest little athlete alive. . . ." RON ARIAS. *People*, June 18, 1990.
"Soccer's little. . . ." GEORGE VECSEY. *New York Times Magazine*, May 27, 1990.
"Prima Dona." RICK TELANDER. *Sports Illustrated*, May 14, 1990.

Marsalis, Branford (1960–)

Jazz saxophonist Branford Marsalis continued to emerge as a leading figure in jazz during 1993, while remaining highly visible to television audiences as bandleader of NBC's "Tonight Show." For his hit album *I Heard You Twice The First Time*, he won a Grammy for best jazz instrumental performance, individual or group, at the 35th Annual Grammy Awards. He also issued the album *Bloomington*, a trio recorded live in 1992 at Indiania University, also featuring bassist Robert Hurst and drummer Jeff "Tain" Watts, with three pieces by Marsalis, one by Hurst, the Thelonius Monk "Friday The 13th," and "Everything Happens to Me." The Marsalis-led trio was the subject of the hour-long music video "The Music Tells You," created by D.A. Pennebaker. Marsalis also hosted a two-part television special on the history of jazz.

New Orleans-born Marsalis is the son of teacher and jazz pianist Ellis Marsalis, and the older brother of trumpeter Wynton Marsalis and trombonist Delfeayo Marsalis. He joined Wynton's band as a saxophonist at the age of sixteen, and while still at school played summers and holidays with the Art Blakey and Lionel Hampton bands. He recorded with Art Blakey in 1981 and from 1982 toured with Wynton's band. In 1985, he toured with Sting, and in 1986 formed his own band. His albums include *Scenes in the City* (1984), *Romances for Saxophone* (1986), *Royal Garden Blues* (1986), *Renaissance* (1987), *Random Abstract* (1988), *Trio Jeepy* (1989), *Music from Mo' Better Blues* (1990), *Crazy People Music* (1990), and *The Beauty Ones Are Not Yet Born* (1991). In 1992, he succeeded Doc Severinsen as bandleader of the NBC "Tonight Show," joining Jay Leno after Johnny Carson retired. He has also appeared in several films. Marsalis attended Southern University, and studied at the Berkley College of Music (1979–81).

FURTHER READING

"Branford Marsalis." *Playboy*, Dec. 1993.
"The reluctant power broker." FRED SHUSTER. *Down Beat*, July 1993.
"The revolution might. . . ." JOSEF WOODARD. *Down Beat*, Sep. 1992.
"The prime of. . . ." JOSEPH HOOPER. *Esquire*, June 1992.
"Here's Branford." PETER WATROUS. *New York Times Magazine*, May 3, 1992.
"Heeere's Branford." MICHAEL BOURNE. *Down Beat*, May 1992.
"Gang of 2. . . ." BILL MILKOWSKI. *Down Beat*, Jan. 1992.
"Marsalis, Branford." *Current Biography*, Sep. 1991.
"Marsalis and Pine." DIMITRI EHRLICH. *Interview*, Nov. 1990.
"Branford Marsalis. . . ." DAVE HELLAND. *Down Beat*, Nov. 1989.
"Wynton and Branford. . . ." A. JAMES LISKA. *Down Beat*, Sep. 1989.
"Branford Marsalis. . . ." CLARENCE WALDRON. *Ebony*, Feb. 1989.

Marsalis, Wynton (1961–) One of the leading jazz composers and trumpet soloists of his time, Wynton Marsalis in 1993 recorded his classic, 132-minute-long composition *Citi Movement*, the product of his 1991 collaboration with choreograper Garth Fagan. The acclaimed work, covering the whole range of jazz history and styles, is also an exploration of the relationship of the music to American 20th-century city life. Marsalis also wrote the music for the Peter Martins ballet "Jazz," which premiered at the New York City Ballet in January. He also continued to tour widely with his jazz septet, and to continue to work with Lincoln Center, notably in his very well received series of children's concerts. Scheduled for 1994 publication was a book, *Sweet Swing Blues on the Road*, written with Frank Stewart.

New Orleans-born Marsalis is the son of pianist and teacher Ellis Marsalis, younger brother of saxophonist Branford Marsalis, and older brother of trombonist Delfeayo Marsalis. After briefly playing with Art Blakey's Jazz Messengers, Wynton Marsalis emerged as one of the leading trumpet soloists of his time, functioning equally well in the classics and in jazz, although he has focused on jazz in the late 1980s and early 1990s. A few of his many notable albums are *Fathers and Sons* (1982), *Wynton Marsalis* (1982), *Trumpet Concertos* (1983), *Black Codes from the Underground* (1985), *Standard Time* (Vol. 1, 1987; Vol. 2, 1990; Vol. 3, 1991, *The Resolution of Romance*), *Majesty of the Blues* (1989), *Soul Gestures in Southern Blue* (1991), *Baroque Duet* (1992; with Kathleen Battle), and *Blue Interlude*, with his own 40-minute title composition. A major work, *In This House On This Morning*, premiered at Lincoln Center's Avery Fisher Hall in 1992. Marsalis studied at the Juilliard School of Music (1979–81).

FURTHER READING

"Wynton Marsalis. . . ." TONY SCHERMAN. *Life*, Aug. 1993.
"Virtuously under the influence." DAVE GELLY. *Observer*, May 23, 1993.
"The cool world." ERIC POOLEY. *New York*, Dec. 21, 1992.
"Wynton's decade." HOWARD REICH. *Down Beat*, Dec. 1992.

"Wynton Marsalis." JAMES BRADY. *Parade*, Aug. 16, 1992.

"Horns of plenty. . . ." THOMAS SANCTON. *Time*, Oct. 22, 1990.

"Wynton. . . ." DAVE HELLAND. *Down Beat*, Sep. 1990.

Outcats: Jazz Composers, Instrumentalists, and Singers. FRANCIS DAVIS. Oxford University Press, 1990.

"Wynton and Branford. . . ." A. JAMES LISKA. *Down Beat*, Sep. 1989.

Marshall, Thurgood (1908–93) Baltimore-born Thurgood Marshall, a historic figure, was a lawyer with the National Association for the Advancement of Colored People (NAACP) from 1936, becoming head of its legal staff (1940–62), and in that position became the most celebrated civil rights lawyer of his time, winning a series of major legal battles, the most notable of them by far the landmark 1954 school desegregation case, *Brown v. Board of Education of Topeka, Kansas* (1954), which destroyed the basis of school segregation and paved the way for the civil rights revolution that soon came. The story of that fight was retold in the telefilm *Separate But Equal* (1991), with Marshall portrayed by Sidney Poitier.

President John F. Kennedy appointed Marshall to the Second Circuit Court of Appeals in 1962. Three years later, in 1965, President Lyndon B. Johnson appointed him United States Solicitor-General. In 1967, Johnson made the historic appointment of Marshall to the Supreme Court, making him the first African-American to serve there. On the Court, Marshall became a leading member of the then-liberal majority; later, in a far more conservative Court, he became a leading liberal dissenter. He retired in 1991. He was survived by his wife, Cecilia Suyat, and two sons. (d. Bethesda, Maryland; January 24, 1993)

FURTHER READING

Making Civil Rights Law: Thurgood Marshall and the Supreme Court, 1936–1961. MARK V. TUSHNET. Oxford University Press, 1994.

"Thurgood Marshall's best years." AUGUST MEIER and JOHN BRACEY. *American Visions*, Oct.-Nov. 1993.

"Thurgood Marshall. . . ." FRANK McCOY. *Black Enterprise*, Apr. 1993.

Obituary. *Current Biography*, Mar. 1993.

" 'The best I could with what I had. . . .' " LISA C. JONES. *Ebony*, Mar. 1993.

"Their amazing grace." JERRY ADLER. *Newsweek*, Feb. 8, 1993.

"Fanfare for an uncommon man." RANDALL KENEDY. *Time*, Feb. 8, 1993.

"A farewell to. . . ." LEWIS LORD. *U.S. News & World Report*, Feb. 8, 1993.

"A just man." *Economist*, Jan. 30, 1993.

Obituary. *The Times* (of London), Jan. 26, 1993.

Obituary. *New York Times*, Jan. 25, 1993.

Dream Makers, Dream Breakers: The World of Justice. CARL T. ROWAN. Little, Brown, 1993.

Thurgood Marshall. JOE NAZEL. Holloway, 1993.

Thurgood Marshall: A Dream of Justice for All. STUART KALLEN. Abdo & Daughters, 1993.

Thurgood Marshall: Justice for All. ROGER GOLDMAN and DAVID GALLEN. Carroll & Graf, 1993.

Thurgood Marshall: Fight for Justice. RAE BAINS. Troll, 1993.

Thurgood Marshall: Champion of Justice. G.S. PRENTZES. Chelsea House, 1993.

Thurgood Marshall: Champion of Civil Rights. ELIZABETH KRUG. Fawcett, 1993.

Thurgood Marshall and Equal Rights. SEAMUS CAVAN. Millbrook, 1993.

Thurgood Marshall: First Black Supreme Court Justice. CAROL GREENE. Childrens, 1991.

Thurgood Marshall: The Fight for Equal Justice. DEBRA HESS. Silver Burdett, 1990.

Thurgood Marshall. LISA ALDRED. Chelsea House, 1990.

Eight Men and a Lady. HERMAN SCHWARTZ et al. National Press, 1990.

Masako (Owada): See Naruhito, Crown Prince and Masako, Crown Princess.

Masterson, Mary Stuart (1966–) Actress Mary Stuart Masterson starred in 1993 in the film *Benny & Joon*, directed by Jeremiah Chechik and co-starring Johnny Depp and and Aidan Quinn. The story, about a sister (Masterson as Joon) and brother (Quinn as Benny), whose lives are changed by a clownlike figure (Depp as Sam). The offbeat, gentle story was very well received, and the film became something of a "sleeper," critically and commercially. Masterson also starred in the not very well received film *Married to It*, about three married couples who become friends; Arthur Hiller directed and Beau Bridges, Stockard Channing, Robert Sean Leonard, Cybill Shepherd, and Ron

Silver co-starred. Forthcoming was a starring role in *Bad Girls*, directed by Tamara Davis and co-starring Madeleine Stowe, Drew Barrymore, Andie MacDowell, and Dermot Mulroney.

New York City-born Masterson made her film debut at the age of 7, in *The Stepford Wives*, as the daughter of her real father, actor Peter Masterson. She worked in the theater and films during the mid-1980s, making her film break-through in 1987, with *Some Kind of Wonderful* and *Gardens of Stone*, then going on to leads and strong supporting roles, in *Mr. North* (1988), *Chances Are* (1989), *Immediate Family* (1989), *Funny About Love* (1990), and *Fried Green Tomatoes* (1991).

FURTHER READING

"A perfect mismatch." RYAN MURPHY. *Entertainment*, May 7, 1993.

"Hot tomatoes." RANDALL KORAL. *Vogue*, Feb. 1992.

"Mary Stuart Masterson." CINDY PEARLMAN. *Seventeen*, Jan. 1991.

"Masterson's 'immediate' success." SHARI ROMAN. *Video Magazine*, July 1990.

"Spellbinding scene stealer. . . ." MICHAEL SEGELL. *Cosmopolitan*, Mar. 1990.

"Will Mary Stuart Masterson. . . ." LAURA MORICE. *Mademoiselle*, Dec. 1989.

"Finding dignity. . . ." CYNTHIA SANZ. *People*, Nov. 13, 1989.

"Hot properties." KATHERINE TURMAN. *Teen*, June 1989.

Masur, Kurt (1927–) In his second full year as music director of the New York Philharmonic, German conductor Kurt Masur was well on his way to becoming a fixture in the life of the city, while at the same time keeping his ties to Germany. He continued such innovative popular programs as the Young Peoples' Concerts; the Philharmonic Forums, in which he met directly with the public to discuss changes and plans; and the brief "rush hour" and Saturday afternoon concerts. In the process, he further placed his musical stamp on, and asserted his control over, the traditionally fractious orchestra, taking that sometimes erratic body of artists onto somewhat more stable-though critics said somethat more bland-ground. In its 151st season, the Philharmonic was to premiere five works commissioned for its 150th anniversary, including works by Tison Street, Ned Rorem,

Barbara Kolb, Stephen Paulus, and Bernard Rands, as well as works by Joan Towers and Alfred Schinittke. An Asian tour was planned for the summer of 1994. In the spring of 1993, the Philharmonic toured Europe, and in the fall, Leipzig's Gewandhaus, Masur's former orchestra, toured the United States, with Masur conducting three of its New York area concerts.

In a wholly different kind of matter, Masur was consistently mentioned as a possible selection for the German presidency, a largely ceremonial post, a position precluded by his acceptance of the New York Philharmonic position.

Masur is one of Germany's leading conductors, developing the bulk of his career in East Germany before unification. He was an opera company director in Erfurt and Leipzig, conductor of the Dresden Philharmonic (1955–58), directed the Mecklenburg State Opera (1958–60), was music director of Berlin's Komische Opera (1960–64), went back to Dresden as music director of the Philharmonic (1967–72), and was director of the Leipzig Gewandhaus (1972–90). He has also toured widely, and has been principal guest conductor of the London Philharmonic. In April 1990, he was named to succeed Zubin Mehta as music director of the New York Philharmonic, one of the most prestigious posts in the world of classical music

Masur was also a major figure in events that led to the peaceful East German revolution of 1990, intervening on several occasions to avert civil war. Afterward, his prestige was so great that there was talk of making him head of the new government, much like the writer Vaclav Havel in Czechoslovakia-but Masur chose to stay with his musical career.

Masur attended the National Musical School at Breslau and the Leipzig Conservatory. He is married to singer Tomoko Sakurai, and has five children.

FURTHER READING

"Kurt Masur." HERBERT KUPFERBERG. *Stereo Review*, May 1992.

"New York's new maestro." ROBERT ANGUS. *Audio*, Dec. 1991.

"New Philharmonic maestro. . . ." PETER G. DAVIS. *New York*, Sep. 23, 1991.

"Maestro of the moment." JOHN ROCKWELL. *New York Times Magazine*, Sep. 8, 1991.

"From Leipzig. . . ." WILLIAM H. YOUNGREN. *World Monitor*, Apr. 1991.

"Masur, Kurt." *Current Biography*, Sep. 1990.

"Matlin, Marlee." *Current Biography*, May 1992.
"The nerve of Marlee!" MICHAEL SEGELL. *Redbook*, Apr. 1992.
"Actress Marlee Matlin. . . ." PATRICIA FREEMAN. *People*, Apr. 10, 1989.
"Marlee Matlin. . . ." MICHAEL LEAHY. *TV Guide*, Apr. 8, 1989.

Walter Matthau (left) and Mason Gamble

Matlin, Marlee Beth (1965–) For her starring role as the deaf prosecutor in the highly regarded television series "Reasonable Doubts," opposite Mark Harmon as her detective and prosecutor partner, Matlin received a Golden Globe nomination as best actress in a television drama. The series concluded in 1993, cancelled for low ratings. Matlin also guest starred on an episode of the "Seinfeld" show, as Jerry's date. Matlin's major work of the year was a starring role as physical trainer Jull Shanahan in the Portland-based thriller *Hear No Evil*, directed by Robert Greenwald. D.B. Sweeney, Martin Sheen, and John C. McGinley co-starred.

Matlin also appeared in a very special role at the Rose Bowl, accompanying Garth Brooks in sign language as he sang the national anthem. On the personal side, she married Los Angeles police officer Kevin Grandalski.

Born in Morton Grove, Illinois, near Chicago, Matlin became deaf as a result of a childhood illness. She began to work on stage as a child in productions done by Chicago's Center for Deafness, and at the age of 21 was cast as the hearing impaired student opposite William Hurt as her teacher in the Randa Haines film version of the Mark Medoff play *Children of a Lesser God*. In 1987, she won a best actress Oscar for her portrayal. She also appeared in the film *Walker* (1988).

FURTHER READING

"In step with. . . ." JAMES BRADY. *Parade*, May 3, 1992.

Matthau, Walter (Walter Matuschanskavasky; 1920–) In 1993, veteran actor Walter Matthau starred opposite Jack Lemmon in the very well received film *Grumpy Old Men*, directed by Donald Petrie. In the film, the two play longtime Minnesota neighbors and friends, who become competitors for the attention of a new woman in town, played by Ann-Margret; Ossie Davis, Burgess Meredith, and Daryl Hannah co-starred. Although very different films, many were reminded of the classic Matthau-Lemmon film collaboration a quarter of a century earlier, in *The Odd Couple*. Matthau also starred as Mr. Wilson, opposite Mason Gamble as Dennis, in the children's film *Dennis the Menace*, directed by Nick Castle.

New York City-born Matthau made his Broadway debut in *Anne of the Thousand Days* (1948), and his film debut in *The Kentuckian* (1955). Among his plays were *Once More With Feeling* (1958), *A Shot in the Dark* (1961), and his Tony-winning lead in *The Odd Couple* (1964), which he recreated on screen in 1968. He won a best actor Oscar for *The Fortune Cookie* (1966); among his many other films are *Charade* (1963), *Fail Safe* (1964), *Kotch* (1971), *Pete n' Tillie* (1972), *Charley Varrick* (1973), *The Sunshine Boys* (1975), *California Suite* (1979), *Hopscotch*

(1980), *First Monday in October* (1980), and *The Couch Trip* (1988). He is married to Carol Marcus, and has had two children, one of whom died.

FURTHER READING

"Rumpled Royalty." LILLIAN ROSS. *New Yorker*, May 31, 1993.
Among the Porcupines: A Memoir. CAROL MATTHAU. Random, 1992.
"He plays a small-town lawyer. . . ." MICHAEL LEAHY. *TV Guide*, Mar. 3, 1990.

Mayle, Peter (c. 1939–)

British expatriate Peter Mayle has made a very comfortable living—and gained a large and still-growing audience—writing about Provence, the region of southern France where he has lived since 1986. First it was *A Year in Provence* (1989), the surprise best-seller, a collection of humorous anecdotes and musings about the first year of Mayle and Jenny Hayes, now his wife, in their new home in the Provence's Luberon Valley; that was followed by an equally popular sequel, *Toujours Provence*. In 1993, while the paperback versions of those two were still on the best-seller lists, Mayle published his first novel, *Hotel Pastis: A Novel of Provence*, similarly humorous in tone, about an ex-advertising man who decides to run a hotel in Provence. The response was equally warm, with some saying the book was like meeting an old friend. Mayle promoted the book on a 16-city tour across North America, also promoting a new line of "Year in Provence" wines. An abridged audio version of the novel, read by Mayle himself, also appeared in 1993. New fans came to Mayle's Provence works when the British-produced television miniseries of *A Year in Provence* aired, dramatized by Michael Sadler and starring John Thaw and Lindsay Duncan, though some felt the adaptation had lost much of the book's appeal. It appeared in four parts, one each season, following the year as does the book; the original work had been similarly serialized, but over 12 months, in London's *Sunday Times*. An earlier book, *Up the Agency: The Funny Busines of Advertising*, was reprinted in the United States, to take advantage of Mayle's now highly recognized name.

Born in Surrey, England, but raised in the West Indies, Mayle made his first career in advertising, most notably at New York's Ogilvy, Bensen & Mather, a period he later humorously recalled in his *Up the Agency* (1990). Tiring of advertising, he became a full-time writer in 1975, publishing numerous books and essays. Among his many children's books were *Where Did I Come From?* (1973), *Grownups and Other Problems: Help for Small People in a Big World* (1982), and *Sweet Dreams and Monsters: A Beginner's Guide to Dreams and Nightmares and Things That Go Bump in the Night* (1987). Adult fare included *How to Be a Pregnant Father* (1977), *Divorce Can Happen to the Nicest People* (1988), and *Wicked Willie's Low-Down on Men* (1987), with cartoonist Gray Jolliffe. Some of his many short pieces, notably for *GQ-Gentlemen's Quarterly*, were collected in *Expensive Habits* (1991) and *Acquired Tastes* (1992). Twice divorced, Mayle is married to former advertising exective Jennie Hayes and has five children.

FURTHER READING

"Peter Mayle. . . ." MICHELE FIELD. *Publishers Weekly*, Oct. 11, 1993.
"How to eat. . . ." PATRICK DUFFY. *Time*, July 22, 1991.

Maynard, Robert (1937–93)

Brooklyn-born Bob Maynard began his newspaper career as teenager reporter for Brooklyn's *New York Age*, and then worked at Baltimore's *Afro-American News* and the *York (Pa.) Gazette and Daily*. He was a Nieman Fellow at Harvard in 1966, and in 1967 won a breakthrough job at the *Washington Post*, becoming a national correspondent and editorial writer. In 1977, he and his wife, Nancy Hicks, founded the Institute for Journalism Education at Berkeley, California, which soon became the leading American training organization for minority journalists. He became chief editor of the Gannett-owned *Oakland Tribune* in 1979, and in 1983 bought the newspaper, with substantial financial help from Gannett. Maynard then became a national figure, with a widely syndicated column and substantial media exposure, especially through his association on the Sunday morning show "This Week with David Brinkley." He was, however, forced to sell his interest in the financially ailing *Tribune* in 1992. He was survived by his wife, a daughter, two sons, and four sisters and brothers. (d. Oakland, California; August 17, 1993)

FURTHER READING

Obituary. *Current Biography*, Oct. 1993.
"Robert Maynard. . . ." *Jet*, Sep. 6, 1993.
" 'Give me a chance to try.' " ELLIS COSE. *Newsweek*,
    Aug. 30, 1993.
Obituary. *The Times* (of London), Aug. 26, 1993.
Obituary. *New York Times*, Aug. 19, 1993.

Mays, Kimberly (1978–) In a case that attracted national interest and media attention, not least for its extension of the concept of children's rights, 14-year-old Kimberly Mays successfully brought suit in Florida to terminate contact with her biological parents, Ernest and Regina Twigg. She had been switched for another child while in the hospital shortly after her birth, and had been raised as the child of Robert and Barbara Mays (the latter since deceased). After the other child, raised by the Twiggs, died in 1988, genetic testing revealed the biological facts, and the Twiggs brought suit to reclaim Kimberly Mays. In 1989, the Twiggs and Robert Mays agreed that Mays would keep custody, and established visitation rights for the Twiggs; but Mays terminated the agreement in 1989, as they upset Kimberly. The custody fight resumed, with Kimberly suing in 1992 to break off all contact with the Twiggs. She was represented by George Russ, who had in 1992 successfully represented Gregory Kingsley in a novel Florida children's rights case. Sarasota Judge Stephen Dakan found for Kimberly Mays, but did not formally sever all legal relations with the Twiggs. How higher courts would find on appeal remained to be seen.

FURTHER READING

"Switched at birth." LORETTA NOBEL-SCHWARTZ. *Ladies
    Home Journal*, Nov. 1992.
" 'Daddy, am I your daughter?' " KATHRYN CASEY.
    Ladies Home Journal, May 1991.
"Update on. . . ." MARIANNE JACOBBI. *Good
    Housekeeping*, Mar. 1990.
"Every parent's nightmare. . . ." MICHELLE GREEN.
    People, Dec. 11, 1989.
"Whose little girl. . . ." MARIANNE JACOBBI. *Good
    Housekeeping*, Mar. 1989.

Merbah, Kasdi (Abdallah Khalaf; 1938–93) On August 21, 1993, Algerian opposition leader and former prime minister Kasdi Merbah was assassinated near Algiers; his son, Hakim, was among those killed in the attack. Merbah became an Algerian independence activist while still in school. He joined the FLN (National Liberation Front) in 1956, as heavy anti-French guerrilla fighting spread throughout the country, becoming a leader of Algerian fighting forces under Houari Boumedienne, and was an FLN peace negotiator (1961–62). After Algerian independence had been won, he became national director of military security, supported Boumedienne's 1965 coup, and remained military security director until Boumedienne's death in 1978. Out of power (1978–88), he was reformist prime minister under President Chadli Benjedid (1988–89). In the early 1990s, Merbah founded the moderate socialist and anti-fundamentalist Movement for Justice and Development, and was actively seeking peace in increasingly embattled Algeria at his death. He was survived by two children.

FURTHER READING

Obituary. *The Times* (of London), Aug. 23, 1993.

Meredith, Scott (1923–93) After World War II military service, New York City-born Scott Meredith and his brother Sidney founded their literary agency in 1946, and in the decades that followed built it into one of the strongest agencies in American publishing, one that powerfully and combatively represented its authors. P.G. Wodehouse was Meredith's first major client and Norman Mailer the most prominent of what became a sizable group of well-known authors. In 1952, Meredith introduced the book auction, a technique that forced publishers to bid against each other for publishing properties. His agency also fostered the practice of charging some authors for advice rendered on manuscripts. Meredith was also a writer and editor, with several published books. He was survived by his wife, Danuta, a daughter, and a son. (d. Manhasset, New York; February 11, 1993)

FURTHER READING

Obituary. *The Times* (of London), Feb. 17, 1993.
Obituary. *New York Times*, Feb. 13, 1993.

Metziner, Alice: See **Power, Katherine Anne.**

Michener, James Albert (1907–) Best-selling author James Michener published no new "big" books in 1993; he has said there will be no more, because of the massive amounts of research they involve. But he did publish three "small" books, two based on earlier work. *Creatures of the Kingdom: Stories of Animals and Nature* was a well-received anthology of selections describing life in the wild, drawn from his many previous works, especially *Centennial*, *Alaska*, and *Chesapeake*, with one new tale. *South Pacific* was Michener's retelling for young people of his *Tales from the South Pacific*, basis for the Rodgers and Hammerstein musical *South Pacific*. *Literary Reflections: Michener on Michener, Hemingway, Capote, and Others* was a potpourri including nine essays, some verse, and Michener's first-published story "Who Is Virgil T. Fry?" (1941). Also, in April, a new musical version of Michener's novel *Sayonara* premiered, at Houston's Music Hall.

Michener was a teacher and editor during the late 1930s and 40s. He emerged as a major U.S. popular author with his Pulitzer Prize-winning first novel *Tales of the South Pacific* (1947); the book was adapted into the musical *South Pacific* (1949). He went on to write many bestsellers, many of them historical novels and several of them adapted into hit movies. Some of his best known novels are *The Bridges at Toko-ri* (1953), *Sayonara* (1954), *The Bridge at Andau* (1957), *Hawaii* (1959), *The Source* (1965), *Iberia* (1968), *Centennial* (1974), *Chesapeake* (1978), *The Covenant* (1980), *Space* (1982), *Texas* (1985), *Alaska*

(1988), *Caribbean* (1989), *The Novel* (1991), and *Mexico* (1992), and the accompanying book *My Lost Mexico* (1992), describing the loss of the manuscript for 30 years and its recovery. He has also written several volumes of essays, edited several art books, and published other nonfiction works, such as *Pilgrimage: A Memoir of Poland and Rome* (1990) and *The World Is My Home: A Memoir* (1992). Michener attended Swarthmore College. He has been married three times, since 1955 to Mari Yoriko Sabusawa.

FURTHER READING

"Novel approach." Helen Thompson. *Texas*, Oct. 1992.
"The man who. . . ." Lynn Rosellini. *U.S. News & World Report*, June 17, 1991.
"The continuing sagas. . . ." Jim Shahin. *Saturday Evening Post*, Mar. 1990.

Midler, Bette (1945–) Singer and actress Bette Midler made her first national tour in a decade in 1993; her tour included a smash hit of four weeks at New York's Radio City Music Hall, to packed houses. She also continued to pursue her film career, starring in the horror-comedy film *Hocus Pocus*, directed by Kenny Ortega and co-starring Sarah Jessica Parker and Kathy Najimy, the three actresses playing the time-travelling Sanderson sisters, "witches" who sucked the "life force" out of children.

Midler also starred as in a television film version of musical *Gypsy*, the 1959 Jule Styne-

Stephen Sondhem Broadway hit musical, based on the Gypsy Rose Lee autobiography, in the role originally created on stage by Ethel Merman. Emile Ardolino directed for television; the cast included Peter Riegert, Cynthia Gibb, and Edward Asner She was also one of the celebrity performers who did readings for Bill Couturie's environmentalist film *Earth and the American Dream.*

Hawaii-born Midler, on stage and screen from 1965, was in the early 1970s the long-running lead singer at New York's Continental Baths, a gay men's health club. She began her recording career with the album *The Divine Miss M* (1973), also recording such albums as *Bette Midler* (1973), *Thighs and Whispers* (1979), *Divine Madness* (1980), and *Some People's Lives* (1990), as well as the soundtrack album for *The Rose* (1980), her first starring film role. Her single "Wind Beneath My Wings" won a 1990 Grammy award for best song. Midler went on to play in such films as *Jinxed* (1982), *Down and Out in Beverly Hills* (1986), *Ruthless People* (1986), *Outrageous Fortune* (1987), *Beaches* (1989), *Stella* (1990), *Scenes From a Mall* (1991), and *For the Boys* (1992), and has also appeared in television. She published *A View from a Broad* (1980). Midler attended the University of Hawaii. She married Martin von Haselberg in 1984; they have one child.

FURTHER READING

" 'Experience the Divine' " RICHARD DAVID. *New York*, Sep. 13, 1993.
"A sure Bette." SALLY OGLE DAVIS. *Ladies Home Journal*, July 1993.
"La belle Bette." KEVIN SESSUMS. *Vanity Fair*, Dec. 1991.
"A fashion fairy tale extravaganza." JONATHAN VAN METER. *Vogue*, Dec. 1991.
"Bette Midler and. . . ." EMILY YOFFE. *Newsweek*, Nov. 25, 1991.
"Bette." VERNON SCOTT. *Good Housekeeping*, Mar. 1991.
"The best Bette yet." CLIFF JAHR. *Ladies Home Journal*, Jan. 1990.
Bette Midler. ACE COLLINS. St. Martin's, 1989.
Bette Midler: Outrageously Divine. MARK BEGO. NAL-Dutton, 1987.

Mikulski, Barbara (1936–) With a
Democratic president in the White House, and the Republican-Democratic legislative deadlock of recent years broken, Maryland Democratic Senator Barbara Mikulski, in her second term, became a highly visible women's rights advocate and liberal in the Senate, moving toward change in such areas as abortion rights, civil rights, job creation, military spending reductions, and homelessness. She also became a strong voice on the Senate's Ethics Committee, which she joined in January, playing a significant role in the Senate's investigation of sexual harassment and other charges against Senator Bob Packwood, and consistently calling for an "open and public" airing of the issues.

On a far wider-ranging sexual harassment matter, Mikulski in March called attention to alleged long-term sexual harassment at an Atlanta veterans hospital, causing Veterans Affairs Secretary Jesse Brown to institute major changes and to institute training seminars throughout the VA system. Her intervention was particularly effective because she chaired the powerful Senate Appropriations subcommittee on veterans affars, housing, and independent agencies. From that vantage point, she was able to make her presence felt in many areas, as when in May she introduced a bill calling for a thorough restructuring of the much-criticized Federal Emergency Management Agency (FEMA).

A social worker, Baltimore-born Mikulski moved into local politics as a community organizer. She served on the Baltimore City Council (1971–76), making an unsuccessful run for the U.S. Senate (1974). She served five terms in the House of Representatives (1976–86), and was elected to her first Senate term in 1986, long the only woman Democrat in the Senate. In 1992, she was elected for second term, by a landslide 71–29 percent majority. She quickly became a leading liberal in the Senate. Her 1958 B.A. was from Mt. St. Agnes College and her 1965 M.S.W. from the University of Maryland.

FURTHER READING

Women in Power: The Secrets of Leadership.
DOROTHY W. CANTOR. Houghton Mifflin, 1992.

Milken, Michael (1946–) On January 4,
1993, Michael Milken was released from prison, having served 22 months of his ten-year sentence for securities fraud. After two months in a halfway house, he was released into the community; he was also scheduled to do 1,800 hours of

community service. Milken had come out of the massive scandal with assets estimated at $500 million and plans to develop an interactive television network. He proceeded to begin work on that project during 1993. He was also a popular guest lecturer in financial management at the University of California at Los Angeles. In September, he contracted publication of his autobiography, to be co-authored by William Novak.

Milken was the central figure in the massive Drexel Burnham Lambert stock scandals of the late 1980s that brought multiple indictments of the Drexel firm in 1988, after a two-year investigation aided by convicted stock market manipulator Ivan Boesky. Drexel pleaded guilty to six felony counts in 1988 and agreed to pay a $650 million fine. Milken was indicted on 98 counts in March 1989, resigned from Drexel in June 1989, and in April 1990 pleaded guilty to six felony counts and agreed to pay a $600 million fine.

Milken's entire career had been with Drexel, Burnham, Lambert. He worked part-time with the firm while in college and joined its bond department in 1970. During the 1970s, he began his long career as a high-yield bond trader, developing the "junk bond" concept. He moved the firm's bond department to Beverly Hills, California in 1978, and vastly expanded junk bond operations throughout the 1980s, using it as a financing technique that raised tens of billions of dollars and earned billions in fees for the firm. He personally earned over $1 billion. But in the mid-1980s, allegations of insider trading and other securities frauds began to surface, and a long series of federal investigations and prosecutions began.

Milken's B.A. was from the University of California, and his M.B.A. from the Wharton School of the University of Pennsylvania. He is married to Lori Anne Hackett.

FURTHER READING

"The predator's fall." Don L. Boroughs. *U.S. News & World Report*, Oct. 25, 1993.
Dangerous Dreamers: The Financial Innovators from Charles Merrill to Michael Milken. Robert Sobel. Wiley, 1993.
"Prose and con. . . ." Joe Queenan. *Barron's*, Nov. 30, 1992.
"My story. . . ." James W. Michaels and Phyllis Berman. *Forbes*, Mar. 16, 1992.
"Den of thieves. . . ." James B. Stewart. *Cosmopolitan*, Feb. 1992.
Fall from Grace: The Untold Story of Michael Milken. Fenton Bailey. Birch Lane/Carol, 1992.
Highly Confident: The True Story of the Crime and Punishment of Michael Milken. Jesse Kornbluth. Morrow, 1992.
The Junk Bond Revolution: Michael Milken, Wall Street and the Roaring Eighties. Fenton Bailey. Fourth Estate/Trafalgar, 1992.
"Insider reporting." Jude Wanniski. *National Review*, Dec. 2, 1991.
"A reversal of misfortune? . . ." Michele Galen. *Business Week*, Nov. 11, 1991.
"Michael Milken. . . ." Tad Friend. *Esquire*, May 1991.
Den of Thieves: The Untold Story of the Men Who Plundered Wall Street and the Chase That Brought Them Down. James B. Stewart. Simon & Schuster, 1991.

Miller, Arthur (1915–   )

Arthur Miller's play, *The Last Yankee*, had its American premiere at the Manhattan Theater Club on January 21, 1993. Directed by John Tillinger, the short play, more character study than full-scale work, starred John Heard in the title role as Leroy Hamilton, Tom Aldredge, Charlotte Maier, Frances Conroy, and Rose Gregorio; it was set in a Connecticut mental hospital, where the two men have met while visiting their institutionalized wives. The play had premiered in London in 1991. A second new Miller play, *Gellburg*, was scheduled to premiere at the Long Wharf Theater in January 1994. The year also saw a television film production of Miller's *The American Clock*, directed by Bob Clark and starring Eddie Bracken, Loren Dean, Mary McDonnell, Darren McGavin, Joanna Miles, and Estelle Parsons. Miller was one of those awarded a National Medal of the Arts by President Bill Clinton in a White House ceremony on October 10.

Miller has been a leading American playwright since the 1947 production of *All My Sons*, which won a New York Drama Critic Award. He became a world figure with his Pulitzer-Prize winning *Death of a Salesman* (1949), in which Lee J. Cobb created the memorable Willy Loman. His most notable further work included the Tony-winning *The Crucible* (1953), the Pulitzer-winning *A View from the Bridge* (1955), *After the Fall* (1963), *Incident at Vichy* (1965), *The Price* (1968), and *The American Clock* (1979). He wrote the screenplay for *The Misfits* (1961), which starred his second wife, Marilyn Monroe, who committed suicide in 1962. His second screenplay was for Karel Reisz's *Everybody Wins* (1990), starring Nick Nolte and Debra Winger. Miller's recent work also includes an Americanized adaptation of Ibsen's *An Enemy of the People* (1990), done in a televised production for PBS's "American Playhouse." In 1987 he published *Timebends: A Life*. Miller attended the University of Michigan. He has been married three times, since 1962 to photographer Inge Morath, with whom he has collaborated on two travel books; he has two children.

FURTHER READING

Arthur Miller in Conversation. STEVE CENTOLA. Contemporary Research, 1993.
Marilyn's Men: The Private Life of Marilyn Monroe. JANE E. WAYNE. St. Martin's, 1992.
"Miller's crossing." JAMES KAPLAN. *Vanity Fair*, Nov. 1991.
Miller the Playwright. DENNIS WELLAND. Heinemann, 1988.
Conversations with Arthur Miller. MATTHEW C. ROUDANE, ed. University Press of Mississippi, 1987.

Milosevic, Slobodan (1941–) As the slaughter of innocents continued in Bosnia-Herzegovina, Serbian President Slobodan Milosevic continued to justify his nickname, "Butcher of the Balkans." Hundreds of thousands were dead, many more had joined the millions in flight, and genocide (now called "ethnic cleansing") continued, while the western democracies continued to ineffectively deplore the mass murders and vaguely threaten some sort of armed action. Although Milosevic continued to deny all responsibility for events in Bosnia-Herzegovina, nobody believed him, as it was perfectly clear that Bosnian Serb forces were being amply supplied by Serbia, including ammunition, tanks, artillery, and other heavy ordnance. On-and-off peace talks continued throughout 1993, with no success, as the Serbs continued their attack on limited United Nations peacekeeping and other international humanitarian operations at will. Nor did international sanctions stop Milosevic; although the Serbian economy was greatly damaged by its economic isolation, and although Serbia experienced a ruinous inflation, Milosevic was returned to power once again, and at year's end faced no effective opposition to his prosecution of the war.

Born in Pozarevac, near Belgrade, Milosevic followed a very orthodox career path in Tito's Communist Yugoslavia. He became a member of the League of Communists of Yugoslavia in 1959, attended Belgrade University, and moved up as a protégé of Serbian Communist leader Ivan Stambolic. Milosevic worked in the Belgrade city administration during the 1960s, and then became deputy director of the government industrial gas monopoly Technogas (1969–73). He ran a state bank (1978–83) and headed the Belgrade Communist organization (1984–86), then becoming president of the League of Communists of Serbia in 1986. In 1987, resurgent Serbian nationalism created an opportunity for him to take a hard line, and gain massive popular and armed forces support. He is married to League of Communists leader Marjana Markovic.

FURTHER READING

"A profile of. . . ." ALESKA DJILAS. *Foreign Affairs*, Summer 1993.
"The butcher of the Balkans." "The world's other newsmakers." JAMES WALSH. *Time*, Jan. 4, 1993. "Man of the Year" issue.
"Mob rule. . . ." CHARLES LAN. *New Republic*, Dec. 28, 1992.
"The butcher of the Balkans." JAMES GRAFF. *Time*, June 8, 1992.
"Conman of the Balkans." IAN TRAYNOR. *Guardian*, June 1, 1992.
"Carving out a greater Serbia." STEPHEN ENGELBERG. *New York Times Magazine*, Sep. 1, 1991.
"Milosevic, Slobodan." *Current Biography*, Apr. 1990.

Mitchell, George John (1933–) Senate Majority Leader George Mitchell, who had functioned within the confines of a Republican-Democratic deadlock during 1991 and 1992, led a far-from-united Democratic majority into a new era in January, and in spite of a major early defeat on the Clinton economic stimulus package was able to negotiate far more victories than defeats in 1993. He played a major role in securing the very narrow passage of the administration's budget bill and the North American Free Trade Agreement (NAFTA), the Brady gun-control bill, "motor-voter" legislation, and campaign finance reform and crime control bills, the latter two still to be completed by Senate-House conference committees after the Congress adjourned in November.

Maine-born Mitchell began his career in Washington as a Justice Department attorney (1960–62) and as an assistant to Maine Democratic Senator Edmund Muskie (1962–65). He went home to practice law and politics in Maine, became a U.S. attorney and then U.S. district judge in the late 1970s, and was elected as a Maine Democratic Senator in 1981, succeeding Muskie. Mitchell rose quickly in the Senate and in his party, becoming majority leader of the Senate in 1988. Until the advent of the Clinton administration, Mitchell's years of leadership were largely years of "gridlock," with a Republican administration and Democratic Congress failing to produce much legislation of significance. During the 1992 election campaign, Mitchell was a leader of the Democratic attack on George Bush, successfully portraying him as a "do-nothing" president, and demanding action on such issues as abortion rights, job creation, civil rights, and comprehensive education and health care reforms. Mitchell was re-elected Senate Majority Leader in November 1992.

With fellow Maine senator William S. Cohen, a Republican, Mitchell has published *Men of Zeal: A Candid Story of the Iran-Contra Hearings* (1988) and *World on Fire: Saving an Endangered Earth* (1991). His 1954 B.A. was from Bowdoin College, and his 1960 LL.B. from Georgetown University. He has one child.

FURTHER READING

"Clinton and Congress...." ERIC FELTEN. *Insight*, Nov. 23, 1992.
"Hill potatoes...." FRED BARNES. *New Republic*, May 20, 1991.
"Mitchell, George John." *Current Biography*, Apr. 1989.

Mitterrand, François Maurice Marie

(1916–   ) French President François Mitterrand's Socialist Party suffered a major electoral defeat in the March 1993 general elections, winning only 54 National Assembly seats, in contrast to the 260 they had won in 1988. Two parties of the Right won a total of 460, or 80 percent of the seats. Mitterrand named Edouard Balladur of the Rally for the Republic party premier, but did not himself resign, leaving France

with a socialist President and a rightist premier, as had been the case when rightist Jacques Chirac had been premier (1986–88).

Mitterrand's second 7-year term was to end in 1995; he announced that he would remain in office, with undiminished responsibity for foreign policy defense matters, as provided by the constitution of the Fifth Republic. For the balance of 1993, he did so, with particular attention to the ongoing Bosnian Civil War, though his meetings with Serbian and Bosnian leaders in an attempt to personally mediate the conflict were unsuccessful. He also visited southeast Asia, pledging French aid to and trade with Vietnam and Cambodia. Mitterrand also resisted the resumption of underground nuclear testing, as urged by the French and other military establishments after the Chinese tests of October 5 had broken the existing undeclared but effective moratorium.

A soldier during World War II, Mitterrand was captured early, but escaped from the Germans and became an active Resistance fighter. He entered politics after the war and was a Socialist Deputy in the national assembly (1946–58; 1962–81), holding many cabinet positions in the early years, when his party held power. At the same time, he rose within the Socialist Party and was its First Secretary (1971–81), while also becoming a vice-president of the Socialist International (1972–81). In 1981, he was elected President of France, and was re-elected to a second seven-year term in 1988. Mitterrand attended the University of Paris. He married Danielle Gouze in 1944; the couple has two children. His brother is general Jacques Mitterrand.

FURTHER READING

Francois Mitterrand: A Study in Political Leadership. ALISTAIR COLE. Routledge, 1994.
"France after la Gloire." DAVID BROOKS. *National Review*, Apr. 26, 1993.
De Gaulle to Mitterrand: Presidential Power in France. MARTIN HARRISON. New York University Press, 1993.
"France turns tetchy." *Economist*, Mar. 7, 1992.
Mitterrand: A Political Biography. WAYNE NORTHCUTT. Holmes & Meier, 1992.
Seven Years in France: François Mitterrand and Unintended Revolution, 1981–1988. JULIUS W. FRIEND. Westview, 1988.
The Black and the Red: François Mitterrand and the Story of an Ambition. CATHERINE NAY. HARCOURT BRACE, 1987.
Mitterrand's France. SONIA MAZEY and MICHAEL NEWMAN, eds. Routledge Chapman & Hall, 1987.

Miyazawa, Kiichi (1919–) On July 18, 1993, the ruling Japanese Liberal Democratic Party (LDP) lost its majority in the lower house of the Japanese parliament, winning only 223 of 511 seats. On July 22 Prime Minister Kiichi Miyazawa resigned, to be replaced by Japan New Party head Morihiro Hosokawa. The fall of the long-dominant LDP came after many years of highly visible and widespread corruption scandals involving its top leadership, together with a deep recession and stock market plunge that greatly shook the confidence of most Japanese voters. During his final months in office, Miyazawa proposed economic stimulus plans and sharply resisted American, Australian, and other attacks on Japanese restrictive trade policies, while attempting to limit the damage of continuing scandals at home, but all to no avail.

Tokyo-born Miyazawa, the child of a prominent Japanese political family, is a graduate of Tokyo Imperial University. He began his five-decades-long political career during World War II, and was with the Finance Ministry (1942–52) through the war and the postwar American occupation of Japan. He became secretary to the Minister of Finance in 1949. A powerful leader of the ruling Liberal Democratic Party (LDP), he became an elected official in 1953, and then

Vice Minister of Education (1959–69), holding a series of Cabinet-level posts for the following three decades. He was chairman of the Executive Council of the LDP (1984–86), and became a key leader of the most powerful of the three LDP factions during that period. He became Prime Minister in 1991, succeeding Toshiki Kaifu, whose proposed reform program had been rejected by the LDP, and quickly brought into his government several politicians tainted by previous scandals. Throughout 1992, the scandals continued and multiplied; they included the Tokyo Sagawa Kyubin Company scandal, which involved $4–7 billion dollars, Japanese organized crime, and many of Japan's leading politicians, including LDP kingmaker Shin Kanemaru, Japan's most powerful politician, who resigned his LDP positions on August 28, though keeping his seat in parliament. He is married to Yoko Miyazawa; they have two children. He also has two brothers, both active in government.

FURTHER READING

"Two for the road. . . ." BILL VAN PARYS. *Rolling Stone*, Oct. 14, 1993.
"Miyazawa, Kiichi." *Current Biography*, Feb. 1992.
"Miyazawa unravels." *Economist*, Dec. 14, 1991.
"Raw and fishy. . . ." JOANNA PITMAN. *New Republic*, Nov. 4, 1991.

Mnouchkine, Alexandre (1908–93) St. Petersburg-born Alexandre Mnouchikine fled from Russia to France after the Bolshevik Revolution, entered the French film industry as a prop assistant to René Clair, and in the early 1930s began his six-decades-long career as a film producer. During World War II, he fought in the Resistance, afterward resuming his film career, forming Films Ariane. Among his scores of films were such classics as Jean Cocteau's *Les Parents Terribles* and Gérard Philipe's *Fanfan the Tulip*. His long association with Philipe de Broca yielded many Jean Paul Belmondo films, including *The Man From Rio*. For Claude Lelouch, he produced *A Man and a Woman*, and for Alain Resnais *Stavisky*. Mnouchkine's later films included *Get Out Your Handkerchiefs*, *The Name of the Rose*, and *Cinema Paradiso*; he was one of the leading figures in the post World War II French cinema. He was survived by two daughters. (d. Paris; April 3, 1993)

FURTHER READING

Obituary. *Variety*, Apr. 12, 1993.
Obituary. *The Times* (of London), Feb. 10, 1993.

Matthew Modine (left) and Julianne Moore

Modine, Matthew (1959–) In 1993, Matthew Modine starred as researcher Don Francis, a central role in Arnold Schulman's film adaptation of Randy Shilts's book about the early days of the AIDS epidemic: *And The Band Played On*, directed by Roger Spottiswoode. Among the others in the very large cast were Alan Alda, Phil Collins, David Dukes, Richard Gere, Glenne Headly, Anjelica Huston, Swoosie Kurtz, Ian McKellen, Steve Martin, and Lily Tomlin. Modine also starred in a dual role in the film *Equinox*, as a pair of twins separated at birth; Alan Rudolph directed. He also appeared in Robert Altman's film *Short Cuts*, based on nine Raymond Carver stories, in another large cast that included Andie MacDowell, Jack Lemmon, Bruce Davison, Julianne Moore, Anne Archer, Fred Ward, Jennifer Jason Leigh, Robert Downey, Jr., Tim Robbins, Lily Tomlin, and Tom Waits. Forthcoming was a remake of *The Browning Version*, directed by Mike Figgis and co-starring Albert Finney, Greta Scacchi, and Ben Silverstone.

California-born Modine emerged as a star in the late 1980s. He made his film debut in *Baby, It's You* (1983), and in the same year won a Venice Film Festival best actor award for his role in *Streamers* (1983). His breakthrough role came in the following year, as a Vietnam War veteran in *Birdy*. Among his further films were *Full Metal Jacket* (1987), *Married to the Mob* (1988), *Gross Anatomy* (1989), *Pacific Heights* (1990), *Memphis Belle* (1990), and *Wind* (1992).

FURTHER READING

"Matthew Modine." RICHARD NATALE. *Cosmopolitan*, Nov. 1990.

Montana, Joe (Joseph C. Montana, Jr.; 1956–) Football great Joe Montana hopes to be the only quarterback ever to lead two different teams to Super Bowl wins. But more fundamentally, he wants to *play*, not watch from the sidelines. With the San Francisco 49ers, he had lost virtually all of the 1991 and 1992 seasons to injuries, returning only briefly in early January 1993-but playing with his old skill and verve. He wanted his starting position back and-despite the fact that replacement Steve Young had been the National Football League's highest-rated quarterback two years running and most valuable player in 1992-Montana's legend and popularity were so great that 49ers' coach George Seifert offered it to him. In the end, however, Montana went to the Kansas City Chiefs.

There, teamed with another future hall-of-famer, Marcus Allen, Montana guided his new team to a division-leading 11–5 season. Montana himself had several nagging injuries, and ended the season with a 87.4 rating, placing him fifth in the league-though his all-time career rating is still slightly ahead of the current leader, Steve Young. With some of his characteristic stirring come-from-behind wins, Montana propelled the Chiefs into the Conference finals in January

1994, but there they were eventually beaten by the Buffalo Bills, who then lost the Super Bowl.

After a notable career as quarterback at the University of Notre Dame, where he received his B.A., Pennsylvania-born Montana became a leading player in professional football during the 1980s. As quarterback of the San Francisco 49ers from 1979, he led his team to four Super Bowl championships (1982; 1985; 1989; 1990) and is the only three-time winner of the ·Super Bowl's most valuable player award (1982; 1985; 1990), in 1990 throwing a record five touchdowns, with no interceptions. Among other Super Bowl records he set were consecutive completions (13), career passes (122), career passing yardage (1142), career completions (83), and pass attempts without an interception (122). Though it looked as if his career might be over in 1986, when he had back surgery, he returned seemingly as strong as ever, and he still has the highest career rating of any quarterback in history. He was named the league's most valuable player and the Associated Press's male athlete of the year in 1989 and *Sports Illustrated*'s Sportsman of the Year in 1990. He has published *Audibles: My Life in Football* (1986), written with Bob Raissman, and *Cool under Fire: Reflections on the San Francisco 49ers-How We Came of Age in the 1980's* (1989), with Alan Steinberg. Twice divorced, Montana married Jennifer Wallace in 1984; they have two children.

FURTHER READING

"No average Joes here." PAUL ATTNER. *Sporting News*, Sep. 13, 1993.
"Joe's a go." RICK REILLY. *Sports Illustrated*, Sep. 13, 1993.
"Second coming. . . ." PAUL ATTNER. *Sporting News*, Sep. 6, 1993.
"Joe Montana." RANDY COVIT. *Sport*, Sep. 1993.
"Joe goes." PAUL ZIMMERMAN. *Sports Illustrated*, Apr. 26, 1993.
"B or not QB?" PETER KING. *Sports Illustrated*, July 27, 1992.
Joe Montana. BOB ITALIA. Abdo & Daughters, 1992.
Sports Great Joe Montana. JACK KAVANAGH. Enslow, 1992.
"Ten living legends. . . ." STEVE WULF. *Sports Illustrated*, Dec. 23, 1991.
"The state of Montana." MIKE LUPICA. *Esquire*, Nov. 1991.
"Joe Montana." *Sporting News*, Sept. 23, 1991.
"Guts and glory. . . ." J. DAVID MILLER et al. *Sport*, July 1991.
Joe Montana. JAMES R. ROTHAUS. Childs World, 1991.

Joe Montana. MARC APPLEMAN. Little, Brown, 1991.
Joe Montana. Scholastic, 1991.

Montoya, Carlos Garcia (1903–93)

Madrid-born Carlos Montoya, a leading flamenco guitarist, began his long career early in his teenage years, playing professionally with flamenco groups in cabaret. He played in the flamenco troupe of La Argentina (Antonia Mercé) from 1928 to 1931, and during the early 1930s with several other flamenco troupes. He joined the troupe of La Argentinita (Encarnación López) from 1938 until her death in 1945, and then became a then-very-unusual guitar soloist, in concert and on records. In the decades that followed he brought flamenco guitar to new worldwide classic and popular music audiences in his own highly improvisational way, in the process becoming a world figure in music. Montoya married American dancer Sally McLean in 1940, and subsequently became an American citizen. He was survived by his wife and two sons. (d. Wainscott, New York; March 3, 1989).

FURTHER READING

"Don Carlos Montoya, 1903–1993." JUAN GUILLERMO CHRISTIE. *Guitar Player*, June 1993.
Obituary. *Current Biography*, May 1993.
Obituary. *The Times* (of London), Mar. 27, 1993.
Obituary. *Billboard*, Mar. 20, 1993.
Obituary. *New York Times*, Mar. 5, 1993.

Moore, Demi (Demi Guynes; 1962–)

Film star Demi Moore's major 1993 movie was *Indecent Proposal*, directed by Adrian Lyne and co-starring Robert Redford and Woody Harrelson. The highly publicized film had as its plot the fantasy that wealthy financier John Gage (Redford) would offer $1 million to spend a night in sexual encounter with Diana Murphy (Moore), the wife of David Murphy (Harrelson). In the film, the Murphys are happily married, but broke. This quintessential male fantasy was a box office smash hit, grossing more than $100 million; both its premise and its great commercial success were at the very least disheartening to many women's rights advocates. At year's end, Moore and her husband, Bruce Willis, were expecting their third child.

New Mexico-born Moore played reporter Jackie Templeton in television's "General Hospital," and appeared in such 1980s films as

Choices (1981), *Parasite* (1982), *St. Elmo's Fire* (1985), *Wisdom* (1986), and *We're No Angels* (1989). Her breakthrough came in 1990 with a starring role opposite Patrick Swayze and Whoopi Goldberg in the fantasy *Ghost*, which became the surprise top-grossing film of the year, thus making her a bankable star. She also starred in *A Few Good Men* (1992).

Having created quite a stir by appearing nude and nine months pregnant on the August 1991 cover of the magazine *Vanity Fair* (though she was not really entirely nude), Moore in August 1992 again appeared on the magazine's cover, this time looking fully clothed, although on this occasion actually nude and wearing a body-painted pin-striped suit. She married Bruce Willis in 1987; they have two daughters.

FURTHER READING

"Moore, Demi." *Current Biography*, Sep. 1993.
"Hollywood's steely lady" MATT WOLF. *Times*, May 19, 1993.
"The last pinup." MICHAEL ANGELI and STEVEN KLEIN. *Esquire*, May 1993.
"Demi Moore. . . ." TRIP GABRIEL. *Us*, May 1993.
"Why Demi wants more." PETER WILKINSON. *Redbook*, Jan. 1993.
"Demi's body language." JENNET CONANT and ANNIE LEIBOVITZ. *Vanity Fair*, Aug. 1992.
"Demi Moore." JOE RHODES. *Harper's Bazaar*, June 1992.
"What she did. . . ." JEFF ROVIN. *Ladies Home Journal*, June 1992.

"Demi's big moment." NANCY COLLINS and ANNIE LEIBOVITZ. *Vanity Fair*, Aug. 1991.
"The haunting magic of. . . ." TOM BURKE. *Cosmopolitan*, Dec. 1990.
"They heard it through. . . ." JEANNIE PARK. *People*, Nov. 12, 1990.

Moore, Garry (Thomas Garrison Morfit; 1915–93) Baltimore-born Garry Moore worked in radio in the 1930s and 1940s, most notably with comedian Jimmy Durante in radio's "Jimmy Durante-Garry Moore Show." He became a star in early television as host of his own long-running afternoon variety series "The Garry Moore Show" (1950–58), and later a nighttime version of the show (1959–61). Moore also hosted the long-running quiz show "I've Got a Secret" (1952–64), with a celebrity panel that included Bill Cullen, Betsy Parker, Henry Morgan, Bess Myerson, Jayne Meadows, and Steve Allen, who succeeded Moore as host of the show. Moore also hosted the syndicated version of the television quiz show "To Tell the Truth" (1969–77). He left television briefly in 1964, and then returned, in 1966 hosting a brief revival of his variety series. He retired in 1977, after contracting throat cancer, and did not return to television after cure was effected. He was survived by his wife, Betsy Moore, two sons, a sister, and a brother. (d. Hilton Head Island, South Carolina; November 29, 1993)

FURTHER READING

Obituary. *New York Times*, Nov. 29, 1993.
Obituary. *Variety*, Nov. 29, 1993.

Morris, Willie (1934–) "I came to the city and it changed my life," Morris began. With *New York Days* (1993), Mississippi writer-editor Willie Morris produced a notable memoir of literary life in the Big Apple during the turbulent late 1960s, and its effect on his own life. In that sense the work was a sequel to his earlier *North Toward Home* (1967). Appointed in 1967 as editor-in-chief of *Harper's*-the youngest in the history of America's oldest magazine-Morris and his staff (including David Halberstam, Larry L. King, Marshall Frady, and Midge Decter) published works by many writers who were or would become America's most noted writers, including

William Styron, Joan Didion, Robert Penn Warren, C. Vann Woodward, Arthur Miller, Elizabeth Hardwick, George Plimpton, James Dickey, Bernard Malamud, Walker Percy, Larry McMurtry, Truman Capote, John Updike, and Norman Mailer, whose 90,000-word 1968 article "Steps of the Pentagon" was the longest piece ever published in any American magazine, and would later become the Pulitzer Prize and National Book Award-winning *Armies of the Night*. Morris's *New York Days* takes his tale (including sidelights such as introducing 21-year-old Oxford-bound fellow Rhodes scholar Bill Clinton to celebrities at Elaine's) to its end in 1971, with his resignation after the explosion of controversy-most notably by his Minneapolis-based owners-that followed publication of Mailer's article "Prisoner of Sex." It would be the best-selling issue in *Harper's* history, and Morris's last as editor.

Born in Jackson, Mississippi, and raised in the Delta's Yazoo City, Morris received his B.A. at the University of Texas in 1956, then, as a Rhodes scholar, a B.A. and M.A. from Oxford University's New College in 1959 and 1960. Returning to Austin, he was associate editor, then editor-in-chief of the *Texas Observer* (1960–62), before coming to New York and *Harper's*, as associate editor (1963–65), executive editor (1965–67), and editor-in-chief and vice president (1967–71). He was later writer-in-residence at the University of Mississippi (1980–91), where his students included bestselling novelists John Grisham and Donna Tartt. Morris's own books include *The South Today, 100 Years After Appomattox* (1965); the autobiographical *North Toward Home* (1967), which won the Houghton Mifflin literary award and the Carr P. Collins non-fiction award; *Yazoo: Integration in a Deep Southern Town* (1971); the children's books *Good Old Boy* (1971) and *Good Old Boy and the Witch of Yazoo* (1989); the novel *The Last of the Southern Girls* (1973); the memoir *James Jones: A Friendship* (1978); *Terrain of the Heart and Other Essays* (1981); *The Courting of Marcus Dupree* (1983), which won the Christopher medal; *Always Stand in Against the Curve* (1983); *Homecomings* (1989), winner of the Mississippi distinguished book award; *Faulkner's Mississippi* (1990); and a book of stories, *After All, It's Only a Game* (1992). Previously married to Celia Ann Buchan (1958–69), Morris married JoAnne Shirley Prichard in 1991. He has one son.

FURTHER READING

"He'll always have Elaine's. . . ." MICHAEL SHNAYERSON. *Vanity Fair*, Oct. 1993.
"The yarn spinner. . . ." GERALD PARSHALL. *U.S. News & World Report*, Sep. 13, 1993.
"The secretaries, the glamour. . . ." TOBIN HARSHAW. *New York Times Book Review*, Sep. 5, 1993.
"The second life of. . . ." RUST HILLS. *Esquire*, Sep. 1993.

Morrison, Toni (Chloe Anthony Wofford; 1931–) In 1993, novelist Toni Morrison became the 90th winner of the Nobel Prize for literature, the first African-American woman and only the second American woman to receive the award, which carries with it a prize of $825,000. The Nobel Committee praised her as a "literary artist of the first rank" whose work portrayed the Black experience "with the luster of poetry." The Swedish Postal Service also honored her by issuing a stamp with her photograph on it. Morrison's Nobel acceptance address, a prose-poem on the value of language, which some compared to William Faulkner's notable Nobel speech in 1950, won a standing ovation. Her six novels were republished as a boxed set, which became a main selection of the Book-of-the-Month Club. On Christmas day, Morrison's home, on the Hudson River north of New York City, was gutted by fire, apparently started from a fireplace ember; most of her manuscripts were saved.

Ohio-born Morrison received her 1953 B.A. from Howard University, and her 1955 M.A. in American literature from Cornell University, then taught English and the humanities at Texas Southern University (1955–57), and back at Howard University (1957–64). Making a major career and location change, she then joined Random House as an editor in 1965, in Syracuse and then New York, then becoming a substantial figure in the publishing world. But it is for her novels-*The Bluest Eye* (1970), *Sula* (1973), *Song of Solomon* (1977), *Tar Baby* (1981), the Pulitzer-Prize winning *Beloved* (1987), and *Jazz* (1992)-that she is by far best known, her focus on the lives of African-American women placing her at the center of the emerging feminist and African-American movements of her time. Her other works include the play *Dreaming Emmett* (1986), *Playing in the Dark: Whiteness and the Literary Imagination* (1992), and as editor, *Race-ing Justice, En-Gendering Power* (1992), a book of essays on the Anita Faye Hill-Clarence Thomas confrontation. After teaching briefly in New York's State University, at Purchase and at Albany, in 1987 Morrison was named Robert F. Goheen Professor of the Humanities at Princeton University, where she has since taught creative writing. Divorced from architect Harold Morrison in 1964, she has two sons.

FURTHER READING

Conversations with Toni Morrison. DANILLE K. TAYLOR-GUTHRIE, ed. University Press of Mississippi, 1994.
Toni Morrison: Author. DOUGLAS CENTURY. Chelsea House, 1994.
"Keep your eyes on the prize." DAVID GATES. *Newsweek*, Oct. 18, 1993.
"Rooms of their own." TONI MORRISON and JACK E. WHITE. *Time*, Oct. 18, 1993.
Fiction and Folklore: The Novels of Toni Morrison. TRUDIER HARRIS. University of Tennessee Press, 1993.
Toni Morrison's World of Fiction. KAREN CARMEAN. Whitston, 1993.
Toni Morrison: Critical Perspectives Past and Present. HENRY L. GATES, JR., and K.A. APPIAH. Amistad Press, 1993.
"Black and right. . . ." CLIVE DAVIS. *Times*, Apr. 28, 1992.
The Voices of Toni Morrison. BARBARA RIGNEY. Ohio State University Press, 1992.
Fiction and Folklore: The Novels of Toni Morrison. TRUDIER HARRIS. University of Tennessee Press, 1991.
Toni Morrison. HAROLD BLOOM, ed. Chelsea House, 1991.
"The divining Ms. Morrison." MAYA ANGELOU. *Savvy Woman*, Aug. 1989.

Mosconi, Willie (1913–93) Philadelphia-born Willie Mosconi, whose father owned a pool hall, became one of the best pool, or "pocket billiards," players of his time. He won his first world pocket billiards championship in 1941, and from then until his retirement from tournament competition in 1956 won 12 more world championships, entirely dominating the game, despite the publicity accorded his chief rival, "Minnesota Fats," who refused to play Mosconi until very late in both their careers. Their ultimate match, which Mosconi won decisively, was played before a national television audience in 1978. Mosconi served as technical advisor and appeared briefly in *The Hustler* (1961), starring Paul Newman and Jackie Gleason as professional pool players. In addition to books on playing pocket billiards, he published *The Willie Mosconi Story* (1959) and *Willie's Game: An Autobiography of Willie Mosconi* (1993), written with Stanley Cohen. He was survived by his wife, Flora, two daughters, and a son. (d. Haddon Heights, New Jersey; September 16, 1993)

FURTHER READING

Obituary. *Current Biography*, Nov. 1993.
Obituary. STEVE RUSHIN. *Sports Illustrated*, Sep. 27, 1993.
Obituary. *New York Times*, Sep. 18, 1993.

Moseley Braun, Carol: See Braun, Carol Moseley.

Mubarak, Hosni (Mohammed Hosni Mubarak; 1928–) Egypt's low-level Islamic guerrilla insurgency continued in 1993, engaging much of Hosni Mubarak's attention, with attacks on tourists and historic sites, especially in southern Egypt, significantly cutting the lucrative tourist trade. Terrorists attacked foreigners, police, and government officials throughout the country, as in the October 26 murders of three foreign tourists at Cairo's Semiramis Intercontinental Hotel. As terrorist attacks grew, the Egyptian government responded by stepping up its mass arrests, military court trials, and in some instances summary executions of fundamentalist militants, although Amnesty International charged the government with torture and other violations of human rights. Mubarak on several occasions accused Iran of fomenting Islamic fundamentalist insurgency in his country.

On October 4, Mubarak was returned to the Egyptian presidency, running unopposed; opposition parties boycotted the election, because they were unable to contest the presidency. He had also run unopposed in 1981 and 1987. Mubarak continued to exert considerable influence in Arab and African affairs, as in his endorsement of the Palestine Liberation Organization-Israeli negotiations and the historic September peace agreement.

Mubarak was a career air force officer who moved up to direct the Air Academy (1967–69), became Air Force chief of staff (1969–72), and was commander in chief (1972–75). He became Anwar Sadat's vice president in 1975 and moved into the presidency in 1981, after Sadat's assassination. He won a second term in the 1987 elections. In 1988, the Mubarak government moved against the fundamentalists, beginning a period of widespread arrests under emergency decrees in effect since the Sadat assassination. Mubarak has been a moderate within the Arab world throughout his presidency, as well a considerable force in the search for Middle East and Arab-Israeli peace. As president of the Organization of African Unity (1989–90), he tried to help settle such regional conflicts as those in Ethiopia, Chad, and Namibia. After the August 1990 Iraqi attack on Kuwait, he led moderate Arab response, convening an Arab summit meeting on August 8 and attempting to convince Saddam Hussein to withdraw. When the Iraqis would not do so, Mubarak led in the formation of the multinational Arab army sent to Saudi Arabia. In the wake of the Persian Gulf War, Egypt received massive infusions of foreign aid and forgiveness of $25 billion in foreign debt, greatly strengthening Mubarak's government, at least for a time. His position in the Arab world was greatly improved as well. Egypt, cast out by hardline anti-Israeli Arab nations after the 1979 Camp David Accords with Israel, had regained some prestige in the late 1980s, and after the Gulf War resumed a major position at the center of the Arab world.

Mubarak attended the Egyptian military and air academies. Little is known of his private life, except that he is married to Suzanne Mubarak and has at least two children.

FURTHER READING

"Who's sitting pretty. . . ." *Business Week*, Mar. 11, 1991.
Hosni Mubarak. JOHN SOLECKI. Chelsea House, 1991.
"A call to negotiate. . . ." DEAN FISHER. *Time*, Sep. 10, 1990.
"The view from Cairo." MORTIMER B. ZUCKERMAN. *U.S. News & World Report*, Apr. 16, 1990.

Mulroney, Brian (Martin Brian Mulroney; 1939–) On February 24, 1993, Canadian Prime Minister Brian Mulroney resigned his leadership of the ruling Progressive Conserv-

ative Party, and by doing so also announced that he would resign as Prime Minister after his party leadership successor was named. Kim Campbell succeeded him as party leader on June 13, and as Prime Minister on June 25, becoming Canada's first woman prime minister. In the October 25 election, in an extraordinary act of repudiation, the Progressive Conservatives lost 151 of their 153 seats, including Campbell's. Liberal Jean Chrétien succeeded her as Prime Minister on November 4. Mulroney himself did not run again.

Mulroney's Progressive Conservatives had come to power in 1984, with 211 of 282 Parliamentary seats; it left power with two, having failed to make any significant impact on Canada's long and deepening depression, accompanied by deep cuts in social services, record deficits, a new value-added tax, and a 1988 Canada-U.S. trade agreement that many felt added to Canadian economic problems. Nor did the Mulroney government make any progress on the central question of the future of Quebec and of the Canadian nation, with Canadian voters in 1990 rejecting the 1987 Meech Lake agreements and in 1992 rejecting the Charlottetown Accord.

Mulroney practiced law in Montreal (1965–76), and then moved into industry, as executive vice president and then president of the Iron Ore Company of Canada (1976–83). He became Progressive Party leader and a Member of Parliament in 1983, and Prime Minister in 1984. He was returned to power in the general election of November 1988, after having made the election a virtual referendum on the recently concluded 1988 Canada-U.S. trade pact. Mulroney attended St. Francis Xavier and Laval Universities. He married Mila Pivnicki in 1973; they have four children.

FURTHER READING

"Hail, Brian, and farewell." MORDECAI RICHLER. *Saturday Night*, June 1993.
"Brian's ladder. . . ." GLEN ALLEN. "Parting shots. . . ." KEVIN DOYLE and ANTHONY WILSON-SMITH. "Governing under siege . . . ." PETER C. NEWMAN. "The Mulroney years . . . ." ANTHONY WILSON-SMITH. *Maclean's*, Mar. 8, 1993.
"Mulroney and Bush. . . ." *U.S. News & World Report*, May 25, 1992.
" 'The basics are right.' " KEVIN DOYLE and ANTHONY WILSON-SMITH. *Maclean's*, Jan. 6, 1992.
"Life of Brian. . . ." JOHN SAWATSKY. *Saturday Night*, Oct. 1991.

"Mulroney revealed. . . ." ANTHONY WILSON-SMITH. *Maclean's*, Oct. 1991.

"Mulroney vs. the unions." ANTHONY WILSON-SMITH. *Maclean's*, Sep. 23, 1991.

"Mulroney up close. . . ." ANTHONY WILSON-SMITH. *Maclean's*, June 10, 1991.

"Under the gun. . . ." BRUCE WALLACE. *Maclean's*, Sep. 24, 1990.

" 'Off to the races'." KEVIN DOYLE and ANTHONY WILSON-SMITH. *Maclean's*, June 25, 1990.

Sacred Trust: Brian Mulroney and the Conservative Party in Power. DAVID BERCUSON. Doubleday, 1987.

Murdoch, Iris (Jean Iris Murdoch; 1919–) Noted British writer Iris Murdoch published two very different books in 1993. Wearing her philosopher's hat, she introduced *Metaphysics as a Guide to Morals: Philosophical Reflections*, a dense and thoughtful book, exploring a modern Platonic view of the universe, in which humanity's moral life is always a striving toward an imperfectly perceived ideal perfection, and examining what that means in art, politics, and daily life. Then, with her fictional hat on, though as usual with strong philosophical overtones, Murdoch published a novel, *The Green Knight*, the title harking back to the medieval legend of Sir Gawain and the Green Knight, though the story of attempted murder takes much from the tale of Cain and Abel. Set in contemporary London, it focuses on two brothers, one of whom attempts to kill the other, but instead seems to kill a Christ-like third man, the work then exploring the resulting changes among the family and friends of those involved. Both books were critically well received and widely reviewed, though-to no one's surprise-neither became a commercial bestseller.

Dublin-born Murdoch was educated at Oxford University's Somerville College. After wartime work for the British government, she studied at Cambridge University's Newnham College (1947–48), then became a fellow of Oxford's St. Anne's College (1948–63). Her first published work was *Sartre: Romantic Rationalist* (1953), but she is best known for her novels, including *Under the Net* (1954); *The Sandcastle* (1957); *A Severed Head* (1961; play 1963), *The Unicorn* (1963), *The Italian Girl* (1964; play 1967), *A Fairly Honorable Defeat* (1970), the James Tait Black fiction prize-winning *The Black Prince* (1973), the Whitbread fiction award-winning *The Sacred and Profane Love Machine* (1974), the Booker Prize-winning *The Sea, the Sea* (1978); *The Book and the Brotherhood* (1987); and *The Message to the Planet* (1989). Among her other writings are the essay collections *The Sovereignty of Good* (1970) and *The Fire and the Sun: Why Plato Banished the Artists* (1978). Murdoch is married to John O. Bayley, long-time professor of English literature at Oxford University.

FURTHER READING

Iris Murdoch: A Sea of Contingency. DOUGLAS A. MACKEY. Borgo, 1994.

"Under Iris Murdoch's net." *Economist*, Sep. 25, 1993.

Understanding Iris Murdoch. CHERYL L. BOVE. University of South Carolina Press, 1993.

."The water is deep. . . ." MADELINE MARGET. *Commonweal*, June 14, 1991.

Murdoch, Rupert (Keith Rupert Murdoch; 1931–) Media baron Rupert Murdoch returned to his acquiring ways in 1993, having apparently handled the impacts of worldwide recession, massive debt service necessitated by his 1980s acquisitions, and direct cash drains from the operations of several of his enterprises. News Corporation stock was up, making it more available for use in acquisitions, interest rates were down, and lenders and investors were accessible.

In March, Murdoch repurchased the ailing *New York Post*, faced down its unions in hard bargaining and with repeated threats to close the paper, got the terms he wanted, as well as the FCC waiver that he had unsuccessfully sought before being forced to sell the newspaper in 1988. In August, he bought a controlling interest in Hong Kong's Star Television group, Asia largest satellite broadcaster, planning to finance the $525 million purchase with News Corporation stock and a stock issue. In September, he announced a considerable series of moves and coming moves, among them the purchase of Delphi Internet and the expansion of Sky Broadcasting, no longer a cash drain.

Australian-American publisher Murdoch started with a small Australian family newspaper in 1952 and by 1990 had built a large worldwide communications company, controlling such publications and companies as Fox Television, 20th Century Fox Films, *The Times* of London, HarperCollins Publishers, Sky Television, *The Australian* and many other publications in Australia, *New York* magazine, and Triangle Publications, purchased for $3 billion in 1988, until then the largest acquisition in publishing history. He became dangerously overextended in 1990, as worldwide advertising revenues fell in a growing recession, existing assets realized less money on sale, and interest rates remained high for a time. His debts exceeded $8 billion by late 1990, and, in the changed atmosphere of the early 1990s, he quickly ran into major problems. Murdoch attended Oxford University. He married Anna Maria Torv in 1967; they have two children.

FURTHER READING

"Paper lions." EDWARD KLEIN. *Vanity Fair*, Oct. 1993.
"Sky is not the limit." ROY GREENSLADE. *New Statesman & Society*, Sep. 10, 1993.
"Murdoch's Asian bet." *Economist*, July 31, 1993.
"The Murdoch touch." ANDREW TANZER. *Forbes*, May 10, 1993.
Murdoch. WILLIAM SHAWCROSS. Simon & Schuster, 1993.
"Uppers and downers." HELEN KAY. *Management Today*, Oct. 9, 1991.
"A chastened man." *Economist*, Jan. 19, 1991.
Outfoxed: Marvin Davis, Barry Diller, Rupert Murdoch and the Inside Story of America's Fourth Television Network. ALEX B. BLOCK. St. Martin's, 1990.
Rupert Murdoch. JEROME TUCCILLE. Donald I. Fine, 1989.

Eddie Murphy (right) and Eartha Kitt

Murphy, Eddie (1961–) Eddie Murphy continued to be a familiar face on American television screens during 1993, as both of his 1992 films, *Boomerang* and *Distinguished Gentleman*, reached the top of the home video rental charts. But neither had done very well at the box office, and Murphy was far from the major film star he had been in the mid-1980s. No new films were released in 1993, and even the announced *Beverly Hills Cop III* was canceled.

Murphy did, however, successfully pursue his parallel career as a popular singer and songwriter, issuing the hit album *Love's Alright*, with nine of its twelve tracks containing new Murphy songs. He also issued three hit singles drawn from the album, including "I Was a King," "Whatzupwitu," and "Desdemona." Murphy also issued the new music video, "Whatzupwitu," performed by Michael Jackson and the Boys Choir of Harlem. Murphy received a special Heritage award at the Soul Train Music Awards. On the personal side, he married model Nicole Mitchell, mother of their daughter and son.

Brooklyn-born Murphy became one of the leading entertainment celebrities of the 1980s, beginning with his regular featured role on television's "Saturday Night Live" (1980–84). His recording career began with the album *Eddie Murphy* (1982), and included *Eddie Murphy Comedian* (1983) and *So Happy* (1989). He began a spectacular film career with *48 Hours* (1982), moving on to such other films as *Trading Places*

(1983), *Beverly Hills Cop* (1983; *II*, 1987), *Coming to America* (1988), *Harlem Nights* (1989), *Another 48 Hours* (1990), *Boomerang* (1992), and *The Distinguished Gentlemen* (1992).

FURTHER READING

"Eddie & Nicole's wedding album." WALTER LEAVY. *Ebony*, May 1993.
"Bye-bye, bad boy. . . ." KAREN S. SCHNEIDER. *People*, Mar. 22, 1993.
"The Us interview. . . ." JON PARELES. *Us*, Jan. 1993.
Eddie Murphy. DEBRAH WILBOURN. Chelsea House, 1993.
"The second coming. . . ." MEREDITH BERKMAN. *Entertainment*, Dec. 18, 1992.
"Eddie Murphy." JOHN CLARK. *Premiere*, Aug. 1992.
"Do you still love Eddie?" RICHARD CORLISS. *Time*, July 6, 1992.
"Trading places." PETER RICHMOND. *GQ-Gentleman's Quarterly*, July 1992.
"The taming of Eddie." JILL NELSON. *Essence*, June 1992.
"Eddie Murphy. . . ." WALTER LEAVY. *Ebony*, Jan. 1990.
Films of Eddie Murphy. EDWARD GROSS. Movie Publications, 1990.
"Eddie Murphy. . . ." BILL ZEHME. *Rolling Stone*, Aug. 24, 1989.

Murray, Bill (1950–) Actor and comedian Bill Murray starred in 1993 in the film *Groundhog Day*, as a weatherman covering Groundhog Day in Punxsutawney, Pennsylvania, who finds himself literally doomed to repeat the day's activities-forever. Andie MacDowell, Chris Elliott, and Stephen Tobolowsky co-starred; Harold Ramis directed.

Murray also starred as Chicago mobster Frank Milo in the film *Mad Dog and Glory*, directed by Bill McNaughton and co-starring Robert De Niro as Chicago police crime scene photographer 'Mad Dog" Dobie and Una Thur-

man as Glory, the woman Milo sends to Dobie, as a "present" for having saved his life. Forthcoming was a starring role in the film *Ed Wood*, directed by Tim Burton and co-starring Johnny Depp, Sarah Jessica Parker, and Martin Landau.

Illinois-born Murray began his career with Chicago's Second City Troupe, and emerged as a television star in the late 1970s, as a regular on *Saturday Night Live*. He has appeared in such films as *Meatballs* (1977), *Caddyshack* (1980), *Stripes* (1981), *Ghostbusters* (1984), *Little Shop of Horrors* (1986), *Scrooged* (1988), *Ghostbusters II* (1989), *Quick Change* (1990; he co-produced, co-directed and starred), and *What About Bob?* (1991). Murray attended Regis College. He married Margaret Kelly in 1980; the couple has two children.

FURTHER READING

"Triumph of the Bill." KATE MEYERS. *Entertainment*, Mar. 19, 1993.
The Rolling Stone Interviews: The 1980s. St. Martin's, 1989.
The Second City. DONNA MCCROHAN. Putnam, 1987.

Prince Naruhito

Princess Masako

Naruhito, Crown Prince (1960–) and Masako, Crown Princess (Masako Owada; 1963–)

On June 9, 1993, the world saw another royal wedding—but only figuratively. When Japan's Crown Prince Naruhito married Masako Owada, not even the groom's parents, Emperor Akihito and Empress Michiko, saw the event. By tradition, the morning ceremony was completely private, held in the *Koshi Kodo Koro* (House of Wisdom), a shrine dedicated to the sun goddess Amatarasu. However, television audiences saw pre-ceremony footage of the couple in traditional garb, Naruhito in an orange silk robe and black crown, and Masako in a twelve-layered kimono, and viewers were also able to watch animated versions of the wedding. For the afternoon celebrations, on what was declared a Japanese holiday, both wore Western-style formal clothes. Indeed, many were surprised at the Prince's choice of a Western-educated wife-and at her choice to marry into the royal family, giving up her diplomatic career.

Heir to Japan's Chrysanthemum Throne, Crown Prince Naruhito graduated from Gakushuin University with a degree in history in 1982, then received a doctorate in economic history from Oxford University's Mereton College in 1985. He has published various historical writings and served as an international goodwill ambassador for his country. Masako Owada, partly raised in Russia and the United States, where her father was stationed as a diplomat, studied economics at Harvard University, graduating with honors in 1985. Back in Japan, she studied law at Tokyo University and worked at the Ministry of Foreign Affairs (1987–88), before going to Oxford's Balliol College, receiving her degree in international relations in 1990. She then returned to the Foreign Affairs Ministry, stationed in the North American section.

FURTHER READING

" 'Virtual reality' wedding." BILL POWELL. *Newsweek*, June 21, 1993.
"Happily ever after?" SCOTT STEELE. *Maclean's*, June 14, 1993.
"The 21st Century Princess." MARTHA DUFFY. *Time*, June 7, 1993.
"Masako's sacrifice." EDWARD KLEIN. *Vanity Fair*, June 1993.
"Crowning achievement." MARGARET SCOTT. *Vogue*, June 1993.
"The career and the kimono." DAVID E. SANGER. *New York Times Magazine*, May 30, 1993.
"The reluctant princess." BILL POWELL, JEAN SELIGMANN, and PETER MCKILLOP. *Newsweek*, May 24, 1993.

Navratilova, Martina (1956–) In her 21st year of competitive tennis play, and still ranked third in the world, Martina Navratilova continued to build on the record number of tournament titles that she had set in 1992, when she surpassed Chris Evert's 158. To the 161 she had garnered through 1992, she added four more titles, for a still-building record of 165, more than any tennis player ever, woman or man. At Wimbledon, where she lost in the quarterfinals to Jana Novotna, she still came away with a title in the mixed doubles, paired with Mark Woodforde, the 55th Grand Slam title in her career. Her record for career prize money also continues to build, to over $19 million, with Steffi Graf's $12 million a distant second. Also in 1993, Navratilova reached a landmark 1400 matches won; she had broken Evert's record of 1309 in 1991. She was aso voted World Team tennis's most valuable female player for the third year in a row (1991–93).

Navratilova was still good enough to end Monica Seles's 34-match winning streak at the Paris Open in February, becoming the oldest player to defeat a top-ranked player. But she is no longer as dominant as she once was—as she herself said, "I've been in the twilight of my career longer than most people have had their career"; her last Grand Slam title was in 1990 at Wimbledon, though she reached the finals at Wimbledon and the U.S. Open in 1991. Wanting to retire on her own terms, she announced that 1994 will be her last year of competitive singles play, though she may continue at doubles. Her plan is to play at three Grand Slam events-the French Open, which she has won twice but has not appeared since 1988; Wimbledon, which she has won a record nine times; and the U.S. Open, where she has four singles titles-and to end her career with the Virginia Slims Championship, where she has won seven singles and ten doubles titles.

During 1993, Navratilova was one of numerous tennis stars who played in the Arthur Ashe Tennis Challenge to benefit the Arthur Ashe Foundation for Defeat AIDS. Looking beyond the tennis court, she has signed a $600,000 contract for at least three mystery novels, to be written with co-author Liz Nickles; publication is scheduled yearly, starting in 1995. In August, Navratilova was honored at a fundraiser for the the Gay Games IV at Madison Square Garden, the tribute raising nearly $250,000. On the personal side, Navratilova's former lover, Judy Nelson, with whom she split acrimoniously in 1991, published a book about their relationship, called *Nelson vs. Navratilova*, written with Sandra Faulkner.

Prague-born Navratilova emerged as a leading Czech tennis player while still in her early teens and was Czech national champion (1972–75). Defecting to the West in 1975, she went on to become the top-ranked woman tennis player in the world for four years in a row (1982–85), enjoying 271 weeks in a row as number one—a record for men *or* women—and 332 weeks overall. She also had a Grand Slam (1983–84) and in 1983 a record annual tally of 86–1. She continued to win major tournaments throughout the later 1980s as well, and in all has won the U.S. Open four times (1983–84; 1986–87), in 1987 with a Triple Crown of singles, doubles, and mixed doubles, and Wimbledon an unprecedented nine times (1978–79; 1982–1987; 1990), with a record six consecutive titles, and 17 overall. Also notable as a doubles player, Navratilova and Pam Shriver won three doubles Grand Slams (1983–84; 1984–85; 1986–1987) and a record 109 consecutive doubles matches (April 24, 1983-July 6, 1985). Navratilova and Gigi Fernandez won the U.S. Open doubles championships in 1990, sweeping the main doubles championships for the year. In that same year, Naratilova had both knees surgically rebuilt. She was named female athlete of the 1980s by *National Sports Review*, UPI, and AP. In 1985 she published *Martina: Autobiography*, written with George Vecsey. Navratilova became a U.S. citizen in 1981.

FURTHER READING

Martina Navratilova. GILDA ZWERMAN. Chelsea House, 1994.

Martina Navratilova: Tennis Star. DENISE WILLI. Blackbirch, 1994.

"Martina Navratilova." MICHELE KORT. *Advocate*, Oct. 5, 1993.

"Martina vs. Colorado." *Ladies Home Journal*, Mar. 1993.

"Martina takes aim. . . ." *Glamour*, Mar. 1993.

Love Match. SANDRA FAULKNER and JUDY NELSON. Birch Lane/Carol, 1993.

"Courting costs." DANA RUBIN. *Texas*, May 1992.

"Martina. . . . " DAVID HIGDON. *Tennis*, Mar. 1992.

Three Female Myths of the 20th Century: Garbo-Callas-Navratilova. IRIS BUNSCH. Vantage, 1992.

"Ten living legends. . . ." STEVE WULF. *Sports Illustrated*, Dec. 23, 1991.

" 'Not obsessed about. . . .' " JIM MARTZ. *Sporting News*, July 2, 1990.

"Postscript to. . . ." ANN SMITH and LEWIS ROTHLEIN. *Women's Sports and Fitness*, Mar. 1990.

Nazarbayev, Nursultan Abishevich

(1940–) Kazakhstan's president, Nursultan Nazarbayev, in 1993 remained a figure of major worldwide interest, because he continued to hold massive numbers of nuclear weapons, part of the huge Soviet nuclear arsenal. Although he had in 1992 agreed to accept the weapons-cutting Strategic Arms Reduction Treaty during a May 1992 meeting with President George Bush in Washington, he did not sign a treaty detailing how $85 million in American aid would be used to dismantle nuclear weapons until late in 1993, and then only under pressure during a visit by American Vice President Al Gore. At year's end, it still seemed quite clear that Nazarbayev wanted to modernize his country and welcomed American and other Western aid and trade-but had no intention of divesting his country of its entire nuclear arsenal. That seemed even more obvious after the strong showing of the Russian fascist and nationalist Vladimir Zhirinovsky in the 1993 Russian elections.

On the economic side, Nazarbayev continued to modernize the Kazakh industrial economy, while making no move to privatize landholding. A major effort was being made to use Kazakhstan's huge natural resources, most notably with the April signing of the joint Kazakh-Chevron Corporation agreement to develop the huge Tengiz oilfield in western Kazakhstan, on the northern shore of the Caspian Sea.

Nazarbayev, who joined the Communist Party in 1962, worked as an economist at the Karaganda Metallurgical Combine (1960–69), and then moved into party work. After holding a series of local posts, he emerged as Kazakh central committee secretary (1979–84), was leader of his party in Kazakhstan from 1984, and was a member of Soviet Communist Party central committee from 1986. He became President of the Soviet republic of Kazakhstan in 1990. While he supported the continued existence of the Soviet Union, he opposed the August 1991 attempted coup, quickly resigning all his Communist Party positions and then leading his country to independence. An economist and economic radical, he quickly and effectively moved toward a market economy with the aid of foreign advisors, and made more than 100 development deals with Western companies during the early 1990s.

FURTHER READING

"A 'temporarily nuclear state.' . . ." MIKHAIL USTIUGOV. "Bridging east and west." VLADIMIR ARDAEV. *Bulletin of the Atomic Scientists*, Oct. 1993.
"The end of the U.S.S.R." GEORGE J. CHURCH. *Time*, Dec. 23, 1991.
"Warily seeking sovereignty." ROBIN KNIGHT. *U.S. News & World Report*, Sep. 23, 1991.
"The khan of Kazakhstan. . . ." CARROLL BOGERT. *Newsweek*, July 8, 1991.
"The war within the corridors. . . ." MARY NEMETH. *Maclean's*, Apr. 1, 1991.

Neeson, Liam (1953–) Actor Neeson emerged as a major Hollywood star in 1993, for his role as Oscar Schindler in *Schindler's List*, directed and produced by Steven Spielberg. In this immediately acclaimed fact-based fictionalized treatment of the Holocaust, set in Nazi-occupied Poland during World War II, Neeson starred as German Catholic businessman Schindler, who comes to Poland to make money by using slave labor, but who ultimately saves 1,100 Polish Jews from the German gas chambers. The large cast includes Ben Kingsley, Ralph Fiennes, Caroline Goodall, Jonathan Sagalle, and Embeth Davidtz. The movie was voted the best film of 1993 by the New York Film Critics Circle and the Los Angeles Film Critics Association.

Neeson also starred in the film thriller *Deception*, directed by Graeme Clifford and co-starring Andie MacDowell as his wife, who goes abroad to investigate his suspicious death in a plane crash. A third film starring role was in *Ethan Frome*, adapted by Richard Nelson from Edith Wharton's novel and directed by John Madden. On stage, he starred in New York opposite Natasha Richardson in Eugene O'Neill's *Anna Christie*.

Belfast-born Neeson began his career in the theater, making his screen debut in *Excalibur* (1981). He moved into substantial screen roles in the late 1980s, in such films as *The Dead Pool* (1988), *The Good Mother* (1988), *Next of Kin* (1989), *Darkman* (1990), and *Leap of Faith* (1991). He studied at the Belfast Players' Theatre and at Dublin's Abbey Theatre.

FURTHER READING

"Liam Neeson puts the kettle on." STEPHANIE MANSFIELD. *GQ*, Dec. 1993.
"A touch of the poet." BARBARA KANTROWITZ. *Newsweek*, Feb. 8, 1993.
"Rugged, romantic. . . ." SUSAN SPILLMAN. *Cosmopolitan*, Dec. 1991.
"Darkman's Liam Neeson. . . ." MARC SHAPIRO. *Video Review*, Mar. 1991.
" 'Man' of the year. . . ." MARTHA FRANKEL. *American Film*, Dec. 1990.

Negulesco, Jean (1900–93) Romanian-born Jean Negulesco began his career as a painter and stage decorator in Paris. He traveled to New York for an exhibition of his works in 1927, stayed on, and began his film career in the early 1930s, working as a production assistant and then assistant director. His feature film directorial debut was *Singapore Woman* (1941), his first major success *The Mask of Dimitrios* (1944), and his final feature film *The Invincible Six* (1970). Among his films were *Three Strangers* (1946), *Nobody Lives Forever* (1946), *Humoresque* (1947), *Johnny Belinda* (1948), *Road House* (1948), *The Mudlark* (1950), *Lydia Bailey* (1952), *How to Marry a Millionaire* (1953), *Three Coins in the Fountain* (1954), *Daddy Long Legs* (1955), *Boy on a Dolphin* (1957), *The Best of Everything* (1959), and *The Pleasure Seekers* (1964). Negulesco published the autobiographical *Things I Did . . . and Things I Think I Did* (1984). He was survived by his wife, Dusty Anderson, and two daughters. (d. Marbella, Spain; July 18, 1993)

FURTHER READING

Obituary. *The Times* (of London), July 22, 1993.
Obituary. *New York Times*, July 22, 1993.
Obituary. *Variety*, July 21, 1993.

Neill, Sam (1947–) Actor Sam Neill starred in 1993 in Steven Spielberg's blockbuster science-fiction special effects film *Jurassic Park*, about modern genetically engineered dinosaurs that break free from a theme park and become a danger to humanity. The film became the commercial picture of the year and decade, the highest grossing film ever released. Directed by Spielberg, with screenplay by Michael Crichton and David Koepp, based on Crichton's novel, the film starred Neill, Jeff Goldbum, Laura Dern, and Richard Attenborough.

Neill also starred in one of the leading art films of the year, Jane Campion's acclaimed *The Piano*, winner of the Cannes Film Festival's Palme d'Or, which was equally well received when it opened in New York late in the year; Holly Hunter and Harvey Keitel co-starred. Neill also starred as a child psychiatrist opposite Anjelica Huston in the two-part television film *Family Pictures*, directed by Philip Saville. Forthcoming was a starring role in the film *Country Life*, co-starring Greta Scacchi and John Hargreaves.

Born in Northern Ireland, Neill made his film debut in *Land Fall* (1976). His breakthrough role came in *My Brilliant Career* (1980); he went on to such films as *Plenty* (1985), *The Good Wife* (1987), *A Cry in the Dark* (1988), *Dead Calm* (1989), *The Hunt for Red October* (1990), *Until the End of the World* (1991), and *Memoirs of an Invisible Man*. He has also appeared in many television films, and starred in the television miniseries *Reilly Ace of Spies* (1986). He attended New Zealand's University of Canterbury. He is married to Noriko Watanabe, and has three children.

FURTHER READING

"Who the heck is Sam Neill?" ANNE THOMPSON. *Entertainment*, July 23, 1993.

"Sam Neill's megalosaurus talent." GRAHAM FULLER. *Interview*, June 1993.

Nelson, Kenneth (1930–93) North Carolina-born Kenneth Nelson developed a wide-ranging Amercan acting career in the 1950s and 1960s, in such diverse roles as that of the title character in the television series "Henry Aldrich" and Matt Hucklebee in *The Fantasticks*. He emerged as a star as Michael in the off-Broadway production of *The Boys in the Band* (1968), Mart Crowley's groundbreaking play on homosexual themes, also starring in the 1969 London production and the 1970 film version of the play. After starring in a 1971 British revival of *Show Boat*, he settled in London, though continuing to work on both sides of the Atlantic, in such plays as *Lover* (1973); the musicals *Cole* (1974) and *Oh! Mr. Porter* (1977), both based on the work of Cole Porter; *Sexual Perversity in Chicago* (1977); and *Annie* (1978). He also appeared in several British television series. Nelson died of an AIDS-related illness. He was survived by his wife, Antoinette Genillard, and a sister. (d. London; October 7, 1993)

FURTHER READING

Obituary. *The Times* (of London), Oct. 9, 1993.
Obituary. *New York Times*, Oct. 9, 1993.

Nelson, Steve (Steven Mesaros; 1903–93) Born in Subocka, Croatia, Steve Nelson emigrated to the United States in 1920, settling in Philadelphia. He became a socialist in 1920 and a communist in 1923. He was a communist activist in Pittsburgh, Detroit, New York City, and Chicago in the 1920s, and went to eastern Pennsylvania as a Communist Party organizer in 1930. He attended Moscow's Lenin School in 1931; he and his wife both worked as couriers for the Comintern (Communist International) in Europe and Asia during the period (1931–33). Nelson then returned to Pennsylvania, working as a Communist Party organizer there (1933–37). In April 1937 he joined the Abraham Lincoln Battalion of the International Brigades in Spain, becoming political commissar of the multinational Fifteenth Brigade, which included the American contingent, was wounded several months later at Belchite, and was invalided home. He was a Communist Party organizer on the West Coast (1938–45), a member of the National Board of his party in New York City (1945–48), and party head in Pittsburgh (1948–56). His 1952 Pennsyvania state sedition conviction was reversed by the state's Supreme Court in 1953; the U.S. Supreme Court upheld that reversal and overturned a federal Smith Act conviction in 1956. In 1957, after the 1956 Nikita Krushchev speech exposing the crimes of Stalinism had split the world's communist parties, Nelson left the U.S. Communist Party. He was a member of the Veterans of the Abraham Lincoln Brigade. He told his story in *Steve Nelson, American Radical* (1981), written with James R. Barrett and Rob Ruck. Nelson was survived by a daughter and a son. (d. New York City; December 11, 1993)

FURTHER READING

Obituary. *New York Times*, Dec. 14, 1993.

Nelson, Willie (1933–) A major figure in American popular music, Willie Nelson had his work seriously disrupted from 1990 to 1992, because of tax problems and the seizure of much of his personal property by the Internal Revenue Service. In February 1993, a settlement was reached on tax matters, and Nelson, who had continued to compose and tour, was fully free to resume his creative life. In April, he released the acclaimed album *Across the Borderline*, which had been in preparation during 1992. Produced by Don Was, Paul Simon, and Roy Halee, and with the collaboration of Bonnie Raitt, Bob Dylan, and Sinead O'Connor, the album was received as an instant classic. During the balance of the year, he also released several singles drawn from the album, including Paul Simon's "Graceland," produced by Simon. In September, Nelson was elected to the Country Music Hall of Fame.

Forthcoming in 1994 was the album *Moonlight Becomes You*, a new collection of standards that includes such classics as "You'll Never Know," "My Blue Heaven," "Sentimental Journey," "Please Don't Talk About Me When I'm Gone," and the title song. Also forthcoming was a starring role in the film *Starlight*, directed and produced by Jonathan Kay, with a cast that includes Rae Dawn Chong and Billy Worth.

Texas-born Nelson began composing and recording in the early 1960s, emerging as a country music star in the mid-1970s, then crossing over to become a major popular music star on records, in concert, and on screen. His first national hit was the song "Blue Eyes Cryin' in the Rain," from his *Redheaded Stranger* album (1975). He went on to become one of the most popular musicians of the the 1970s and 1980s with such songs as "Georgia on My Mind," "Stardust," "On the Road Again," "Always on My Mind," and "Blue Skies," and such albums as *Waylon and Willie* (1978), *Stardust* (1978), and *Honeysuckle Rose*, the soundtrack album of his 1980 film of that name. He has also appeared in such films as *Barbarossa* (1982), *Red-Headed Stranger* (1986), and *Pair of Aces* (1990). In 1990, he, Johnny Cash, Waylon Jennings, and Kris Kristofferson began touring as The Highwaymen. Nelson ran into severe tax difficulties in 1990, and much of what he owned was seized and auctioned off by the U. S. Internal Revenue Service, generating his album *Who'll Buy My Memories (The I.R.S. Tapes)*. In 1988 he published his autobiographical *Willie*. Nelson attended Baylor University. He has been married three times and has five children, one of whom, Billy, was a probable suicide late in 1991.

FURTHER READING

"20 questions with. . . ." MICHAEL BANE. *Country Music*, Mar.-Apr. 1993.
"Willie Nelson." MICHAEL BANE. *Country Music*, Mar.-Apr. 1992.

"Willie Nelson's heartbreak." *People*, Jan. 13, 1992.

"The ballad of. . . ." RON ROSENBAUM. *Vanity Fair*, Nov. 1991.

"Willie the actor. . . ." GARY CARTWRIGHT. "Poor Willie. . . ." ROBERT DRAPER. *Texas*, May 1991.

Country Musicians . . . Other Great American Artists-Their Music and How They Made It. JUDIE EREMO, ed. Grove-Weidenfeld, 1987.

Heart Worn Memories: A Daughter's Personal Biography of Willie Nelson. SUSIE NELSON. Eakin Press, 1987.

Nicholson, Jack (1937–) For his role as the Guantanamo Bay base commander who is Tom Cruise's chief courtroom opponent in the 1992 hit film *A Few Good Men*, Nicholson won yet another Oscar nomination, this one as best supporting actor. In home video rentals during 1993, the film was a smash hit. Nicholson also won a best actor Golden Globe nomination, for his starring role as Teamsters' boss Jimmy Hoffa in *Hoffa*, which also did very well in home video rentals. That was far from all: late in 1993, he was announced winner of the 1994 American Film Institute's 22nd Life Achievement Award.

Forthcoming was a starring role in the film *Wolf*, directed by Mike Nichols and co-starring Michelle Pfeiffer, Kate Nelligan, James Spader, and Richard Jenkins. Also forthcoming was participation in Mel Gibson's public television family radio show "Rabbit Ears Radio;" he and Bobby McFerrin were slated to read the children's classic "The Elephant's Child."

New Jersey-born Nicholson played strong supporting roles beginning in the late 1950s, most notably in *Easy Rider* (1969), and then moved into the powerful dramatic roles that made him a major figure for the next two decades in such films as *Five Easy Pieces* (1970), *Chinatown* (1974), *One Flew Over the Cuckoo's Nest* (1975; he won a best actor Oscar), *The Postman Always Rings Twice* (1981), *Reds* (1981), *Terms of Endearment* (1983; he won a best supporting actor Oscar), *Prizzi's Honor* (1985), *Heartburn* (1986), *Ironweed* (1987), *Batman* (1989), *A Few Good Men* (1992), *Hoffa* (1992), and *Man Trouble* (1992). In 1990, he directed and starred in *The Two Jakes*, a sequel to *Chinatown*. Nicholson was formerly married to Sandra Knight; they had one daughter. He had a 17-year relationship with actress Anjelica Huston that ended in 1990. He and actress Rebecca Broussard have two children, a daughter born in 1990 and a son born in 1992; the couple separated in 1992.

FURTHER READING

Jack's Life: A Biography of Jack Nicholson. PATRICK McGILLIGAN. Norton, 1994.

"Jack in the box." TY BURR. "King leer." JAMES KAPLAN. *Entertainment*, Jan. 8, 1993.

"The sexy legend. . . ." MICHAEL SEGELL. *Cosmopolitan*, Aug. 1992.

"Happy Jack." NANCY COLLINS. *Vanity Fair*, Apr. 1992.

Jack Nicholson: An Unauthorized Biography. DONALD SHEPERD. St. Martin's, 1991.

Jack Nicholson: The Unauthorized Biography. BARBARA SIEGEL and SCOTT SIEGEL. Avon, 1991.

"The myth that Jack built." STEVE ERICKSON. *Esquire*, Sep. 1990.

"Hollywood's wild card." BRIAN D. JOHNSON. *Maclean's*, Aug. 20, 1990.

"Jake Jake. . . ." JULIAN SCHNABEL. *Interview*, Aug. 1990.

"Forget it, Jack. . . ." JAMES GREENBERG. *American Film*, Feb. 1990.

The Films of Jack Nicholson. DOUGLAS BRODE. Carol, 1990.

Nicklaus, Jack William (1940–) Golf's "Golden Bear" made it to the top once again in 1993. In June, Jack Nicklaus had hopes of winning the U.S. Open, which was played at the Baltusrol Golf club in Springfield, New Jersey, site of his notable 1967 and 1980 wins, the latter with a record 272. But it was not to be. Winner

Lee Janzen tied that 1980 record, and won the tournament. However, in July, at the Cherry Hills Country Club in Englewood, Colorado, Nicklaus posted a tournament-winning, six-under-par 278, with a stirring one-shot finish over his old golf rival Tom Weiskopf. Nicklaus said the victory was especially meaningful because his poor showings of the previous year had left him on the verge of quitting competition, for the year—possibly for good—before he embarked on a program to increase his fitness and recapture his golf swing. Nicklaus also continued to act as a course design consultant around the world.

Born in Columbus, Ohio, Nicklaus attended Ohio State University, winning the U.S. Amateur title twice (1959; 1961), before turning professional in 1961. He joined the Professional Golfers Association (PGA) Tour in 1962, winning his first U.S. Open. Through 1992, he won a total of 70 PGA tournaments, 18 international titles, and five titles on the Senior PGA Tour, which he joined in 1990. Among his major titles were the U.S. Open (1962; 1967; 1972; 1980), Masters (1963; 1965; 1966; 1972; 1975; 1986), PGA Championship (1963; 1971; 1973; 1975; 1980), Tournament of Champions (1963; 1964; 1971; 1973; 1977), Australian Open (1964; 1968; 1971; 1975; 1976; 1978), British Open (1966; 1970; 1978), World Golf Classic (1971; 1972; 1973), Tournament of Players Championship (1974; 1976; 1978), PGA Seniors Championship (1991), and U.S. Senior Open (1991). Among his

many honors were PGA Player of the Year five times (1967; 1972; 1973; 1975; 1976), Byron Nelson award (1964; 1965; 1972; 1973), Dunlop Professional Athlete of the Year (1972), Golfer of the Year (1973), Bob Jones Award (1975), *Sports Illustrated*'s Sportsman of the Year (1978), Golfer of the 1970's (1979), Athlete of the Decade (1979), and Golfer of the Century (1988); he has also been named to the World Golf Hall of Fame. Nicklaus has also published numerous books, including *The Greatest Game of All* (1969), *The Full Swing* (1982), and *My Most Memorable Shots in the Majors* (1988). He married Barbara Bash in 1960 and has five children.

FURTHER READING

"Shooting for seven." TIM ROSAFORTE. *Sporting News*, Apr. 13, 1992.
"Ten living legends. . . ." STEVE WULF. *Sports Illustrated*, Dec. 23, 1991.
"Long live the king. . . ." E. M. SWIFT. *Sports Illustrated*, Apr. 9, 1990.
"The glow of the bear." ROBERT LEWIS. *Maclean's*, Apr. 10, 1989.

Nicolais, Alwin (1910–93) Connecticut-born Alwin Nicolais began his career as a pianist and puppeteer, turning to the study of dance in 1933, and beginning to choreograph in 1936. He studied with Hanya Holm at Bennington's summer dance school (1938–40), and became an assistant to Holm after military service during World War II. He became musical director of the Henry Street Settlement Playhouse in 1948, retired as a dancer in 1950, and began his emergence as a multi-media oriented choreographer, designer, and composer, beginning with "Masks, Props, and Mobiles" (1953), followed by such works as "Kaleidoscope (1956), "Imago" (1963), "Scenario" (1971), and "Crucible" (1985). His dance company toured widely in the United States from the 1960s, and in Europe from 1968. Nicolais was artistic director of the French national center for contemporary dance (1979–81), afterward receiving several honors; his many awards included an American National Medal of the Arts. He was survived by his companion, choreographer Murray Louis, and two sisters. (d. New York City; May 8, 1993)

FURTHER READING

Obituary. *The Times* (of London), May 12, 1993.
Obituary. *New York Times*, May 10, 1993.

Nixon, Patricia (Thelma Catherine Ryan; 1912–93)

Nevada-born Pat Nixon worked as a secretary, studied merchandising at the University of Southern California, and was a high school teacher before her 1940 marriage to Richard M. Nixon, then a young lawyer. Early in her husband's career, she actively supported his political campaigns, but later limited her political work to the essentially ritual public appearances required of a candidate and officeholders' wife. There is no evidence that she enjoyed the celebrity that inevitably accompanied her husband's tenure in the White House any more than the massive publicity that accompanied his fall. From 1974, back in private life for the first time in almost three decades, she was able to shield herself more effectively from unwanted public attention. She was survived by her husband and two daughters, one of whom, Julie Nixon Eisenhower, wrote *Pat Nixon: The Untold Story* (1986). (d. Park Ridge, New Jersey; June 22, 1993)

FURTHER READING

Obituary. *Current Biography*, Aug. 1993.
" 'Love bears all things'. . . ." MELINDA BECK. *Newsweek*, July 5, 1993.
"The woman in the cloth coat." BONNIE ANGELO. *Time*, July 5, 1993.
"Forged of hidden steel. . . ." PAM LAMBERT. *People*, July 5, 1993.
Obituary. *The Times* (of London), June 23, 1993.
Obituary. *New York Times*, June 23, 1993.
"Pat Nixon. . . ." CARL SFERRAZZA ANTHONY. *Good Housekeeping*, Jan. 1991.

Nixon, Richard Milhous (1913–)

Former President Richard Nixon, existing permanently under the shadow of Watergate and his forced resignation to avoid impeachment, nonetheless continued to play a public role in 1993. In January, the shadow of the lost Vietnam War also pursued him, in the form of the final report of the Senate Select Committee on POW-MIA Affairs. It was highly critical of his administration's role as the Vietnam War was ending and afterward, in regard to POW's possibly left behind at the end of the war, though finding no convincing evidence that any were still being held.

Nixon in 1993 continued his campaign for increased American aid to Russia, visited Moscow in February, and on March 8 met with President Clinton in the White House to discuss Russian aid. He also announced support of the North American Free Trade Agreement (NAFTA), but did not join former presidents Carter, Ford, and Bush at the September 14 White House signing ceremony. A new book, *Beyond Peace*, was scheduled for 1994 publication. On the personal side, his wife, Pat, died on June 22.

California-born Nixon became the 37th President of United States in 1969 and resigned to avoid impeachment in 1974, after his complicity in the Watergate scandal was exposed. He had previously been a leading member of the House Un-American Activities Committee while a California Congressman (1947–51), senator from California in the early 1950s, and Dwight D. Eisenhower's vice-president (1953–61). He was defeated for the presidency by John F. Kennedy in 1960, but came back to defeat Hubert Humphrey in 1968 and George McGovern in 1972. He presided over the last stages of his country's defeat in Vietnam and played a key role in reestablishing U.S.-Chinese relations, but is in the long run chiefly notable for his multiple illegal attacks on domestic political opponents, which climaxed with the Watergate Democratic National Committee break-ins by his "plumbers," and the subsequent attempted coverup, which together ultimately destroyed his career and reputation.

His written works include *RN: Memoirs of Richard Nixon* (1978); *The Memoirs of Richard Nixon* (2 vols.; 1978–79); *1999: Victory Without War* (1988); *In the Arena: A Memoir of Victory, Defeat, and Renewal* (1990), and *Seize the Moment* (1992). Nixon's 1934 B.A. was from Whittier College, and his 1937 LL.B. from Duke. Nixon and Thelma Catherine "Pat" Ryan married in 1940; they had two children.

FURTHER READING

Cold War Patriot and Statesman: Richard M. Nixon. LEON FRIEDMAN and WILLIAM F. LEVANTROSSER, eds. Greenwood, 1993.
"How Nixon came in. . . ." MICHAEL BESCHLOSS. *Vanity Fair*, June 1992.
"He's back again." DAVID POSTMAN. *New Republic*, Apr. 6, 1992.
George Wallace, Richard Nixon, and the Transformation of American Politics. DAN T. CARTER. Baylor University Press, 1992.
The Limits of Power: The Nixon and Ford Administrations. JOHN R. GREENE. Indiana University Press, 1992.

The Great Cover-up: Nixon and the Scandal of Watergate. BARRY SUSSMAN. Stephanus, 1992.

The Nixons. CASS R. SANDAK. Crestwood/Macmillan, 1992.

Watergate and Afterward: The Legacy of Richard M. Nixon. LEON FRIEDMAN and WILLIAM F. LEVANTROSSER, eds. Greenwood, 1992.

Richard M. Nixon Oral History Project. CALIFORNIA STATE UNIVERSITY-FULLERTON ORAL HISTORY OFFICE STAFF, ed. Meckler, 1992.

Nixon: Ruin and Recovery, 1973–1990, 1991. *Nixon: The Triumph of a Politician, 1962–1972,* 1989. *Nixon: The Education of a Politician, 1913–1962,* 1987. STEPHEN E. AMBROSE. Simon & Schuster.

Silent Coup: The Removal of Richard Nixon. LEN COLODNY and ROBERT GETTLIN. St. Martin's, 1991.

Richard M. Nixon: Politician, President, Administrator. LEON FRIEDMAN and WILLIAM F. LEVANTROSSER, eds. Greenwood, 1991.

One of Us: Richard Nixon and the American Dream. TOM WICKER. Random, 1991.

Richard Nixon. RICHARD M. PIOUS. Silver Burdett, 1991.

The Great Stream of History: A Biography of Richard M. Nixon. LAURIE NADEL. Macmillan, 1991.

Richard Nixon: The Making and Unmaking of a President. REBECCA LARSEN. Watts, 1991.

Richard Nixon and His America. HERBERT S. PARMET. Little, Brown, 1990.

Richard M. Nixon, President. SALLIE RANDOLPH. Walker, 1989.

Richard Milhous Nixon: The Rise of an American Politician. ROGER MORRIS. Holt, 1989.

Nolte, Nick (1942–) During 1993, Nick Nolte's *Lorenzo's Oil* (1992) enjoyed a successful theatrical run and then went into home video rentals, while Nolte made the comedy *I'll Do Anything*, co-starring Albert Brooks and directed by James L. Brooks. The $40 million film was made as a musical, but test screenings that began during the summer made it clear that major surgery was in order, and the film, originally scheduled for Christmas release, was rescheduled for early 1994.

Forthcoming was a starring role as a college basketball coach in *Blue Chips*, directed by William Freidkin, with a cast that included Mary McDonnell, Shaquille O'Neal, Bob Cousy, and Ed O'Neill. Also forthcoming was a starring role opposite Greta Scacchi in *Jefferson in Paris*, directed by James Ivory, written by Anthony Chase, Ruth Prawer Jhabvala, and James Ivory, and produced by Ismail Merchant.

Nebraska-born Nolte spent years in regional theater before emerging as a film star in the mid-1970s in *The Deep* (1977), and went on to star in such films as *Who'll Stop the Rain* (1978), *North Dallas Forty* (1979), *Cannery Row* (1982), *48 Hours* (1982), *Under Fire* (1983), *Down and Out in Beverly Hills* (1986), *Three Fugitives* (1989), *Everybody Wins* (1990), *Another 48 Hours* (1990), *Q&A* (1990), *Cape Fear* (1991), *The Prince of Tides* (1991), and *Lorenzo's Oil* (1992). He has also appeared in television, most notably in *Rich Man, Poor Man* (1976). Nolte attended Pasadena College. He has been married three times, since 1984 to Rebecca Linger; they have one child.

FURTHER READING

"The time of Nick Nolte." SUSAN SCHINDEHETTE. *People,* Mar. 16, 1992.

"Nick's time." LISA SCHWARZBAUM. *Entertainment,* Jan. 24, 1992.

"Nick Nolte." TRIP GABRIEL. *US,* Jan. 1992.

"Off-balance heroes." PETER DE JONGE. *New York Times Magazine,* Oct. 27, 1991.

"Nick Nolte. . . ." STEPHANIE MANSFIELD. *GQ-Gentlemen's Quarterly,* Oct. 1991.

"Prince of Hollywood." MEREDITH BRODY. *Connoisseur,* Sep. 1991.

"Nick Nolte." PETER BECKER. *M Inc.,* Sep. 1991.

"The passions of. . . ." ERIC GOODMAN. *McCall's,* Sep. 1991.

Norman, Gregory John (1955–) Australian golfer Greg Norman completed his rebound back to the top in 1993. In 1990–92, he had gone 27 months without a win, breaking a 15-year run of winning at least one tournament a year and falling to 53rd on the PGA money list; several times over the years he had led in the final round, only to lose. But after winning the Canadian Open in 1992, Norman posted an extraordinary year in 1993. Most notable was his win at the 122nd British Open, at the Royal St. George, in Sandwich, where he beat the then-top-ranked defending champion Nick Faldo by two strokes; Norman's total of 267 was the lowest four-round total every posted for the Open, and Norman himself described his final 64 as the "first perfect round" he had ever played. In 1993, Norman also won two other titles, the Doral Open and Japan's Taiheiyo Masters, finishing third on the PGA money list with $1.3 million. In December, he was voted World Player of the Year by *Golf Digest* magazine's editors.

Two key disappointments in 1993 were lost leads at the Tour Championship, where he bogeyed two of the last three holes to lose the lead, and the PGA Championship, where he missed a birdie putt that would have forced a playoff. The golfer nicknamed the "Great White Shark" also hosted his annual televised *Shark Shootout*. In 1993, he also published *Greg Norman's Instant Lessons*, written with George Peper.

Born in Queensland, Australia, but now based in Florida, Norman turned professional in 1976, winning his first victory that year in Australia's West Lakes Classic, and joining the Professional Golfers Association (PGA) Tour in 1983. He built a total of 60 international tournament wins through 1992, among them the Martini International (1977; 1979; 1981), French Open (1980), Australian Open (1980; 1985; 1987), Dunlop Masters (1981; 1982), Australian Masters (1981; 1983; 1984; 1987; 1989; 1990), Kemper Open (1984; 1986), Canadian Open (1984; 1992), British Open (1986), European Open (1986), Australian Tournament Players Championship (1988; 1989), Italian Open (1988), Doral Ryder Open (1990), and Memorial Tournament (1990). Norman was the leading PGA money-winner in 1986 and 1990, when he also led all four major tournaments going into the final round; he won the 1989 and 1990 Vardon Trophies. Norman has also played on numerous Australian national teams, winning two Dunhill Cups. He published *Shark Attack!: Greg Norman's Guide to Aggressive Golf* (1988), written with George

Peper. He is married to Laura Norman and has two children.

FURTHER READING

"Greg's new swing." CLAUDE HARMON, JR. *Golf Magazine*, Oct. 1993.
"Return of the shark." JAMES DEACON. *Maclean's*, Sep. 13, 1993.
"Shark attack." RICK REILLY. *Sports Illustrated*, July 26, 1993.
"Greg Norman." JOHN GARRITY. *Sports Illustrated*, Oct. 28, 1991.
"Georgia on our minds." GEORGE PEPER. *Golf Magazine*, Apr. 1991.
"Shark bites back." MIKE LUPICA. *Esquire*, June 1990.
"Norman, Greg." *Current Biography*, Aug. 1989.
A Victory for Jamie: The Story of Greg Norman and Jamie Hutton. LAWRENCE LEVY and GORDON S. WHITE, JR. International Merc (OH), 1989.
Greg Norman. SUSAN CREIGHTON. Crestwood/Macmillan, 1988.

Norman, Leslie (1911–93) British film producer and director Leslie Norman worked as a film editor at Ealing Studios in the late 1930s. He saw military service in Burma during World War II, until Ealing requested his return to edit *The Overlanders*, released in 1946. During the postwar period, he produced *Eureka Stockage* (1948), *Where No Vultures Fly* (1951; he also wrote the screenplay), *Mandy* (1952), and the classic *The Cruel Sea* (1953). He directed *The Night My Number Came Up* (1955), *X the Unknown* (1956), *The Shiralee* (1957), *Dunkirk* (1958), *Summer of the Seventeenth Doll* (1959), *The Long and the Short and the Tall* (1961), and *Mix Me a Person* (1962). He was survived by his wife, Elizabeth, and two sons. (d. Knebworth, England; February 18, 1993)

FURTHER READING

Obituary. *The Times* (of London), Feb. 22, 1993.

North, Henry Ringling (1910–93) With his older brother, John, Chicago-born Henry North took over the management of the financially ailing Ringling Brothers and Barnum and Bailey Circus after the death of John Ringling in 1936. John Ringling had been one of the five founders of the Ringling Brothers Carnival in 1884; they had taken control of the Barnum and

Bailey circus in 1908 and combined the two into "The Greatest Show on Earth" in 1919. Henry and John North took the circus through the remainder of the Great Depression, managed it back into financial health, and ran it until 1967, in the process retiring the canvas "big top" in favor of playing in arenas in the cities they visited; Henry stayed on as consultant after the selling the circus. Henry and Alden Hatch wrote *The Circs Kings: Our Ringling Family Story* (1960). He was survived by his wife, Gloria de la Feld, and a son. (d. Geneva, Switzerland; October 2, 1993)

FURTHER READING

Obituary. *The Times* (of London), Oct. 5, 1993.
Obituary. *New York Times*, Oct. 3, 1993.

North, Oliver (1943–)

On September 12, 1993, former Marine officer, White House aide, and Iran-Contra scandal figure Oliver North declared his candidacy for the seat held by Virginia Democratic Senator Charles Robb. North, a conservative Republican, had been moving toward a Virginia senatorial run since early 1992, had engaged in substantial fundraising activities, and had publicly declared his interest in August of that year. Always a controversial figure, he had attacked Governor L. Douglas Wilder as "King Douglas, the Wilder," singling out Wilder's support of abortion rights.

North remained highly controversial, sometimes in ways not to the liking of many of his fellow Republicans. He reportedly joined several other Republicans in "jokingly" vilifying gays at a March 12, 1993 Republican Party dinner at Tysons Corners, Virginia, a dinner at which African-Americans were also vilified. In 1993, North also published a new book, *One More Mission: Oliver North Returns to Vietnam*, written with David Roth.

North, a career Marine officer, was on active service in Vietnam (1968–69). He was deputy director of the military affairs bureau of the U.S. National Security Council (1981–86), working directly out of the White House; he became a Marine lieutenant-colonel in 1983. North was involved in developing several covert operations during his White House years. One of them blew up in late 1986, becoming the Iran-Contra affair, a set of scandals that resulted in North's dismissal from his White House post, though not from the Marines, in November 1986. North then became an international figure, testifying on television before congressional committees. He was indicted on Iran Contra-related charges on March 14, 1988 and convicted on three felony counts in May 1989. He had one of three counts overturned and two sent back to the trial court on appeal in 1990. All charges against North were dropped on September 16, 1991, after testimony by former National Security Advisor Robert C. McFarlane made it clear that the Iran-Contra hearings had fatally tainted the prosecution's case. North has published the bestseller *Under Fire: An American Story* (1991), written with William Novak. He is a graduate of the U.S. Naval Academy at Annapolis. He is married to Betsy (Frances Elizabeth) Stuart; they have three children.

FURTHER READING

"Oliver North's next war." PHILIP WEISS. *New York Times Magazine*, July 4, 1993.
"North, Oliver." *Current Biography*, Mar. 1992.
"Oliver North. . . ." *Christianity Today*, Nov. 25, 1991.
"The unsinkable. . . ." BARRETT SEAMAN. *Time*, Oct. 28, 1991.
Opening Arguments: A Young Lawyer's First Case: United States v. Oliver L. North. JEFFREY TOOBIN. Viking Penguin, 1991.
Guts and Glory: The Oliver North Story. BEN BRADLEE, JR. Fine, 1988.
The Secret Government. BILL MOYERS. Seven Locks, 1988.
Men of Zeal: A Candid Story of the Iran-Contra Hearings. WILLIAM S. COHEN and GEORGE J. MITCHELL. Viking Penguin, 1988.
Defiant Patriot: The Life and Exploits of Lieutenant Colonel Oliver North. PETER MEYER. St. Martin's, 1987.
Taking the Stand: The Testimony of Lieutenant Colonel Oliver L. North. DANIEL SCHORR, ed. Pocket Books, 1987.

Nosaka, Sanzo (1892–1993)

As a student in London, Sanzo Nosaka joined the new British Communist Party in 1920. Returning to Japan, he was a founder of the Japanese Communist Party in 1922, and for almost seven decades was Japanese communism's leading figure, becoming a legendary figure as he moved into his 80s and 90s. With the ascendancy of Japanese militarism and fascism in the 1930s, Nosaka was imprisoned and then went into exile, in the late 1930s fighting with Chinese Communist forces in north China. He returned to Japan in 1946, and was, until his retirement in 1982 at the age of 90, head of the Central Committee of the Japanese Communist Party, then becoming honorary chairperson of his party. In September 1992, documents from recently opened Soviet-period archives revealed that he had in the late 1930s falsely accused another leading Japanese communist, Kenzo Yamamoto, then a resident of the Soviet Union and working with the Comintern (Communist International), of being a spy for the Japanese goverment. Yamamoto was executed by the Soviets in 1939. Nosaka was removed as honorary chairperson in September 1992, and expelled from his party in December 1992. There were no survivors. (d. Tokyo; November 14, 1993)

FURTHER READING

Obituary. *The Times* (of London), Nov. 18, 1993.
Obituary. *New York Times*, Nov. 15, 1993.

Nunn, Sam (Samuel Nunn, Jr.; 1938–   )
Senate Armed Forces Committee chairman Sam Nunn, a conservative Georgia Democrat, went into sharp opposition to his own party's new President a few days after Bill Clinton's inauguration, publicly breaking with Clinton over his proposed ban on discrimination against gay men and lesbians in the armed forces. Clinton and Nunn worked out a compromise that was far short of Clinton's campaign promise to end such discrimination, but defused the confrontation, which had been very damaging to the new Democratic administration. Ultimately, the September defense appropriation bills established "don't ask, don't tell, don't pursue" as policy, providing that the question of sexual preference not be asked by the military. Nunn continued to oppose Clinton on a series of other issues during the first year of the new administration, perhaps most notably on the amounts of defense appropriations to be cut and on the amounts to be spent on economic stimulus.

Georgia-born Nunn was a Georgia state legislator (1968–72) and began his long career in the Senate in 1973. He became chairman of the Senate Armed Services Committee in 1986, was regarded as a possible 1988 Democratic presidential and then vice-presidential candidate during the run-up to the Dukakis nomination, but refused the vice-presidential nomination when it was offered. During the late 1980s, as the Cold War wound down, Nunn moved from general support of military spending plans toward a call for large cuts in spending, armaments, and force levels. In late July 1990, his committee reported out the first large Senate defense-cuts bill in decades. Nunn continued to support substantial cuts during 1991 and 1992. His B.A. and LL.B. were from Atlanta's Emory University. He married Colleen O'Brien in 1964; they have two children.

FURTHER READING

"Washington Nunn sense. . . ." *National Catholic Reporter*, May 21, 1993.
"The mystique of. . . ." SIDNEY BLUMENTHAL. *New Republic*, Mar. 4, 1991.
"Wanted. . . . " DOUGLAS HARBRECHT. *Business Week*, Nov. 19, 1990.
"Born to be mild. . . ." TIMOTHY NOAH. *Washington Monthly*, Dec. 1989.
"Smart, dull and very powerful." MICHAEL KRAMER. *Time*, Mar. 13, 1989.

Nureyev, Rudolf Hametovich

(1938–93) Born near Lake Baikal, the great dancer Rudolf Nureyev grew up in Moscow and Ufa, in Bashgiria, where he became an apprentice in the Ufa Opera ballet company. He trained with the Kirov Ballet in St. Petersburg (then Leningrad), and joined the Kirov in 1958, immediately being put into solo roles and quickly emerging as one of the leading Soviet dancers of his time. Three years later, in 1961, he defected to the West, and within a year was a world figure in the ballet, very notably as Margot Fonteyn's partner at London's Royal Ballet. During the next quarter century, he danced as a guest artist in many countries, and became a leading choreographer, as well, of such works as *Tancredi* (1966), *Romeo and Juliet* (1977), and *Washington Square* (1985). He was artistic director of the Paris Opera Ballet (1983–89) and became its principal choreographer in 1989, while continuing to dance throughout the world. He starred on stage in musical theater for the first time in a U.S. tour of *The King and I* (1989–90). He has also appeared in several films, including *Valentino* (1977) and *Exposed* (1982). He made his conducting debut in July 1991, leading a Vienna chamber orchestra, and continued in the year that followed, conducting in Europe, making his American debut with the American Ballet Theater in May 1992, and leading the University of California at San Francisco Orchestra in July. But as the year progressed, it became clear that Nureyev was very ill, and then desperately so. He died of AIDS-related illness. There were no survivors. (d. Paris; January 6, 1993)

FURTHER READING

"Nureyev, documented." ROSE ANNE THOM. *Dance Magazine*, July 1993.
"Fugitive glimpses. . . ." CLIVE BARNES. *Dance Magazine*, Apr. 1993.
"Nureyev dies in Paris." ROBERT JOHNSON. *Dance Magazine*, Mar. 1993.
"Memories of Nureyev." JOAN ACOCELLA. *Vogue*, Mar. 1993.
"The last days of Nureyev." BOB COLACELLO. *Vanity Fair*, Mar. 1993.
Obituary. *Current Biography*, Feb. 1993.
"Quantum leaper." LAWRENCE O'TOOLE. *Entertainment*, Jan. 22, 1993.
"Lord of the dance. . . ." MICHAEL CRABB. *Maclean's*, Jan. 18, 1993.
"The daring young man." LAURA SHAPIRO. *Newsweek*. Jan. 18, 1993.
"Two who transformed their worlds. . . ." MARTHA DUFFY. *Time*, Jan. 18, 1993.
Obituary. *Variety*, Jan. 11, 1993.
Obituary. *The Times* (of London), Jan. 7, 1993.
Obituary. *New York Times*, Jan. 7, 1993.
"At the bedside of. . . ." ETTORE MO. Dec. 8, 1992.
"And now, superstar?" IRIS M. FANGER. *World Monitor*. June 1991.
"Nureyev. . . ." ELIZABETH KAYE. *Esquire*, Mar. 1991.

O

Oates, Joyce Carol (1938–) Noted and prolific author Joyce Carol Oates published two major works in the 1993. The first was her 22nd novel, *Foxfire: Confessions of a Girl Gang*, the powerful adult reflections of Madeleina Faith Wirtz who, as one of five teenage girls, led by Legs Sadovsky, took sometimes murderous revenge on adult males who had used and tyrannized them. The other was a collection of 25 early short works, *Where Are You Going, Where Have You Been? Selected Early Stories*, generally drawn from her short story collections of the 1960s and 1970s, but including some stories that had never appeared in book form. One offering is

her own twist on Henry James's *Turn of the Screw*. Also in 1993, Oates was one of 19 authors whose stories were collected in *The Literary Lover: Great Contemporary Stories of Passion and Romance*, edited by Larry Dark; she described the early impact on her of Tod Browning's *Dracula* for *The Movie That Changed My Life*, edited by David Rosenberg; and she submitted and discussed various drafts of a work for *A Piece of Work: Five Writers Discuss Their Revisions*, edited by Jay Woodruff. Scheduled for 1994 publication was *Haunted: Tales of the Grotesque*.

Oates emerged as a major American novelist in the mid-1960s, with a group of powerful novels that had in common their view of the United States as an insane place inhabited by people on or over the edge of madness; these included *With Shuddering Fall* (1964), *A Garden of Earthly Delights* (1967), and *them* (1969), which won a National Book Award. She later wrote such novels as *Childworld* (1976), *Son of the Morning* (1978), *Bellefleur* (1980), *Solstice* (1985), and *Black Water* (1992). She has also written, by her own estimate, over 400 short stories, which appeared in various magazines and collections, including 16 of her own collections, from *By the North Gate* (1963) through *Where Is* Here?: Stories (1992). Other works include several poetry collections, beginning with *Women in Love* (1968); several plays, including *Miracle Play* (1974) and *In Darkest America* (1990); and several volumes of essays, including *Woman Writer: Occasions and Opportunities* (1988). She has also edited numerous works, most notably *The*

Oxford Book of American Short Stories (1992). Oates taught at the University of Detroit (1961–67), the University of Windsor at Ontario (1967–87), and Princeton University (1987–). Her B.A. was from Syracuse University, and her M.A. from the University of Wisconsin. She is married to Raymond Smith.

FURTHER READING

Joyce Carol Oates. GREG JOHNSON. Twayne/Macmillan, 1994.
"Playboy interview. . . ." LAWRENCE GROBEL. *Playboy*, Nov. 1993.
Broken Silences: Interviews with Black and White Women Writers. SHIRLEY M. JORDAN, ed. Rutgers University Press, 1993.
"Princeton pastoral. . . ." *House & Garden*, June 1990.
Conversations with Joyce Carol Oates. LEE MILAZZO, ed. University Press of Mississippi, 1989.
Understanding Joyce Carol Oates. GREG JOHNSON. University of South Carolina Press, 1987.
Joyce Carol Oates. HAROLD BLOOM, ed. Chelsea House, 1987.
Joyce Carol Oates, Artist in Residence. EILEEN T. BENDER. Indiana University Press, 1987.

O'Brien, Conan (1963–) After the May 1993 announcement that Conan O'Brien was taking over the late-night television talk-show slot being vacated by David Letterman, O'Brien cracked to a reporter who described him as a relative unknown, "Let's have none of that. I am a complete unknown." In truth, this young comedian with his roots in the *Harvard Lampoon* had virtually no on-the-air television experience, beyond acting in a few sketches on "Saturday Night Live." But his quirky charm attracted NBC executives who saw a 40-minute mock segment with Mimi Rogers and "Seinfeld" 's Jason Alexander taped on Jay Leno's "Tonight" set. After negotiations with Garry Shandling fell through, they chose him over better known candidates, including Dana Carvey and Dennis Miller, reminding observers that David Letterman had been largely unknown when he started "Late Night" a decade earlier. Max Weinberg, longtime drummer from Bruce Springsteen's E Street Band, was named music director for the show, leading O'Brien to quip, "This is the first time in television history where the music director is better known than the host." By year's end, NBC had to be reasonably satisfied. After his initial show on September 13th, opening with John Goodman, George Wendt, Drew Barrymore, and Tony Randall, O'Brien built a solid audience, especially among the younger viewers so desired by networks.

Born in Brookline, Massachusetts, O'Brien received his B.A. in American History and Literature from Harvard University in 1985. While there, he worked on *The Harvard Lampoon* (1981–85), as president (1983–84). He was a writer for HBO's "Not Necessarily the News" (1985–87), in the same period appearing on-stage with the comedy troupe The Groundlings in Los Angeles; was writer and producer of the syndicated "The Wilton North Report" (1987); was a performer and writer with "The Happy Happy Good Show" in Los Angeles and Chicago (1988); then became a writer for "Saturday Night Live" (1988–91), sharing an Emmy for outstanding writing in comedy series (1989), also working as a writer on "Lockwell" (1991). He then became writer and producer on Fox's "The Simpsons" (1991–93), and on his own "Late Night with Conan O'Brien" (1993–).

FURTHER READING

"Conan." TOM FIELDS-MEYER. *TV Guide*, Aug. 28, 1993.
"Can Conan cut it?" RICK MARIN. *Vogue*, Aug. 1993.
"Conan O'Brien." THOMAS FIELDS-MAYER. *Esquire*, July 1993.
"Educating Conan" LYNN HIRSCHBERG. *Vanity Fair*, July 1993.

Ochoa, Severo (1905–93) Born in northern Spain, Severo Ochoa did not practice as a doctor after his 1929 graduation from the University of Madrid medical school, instead going into research in the life sciences. He worked with Otto Meyerhoff in Germany (1929–31), and taught and researched at the University of Madrid medical school (1931–36). Ochoa left Spain at the onset of the civil war, and worked in Germany and Britain before emigrating to the United States. He taught at Washington University and settled at New York University, where he taught biochemistry from 1942 until his retirement in 1986. He then returned to Spain. A leading figure in biochemistry, Ochoa in 1959 shared a Nobel prize for medicine with Arthur Kornberg, for their complementary work on RNA and DNA, which made a major contribution to the discovery of the genetic code. Ochoa in 1956 cooperated with Wendell Stanley in using RNA to synthesize an artificial virus. There were no survivors. (d. Madrid; November 3, 1993)

FURTHER READING

Obituary. *The Times* (of London), Nov. 6, 1993.
Obituary. *New York Times*, Nov. 3, 1993.

O'Connell, Helen (1920–93) Big band singer Helen O'Connell left high school in Lima, Ohio to become a singer in the mid-1930s. Her big break came in 1939, when she was "discovered" by bandleader Jimmy Dorsey while singing with Larry Funk's band at New York's Village Barn. She became nationally known in the early 1940s, for her recordings of "Green Eyes," "Amapola," and "Tangerine," all duets with Bob Eberly for the Dorsey band, and for her solos in such songs as "You've Got Me This Way" and "Arthur Murray Taught Me Dancing in a Hurry." O'Connell appeared on television and recorded during the 1950s, although her career sagged as styles in popular music changed. She made a considerable comeback in 1978–79, touring widely with Rosemary Clooney, Margaret Whiting, and Rose Marie in "4 Girls 4." She was survived by her husband, Frank DeVoi, and four daughters. (d. San Diego; September 9, 1993)

FURTHER READING

Obituary. *Down Beat*, Dec. 1993.
Obituary. *Billboard*, Sep. 25, 1993.

Obituary. *New York Times*, Sep. 19, 1993.
Obituary. *The Times* (of London), Sep. 16, 1993.

O'Connor, Sandra Day (1930–   ) Speaking for a unanimous Court, Sandra Day O'Connor, the first woman to become a justice of the Supreme Court, wrote the landmark opinion in *Harris v. Forklift Systems*, ruling that workers need not prove that they had suffered psychological damage or were unable to perform their tasks to successfully charge sexual harassment, instead applying the rule of "workplace equity." She also wrote the majority opinion in *Shaw v. Reno*, ruling that "bizarrely" shaped voting districts created to provide minority representation could be constitutionality challenged. She also wrote a concurring dissenting opinion in *Bray v. Alexandria Women's Health Clinic*, which allowed Operation Rescue to blockade abortion clinics. O'Connor voted with the majority on several other major cases, including *Church of the Lukumi Babalu Aye v. City of Hialeah*, ruling unconstitutional three city ordnances banning ritual animal sacrifice; *Herrera v. Collins*, which sharply limited the ability of those on death row to gain stays of execution on the basis of alleged later discovery of new evidence; *Sale v. Haitian Centers Council*, which ruled that Haitian refugees could be intercepted in international waters and forcibly returned to Haiti without violating American and international law; *Zobrest v. Catalina Foothills School District*, ruling that local governments could pay for special services to the disabled in parochial schools, as compliance with federal equal educational opprtunities for the disabled laws; *St. Mary's Honor Center v. Hicks*, ruling that workers must provide proof of specific discrimination against them to claim protection of civil rights laws; *Wisconsin v. Mitchell*, ruling that states could prescribe increased sentences for hate-motivated crimes; *Alexander v. Reno*, which ruled that the First Amendment did not protect $25 million of books and movies destroyed, many of them not obscene, after a seller had been convicted as a pornographer; and *Lamb's Chapel v. Center Moriches Union Free School District*, in which the Court ruled unanimously that religious groups had equal access to school facilities as other organizations in the community.

El Paso-born O'Connor made history in 1981 when she became the first woman Supreme

Court justice, the climax of long careers in law and politics. She had moved from private practice to become Arizona assistant attorney general (1965–69), into politics as an Arizona state senator (1969–75), and then back into a series of Arizona judicial posts, ultimately becoming a state court of appeals judge (1979–81). O'Connor's 1950 B.A. and 1952 LL.B. were from Stanford. She married John Jay O'Connor in 1952; they have one child.

FURTHER READING

Sandra Day O'Connor: Justice for All. BEVERLY GHERMAN. Puffin, 1993.
Sandra Day O'Connor: American Women of Achievement. PETER HUBER. Chelsea House, 1992.
Sandra Day O'Connor. PAUL DEEGAN. Abdo & Daughters, 1992.
Sandra Day O'Connor. NORMAN L. MACHT. Chelsea House, 1992.
"A new day in court." LAUREN TARSHIS and JAMES EARL HARDY. *Scholastic Update*, Nov. 1, 1991.
Sandra Day O'Connor: A New Justice, a New Voice. BEVERLY BERWALD. Fawcett, 1991.
Sandra Day O'Connor. BEVERLY GHERMAN. Viking Penguin, 1991.
Sandra Day O'Connor. PETER HUBER. Chelsea House, 1990.
Eight Men and a Lady. HERMAN SCHWARTZ et al. National Press, 1990.

Olajuwon, Hakeem Abdul (1963–)

Houston Rockets basketball star Hakeem Olajuwon may be headed for MVP status. In the 1992–93 season, he was runner-up (by a vote of 10–9) to Charles Barkley for National Basketball Association (NBA) most valuable player in the 1992–93 season, coming in ahead of three-time MVP Michael Jordan. Many observers think him to be the best all-around center in the game today; at season's end, he had bested his main rivals at that position-Patrick Ewing, Shaquille O'Neal, and David Robinson-in every key area, in scoring (at 26.1 points, 4th in the league), rebounding (13.0, also 4th), field-goal percentage (.529, 13th overall), and blocks (4.17 a game, tops in the league, for the third time in four years). Not surprisingly, he was named to the NBA All-Defensive team, as the league's top defender. He also became one of only three players ever (Kareem Abdul-Jabbar in 1975–76 and David Robinson 1990–91) to have over 2000 points, 1000 rebounds, and 300 blocks in a single season, and only the second (after Abdul-Jabbar in 1975–76 and 1978–79) to record over 250 assists and 300 blocks in the same season.

Then, at the start of the 1993–94 season, with his team following the strong defensive strategy laid out by coach Rudy Tomjanovich, Olajuwon led his Houston Rockets team to a remarkable 15–0 start to the season, tying a 45-year-old league record. By the new year, 1994, the team had a league-leading 24–4 record. On the personal side, Olajuwon became a United States citizen in April 1993.

Born in Lagos, Nigeria, Olajuwon came late to basketball, in 1978, having started as a soccer and handball player. Even so, he quickly became a dominant force on the basketball court, first as a student at the University of Houston (1980–84), leading his team to three straight NCAA semifinals (1982–1984), then professionally with the Houston Rockets (1984–), as the top pick in the NBA college draft. He was named to the NBA All-Star Team six times (1985–90; 1992) and the NBA All-Defensive First Team four times (1987–88; 1990; 1992). Earlier called Akeem Olajuwon, he added the H to his first name in 1991.

FURTHER READING

"Olajuwon, Hakeem." *Current Biography*, Nov. 1993.
"Sweet dream." MICHAEL KNISLEY. *Sporting News*, May 24, 1993.

"A dream of a season." ROBERT FALKOFF. *Sporting News*, Apr. 12, 1993.

Hakeem Olajuwon: Tower of Power. GEORGE R. REKELA. Lerner, 1993.

Sports Great Hakeem Olajuwon. RON KNAPP. Enslow, 1992.

Oldman, Gary (1958–   ) Highly visible after his 1992 roles as presidential assassin Lee Harvey Oswald and Dracula, actor Gary Oldham continued to star in character leads in 1993. His major role of the year was as a corrupt New York police sergeant in the film *Romeo Is Bleeding*, directed by Peter Medak and co-starring Lena Olin, Annabella Sciorra, Juliette Lewis, and Roy Scheider. Oldman also starred as a pimp in the film thriller *True Romance*, directed by Tony Scott, in a cast that included Christian Slater, Patricia Arquette, Dennis Hopper, Brad Pitt, Christopher Walken, and Val Kilmer

Forthcoming was a starring role in the film *Leon*, written, produced, and directed by Luc Besson, and co-starring Jeanne Reneau. Also forthcoming was a starring role in the film *Murder in the First*, directed by Marc Rocco and co-starring Christian Slater and Kevin Bacon.

London-born Oldman spent several years in the British theater before making his film debut as Sid Vicious in *Sid and Nancy* (1986), which he followed with a starring role as playwright Joe Orton in *Prick Up Your Ears* (1987). He con-

tinued to emerge as a star in *Track 29* (1988), *We Think the World of You* (1988), *Criminal Law* (1988), *Paris by Night* (1989), *Chattahoochee* (1990), *State of Grace* (1990), *Rosencrantz and Guildenstern Are Dead* (1991), JFK (1991), and *Bram Stoker's Dracula* (1992). He has also appeared in several television films. He attended Rose Buford Dramatic College. He has been married twice, and has one child.

FURTHER READING

"Neck romance." RACHEL ABRAMOWITZ. *Premiere*, Dec. 1992.

"Gary Oldman." TRISH DEITCH ROHRER. *Entertainment*, Nov. 20, 1992.

"A vicious undertaking. . . ." SUSAN DWORKIN. *New York Times Magazine*, Nov. 8, 1992.

"Gary Oldman." DENNIS HOPPER. *Interview*, Jan. 1992.

"Gary Oldman. . . ." FRED SCHRUERS. *Rolling Stone*, Oct. 18, 1990.

O'Leary, Hazel Rollins (1947–   ) Secretary of Energy Hazel O'Leary, like her predecessors, spent much of her first year attempting to deal with the intractable problems associated with nuclear energy, while at the same time trying to initiate a reorganization of her department. In February, her department was forced by Congressional exposure to reveal a July 1992 internal report indicating major environmental pollution hazards stemming from continuing leaks in the storage tanks at the Hanford, Washington nuclear site; while major problems continued at other major atomic installations, such as at the Savannah River plant in South Carolina, where the tritium-producing K reactor, was permanently closed down for safety reasons. On May 5, after years of resistance on the part of the Energy Department, O'Leary announced acceptance of Occupational Safety and Health Administration (OSHA) worker safety monitoring of nuclear plants. And while the Energy Department in July announced acceptance of foreign reactor fuel, a decision quickly challenged by environmentalist legal actions, no national repository for nuclear waste yet had gone into operation.

On December 28, O'Leary opened a major effort to expose more than two decades of radiation experiments that had been done on humans by the United States government, often without their consent or informed consent; many hundreds and perhaps thousands of people were involved, some of them children and others prisoners, most of them victims of a Cold War scientific establishment that clearly thought itself above law and morality. In beginning to expose what had happened, she also called for compensation to the victims and their families. The matter immediately became a national scandal, many comparing the experimenters to the infamous German doctors of the Nazi period, and calling their actions crimes against humanity. President Clinton immediately welcomed O'Leary's action, called for full disclosure, and set several federal departments to the task of learning what had been done, to whom, and by whom.

Virginia-born O'Leary's 1959 B.A. was from Nashville's Fisk University, and her 1966 J.D. from New Jersey's Rutgers University. She was a New Jersey assistant attorney general, an assistant Essex County, New Jersey prosecutor, and a partner in the Coopers and Lybrand accounting firm, before entering federal energy regulation with the Department of Energy during the Ford administration. She also worked in the U.S. Department of Energy during the Carter administration. In 1981, she joined O'Leary Associates, a consulting firm in the energy field operated by her husband, John O'Leary, now deceased, who was a deputy Energy Secretary during the Carter administration. She became executive vice president of the Minneapolis-based Northern States Power Company in 1989. She has one son.

FURTHER READING

"Black clout in the Clinton administration." *Ebony*, May 1993.
"Clinton picks. . . ." *Jet*, Jan. 11, 1993.
"Words of advice. . . ." *MPLS-St. Paul*, Apr. 1991.

O'Neal, Shaquille (1972–) Basketball fans continued to see newcomer Shaquille O'Neal as one of the emerging stars of the game. Indeed, among card collectors, "Shaq" was in 1993 overtaking Michael Jordan, even spurring the sale of counterfeit cards, and helping to make basketball the most popular sport for collectors, as baseball has traditionally been. Fans also voted O'Neal onto the starting team in the National Basketball Association (NBA) All-Star game, ahead of seven-time All-Star and three-time starting center, Patrick Ewing, making him the first rookie since Michael Jordan in 1985 to be elected to the starting lineup. O'Neal was philosophical about the choice, noting: "It's a fan thing. If it were a coach thing, the coaches probably would've put Ewing first and me second." In the end, both played well, O'Neal with 21 points, 9 rebounds, and 9 blocks, also making two free throws to send the game into a second overtime—especially sweet since free throws are usually the weakest part of his game. To no one's surprise, he was almost unanimously named NBA Rookie of the Year.

O'Neal's team, the Orlando Magic, had a chance to squeak into the Eastern Conference playoffs, but failed in the end. In the new 1993–94 season, O'Neal was by year's end leading the league in scoring, with a 28.3 average per game. He helped his team to its best December ever, at 10–7, and was named NBA Player of the Month. Meanwhile, O'Neal was also widely seen in commercials; taking the side of one sponsor, Pepsi, in a dispute with USA Basketball, apparently cost him a spot on the World Championship team, and possibly therefore on the 1996 Olympic team. He also recorded a rap album, *Shaq Diesel*, that got wide attention and, at year's end, was rising in the charts, and published a book, *Shaq Attaq!*, written by Jack McCallum.

An "Army brat," New Jersey-born O'Neal and his family lived in various places, including Germany twice, where Louisiana State University (LSU) coach Dale Brown spotted him in a basketball clinic. He attended Cole High School in San Antonio, Texas, then moved on to LSU, where he was named national player of the year by AP, UPI, and Sports Illustrated after his sophomore season, during which he broke his leg and was a two-time consensus first-team All-American. Leaving LSU after his junior season in 1992, O'Neal was the top pick in the NBA college draft, going to the Orlando Magic, with a seven-year, $40 million contract.

FURTHER READING

Shaquille O'Neal. KEN RAPPOPORT. Walker, 1994.

Shaquille O'Neal, Center of Attention. BRAD TOWNSEND. Lerner, 1994.

Shaquille O'Neal. ELLEN E. WHITE. Scholastic, 1994.

Meet Shaquille O'Neal. PUBLICATIONS INTERNATIONAL STAFF. NAL-Dutton, 1993.

Shaquille O'Neal: Shaq Attack. TED COX. Childrens, 1993.

Shaquille O'Neal. NEIL COHEN. Bantam, 1993.

Shaq Impaq: The Unauthorized Untold Story of the NBA's Newest Superstar Shaquille O'Neal. BRUCE HUNTER. Bonus Books, 1993.

Meet Shaquille O'Neal. STEPHANIE ST. PIERRE. Random, 1993.

"The next superstar." *New York Times Magazine*, Nov. 15, 1992.

"Shaq attack!" WILLIAM PLUMMER and RON RIDENHOUR. *People*, Dec. 16, 1991.

"College's biggest deal? . . ." BRUCE SCHOENFELD. *Sporting News*, Feb. 4, 1991.

"Shack attack." CURRY KIRKPATRICK. *Sports Illustrated*, Jan. 21, 1991.

Owada, Masako: See Naruhito, Crown Prince and Masako, Crown Princess.

Ozal, Turgut (1927–93) Turkish premier Turgut Ozal was born and grew up in Malatya, in central Anatolia. An engineer and economist, he worked as an economist with the World Bank and with Turkey's state planning office in the 1970s. He was a deputy prime minister (1980–82), during the period of military government. Ozal became prime minister after his Motherland Party won the 1983 elections, resigning in 1989 when facing difficult elections, and instead having his parliament elect him to a seven-year term as president of Turkey. Although the post had been largely ceremonial, he took a series of activist international positions, becoming especially visible during the Persian Gulf War, when he led his country into the anti-Iraq alliance. He also voiced strong support for the emerging Muslim countries of the former Soviet Union, most recently supporting Azerbaijan in its war with Armenia. He was survived by his wife, Semra, a daughter, and two sons. (d. Ankara; April 17, 1993)

FURTHER READING

Obituary. *Current Biography*, June 1993.

"After Ozal. . . ." *Economist*, Apr. 24, 1993.

Obituary. *The Times* (of London), Apr. 19, 1993.

Obituary. *New York Times*, Apr. 18, 1993.

"Losing a staunch friend." FREDERICK PAINTON. *Time*, Nov. 4, 1991.

"Hoping Saddam Hussein. . . ." DAVID AIKMAN. *Time*, May 13, 1991.

"Any takers?" DONALD KIRK. *National Review*, Apr. 15, 1991.

"Atta Turk. . . ." AMY E. SCHWARTZ. *New Republic*, Apr. 15, 1991.

"An ally deserves better." STROBE TALBOTT. *Time*, Jan. 28, 1991.

" 'Bridge between two worlds'. . . ." CARLA ANNE ROBBINS. *U.S. News & World Report*, Aug. 20, 1990.

P

Pacino, Al (Alfredo Pacino; 1940–   ) For his portrayal of blind lieutenant colonel Frank Slade in Martin Brest's *Scent of a Woman*, Pacino was awarded the 1993 best actor Academy Award. He had also been nominated in the best supporting actor category for his role as unscrupulous real estate boiler room salesman Ricky Roma, in James Foley's *Glengarry Glen Ross*, adapted by David Mamet from his play. Pacino also won a best actor Golden Globe award for *Scent of a Woman*, and received a career award from New York's American Museum of the Moving Image.

Pacino's major work of 1993 was the title role in the film *Carlito's Way*, directed by Brian De Palma and co-starring Sean Penn and Penelope Ann Miller. Forthcoming was a starring role in the film *Two Bits*, directed by James Foley and co-starring Mary Elizabeth Mastrantonio and Gerlando Barone.

New York-born Pacino is one of the leading alumni of the Actor's Studio, beginning his long association with the group in 1966 and becoming one of its artistic directors (1982–84). He worked in the theater through the 1960s, and in the early 1970s emerged as a major film star, breaking through as Michael Corleone in *The Godfather* (1972). He went on to star in such films as *Serpico* (1973), *The Godfather, Part II* (1974), *Dog Day Afternoon* (1975), *Cruising* (1980), *Scarface* (1983), *Sea of Love* (1989), *Dick Tracy* (1990), *The Godfather, Part III* (1990), and *Frankie and Johnny in the Clair De Lune* (1991). He also continued to work in the theater, in such plays as *Camino Real* (1973), *Richard III* (1973), *American Buffalo* (1981), *Salome* (1992), and *Chinese Coffee* (1992).

FURTHER READING

". . . And justice for all." Bronwen Hruska. *Entertainment Weekly*, Nov. 12, 1993.
"Conquest of space." David Denby. *New York*, Dec. 21, 1992.
"Al alone." Maureen Dowd. *GQ-Gentleman's Quarterly*, Sep. 1992.
Bomb: Interviews. Betsy Sussler, ed. City Lights, 1992.
"Al Pacino." Julian Schnabel. *Interview*, Feb. 1991.

"Pacino powers. . . ." JOHN PODHORETZ. *Insight*, Jan. 14, 1991.

Life on the Wire: The Life and Art of Al Pacino. ANDREW YULE. Fine, 1991.

Packwood, Bob

Packwood, Bob (1932–   ) Oregon Senator Bob Packwood was pursued throughout 1993 by sexual harassment charges brought against him late in 1992 by 10 women, most of them former employees. Packwood denied all sexual harassment, but did state that he had an alcohol problem, for which he was seeking treatment, and made a general apology for any possibly offensive behavior. His accusers were not placated; by early February 1993, the number of women accusing him of sexual harassment had grown to 23, and would reach 26. A year-long Senate Ethics Committee investigation proceeded.

The Senate Rules Committee on May 20 rejected an Oregon residents' petition to unseat Packwood on the basis of alleged election fraud, consisting of campaign trail denials that he was being charged with sexual harassment.

The case took a bizarre turn, when in his October 5–6 testimony before the Ethics Committee Packwood revealed that his detailed diaries, kept since 1969, contained relevant material. Packwood allowed the committee to examine his earlier diaries, but refused access past 1989; he then resisted a committee subpoena of the diaries, but was forced by the full Senate to give them up. During the course of the dispute, Ethics Committee chairman Richard Bryan suggested publicly that there might be criminal violations revealed in the diaries. At year's end, with Congress in recess, Packwood was back home in Oregon, pursued everywhere by his accusers and other opponents, with speculation growing as to when and if he might resign.

Portland-born Packwood served in the Oregon House of Representatives (1963–69), and in 1968 scored a major upset victory over long-time Democratic Senator Wayne Morse, becoming at 36 the youngest Senator of his day. A thoroughly independent Republican liberal, he often voted in opposition to his party's positions, although equally often voted with his party. In 1985–86, he was chairman of the Senate's Finance Committee, and was a key figure in the passage of the 1986 tax law revision. Ironically, he was for many years one of the Senate's most vocal and effective women's rights advocates, and was only one of two Republicans to vote against the confirmation of Clarence Thomas to be Supreme Court justice, after the Thomas-Anita Faye Hill confrontation. In 1992, Packwood won another Senate term, defeating Democrat Les AuCoin 52–46 percent. Packwood's B.A. was from Williamette University, and his LL.B. from New York University. Formerly married, he has two children.

FURTHER READING

"The trials of Bob Packwood." TRIP GABRIEL. *New York Times Magazine*, Aug. 29, 1993.

Panetta, Leon

Panetta, Leon (1938–   ) Office of Management and Budget (OMB) Director Leon Panetta during 1993 played a major role in defending proposed Clinton administration spending cuts and deficit reduction plans, beginning immediately after Clinton's February 17 Congressional address, in which he explained his five-year economic plan. Panetta's major work was the detailed $1.52 trillion proposed budget sent to Congress on April 8, which stressed deficit reduction, long Panetta's chief preoccupation. Foreseeing a long, difficult budget fight in Congress, he was one of those who successfully advised Clinton to hold his massive health care reform plan until after the budget was passed. Elsewhere, however, he underestimated Clinton's political skills, in late April calling the

North American Free Trade Agreement (NAFTA) "dead" because of lack of support in Congress. During the hard budget fight, he played a key final role in helping craft compromises that won vital conservative support.

California-born Panetta began his political career as a Congressional assistant after his Navy service (1964–66). He was director of the U.S. Office of Civil Rights in the Department of Health, Education, and Welfare (1969–70), but was fired by the Nixon administration for his strong civil rights advocacy. He then served as executive assistant to New York Mayor John Lindsay (1970–71). After practicing law (1971–76), he successfully ran for Congress, and was an eight-term California Democratic Congressman (1976–92), leaving to become Clinton's budget director. While in Congress, he was on the House of Representatives Budget Committee for 12 years, four of them as committee chairman. During the Reagan and Bush administrations, he was a key Congressional critic of the often-understated budgets submitted to Congress, and a leading liberal who was especially concerned about the environmental threats posed by offshore oil drilling in his California coastal district. He sponsored the establishment of a national marine sanctuary at Monterey Bay.

Panetta's 1960 B.A. was from the University of Santa Clara, and his 1963 J.D. from the University of Santa Clara Law School. He is married to the former Sylvia Marie Varni; they have three sons.

FURTHER READING

"Leon lays it on the line." KEN KELLEY. *Mother Jones*, Sep.-Oct. 1993.
"Panetta, Leon E." *Current Biography*, June 1993.
"Clinton team. . . . " THOMAS FRIEDMAN. *New York Times*, Dec. 11, 1992.
"Clinton's team. . . . " DAVID WESSEL and JEFFREY H. BIRNBAUM. *Wall Street Journal*, Dec. 10, 1992.
"To omb or not to omb?" PAUL HOUSTON. *Los Angeles Times*, Nov. 30, 1992.

Parish, Mitchell (1900–93) Born in

Lithuania, Mitchell Parish grew up on New York's East Side, and went work as a lyricist and song plugger when still in his mid-teens. He became one of the most notable popular song lyricists of his day, creating song lyrics for more than 600 songs. "Star Dust" was his best-known work; written as an instrumental piece by Hoagy Carmichael in 1927, Parish added its lyrics in 1929. The song became a popular hit in the early 1930s, and since been revived again and again, by among others Tommy Dorsey, Frank Sinatra, Nat "King" Cole, and Willie Nelson. The 1986 Broadway musical *Star Dust* was a retrospective of the many songs with Parish's lyrics. Among his other most popular standards were "Sophisticated Lady," "Stars Fell on Alabama," "Moonlight Serenade," "Volare," "Tzena, Tzena, Tzena," "Deep Purple," " Dream, Dream, Dream," "Sweet Lorraine," and "Stairway to the Stars." He was survived by a daughter and a son. (d. New York City; April 30, 1993)

FURTHER READING

Obituary. *Billboard*, Apr. 10, 1993.
Obituary. *New York Times*, Apr. 2, 1993.

Parker, Cecilia (1905–93) Born in Fort

William, Canada, Cecilia Parker trained as an opera singer at the Toronto Academy of Music. Instead, she became a sometime Hollywood star and very durable supporting player in the 1930s, appearing in such films as *The Rainbow Trail* (1932), *Gun Justice* (1933), Greta Garbo's *The Painted Veil* (1934), and *Ah Wilderness!* (1935). In 1937, she appeared as Mickey Rooney's older sister, Marion, in *A Family Affair*, the first of the hugely successful Andy Hardy films, and went on to appear in the series for two decades, in 1958 playing in *Andy Hardy Comes Home*. She was survived by her husband, Richard Baldwin, a daughter, and two sons. (d. Ventura, California; July 25, 1993)

FURTHER READING

Obituary. *The Times* (of London), Aug. 12, 1993.

Parkinson, C(yril) Northcote

(1909–93) British author and historian C. Northcote Parkinson became famous for his invention (he called it "discovery") of "Parkinson's Law," that "work expands so as to fill the time available for its completion," first published in an article for *The Economist* magazine in 1955, and then in his bestselling 1958 book *Parkin-*

son's Law. In a world increasingly beset by aggressive bureaucracies, his additional comment-that work expands to occupy the people available for its completion-was equally well received, even by the bureaucrats who were his targets, though with no apparent lasting impact on the people and practices being criticized. After World War II naval service, Parkinson lectured on naval history at the University of Liverpool, in 1950 became Raffles Professor of History at the University of Malaya, and after the success of his book focused on his diverse body of writings, expanding already well established interests. Among his works were books on the British in Malaya, several business books, novels, and many essays. He was survived by his wife, Iris Hilda Waters, two daughters, and three sons. (d. Canturbury, England; March 9, 1993)

FURTHER READING

Obituary. *Current Biography*, May 1993.
Obituary. *New York Times*, Mar. 12, 1993.
Obituary. *The Times* (of London), Mar. 11, 1993.
"How do you cure injelitance?" PETER BRIMELOW. *Forbes*, Aug. 7, 1989.

Parton, Dolly Rebecca (1946–) In 1993, country singer Dolly Parton issued the hit album *Slow Dancing With The Moon*, which she co-produced with Steve Buck. Among its hit songs were "Put A Little Love In Your Heart,"

"I'll Make Your Bed," and "Full Circle"; the latter also became a hit single. A second album was *Honkey Tonk Angels*, a hit collection of country classics sung with Loretta Lynn and Tammy Wynette.

Among Parton's other hit singles of the year were "The Day I Fall in Love;" "Romeo," with Billy Ray Cyrus, Tanya Tucker, Mary-Chapin Carpenter, Kathy Mattea, and Pam Tillis; "More Where That Came From;" and "You've Lost That Lovin' Feelin'," a duet with Neil Diamond from Diamond's album *Songs from the Brill Building.*

Forthcoming was the Chicago-set CBS television comedy series, "Dixie Fixin's," in which Parton plays the host of a cable television cooking show. Scheduled for 1994 publication was an autobiography, tentatively titled *Coat of Many Colors.*

Tennessee-born Parton began her country music singing and composing career in the mid-1960s, and emerged as a leading figure in country music in the early 1970s, with such well-received albums as *Coat of Many Colors* (1971), *My Tennessee Mountain Home* (1973), and *Jolene* (1974). In the late 1970s, she began to reach large rock music audiences as well, merging country and rock in the album *New Harvest . . . First Gathering* (1977). Among her other albums were the Grammy-winning *Here You Come Again* (1978), *Real Love* (1985), the Grammy-winning *Trio* (1986; with Emmylou Harris and Linda Ronstadt), *Rainbow* (1988), and *Eagle When She Flies* (1991). Her many songs included the Grammy-winning "Nine to Five." Her films include *Nine to Five* (1980), *The Best Little Whorehouse in Texas* (1982), *Rhinestone* (1984), *Steel Magnolias* (1989), and *Straight Talk* (1991). Among her other honors were Grammys as best female country vocalist (1978; 1981), a Country Music Association entertainer of the year award (1978), and an Academy of Country Music female vocalist award (1980). She is married to Carl Dean.

FURTHER READING

"Dolly Parton." MARY MURPHY. *TV Guide*, Nov. 27, 1993.
"Dolly. . . ." ALAN W. PETRUCELLI and MINDY HERMANN. *First for Women*, June 28, 1993.
"20 questions with. . . ." MICHAEL BANE. *Country Music*, May-June 1993.
" 'My toughest moment. . . .' " GLENN PLASKIN. *Ladies Home Journal*, Nov. 1992.

"What Dolly wants now." JOYCE MAYNARD. *McCall's*, May 1992.

"Good golly, Miss Dolly!" KEVIN SESSUMS. *Vanity Fair*, June 1991.

"Dolly Parton. . . ." HOLLY GLEASON. *Saturday Evening Post*, Oct. 1989.

"The quotable Dolly." KAREN JAEHNE. *Film Comment,* Sep.-Oct. 1989.

"Dolly Parton. . . ." PATRICK CARR. *Country Music*, Sep.-Oct. 1989.

"Daisy Mae in Hollywood." WILLIAM STADIEM and HERB RITTS. *Interview*, July 1989.

Behind Closed Doors: Talking with the Legends of Country Music. ALANNA NASH. Knopf, 1988.

Peale, Norman Vincent (1898–93)

Protestant religious leader Norman Vincent Peale was ordained in the Methodist Episcopal Church in 1922, and held ministries in Rhode Island and Brooklyn in the mid-1920s. In 1927, he became pastor of the University Methodist Church in Syracuse, New York, in that period making his first radio appearances. In 1932, he became minister of New York's Marble Collegiate Church, changing denominations from Methodist to Reformed Church. In 1935, he began his very popular radio ministry, his weekly sermons reaching millions of listeners. During this period, he also introduced church-based psychiatric services, and published the books *The Art of Living* (1937) and *You Can Win* (1939). In 1947, he published the bestseller *A Guide for Confident Living*, and in 1951 the worldwide bestseller *The Power of Positive Thinking*, continuing to publish on similar themes through the early 1990s. A leading Republican conservative, Peale opposed the election of Catholic John F. Kennedy on religious grounds. He was survived by his wife, Ruth, two daughters, and a son. (d. Pawling, New York; December 24, 1993)

FURTHER READING

Obituary. *New York Times*, Dec. 29, 1993.

Obituary. *The Times* (of London), Dec. 26, 1993.

God's Salesman: Norman Vincent Peale and the Power of Positive Thinking. CAROL V. R. GEORGE. Oxford University Press, 1992.

The Positive Thinkers: Popular Religious Psychology from Mary Baker Eddy to Norman Vincent Peale and Ronald Reagan. DONALD MEYER. Wesleyan/University Press of New England, 1988.

Peck, James (1915–93)

New York City-born James Peck dropped out of Harvard College after a year, in the mid-1930s, and went to Paris and then to sea, in that period helping to organize the National Maritime Union and becoming a journalist. A lifelong pacifist and civil rights activist, he was an active member of the War Resisters League and a conscientious objector during World War II, who was imprisoned for two years. During the postwar period, he continued to work with the War Resisters League, and also became editor of the Congress of Racial Equality (CORE) publication *The CORErelator*, holding that position through the major portion of the civil rights movement of the 1950s and 1960s. He was seriously injured by a Birmingham, Alabama mob during a 1961 Freedom Ride. Peck became a leading anti-Vietnam War activist during the 1960s and early 1970s. He was also a prolific essayist. He was survived by two sons. (d. Minneapolis; July 12, 1993)

FURTHER READING

Obituary. *New York Times*, July 13, 1993.

Perot, H. Ross (Henry Ross Perot; 1930–)

During 1993, billionaire Ross Perot carried forward the themes of his failed 1992 presidential campaign, sharply and continually criticizing a wide range of political leaders, practices, and policies. He began a renewed call for widespread federal government reforms in January, and continued to attack members of Congress of both parties, lobbyists, and appointed officials throughout the year. He criticized incoming President Bill Clinton's economic stimulus policies, called his deficit reduction package inadequate, and opposed his budget. Perhaps most visibly, he opposed the North American Free Trade Agreement (NAFTA), publishing the books *Save Your Job, Save Our Country: Why NAFTA Must Be Stopped Now* and *Not for Sale at Any Price: How We Can Save America for Our Children*; he was widely thought to have "lost" a nationally televised NAFTA debate with Vice President Al Gore on "Larry King Live." He also attempted to build his organization United We Stand into a major national force, with mixed results. Whether Perot was, during 1993, positioning himself for another presidential run in 1996 was a matter of conjecture;

beyond question, though, his was a major independent voice in American politics, to be taken into account by the leaders of both parties.

Born in Texarkana, Perot graduated from the U.S. Naval Academy in 1953, afterwards serving four years in the navy. He worked as an IBM salesperson (1957–62), then founded Electronic Data Systems in 1962, and in the decades that followed built it into a major company, selling it to General Motors for $2.5 billion in 1984, and in doing so, becoming GM's major stockholder. He resigned from the GM board of directors in 1986, and in 1988 founded Perot Systems. He has long been associated with attempts to secure more information about and possible release of U.S. prisoners of war thought to be held in Vietnam.

In 1992, Perot used substantial sums of his own money to build what seemed in the spring to be a promising run for the presidency, making the campaign a three-way race. But his campaign faded in June and July, and he withdrew from the race on July 17, shocking and dismaying thousands of active campaigners and millions of supporters. On October 1, Perot reversed course again, announcing that he was once again a presidential candidate. He then proceeded to actively campaign, spending tens of millions of dollars on television advertising, and becoming a full participant in the Clinton-Bush-Perot televised presidential debates. But his candidacy had been fatally compromised by his earlier withdrawal, and although he won 19 percent of the popular vote on November 3, he won no electoral votes. He and Margot Birmingham married in 1956; they have five children.

FURTHER READING

"Does the Sphinx. . . ." WICK ALLISON. *National Review*, Sep. 20, 1993.

"Loving too much. . . ." FRED BARNES. *New Republic*, Aug. 9, 1993.

"Perot and con." CHRISTOPHER GEORGES. *Washington Monthly*, June 1993.

"Perot keeps going and going." GLORIA BORGER and JERRY BUCKLEY. "Not thinking big enough." PAUL GLASTRIS. "The magnificent obsession." KENNETH T. WALSH and STEVEN V. ROBERTS. "A diversionary 'little war.'" DAVID R. GERGEN and GLORIA BORGER. *U.S. News & World Report*, May 17, 1993.

H. Ross Perot: The Man Who Woke up America. BOB ITALIA. Abdo & Daughters, 1993.

H. Ross Perot. GENE BROWN. Rourke, 1993.

The Big Bio of Ross Perot. CAROLE MARSH. Gallopade, 1992.

Ross Perot: the Candidate: A Portrait of the Man

and His Views. CECIL JOHNSON. Summit (TX), 1992.

Ross Perot: In His Own Words. TONY CHIU. Warner, 1992.

Ross Perot Speaks Out: In His Own Words. JAMES W. ROBINSON. Prima, 1992.

Ross Perot: The Man Behind the Myth. KEN GROSS. Random, 1992.

Petrovic, Drazen (1964–93)

On June 7, 1993, Croatian basketball star Drazen Petrovic was killed in a motor vehicle accident near Ingolstadt, Germany, when the car in which he was riding smashed into a truck that had jumped the lane divider and stopped in the path of ongoing traffic. Petrovic became a Yugoslav national team star in the 1980s, winning world attention in the 1988 Olympics. He played for the National Basketball Association (NBA) Portland Trail Blazers for a season and a half (1989–91), was traded to the New York Nets in 1991, and there became an American basketball star, who led the Nets in scoring during the 1992–93 season. Petrovic also led the Croatian national team at the 1992 Barcelona Olympics.

FURTHER READING

Obituary. *New York Times*, June 8, 1993.

Pfeiffer, Michelle (1959–)

For her starring role in the 1992 film *Love Field*, Michelle Pfeiffer was nominated for a 1993 best actresss Academy Award and a Golden Globe best actress award. In 1993, she scored a triumph in the acclaimed film *The Age of Innocence*, a faithful screen adaptation of the Edith Wharton novel, set in 1870s New York high society. The film starred Daniel Day-Lewis as Newland Archer, a rich young lawyer, Winona Ryder as May Welland, his proper provincial fiancée, and Pfeiffer as sophisticated Elena Olenska, who has just returned to New York from her marriage to a Polish Count; the film was written by Jay Cocks and Martin Scorsese, and directed by Scorsese. Also in the cast were Alec McCowen, Alexis Smith, Geraldine Chaplin, Michael Gough, and Jonathan Pryce, with Joanne Woodward narrating.

Forthcoming for Pfeiffer were starring roles opposite Jack Nicholson in the film *Wolf*, directed by Mike Nichols and co-starring Mia Farrow, James Spader, and Richard Jenkins; and opposite Richard Gere in the film *Higgins and Beach*, directed by Jon Amiel.

On the personal side, Pfeiffer, in March adopted a baby daughter, Claudia Rose Pfeiffer.

California-born Pfeiffer very quickly emerged as one of the leading film players of the 1980s, starring in such films as *Grease 2* (1982), *Scarface* (1983), *Into the Night* (1984), *Ladyhawke* (1985), *Sweet Liberty* (1986), *The Witches of Eastwick* (1987), *Married to the Mob* (1988), *Tequila Sunrise* (1988), *Dangerous Liaisons* (1989), *The Fabulous Baker Boys* (1989; she was nominated for an Oscar), *The Russia House* (1990), *Frankie and Johnny* (1991), *Batman Returns* (1992), and *Love Field* (1992). In the summer of 1989, she appeared as Olivia in *Twelfth Night* at the New York Shakespeare Festival. She was formerly married to actor Peter Horton.

FURTHER READING

"Belle Michelle." LESLIE BENNETTS. *Vanity Fair*, Sep. 1993.
"Blond ambivalence." JAMES KAPLAN and TY BURR. *Entertainment*, Jan. 29, 1993.
"The bat's meow. . . ." GERRI HIRSHEY. *Rolling Stone*, Sep. 3, 1992.
"The two lives of Catwoman." MICHAEL LIPTON. *People*, July 13, 1992.
"What she did. . . ." JEFF ROVIN. *Ladies Home Journal*, June 1992.
"Tough guise." JONATHAN VAN METER. *Vogue*, Oct. 1991.
"Queen for a decade." MARC ELIOT. *California*, Sep. 1991.
"The fabulous Pfeiffer girl." ROBERT SEIDENBERG. *American Film*, Jan. 1991.
"Michelle Pfeiffer as. . . ." HAL HINSON. *Esquire*, Dec. 1990.
"Pfeiffer, Michelle." *Current Biography*, Mar. 1990.

Phillips, Lou Diamond (1962–) In 1993, actor Lou Diamond Phillips starred in the film *Shadow of the Wolf*, set in an Eskimo culture in the mid-1930s Canadian north. Directed by Jacques Dorfmann and written by Rudy Wurlitzer and Evan Jones, the film was based on the novel *Agaguk* by Yves Theriault; Toshiro Mifune, Jennifer Tilly, and Donald Sutherland co-starred. Phillips also starred in the television film *Extreme Justice*, directed by Mark Lester,

as a detective in the mystery-shrouded Los Angeles Police Department Special Investigation Section, noted for its violent sting operations.

Forthcoming was a starring role in the film *Sioux City*, to be directed by Phillips. Also forthcoming-some day-is the film *The Dark Wind*, made in 1991, and starring Phillips in what was widely expected to be his breakthrough role, as Navajo tribal policeman Jim Chee, in the film version of the Tony Hillerman mystery novel. The film, caught in the 1992 Carolco Pictures financial disaster, was still in the can during 1993.

After playing in cabaret as a comedian, and in small roles in theater and television, Phillips suddenly emerged as one of the leading young film stars of the late 1980s, beginning with his role as Mexican-American rock star Richie Valens in the Luis Valdez film *La Bamba* (1987). He went on to appear in such films as *Stand and Deliver* (1987), *Young Guns* (1988; and the 1990 sequel *Young Guns II*), *Disorganized Crime* (1989), *Renegades* (1989), *First Power* (1989), *Show of Force* (1989), and *Ambition* (1991). Texas-born Phillips attended the University of Texas. He is married to actress Julie Cypher.

FURTHER READING

"Does Lou Diamond Phillips. . . ." Alice Lane. *Mademoiselle*, Feb. 1990.
"Lou Diamond Phillips. . . ." *Teen*, Sept. 1989.

Phoenix, River (1970–93) On October 31, 1993, actor River Phoenix collapsed and died after leaving a Los Angeles nightclub. A postmortem examination indicated that he had died of a massive, accidental drug overdose. Oregon-born Phoenix, child of a missionary family, spent most of his early life in Venezuela, then moved with his family to Los Angeles. He began his stage and screen career with a role in the television series "Seven Brides for Seven Brothers" (1982). He emerged as a film star as an abused child in Rob Reiner's *Stand By Me* (1986), and was featured in several other films, among them *Mosquito Coast* (1986), *Running On Empty* (1988), *Little Nikita* (1988), *Indiana Jones and the Last Crusade* (1989), *My Own Private Idaho* (1991), and *Sneakers* (1992). He was filming *Dark Blood* when he died. He was survived by his parents, three sisters, and a brother.

FURTHER READING

"The sad and sudden end. . . ." JEFF GILES. *Newsweek*, Nov. 15, 1993.

"His own private agony." RICHARD CORLISS. *Time*, Nov. 15, 1993.

"River's end." SHELLEY LEVITT. *People*, Nov. 15, 1993.

"River's edge." DANA KENNEDY. *Entertainment Weekly*, Nov. 12, 1993.

Obituary. *The Times* (of London), Nov. 3, 1993.

Obituary. *New York Times*, Nov. 1, 1993.

Obituary. *Variety*, Nov. 1, 1993.

"My own private interview." MALISSA THOMPSON. *Seventeen*, Aug. 1993.

"River Phoenix, Keanu Reeves." GINI SIKES. *Interview*, Nov. 1991.

" 'Stand By Me'. . . ." *Seventeen*, July 1991.

River Phoenix: Hero and Heartthrob. GRACE CATALANO. Bantam, 1988.

Pinter, Harold

Pinter, Harold (1930–) Fifteen years after his last full-length play (*Betrayal*), Harold Pinter brought his very favorably received 80-minute-long one act play *Moonlight* to the London stage. Ian Holm starred as Andy, the dying father, in a cast that co-starred Claire Skinner as Bridget, Anna Massey as Bel, Michael Sheen as Fred, Douglas Hodge as Jake, Jill Johnson as Maria, and Edward de Souza as Ralph. Pinter also wrote the screenplay for the film *The Trial*, based on the 1913 Franz Kafka novel; directed by David Jones, the film starred Kyle McLachlan, Anthony Hopkins, Jason Robards, Polly Walker, and Juliet Stevenson. Forthcoming was a New York revival of Pinter's play *No Man's Land*, directed by David Jones, and starring Jason Robards and Christopher Plummer, with John Seitz and Tom Wood.

London-born Pinter began his career as an actor, from 1949 working largely in repertory. He moved into playwriting in the late 1950s, scoring his first major success with *The Caretaker* (1960; he also adapted it into the 1964 film), and went on to such works as *The Homecoming* (1965; and the 1973 film), *Old Times* (1970), *No Man's Land* (1975), *Family Voices* (1980), and *Party Time* (1991). He has also directed such plays as *Exiles* (1970), *Butley* (1971; and the 1973 film), *Otherwise Engaged* (1975), and *The Common Pursuit* (1984), and has written many screenplays, including *The Servant* (1962), *The Quiller Memorandum* (1965), *The Go-Between* (1969), *The French Lieutenant's Woman* (1980), *The Turtle Diary* (1984), *The Handmaid's Tale* (1990), *The Heat of the Day* (1990), *Reunion* (1991), and *The Comfort of Strangers* (1991). Pinter has been married twice, first to actress Vivien Merchant and since 1980 to the writer Antonia Fraser. He has one child.

FURTHER READING

Pinter at Sixty. KATHERINE H. BURKMAN et al, eds. Indiana University Press, 1993.

Harold Pinter: The Dramatist. CHITRANJAN MISRA. Advent (NY), 1993.

File on Pinter. PAGE. Heinemann, 1993.

"The Pinter principle." DONALD CHASE. *American Film*, Oct. 1990.

Harold Pinter, 2nd ed. BERNARD F. DUKORE. St. Martin's, 1990.

Harold Pinter. LOIS GORDON, ed. Garland, 1990.

Pinter the Playwright, 4th ed. MARTIN ESSLIN. Heinemann, 1988.

Harold Pinter. HAROLD BLOOM, ed. Chelsea House, 1987.

Plaidy, Jean: See Hibbert, Eleanor.

Pleven, René

Pleven, René (1902–93) French politician René Pleven spent much of his career in business. A law graduate of the University of Paris, he failed a civil service examination and became a telephone company manager in Canada and the United States before joining the London-based Free French forces of Charles De Gaulle. He became a member of De Gaulle's government in exile, was a member of the postwar constituent assembly and national assembly, and was a founder and chairman of the Democratic and Socialist Union of the Resistance. Pleven was minister of the economy and finance in the postwar French government. He broke with De Gaulle in 1947, joined the 1950 government as defense minister, and became prime minister (July 1950-Feb. 1951). He was prime minister again (Aug. 1951-Jan. 1952), defense minister again (1952–54), and for a short time in 1958 foreign minister. He was survived by his daughters. (d. Paris; January 13, 1993)

FURTHER READING

Obituary. *Current Biography*, Mar. 1993.

Obituary. *New York Times*, Jan. 20, 1993.

Obituary. *The Times* (of London), Jan 16, 1993.

Pontecorvo, Bruno (1913–93) Italian-born physicist Bruno Pontecorvo worked with Irène Joliot-Curie in Paris during the 1930s. He and his wife, Marianne Nordbloom, fled France to the United States in 1940, after the German invasion. He worked in Canadian atomic research (1943–48), at Montreal and later at the Chalk River nuclear establishment. Moving to Britain in 1949, he worked at the Harwell nuclear establishment. He and his family went to Rome on holiday in 1950, and from there traveled to the Soviet Union, where he spent the rest of his life. His "defection," if that is what it was, caused a major Cold War espionage scare at the time, for it was feared that he had taken atomic weapons information with him, and much was made of his statement to a security officer at Harwell that his brother was an Italian communist, though Pontecorvo himself had not been a "political" of any kind. He denied that he had ever worked on atomic weapons, east or west. He was survived by his wife and three sons. (d. Dubna, Russia; September 25, 1993)

FURTHER READING

Obituary. *The Times* (of London), Sep. 27, 1993.

Popp, Lucia (Uhorska Ves; 1939–93) Czech-born Lucia Popp, a leading lyric soprano, made her debut at the Bratislava Opera in 1963. Later that year, she also debuted at the Vienna State Opera, as Barbarina in Mozart's *The Marriage of Figaro*, beginning her long assocation with the composer and the theater. Also in 1963, she recorded *The Magic Flute*, conducted by Otto Klemperer. In a single year, she had established herself as a major figure in opera, a position she was to hold for the rest of her life; in all of the major roles in her range, in recital, and as an international recording star of the first rank, throughout her career taking on newly appropriate roles as her voice matured and changed. She was particularly associated with the operas of Mozart and Richard Strauss. She was survived by her husband, singer Peter Sieffert, and by her father. (d. Munich; November 16, 1993)

FURTHER READING

Obituary. *The Times* (of London), Nov. 18, 1993.
Obituary. *New York Times*, Nov. 17, 1993.

Powell, Colin Luther (1937–) Early in 1993, Lieutenant General Colin Powell, in his final year as chairman of the Joint Chiefs of Staff, strongly and publicly opposed incoming President Bill Clinton's proposed ban on discrimination against gay men and lesbians in the armed forces, and with Senator Sam Nunn won the far different "don't ask, don't tell, don't pursue" policy, providing that the question of sexual orientation not be asked by the military.

His main effort, however, seemed to be protection of the armed forces against what he considered too-deep budget cuts, and his main contribution the rather modest set of changes proposed in his "military roles and missions" report of February 12. On September 1, he joined Defense Secretary Les Aspin in announcing substantial cuts in the military, but far short of original Clinton administration goals. On questions of possible armed intervention, he continued to exert a cautionary influence, as in Bosnia, Somalia, and Haiti. Powell's formal retirement date was September 30; he was replaced by General John Shalikashvili.

On August 17, Random House announced that it would be publishing Powell's autobiography, reportedly for a $6.5 million advance.

New York-born Powell began his long military career in 1958. He has held a series of line and staff posts in Europe and the United States, including command posts in the 101st Airborne and 4th Infantry divisions. He was National Security Affairs assistant to President Reagan (1987–89). He was then appointed chairman of the Joint Chiefs of Staff by President George Bush on August 10, 1989; it was a historic "first," as he was the first African-American to hold the post. One of his earliest major tasks was the organization of the December 1989 Panama invasion. He also sent American forces into El Salvador, Liberia, and The Philippines, and played a major role in the Persian Gulf War.

Powell's 1958 B.S. was from the City University of New York, and his 1971 M.B.A. from George Washington University. Most unusually for one who went so far in the U.S. Army, he is not a West Point graduate, instead having become an officer through the Reserve Officer Training Corps (ROTC). He married Alma Johnson in 1962; they have three children.

FURTHER READING

"Colin Powell. . . ." STEVEN V. ROBERTS et al. *U.S. News & World Report*, Sep. 20, 1993.

"Everybody's dream candidate." HOWARD FINEMAN et al. *Newsweek*, Aug. 23, 1993.

"The demobilization. . . ." CLAUDIA GLENN DOWLING and DAVID HUME KENNERLY. *Life*, July 1993.

Sacred Honor: Colin Powell: The Inside Account of His Life and Triumphs. DAVID ROTH. Zondervan, 1993.

Colin Powell. DAVID ROTH and LINDA L. MAIFAIR. Zondervan, 1993.

Colin Powell: Soldier-Statesman-Statesman-Soldier. HOWARD MEANS. Fine, 1992.

Colin Powell: A Man of War and Peace. CARL SENNA. Walker, 1992.

Colin Powell. CATHERINE REEF. Twenty-First Century Books (MD), 1992.

Colin Powell: A Biography. JAMES HASKINS. Scholastic, 1992.

Colin Powell. WARREN BROWN. Chelsea House, 1992.

Story of Colin Powell and Benjamin Davis. KATHERINE APPLEGATE. Dell, 1992.

Colin Powell: Straight to the Top. ROSE BLUE. Millbrook, 1992.

" 'Nobody knows my politics' " TOM MATHEWS. "The reluctant warrior. . . ." EVAN THOMAS. *Newsweek*, May 13, 1991.

"America's Black Eisenhower. . . ." JOHN RANELAGH. *National Review*, Apr. 1, 1991.

"What next. . . ." STEVEN V. ROBERTS. *U.S. News & World Report*, Mar. 18, 1991.

"In the footsteps. . . ." BRUCE B. AUSTER. *U.S. News & World Report*, Feb. 4, 1991.

Colin Powell. JONATHAN EVERSTON. Bantam, 1991.

Colin Powell: Four Star General. ELAINE LANDAU. Watts, 1991.

Powell, Laurence M.: See King, Rodney.

Power, Katherine Ann

(c. 1949–) On September 23, 1970, Katherine Power, then a senior at Brandeis University and an anti-Vietnam war radical activist, drove the getaway car in the $26,000 armed robbery of Boston's State Street Bank and Trust Company. Boston police officer Walter A. Schroeder, Sr. was murdered during the robbery. Power then went into hiding, changed her name to Alice Metzinger in 1977, and settled under that name in Corvallis, Oregon, where she built a restaurant business and taught cooking.

On September 15, 1993, after plea bargaining with law enforcement authorities, she surren-dered, pleading guilty to manslaughter and armed robbery, rather than to murder. The case drew great national attention, as she was one of the last of the underground radical fugitives of her time. On October 6, Massachusetts state judge Robert Banks sentenced her to 8 to 12 years in prison, followed by a 20-year period of probation, and ordered that she not be able to profit from the sale of her story. Sentencing was accompanied by condemnatory statements from the oldest of murdered police officer Schroeder's nine children, Waltham, Massachusetts police sergeant Claire Schroeder. On November 23, 1993, Power was sentenced to a 5-year concurrent term on federal charges.

Power married longtime companion Ron Duncan in 1992; she has a 14-year-old son.

FURTHER READING

"Alice doesn't live here anymore." PAM LAMBERT. *People*, Oct. 4, 1993.

"The fugitive." BARBARA KANTROWITZ. *Newsweek*, Sep. 27, 1993.

Premadas, Ranasinghe

(1923–93) On May 1, 1993, Sri Lankan president Ranasinghe Premadas was assassinated, becoming yet another casualty of the long Sri Lankan Civil War. A Sinhalese born poor in Colombo, Premadas began his political career as a Labour member of the Colombo municipal council in 1950, and became deputy mayor of the city in 1955. Joining the United National Party in 1956, he rose to cabinet level rank in 1968, becoming housing minister in 1977. Premadas initially strongly opposed 1987 Indian intervention in the Sri Lankan civil war, but changed his position, going on to win the presidency in 1988. As president, he strongly prosecuted a campaign against terrorist Sinhalese guerrillas while attempting to negotiate with Tamil separatists; but the civil war continued. He was survived by his wife, Hema, a daughter, and a son.

FURTHER READING

Obituary. *The Times* (of London), May 3, 1993.

Price, Nick

(Nicholas Raymond Leige Price; 1957–) In golf, Nick Price is considered something of a late bloomer, but bloom he has. In 1992, he won his first major championship, the

Professional Golfers Association (PGA) Championship, as well as the Texas Open, and was one of four PGA Tour golfers to win more than $1 million for the year, bringing his career earnings to over $3.7 million. In 1993, he did even better, becoming one of the hottest golfers on the PGA Tour, ending up the leading money-winner and winning the prestigious Vardon trophy. His major 1993 win was the Players Championship in March, followed by the Greater Hartford Open in June, the Western Open in July, and the Federal Express-St. Jude Classic in Memphis in August. In all, he had an astonishing six wins in eleven months.

Born in South Africa to British parents, Price was raised in Rhodesia (now Zimbabwe) and joined the air force there in 1976, serving for two years. After winning the Junior World championship in California at age 17, he played on amateur tours in South Africa and Europe, before turning professional in 1977. He won the Swiss Open in 1980 and the World Series of Golf, his first victory on the PGA Tour, in 1983. Then came a long drought; his next win was not until 1991, when he captured the Byron Nelson Classic and the Canadian Open. He is married to Sue Price and has one son.

FURTHER READING

"Stymied no more." RICK REILLY. *Sports Illustrated*, Apr. 5, 1993.
"First Price." DAVID BARRETT. *Golf Magazine*, Oct. 1992.

"The Price is right." JOHN GARRITY. *Sports Illustrated*, Aug. 24, 1992.

Price, Vincent (1911–93)

St. Louis-born Vincent Price made his London stage debut in 1935, and in the same year starred opposite Helen Hayes in *Victoria Regina*. His later theater work included *Angel Street* (1941), a revival of Jean Anouilh's *Ardéle* (1975; he co-starred with his third wife, Coral Browne), and a long tour as Oscar Wilde in the one-man *Diversions and Delights* (1977–82). He made his film debut in *Service de Luxe* (1938), and appeared in more than 100 films, among them *The Private Lives of Elizabeth and Essex* (1939), *The Song of Bernadette* (1944), *Laura* (1944), and *The Three Musketeers*(1948). He emerged as the leading horror film star of his time in *The House of Wax* (1953), which was succeeded by *The Fly* (1958), *The House of Usher* (1958), *The Pit and the Pendulum* (1961), *Diary of a Madman* (1962), *The Raven* (1963), *The Masque of the Red Death* (1964), and *Theater of Blood* (1973). In a far different vein was *The Whales of August* (1987). Price was also a well-known art collector, lecturer, and writer, whose books included *The Drawings of Delacroix* (1966) and *The Vincent Price Treasury of American Art*. He also co-wrote several cookbooks with his second wife, Mary Grant. His autobiography was *I Like What I Know: A Visual Autobiography* (1959). He was survived by a daughter and a son. (d. Los Angeles; October 25, 1993)

FURTHER READING

Obituary. *Variety*, Nov. 15, 1993.
"The gable of gothic." *People Weekly*, Nov. 8, 1993.
Obituary. *The Times* (of London), Oct. 27, 1993.
Obituary. *New York Times*, Oct. 27, 1993.
Obituary. *Variety*, Oct. 26, 1993.
Price of Fear: The Film Career of Vincent Price. JOEL EISNER. Windsong (VA), 1993.
"Vincent Price. . . ." JEAN BARRETT. *Wine Spectator*, Dec. 15, 1990.
"Tim Burton and. . . ." GRAHAM FULLER and RODDY MCDOWALL. *Interview*, Dec. 1990.

Prince (Prince Rogers Nelson; 1958–)

In 1993, pop star Prince issued a 3-CD collection of his songs, "The Hits," which included some material never before released. One new work was

the well received "Peach;" another was "Pink Cashmere," also released as a hit single. He also released the hit rock single "The Morning Papers." Prince also issued the music video *The Hits Collection*, with 16 videos, some of them until then not commercially available. One of Prince's best received works of recent years was his music for the full-length ballet *Billboards*, premiered by the Joffrey Ballet in August.

In late April, Prince announced that he was "retiring from studio recording," in favor of other projects. But although his record sales and recording career had been sagging, most felt that his retirement was far more likely to become a rest, followed by an attempt to restart his career at a higher level.

Minneapolis-born Prince emerged as a recording star in the late 1970s and early 1980s, and in 1984 starred in the film *Purple Rain*, winning a 1985 Oscar for best original score. He also won three Grammys in 1985. His albums include *For You* (1978), *Dirty Mind* (1979), *Controversy* (1981), *Purple Rain* (1984), *Around the World in a Day* (1985), *Parade* (1986), *Sign O' the Times* (1987), *Lovesexy* (1988), *Batman* (1989), and *Diamonds and Pearls* (1991). Prince has also appeared in the films *Under the Cherry Moon* (1986), *Sign O' the Times* (1987), and *Graffiti Bridge* (1990).

FURTHER READING

"Prince talks." NEAL KARLEN. *Rolling Stone*, Oct. 18, 1990.

"Twin citians of the decade. . . ." ELIZABETH KAIBEL. *MPLS-St. Paul Magazine*, Jan. 1990.
Rock Lives: Profiles and Interviews. TIMOTHY WHITE. Holt, 1990.

Pryce, Jonathan (1947–) British stage and screen star Jonathan Pryce appeared in 1993 as corporate raider Henry Kravis in the fact-based, very well received television film; *Barbarians at the Gate*, the story of the 1980s RJR Nabisco takeover, directed by Glen Jordan and written by Larry Gelbart. James Garner also starred, in a cast that included Joanna Cassiday, Fred Dalton Thompson, Leilani Ferrer, Matt Clark, Jeffrey DeMunn, David Rasche, and Tom Aldredge. Pryce received an Emmy nomination for best supporting actor in miniseries or special and a CableAce nomination for best supporting actor in a movie or miniseries.

Pryce also appeared in the acclaimed film *The Age of Innocence*, adapted from the Edith Wharton novel, directed by Martin Scorsese, and starring Daniel Day-Lewis, Michelle Pfeiffer, and Winona Ryder. A third film appearance was in *A Business Affair*, directed by Charlotte Brandstrom, and co-starring Christopher Walken and Carole Bouquet.

A leading British actor, Pryce has played in a series of major stage roles from the mid-1970s. He won a Tony for *The Comedians* (1976), a production originating in England that transferred to New York. His 1980 *Hamlet* won Britain's Olivier Award. His plays include *The Caretaker* (1981), *Accidental Death of an Anarchist* (1984), *The Seagull* (1985), *Macbeth* (1986; he played the title role), and *Uncle Vanya* (1988). Pryce was widely acclaimed for his portrayal of the Eurasian pimp in the musical *Miss Saigon* (1989), with which he moved from London to Broadway, where he won a 1991 Tony as leading actor in a musical. He has also appeared in such films as *The Ploughman's Lunch* (1983), *Brazil* (1985), *The Doctor and the Devils* (1986), *Consuming Passions* (1988), *The Adventures of Baron Munchausen* (1988), *The Rachel Papers* (1989), *The Man from the Pru* (1991), and *Glengarry Glen Ross* (1992); in several television films; and in the television series "Roger Doesn't Live Here Any More" (1981). He attended the Royal Academy of Dramatic Art.

FURTHER READING

"Mr. Saigon." MICHAEL BILLINGTON. *Interview*, Apr. 1991.
"Mr. Saigon. . . ." CHRIS SMITH. *New York*, Mar. 11, 1991.

Pulitzer, Joseph, Jr. (1913–93) Actually

the third Joseph Pulitzer, newspaper publisher and art collector Pultizer was the grandson of the first Joseph Pulitzer, who founded the St. Louis *Post-Dispatch* in 1878 and established the Pulitzer Prizes in 1917.

Joseph Pulitzer, Jr., joined the *Post-Dispatch* in 1936, after his graduation from Harvard, and took over the newspaper and other family holdings in 1955, after his father's death. During his tenure, he expanded the publishing company's newspaper, television, and radio holdings greatly, while at the same time maintaining the position of the *Post-Dispatch* as a leader in American journalism. He also chaired the Pulitzer Prize board of directors (1955–80). Privately, Pulitzer was also a major modern art collector, who started collecting while still a student at Harvard, and who often lent large parts of collection to museums for public viewing. He was survived by his son, two sisters, and a brother. (d. St. Louis; May 26, 1993)

FURTHER READING

Obituary. *Variety*, June 7, 1993.
Obituary. *The Times* (of London), June 4, 1993.
Obituary. *New York Times*, May 27, 1993.

Q

Quaid, Dennis (Dennis William Quaid; 1954–) Dennis Quaid starred in 1993 opposite his wife, Meg Ryan, and James Caan in the film *Flesh and Bone*, written and directed by Steve Kloves. Quaid played a man who, as a boy, had been abused by his father, played by Caan. In a year in which child abuse continued to be a mounting national preoccupation, the film was timely.

Quaid also starred in the film *Wilder Napalm*, directed by Glenn Gordon Caron and co-starring Arliss Howard as his brother and Debra Winger as his brother's wife. The very poorly received film told the standard story of a battle between brothers over the wife of one of them; the twist introduced was that both brothers had the ability to create fires by willing them, which created an opportunity for special effects. Forthcoming was a starring role opposite Kevin Costner in the film *Wyatt Earp* written and directed by Lawrence Kasdan.

Houston-born Quaid played a lead as one of the four young men in *Breaking Away* (1979), and went on to roles in such 1980s films as *Longriders* (1979), *The Right Stuff* (1983), *Dreamscape* (1984), *Enemy Mine* (1985), and *The Big Easy* (1987). He starred as singer Jerry Lee Lewis in the film biography *Great Balls of Fire* (1989), and began the 1990s with *Come and See the Paradise* (1990) and *Postcards from the Edge* (1990). Quaid attended the University of Houston. He and his wife, actress Meg Ryan have a son. He is the brother of actor Randy Quaid.

FURTHER READING

"When Dennis met Meg." GEORGE KALOGERAKIS. *Vogue*, Nov. 1993.

"The devil and. . . ." JAN HOFFMAN. *Premiere*, Aug. 1989.

"Playing the killer." NICK TOSCHES. *Vogue*, July 1989.

"Simmer down, son." ROBERT PALMER. *American Film*, June 1989.

"Goodness gracious." JOHN ED BRADLEY. *Esquire*, Mar. 1989.

"Whole lotta shakin'." HERB RITTS and KEVIN SESSUMS. *Interview*, June 1989.

Dennis Quaid. GAIL BIRNBAUM. St. Martin's, 1988.

Quennell, Peter (1905–93) British literary figure Peter Quennell began his long career as a writer and essayist with several poems published while he still a student, and in 1926 published *Poems*, his debut book. In the seven decades that followed, he published a very wide variety of works, was a magazine editor and literary critic. He also became a very durable and much-sought man-about-London. His five marriages and numerous liaisons were a source of considerable media attention. He was a book critic with the *Daily Mail* (1943–56), edited *Cornhill* magazine (1944–51), and co-edited *History Today* (1951–79). His best-known body of work was on Byron, and included two biographies: *Byron* (1934) and *Byron, the Years of Fame* (1935). Among his other books were studies of John Ruskin, Alexander Pope, Samuel Johnson, and Vladimir Nabokov. He was survived by his wife, Marilyn, a daughter, and a son. (d. London; October 27, 1993)

FURTHER READING

Obituary. MICHAEL GRANT. *History Today*, Dec. 1993.
Obituary. *New York Times*, Oct. 31, 1993.
Obituary. *The Times* (of London), Oct. 29, 1993.
"Mr. and Mrs. Peter. . . ." DUNCAN FALLOWELL.
 American Scholar, Autumn 1992.

Quindlen, Anna (1953–) *New York Times* "Op-Ed" columnist Anna Quindlen published a collection of her columns in 1993, under the title *Thinking Out Loud: On the Personal, the Political, the Public and the Private*. In doing so, she brought to wider audiences her clear-eyed, compassionate, skeptical explorations of personal and political aspects of the key issues of the 1990's, from Anita Hill and Bill Clinton to abortion and AIDS to homelessness and rape, and showed why she received the Pulitzer Prize for Commentary in 1992. Quindlen was widely

seen publicizing the book, not least on Oprah Winfrey's popular talk show.

Quindlen began her career as a reporter for the *New York Post*. Moving to *The New York Times*, she wrote the popular "About New York" and "Life in the 30's" columns, becoming deputy metropolitan editor of the *Times*. She emerged as a nationally respected syndicated columnist in the late 1980s. Her books include *Living Out Loud* (1988), the novel *Object Lessons* (1991), and the children's book *The Tree That Came to Stay* (1992). Quindlen attended Barnard College. She is married to Gerald Krovatin, and has three children.

FURTHER READING

"Quindlen, Anna." *Current Biography*, Apr. 1993.
"Reporting the details of life." ROSE A. ADKINS.
 Writer's Digest, Mar. 1993.
She Said What?: Interviews with Women
 Columnists. MARIA BRADEN. University Press of Kentucky, 1993.
"Anna Quindlen. . . ." ALEXANDER M. SANTORA.
 Commonweal, Feb. 14, 1992.
"Anna Quindlen. . . ." SYBIL STEINBERG. *Publishers Weekly*, Mar. 15, 1991.

R

Ra, Sun (Herman Sonny Blount; 1914–93) Jazz musician Sun Ra, a bandleader, composer, and arranger, worked as a backup musician in Nashville and on tour before joining Fletcher Henderson's band in Chicago's Club De Lisa in 1946. Ra formed his own band, the Solar Arkestra, moving from bop to a wide variety of African ethnic and highly experimental jazz forms, instruments, and multimedia presentations, and was a pioneer in the development of "free" jazz. He also developed his own Saturn recording label. Though never drawing a great popular following, his work did develop a cult following in his lifetime, and in his later years he became a historic figure in jazz. No information was available on survivors. (d. Birmingham, Alabama; May 30, 1993)

FURTHER READING

"Inherit the Sun." JOHN CORBETT. *Down Beat*, Sep. 1993.
Obituary. *Down Beat*, Aug. 1993.
Obituary. *Rolling Stone*, July 8, 1993.
"Jazz innovator. . . ." *Jet*, June 21, 1993.
Obituary. *Variety*, June 14, 1993.
Obituary. *Billboard*, June 12, 1993.
Obituary. *The Times* (of London), June 2, 1993.
Obituary. *New York Times*, May 31, 1993.
"Orbiting with Sun. . . ." JOHN DILIBERTO. *Down Beat*, Feb. 1993.

Rabin, Yitzhak (1922–) On September 13, 1993, Israeli prime minister Yitzhak Rabin and Palestine Liberation Organization (PLO) chairman Yasir Arafat shook hands on the White House lawn, approving the historic declaration of principles that had a few minutes earlier been signed by Shimon Peres and Mahmoud Abbas, establishing a basis for Palestinian self-rule, beginning in the Gaza Strip and Jericho. The agreement was the product of a series of negotiations initiated by Rabin soon after becoming prime minister, in August 1992, and had been preceded by four months of secret negotiations in Norway, mediated by Norwegian foreign minister Johan Jorgen Holst. A preliminary agreement had been announced by both sides on August 30–31.

The road to the peace agreement had been far from smooth for Rabin. In Israel, he had been sharply opposed by the opposition Likud Party, now out of power, but strong enough to pose a constant threat to the future of the Rabin government. He also faced the fruit of Likud policies, in the form of tens of thousands of Gaza Strip and West Bank Israeli settlers, encouraged by their government to settle in areas now to be under PLO administration, many of whom seemed ready to fight to the death to upset the peace settlement, as were many radical Palestinians, some of them Iranian-financed Hezbollah (Party of God) activists, who called the settlement a betrayal. Violence escalated after the peace agreement. Israeli and PLO negotiators also found it very difficult to agree on the specifics of Israeli withdrawal, and on such matters as control of border crossing points and the exact size of the Jericho enclave, and had not reached agreement by year's end, although agreement seemed near. As 1994 began, the fate of the peace settlement and of the Rabin government was still far from clear.

Jerusalem-born Rabin has spent all of his adult life involved in war and politics. He was an officer in the Israeli frontline fighting force, the Palmach (1943–48), through the Israeli War of Independence (First Arab-Israeli War), and remained a soldier, rising to become commander in chief of the Northern Command (1956–59), Deputy Chief of Staff (1960–64), and Chief of Staff (1964–68), achieving the rank of major-general. He was later Israeli ambassador to the United States (1968–73). Rabin entered the Knesset (parliament) in 1974, in that year briefly serving as Minister of Labour, and then becoming head of the Labour Party and Prime Minister, holding both posts until 1977. He became Defense Minister in the 1984 coalition government, taking personal responsibility for the repression of the Palestinian Intifida (Uprising) that began in 1988. He became leader of the Labour Party in February 1992 and prime minister after the Labour Party's victory in June 1992. He has published *The Rabin Memoirs* (1979) and, with Uri Lubrani, *Israel's Lebanon Policy: Where To?* (1984). He was educated at the Kadoorie Agricultural School and at military colleges. He married Leah Schlossberg, and has two children.

FURTHER READING

" 'I oppose. . . .' " LISA BEYER. *Time*, Sep. 27, 1993.
"Peace at last?" RUSSELL WATSON. *Newsweek*, Sep. 13, 1993.
"The breakthrough, maybe." *Economist*, Sep. 4, 1993.
"Can this man . . .?" ROWLAND EVANS and ROBERT NOVAK. *Reader's Digest*, Jan. 1993.
Rabin of Israel. ROBERT SLATER. St. Martin's. 1993.
"Yitzhak Rabin. . . ." *Time*, Nov. 30, 1992.
"The view from Jerusalem." *U.S. News & World Report*, Apr. 16, 1990.

Rafsanjani, Ali Akbar Hashemi

(1934–   ) On June 11, Iranian President Ali Akbar Rafsanjani was elected to a second four-year term, gaining 63 percent of the vote in an election in which three opposing candidates were not allowed to campaign. He had received 95 percent of the vote four years earlier, and voter turnout was lighter in 1993. The election was widely interpreted as an indication of Rafsanjani's lack of popularity, as Iran's growing economic problems generated mass dissatisfaction, unrest, and some demonstrations.

During 1993, in spite of foreign trade imbalances and a shortage of hard currency, Iran continued to arm itself, and to finance, train, and arm Islamic fundamentalist movements, perhaps most notably in Sudan, southern Lebanon, Egypt, Algeria, and Turkey, though it sponsored such movements throughout the Muslim world. As always, Iranian-Iraqi hostilities were a constant threat; in May, Iranian warplanes bombed Iranian exile bases in Iraq, allegedly in retaliation for stepped up guerrilla attacks from Iraq into Iran. Iranian forces also attacked Kurdish forces raiding into Iran from Iraq.

Despite international pressures, Rafsanjani also reaffirmed the death sentence placed on author Salman Rushdie by the late Ayatollah Ruhollah Khomeini.

Rafsanjani was long associated with Ayatollah Khomeini. He became a key figure in Iranian politics as speaker of the national assembly during the 1980s. As speaker, he sometimes played the role of hard-line Iranian politician, as in 1989 when he called for the assassination of the author Salman Rushdie for writing *The Satanic Verses*, but sometimes functioned as a relative moderate, who made very tentative overtures to the West in a bid to re-establish broken relationships. He became president of Iran in August 1989, during the period of maneuvering that followed the death of Khomeini. Facing a mounting economic crisis at home and growing American power in the Middle East, he took a markedly conciliatory attitude after the Persian Gulf War defeat of Iraq, calling for economic ties with the West and other Gulf nations. This also extended to the American and other European hostages held in Lebanon by the Iranian-controlled Hezbollah (Party of God). In the autumn of 1991, following a September 10–13 Teheran meeting between United Nations Secretary-General Javier Pérez de Cuéllar and Rafsanjani, nine of the eleven remaining Lebanon Western hostages were released. Rafsanjani's personal life has been kept very private, but it is known that he is married and has several children.

FURTHER READING

"Rafsanjani's advice. . . ." JAMES R. GAINES and KARSTEN PRAGER. *Time*, May 31, 1993.

"Who's sitting pretty. . . ." *Business Week*, Mar. 11, 1991.

"Rafsanjani, Ali Akbar Hashemi." *Current Biography*, Nov. 1989.

" 'Rafsanjani would have. . . .' " ALFRED BALK. *World Press Review*, Aug. 1989.

"Iran without Khomeini." MICHAEL LEDEEN. *American Spectator*, Aug. 1989.

"Burying the passions. . . ." BILL HEWITT. *Newsweek*, June 19, 1989.

"Santa satan?. . . ." MAGGIE MAHAR. *Barron's*, Jan. 16, 1989.

Rahman, Omar Abdel (1938–) Egyptian Islamic fundamentalist cleric Omar Abdel Rahman, blind since childhood, began his long career as an anti-government activist in the late 1960s. Arrested several times by the Nasser and Sadat governments, he was believed to have been a leading influence in the terrorist Islamic Jihad, though his exact status vis-a-vis that organization and other terrorist groups has never been clear. He fled Egypt in 1976, returning in 1980. In 1981, he was charged with complicity in the assassination of President Anwar Sadat, but was acquitted in 1984, held under house arrest, and then allowed to travel abroad. He arrived in the United States in 1990, was accused of complicity but not indicted in connection with the 1991 murder of Rabbi Meir Kahane, and was involved in a series of government hearings as to his immigration and possible asylum status through 1992, while at the same time building a following at Jersey City's Magjid-al-Salaam mosque.

On February 26, 1993, Muslim fundamentalist terrorists bombed New York's World Trade Center, killing six people, injuring at least 1,000, and causing enormous damage. As law enforcement agencies began to arrest and charge Muslim militants, Abdel Rahman consistently denied all complicity in the bombing. He was ordered deported in March, and detained on July 2, pending appeal of his deportation order. Although he lost that appeal, he was not deported, but was instead, on August 25, indicted with 14 others by a federal grand jury on a wide range of charges. These included leadership of conspiracies to commit the World Trade Center bombing, an aborted bombing of the United Nations, and the 1990 Kahane murder, as well as a considerable range of other terrorist plans, including a projected assassination of Egyptian president Hosni Mubarak. He denied all charges. At year's end, he was in prison, awaiting trial.

Abdel Rahman attended the Cairo University theology school and Cairo's Al Azhar University. He is reportedly married, with ten children.

FURTHER READING

"Scouring the Koran. . . ." JEFFERY L. SHELER. *U.S. News & World Report*, Aug. 16, 1993.

"The terror within." GREGORY J. CHURCH and SOPHFRONIA SCOTT. *Time*, July 5, 1993.

"How the Sheik got in." JAY PETERZELL. *Time*, May 24, 1993.

"The trail of the sheikh. . . ." MARY ANNE WEAVER. *New Yorker*, Apr. 12, 1993

"Bloody Sheikh. . . ." JUDITH MILLER. *New Republic*, Mar. 29, 1993.

"Sheik Omar speaks out." JILL SMOLOWE. *Time*, Mar. 15, 1993.

"A voice of holy war." JILL SMOLOWE. *Time*, Mar. 15, 1993.

Randall, Tony (Leonard Rosenberg; 1920–) For New York's National Actors Theater, founded by Tony Randall in 1991, the year 1993 provided something of a turnaround. After two seasons of fair-to-poor reviews, the theater produced a strong revival of George Bernard Shaw's *St. Joan*, with Maryann Plunkett's powerful portrayal of Joan at the center of the work.

Randall himself starred opposite Jack Klugman and Julie Hagerty in the National Actors Theater revival of the comedy *Three Men on a Horse*, by John Cecil Holm and George Abbott. Randall and Klugman also starred as Felix Unger and Oscar Madison in a television film version of *The Odd Couple*, reprising their roles from the popular television series; Robert Klane wrote and directed.

Tulsa-born Randall has played in a wide variety of stage and screen roles during his five-decades-long career. He is best known by far for his role as Felix opposite Jack Klugman in the long-running television series "The Odd Couple" (1970–75) developed from Neil Simon's 1965 play and 1968 film; Randall won a 1975 Emmy award for his performance in the series. He also starred in "Mr. Peepers" (1952–55), "The Tony Randall Show" (1976–77), and "Love Sydney" (1981–83). Much of his work on stage was in the 1940s and early 1950s. His many films include *Oh Men Oh Women* (1957), *Pillow Talk* (1959), *Send Me No Flowers* (1964), and *The Alphabet*

Murders (1966). His autobiographical reminiscences were published in *Which Reminds Me* (1989). Randall attended Northwestern University, Columbia, and the Neighborhood Playhouse. Randall's wife, Florence Mitchell, died in 1992.

FURTHER READING

The Magic of Theater. DAVID BLACK. Macmillan, 1993.
Sing Out Louise! 150 Stars of the Musical Theatre Remember 50 Years on Broadway. DENNIS McGOVERN and DEBORAH G. WINER. Schirmer, 1993.
"Tony Randall. . . ." JOHN HEILPERN. *Vogue*, Jan. 1992.

Rao, P. V. Narasimha (Pamulaparti Venkate Narasimha Rao; 1921–) Indian Prime Minister P.V. Rao's government faced continuing ethnic and religious problems during 1993, though late in the year there was some easing in the size and scope of the Hindu-Muslim clashes. Nor was there an inflammatory incident comparable to the December 1992 Hindu fundamentalist destruction of the historic Ayodhya mosque, which ignited Hindu attacks on Muslims throughout India, and answering attacks on Hindus in Pakistan and other Muslim countries. Rao's government moved decisively against massive impending violence in early February, arresting an estimated 50,000–100,000 demonstrators preparing to march on New Delhi, and 25,000–45,000 already in the city. Gains were minor, though; civil war continued in Kashmir, Jammu, and the northeastern states throughout the year, and Hindu mobs attacked Muslims in many parts of the country. In March, a series of massive bombings killed more than 300 people in Bombay and Calcutta, and lesser bombings continued throughout the year.

During 1993, Rao and his government also survived financial corruption charges, stock market scandals, and significant economic problems, as Rao continued to bring forward his market economy program and attempted to dismantle more of India's state-owned enterprises.

Born in Uttar Pradesh, Rao is a long-time Congress Party leader, who supported Indira Gandhi during her rise to power, and went with her faction when the party split in 1969. He was chief minister of the state of Andra Pradesh

(1971–73), and held several cabinet positions thereafter, including four years as Indian foreign minister (1980–84). Rao was named Prime Minister on June 20, 1991, after the assassination of Indian Prime Minister Rajiv Gandhi. Initially expected to serve as a caretaker, Rao held onto power once he had it, introducing major economic changes that changed India's socialist and central planning commitment to one focused on the development of a market economy. This impacted adversely on the great masses of India's poor, who lost some of what was already a very slim social services support network. Rao is also a well known translator and writer. He attended the universities of Bombay and Nagpur. He has eight children.

FURTHER READING

"Moon-faced matador. . . ." DONALD TRELFORD. *Observer*, Feb. 7, 1993.
"Doing the splits. . . ." *Economist*, Aug. 22, 1992.
"The accidental prime minister." SUBRATA CHAKRAVARTY. *Forbes*, July 20, 1992.
"Rao, P.V. Narasimha." *Current Biography*, Jan. 1992.
Prime Minister P. V. Narasimha Rao: The Scholar and the Statesman. South Asia Books, 1991.

Rather, Dan (1931–) Settling in for the rest of the century, Dan Rather in 1993 signed a contract that would keep him as anchor on the "CBS Evening News" into the year 2000. But after 12 years as sole anchor, he was joined on June 1 by Connie Chung, the first Asian-American anchor, the first woman co-anchor since Barbara Walters (ABC; 1976–78) and the first co-anchor in CBS history. Clearly the aim was to boost CBS's evening news ratings, closing the gap with the leader, ABC. However, by late 1993, CBS continued to lag behind ABC and often NBC as well, though the partnership and the format of the show were still in a shaking-down stage. Beyond ratings, Rather has long expressed a strong desire to report more from the field, especially after his trip to Somalia in December 1992; his hope is that Chung's presence as co-anchor will allow him the freedom to report from around the world.

Meanwhile, Rather continued hosting his own highly rated prime-time news magazine program "48 Hours," in an April edition, *All Night Long*, exploring New York's after-dark life. In

March, he had a one-hour prime-time television interview with President Bill Clinton. As interviewee, Rather appeared in March on the "David Letterman Show," then still on NBC. It was the first time a news anchor from a rival network had appeared on the show. In October, speaking to the Radio and Television News Directors Association, Rather was sharply critical of television news for focusing on ratings more than responsible journalism, especially for focusing on sensationalist stories or, in a phrase he had introduced years earlier, "fuzz and wuzz."

Texas-born Rather became CBS news anchor in 1981, climaxing a long career that began in Houston in the early 1950s. His breakthrough came when, as a young CBS correspondent in Dallas, he reported live to the nation the November 22, 1963 assassination of President John F. Kennedy. After working as a CBS White House correspondent in 1964, and then going abroad, he returned to Washington as CBS White House correspondent (1966–74), playing a substantial role as an investigative reporter during the unfolding Watergate affair and the resignation of Richard Nixon, before succeeding Walter Cronkite as one of the three chief American reporters and interpreters of the news. Rather's "CBS Evening News" dominated the ratings in the 1980's, and was number one for 211 weeks in a row (1982–86), until ABC took the lead in 1989. Rather's written works include *The Palace Guard* (1974), with Gary Gates; *The Camera Never Blinks* (1977), with Mickey Herskowitz; and his personal memoirs *I Remember: Fifty Years Ago in America* (1991), with Peter Wyden. Rather's B.A. was from Sam Houston State College, in 1951. He is married to Jean Goebel; they have two children.

FURTHER READING

"Over to you, Dan. . . ." Jon Katz. *Rolling Stone*, Oct. 14, 1993.

"Dan Rather is. . . ." Robert Draper. *Texas*, Nov. 1991.

Anchors: Brokaw, Jennings, Rather and the Evening News. Robert Goldberg and Gerald J. Goldberg. Carol, 1990.

Dan Rather and Other Rough Drafts. Martha A. Turner. Eakin, 1987.

Reagan, Ronald Wilson (1911–)

Former President Ronald Reagan saw many of his policies reversed and superseded by those of the new Clinton administration during 1993; still moderately active in politics, he protested early and rather often, giving support as a Republican "elder statesman" to Republican efforts to block Clinton programs. On January 22, by executive order, Clinton reversed four key abortion and family planning restrictions instituted by Reagan, including Reagan's withholding of American aid to foreign family planning programs that included abortion counseling; Reagan's "gag rule," prohibiting all but doctors at federally funded family planning clinics to even discuss abortion with patients; Reagan's prohibition on using electively aborted fetuses in medical research; and Reagan's ban on abortions in American military hospitals abroad. In February, Reagan sharply criticized Clinton's budget and in May, his ending of the SDI (Strategic Defense Initiative) program, continuing to attack Democratic policies during the balance of the year. Clinton also reversed a wide range of other Reagan policies, as in his approving the re-hiring of air traffic controllers fired and banned by Reagan after their 1981 strike. Along with the other ex-presidents, Reagan did, however, support Clinton's position on adoption of the North American Free Trade Agreement (NAFTA).

For Illinois-born Reagan, the presidency was the culmination of his second major career. After briefly working as a sportscaster in the Midwest, he had became a film actor in the late 1930s and early 1940s playing in such movies as *Knute Rockne-All American* (1940) and *King's Row* (1942). He headed the Screen Actors Guild (1947–52). He was governor of California (1967–75), and after two unsuccessful runs for the Republican presidential nomination was ultimately nominated and defeated Jimmy Carter in the 1980 election. He notably began his presidency with the hardline anti-communism of his "evil empire" speech and ended with the series of treaties and Reagan-Gorbachev meetings that, under his successor George Bush, brought the long Cold War to a close. Reagan also presided over the build-up of a national debt that approached two trillion dollars by the time he left office.

Reagan's latter years were shadowed by the Iran-Contra affair, but after leaving office, Reagan was largely able to put that behind him, successfully claiming executive privilege as to his diaries during the trial of John Poindexter, and limiting his involvement to videotaped testimony at that trial. November 1990 saw publication of his bestselling autobiography *An American Life*; his wife had published her view in 1989 in *My Turn: The Memoirs of Nancy Reagan*. The Reagan Presidential library at Simi Valley, California, opened on November 4, 1991. Reagan's B.A. was from Eureka College in 1932. He was previously married to actress Jane Wyman (1940–48); they had two children. He married Nancy Davis Reagan in 1952; they had two more children.

FURTHER READING

The Public Speeches of Ronald Reagan. AMOS KIEWE and DAVIS W. HOUCH, eds. Greenwood, 1993.

The Reagans. CASS R. SANDAK. Crestwood/Macmillan, 1993.

"The Real Reagan Record." *National Review*. Aug. 31, 1992. Special Issue.

Reckoning with Reagan: America and Its President in the 1980s. MICHAEL SCHALLER. Oxford University Press, 1992.

The Reagan Presidency: An Actor's Finest Performance. WILBUR EDEL. Hippocrene, 1992.

The Bully Pulpit: The Presidential Leadership of Ronald Reagan. WILLIAM K. MUIR. ICS Press, 1992.

Ronald Reagan: The Great Communicator. KURT RITTER and DAVID HENRY. Greenwood, 1992.

"Ronald Wilson Reagan." A. ROYCE DALBY. *Ad Astra*, July-Aug. 1991.

"Ronald and. . . ." DANIEL WATTENBERG. *Insight*, July 22, 1991.

President Reagan: A Role of a Lifetime. LOU CANNON. Simon & Schuster, 1991.

A Shining City on a Hill: Ronald Reagan's Economic Rhetoric, 1951–1989. AMOS KIEWE and DAVIS W. HOUCK. Greenwood, 1991.

Ronald Reagan. RENEE SCHWARTZBERG. Chelsea House, 1991.

Ronald Reagan. JOHN DEVANEY. Walker, 1990.

Reagan As President: Contemporary Views of the Man, His Politics, and His Policies. PAUL BOYER, ed. I. R. Dee, 1990.

The Reagan Years. HODDING CARTER. Braziller, 1988.

Early Reagan: The Rise to Power. ANNE EDWARDS. Morrow, 1987.

Redford, Robert (Charles Robert Redford, Jr.; 1937–)

In 1993, Robert Redford's major film was *Indecent Proposal*, directed by Adrian Lyne and co-starring Demi Moore and Woody Harrelson. The highly publicized and rather controversial film unfolded what turned out to be a commercially successful male fan-

tasy, involving an offer of $1 million from wealthy financier John Gage (Redford) for a night of sexual encounter with Diana Murphy (Moore), the wife of David Murphy (Harrelson). In the film, the Murphys are happily married, but broke. The film grossed more than $100 million, also outraging many women's rights advocates, who saw in it proof that vast numbers of men still regarded women primarily as sex objects.

Redford was nominated for a 1993 best director Golden Globe award for *A River Runs Through It*. Forthcoming was the film *Quiz Show*, directed by Redford and starring John Turturro, Rob Morrow, and Ralph Fiennes.

California-born Redford began his spectacular film career in the late 1960s. His first starring role was in *Barefoot in the Park* (1967), a role he had played on Broadway in 1963. He went on to star in such classics as *Butch Cassidy and the Sundance Kid* (1969), *Jeremiah Johnson* (1972), *The Way We Were* (1973), *The Sting* (1973), and *All the President's Men* (1976). He later directed the Oscar-winning *Ordinary People* (1980), directed and starred in *The Natural* (1984), starred in *Out of Africa* (1985), directed and produced *The Milagro Beanfield War* (1988), starred in *Havana* (1990), directed and produced *A River Runs Through It* (1992), and starred in *Sneakers* (1992). During the 1980s and early 1990s, his film institute at Sundance, Colorado, became a mecca for moviemakers from all over the world. Redford attended the University of Colorado, Pratt Institute, and the American Academy of

Dramatic Arts. He married Lola Jean Van Wagenen in 1958; they later separated. They have two children.

FURTHER READING

"Portrait. . . ." JUDITH THURMAN. *Architectural Digest*, June 1993.
"Robert Redford." TRIP GABRIEL. *US*, Nov. 1992.
"Robert Redford. . . ." PHILIP CAPUTO. *Esquire*, Sep. 1992.
"Redford talks. . . ." NEIL GABLER. *New York*, Dec. 10, 1990.
"Hollywood goes. . . ." MERLE LINDA WOLIN. *New Republic*, Apr. 16, 1990.

Redgrave, Lynn (1943–) British stage and screen star Lynn Redgrave spent much of 1993 touring and playing on Broadway in her very well received one-woman play *Shakespeare for My Father*, a two-act autobiographical work she wrote, presented, and performed. For her audiences, the work was a rare opportunity to see firsthand into the lives of Redgrave and her famous parents and siblings, and also into the life and people of the British theater. At its center, the work was an exploration of her complex relationship with her father, Michael Redgrave, one of the great figures of the 20th century English-speaking theater. Lynn Redgrave won a Tony nomination in the role.

Redgrave also starred in the BBC television film *Calling the Shots*, as a journalist whose drive toward an exclusive story leads to unforeseen hazards and fatal consequences.

London-born Redgrave quickly emerged as a star in the film *Georgy Girl* (1966; she was nominated for an Oscar), and went on to pursue a very diverse career on both sides of Atlantic, in theater, films, and television, acting in such works as *Tom Jones* (1963) and *The Happy Hooker* (1975) on screen; *St. Joan* (1977) and *Sweet Sue* (1987) on stage; and "Centennial" (1978), "House Calls" (1984) and "Chicken Soup" (1989) in television. She appeared on stage in a notable 1990–91 London production of *The Three Sisters*, and in 1992 in the National Actors Theater productions of *Little Hotel on the Side* and *The Master Builder*. In 1992 she published *This Is Living: How I Found Health and Happiness*.

Redgrave attended London's Central School of Speech and Drama. She is the daughter of actress Rachel Kempson and actor Michael Redgrave, the sister of actress Vanessa Redgrave and actor-director Corin Redgrave, and the aunt of actresses Natasha Richardson, Joely Richardson, and Jemma Redgrave. She married director John Clark in 1967; they have three children.

FURTHER READING

"Double blessing." LIZ GEORGE. *Weight Watchers Magazine*, Oct. 1993.
" 'I couldn't bear the silence.' " MICHAEL RYAN. *Parade*, Sep. 26, 1993.
"Fuming over. . . ." KAREN S. SCHNEIDER. *People*, Mar. 11, 1991.
"The Redgrave sisters." RODDY McDOWALL. *Interview*, Feb. 1991.
"Catching up with. . . ." LEE RANDALL. *Weight Watchers Magazine*, Aug. 1990.
Life among the Redgraves. RACHEL KEMPSON. NAL-Dutton, 1988.

Redgrave, Vanessa (1937–) A major figure in the English-speaking theater, as was her father, Michael Redgrave, Vanessa Redgrave again won recognition from her peers in 1993, with a best supporting actress nomination for her role in James Ivory's 1992 film *Howard's End*. In 1993, she starred as a blind spiritualist opposite Patrick Bergin in the television film *They*, set in the American south. She also starred in the film *Mother's Boys*, directed by Yves Timoneau and co-starring Jamie Lee Curtis and Joanne Whalley-Kilmer.

Vanessa Redgrave is one of the most celebrated stage and screen actresses of her time, emerging in the early 1960s in the classics and then in her very notable starring role in the stage version of Muriel Spark's *The Prime of Miss Jean Brodie* (1966). She reached world audiences on screen in such films as *Isadora* (1968), *Julia* (1977), *Agatha* (1978), and in television's *Playing For Time* (1979), *The Bostonians* (1983), and *Comrades* (1986). Her recent work includes Peter Hall's acclaimed revival of Tennessee Williams's *Orpheus Descending* (1989 on Broadway; 1990 on television); a London stage version of *The Three Sisters* (1990–91); and the films *Howard's End* (1992), *Di Ceria dell'Unore* (*The Plague Sower*) (1992), and *Stalin's Funeral* (1992). Active in far-left politics for many years, and notably as a supporter of the Palestine Liberation Organization, she also produced and narrated *The Palestinians* (1977).

Vanessa Redgrave attended the Central School of Speech and Drama (1955–57). She is the daughter of actor Michael Redgrave and actress Rachel Kempson, and the sister of Lynn Redgrave and actor-director Corin Redgrave, father of Jemma Redgrave. She was formerly married to the late director Tony Richardson, and has a son and two daughters, the actresses Natasha Richardson and Joely Richardson.

FURTHER READING

"A woman of conscience." NICHOLAS WROE. *New Statesman and Society*, Oct. 4, 1991.
"Who's afraid of. . . ." STEPHEN SCHIFF. *Vanity Fair*, July 1991.
"Fuming over. . . ." KAREN S. SCHNEIDER. *People*, Mar. 11, 1991.
"The Redgrave sisters." RODDY MCDOWALL. *Interview*, Feb. 1991.
"Vanessa ascending. . . ." WILLIAM A. HENRY, III. *Time*, Oct. 9, 1989.
Life among the Redgraves. RACHEL KEMPSON. NAL-Dutton, 1988.

Reeve, Christopher (1952–) His 1978 *Superman* still a fixture on the world's television screens, Christopher Reeve continued to pursue quite a different kind of stage and screen career in 1993. He starred opposite Deborah Raffin in the film *Morning Glory*, an offbeat love story, he as a desperately poor ex-convict who answers an ad for a husband, she as a pregnant, poor widow who is seeking someone to work her farm; Steven Hilliard Stern directed.

Reeve also appeared in a strong supporting role in the film *The Remains of the Day*, directed by James Ivory, and written by Ruth Prawer Jhabvala, based on the novel by Kazuo Ishiguro, which starred Anthony Hopkins and Emma Thompson. He also starred opposite Charles Bronson in the television film *The Sea Wolf*, based on the Jack London novel and directed by Michael Anderson, and was the host of the travel series *Earth Journey with Christopher Reeve*. He was one of the celebrity actors who did readings for Bill Couturie's environmentalist film *Earth and the American Dream*.

New York City-born Reeve has appeared on Broadway in *A Matter of Gravity* (1978) and

Fifth of July (1980), and has played a wide range of roles in regional theater, also working in London opposite Vanessa Redgrave and Wendy Hiller in *The Aspern Papers* (1984). His recent work in the theater includes a New York Shakespeare Festival production of Shakespeare's *Winter's Tale* (1989) and a London stage production of Chekhov's *The Three Sisters* (1990–91), with Lynn and Vanessa Redgrave. He has also appeared in such films as *Somewhere in Time* (1980), *Deathtrap* (1982), *Monsignor* (1982), *The Bostonians* (1984), *Switching Channels* (1988), and *Noises Off* (1992), as well as in several television films, including *The Great Escape* (1988), *Bump in the Night* (1991), *Death Dreams* (1991), and *The Last Ferry Home* (1992). Reeve attended the Juilliard School; his B.A. was from Cornell University. He has two children.

FURTHER READING

The Magic of Theater. DAVID BLACK. Macmillan, 1993.

Rehnquist, William Hubbs (1924–) Chief Justice William Rehnquist powerfully influenced the actions of the Supreme Court during 1993. He wrote several key majority opinions, including those in *Herrera v. Collins*, which sharply limited the ability of those on death row to gain stays of execution on the basis of alleged later discovery of new evidence; *Alexander v. Reno*, which ruled that the First Amendment did not protect $25 million of books and movies destroyed, many of them not obscene, after a seller had been convicted as a pornographer; *Zobrest v. Catalina Foothills School District*, ruling that local governments could pay for special services to the disabled in parochial schools, as compliance with federal equal educational opprtunities for the disabled laws; and *Wisconsin v. Mitchell*, ruling that states could proscribe increased sentences for hate-motivated crimes. He also voted with the majority on several other key cases including *Church of the Lukumi Babalu Aye v. City of Hialeah*, ruling unconstitutional three city ordinances banning ritual animal sacrifice; *Harris v. Forklift Systems*, in which the Court ruled unanimously that workers need not prove that they had suffered psychological damage or were unable to perform

their tasks to successfully charge sexual harassment, instead applying the rule of "workplace equity"; *Sale v. Haitian Centers Council*, which ruled that Haitian refugees could be intercepted in international waters and forcibly returned to Haiti without violating American and international law; *Bray v. Alexandria Women's Health Clinic*, which allowed abortion protestors to legally block abortion clinics; *Shaw v. Reno*, which made it possible to challenge "bizarrely" shaped voting districts formed to provide minority representation as unconstitutional; *St. Mary's Honor Center v. Hicks*, ruling that workers must provide proof of specific discrimination against them to claim protection of civil rights laws; and *Lamb's Chapel v. Center Moriches Union Free School District*, in which the Court ruled unanimously that religious groups had equal access to school facilities with other organizations in the community.

Milwaukee-born Rehnquist clerked with Supreme Court Justice Robert Jackson (1952–53), and then practiced law in Phoenix until 1969. He was a Washington-based assistant attorney-general (1969–71), was named to the Supreme Court by then-president Nixon in 1971, and was confirmed only after a sharp Senate battle over his allegedly extremely conservative views. President Reagan appointed him Chief Justice in 1986; he was confirmed after another Senate battle. Rehnquist's 1948 B.A. was from Stanford, his 1949 M.A. from Harvard, and his 1952 LL.B. from Stanford. In 1987, he published *The Supreme Court: The Way It Was-the Way It Is*, and in 1992 *Grand Inquests: The Historic Impeachments of Justice Samuel Chase and President Andrew Johnson*. He married Natalie Cornell in 1953; they have two children.

FURTHER READING

Turning Right: The Making of the Rehnquist Supreme Court. DAVID G. SAVAGE. Wiley, 1993.
"Dead end. . . ." JOHN TUCKER. *New Republic*, May 4, 1992.
Chief Justice William Rehnquist. BOB ITALIA. Abdo & Daughters, 1992.
"A new day in court." LAUREN TARSHIS and JAMES EARL HARDY. *Scholastic Update*, Nov. 1, 1991.
Original Intent: Chief Justice Rehnquist and the Course of American Church State Relations. DEREK DAVIS. Prometheus, 1991.
Eight Men and a Lady. HERMAN SCHWARTZ et al. National Press, 1990.
Packing the Courts: The Conservatives' Campaign to Rewrite the Constitution. HERMAN SCHWARTZ. Scribner/Macmillan, 1988.

Robert Reich (left) and Bill Clinton

Reich, Robert Bernard (1946–)

Secretary of Labor Robert Reich spoke before the executive council of the AFL-CIO on February 16, and was apparently well received, although differences were beginning to appear over the incoming Clinton administration's handling of the North American Free Trade Agreement (NAFTA). He and his president continued to be well received by labor for several months beyond that, although most of their campaign promises went unfulfilled, some of them because of the defeat of the Clinton economic stimulus plan, and some of them, like the increased minimum wage, deferred by the administration. Reich's own strongly sponsored labor-management committees approach was declared illegal by the National Labor Relations Board on June 28, as impermissibly anti-union. Reich very strongly supported NAFTA, sharply criticizing labor's anti-NAFTA campaign in September, as the split between labor and the Clinton adminstration grew into the bittler labor denunciations that followed passage of the pact.

Reich is a leading political economist, author, and commentator. He and President Bill Clinton became close friends while both were Rhodes Scholars at Oxford in the late 1960s and then classmates at Yale Law School. Reich went on to a career in government and education. He was an assistant solicitor general in the U.S. Justice Department (1974–76), and during the Carter years served as director of policy planning for the Federal Trade Commission (1976–81). He then taught at Harvard University's John F. Kennedy School of Government (1981–92). He became a senior advisor to the Clinton-Gore campaign and was transition team Director of Economic Policy.

Pennsylvania-born Reich's 1968 B.A. was from Dartmouth College, his 1970 M.A. from Oxford University, and his 1973 J.D. from Yale University. His books include *Minding America's Business: The Decline and Rise of the American Economy* (1982; with Ira C. Magaziner), *The Next American Frontier* (1983), *New Deals: The Chrysler Revival and the American System* (1985; with John D. Donahue), *Tales of a New America* (1987), *The Power of Public Ideas* (1987; as co-author), *Public Management in a Democratic Society* (1989), *Resurgent Liberal and Other Unfashionable Prophecies* (1989), and *The Work of Nations: Preparing Ourselves for 21st Century Capitalism* (1991). He has been a contributing editor of *The New Republic* since 1982, and chairman of the editorial board of *The American Prospect* since 1990. He is also a widely seen television commentator, whose work included hosting and co-authoring the PBS series "Made In America" (1992). He is married to Clare Dalton; they have two children.

FURTHER READING

"Labor's man in Washington." JAMES RISEN. *Financial World*, Aug. 3, 1993.
"Clinton's brain trusters." HOWARD FINEMAN. *Newsweek*, Apr. 19, 1993.
"Reich, Robert B." *Current Biography*, Apr. 1993.
"Clinton's dismal scientists." STEPHEN MOORE. *National Review*, Mar. 15, 1993.
"The Labor Secretary speaks. . . ." *Fortune*, Mar. 8, 1993.
" 'Nobody is safe.' " JANICE CASTRO. *Time*, Mar. 29, 1993.
"New dealer." RANDALL LITCHFIELD. *Canadian Business*, Jan. 1993.
"The policy hustler. . . ." MICKEY KAUS. *New Republic*, Dec. 7, 1992.
"Clinton's economic idea man." DAN GOODGAME. *Time*, Nov. 23, 1992.
"In education, he trusts." VICTORIA LYTLE. *NEA Today*, Nov. 1991.
"25 who help. . . ." LOUIS KRAAR. *Fortune*, Spring-Summer 1991.
"Harnessing human capital. . . ." SUSAN DENTZER. *U.S. News & World Report*, Apr. 22, 1991.
"American society. . . ." RICHARD SMITH and DEBORAH SINGER. *Society*, Nov.-Dec. 1990.

Reichenbach, François (1921–93)

French documentary filmmaker François Reichenbach began his career as an art dealer in the United States, and began to make documentaries in the mid-1950s, beginning with *Impressions de New York* (1955). He generated international attention with his first feature-length documentary, *L'Amérique Insolite* (*Unusual America*; or *America Through the Keyhole*; 1960), which won a prize at the Cannes Film Festival. His *La Douceur de village* (1964) also won a prize at Cannes, as did what became his best known film, the feature-length *Arthur Rubinstein, l'amour de la vie* (1969), which won a best feature-length documentary Oscar. His many documentaries also included *Marines, Mexico, Mexico, Voyage de Brigitte Bardo aux USA, Entends-tu les chiens aboyer?*, and *Le Japon insolite*. There were no survivors. (d. Paris; February 2, 1993)

FURTHER READING

Obituary. *Variety*, Feb. 8, 1993.
Obituary. *The Times* (of London), Feb. 5, 1993.

Reid, Kate (1930–93)

London-born Kate Reid grew up in Toronto and studied acting with Uta Hagen in New York City. She made her debut in repertory, playing a good deal of Shakespeare at the Stratford, Ontario festival, and made her Broadway debut as Martha in *Who's Afraid of Virginia Woolf* (1962). Reid went on to play in a wide range of stage, film, and television roles, winning Tony nominations for *Dylan* (1964) and *Slapstick Tragedy* (1965), and very notably playing opposite Dustin Hoffman in the stage and screen revivals of *Death of a Salesman* (1984; 1985). Reid won Emmy nominations for her Queen Victoria in *The Invincible Mr. Disraeli* (1963) and her Mary Todd Lincoln in *Abe Lincoln in Illinois* (1964). As Aunt Lil in "Dallas," she became a very well known figure on both sides of the Atlantic. Her films also included *The Andromeda Strain* (1971), *A Delicate Balance* (1973), *Equus* (1977), and *Atlantic City* (1981). She was survived by a daughter and a son. (d. Stratford, Ontario; March 27, 1993)

FURTHER READING

Obituary. *Current Biography*, May 1993.
Obituary. *Variety*, Apr. 5, 1993.

Obituary. *The Times* (of London), Mar. 31, 1993.
Obituary. *New York Times*, Mar. 29, 1993.

Rob Reiner (right) and Jack Nicholson

Reiner, Rob (1945–) To the world's television audiences, film director Rob Reiner is still a 20-years-younger Meathead in the series "All in the Family" (1974–78), a role for which he won two Emmys (1974; 1978). But Reiner has long since moved into directing, becoming a top-ranked Hollywood film writer and director in the late 1980s. In 1993, he received a best director nomination from the Directors Guild of America for his 1992 smash hit, the naval courtroom drama *A Few Good Men*, starring Tom Cruise, Demi Moore, and Jack Nicholson. The film ran its highly successful course during the year, from theatrical release to top home video rental to cable reruns. Forthcoming was the film *North* directed by Reiner and starring Elijah Wood, Kathy Bates, and Bruce Willis.

On the personal side, Reiner and his wife, photographer Michelle Singer, became the parents of a second child, Nick.

New York City-born Reiner became a television scriptwriter in the late 1960s. He moved into film direction in the mid-1980s with the documentary *This Is Spinal Tap* (1984), and then directed several well-received feature films, including *The Sure Thing* (1985), *Stand By Me* (1986), and *The Princess Bride* (1987). His breakthrough film was *When Harry Met Sally . . .* (1989), which he directed and co-produced; the film starred Billy Crystal, Meg Ryan, and Carrie Fisher. He also directed *Misery* (1990) and the television series "Morton and Hayes" (1991). Reiner attended the University of California at Los Angeles. Son of actor-writer-director Carl Reiner, he has been married

twice, first to actress-director Penny Marshall, then to Michele Singer in 1989, and has two children.

FURTHER READING

"Pals." ROBERT LLOYD. *American Film*, July-Aug. 1989.
"Reiner's reason." APRIL BERNARD and MICHELLE SINGER. *Interview*, July 1989.

Reno, Janet (1938–) On March 11, the U.S. Senate unanimously confirmed President Bill Clinton's nomination of Dade County, Florida state prosecutor Janet Reno as U.S. Attorney General, at the head of the Justice Department, the first woman to hold that position. The popular appointment was something of a triumph for Clinton, after the withdrawals of Zoö Baird and Judge Kimba Wood.

During her first year in office, Reno faced some appointments of her own, one of them the nomination of Lani Guinier as head of the civil rights division of the Justice Department, which was withdrawn on June 3 after conservatives threatened a confirmation fight. The other was the July 19 firing of FBI director William Sessions. The defining event in Reno's first year came with the Waco, Texas Branch Davidian siege and disaster; she entirely and very publicly took full blame for the series of government law enforcement actions that led up to the disaster, refused to criticize the FBI for its role, and in the process won the respect of the public and government law enforcement personnel. Reno emerged as one of the strongest and most popular figures in the Clinton administration, even though she embarked on no new major law enforcement initiatives during the year, limiting her role largely to support of Clinton's initiatives.

Miami-born Reno's 1960 B.A. was from Cornell University, and her 1963 LL.B. from Harvard Law School. After being in private practice in Miami (1963–71), she became staff director for the Florida House of Representatives Judiciary Committee (1971–72) and worked in the Dade County (including Miami) state attorney's office (1973–76), and went back into private practice for 2 years (1976–78). She was appointed Dade County state prosecutor in 1978, becoming the first woman in that position, and stayed in office through five re-elections (1978–93).

FURTHER READING

Janet Reno: First Woman Attorney General.
    CHARNAN SIMON. Childrens, 1994.
"Gambling on Reno." RICH LOWRY. *National Review,*
    Nov. 15, 1993.
"Reno, Janet." *Current Biography,* Sep. 1993.
"The unshakable Janet Reno." ELAINE SHANNON.
    Vogue, Aug. 1993.
"Truth, justice and. . . ." NANCY GIBBS and ELAINE
    SHANNON. *Time,* July 12, 1993.
"Janet Reno. . . ." LAURA BLUMENFELD. *Cosmopolitan,*
    July 1993.
"Rough rider." TED GEST. *U.S. News & World
    Report,* June 7, 1993.
"The reluctant star." MELINDA LIU and BOB COHN.
    Newsweek, May 17, 1993.
"Standing tall." STANLEY W. CLOUD. *Time,* May 10,
    1993.
"General Reno. . . ." ARIC PRESS. *Newsweek,* May 3,
    1993.
"Will she be a force for change?" BARBARA GORDON.
    Parade, May 2, 1993.
"Janet Reno. . . ." DAVID A. KAPLAN. *Newsweek,* Feb.
    22, 1993.

Renoir, Claude (1914–93) French cinematographer Claude Renoir, the grandson of painter Auguste Renoir, son of actor Pierre Renoir, and the nephew of film director Jean Renoir, filmed his uncle's classic *The River* (1951), and that alone make him a substantial figure in cinema history. Paris-born Claude

Renoir began his long career as co-photographer of Jean Renoir's *Toni* (1935); he also co-photographed several other Jean Renoir film of the 1930s, including the classic *Grand Illusion* (1937). He went on to created a substantial body of work, including *Monsieur Vincent* (1947), *Rendez-vous de Juillet* (1949), *Mystère Picasso* (THE PICASSO MYSTERY, a documentary), *Crime and Punishment* (1956), *The Witches of Salem* (1957), *The Lovers of Teruel* (1962), *Barbarella* (1968), *The French Connection II* (1975), and *The Spy Who Loved Me* (1977). He was survived by a daughter and a son. (d. Troyes, France; September 5, 1993)

FURTHER READING

Obituary. *Variety,* Sep. 29, 1993.
Obituary. *New York Times,* Sep. 13, 1993.
Obituary. *The Times* (of London), Sep. 8, 1993.

Reynolds, Burt (1936–) Burt Reynolds's hit television series "Evening Shade" remained a top-rated show during 1993, and the veteran stage, screen, and film star therefore continued to be a focus of media attention. For his role in the series, Reynolds received a Golden Globe nomination as best actor in a television musical or comedy. Reynolds also starred as a case-hardened detective in the film *Cop and a Half,* directed by Henry Winkler, and co-starring Norman D. Golden as an 8-year-old who wants to be

a police officer, witnesses a murder, and "partners" with Reynolds; Ruby Dee co-starred. Reynolds also directed, co-produced, and starred in the television film *The Man From Left Field*, as a loner who becomes a Little League coach, in a cast that included Reba McEntire, Kuawela Acocella, and Derek Baxter.

On the personal side, Reynolds and actress Loni Anderson, who had been married for five years, went through a very highly publicized divorce.

Georgia-born Reynolds became a very popular film star in the 1970s, acting in such films as *Deliverance* (1972), *The Man Who Loved Cat Dancing* (1973), *White Lightning* (1973), *The Longest Yard* (1974), *W.W. and the Dixie Dance Kings* (1975), *Nickelodeon* (1976), the two *Smokey and the Bandit* films (1977; 1980), *Hooper* (1978), *Sharkey's Machine* (1981), the two *Cannonball Run* films (1981; 1984), *Physical Evidence* (1989), and *Breaking In* (1989). On television, he appeared in many episodes of "Gunsmoke" (1965), and starred in the series "Hawk" (1966), "Dan August" (1970–71), "ABC Mystery Movie" (1988–89; as B. L. Stryker), and "Evening Shade" (1990–   ). Reynolds attended Palm Beach Junior College and Florida State University. Previously married to Judy Carne, he is separated from Loni Anderson; he and Anderson have one child.

FURTHER READING

"What a mess!" SUSAN SCHINDEHETTE. *People*, Sep. 13, 1993.

"Coastal disturbance. . . ." SUSAN SCHINDEHETTE. *People*, June 28, 1993.

"Burt Reynolds." MARY MURPHY. *TV Guide*, Apr. 25, 1992.

"Reynolds unwrapped." JESS CAGLE. *Entertainment*, Mar. 27, 1992.

Burt Reynolds. LISA SMITH. Magic Light, 1992.

"What's hot. . . ." DAVID WALLACE. *Ladies Home Journal*, Sept. 1991.

Rice, Anne (Howard Allen O'Brien; 1941–   ) In what was described as a "killer deal," novelist Anne Rice in 1993 signed a contract with Knopf to publish three new books in her "Vampire Chronicles" series, for a reported, though unconfirmed, $17 million, plus an additional $1.5 million for paperback rights to *Interview with the Vampire*. After 17 years of "development" at five different studios, a film of that 1976 cult-classic novel, for which Rice herself had written three screenplays, went into production in late 1993, directed by Neil Jordan and starring Tom Cruise, Brad Pitt, and Stephen Rea. Rice expressed concern (as did many of her fans) that Cruise was miscast as the French-speaking 19th-century-style world-traveling vampire Lestat, but said the film was out of her hands.

Rice's most current novel, published in 1993, was *Lasher*, a sequel to *The Witching Hour*, focusing on the Mayfair family of witches, who, like Lestat, were based in New Orleans. During her 20-city publicity tour, *Lasher* hit the best-seller lists, as did several previous novels.

New Orleans-born Rice attended Texas Women's University, later receiving her B.A. and M.A. from San Francisco State College in 1964 and 1971. Her novels include *Interview with the Vampire* (1976), *The Feast of All Saints* (1980), *Cry to Heaven* (1982), *The Vampire Lestat* (1985), *The Queen of the Damned* (1988), *The Mummy or Ramses the Damned* (1989), *The Witching Hour* (1990), and *Tale of the Body Thief* (1992). Some other novels were published pseudonymously: as A.N. Roquelaure, *The Claiming of Sleeping Beauty* (1983), *Beauty's Punishment* (1984), *Beauty's Release: The Continued Erotic Adventures of Sleeping Beauty* (1985), and as Anne Rampling, *Exit to Eden* (1985) and *Belinda* (1986). She married Stan Rice in 1961; she has one son; a daughter died.

FURTHER READING

"Anne Rice." *Playboy*, Mar. 1993.

The Vampire Companion: The Official Guide to Anne Rice's The Vampire Chronicles. KATHERINE RAMSLAND. Ballantine, 1993.

"Rice, Anne." *Current Biography*, July 1991.

"An interview with. . . ." RONNIE VIRGETS and TOBY ARMSTRONG. *New Orleans Magazine*, June 1991.

Prism of the Night: A Biography of Anne Rice. KATHERINE RAMSLAND. NAL-Dutton, 1991.

A Checklist of Anne Rice. CHRISTOPHER P. STEPHENS. Borgo, 1991.

Anne Rice's The Vampire Lestat: The Graphic Novel. FAYE PEROZICH, ed. Ballantine, 1991.

"Anne Rice." JOHN PRESTON and SILVIA TACCANIL *Interview*, Dec. 1990.

"Novels you can. . . ." SUSAN FERRARO. *New York Times Magazine*, Oct. 14, 1990.

"A strange and timeless place." LIZ SCOTT. *New Orleans Magazine*, June 1989.

Rice, Jerry Lee (1962–) It was a frustrating year for wide receiver Jerry Rice. In January 1993, his San Francisco 49ers were beaten in the Conference championship game by the Dallas Cowboys, who went on to win the Super Bowl. In a regular season rematch, Dallas won again, and then in January 1994, the same thing happened. In between, Joe Montana, perhaps the greatest quarterback ever, with whom Rice had won three Super Bowls, left the 49ers; his replacement, Steve Young, has been the National Football League's top-rated quarterback three years running, and he and Rice have piled up a good many receptions and yards between them. But the Young-Rice duo has yet to win a Super Bowl.

Meanwhile Rice himself continued to climb in the record books. In 1992, he had broken the NFL career record for number of receiving touchdowns, and continued to add to it in 1993, with 15, his regular season record now standing at 118 after only 8 years; the previous record-holder, Steve Largent, had reached 100 in 14 years. In 1993, Rice also led the league in receiving yards, at 1503, his nearest competitor at 1330.

Mississippi-born Rice was a football, basketball, and track star at Crawford Moor High School before moving on to Mississippi Valley State, where he was a consensus All-American, with over 100 receptions in both his junior and senior years and over 1000 yards in three consecutive years; he set numerous National Collegiate Athletic Association (NCAA) records. A first-round draft pick in 1985, Rice exploded in 1986 to lead the league with 86 receptions, 15 receiving touchdowns, and 1,570 receiving yards; he was named *Sports Illustrated's* NFL Player of the Year. In 1987, he was named the NFL's most valuable player, gathering 138 points and setting records by catching a total of 22 receiving touchdowns, and also by catching receiving touchdowns in 13 consecutive games. He again led the league in number of receptions in 1989 and 1990, and in receiving yardage in 1990, when he was once more named *Sports Illustrated's* NFL Player of the Year. He has helped win three Super Bowls (1985; 1989; 1990), in 1989 being named Super Bowl MVP, tying post-season league records for number of touchdowns (6) and most receiving touchdowns in a single game (3), which he did again in 1990. With eight consecutive years of over 1000 reception yards, Rice has been named to nine consecutive Pro Bowls. He and his wife, Jackie, have a son and a daughter.

FURTHER READING

"A player for the ages." PAUL ATTNER. *Sporting News*, Dec. 20, 1993.
Jerry Rice. JOHN ROLFE. Bantam, 1993.
Jerry Rice: Touchdown Talent. J. EDWARD EVANS. Lerner, 1993.
Sports Great Jerry Rice. GLENN DICKEY. Enslow, 1993.
Jerry Rice: Touchdown Talent. NATHAN AASENG. Lerner, 1993.
"Rice, Jerry." *Current Biography*, Apr. 1990.
"Why I wear. . . ." STEVE KETTMANN. *GQ-Gentleman's Quarterly*, Oct. 1989.

Richardson, Natasha Jane (1963–) Actress Natasha Richardson starred on both stage and screen in 1993. On Broadway, she played opposite Liam Neeson in a well-received revival of Eugene O'Neill's classic play *Anna Christie*, directed by David Leveaux and co-starring Rip Torn and Anne Meara. Richardson received a Tony nomination for her performance in the title role.

On screen, she starred as Zelda Fitzgerald opposite Timothy Hutton as F. Scott Fitzgerald in the not-very-well-received television film *Zelda*, directed by Pat O'Connor. She also starred in a television version of Tennessee Williams's play *Suddenly, Last Summer*, directed by Richard Eyre and co-starring Maggie Smith and Rob Lowe. A third television role was in the fact-based drama *Hostages*, about British and American hostages in Lebanon; Jay O. Sanders, Josef Sommer, Colin Firth, Ciaran Hinds, Harry Dean Stanton, and Kathy Bates co-starred. Forthcoming was a starring role in the film *Widow's Peak*, directed by John Irvin and co-starring Mia Farrow, Joan Plowright, Adrian Dunbar, and Jim Broadbent.

A member of the third generation of a distinguished British stage family, Richardson is the daughter of actress Vanessa Redgrave and director Tony Richardson, and the granddaughter of actors Michael Redgrave and Rachel Kempson. She made her stage debut in *On The Razzle* (1983); among her plays were *Hamlet* (1985), *The Seagull* (1985), *China* (1985), and *High Society* (1987). Her films include *Every Picture Tells a Story* (1984), *Gothic* (1987), *A Month in the Country* (1987), *Patty Hearst* (1988), *Fat Man and Little Boy* (1989), *The Handmaid's Tale* (1990), *The Comfort of Strangers* (1991), and *The Favor, The Watch and the Very Big Fish* (1992). She has also appeared in several television films.

FURTHER READING

"Natasha Richardson and. . . ." PETER CONRAD. *New York Times Magazine*, June 6, 1993.
"Natasha center stage." JOHN HEILPERN. *Vogue*, Jan. 1993.
"Natasha Richardson." GRAHAM FULLER. *Interview*, Mar. 1991.
Life among the Redgraves. RACHEL KEMPSON. NAL-Dutton, 1988.

Ridgway, Matthew Bunker (1895–1993)

The son of an army colonel, Matthew Ridgway was born at Fort Monroe, Virginia. He graduated from West Point in 1917, but did not see service during World War I. During the interwar period, he held a series of army positions, ultimately becoming a protegé of General George C. Marshall. In 1942, then a brigadier general, he took command of the army's 82nd Infantry Divison, which became one of its first airborne divisions, taking its first, extremely costly jump into Sicily in 1943. He joined his soldiers in the jump into Normandy on D-Day, and commanded the 18th Airborne Corps during the advance into Germany. In 1950, he took command of the 8th Army and United Nations forces in Korea, and took overall command in the theater after President Harry Truman fired General Douglas MacArthur. Ridgway was army chief of staff (1953–55), retiring a few months early because of disputes over military policy. Ridgway wrote *Soldier* (1956), with Harold H. Martin, and *The Korean War* (1967). He was survived by his wife, Mary, and two daughters. (d. Pittsburgh; July 26, 1993)

FURTHER READING

Obituary. *Current Biography*, Sep. 1993.
Obituary. *The Times* (of London), July 27, 1993.
Obituary. *New York Times*, July 27, 1993.
General Matthew B. Ridgway: An Annotated Bibliography. PAUL M. EDWARDS, ed. Greenwood, 1993.
Ridgway Duels for Korea. ROY E. APPLEMAN. Texas A & M University Press, 1990.

Ridley, Nicholas (1929–93)

The grandson of architect and artist Edwin Luytens, Nicholas Ridley went into British politics after a career as a civil engineer. He won a Conservative seat in the House of Commons in 1959, and was in the House for the rest of his long political career. He rose to cabinet level positions in the early 1970s, and was an early backer of Margaret Thatcher. Ridley served in Thatcher's cabinet (1983–90), as Transport Secretary, Secretary for the Environment, and Secretary for Commerce and Industry. His tenure in all three positions was marked by intense controversy, some occasioned by his unswerving support for Thatcher's policies, however unpopular at the moment, but much of it stemming from his sharply abrasive style. His final major controversy came in 1990, when in an interview with *The Spectator* he publicly and very intemperately attacked the Germans, the French, the European Commission, and other targets. The subsequent storm forced him from office. His memoirs were *My Style of Government: The Thatcher Years*. He was survived by his wife, Judy Kendall, and three daughters. (d. March 4, 1993)

FURTHER READING

Obituary. *The Times* (of London), Mar. 6, 1993.
Obituary. *New York Times*, Mar. 6, 1993.

Rifkin, Joel (c. 1959–)

On June 28, 1993, for a minor traffic violation, New York state police tried to pull over a pickup truck driven by unemployed landscape worker Joel Rifkin, of East Meadow, Long Island. Rifkin fled instead, and was captured in Mineola after a high speed chase. He turned out to have been transporting the body of 22-year-old Tiffany Bresciani. On that day, the police reported that Rifkin had admitted killing Ms. Bresciani and 16 other women, many of them prostitutes. Investigators later believed that he had killed at least one more woman. Rifkin's information led to the burial places of 13 murdered women, throughout the New York metropolitan area, raising the strongest possible presumption that the 34-year-old man, without any previous criminal record, was a serial killer who had murdered them all. Rifkin was indicted for Ms. Bresciani's murder in July, and jailed without bail, while prosecutors in nine counties wrangled over who would prosecute the first of multiple trials or who would prosecute a single consolidated trial.

FURTHER READING

"The bad seed. . . ." JEANIE RUSSELL KASINDORF. *New York*, Aug. 9, 1993.
"The landscaper's secrets." KEVIN FEDARKO. *Time*, July 12, 1993.

Riley, Pat (Patrick James Riley; 1945–) As basketball coach Pat Riley puts it, "Playing in June is what it's all about"-June being when the playoffs reach their peak in the National Basketball Association (NBA) championships. No one knows that better than Riley, who has won more playoff games than any NBA coach ever; by the end of the 1992–93 season he had racked up over 117, while no one else had ever reached 100. In June 1993, continuing his hard-driving, meticulous coaching style, strongly emphasizing physical defense, he again guided his New York Knicks to the Eastern Conference playoffs, though they lost there to the Chicago Bulls, who went on to win their third straight league championship.

Riley's achievement was honored when he was named NBA coach of the year for the second time. He also coached the Eastern Conference team in the All-Star game, Chicago coach Phil Jackson being barred by the rules from repeating. Nor did Riley come away from the champi-onship empty-handed; back in 1989, when his Los Angeles Lakers were going for a third straight championship, Riley had legally registered the term "Three-peat" as a trademark and so got a royalty from all commercial merchandise using the term sold after the Bulls' third victory.

After Michael Jordan's retirement, many people thought that the Knicks would be the likely 1993–94 champions, but injuries to key players, including a season-ending injury to point guard Doc Rivers, put that into question at year's end. During 1993, Riley also published a new book, *The Winner Within: A Life Plan for Team Players*. He has built a second career as a motivational speaker for major corporations, also producing video games and motivational videos.

Born in Schenectady, New York, Riley has spent his whole career in and around basketball. During his eight-year career as a professional basketball player, he was a guard with the San Diego Rockets (1967–70), the Los Angeles Lakers (1970–75), and the Phoenix Suns (1975–76). He was an assistant coach of the Lakers (1979–81), and then began his extraordinarily successful nine-year run as Laker head coach (1981–90). Under Riley, the Lakers had a won-lost record of 533–194, and won four NBA championships (1982; 1985; 1987; 1988). He is only the fifth coach ever to be named coach of the year twice (1990; 1993). In June 1990, after a winning season but an early elimination in the playoffs, Riley resigned from the Lakers. At that point, he led all coaches in NBA history, including the great Red Auerbach, in percentage of regular-season games won, at .733, and total number of playoff victories, at 102. Riley had broadcast Laker games (1977–79), and returned to broadcasting, at NBC television for the 1990–91 season. Then in 1991, he returned to coaching with the New York Knicks, taking them to the top of their division and into the Eastern Conference finals (1992; 1993). In 1988 he published *Show Time: Inside the Laker's Breakthrough Season*. He also hosted HBO's special *The History of the NBA* (1992). He is married to Chris Riley; they have two children.

FURTHER READING

"Character study." DAVID HALBERSTAM. *New York*, Dec. 21, 1992.
"Pat Riley. . . ." JOE MCDONNELL. *Sport*, Oct. 1992.
"The life of Riley." KEN AULETTA. *Vanity Fair*, Apr. 1992.

"A whole new ball game. . . ." MICHAEL STONE. *New York*, Nov. 25, 1991.
"Coach Pat Riley brings. . . ." ERIC POOLEY. *New York* Sep. 23, 1991.
" 'Call me Mister Riley.' " AL STUMP. *Los Angeles Magazine*, Oct. 1989.
"The transformation. . . ." DIANE K. SHAH. *GQ-Gentlemen's Quarterly*, Jan. 1989.

Rivers, Larry (Yitzroch Loiza Grossberg; 1923–) Larry Rivers provided a rare look at the life of a modern artist when he published, at the beginning of 1993, *What Did I Do? The Unauthorized Autobiography of Larry Rivers* (1992), written with his friend, poet and playwright Arnold Weinstein. Appropriately for a card-carrying member of the post-war avantgarde, one of the 1950s and 1960s hippest artists, sometimes dubbed "the father of pop art," the confessional tome was controversial and nontraditional. As Rivers commented, "I took seriously the calling to make life seem absurd. The book is in some way about that." It is indeed very much about the art world, but less the glossy, celebrity life than its sexual and social-climbing subtext. Rivers continues to be active, an artist whose reputation varies with critical fashions, though in the book he himself opines that he is no longer one of the hottest artists around.

After outgrowing an early ambition to be a jazz saxophonist, which spawned Larry Rivers and His Mudcats, Bronx-born Rivers studied painting with Hans Hofmann and graduated from New York University. His first show, at age 25, brought him wide attention; among his best known early works was his version of "Washington Crossing the Delaware" (1953) and "Double Portrait of Berdie" (1955), his elderly mother-in-law portrayed in two views in the nude. An artistic rebel, Rivers was considered a key influence on artists such as Jasper Johns, Robert Rauschenberg, and Andy Warhol, turning their Pop sights toward Americana. Rivers's works have been exhibited in galleries and museums throughout the world; a special exhibition of his work traveled the world (1979–80). Among his many honors are special awards from the Corcoran Gallery of Art (1954) and the Arts Festival of Spoleto, Italy (1958). An earlier book, also written with Arnold Weinstein, was *Drawings and Digressions* (1979). His 1945 marriage to Augusta Berger ended in divorce; he married Clarice Price in 1961; he has five children.

FURTHER READING

"Larry Rivers." *Interview*, Nov. 1992.
"How to face a firing squad." GEORGE PLIMPTON. *Esquire*, June 1991.
Larry Rivers. SAM HUNTER. Rizzoli, 1990.
"Larry Rivers at Marlborough." BROOKS ADAMS. *Art in America*, Apr. 1989.
"Larry Rivers." RUTH BASS. *ARTnews*, Mar. 1989.

Robards, Jason, Jr. (Jason Nelson Robards, Jr.; 1922–) Distinguished American stage and screen star Robards had another varied, productive year in 1993. In the film *Philadelphia*, directed by Jonathan Demme, Robards played a leading member of an old Philadelphia law firm, mentor of a rising young lawyer (Tom Hanks), who turns on and fires the young lawyer upon learning that his protegé has AIDS. Denzel Washington co-starred as Hanks's lawyer and Robards's adversary in the discrimination case brought by Hanks against the firm. Robards also starred in the film *The Trial*, directed by David Jones, with screenplay by Harold Pinter, based on the 1913 Franz Kafka novel; co-starring were Kyle McLachlan, Anthony Hopkins, Polly Walker, and Juliet Stevenson.

In television, Robards starred as the mountaineer grandfather opposite Noley Thornton as Heidi in the two-part film *Heidi*, directed by Michael Rhodes, with a cast that included Jane

Seymour, Lexi Randall, Sîan Phillips, and Patricia Neal. He also narrated the television special *All Aboard! Riding the Rails of American Film*. Forthcoming was a New York revival of Harold Pinter's play *No Man's Land*, directed by David Jones and starring Robards and Christopher Plummer, with John Seitz and Tom Wood. Also forthcoming were starring roles in the film *Little Big League*, directed by Andrew Scheinman, and in the Stephen Sommers film *The Adventures of Huck Finn*.

Chicago-born Robards became a leading player on the American stage in 1956 as Hickey in Eugene O'Neill's *The Iceman Cometh*, a role he repeated in 1976 and 1988. His work in O'Neill included *Long Day's Journey Into Night* (1956; 1976; 1986), *A Moon for the Misbegotten* (1973), and *A Touch of the Poet* (1977). He won a Tony in *The Disenchanted* (1958), and also starred in such plays as *A Thousand Clowns* (1962; and the 1965 film), *After the Fall* (1964), *The Country Girl* (1972), and *Park Your Car in Harvard Yard* (1991). On screen, he appeared in many films, largely in strong supporting roles. His most notable films include *The Loves of Isadora* (1969), *All the President's Men* (1976; he won a best supporting actor Oscar), *Julia* (1977; and a second best supporting actor Oscar), *Melvin and Howard* (1979), *Parenthood* (1989), *Black Rainbow* (1990), and *Reunion* (1990), as well as many television films, most notably in *The Iceman Cometh* (1961), *One Day in the Life of Ivan Denisovitch* (1963), *Haywire* (1980), *The Day After* (1983), *Sakharov* (1984), *Inherit the Wind* (1988), *Chernobyl: The Final Warning* (1991), *The Perfect Tribute* (1991), and *Mark Twain and Me* (1991). Robards attended the American Academy of Dramatic Arts. He has been married four times and has seven children. He is the son of actor Jason Robards.

FURTHER READING

"The players." ANDREW CORSELLO and AMY DONOHUE. *Philadelphia Magazine*, Dec. 1993.

Robbins, Tim (1958–) Emerging film star Tim Robbins followed up his smash hit in the title role of Robert's Altman's 1992 film *The Player* with a starring role as a Los Angeles police officer in Altman's 1993 film *Short Cuts*,

Tim Robbins (left) and Frances McDormand

based on eight stories and a poem by Raymond Carver, as adapted for film by Altman and Frank Barhydt. The large cast also included Fred Ward, Anne Archer, Robert Downey, Jr., Jennifer Jason Leigh, Jack Lemmon, Andie MacDowell, Matthew Modine, Lily Tomlin, and Tom Waits. Forthcoming were starring roles in the films *The Hudsucker Proxy*, written and directed by Joel Coen and co-starring Paul Newman and Jennifer Jason Leigh, and *Rita Hayworth and The Shawshank Redemption*, directed by Frank Darabont and co-starring Morgan Freeman. On the business side, Robbins signed a three-year agreement with Polygram Filmed Entertainment for the financing of films developed by his Chaos Productions.

California-born Robbins grew up in New York's Greenwich Village, the child of a theater family (his father, Gil Robbins, was a folksinger and cabaret manager). He made his stage debut in his early teens, studied theater at the Plattsburgh campus of the State University of New York and the University of California at Los Angeles, and while still in school was a founder of the Actors' Gang; he is still artistic director of the group. He has written several experimental plays. He made his film debut in *No Small Affair* (1984), and went on to roles in such films as *The Sure Thing* (1985), and *Five Corners* (1987), his breakthrough role coming in *Bull Durham* (1988), followed by such films as *Eric the Viking* (1989), *Cadillac Man* (1990), *Jacob's Ladder* (1990), *The Player* (1992), and *Bob Roberts* (1992; he wrote script and songs, directed, and starred). Robbins and Susan Sarandon have two children, one born in 1992.

FURTHER READING

"A dangerous man." STEPHANIE MANSFIELD. *GQ-Gentleman's Quarterly*, Oct. 1992.

"Tim Robbins." *Playboy*, Oct. 1992.

"Renaissance radical." JONATHAN ALTER. *Vogue*, Sep. 1992.

"Tim Robbins." MARK HARRIS. *Entertainment*, June 26, 1992.

"Two-coast man." JACK KROLL. *Newsweek*, Nov. 12, 1990.

Roberts, Julia (Julie Roberts; 1967–) After having taken most of a year off from the business of making movies, film star Julia Roberts re-emerged in late 1993, starring in the blockbuster hit *The Pelican Brief*, written and directed by Alan Pakula, based on John Grisham's best-selling novel about assassination and intrigue in high places. Roberts played law student Darby Shaw, who uncovers damning assassination evidence, opposite Denzel Washington as newspaper reporter Gray Grantham, Sam Shepard, John Heard, Hume Cronyn as assassinated Supreme Court Justice Abraham Rosenberg, Robert Culp, and John Lithgow. Forthcoming was a starring role as a journalist opposite Nick Nolte as a competing journalist in *I Love Trouble*. On the personal side, Roberts married singer Lyle Lovett in June.

Georgia-born Roberts began her acting career with a small role as sister to her actor-brother, Eric, in the western *Blood Red* (1986; released in 1989). After a single 1986 guest role on the television series "Crime Story," followed by a role in the HBO telefilm *Baja, Oklahoma* (1987), she very quickly moved into feature films, in *Satisfaction* (1988) playing guitar in an all-female rock band; in her breakthrough role as the highly sexual waitress in *Mystic Pizza* (1988); and in *Steel Magnolias* (1989) as diabetic Shelby, winning a Golden Globe award and an Oscar nomination for best supporting actress. Her starring role in *Pretty Woman* (1990) brought her a 1991 Academy Award nomination and a Golden Globe Award as best actress. She has also starred in *Flatliners* (1990), *Sleeping With the Enemy* (1991), *Dying Young* (1991), and *Hook* (1991). She is also the sister of actress Lisa Roberts.

FURTHER READING

"The crown Julia." KEVIN SESSUMS. *Vanity Fair*, Oct. 1993.

"Lovett first sight. . . ." SHELLEY LEVITT. *People*, July 12, 1993.

"Hidden star." SHELLEY LEVITT. *People*, Feb. 8, 1993.

"Julia Roberts. . . . " ANN TREBBE. *McCall's*, Sep. 1992.

"Julia Roberts." JOHN CLARK. *Premiere*, Dec. 1991.

"Hooked on Julia!" *Teen*, Nov. 1991.

"20 questions. . . ." *Playboy*, Nov. 1991.

"Queen for a decade." MARC ELIOT. *California*, Sep. 1991.

"Miss Roberts regrets." LOUISE LAGUE. *People*, July 1, 1991.

"Julia Roberts. . . ." SALLY OGLE DAVIS. *Ladies Home Journal*, July 1991.

"Roberts, Julia." *Current Biography*, May 1991.

"Bare-foot girl. . . ." JOHANNA SCHNELLER. *GQ-Gentlemen's Quarterly*, Feb. 1991.

Julia Roberts. ROSEMARY WALLNER. Abdo & Daughters, 1991.

"The jewel who's Julia." SUSAN SCHINDEHETTE. *People*, Sep. 17, 1990.

"Suddenly, Julia." ROBERT PALMER. *American Film*, July 1990.

"The barefoot principessa. . . ." MICHAEL REESE. *Newsweek*, Mar. 26, 1990.

"Julia Roberts." CATHERINE SEIPP. *Harper's Bazaar*, Sep. 1989.

"Family ties. . . ." DOUG GARR. *Harper's Bazaar*, Feb. 1989.

Robinson, Roscoe (1928–93) St. Louis-born Roscoe Robinson, who became the first African-American U.S. army general, graduated from West Point in 1951, and began his career as a second lieutenant in command of a frontline unit in Korea. After a series of peacetime assignments, a period in which he also earned a master's degree in international relations at the University of Pittsburgh, he went into combat again, this time as a battalion commander in Vietnam. He later became deputy chief of staff for logistics in Korea, commanded the 82nd Airborne Division, and commanded the IX Corps in Japan. General Robinson's fourth star came in 1982. He retired in 1985, and went into private industry. He was survived by his wife, Mildred E. Sims, a daughter, and a son. (d. Washington, D. C.; July 22, 1993)

FURTHER READING

Obituary. *Jet*, Aug. 9, 1993.
Obituary. *The Times* (of London), July 30, 1993.
Obituary. *New York Times*, July 24, 1993.

Rogers, Will, Jr. (1911–93) New York City-born Will Rogers, Jr., the son of entertainer Will Rogers, began his career as a journalist, and owned the *Beverly Hills Citizen* (1935–53). He ran for a House of Representatives seat in 1942, was elected while in military service, served briefly in Congress (1943–44), and resigned to go back into active service, then seeing battle as a tank commander during the invasion of Europe. He was an unsuccessful Democratic senatorial candidate in 1946. Rogers starred in two film biographies of his father, *The Story of Will Rogers* (1952) and *The Boy from Oklahoma* (1954). He also hosted the CBS "Good Morning Show" (1957–58). Rogers, who was partly Cherokee, was an assistant to the Commissioner of Indian Affairs (1967–69). He was survived by two sons and a brother. (d. Tubac, Arizona; July 10, 1993)

FURTHER READING

Obituary. *Current Biography*, Sep. 1993.
Obituary. *Variety*, July 12, 1993.
Obituary. *New York Times*, July 11, 1993.

Rome, Harold (1908–93) Hartford-born Harold Rome, a leading songwriter, studied law and graduated from Yale University in 1934 with a degree in architecture, but turned almost immediately to music, earning his living in the mid-1930s as a pianist and arranger. His breakthrough came in 1937, with the long-running hit musical *Pins and Needles*, sponsored by the International Ladies Garment Workers Union. Among its songs was Rome's first popular hit, "Sunday in the Park." A second 1930s topical revue was *Sing Out the News*, with the hit "Franklin D. Roosevelt Jones." His further musicals included *The Little Dog Laughed* (1940); *Call Me Mister* (1946), with its hit song "South America, Take It Away;" *Wish You Were Here* (1952), with its hit title song; *Fanny* (1954), with another hit title song; and *I Can Get It for You Wholesale* (1962), with Barbara Streisand's debut showstopper "Miss Marmelstein." He also wrote the musical *Scarlett* (1970), an adaptation of *Gone With the Wind* (1970). He was survived by his wife, Florence, a daughter, a son, and two sisters. (d. New York City; October 26, 1993)

FURTHER READING

Obituary. *Billboard*, Nov. 6, 1993.
Obituary. *Variety*, Oct. 29, 1993.
Obituary. *New York Times*, Oct. 27, 1993.

Ronson, Mick (1944–93) British rock guitarist, singer, songwriter, and producer Mick Ronson began his career while in his teens. He was best known for playing in the band backing David Bowie in five hit Bowie albums: *The Man Who Sold the World* (1970), *Hunky Dory* (1971), *The Rise and Fall of Ziggy Stardust and the Spiders from Mars* (1972) *Aladdin Sane* (1973), and *Ups* (1973). Ronson's first solo album was *Slaughter on Tenth Avenue* (1974); his second *Play Don't Worry* (1975). He later played with and sometimes produced a wide range of rock artists, including Bob Dylan, and recorded and performed with Ian Hunter on record and on tour. He was working on a solo album when he died. He was survived by his wife, Suzy Fussey, and a daughter. (d. London; April 30, 1993)

FURTHER READING

Obituary. JOE GORE. *Guitar Player*, Aug. 1993.
"Ziggy's axeman . . ." DAVID SINCLAIR. *Rolling Stone*, June 24, 1993.
Obituary. *Rolling Stone*, June 10, 1993.
Obituary. *Billboard*, May 15, 1993.
Obituary. *The Times* (of London), May 4, 1993.

Ronstadt, Linda Marie (1946–) Popular music star Linda Ronstadt's long exploration of her Latin roots brought her two Grammys at the 35th Annual Grammy Awards. She won the best tropical latin album Grammy for her album *Frenesi*, a mambo record in which she sang many Afro-Cuban-influenced Mexican popular songs of the 1940s and 1950s; and for her album *Mas Canciones* (*More Songs*), she won the best Mexican-American album Grammy.

As had been hoped by her fans, she also released her first wide-ranging popular album in four years, the very well received *Winter Light*; and from it the hit single "Heartbeats Accelerating." More singles from the album were expected in 1994. Her late-1992 single "Entre Abismos" continued to sell well, while her two Grammy-winning albums enjoyed a considerable assist from the awards.

Tucson-born Ronstadt began her recording and touring career in the late 1960s, and emerged in mid-1970s as a very versatile popular and country star. Her first hit album was *Heart Like a Wheel* (1974), containing two of her most popular songs: "You're No Good" and "I Can't Help It If I'm Still in Love with You." She went on to record such albums as *Different Drum* (1974), *Prisoner In Disguise* (1975), *Hasten Down the Wind* (1976), *Blue Bayou* (1977), *Living in the U.S.A* (1978), *Mad Love* (1980), *Lush Life* (1984), the Grammy-winning *Trio* (1986; with Dolly Parton and Emmylou Harris), *'Round Midnight* (1987), *Canciones de Mi Padre* (1987), *Cry Like a Rainstorm-Howl Like the Wind*(1989), and *Warm Your Heart* (1991). On stage, she starred in *Pirates of Penzance* (1981; on film, 1983), and off Broadway in *La Bohème* (1984).

FURTHER READING

Linda Ronstadt: Mexican-American Singer. RICHARD AMDUR. Chelsea House, 1994.
"Skylark." JONATHAN SCHWARTZ. *GQ-Gentlemen's Quarterly*, Feb. 1990.
Linda Ronstadt. MARK BEGO. Eakin, 1990.

Ross, Diana (1944–) Diana Ross issued a very well received new album in 1993: *Live-Stolen Moments: The Lady Sings . . . Jazz And Blues*, recorded during a 1992 show in New York City. Singing with backup bands, Ross performs several jazz standards, several of them identified with Billie Holliday; among the songs are "Love Is Here To Stay," "Ain't Nobody's Bizness If I Do," and "God Bless The Child." She also issued a companion *The Lady Sings . . . Jazz and Blues*, featuring many of the same songs. Ross also was among the headliners in the Inauguration Eve celebrations at the Lincoln Memorial for President Bill Clinton. Although her long-awaited film biography of Josephine Baker seemed no nearer fruition, Ross did move to restart her film career, signing an agreement with ABC to produce and star in two television films. Late in 1993, Ross published an autobiography, *Secrets of a Sparrow*, which also included many of her poems, and a 30-year retrospective collection, *Forever Diana*.

In 1960, then-teenager Ross and her friends Mary Wilson and Florence Ballard formed the Supremes, with Ross as lead singer. The trio became one of the leading vocal groups of the 1960s. Ross left to go solo in 1969, and has been a popular music superstar ever since, with such albums as *Diana Ross* (1970), *Lady Sings the Blues* (1972; and the film, with Ross in an Oscar-nominated performance as Billie Holiday), *Touch Me in the Morning* (1973), *The Wiz* (1978; she starred in the film version of the play), *Diana* (1981), *Why Do Fools Fall in Love?* (1981), *Ain't No Mountain High Enough* (1989), and *The Force Behind the Power* (1991). Detroit-born Ross has been married twice, and has five children.

FURTHER READING

Call Her Miss Ross: The Unauthorized Biography of Diana Ross. J. RANDY TARABORRELLI. Ballantine, 1991.
All That Glittered: My Life with the Supremes. TONY TURNER and BARBARA ARIA. NAL-Dutton, 1990.

Rossi, Bruno Benedetto (1905–93) Venice-born Bruno Rossi, a central figure in the study of cosmic ray physics and development of space exploration, received his doctorate in physics at the University of Bologna in 1927, and then taught physics in Italy until dismissed from his professorial chair at Padua by the fascist regime in 1938. He then fled abroad, teaching in Europe and then in the United States, at Cornell University from 1940. He worked on atomic

bomb development at Los Alamos (1943–46). In 1929, he developed the Rossi coincidence circuit, the first of his many major contributions to research, and continued to work in space exploration and cosmic ray research, his work in the early 1960s strongly contributing to the development of X-ray astronomy. Rossi published *Moments in the Life of a Scientist* (1990). He was survived by his wife, Nora Lombroso Rossi, two daughters, and a son. (d. Cambridge, Massachusetts; November 21, 1993)

FURTHER READING

Obituary. *New York Times*, Nov. 24, 1993.

Rostenkowski, Dan (1928–) The powerful Democrat Dan Rostenkowski, from 1981 chairman of the tax-writing House Ways and Mean Committee and also chairman of the Joint Committee on Taxation, played a major role in moving Clinton administration initiatives through an often-reluctant Congress during 1993. In May, he moved Clinton's entire tax package through his committee, and he continued to play a major role in the long, complex tax and budget fight that ultimately passed, by the narrowest possible margin. On this and many other issues, Rostenkowski was one of Clinton's staunchest and most consistent supporters.

During the same period, Rostenkowski continued to face the grand jury investigation that had begun in May 1992, focusing on his possible in-

volvement in the House post office scandal and other possible financial irregularities. In July 1993, the former House postmaster, Robert V. Rota, was widely reported to have implicated Rostenskowski, while Rota pleaded guilty to conspiracy and embezzlement charges. Rostenskowski continued to deny all wrongdoing, and was not indicted on any charges, despite repeated media reports of impending indictments.

Chicago-born Rostenkowski built his long political career in the rough and tumble of Chicago Democratic politics. He served as an Illinois state representative from a Chicago district (1953–55), and was an Illinois state senator (1955–59). He has served uninterruptedly in Congress since 1959. Rostenkowski attended Loyola University. He is married to LaVerne Pirkins, and has four children.

FURTHER READING

"Power drive." Iris Krasnow. *Chicago*, Nov. 1991.

Roth, Philip (1933–) In his 1993 novel *Operation Shylock: A Confession*, author Philip Roth plays with the venerable *doppelgänger* (double) theme, introducing a narrator named Philip Roth, who has a nervous breakdown (as the real Roth has described in his autobiographical *The Facts*), and travels to Israel, where he meets an imposter with the Yiddish folk name Moishe Pipik, who is passing himself off as the real Philip Roth. Roth the writer elaborates on these themes with notable dexterity, having Roth the character at one point even taking Pipik's identity in return, producing multiple double visions, including the author himself. In a surprise move, considering the furor aroused in much of the Jewish community over Roth's early works, especially *Portnoy's Complaint*, the Kafkaesque *Operation Shylock* was excerpted in *The Forward*, the national weekly Jewish newspaper. Roth himself broke with his past practice to go on a publicity tour for the new book.

Newark-born Roth, much of whose work is rooted in Jewish-American life, emerged as a leading novelist in the late 1950s, with the novella *Goodbye, Columbus* (1959), which won a National Book Award, and became the basis of the 1969 film, starring Richard Benjamin and directed by Larry Peerce. Among his novels are *Letting Go* (1962), *Portnoy's Complaint* (1969), *The Breast* (1972), *The Great American Novel* (1973), *The Professor of Desire* (1977), *The Ghost Writer* (1979), *Zuckerman Unbound* (1981), *The Anatomy Lesson* (1983), *Zuckerman Bound* (1985), *The Prague Orgy* (1985), *The Counterlife* (1987; it won the National Book Critics Circle award), and *Deception* (1990). Roth is also a prolific short story writer. His other works include *Reading Myself and Others* (1975), *The Facts: A Novelist's Autobiography* (1988), and *Patrimony* (1991), about his father, which won the National Book Critics Circle award for biography or autobiography. He has taught at several colleges and universities and received numerous honors, including a Guggenheim fellowship (1959–60), National Institute of Arts and Letters award (1960), Rockefeller fellowship (1966), and the National Arts Club's Medal of Honor for Literature (1991). His B.A. was from Bucknell University, and his M.A. from the University of Chicago. Previously married to Margaret Martinson (1959–68), he married actress Claire Bloom in 1990.

FURTHER READING

Beyond Despair: Three Lectures and a Talk with Philip Roth. AHARON APPELFORD. Fromm International, 1994.
Philip Roth Revisited. JAY L. HALIO. Twayne/Macmillan, 1992.
Conversations with Philip Roth. GEORGE J. SEARLES, ed. University Press of Mississippi, 1992.
"Roth, Philip Milton." *Current Biography*, May 1991.
" 'All new to me. . . .' " BARTH HEALEY. *New York Times Book Review*, Jan. 6, 1991.
Understanding Philip Roth. MURRAY BAUMGARTEN and BARBARA GOTTFRIED. University of South Carolina Press, 1990.
Reading Philip Roth, ASHER Z. MILBAUER and DONALD G. WATSON, eds. St. Martin's, 1988.

Rowan, Chad: See Akebono.

Rudé, George (1910–93) Oslo-born George Rudé, who grew up in Britain, became a Marxist historian during the 1930s, whose major interest was in the dynamics of revolutionary mass movements. Rudé, who had joined the British Communist Party in the mid-1930s, left it in the late 1950s, after the crimes of the Stalin era had been exposed, and left Britain, as well, teaching in Australia and later in Canada. Among his many major works were *The Crowd in the French Revolution* (1935), *Wilkes and Liberty* (1962), *The Crowd in History* (1964), *Revolutionary Europe* (1964), *Robespierre* (1967), *Europe in the Eighteenth Century* (1972), and *Paris and London in the Eighteenth Century* (1972). He was survived by his wife, Doreen de la Hovde. (d. Rye, England; January 8, 1993)

FURTHER READING

Obituary. *New York Times*, Jan. 30, 1993.
Obituary. *The Times* (of London), Jan. 27, 1993.

Ruehl, Mercedes (c. 1950-55–) In 1993, Mercedes Ruehl took her Tony-winning stage role as Aunt Bella, from Neil Simon's 1991 Pulitzer Prize-winning play, into the film version of *Lost in Yonkers*, adapted by Simon and directed by Martha Coolidge. Co-starring were Richard Dreyfuss as Uncle Louie and Irene Worth as Grandma Kurnitz. Ruehl also appeared in *The Last Action Hero*, a poorly received movie starring Arnold Schwarzenegger that cost $80 million to produce. Directed by John McTiernan, the film's huge cast also included F. Murray Abraham, Art Carney, Charles Dance; Anthony Quinn, Ian McKellen, Joan Plowright, and Tina Turner.

New York City-born Ruehl has spent much of her career in the theater, starting in the mid-1970s. She played substantial stage roles in *The Marriage of Bette and Boo* (1985), *I'm Not Rappaport* (1985; she won a Obie award), *American Notes* (1988), *Other People's Money* (1989), and *Lost in Yonkers* (1991; she won a best actress Tony award). She made her film debut in *The Warriors* (1979), and moved into substantial roles in *Married to the Mob* (1988), *Slaves of New York* (1989), *Crazy People* (1990), *Another You* (1991), and *The Fisher King* (1991; she won a best supporting actress Oscar). Ruehl's B.A. was from the College of New Rochelle; she studied acting with Uta Hagen.

FURTHER READING

" 'Finally a simple thing. . . .' " GAIL BUCHALTER. *Parade*, June 6, 1993.
"Why is Mercedes . . .?" JESSE CAGLE. *Entertainment Weekly*, June 4, 1993.
"Slow and steady. . . ." HAP ERSTEIN. *Insight*, Oct. 28, 1991.
"Irene Worth and. . . ." JOHN HEILPERN. *Vogue*, Mar. 1991.

Rushdie, Salman (Ahmed Salman Rushdie; 1947–   ) Salman Rushdie remained under extremely heavy security; since February 14, 1989, he has been in hiding from potential assassins, outraged by his 1988 novel, *The Satanic*

Verses. But he was seen more often in public during 1993, in a deliberate bid to gain more support for his cause. In his most public appearance, in August, he was a warmly welcomed surprise guest at a U2 concert at London's Wembley Stadium. On November 24, at what had for security reasons been billed as a reading by author Susan Sontag, Rushdie appeared at the Massachusetts Institute of Technology, to accept the honorary post of visiting professor of the humanities, the first such university honor he has received.

The next day, Rushdie had an hour-long conversation with Secretary of State Warren Christopher and National Security Adviser Anthony Lake, and a brief surprise meeting with President Bill Clinton-though the occasion was regarded as so sensitive that no photographs were allowed. It was his first meeting with an American president; in April 1992 the Bush administration refused to meet with or support Rushdie, and pressured some senators not to do so; in February 1993, however, the new Clinton administration had issued an unequivocal condemnation of the death sentence.

In February 1993, Rushdie had also met with high-level British officials, for the first time at the Foreign Office itself, which ruled out full diplomatic relations with Iran unless the death sentence was retracted. This was followed by a meeting with Prime Minister John Major in May. Rushdie also visited nine other countries seeking support. The United Nations Commission on Human Rights, meeting in Geneva in

March, for the first time included Rushdie's case in its resolution on Iran's human rights record.

In 1993, Rushdie also received notable support from other writers, with publication of *The Rushdie Letters: Freedom to Speak, Freedom to Write*, letters from 26 noted international writers, on the case and on censorship in general, and *For Rushdie*, a collection of brief works, generally poems and essays, by 100 Muslim writers and intellectuals-many unhappy about Rushdie's treatment of Islam, but all insisting that no death threat could properly be imposed under Islamic law, and putting themselves at risk by taking this public stand. Also, the Rushdie Defense Committee USA was formed by various American organizations to mobilize public opinion on his behalf, working with the International Committee to Support Salman Rushdie and a dozen other organizations. Rushdie himself wrote an "Op-Ed" piece for the *New York Times*, "The Struggle for the Soul of Islam," about the danger throughout the Muslim world of letting fundamentalists set the agenda.

Though Rushdie in September expressed optimism that the death sentence (*fatwa*) would be lifted within the year, the threat was renewed in 1993 by Ayatollah Ali Khamenei and Iranian president Ali Akbar Heshemi Rafsanjani said it could never be lifted because Ayatollah Khomeini, who imposed it, is now dead. Those associated Rushdie still faced danger as well. In July an angry mob torched a hotel in Istanbul; their target, Aziz Nesin, Rushdie's translator, escaped, but 35 others were killed. William Nygaard, publisher of the Norwegian translation, was shot three times and seriously wounded in October. These were the most recent such incidents; in 1991, Rushdie's Japanese translator was murdered and his Italian translator badly wounded.

On the personal side, Rushdie's marriage to American novelist Marianne Wiggins ended in divorce after over two years of separation; he can only communicate with his 15-year-old son, Zafar, by phone. Rushdie was working on another novel, tentatively titled *The Moor's Last Sigh*, scheduled for publication in autumn 1994. Late in 1993, Rushdie's 1981 novel *Midnight's Children* won the "Booker of Bookers," as the best of the Booker-winners in the award's 25-year history.

Rushdie's *The Satanic Verses* became a worldwide best-seller in 1988, after many fundamentalist Muslims protested its publication, rioting, publicly burning the book, and threatening the life of its author and publishers. In February 1989, Iran's Ayatollah Khomeini publicly sentenced Rushdie to death and offered $1 million to anyone who would murder him, a threat since repeated by others. Rushdie continued to deny any intent to insult those of Muslim faith, while calling for free speech for those would murder him; he also publicly apologized to any who may have been offended by his book, opposed its issuance in paperback, and affirmed his allegiance to Islam, all to no immediate avail. After much delay and hesitation, a paperback edition of *The Satanic Verses* was released in 1992 by a consortium of publishers, writers, and human-rights organizations.

Bombay-born but long resident in Britain, Rushdie is a leading novelist, whose works also include the Booker Prize-winning *Midnight's Children* (1981) and *Shame* (1983). His *Haroun and the Sea of Stories* was named best children's novel of 1990 by the Writers' Guild of Great Britain. During 1991, Rushdie published *Imaginary Homelands: Essays and Criticisms 1981–1991*. He attended King's College, Cambridge. He has been married twice, and has one child.

FURTHER READING

"The fundamental lesson. . . ." FRED HALLIDAY. *New Statesman & Society*, Feb. 12, 1993.

"The martyr." PHILIP WEISS. *Esquire*, Jan. 1993.

The Rushdie Letters: Freedom to Speak, Freedom to Write. STEVE MACDONOGH, ed. University of Nebraska Press, 1993.

"Salman Rushdie. . . ." GERALDINE BROOKS. *New Republic*, July 27, 1992.

" 'Free speech is life itself.' " KARSTEN PRAGER. *Time*, Dec. 23, 1991.

"The fugitive. . . ." MARK ABLEY. *Saturday Night*, May 1991.

"Keeping up with. . . . " JAMES FENTON. *New York Review of Books*, Mar 28, 1991.

Bomb: Interviews. BETSY SUSSLER, ed. City Lights, 1992.

Salman Rushdie. JAMES HARRISON. Macmillan, 1991.

A Satanic Affair: Salman Rushdie and the Rage of Islam. MALISE RUTHVEN. Trafalgar Square, 1991.

The Novels of Salman Rushdie. R.K. DHAWAN and G.R. TANEJA, eds. Advent (NY), 1991.

Salman Rushdie: Sentenced to Death. W.J. WEATHERBY. Carroll & Graf, 1990.

The Rushdie Affair: The Novel, the Ayatollah, and the West. DANIEL PIPES. Carol, 1990.

The Rushdie File. SARA MAITLAND, ed. Syracuse University Press, 1990.

The Salman Rushdie Controversy in Inter-Religious Perspective. DAN COHN-SHERBOK, ed. E. Mellen, 1990.

Salman Rushdie and the Third World: Myths of the Nation. TIMOTHY BRENNAN. St. Martin's, 1989.

Rutskoi, Aleksandr Vladimirovich

(1947–) Air general and Russian vice president Aleksandr Rutskoi was originally allied with Russian president Boris Yeltsin, but broke with Yeltsin in late March 1993, as the struggle between conservative and reform forces intensified. Rutskoi and parliamentary speaker Ruslan Khasbulatov charged electoral fraud after the April 25 Yeltsin referendum victory, and then became co-leaders of the opposition. Ultimately, Rutskoi and Khasbulatov led the unsuccessful armed insurrection of October 3–4, and it was Rutskoi who on October 3 publicly called for the formation of military units and armed insurrection against the Yeltsin government. But hoped-for armed forces support did not materialize, despite Rutskoi's ties with the military, and Rutskoi surrendered after the October 4 armored attack on the White House that ended the brief revolt. On October 15, Rutskoi, Khasbulatov, and several other leaders of the insurrection were charged with organizing mass disturbances against the government.

Kursk-born Rutskoi was a career military officer before going into politics. He is a graduate of the Air Force College and Air Force Academy, who became a highly respected and popular air general during the Afghan-Soviet War. He was a regimental commander (1985–86) and an Army Air Force deputy commander (1988) before becoming a member of the Supreme Soviet and head of the People's Party of Free Russia (1990–91). Rutskoi became vice president of the Soviet Union's Russian Republic in 1991, and continued on as vice president after it became Russia.

FURTHER READING

"Aleksandr the great." ROY MEDVEDEV. *New Statesman & Society*, Apr. 23, 1993.
"Aleksandr Rutskoi, vice-king?" PAVEL GUTIONTOV. *Bulletin of the Atomic Scientists*, Jan.-Feb. 1993.

Ryan, Nolan (1947–) His body told him it

was time to go. Nolan Ryan knew from the start of the 1993 season that it would be his last, after an astounding 27 years at the top. His fastball,

which had sometimes surpassed 100 miles per hour, was still clocked at 94 mph or more during his final months. But even as he made his farewell tour, Ryan was plagued with injuries. He was on the disabled list three times during the year with hip and rib injuries, coming off on September 20 for Nolan Ryan Appreciation Day at Arlington Stadium. A torn ligament in his right elbow against Seattle on September 22 finally ended his playing career two weeks before season's end. Ryan's final, non-playing farewell appearance was at Cleveland Stadium, where none other than Bob Hope sang "Thanks for the Memories."

Texas-born Ryan is far and away the leading strikeout artist in the history of baseball, with 5,714 strikeouts to his credit, with a record 383 in a single season (1973), having 15 years with over 200 strikeouts and 6 years with over 300 strikeouts, both records, not to mention his record 7 no-hitters. Ryan had a career record of 324–292 and an ERA of 3.19, reaching his 300th career victory on August 1, 1990, the youngest pitcher to do so. He pitched for the New York Mets (1966–71), the California Angels (1972–79), and the Houston Astros (1979–88), before moving to the Texas Rangers (1989–1993), and was a member of seven All-Star teams. His books include *Throwing Heat: The Autobiography of Nolan Ryan* (1988), written with Harvey Frommer; *Nolan Ryan: The Authorized Pictorial History*, and *Nolan Ryan's Pitcher's Bible: The Ultimate Guide to Power, Precision, and Long-Term Performance* (both 1991), with Tom House; *Miracle Man: Nolan Ryan: The Autobiography* (1992), with Jerry Jenkins; and *King of the Hill: An Irreverent Look at the Men on the Mound* (1992), with Mickey Herskowitz. He attended Alvin Junior College (1966–69). He married Ruth Elsie Holdruff in 1967; they have three children.

FURTHER READING

The Meaning of Nolan Ryan. NICK TRUJILLO. Texas A & M University Press, 1994.
Nolan Ryan. KEITH GREENBERG. Rourke, 1993.
Nolan Ryan: Strikeout King. HOWARD REISER. Children's, 1993.
Sports Great Nolan Ryan. WILLIAM W. LACE. Enslow, 1993.
" 'First, respect yourself.' " MICHAEL RYAN. *Parade*, Apr. 26, 1992.
Nolan Ryan. JOHN ROLFE. Little, Brown, 1992.
Nolan Ryan Sports Shots. Scholastic, 1992.

Nolan Ryan: The Ryan Express. KEN RAPPOPORT. Dillon/Macmillan, 1992.
"Ten living legends. . . ." STEVE WULF. *Sports Illustrated*, Dec. 23, 1991.
"Sales pitcher." JOHN ANDERSON. *Texas*, Sep. 1991.
"Nolan Ryan." *Sporting News*, May 13, 1991.
"Citizen Ryan. . . ." LEIGH MONTVILLE. *Sports Illustrated*, Apr. 15, 1991.
"Man of the Year." DAVE NIGHTINGALE. *Sporting News*, Jan. 7, 1991.

Ryder, Winona

(Winona Laura Horowitz; 1971–) Winona Ryder appeared in 1993 in the extremely well received film *The Age of Innocence*, adapted from the classic Edith Wharton novel, set in 1870s New York high society. She played Edith Welland, the rather provincial fiancée of Newland Archer, a rich young lawyer (Daniel Day-Lewis); Michelle Pfeiffer co-starred as her rival, sophisticated Elena Olenska, who has just returned to New York from her marriage to a Polish Count. The film was written by Jay Cocks and Martin Scorsese, and directed by Scorsese. Among the others in the cast were Alec McCowen, Alexis Smith, Geraldine Chaplin, Michael Gough, and Jonathan Pryce; Joanne Woodward narrated.

Forthcoming was a starring role in the film *Reality Bites*, directed by Ben Stiller and co-starring Ethan Hawke and Stiller. Still forthcoming was a starring role in the film *House of the Spirits*, based on the Isabel Allende novel and set in Chile; co-starring are Meryl Streep, Glenn Close, Jeremy Irons, and Anthony Banderas.

Minnesota-born Ryder became a teenage film star in the late 1980s, making her debut in *Lucas* (1986). She appeared in *Beetlejuice* (1988), played a breakthrough role as Veronica in *Heathers* (1989), and went on to star in such films as *Great Balls of Fire* (1989), *Welcome Home Roxy Carmichael* (1990), *Mermaids* (1991), *Edward Scissorhands* (1991), and *Bram Stoker's Dracula* (1992). She studied at the American Conservatory Theater.

FURTHER READING

"Riding high." DAVID HANDELMAN. *Vogue*, Oct. 1993.
"Winona among the grown-ups." MICHAEL HIRSCHORN. *Esquire*, Nov. 1992.
Winona Ryder. EVAN KEITH. Dell, 1992.
"Winona." *Harper's Bazaar*, Jan. 1991.
"Winona." CLAIRE CONNORS. *Seventeen*, Dec. 1990.
"Winona Ryder. . . ." JEFF GILES and MICHEL HADDI. *Interview*, Dec. 1990.
"Wise child." PHOEBE HOBAN. *Premiere*, June 1989.
"Hot actress. . . ." DAVID HANDELMAN. *Rolling Stone*, May 18, 1989.

Sabin, Albert Bruce (1906–93) Born in Poland, Dr. Albert Sabin emigrated to the United States with his family in 1921. After his graduation from the New York University Medical School in 1931, he was on the staff of Bellevue Hospital, then moving into research at London's Lister Institute and back to New York as a researcher at the Rockefeller Institute in 1935. In 1939, he moved to the University of Cincinnati, to do viral research. As an armed forces consultant during World War II, he developed vaccines against dengue fever and a form of encephalitis, and isolated several disease viruses. He became a world figure in 1955, with his development of the Sabin live-virus polio vaccine, which by the early 1960s had largely replaced Dr. Jonas Salk's earlier dead-virus polio vaccine. Later in his career, Sabin focused the fight against cancer, while continuing to work on several other vaccines. He was president is Israel's Weizmann Institute of Science (1970–72). He was survived by his wife, Heloisa Dunsha de Abranches, and two daughters. (d. Washington, D.C.; March 2, 1993)

FURTHER READING

Obituary. *Current Biography*, Apr. 1993.
Obituary. *The Times* (of London), Mar. 4, 1993.
Obituary. *New York Times*, Mar. 4, 1993.

Sachar, Abram Leon (1899–1993) New York City-born Abram Sachar grew up in St. Louis, earned bachelor's and master's degrees at Washington University, and his doctorate from Cambridge University in 1923. He taught history at the University of Illinois for 24 years, retiring to found Brandeis University in 1948. He was the driving force behind the subsequent growth of that institution into a major university during the 20 years of his presidency. Sachar's books include *A History of the Jews* (1929), *Sufferance Is the Badge* (1939), *The Course of Our Times* (1972), *A Host At Last* (1977), and *The Redemption of the Unwanted* (1983). A much honored educator and Jewish leader, he served on many boards and commissions, and was awarded many honorary degrees. He was survived by his wife, Thelma Horowitz, and two sons. (d. Newton, Massachusetts; July 24, 1993)

FURTHER READING

Obituary. *Current Biography*, Sep. 1993.
Obituary. *The Times* (of London), Aug. 11, 1993.
Obituary. *New York Times*, July 25, 1993.

Salant, Richard S. (1914–93) New York City-born Richard Salant was a communications industry lawyer who ultimately made a major contribution to the evolution of modern broadcast news. After his 1938 graduation from Harvard Law School, he worked in several federal agencies as a lawyer until seeing naval service as a lieutenant commander in World War II. After the war, he went into private practice in New York, worked for a firm that had CBS as a client, and joined CBS as a vice-president in 1952. In 1961, he became the first non-journalist president of CBS News (1961–64; 1966–79), and for two volatile decades helped CBS become the leading organization in its field, resisting censorship attempts, expanding nightly national news coverage to 30 minutes, fostering the introduction of many often controversial news specials, and developing such continuing news programs as "60 Minutes" and "Sunday Morning." He was survived by his wife, Frances Trainer, four daughters, a son, and a sister. (d. Southport, Connecticut; February 18, 1993)

FURTHER READING

Obituary. *Current Biography*, Apr. 1993.
Obituary. *New York Times*, Feb. 19, 1993.

Salinas de Gortari, Carlos (1948–)

Mexican President Carlos Salinas scored a major victory in 1993, his final year in office, with U.S. ratification of the Mexican-U.S.-Canadian North American Free Trade Agreement (NAFTA), which provided for elimination of a wide range of tariff barriers, some immediately and some over a fifteen-year period, and which contained many other provisions aimed at essentially merging the economies of the three countries. He had banked heavily on ratification, hoping for the creation of hundreds of thousands of Mexican jobs and the accretion of other great benefits to Mexico, even though he had been forced to made potentially expensive "side agreements" on minimum wages, workers' health and safety standards, and environmental protection.

In politics, Salinas continued to combat corruption in his own Institutional Revolutionary Party, which has ruled Mexico since 1929, to call for electoral reforms, and to prepare his party for the August 1994 elections. In late November, he named Luis Donaldo Colosio Murrieta as his party's presidential candidate; although favored to win, Colosio Murrieta faced a strong challenge from Democratic Revolutionary Party candidate Cuauhtemoc Cárdenas, 1988 presidential candidate and the son of revered 1930s Mexican president Lázaro Cárdenas del Rio.

Salinas has spent his whole career in a series of increasingly responsible Mexican federal gov-

ernment financial planning posts, beginning with his term as Assistant Director of Public Finance in the finance ministry (1971–74). Before his 1987 presidential nomination, he was minister of planning and the federal budget (1982–87). Salinas attended the National University of Mexico and Harvard. He married Yolanda Cecilia Occelli González; they have three children.

FURTHER READING

"A talk with. . . ." GERI SMITH. *Business Week*, Dec. 6, 1993.
"Salinas. . . ." GERI SMITH and FRANK J. COMES. *Business Week*, Feb. 1, 1993.
"The real revolutionary." "The world's other newsmakers." JAMES WALSH. *Time*, Jan. 4, 1993.
"Salinas speaks. . . ." MARSHALL LOE. *Fortune*, Dec. 28, 1992.
" 'We are talking. . . .' " JONATHAN FISHER. *International Wildlife*, Sep.-Oct. 1992.
"Salinas's Mexican standoff." DEIRDRE McMURDY. *Maclean's*, Sep. 7, 1992.
"Interview with. . . ." ALFREDO J. ESTRADA. "A man for all seasons." MICHELE HELLER. *Hispanic*, Sep. 1992.
"Behind Mexico's. . . ." *Reader's Digest*, Aug. 1992.
" 'We had to react quickly.' " MALCOLM S. FORBES, JR. and JAMES W. MICHAELS. *Forbes*, Aug. 17, 1992.
" 'We have to get together.' " *Newsweek*, Feb. 3, 1992.
"President Salinas. . . ." STEPHEN B. SHEPARD. *Business Week*, Aug. 12, 1991.
"Mexico according to. . . ." MORTIMER B. ZUCKERMAN. *U.S. News & World Report*, July 8, 1991.
"North American. . . ." NATHAN GARDELS. *New Perspectives*, Winter 1991.
"The man behind the mask. . . ." JOHN MOODY. *Time*, Nov. 19, 1990.
"Salinas de Gortari, Carlos." *Current Biography*, Mar. 1989.

Salisbury, Harrison (1908–93) Minneapolis-born Harrison Salisbury began his career as a reporter on the Minneapolis *Journal* in 1928, after his graduation from the University of Minnesota. He was with UPI (United Press International) for 18 years before joining the *New York Times* in 1949. He emerged as a central figure in postwar American journalism during his years in Moscow (1949–54), early, very dangerous Cold War years that also saw the death of Stalin. He won a 1955 Pulitzer Prize for

his 14-part series "Russia Reviewed," and in the same year published *Stalin's Russia*. Salisbury became a roving national and international reporter for the *Times* (1956–64), continuing to undertake special assignments after becoming assistant editor (1964–72) and associate editor (1972–74). He reported on the civil rights struggle from Birmingham and on the American bombing of Hanoi from that city, and travelled and reported throughout Asia. Among his many other books were *Orbit of China* (1967), *The Siege of Leningrad* (1969), *A Time of Change: A Reporter's Tale of Our Time* (1988), *The Long March* (1989), *Tiananmen Diary: Thirteen Days in June* (1989), *The New Emperors: China in the Era of Mao and Deng* (1992), and *Heroes of My Time* (1993). He was survived by his wife, Charlotte, and two sons. (d. Providence, Rhode Island; July 8, 1993)

FURTHER READING

Obituary. *Current Biography*, Sep. 1993.
Obituary. *New York Times*, July 9, 1993.
Obituary. *The Times* (of London), July 8, 1993.

Sampras, Pete (1971–) After an uncertain year in 1992, Pete Sampras came on strong in 1993, in April taking the number one world ranking from Jim Courier by winning the Japan Open. The two traded the top spot for several months, as in August, with wins by Courier, but Sampras took it back definitively with two con-

secutive Grand Slam wins. In July he took the Wimbledon, defeating Courier in four sets, despite a recurring right shoulder problem. Then in September, at the U.S. Open, he defeated French player Cédric Pioline, who had earlier upset Courier at the French Open. At that point, though he had just turned 22 on August 12th, Sampras had already won 19 tournament titles in his brief career. Many observers, and indeed Sampras, himself were wondering whether he might be on a roll toward a Grand Slam of the world's four top titles.

In August, Sampras was one of many tennis stars who played at the Arthus Ashe Tennis Challenge to benefit the Arthur Ashe Foundation to Defeat AIDS, opposite Courier in a match chaired by boxer Evander Holyfield. In November, he also won the European Community Championships held at Antwerp, Belgium, for his 8th title of the year.

Maryland-born Sampras grew up in Palos Verdes, California, where he was groomed for tennis stardom from second grade. He dropped out of Palos Verdes High School after his junior year to turn professional, at 19 becoming the youngest male ever to win the U.S. Open, in 1990, when he was ranked 81st in the world.

FURTHER READING

" 'Sweet Pete' swings. . . ." CURRY KIRKPATRICK. *Newsweek*, Sep. 6, 1993.
"The sweet one." David Higdon. *Tennis*, Sep. 1993.
"Sampras: King of Aces." HAL HIGDON. *Boys' Life*, Sep. 1991.
"The Sampras stakes." PETER M. COAN. *World Tennis*, July 1991.
"Pete Sampras. . . . " DAVID HIGDON. *Tennis*, Jan. 1991.
"Calm, cool and collecting." CINDY SHMERLER. *World Tennis*, Nov. 1990.
"Open for debate." STEVE FLINK. *World Tennis*, Nov. 1990.
"Focused. . . ." BRUCE NEWMAN. *Sports Illustrated*, Oct. 22, 1990.
"Clean-cut Sampras. . . ." JOE GERGEN. *Sporting News*, Sept. 24, 1990.
"Float like a butterfly. . . ." ANDREW ABRAHAMS. *People*, Sept. 24, 1990.
"Now playing. . . ." TOM CALLAHAN. *U.S. News & World Report*, Sept. 24, 1990.
"Upset time. . . ." ALEXANDER WOLFF. *Sports Illustrated*, Sept. 17, 1990.
"Sampras. . . ." JIM MARTZ. *Sporting News*, Sept. 17, 1990.

Sanders, Deion Luwynn (1967–)

Super-athlete "Neon" Deion Sanders is a rare two-sport player, who has managed to arrange his life so that he can play both sports in the same city, Atlanta, with baseball's Braves and football's Falcons. During 1992, when the Braves post-season play overlapped with the football season, he sometimes played both at once, on one weekend jetting to Miami for a football game between two baseball playoff games in Pittsburgh.

In 1993, both teams tussled for his time, and expressed unhappiness about playing time given to the other sport. Though with his stunning play as cornerback and punt returner, Sanders was probably more important to the Falcons than to the Braves, for whom he was often not in the starting lineup, in May 1993 he signed a new three-year $11 million baseball contract. Under it, he received a $1.75 million bonus for not playing football until the end of baseball's post-season. That meant Sanders missed the first few games of the football season, part of the Falcons's abysmal start; but as soon as Sanders returned to football, he helped spark a turnaround, the Falcons winning four of their next five, though the team ended with a record of 6–10 and out of the playoffs. For the 1993 season, Sanders himself led the league in interceptions with seven; he was named NFL defensive player for December and was again named to the Pro Bowl as a cornerback.

Florida-born Sanders attended Florida State University, where he was named to the *Sporting News* Collegiate All-American football team (1986–88). He joined the New York Yankees baseball team (1989–90), then moved to the Atlanta Braves (1991–   ), while also playing football with the Atlanta Falcons (1989–   ). He was three times named to the Pro Bowl (1991–93) and also was named to the *Sporting News* All-Pro football team (1991). In 1992, he was kickoff return leader of the National Football League, while also leading baseball's National League in triples.

FURTHER READING

Deion Sanders. CARL R. GREEN and M. ROXANNE FORD. Crestwood/Macmillan, 1994.
Deion Sanders: Prime Time Player. STEW THORNLEY. Lerner, 1993.
"Time for a game plan." PETER KING. *Sports Illustrated*, Aug. 24, 1992.
"The neon nineties." MIKE LUPICA. *Esquire*, June 1992.

" 'They don't pay. . . .' " CURRY KIRKPATRICK. *Sports Illustrated*, Nov. 13, 1989.

Sarandon, Susan (Susan Abigail Tomalin; 1946–   )

Film star Susan Sarandon was again honored by her peers during 1993. She received Academy Award and Golden Globe best actress nominations for her role as Michaela Odone opposite Nick Nolte as Augusto Odone in *Lorenzo's Oil*, George Miller's 1992 film study of a couple who successfully struggle to save their five-year-old son from what was considered incurable ALD (adrenoleukodystrophy). The film, which had done well in theatrical release, was also a hit in home video release. Forthcoming were starring roles in the films *The Client*, directed by Joel Schumacher and co-starring Tommy Lee Jones, Anthony LaPaglia, and Brad Renfro, and *Safe Passage*, directed by Robert Ackerman.

Sarandon also continued to be active on many social issues. She and her companion, Tim Robbins, used their appearances as presenters at the 1993 Academy Awards ceremonies to comment on the need to spend more and do more to combat the scourge of AIDS.

New York City-born Sarandon began her film career with *Joe* (1970), and went on to play a wide variety of roles in the next two decades, in such films as *The Rocky Horror Picture Show* (1974), *Pretty Baby* (1978), *Loving Couples* (1980), *Atlantic City* (1981), *The Hunger* (1983), *Compromising Positions* (1985), *The Witches of Eastwick* (1987), *Bull Durham* (1988), *A Dry White Season* (1989), *White Palace* (1990), and *Light Sleeper* (1992). She has also appeared in several plays and on television. Her B.A. was from Catholic University of America. She and actor-director Tim Robbins have two children, one of whom was born in 1992; she also has a third child. She was formerly married to actor Chris Sarandon.

FURTHER READING

"Susan Sarandon. . . ." GAVIN SMITH. *Film Comment*, Mar.-Apr. 1993.
"Rebel, rebel." NUALA BOYLAN. *Harper's Bazaar*, Jan. 1993.
"Most of all. . . ." OVID DEMARIS. *Parade*, Mar. 1, 1992.
"Susan Sarandon. . . ." DONNA MINKOWITZ. *Advocate*, June 4, 1991.
"Susan Sarandon." GRAHAM FULLER. *Interview*, June 1991.

"The prime of. . . ." BEN YAGODA. *American Film*, May 1991.

"Susan Sarandon." ROD LURIE. *Los Angeles*, May 1991.

"Sarandon, Susan." *Current Biography*, Sep. 1989.

Savimbi, Jonas (1934–)

The peace treaty of May 1991, between Jonas Savimbi, as leader of the National Union for the Total Independence of Angola (UNITA), and José Eduardo Dos Santos, as leader of the Popular Movement for the Liberation of Angola (MPLA), did not hold. The long Angolan civil war resumed on October 30, 1992, after Savimbi refused to accept the electoral victory of Dos Santos, charging massive fraud. A United Nations-sponsored truce in early November 1992 also failed to hold, as fighting intensified throughout the country. In January, government forces successfully attacked UNITA forces in many cities, but UNITA soon retook much of the territory it had held during the civil war, in March capturing Huambo, Angola's second largest city, while the fighting claimed tens of thousands of lives. On May 19, the United States recognized the Dos Santos government, ending its long support for UNITA, but the fighting continued. By mid-September, when the UN voted to impose sanctions on UNITA, Savimbi's forces held an estimated two thirds of the country; the fighting continued. In October, both sides stated their willingness to resume peace talks, while the war continued, by then having claimed an estimated 50,000–100,000 lives in 1993 alone.

Savimbi became active in the anti-Portuguese Angolan revolutionary movement in the early 1960s. In 1966, he founded UNITA, and has led it through 25 years of revolution and civil war. From 1975, he led a guerrilla war against the Soviet and Cuban-backed Angolan government of the MPLA, being substantially helped by Portuguese exiles from Angola and by the South African government. Savimbi attended the University of Lausanne. Though his personal life has been kept very private, it is known that he has been married and has several children.

FURTHER READING

The Cold War Guerrilla: Jonas Savimbi, the U.S. Media and the Angolan War. ELAINE WINDRICH. Greenwood, 1992.

Jonas Savimbi: A Key to Africa. FRED BRIDGLAND. Paragon House, 1987.

Scalia, Antonin (1936–)

Justice Antonin Scalia, with Chief Justice William Rehnquist and Justice Clarence Thomas, formed the most conservative group in a generally conservative U.S. Supreme Court during 1993. Scalia wrote the majority opinions in *St. Mary's Honor Center v. Hicks*, ruling that workers must provide proof of specific discrimination against them to claim protection of civil rights laws and in *Bray v. Alexandria Women's Health Clinic*, which allowed abortion protestors to legally block abortion clinics. He wrote a concurring opinion in *Harris v. Forklift Systems*, in which the Court ruled unanimously that workers need not prove that they had suffered psychological damage or were unable to perform their tasks to successfully charge sexual harassment. He joined the majority in several other key cases, including *Church of the Lukumi Babalu Aye v. City of Hialeah*, ruling unconstitutional three city ordinances banning ritual animal sacrifice; *Herrera v. Collins*, which sharply limited the ability of those on death row to gain stays of execution on the basis of alleged later discovery of new evidence; *Sale v. Haitian Centers Council*, which ruled that Haitian refugees could be intercepted in international waters and forcibly returned to Haiti without violating American and international law; *Zobrest v. Catalina Foothills School District*, ruling that local governments could pay for special services to the disabled in parochial schools, as compliance with federal equal educational opportunities for the disabled laws; *Shaw v. Reno*, which made it possible to challenge "bizarrely" shaped voting districts formed to provide minority representation as unconstitutional; *Alexander v. Reno*, which ruled that the First Amendment did not protect $25 million of books and movies destroyed, many of them not obscene, after a seller had been convicted as a pornographer; *Lamb's Chapel v. Center Moriches Union Free School District*, in which the Court ruled unanimously that religious groups had equal access to school facilities with other organizations in the community; and *Wisconsin v. Mitchell*, ruling that states could prescribe increased sentences for hate-motivated crimes.

New Jersey-born Scalia taught law at the University of Virginia (1967–74), was an assistant attorney-general (1974–82), and taught law again at the University of Chicago (1977–82). He was appointed to the District of Columbia U.S. Court of Appeals by President Ronald Reagan in 1982, and to the Supreme Court by

Reagan in 1986. Scalia's 1957 B.A. was from Georgetown University, and his 1960 LL.B. from Harvard Law School. He married Maureen McCarthy in 1960; they have nine children.

FURTHER READING

"Scalia the terrible." JOE MORGENSTERN. *Playboy*, July 1993.
"The leader of the opposition. . . ." JEFFREY ROSEN. *New Republic*, Jan. 18, 1993.
Justice Antonin Scalia and the Supreme Court's Conservative Moment. CHRISTOPHER E. SMITH. Greenwood, 1993.
Antonin Scalia. BOB ITALIA. Abdo & Daughters, 1992.
"A new day in court." LAUREN TARSHIS and JAMES EARL HARDY. *Scholastic Update*, Nov. 1, 1991.
"Top gun on the high court." FRED BARNES. *Reader's Digest*, July 1991.
Eight Men and a Lady. HERMAN SCHWARTZ et al. National Press, 1990.
Packing the Courts: The Conservatives' Campaign to Rewrite the Constitution. HERMAN SCHWARTZ. Scribner/Macmillan, 1988.

Scheider, Roy (Roy Richard Bernhard; 1935–)

During the 1993–94 television season, Roy Scheider starred in the prime-time high-budget television series "seaQuest DSV," an underwater science fiction series set in the year 2018, and featuring the huge seaQuest Deep Submergence Vehicle, a combined research and military vessel captained by Scheider that travels Earth's oceans at a time in which they are being settled by rival imperial powers. The similarities between this setting and that of "Star Trek" were inescapable, and drew much comment. Scheider also starred in the film *Romeo Is Bleeding*, directed by Peter Medak, and co-starring Gary Oldman, Lena Olin, Annabella Sciorra, and Juliette Lewis.

Scheider emerged as a film star in the 1970s, in strong supporting roles in such movies as *The French Connection* (1971), *Klute* (1971), and then as the star of the worldwide hit *Jaws* (1975; and the 1978 sequel), as well as *Marathon Man* (1976), *Sorcerer* (1977), *All That Jazz* (1979), *The Men's Club* (1986), *Night Game* (1989), *Listen to Me* (1989), *The Fourth War* (1990), *Russia House* (1990), *Somebody Has to Shoot the Picture* (1990), and *Naked Lunch* (1991). He has also appeared in such plays as *The Chinese Prime Minister* (1963), *The Alchemist* (1964),

and *Stephen D* (1968), for which he won an Obie award. Scheider's B.A. was from Franklin and Marshall College, in 1955. He has been married twice and has two children.

FURTHER READING

"Recognizing Roy Scheider." PETE HAMILL. *New York*, May 23, 1983.

Schmidt, Anna Lee, Cara, and Daniel: See DeBoer, Jessica.

Schneider, Alexander (1908–93)

Lithuania-born Alexander Schneider, a leading violinist and conductor, studied at the Vilnius Conservatory and at the Hoch Conservatory in Frankfurt, there quickly becoming concertmaster of the Frankfurt Museum Orchestra. He became the second violinist of the Budapest String Quartet in 1932; his brother Mischa was cellist. The quartet came to America in 1938; Schneider left the quartet in 1944, playing in several New York-based chamber groups, co-founding the New York Quartet, and helping Casals to found his Prades festival, playing with Casals there and on many other occasions. Schneider began conducting in 1944, with the Dumbarton Oaks Chamber Orchestra, and guest conducted with many orchestras. He rejoined the Budapest String Quartet from 1955 until it disbanded in 1964. He founded the New York String Orchestra in 1968, and performed with it until shortly before his death. There were no survivors. (d. New York City; February 2, 1993)

FURTHER READING

Obituary. *Current Biography*, Mar. 1993.
Obituary. *The Times* (of London), Feb. 5, 1993.
Obituary. *New York Times*, Feb. 3, 1993.
Con Brio: Four Russians Called the Budapest String Quartet. NAT BRANDT. Oxford University Press, 1993.

Schott, Marge Unnewehr (1928–)

Effective March 1, 1993, baseball's executive council suspended Cincinnati Reds owner Marge Schott from participation in the sport for a year (in fact, until November, given "good behavior"), fined her $25,000, and ordered her to attend multicultural "sensitivity classes," for making blatant racial and ethnic slurs, such as talking about her "million-dollar niggers" and displaying the Nazi swastika. Schott had long been known for her idiosyncratic, even eccentric behavior; many felt that once the slurs became widely known, the suspension was too long in coming, while others argued that such speech, however undesirable, is protected by the First Amendment. Some even charged that Schott was a "designated racist" in a sport riddled with racism at the ownership level. Schott herself denied being racist or anti-Semitic, calling the action a "witch hunt." Schott was also barred from favorite field-level seat, but was allowed to watch games from a box seat behind the Reds' dugout, and was sometimes observed passing notes to Reds' manager, Davey Johnson. Her popular St. Bernard, Schottzie, was also barred from the field. The controversy was aired widely in a book by *Cincinnati Post* journalist Mike Bass, called *Marge Schott . . . Unleashed*. The Schott affair once again spurred the baseball owners into discussing more plans to end discrimination and increase minority involvement in the sport; results remained to be seen.

Marge Unnewehr was married to Charles J. Schott from 1952 until his death in 1968. As owner of Schottco, she became first a limited partner of the Cincinnati Reds (1981–84), then a general partner (1984–85), finally owner and president (1985–   ), and until her banning, the chief executive officer.

FURTHER READING

"To each her own. . . ." Wendy Cole. *Time,* Fall 1993.
"Bumbling Schott was. . . ." Mike Bass. *Sporting News,* July 19, 1993.
"Marge Schott suspended. . . ." *Jet,* Feb. 22, 1993.
"Schott out of the park." *Time,* Feb. 15, 1993.
"Cincy owner Schott. . . ." *Jet,* Dec. 28, 1992.
"Big red embarrassment. . . ." William Plummer. *People,* Dec. 14, 1992.
"Marge strikes out. . . ." *Economist,* Dec. 12, 1992.

Schroeder, Pat (Patricia Scott Schroeder; 1940–   )

The senior woman in Congress, Colorado Democratic Congresswoman Pat Schroeder, found herself in a new legislative situation dur-

ing the first year of the Clinton administration, and on the adjournment of Congress called it the most productive year she had encountered. The Congressional Caucus for Women's Issues, co-chaired by Schroeder, pointed to passage of legislation on a wide range of matters affecting women and families, although also calling attention to some battles unwon, and to the dissolution of the House Select Committee on Children, Youth, and Families, which Schroeder had chaired. During the year, Schroeder continued to take up a series of women's rights issues, among the most highly visible the reversal of the announced ban on the enlistment of married people into the Marines, and the expansion of the right of women in the military to serve in combat.

Portland-born Schroeder's 1961 B.A. was from the University of Minnesota, and her 1964 J.D. from Harvard Law School. She was a field attorney with the National Labor Relations Board (1964–66), and an attorney and teacher until her first election to the House of Representatives in 1972. She won re-election to her eleventh congressional term in 1992, with a landslide 69–31 percent victory, becoming part of the story of "The Year of the Woman"-although it is likely that she would have won handily in any event. Schroeder was also greatly involved in sexual discrimination issues, as in the aftermath of the 1991 Navy Tailhook scandal. A member of the House Armed Services Committee, she was unpopular with some in the military for this, and for advocating women's entry into combat functions. In one notable incident, three senior Navy fliers, all Fighter Squadron commanders, were relieved of command for not taking action when a group of fighter pilots put on a sexually offensive skit referring to Schroeder.

Among her written works are *Champion of the Great American Family: A Personal and Political Book* (1989), co-authored with Andrea Camp and Robyn Lipner. She is married to James White Schroeder; they have two children.

FURTHER READING

Women in Power: The Secrets of Leadership. DOROTHY W. CANTOR. Houghton Mifflin, 1992.
"Women of the House." MARIANNE WAIT. *Ladies Home Journal*, Nov. 1991.

Schwarzenegger, Arnold Alois

(1947–) Film star Arnold Schwarzenegger in 1993 starred in *The Last Action Hero*, $80 million would-be blockbuster aimed at the worldwide action film audiences that had paid $450–500 million to see his *Terminator 2: Judgment Day*. Directed by John McTiernan, the film's huge cast included F. Murray Abraham, Art Carney, Charles Dance; Anthony Quinn, Mercedes Ruehl, Ian McKellen, Joan Plowright, and Tina Turner. However, the film drew adverse reviews, poor word-of-mouth referrals, and did not do very well at the box office, considering its enormous cost. Published simultaneously was *Last Action Hero: The Making of the Arnold Schwarzenegger Film-The Official Moviebook*, by Steve Newman and Ed Marsh. Schwarzenegger himself published a trilogy of books, including *Arnold's Fitness for Kids Ages Eleven to Fourteen: A Guide to Health, Exercise, and Nutrition*, written with Charles Gaines, and appropriately tailored volumes for children from birth to age 5 and from ages 6–10.

Forthcoming was another action film, again in the $80 million cost range: *True Lies*, written and directed by James Cameron, with Jamie Lee Curtis and Tom Arnold.

On the personal side, Schwarzenegger won damages and court costs in a London court from a reporter who had supplied false information for a 1988 article that wrongly alleged he held pro-Nazi and anti-Semitic views.

Austrian-born Schwarzenegger was a champion bodybuilder (1969–75), then turning to films. He played in such films as *Stay Hungry*

(1976) and *Pumping Iron* (1977), emerged as an action film star in *Conan the Barbarian* (1982; and the 1983 sequel), and went on to such very popular films as *The Terminator* (1984), *Commando* (1985), *Raw Deal* (1986), *Predator* (1987), *Red Heat* (1988), *Twins* (1988), *Total Recall* (1990), *Kindergarten Cop* (1990), and *Terminator 2: Judgment Day* (1991). He directed the film *Christmas in Connecticut* (1992). He has also written several bodybuilding books and the autobiographical *Arnold: The Education of a Bodybuilder* (1992), written with Douglas K. Hall. He attended the University of Wisconsin. He married newscaster Maria Owings Shriver in 1986; the couple have two children.

FURTHER READING

"Some kind of hero." STEVE POND. *US*, July 1993.
"Arnold Schwarzenegger. . . ." *Ladies Home Journal*, July 1993.
"What, me worry?" BENJAMIN SVETKEY. *Entertainment Weekly*, June 11, 1993.
"Fire & reign." NANCY GRIFFIN. *Premiere*, June 1993.
Arnold Schwarzenegger: Larger Than Life. CRAIG DOHERTY and CATHERINE DOHERTY. Walker, 1993.
Arnold Schwarzenegger: Hard Work Brought Success. CHRISTOPHER MEEKS. Rourke, 1993.
Arnold Schwarzenegger: Hercules in America. ROBERT LIPSYTE. HarperCollins, 1993.
Films of Arnold Schwarzenegger. JOHN L. FLYNN. Citadel/Carol, 1993.
Arnold Schwarzenegger. SUE HAMILTON. Abdo & Daughters, 1992.
Arnold Schwarzenegger. BROOKS ROBARDS. Smithmark, 1992.
"Schwarzenegger, Arnold." *Current Biography*, Oct. 1991.
"Mr. Big Shot." BILL ZEHME. *Rolling Stone*, Aug. 22, 1991.
"Arnold Schwarzenegger. . . ." JEFF ROVIN. *Ladies Home Journal*, Aug. 1991.
"Rnld Schwzngr." PAT H. BROESKE and HERB RITTS. *Interview*, July 1991.
Schwarzenegger. NAL-Dutton, 1991.
Arnold Schwarzenegger: A Portrait. GEORGE BUTLER. Simon & Schuster, 1990.
Arnold: The Unauthorized Biography. WENDY LEIGH. Congdon & Weed, 1990.

Scorsese, Martin (1942–) Director Martin Scorsese's major film of the year was *The Age of Innocence*, made in 1992 and released in late 1993. Scorsese directed and with Jay Cocks co-wrote the screenplay, adapted from the classic

Edith Wharton novel, set in 1870s New York high society. Daniel Day-Lewis starred as Newland Archer, a rich young society lawyer, opposite Winona Ryder as May Welland, his very young fiancée, and Michelle Pfeiffer as a sophisticated Elena Olenska, a New Yorker recently returned from Europe a Countess after a failed marriage to a Polish Count. The cast also included Alec McCowen, Alexis Smith, Geraldine Chaplin, Michael Gough, and Jonathan Pryce; Joanne Woodward narrated. The film was generally very favorably reviewed, though some reported finding its comedy of manners less than fully engaging. The National Board of Review named Scorsese best director of the year for the film. Scorsese and Cocks also published the accompanying book *Age of Innocence: A Portrait of the Film Based on the Novel by Edith Wharton*.

Scorsese also produced *Mad Dog and Glory*, directed by John MacNaughton and starring Robert De Niro, Una Thurman, and Bill Murray. Forthcoming was the film comedy *Clockers*, directed by Spike Lee and produced by Scorsese.

New York-born Scorsese scored his first major success with *Mean Streets* (1973), set on the underside of New York life. He went on to become one of the major directors of the modern period, with such films as *Alice Doesn't Live Here Anymore* (1974), *Taxi Driver* (1976), *New York, New York* (1977), the classic *Raging Bull* (1980), *The Color of Money* (1986), the highly controversial *The Last Temptation of Christ* (1988), *GoodFellas* (1990), and *Cape Fear* (1991). He also appeared as an actor in a small but key role as Van Gogh in *Akira Kurosawa's Dreams* (1990). Scorsese's 1964 B.S. and 1966 M.A. in film communications was from New York University. He has been married four times and has two children.

FURTHER READING

"Martin Scorsese interviewed." GAVIN SMITH. "Artist of the beautiful." KATHLEEN MURPHY. *Film Comment*, Nov.-Dec. 1993.
"Martin Scorsese's mortal sins." MARCELLE CLEMENTS. *Esquire*, Nov. 1993.
"A beautiful present from the past...." GRAHAM FULLER. *Interview*, Oct. 1993.
Martin Scorsese: An Analysis of His Feature Films, with a Filmography of His Entire Directorial Career. MARIE K. CONNELLY. McFarland, 1993.
The Scorsese Picture: The Art and Life of Martin Scorsese. DAVID EHRENSTEIN. Birch Lane/Carol, 1992.
Martin Scorsese. LESTER KEYSER. Twayne/Macmillan, 1992.
"Martin Scorsese." GRAHAM FULLER. *Interview*, Nov. 1991.
"Slouching toward Hollywood. . . ." PETER BISKIND. *Premiere*, Nov. 1991.
"Playboy interview. . . ." DAVID RENSIN. *Playboy*, Apr. 1991.
Martin Scorsese: A Journey. MARY P. KELLY. Thunder's Mouth, 1991.
The Future of the Movies: Interviews with Martin Scorsese, George Lucas, and Steven Spielberg. ROGER EBERT and GENE SISKEL. Andrews & McMeel, 1991.
"Blood and pasta." AMY TAUBIN. *New Statesman & Society*, Nov. 9, 1990.
"Martin Scorsese." ANTHONY DeCURTIS. *Rolling Stone*, Nov. 1, 1990.
"Made men." KATHLEEN MURPHY and GAVIN SMITH. *Film Comment*, Sep.-Oct. 1990.
" 'God's lonely man'. . . ." RICHARD GEHR. *Video Magazine*, Mar. 1990.
Martin Scorsese: A Guide to References and Resources. MARION WEISS. G.K. Hall, 1987.

Scott, George C. (George Campbell Scott; 1927–) Stage, screen, and television star George C. Scott played in all three forms during 1993. On stage, he starred in New York in *Wrong Turn at Lungfish*, by Garry Marshall and Lowell Ganz; directed by Marshall. Scott played former college dean Peter Ravenswaal, blind and dying alone, opposite Jami Gertz as uneducated Anita Merendino, a volunteer reader to the blind.

Scott also starred as a former ship captain turned bar owner in Curaçao, who has a secret, in the television mystery *It's Showtime: Curaçao*, directed by Carl Schultz and co-starring William Petersen, Julie Carmen, Philip Anglim, Maria Ellengsen, and Trish Van Devere. He also played a strong supporting role in the film thriller *Malice*, directed by Harold Becker and starring Alec Baldwin and Nicole Kidman.

Virginia-born Scott suddenly emerged as a star with his 1957 *Richard III* at the New York Shakespeare Festival. He went on to appear in Shakespeare, Chekhov, O'Neill, Coward, and several contemporary works, as well, very notably as Willy Loman in the 1975 Broadway revival of *Death of a Salesman*, and a year later in *Sly Fox*; he directed both plays. He later appeared in *Present Laughter* (1982), which he also directed, and *The Boys of Autumn* (1988). He played strong supporting roles in such films as *The Hanging Tree* (1959) and *Dr. Strangelove*

(1964), moving into leads with his best actor Oscar-winning role as *Patton* (1969; he refused the award as a matter of principle), and leads in such other films as *Jane Eyre* (1971), *The Hospital* (1971), *The Day of the Dolphin* (1973), *Movie, Movie* (1978), *Firestarter* (1984), *Exorcist III: Legion* (1990), and *Descending Angel* (1990). He has also appeared in many telefilms, and in the series "East Side, West Side" (1963–64) and "Mr. President" (1989). His later work included the television films *Finding the Way Home* (1991) and *Mittleman's Hardware* (1991). Scott attended the University of Missouri. He has been married four times, twice to Colleen Dewhurst, and from 1972 to Trish Van Devere. He has six children, one of them actor Campbell Scott.

FURTHER READING

"This time. . . ." Bill Davidson. *TV Guide*, Sept. 6, 1986.

Seinfeld, Jerry (1955–) In its three seasons, comedian Jerry Seinfeld's television situation comedy, "Seinfeld," has built up a strong following, especially after it was moved into a position following "Cheers" in February 1993. By the first week of the 1993–94 season, "Seinfeld" was the second-highest-rated program overall. The quirky prime-time series, on which Seinfeld is joined by Julia Louis-Dreyfus as his ex-girl friend Elaine, Jason Alexander as George, and Michael Richards as Kramer, is talk-driven, not plot-driven, and takes up topics rarely found in sitcom-land, such as masturbation, breast implants, neo-Nazis, and body odor. Late 1993 saw the publication of *The Entertainment Weekly Seinfeld Companion*, a compendium of favorite comedic turns, along with biographies of each character and a synopsis of over 60 episodes. Seinfeld published his own book, *SeinLanguage*, which chapters such as "Freeway of Love" and "Shut Up and Drive"; after its August publication-in time for the new television season-it quickly shot onto the bestseller lists.

Seinfeld and crew were also honored by their peers in September 1993, when "Seinfeld"—which had received 11 nominations—won an Emmy as the best comedy series of the 1992–93 season; also winning were Michael Richard for best supporting actor on a comedy series and Larry David for best comedy writing; Seinfeld himself lost out to Ted Danson for "Cheers" for best actor in a comedy series. At the American Television Awards in May, top honors were won by the show, by Seinfeld as leading male performer, and by Alexander and Louis-Dreyfus as supporting players. In March, the same three had won top honors at the American Comedy Awards.

Brooklyn-born Seinfeld received his B.A. from Queens College. He began his career as a stand-up comedian in 1976, writing his own material and creating material for other comedians, as well. He was a writer with the television series "Benson" in 1980. He became the star of his enormously successful "Seinfeld" television series in 1990.

FURTHER READING

"Jerry Seinfeld. . . ." BRUCE FRETTS. *Entertainment Weekly*, Dec. 31, 1993.
"The war of neuroses." STEVE POND. *US*, Dec. 1993.
"Playboy interview. . . ." *Playboy*, Oct. 1993.
"Much ado about nothing." LISA SCHWARZBAUM. *Entertainment Weekly*, Apr. 9, 1993.
"Jerry Seinfeld. . . ." PEGGY MULLOY. *Cosmopolitan*, Mar. 1993.
Jerry Seinfeld: A Life in Comedy. JOSH LEVINE. InBook, 1993.
"Jerry Seinfeld." MARK MORRISON. *US*, Sep. 1992.
"Seinfeld, Jerry." *Current Biography*, Aug. 1992.
"Stand-up Seinfeld. . . ." STEWART WEINER. *TV Guide*, May 23, 1992.
"You're a comic." ALAN RICHMAN. *GQ-Gentleman's Quarterly*, May 1992.
"Comedy abounds." MARK GOODMAN and LORENZO BENET. *People*, Dec. 2, 1991.
"Jerry Seinfeld's. . . ." STEPHEN RANDALL. *Playboy*, Aug. 1990.

Seles, Monica (1974–) The violence and madness of the streets penetrated onto the tennis court in April 1993, when a German man obsessed with tennis star Steffi Graf reached over the spectator's fence during a changeover and stabbed Seles high in the back, between the shoulder blades, narrowly missing the spinal column, his attempt apparently being not to kill her but to injure her and keep her from playing so Graf could regain tennis' top ranking. The incident at the WTA Citizen Cup in Hamburg,

Germany shook the tennis world, and resulted in much increased security precautions in a sport that has felt little need for them in the past. The man was given only two years' probation, but the Women's Tennis Association and other groups were pressing for review of the case in 1994.

Before Hamburg, Seles had been out of competition for over two months battling a virus. Even so, the knifing came when Seles was firmly number one in the world, having defeated Graf to take her third straight Australian Open in January; it was her eighth major championship, and many observers gave her a good chance to take the other three majors in 1993 for a Grand Slam. Instead, she was out indefinitely. First reports indicated that she might be out for 3–4 weeks, but at year's end, Seles was still not back in tournament play. In a "Prime Time Live" interview with Diane Sawyer, she was critical of the fact that her ranking has fallen from first to tenth, through no fault of her own, feeling there should have been special provision made; Women's Tennis Association officials said it would not have been right to "hold" the ranking for her, but that the circumstances would be taken into account in tournament seedings when she returns.

Ethnically Hungarian, born in the Serbian part of the former Yugoslavia, Seles became a leading amateur tennis player in Yugoslavia and throughout Europe, before emigrating to America with her family at age 11 to train at the Bradenton Tennis Academy in Florida under Nick Bollettieri; she was also coached by her father, cartoonist and documentary filmmaker Xarolj Seles. She turned professional in 1989, and emerged in 1990 as a dominating presence on the women's tennis scene, winning the Italian and German Opens, and defeating then-top-ranked Graf at the French Open, becoming the youngest player since 1887 to win a Grand Slam event. She won the French Open twice again (1991; 1992); her other Grand Slam titles include the U.S. Open (1991; 1992) and the Australian Open (1991; 1992; 1993). She reached the finals of all 16 events she entered in 1991 and all but 1 of 15 in 1992, including a string of 22 consecutive finals, second only to Navratilova's earlier 23. In that period winning 10 tournaments, including six Grand Slams, she set two successive single-year earnings records, with over $2.4 million in 1991 and over $2.6 million in 1992, broken by Graf in 1993.

FURTHER READING

"Bloody obsessions. . . ." DAVID ELLIS. *People*, May 17, 1993.
"Savage assault." SALLY JENKINS. *Sports Illustrated*, May 10, 1993.
"Women's tour '92. . . ." CINDY HAHN. *Tennis*, Feb. 1992.
"Mystery women or material girl?" PETER BODO. *Tennis*, Nov. 1991.
"Madonna is the model." PETER NEWCOMB. *Forbes*, Aug. 19, 1991.
"Steppin' out. . . ." CURRY KIRKPATRICK. *Sports Illustrated*, May 27, 1991.
"Monica Seles. . . ." PETER BODO. *Tennis*, Jan. 1991.
"Grunts, giggles. . . ." JIM MARTZ. *Sporting News*, Aug. 27, 1990.
"Hitting out in all directions." CINDY SHMERLER. *World Tennis*, Aug. 1990.
"Yiii! Can this be. . . ." SUSAN REED. *People*, July 2, 1990.

Selig, Bud (Allan H. Selig; 1934–) Though still officially "interim" commissioner of baseball, since the ousting of former commissioner Fay Vincent in 1991, Selig had by the end of 1993 served as head of baseball for 16 months. The job had been offered to him permanently, but Selig declined, so the search for an acceptable person continued. Appointment of a new commissioner was promised for early 1994, but meanwhile Selig was in the hot seat while baseball's owners were attempting to restructure the league. The concern for many is that the restructuring will weaken the commissioner's post, which was originally intended as an independent power and guarantor of fairness and incorruptibility of the sport, overseeing but not *of* the owners. In fact, the House Judiciary Committee, which expressed displeasure at the forcing out of Vincent, notified the owners that it considered the appointment of an independent commissioner crucial to continuation of baseball's antitrust exemption, which was criticized by some in House hearings.

During 1993 Selig and his staff oversaw the signing of major league baseball's new national television contract, with fewer games televised and, for the first time, with no guaranteed revenue. But numerous policy questions remained to be settled, including equitable revenue-sharing between big-market and small-market owners, a proposed realignment of teams into six divisions, and the addition of a post-season round of playoffs, akin to those in basketball or football, possibly to start as early as 1994. Difficult questions, over which Vincent had foundered and contracts with the players' union had stalled, since any structural changes required their approval; no small matter, since player's contracts were expiring at year's end. Selig also presided over the executive council's decision to reprimand Cincinnati Red owner Marge Schott for racist remarks and restrict her baseball activities during the 1993 season.

Milwaukee-born Selig graduated from the University of Wisconsin at Madison in 1956. After service in the U.S. Army (1956–58), he worked in automobile leasing and sales (1959–90), as owner from 1966. He was part-owner of the Milwaukee Braves (1963–65), until their move to Atlanta, and co-owner and president of the Milwaukee Brewers (1970–   ), becoming interim commissioner of baseball (1991–   ). He has also served on the board of the Green Bay Packers football team, was co-founder of the Child Abuse Prevention Fund (1988), and has received numerous awards. Selig married Suzanne Lappin Steinman in 1977 and has two daughters.

FURTHER READING

"A healthy game. . . ." JOHN RAWLINGS. *Sporting News*, Oct. 25, 1993.

Sendak, Maurice Bernard (1928–   ) In 1993, Maurice Sendak dug back into his own history, to two Mother Goose nursery rhymes he had been planning for over 20 years to make into a book, and further back into Dickensian images, linked with modern-day images of poverty and homelessness, especially focusing on children. The result was his first wholly new book in over ten years: *We Are All Down in the Dumps with Jack and Guy*. The visual style of the book, and the crush of characters running around on the pages, were also much affected by his decade of designing sets for operas; indeed, Sendak said he even heard the characters singing as he drew them. He said he was also inspired by working with Iona Opie on *I Saw Esau* (1992), which he illustrated. As usual with Sendak books, the themes have raised controversy among adults; children remain to be heard from.

Sendak also continued to run the Night

Kitchen, the national children's theatre he founded in 1990 with Arthur Yorinks to produce original plays, musical, ballets, and operas for children. Among their 1993 productions was Sendak's *Really Rosie*, with music by Carole King, which he was also producing as a film for Wild Things productions, under a long-term film-production contract that he and his partner John Carls have with TriStar Pictures.

Sendak has been a prolific author and illustrator of children's books since the early 1950s, illustrating such books as *A Hole Is to Dig* (1952), *I'll Be You and You Be Me* (1954), *Charlotte and the White Horse* (1955), *Hector Protector* (1965), *Zlateh the Goat* (1966), *In the Night Kitchen* (1970), *Outside Over There* (1981), *The Love For Three Oranges* (1984), and *Dear Mili* (1988), and writing and illustrating such books as *Kenny's Window* (1956), *The Nutshell Library* (1963), and the Caldecott Award-winning *Where the Wild Things Are* (1963), one of the top ten all-time best-selling children's books. He has also written for television and done several stage designs, in opera and ballet. He attended the Art Students League.

FURTHER READING

Angels and Wild Things: The Archetypal Poetics of Maurice Sendak. JOHN CECH. Pennsylvania State University Press, 1994.
"Why is Maurice Sendak. . . ." LEONARD S. MARCUS. *Parenting*, Oct. 1993.

"Seriously Sendak." JED PERL. *Vogue*, Sep. 1993.

Maurice Sendak. JULIE BERG. Abdo & Daughters, 1993.

Writers Dreaming-Dreamers Writing: 25 Writers Discuss Dreams and the Creative Process. NAOMI EPEL. Crown, 1993.

"The wild world. . . ." SARA EVANS. *Parents' Magazine*, Nov. 1992.

Maurice Sendak. AMY SONHEIM. Twayne/Macmillan, 1992.

"Reflections." *Life*, Spring 1990.

"Maurice Sendak. . . ." GLENN EDWARD SADLER. *Horn Book Magazine*, Sep.-Oct. 1989.

"Sendak, Maurice (Bernard)." *Current Biography*, June 1989.

Sessions, William Steele (1930–)

On July 19, 1993, President Bill Clinton fired Federal Bureau of Investigation (FBI) director William Sessions, on the recommendation of Attorney General Janet Reno. Sessions had refused to resign midway through his ten-year term, although Administration pressure to do so had been building ever since a January 1993 Justice Department Office of Professional Responsibility report that had sharply criticized his handling of expenses and prerogatives while in office. He had also been hurt by criticisms of his leadership style, and by the Branch Dravidian debacle at Waco, Texas, though his defenders pointed out that some of those criticizing him had reacted adversely to his campaign to open up the FBI to women and minorities, and that many in the outgoing Republican administration felt that the Bush candidacy had been hurt by FBI actions late in the 1992 presidential campaign.

Arkansas-born Sessions began his long legal career in Waco, Texas, as a partner in McGregor and Sessions (1959–61), and continued to practice in Waco until 1969. He moved to Washington as head of the government operations section of the criminal division of the Justice Department (1969–71) and then back to Texas as a U.S. Attorney in San Antonio (1971–74). He was appointed a U.S. District Judge for western Texas (1974–80) and was later chief judge for that district court (1980–87). He was appointed head of the Federal Bureau of Investigation in 1987. His B.A. and J.D. were from Baylor University. He is married to Alice Lewis, and has four children.

FURTHER READING

"Cleaning up a messy bureau." BILL TURQUE. *Newsweek*, July 26, 1993.

"Unthinkable befalls. . . ." COLIN SMITH. *Observer*, July 25, 1993.

"Why not just fire him?" SOPHFRONIA SCOTT GREGORY. *Time*, July 12, 1993.

"Wanted! by the FBI. . . ." JAN JARBOE. *Texas Monthly*, May 1993.

"Bill and Alice. . . ." CHUCK CONCONI and HARRY JAFFE. *Washingtonian*, Mar. 1993.

"Under fire at the FBI." ANDREA SACHS. *Time*, Feb. 22, 1993.

"Is America's top cop. . . ." DAVID A. KAPLAN. *Newsweek*, Feb. 1, 1993.

Seth, Vikram (1952–)

The year 1993 saw the publication of a new novel notable for several reasons. *A Suitable Boy*, the first prose novel of Indian poet and travel writer Vikram Seth, was the longest single-volume fictional work published in English since Samuel Richard's *Clarissa* in 1747; Seth's typed manuscript ran 5000 pages and the printed book 1349 pages—though for all its length at least one reviewer lauded it as "not bloated, but spare," and many praised it as having the sweep of the great 19th-century novels. The book also won a £250,000 advance from its British publisher, Orion, the largest ever paid in Britain for a first novel, with Seth's American advance bringing the total to a million dollars.

Because of its length, and because Seth was based in India, the book was produced there in a single uniform edition for Indian, English, and

American buyers, all three groups making the work a best-seller; in America, it was a main selection of the Book-of-the-Month club. Seth had returned to India in 1985 to write the saga, which focuses on four families-the Mehras, the Kapoors, the Chatterjis, and the Khans-in the imaginary northern city of Brahmpur, in the newly independent India of the early 1950s, with the background of all the social changes that entailed. The book's central character is Lata Mehra, a law student (Seth's own mother is a lawyer and magistrate), whose parents attempt to find and convince her to marry the title's "suitable boy."

Also in 1993, Seth published *Three Chinese Poets*, his translations of three T'ang dynasty poets: Du Fu, Li Bai, and Wang Wei. He had in 1992 also written an opera libretto about dolphins, *Arion and the Dolphin*, commissioned by the English National Opera, expected to premiere in 1994.

Born in Calcutta, Seth (pronounced "sate") was raised and educated in India, winning a scholarship to Oxford University, where he took his M.A. in philosophy, politics, and economics from Corpus Christi College in 1975. He received another M.A. in economics from Stanford University in 1977, and was based at Nanjing University, China, in 1982 while doing research in Chinese villages studying toward a further degree in economic demography. Seth later worked as senior editor of Stanford University Press (1985–86). After publication of a first volume of

poetry, *Mappings* (1980), Seth came to wide literary notice with *From Heaven Lake: Travels Through Sinkiang and Tibet* (1983), which won Britain's prestigious Thomas Cook Travel Book award. Further works of poetry followed, including *The Humble Administrator's Garden* (1985) and *All You Who Sleep Tonight* (1990). Inspired by Pushkin's *Eugene Onegin*, but using contemporary themes and language, he also wrote a widely praised novel-in-verse, *The Golden Gate* (1986), which won the Commonwealth Poetry Prize for the Asian Region and later the Quality Paperback Book Club's New Voice award on its American paperback publication (1990). Other awards include an Ingram Merrill fellowship (1985–86) and a Guggenheim fellowship (1986–87).

FURTHER READING

"A suitable sensation." CHRISTOPHER HITCHENS. *Vanity Fair*, June 1993.
"Vikram Seth. . . ." MICHELE FIELD. *Publishers Weekly*, May 10, 1993.
"Vikram Seth's big book." RICHARD B. WOODWARD. *New York Times Magazine*, May 2, 1993.

Shalala, Donna Edna (1941–) U.S. Secretary of Health and Human Services Donna Shalala during 1993 played a substantial role in developing and then in trying to "sell" the Clinton universal health care plan to Congress and the American people, while at the same time dealing with the host of matters generated by her enormous federal department, greatly burdened by inadequate funding. Among the most notable of the few concrete, positive new accomplishments of Shalala and her department were the provision of free flu vaccinations for Medicare recipients and a plan to provide free vaccines for children who were uninsured or Medicaid recipients. In March, she approved Oregon's experimental health care rationing plan, to go into effect in 1994. On December 1, Shalala announced the formation of another task force to foster development of AIDS drugs.

Cleveland-born Shalala began her long career in education as a Peace Corps teacher in Iran (1962–64). She worked at Syracuse University (1965–70), was assistant professor of political science at City University of New York (CUNY) (1970–72), and was an associate professor at Teachers College of Columbia University (1972–79). She moved into goverment as an assistant secretary for policy development and research at the Department of Housing and Urban Development (1977–80). Shalala emerged as a major figure as president of Hunter College (1980–88), and then as the highly visible chancellor of the University of Wisconsin (1988–92), in that position stressing multicultural education and ethnic and women's studies and rights. Among her many advisory board and board of director posts is that of chairman of the board of the Children's Defense Fund. Her 1962 A.B. was from Western College, and her 1968 M.S.S.C. from Syracuse University, as was her 1970 Ph.D.

FURTHER READING

"The Shalala strategy. . . ." JEFFREY TOOBIN. *New Yorker*, Apr. 26, 1993.
"Campus CEO." CEIL CLEVELAND. *Working Woman*, Dec. 1991.
"Shalala, Donna Edna." *Current Biography*, Mar. 1991.
"Big campus, big issues. . . ." BONNIE ANGEL. *Time*, Apr. 23, 1990.
"Tackling the Big Ten. . . ." LINDSY VAN GELDER. *Savvy Woman*, Dec. 1989.

Shalikashvili, John Malchase David

(1936–) On August 11, 1993, President Bill Clinton selected General John Shalikashvili to head the Joint Chiefs of Staff, to succeed retiring

general Colin Powell. Warsaw-born Shalikashvili, who had emigrated to the United States with his family after World War II, began his military career as a draftee, attended Officers Candidate School, and emerged a second lieutenant in 1959. He served in Vietnam (1968–69), and began moving up in earnest after earning an M.A. in international affairs from George Washington University in 1970. He was later a divisional commander, commanded Allied forces in Kurdish-held northern Iraq after the Persian Gulf War, and became supreme Allied commander in Europe in 1992. That his father, Dimitri Shalikashvili, had fought with Nazi-organized Georgian units during World War II, did not impede his acceptance as Joint Chiefs head.

FURTHER READING

"Globo-cops. . . ." TOM MORGANTHAU and JOHN BARRY. *Newsweek*, Aug. 23, 1993.
"The rules of the game. . . ." BRIAN DUFFY. *U.S. News & World Report*, Aug. 23, 1993.
"Army man named. . . ." *Facts on File*, Aug. 12, 1993.

Sharaff, Irene (1910–93) Boston-born

Irene Sharaff began her career as a fashion illustrator, emerging in the early 1930s as a leading theater and cinema costume designer, who ultimately designed clothes for approximately

60 shows and 40 musicals. Her breakthrough came in 1932, with Eve Le Gallienne's Civic Repertory Theater production of *Alice in Wonderland*, followed by more plays and by costumes for the Ballet Russes de Monte Carlo, American Ballet Theater, and New York City Ballet. Sharaff won 15 Oscar nominations and 5 Oscars, for *An American in Paris* (1951), *The King and I* (1956), *West Side Story* (1961), *Cleopatra*(1963), and *Who's Afraid of Virginia Woolf?* (1966). On Broadway, she won a Tony and two Donaldson awards. There were no survivors. (d. New York City; August 16, 1993)

FURTHER READING

"Irene Sharaff." *Dance Magazine*, Nov. 1993.
Obituary. *The Times* (of London), Aug. 19, 1993.
Obituary. *Variety*, Aug. 18, 1993.
Obituary. *New York Times*, Aug. 17, 1993.
"Costume drama." MEREDITH BRODY. *Interview*, Aug. 1989.

Shatner, William (1931–) Boldly going

Shatner, William (1931–) Boldly going where few of his colleagues had gone before, William Shatner-better known as Captain James Kirk-produced his memoirs of the early days of the cult television series "Star Trek," in *Star Trek Memories*, written with Chris Kreski. As part of a major publicity campaign, Shatner was seen on numerous television shows, and made a nationwide publicity tour. Sold in bookstores as usual, the book also appeared in audio form and in a specially autographed, leatherbound edition, some of which were sold on the QVC home shopping network. A seventh *Star Trek* film was in the offing, but this one was to focus on the "next generation;" Shatner and co-star Leonard Nimoy had said the sixth would be their last.

Benefitting from all this publicity was Shatner's futuristic detective series; his fifth novel, *Tek Secret*, was published in November 1993; Shatner was scheduled to direct and act as executive producer for a series of television movies based on his novels. In May 1993, Shatner hosted the first "Tekwar" Symposium, held in Los Angeles, exploring life in the future, specifically in 2043, when *Tekwar* was set.

Shatner was also scheduled to be grand marshal of the 105th Rose Bowl Parade in Pasadena on New Year's Day 1994, the parade's theme being "Fantastic Adventure." In February 1993,

he appeared in a television movie, *A Family of Strangers*, playing an adoptive parent.

Montreal-born Shatner graduated from McGill University in 1952, the same year he made his stage debut at the Montreal Playhouse. He performed at Ottawa's Canadian Repertory Theatre (1952–54), primarily in juvenile roles, and the Stratford Shakespeare Festival in Ontario (1954–56), receiving the Tyrone Guthrie award in 1956, before appearing on Broadway in *Tamburlaine the Great* (1956), *The World of Suzie Wong* (1958), and *A Shot in the Dark* (1961). Early film appearances include *The Brothers Karamazov* (1958), *The Explosive Generation* (1961), *Judgment at Nuremburg* (1961), *The Intruder* (1962), and *The Outrage* (1964), but it was "Star Trek" (1966–69) that brought him lasting fame. Much other television work followed, including the animated "Star Trek" series (1973–75), "Barbary Coast" (1975–76), "T.J. Hooker" (1982–86), and as host, "Rescue 911" (1989–). But his film career became dominant with the enormous success of the film *Star Trek* (1979), and its successors: *The Wrath of Khan* (1982), *The Search for Spock* (1984), *The Voyage Home* (1986), *The Final Frontier* (1989), which he also directed, and *The Undiscovered Country* (1991). He also appeared in *National Lampoon's Loaded Weapon* (1992). Shatner has also written several novels in a science fiction detective series, including *TekWar* (1989), *TekLords* (1991), *TekLab* (1991), and *Tek Vengeance* (1992). Previously divorced, he married Marcy Lafferty in 1973 and has three daughters.

FURTHER READING

William Shatner: A Bio-Bibliography. DENNIS WILLIAM HAUCK. Greenwood, 1994.
"Warp speed ahead." RICK MARIN and MICHAEL LOGAN. *TV Guide*, July 24, 1993.
"I'm typing. . . ." BENJAMIN SVETKEY. *Entertainment Weekly*, Jan. 15, 1993.
"20 questions. . . ." DAVID RENSIN. *Playboy*, July 1989.

Sheehan, George (1918–93)

Sheehan, George (1918–93) Brooklyn-born George Sheehan, a cardiologist, began his practice of medicine in the mid-1940s. He had been a runner in college, but had given running up in favor of other sports. In 1962, he broke his hand, could not then participate in his favorite sports, and took up running again, finding personal salvation in the process. He became a philosophical leader of the running movement, speaking widely and writing prolifically on the virtues of running; among his books were *This Running Life* (1980), *Personal Best* (1989) and *Dr. Sheehan on Running to Win* (1992). He discontinued his medical practice in 1984, then devoting full-time to the sport. During several years of treatment for the prostate cancer that ultimately took his life, he continued running, speaking, and writing. He was survived by his wife, Mary, five daughters, and seven sons. (d. Ocean Grove, New Jersey; November 5, 1993)

FURTHER READING

Obituary. *The Times* (of London), Nov. 13, 1993.
Obituary. *New York Times*, Nov. 2, 1993.

Sheen, Martin (Ramon Estevez; 1940–) Veteran actor Martin Sheen played in a variety of roles during 1993. In the film *Hear No Evil*, directed by Robert Greenwald, he played a crooked Portland cop, opposite Marlee Matlin, D.B. Sweeney, and John C. McGinley. In Ted Turner's 4-hour-plus television epic *Gettysburg*, written and directed by Ronald F. Maxwell, Sheen played Confederate general Robert E. Lee. In the television film *A Matter of Justice*, directed by Michael Switzer, he played opposite Patty Duke as her husband in a smalltown family drama. In the television mini-series *Alex Haley's "Queen"*, directed by John Erman, and co-

starring Halle Berry, Ann-Margret, and Jasmine Guy in a large cast, he played an Alabama plantation owner during slavery days. He also hosted the television music film series "Played in the U.S.A." Forthcoming was a starring role in the film *The Break*, co-starring Ren Jorgenson, Rae Dawn Chong, Valerie Perrine, and Vince Van Patten.

Ohio-born Sheen played on stage with the Living Theatre from 1959, on Broadway in *The Subject Was Roses* (1964; and in the 1968 film version) and at the New York Shakespeare Festival in the late 1960s. On screen, he appeared in such films as *Catch-22* (1970), *Apocalypse Now* (1979), *Gandhi* (1982), *Wall Street* (1987), and *The Maid* (1991), and such telefilms as *The Execution of Private Slovik* (1974), *The Missiles of October* (1974; as Robert Kennedy), *Blind Ambition* (1979; as John Dean), *Kennedy* (1982; as John F. Kennedy), *Samaritan: The Mitch Snyder Story* (1986; as homeless activist Snyder), and *Guilty Until Proven Innocent* (1991). In 1992, he starred on Broadway opposite Maryann Plunkett in the National Actors Theater production of *The Crucible*. He married Janet Sheen in 1961; they have four children, two them the actors Charlie Sheen and Emilio Estevez.

FURTHER READING

Martin Sheen: Actor and Activist. Jim Hargrove. Childrens, 1991.

Shevardnadze, Eduard Amvroslyevich (1928–) As the conflict in the Georgian Black Sea region of Abkhazia intensified, Georgian leader Eduard Shevardnadze appealed to Russian president Boris Yeltsin to stop the fighting and negotiate an end to what had become an undeclared Georgian-Russian war. But the fighting went on, through several broken ceasefires, a United Nations-brokered peace agreement in July, and an August Georgian-Russian friendship treaty. Georgian forces began to withdraw from Abkhazia during the summer, and Abkhazian rebel forces then broke the ceasefire, successfully attacked, and took the province in September, taking the Abkhazian capital, Sukhumi, on September 27. Shevardnadze, who had gone to Sukhumi, was forced to flee. Insurrection also continued in western Georgia, led by former president Zviad K. Gam-

sakhurdia. On October 22, Shevardnadze reluctantly took Georgia into the Commonwealth of Independent States (CIS), secured Russian armed intervention against Gamsakurdia's forces, and then quickly defeated Gamsakurdia. The question of Abkhazia remained open.

Until he went home to Georgia in 1992 Shevardnadze had spent his whole life in Communist Party and Soviet government work, beginning his career in the late 1940s, and rising through a series of Communist Party positions in his native Georgia through the early 1970s. His first major move came in 1972, when he led an anticorruption campaign in Georgia and replaced the Republic's party leader. He was first secretary of the Georgian Communist Party (1972–85), becoming a Soviet Central Committee member in 1976. Long associated with Mikhail Gorbachev, Shevardnadze replaced Andrei Gromyko as Soviet foreign minister in 1985 and remained in that position throughout most of the extraordinary Gorbachev era. He broke with Gorbachev and resigned as foreign minister on December 20, 1990, because of the too-slow pace of reform and Gorbachev's appointment of hard-line conservative Communists to key positions; at the time, he warned against a restoration of right-wing Communist dictatorship, raising the prospect of a disastrous civil war should that happen. He then founded the Soviet Foreign Policy Association and the Democratic Reform Movement. In December 1991, he served briefly as the last Soviet foreign minister.

Shevardnadze was chosen to head the Georgia's State Council in March 1992, and then tried to unify his fragmented country, with armed secession movements in South Ossetia and Abkhazia, and the armed forces of deposed Georgia President Gamsakhurdia in western Georgia. On October 11, 1992, Shevardnadze was elected parliamentary Speaker, and as such effectively president of Georgia. He immediately moved to deal with the civil war in Abkhazia. He and Yeltsin had arranged a ceasefire in that war on September 3, followed by major Georgian force reductions in the area. But Abkhazian rebel forces, helped by Russian "volunteers" and armed with Russian weapons and supplies, then quickly moved in to take much of Abkhazia, while Yeltsin ordered Russian forces in Abkhazia to protect Russians there.

Shevardnadze attended the Kutaisi Pedagogical Institute. He has published *The Future Be-*

longs to Freedom: World Peace and Democracy in the U.S.S.R. (1991).

FURTHER READING

" 'The dark forces. . . .' " *Time*, Oct. 5, 1992.
"Georgia preying. . . ." PETER PRINGLE. *Independent*, Sep. 24, 1992.
"Curious Georgia." SIMON SEBAG MONTEFIORE. *New Republic*, June 29, 1992.
" 'Mikhail Gorbachev has. . . .' " *U.S. News & World Report*, Sep. 2, 1991.
"A growing momentum. . . ." PIERRE BOCEV. *World Press Review*, Sept. 1991.
"Shevardnadze . . . ." *Time*, May 13, 1991.
"Shevardnadze. . . ." *Fortune*, May 20, 1991.
"The alternative is dictatorship." *Time*, Apr. 16, 1990.
"Falcon of the Kremlin." E. KAYE FULTON. *Maclean's*, Feb. 26, 1990.

Shilts, Randy (1951–) Journalist-author Randy Shilts continued to work on the edge of controversy in 1993. He worked as consultant on the film of his 1987 book, *And the Band Played On*, chronicling the early years of the AIDS crisis, from the first obscure, largely ignored contacts with the newly discovered disease to its emergence as a widespread epidemic. The controversial work, highly critical of those who might have had a chance to halt the spread of the deadly disease, had been in development for several years, but was finally completed in 1992 when several major actors signed to do the film, including Richard Gere, Alan Alda, Lily Tomlin, B.D. Wong, Saul Rubinek, Steve Martin, Anjelica Huston, Phil Collins, David Dukes, Swoosie Kurtz, Richard Masur, Stephen Spinella, Nathalie Baye, and Glenne Headly, many appearing in cameos, and two central figures, Matthew Modine and Ian McKellen. Directed by Roger Spottiswoode from a final script by Arnold Schulman, it first aired in September 1993 on HBO, to an estimated audience of over 3 million, and was bought for later network showing by NBC, which had originally planned to film the work, but then passed.

Shilts also had a new controversial work, *Conduct Unbecoming: Lesbians and Gays in the U.S. Military, Vietnam to the Persian Gulf*, detailing participation of and discrimination against homosexuals in the military, actually back to the Revolutionary War. The work was published in

April 1993, while the Clinton administration and the military were publicly at odds over the role of gays and lesbians in the armed forces. In 1993, HBO Pictures announced plans to film *Conduct Unbecoming*; Oliver Stone was also set to direct for HBO an earlier work, *The Mayor of Castro Street*, about murdered gay San Francisco supervisor Harvey Milk. Shilts himself was widely interviewed and profiled in the print, radio, and screen media, and *Conduct Unbecoming* quickly became a best-seller. Most interviews were conducted from San Francisco, where Shilts lives, because his illness prevented him from traveling.

Shilts had earlier, in February 1993, announced that he was himself infected with the HIV virus that causes AIDS; he learned this just as he finished writing *And the Band Played On*, in March 1987, and a collapsed lung almost prevented him from finishing *Conduct Unbecoming*. He explained that he had not gone public before because he wanted to remain a reporter, not be forced into the role of activist. He also announced that he was endowing a journalism scholarship at the University of Oregon, his alma mater. In 1993, Shilts married his lover, Barry Barbieri.

Born in Davenport, Iowa, Shilts received his B.S. from the University of Oregon in 1975. He worked as a reporter for San Francisco's station KQED (1977–80) and Oakland's KTVU (1979–80), before joining the *San Francisco Chronicle* in 1981 as staff reporter and then, from 1988, national correspondent. His books, inspired by his reporting on current issues, include *The Mayor of Castro Street: The Life and Times of Harvey Milk* (1982) and *And the Band Played On: Politics, People, and the AIDS Epidemic* (1987). He has received numerous awards, including the Media Alliance award for outstanding non-fiction author (1982), Outstanding Communicator award from the Association of Educational Journalism and Mass Communication (1988), and Outstanding Author award from the American Society of Journalists (1988).

FURTHER READING

"Shilts, Randy." *Current Biography*, Oct. 1993.
"Randy Shilts. . . ." GARRY WILLS. *Rolling Stone*, Sep. 30, 1993.
"The life and times. . . ." JEFF YARBROUGH. *Advocate*, June 15, 1993.
"AIDS and the media . . ." JOHN KATZ. *Rolling Stone*, May 27, 1993.

"Writer of wrongs." DAVID ELLIS. *People*, Apr. 26, 1993.

Shirer, William L(awrence) (1904–93)

Born in Chicago and raised in Iowa, Shirer began his long career in journalism as a reporter for the *Cedar Rapids Republican*, while still a student at Coe College. After graduation, he went to Paris, where he worked for several newspapers and freelanced, reporting on the rise of Naziism as Berlin correspondent of Univeral News Service (1935–37). In 1937, he became a broadcaster, hired by London-based Edward Murrow to open the CBS Vienna office, and continued to report from Europe on the rise of fascism (1937–41). His work in the 1930s resulted in the books *Berlin Diary* (1941) and his massive worldwide best-seller *The Rise and Fall of the Third Reich: A History of Nazi Germany* (1960), the work for which he became a world figure. He later reported that he had found the time to write the latter book because he had been blacklisted by the networks after having been falsely accused of being a Communist during the McCarthy era. Among his other books were *End of a Berlin Diary* (1947), *The Consul's Wife* (1956), *The Collapse of the Third Republic* (1969), *Gandhi: A Memoir* (1980), and the autobiographical trilogy *Twentieth Century Journey: Start: 1904–1930* (1976), *The Nightmare Years: 1930–1940* (1984), and *A Native's Return: 1945–1988* (1990). His final work was *Love and Hatred: The Troubled Marriage of Leo and Sonya Tolstoy* (1994). He was survived by his wife, Irina Lugovskaya Shirer, and two daughters. (d. Boston; December 28, 1993)

FURTHER READING

Obituary. *New York Times*, Dec. 30, 1993.
"Fear of reunification." BARTH HEALY. *New York Times Book Review*, Jan. 21, 1990.
"The lessons of history." JAMES DODSON. *Yankee*, Jan. 1990.

Shirley, Anne (Dawn Paris; 1918–93)

New York City-born Anne Shirley began her movie career at the age of five, as Dawn O'Day, making her debut in *Moonshine Valley* (1922). Among her early films were *Riders of the Purple Sage* (1925), *Night Life* (1927), *Liliom* (1930), and *So

Big (1932). In 1934, she starred in a film version of *Anne of Green Gables* as Anne Shirley, taking that as her stage name. She also starred in the sequel, *Anne of Windy Poplars* (1940). Shirley received a best supporting actress nomination for her role in *Stella Dallas* (1937), also appearing in more than a score of other films, among them *Steamboat 'Round the Bend* (1935), *Chatterbox* (1936), *All That Money Can Buy* (1941), and *Murder My Sweet* (1944). She retired in 1945, after marrying producer Adrian Scott, her second husband. Her first and third husbands were actors John Payne and Charles Lederer. She was survived by a daughter and a son. (d. Los Angeles; July 4, 1993)

FURTHER READING

Obituary. *The Times* (of London), July 9, 1993.
Obituary. *Variety*, July 8, 1993.

Shula, Don Francis (1930–) On November 14, 1993, Miami Dolphins coach Don Shula passed one of football's major milestones: He became the winningest coach ever in the history of football, his team's 19–14 victory over the Philadelphia Eagles being the 325th of Shula's career. That win broke the record held by the great Chicago Bears coach George Halas, whose 324 career wins Shula had tied just two weeks earlier. To put Shula's achievement in perspective, when he won his 324th game, his closest competitors among coaches still currently active in the National Football League were Chuck Knox with 186 wins and Dan Reeves with 122. *Sports Illustrated* named Shula its Sportsman of the Year.

Despite his achievements, 1993 was not an easy year. Miami's star quarterback, Dan Marino, had a season-ending injury early in the year, and was replaced by Scott Mitchell, who was himself injured during Shula's record-breaking game. After that Shula brought out of retirement veteran quarterback Steve DeBerg, who served well until Mitchell was able to return. At one point Miami was tied for the best record in the league, but it all unraveled late in the season, as a series of losses kept them out of the playoffs; the team finished with a record of 9–7. On the personal side, Shula married for the second time in 1993, to Mary Anne Shula.

Ohio-born Shula received his B.S. from Cleveland's John Carroll University in 1951 and his M.A. from Case Western Reserve University in 1953. He began his professional career as a defensive back with the Cleveland Browns (1951–52), moved to the Baltimore Colts (1953–56), and the Washington Redskins (1957), and then became an assistant coach at the University of Virginia (1958) and the University of Kentucky (1959). He moved back into the professional ranks as assistant coach of the Detroit Lions (1960–62), head coach of the Baltimore Colts (1963–69), the youngest NFL head coach ever, and finally head coach of the Miami Dolphins (1970–). He took six teams to the Super Bowl, one from Baltimore (1969) and five from Miami (1972; 1973; 1974; 1983; 1985), winning back to back in 1973 and 1974, the former after the only perfect season in NFL history (17–0). He was named Coach of the Year five times (1964; 1966; 1970; 1971; 1972), and Coach of the Decade (1980) by the Pro Football Hall of Fame. He published *The Winning Edge* (1972). Shula's first wife, Dorothy, died of cancer in 1991; they had five children, one of whom, David, is also a professional football coach, for the Cincinnati Bengals.

FURTHER READING

"Don Shula." PAUL ZIMMERMAN. *Sports Illustrated*, Dec. 20, 1993. "Sportsman of the Year" issue.

Sihanouk, Norodom (1922–) King Norodom Sihanouk came close to completing his historic task in 1993-the creation of an independent multiparty democracy in Cambodia. In 1991, he had been the prime mover in negotiating the Treaty of Paris, sponsored by the United States, the Soviet Union, and China, under United Nations auspices. The treaty, which ended the long Cambodian Civil War, provided for an immediate ceasefire, the return home of an estimated 350,000 refugees, and the posting of thousands of UN trooops and civilian personnel to keep the peace, help set up a new government, and prepare for free elections to be held in 1993. Despite continuing Khmer Rouge refusal to surrender its arms and demobilize, and escalating Khmer Rouge armed actions that came close to reopening the civil war, Sihanouk saw the treaty through during 1993. Although the Khmer Rouge boycotted the May national elec-

tions, 90 percent of the country's registered voters turned out to vote. The royalist coalition party (Funcinpec) defeated the Cambodian People's Party (CPP) in the free election; the two parties then joined in a government of national unity. The 22,000 UN peacekeepers then began to leave the country, and almost all had left by year's end. Despite continuing opposition, Khmer Rouge forces weakened.

On September 24, Sihanouk once again took the Cambodian throne he had renounced in 1955, ruling as a constitutional monarch, with his son, Prince Norodom Ranariddh as first premier and CPP leader Hun Sen as second premier. Sihanouk then moved against the Khmer Rouge, still holding 20 percent of the country with an estimated force of 10,000. Cambodian government forces attacked and took several Khmer Rouge bases in November and December, driving Khmer Rouge forces toward their established sanctuaries in Thailand. What remained to be seen was whether a long, continuing guerrilla war would develop, or whether Cambodian and international pressure would cause the Thai military to withdraw its support of the Khmer Rouge.

Eighteen-year-old Prince Sihanouk was named King of Cambodia by the French colonial occupiers of his country in 1941, and remained a nominal ruler under Vichy French collaborationist rule during much of the Japanese World War II occupation. Late in the war, the Japanese took control of Cambodia; Sihanouk then declared Cambodian independence, and led the national independence movement until Cambodian independence was won in 1953. He quit the throne in 1955, was prime minister of democratic Cambodia in the mid-1950s, and was the elected head of his country from 1960 to 1970. In 1970, his government was deposed by the Lon Nol military dictatorship, and Cambodia then endured the civil war that ended with the 1975 victory of the Khmer Rouge. Under Khmer Rouge house arrest, Sihanouk cooperated with the murderous new government and its Chinese allies, going into Chinese exile. He remained in exile through the balance of the Cambodian Holocaust and the 1979 Vietnamese invasion. In 1982, he became head of a new coalition government in exile, resigning after Khmer Rouge attacks on other Cambodian guerrilla groups. He returned to coalition leadership in 1988, and in 1989 started the long process of negotiation that led to the Vietnamese troop withdrawals that began in 1989, and the on-and-off negotiations during 1990 and 1991 that resulted in the 1991 peace treaty.

In 1980, Sihanouk published *War and Hope: The Case for Cambodia.* He is married and has had fourteen children.

FURTHER READING

The Terrible but Unfinished Story of Norodom Sihanouk, King of Cambodia. HELEN CIXOUS. University of Nebraska Press, 1994.
"Sihanouk becomes. . . ." *Facts on File*, Sep. 30, 1993.
"Sihanouk, Norodom." *Current Biography*, Aug. 1993.
"Crazy in Cambodia." ROBERT SAM ANSON. *Esquire*, Aug. 1992.
"The man who. . . ." *Economist*, Sep. 29, 1990.
Prince Sihanouk. MADHARI KUCKREJA. Chelsea House, 1990.
"The prince presses on." *Time*, Dec. 11, 1989.
"Sihanouk on the high wire. . . ." ADAM PLATT. *Newsweek*, May 15, 1989.
"An exiled leader. . . ." *Insight*, Jan. 20, 1989.

Simon, Neil (Marvin Neil Simon; 1927–) Simon had a hit and a flop on stage in 1993, as well as a hit on film. His hit came in late November, with the Broadway opening of his acclaimed autobiographical comedy *Laughter on the 23rd Floor*, hailed as one of the funniest plays to come to Broadway in many years. In this play, Simon returned to his television-writing days of the 1950s, the Sid Caesar shows, and the era of creative freedom that would end with the triumph of McCarthyism. Jerry Zaks directed a cast that included Nathan Lane, Mark Linn-Baker, John Slattery, Stephen Mailer, Lewis J. Stadlin, J.K. Simmons, Randy Graff, Billy Schram, and Ron Orbach. Simon's flop came earlier, with the failure of the $7 million musical *The Goodbye Girl*, based on his 1977 film; Bernadette Peters and Martin Short starred, and Michael Kidd directed.

His film success came with the well-received film version of his 1991 Pulitzer Prize and Tony-winning play *Lost in Yonkers*. Simon adapted the play for the film, which was directed by Martha Coolidge and starred Richard Dreyfuss, Mercedes Ruehl, and Irene Worth. The illustrated screenplay was published in book form, with commentary by Simon.

New York City-born Simon worked as a radio and television comedy writer in the 1950s, most notably for Phil Silvers and Sid Caesar, and began his long career as a leading playwright with *Come Blow Your Horn* (1961). That work was followed by more than a score of other plays, including such hits as *Barefoot in the Park* (1963; and the 1967 film adaptation), *The Odd Couple* (1965; and the 1968 film), *The Star-Spangled Girl* (1966), *Plaza Suite* (1968; and the 1971 film), *Last of the Red Hot Lovers* (1969), *The Prisoner of Second Avenue* (1971; and the 1975 film), *The Sunshine Boys* (1972; and the 1975 film), and *California Suite* (1976; and the 1978 film), and *Jake's Women* (1992). Much of Simon's work is to some extent autobiographical, and five plays are directly so: *Chapter Two* (1977; and the 1979 film), *I Ought to Be in Pictures* (1980; and the 1982 film), *Brighton Beach Memoirs* (1983; and the 1986 film), the Tony-winning *Biloxi Blues* (1985; and the 1988 film), and *Broadway Bound* (1986). He has also written the books for several musicals, including *Little Me* (1962), *Sweet Charity* (1966), and *Promises, Promises* (1968); and has written several filmscripts, most notably the *The Goodbye Girl* (1977), which starred his second wife, Marsha Mason. Simon attended New York University. He has been married three times, and has two children.

FURTHER READING

"King of comedy's. . . ." HAP EPSTEIN. *Insight*, Mar. 18, 1991.
"The last of the. . . ." DAVID RICHARDS. *New York Times Magazine*, Feb. 17, 1991.
"Simon, Marvin Neil." *Current Biography*, Mar. 1989.

Simon, Norton Winfred (1907–93)

Portland-born Norton Simon, a leading American art collector and former industrialist, began his business career in the late 1920s, after dropping out of the University of California. He began with a small cannery, which he sold to the Hunt Brothers Packing Company in the early 1940s. He than gained control of Hunt, spent most of the next three decades building a highly diversified conglomerate, selling out and leaving business in 1969 to devote full time to art collecting. He began collecting artworks in 1954, and for almost four decades was one of the world's most active collectors, spending an estimated $100 million in that period to amass one of the world's most substantial private collections, ultimately showing it in Pasadena's Norton Simon Museum of Art. Simon was survived by his wife, the actress Jennifer Jones, and by a son and a sister. (d. Los Angeles; June 2, 1993)

FURTHER READING

Obituary. *Current Biography*, Aug. 1993.
Obituary. *The Times* (of London), June 30, 1993.
Obituary. *New York Times*, June 4, 1993.

Simon, Paul (1941–)

Paul Simon did a massive retrospective of his whole body of work in 1993. In the spring, the documentary video *Born At The Right Time* aired, following him throughout his long career, beginning as a teenager in Brooklyn and ending with his 1992 South African tour, complete with his own commentary and interviews with those close to him and many other musicians, and including much concert and other material shot on the road.

In September, Simon issued a three-CD collection consisting of most of his work, and during October he appeared at New York's Paramount Theater in series of concerts that presented his body of work live, including a reunion concert with Art Garfunkel. He then toured extensively. A major new project is a coming collaboration with poet Derek Walcott to create a Broadway musical.

On the personal side, Simon and his wife, singer Edie Brickell, became the parents of Adrian Edward Simon.

Newark-born Simon and Art Garfunkel were one of the leading folk-rock groups of the 1960s, beginning with their album *Wednesday Morning 3 A.M* (1965), with Simon's hit song "Sound of Silence," and ending with the extraordinarily popular Grammy-winning album *Bridge Over Troubled Water* (1970), its title song still a worldwide favorite. Their work together included the albums *Parsley, Sage, Rosemary, and Thyme* (1967), *Bookends* (1968), and the score of the film *The Graduate* (1968), with its Grammy-winning song "Mrs. Robinson." After 1971, Simon went solo, creating such albums as *Paul Simon* (1972), *Still Crazy After All These Years* (1975), *Hearts and Bones* (1983), the Grammy-winning *Graceland* (1986), and *The Rhythm of the Saints* (1990). He wrote, scored, and starred in the film *One Trick Pony* (1980), and has written the children's book *At the Zoo* (1991). Simon attended Queens College. Previously twice married, the second time to actress-writer Carrie Fisher, Simon married Edie Brickell in 1992; they have one son.

FURTHER READING

"Homeward bound." JEFF GILES. *Newsweek*, Oct. 11, 1993.

"Profile. . . ." JESSE NASH and GEORGE FLOWERS. *Guitar Player*, Feb. 1991.

"In praise of midlife crisis. . . ." DAVID GATES. *Newsweek*, Jan. 14, 1991.

"Songs of a thinking man. . . ." JAY COCKS. *Time*, Nov. 12, 1990.

"Flying down to Rio . . ." BRIAN D. JOHNSON. *Maclean's*, Nov. 12, 1990.

Paul Simon: Still Crazy after All These Years. PATRICK HUMPHRIES. Doubleday, 1989.

Sinatra, Frank (Francis Albert Sinatra; 1915–)

In his 78th year, legendary and very live singer Sinatra went back to Capitol Records, where he had more than 30 years earlier generated so many hit records, and scored again, this time with the album *Duets*, a collection of 13 classic pairings with a wide range of partners, including a Sinatra-Barbara Streisand rendition of "I've Got a Crush on You," which also became a hit single, along with duets with Carly Simon, Julio Iglesias, Charles Aznavour, and others. *Duets* was to be the first of three Sinatra recordings with Capitol, unusual in that the duets were mixed electronically, with Sinatra and his partners not even singing in the same studio.

Capitol also issued a 19-song Sinatra retrospective collection, *Frank Sinatra at the Movies*. Sinatra himself appeared in concert throughout the year, and planned to do so into 1994. And, in a rare foray into televison, he appeared as himself in an episode of the the television comedy series "Daddy Dearest."

Sinatra began his singing career in cabaret in 1935. He became a popular singer and recording artist in 1940, while appearing with Tommy Dorsey's band. In January 1943, at a four-week engagement at New York's Paramount Theater, he became the first of the modern teenage idols, whose fans "swooned" and rioted over him. He also became a radio and film star on "Your Hit Parade," and in such musicals as *Anchors Aweigh* (1945) and *On the Town* (1949), and won a special Oscar for his role in *The House I Live In* (1945), a plea for tolerance. But he ran into serious throat problems in 1952, and his career all but vanished. He then made an extraordinary comeback as a dramatic actor, winning a best supporting actor Oscar as Maggio in *From Here to Eternity* (1953), and went on to such films as *Guys and Dolls* (1955), *The Joker Is Wild* (1957), *The Manchurian Candidate* (1962), and *The Detective* (1968). His vocal problems eased as well; he re-emerged as one of the leading song stylists of his time, continuing to tour into his mid-70s. He celebrated his 75th birthday in performance on television in December 1990 before a nationwide audience, and began his year-long world tour in the same month. He has also written a book about his other vocation: *A Man and his Art* (1990), in 1991 retitled *Paintings: A Man and his Art*. Sinatra has been married four times, and has three children, including singers Nancy Sinatra and Frank Sinatra, Jr.

FURTHER READING

"Secrets of. . . ." BUDD SCHULBERG. *New Choices for Retirement Living*, Dec.-Jan. 1993.

"Sinatra. . . ." SUSAN LITTWIN. *TV Guide*, Nov. 7, 1992.

"Really Frank? . . ." MARK HARRIS. *Entertainment*, Nov. 6, 1992.

"The man who was Sinatra." JOSEPH SOBRAN. *National Review*, Feb. 17, 1992.

Frank Sinatra. JESSICA HODGE. Outlet, 1992.
"Frank Sinatra. . . ." WALTER THOMAS. *Interview*, July 1991.
"Sinatra 101." CHRISTIAN LOGAN WRIGHT. *Mademoiselle*, Apr. 1991.
Frank Sinatra: A Complete Recording History . . . 1939–1984. RICHARD W. ACKELSON. McFarland, 1991.
"Still good and saucy. . . ." CHARLES LEERHSEN. *Newsweek*, Dec. 17, 1990.
"Under my skin." WILLIAM KENNEDY. *New York Times Magazine*, Oct. 7, 1990.
His Way: The Unauthorized Biography of Frank Sinatra. KITTY KELLEY. Bantam, 1987.
Sinatra: The Man and the Myth (An Unauthorized Biography). B. ADLER. NAL-Dutton, 1987.

Slayton, Deke (Donald Kent Slayton; 1924–93)

Wisconsin-born Deke Sleyton was a B-25 bomber pilot during World War II, and became an aeronautical engineer after the war. He returned to active duty as a fighter pilot during the Korean War, and then became air force test pilot. In 1959, he became one of the Mercury Seven, the first seven American astronauts, but was grounded because a heart condition shortly before he was to fly the second Earth-orbital mission. Sleyton then became the non-flying director of flight operations at the Johnson Space Center. Ultimately, his heart condition having apparently cured itself, he was one of the astronauts to fly the last Apollo mission, in 1971. He later worked in space-related private industry. Scheduled for publication in 1994 were his autobiography, *Deke!*, written with Michael Cassutt, and *Moon Shot: The Inside Story of America's Race to the Moon*, co-authored with Alan Shepard. He was survived by his wife, Bobbie Osborn, a son, two sisters, and two brothers. (d. League City, Texas; June 13, 1993)

FURTHER READING

Obituary. *Current Biography*, Aug. 1993.
"Donald Kent Slayton." KAREN BOEHLER. *Ad Astra*, July-Aug. 1991.
Obituary. *The Times* (of London), June 15, 1993.
Obituary. *New York Times*, June 14, 1993.

Smith, Alexis (Gladys Smith; 1921–93)

Canadian-born Alexis Smith grew up in Los Angeles, was "discovered" while appearing in a Los Angeles City College production, and signed to a Warner's contract. Her film debut came in *The Girl With Red Hair* (1940). Among her dozens of films in the two decades that followed were *The Constant Nymph* (1943), *The Adventures of Mark Twain* (1944), *Rhapsody in Blue* (1945), *Night and Day* (1946; as Cole Porter's wife), *The Two Mrs. Carrolls* (1948), *Any Number Can Play* (1949), *The Turning Point* (1952), *The Sleeping Tiger* (1954), and *The Young Philadelphians* (1959). She retired from films in 1960, though continuing to work on stage and in television. In 1971, she starred on Broadway in Stephen Sondheim's musical *Follies*, winning a Tony award as best actress in a musical. She also had a continuing role in the television series "Dallas." She was survived by her husband, actor Craig Stevens. (d. Los Angeles; June 9, 1993)

FURTHER READING

Obituary. *The Times* (of London), June 14, 1993.
Obituary. *New York Times*, June 10, 1993.
Obituary. *Variety*, June 10, 1993.
"Inventing Alexis Smith." MARTIN FILLER. *House & Garden*, Dec. 1991.

Smith, Emmitt J., III (1969–)

Three words say it all: Most Valuable Player. That's what Dallas Cowboys' running back Emmitt Smith was named for the National Football League's 1993 season. The Cowboys started 1993 on a high, defeating Buffalo handily, 52–17, in the Super Bowl in January. In the new fall 1993 season, Smith missed the first two games in a contract dispute, and then a third game in November due to injuries—all three of which the Cowboys lost. Despite that, Smith won his third straight NFL rushing title and was only 14 yards short of having three consecutive 1500-yard seasons, something no one has ever done; he also led the league in total yards from scrimmage (rushing and receiving), at 1900, and in yards per carry, at 5.3. The Cowboys ended the regular season with a 12–4 record and at year's end, although Smith had suffered a separated shoulder in the final game, were pointed toward another Super Bowl, having the home field advantage and being heavy favorites to win again. Not surprisingly, Smith was named to the Pro Bowl; he was also offensive player of the month for December. Smith's new four-year contract was worth $13.6 million, making him, temporarily, the highest-paid player at his position.

While still in high school, Florida-born Smith was a consensus All-America running back and was named Player-of-the-Year by *Parade* and *USA Today*. During his three seasons at the University of Florida, he reached 1000 rushing yards in only his seventh game, faster than anyone in college football history. In 1990, his first season with the Cowboys, he was named Offensive Rookie of the Year by AP and various sports publications, and was also named to the all-Rookie Team by UPI and several publications. He is one of only four players ever to go the Pro Bowl in their first three NFL seasons.

FURTHER READING

Emmitt Smith: Finding Daylight. TED COX. Children's, 1994.
"The quest." PETER KING. *Sports Illustrated*, Oct. 18, 1993.
"America's running back. . . ." RANDY GALLOWAY. *Sport*, Aug. 1993.
"Lapping the field." PETER KING. *Sports Illustrated*, Sep. 14, 1992.
"Who's hurting whom?" PETER KING. *Sports Illustrated*, Dec. 9, 1991.
"The 100-yard dasher." PAUL ZIMMERMAN. *Sports Illustrated*, Oct. 21, 1991.
"Beware the 'boys.' " PETER KING. *Sports Illustrated*, Dec. 24, 1990.
" 'Nothing bothers Emmitt'. . . ." NICK PUGLIESE. *Sporting News*, Nov. 13, 1989.

Smith, Maggie (Margaret Natalie Smith; 1934–) In the 1993 film *Sister Act II*, celebrated British actress Maggie Smith once again played the Mother Superior of the convent in which singer Deloris, played by Whoopi Goldberg, had hidden in *Sister Act* (1992). This time, Deloris returns to teach at the convent high school at the Mother Superior's request. Bill Duke directed; the cast included Kathy Najimy, Mary Wickes, Barnard Hughes, James Coburn.

Smith also starred as Mrs. Venable in a television film version of Tennessee Williams's *Suddenly, Last Summer*, directed by Richard Eyre, and co-starring Natasha Richardson, Rob Lowe, and Moira Redmond. She won an Emmy nomination as best lead actress in miniseries or special for the role. She also starred as the housekeeper in Agnieszka Holland's film version of Frances Hodgson Burnett's children's story *The Secret Garden*, opposite ten-year-old British actress Kate Maberly. Still forthcoming was a starring role in Lindsay Anderson's film adaptation of Anton Chekhov's *The Cherry Orchard*, opposite Alan Bates and Bob Hoskins, with a screenplay by Anderson and Frank Grimes.

Smith has been one of the leading actresses of the English-language theater since the mid-1960s. She played Desdemona to Laurence Olivier's Othello at the National Theatre in 1964, and went on to a long series of classic and modern roles, as in *Miss Julie* (1965), *Hedda Gabler* (1970), and *Private Lives* (1972). She won a 1990 Tony as best actress in a Broadway play, in Peter Shaffer's *Lettice & Lovage*, a role she had created on the London stage. She won a best actress Oscar in the title role of *The Prime of Miss Jean Brodie* (1969), a best supporting actress Oscar for *California Suite* (1978), and starred in the telefilm *The Lonely Passion of Judith Hearne* (1987), as well as appearing in many key character roles on screen. She played Granny Wendy in Stephen Spielberg's 1991 *Hook*. She married playwright Beverley Cross in 1975. She has two children from her earlier relationship with actor Robert Stephens.

FURTHER READING

"Filmographies." JOHN CLARK and HENRY S. HAMPLE. *Premiere*, Sep. 1993.
Maggie Smith: A Bright Particular Star. MICHAEL COVENEY. Trafalgar, 1993.
"The prime of Maggie Smith." MICHAEL COVENEY. *Observer*, Sep. 6, 1992.
"There's nothing. . . ." GEORGINA HOWELL. *Vogue*, Apr. 1990.
"English accents." MARK MATOUSEK. *Harper's Bazaar*, Apr. 1990.

"There is nothing. . . ." MATT WOLF. *New York Times Magazine*, Mar. 18, 1990.

Snipes, Wesley (1962–) Rising actor Wesley Snipes starred in four action films during 1993. In the film *Rising Sun*, he and Sean Connery starred as Los Angeles Police Department detectives investigating the suspicious death of a young woman at a party in a Japanese corporate headquarters. The film, based on Michael Crichton's novel, was directed by Philip Kaufman, and written by Kaufman and Crichton. Co-starring were Harvey Keitel, Hiryuki Tagawa, and Tatjana Patitz, whose murder provided the event from which the plot unfolded.

Snipes also starred in the science fiction special effects thriller *Demolition Man*, directed by Marco Brambilla, and co-starring Sylvester Stallone and Sandra Bullock. Snipes was a psychopathic mass murderer, opposite Stallone as a Los Angeles police officer; both ultimately find themselves 70 years in the future; Bullock plays a police officer of that time.

His third starring role was as a Treasury agent in the cops-and-robbers film *Boiling Point*, written and directed James B. Harris, based on Gerald Petievich's novel *Money Men*, and co-starring Dennis Hopper and Lolita Davidovich. His fourth starring role was as a Harlem drug dealer in the film *Sugar Hill*, directed by Leon Ichaso and co-starring Michael Wright and Theresa Randle.

Florida-born Snipes appeared in several New York plays in the late 1980s, including *The Boys of Winter*, *Death and the King's Horsemen*, and *Execution of Justice*. His film debut came in *Street of Gold* (1986), which was followed by an ACE Award-winning appearance in the television film *Vietnam Story* (1987). In 1987, he also appeared in Michael Jackson's music video "Bad." After playing in several small supporting film roles, he emerged as a rising young film star as jazz saxophonist Shadow Henderson in Spike Lee's *Mo' Better Blues* (1989), followed by major roles in *New Jack City* (1991), *Jungle Fever* (1991), *White Men Can't Jump* (1992), and *Passenger 57* (1992). Snipes is divorced.

FURTHER READING

"20 questions. . . ." *Playboy*, Oct. 1993.
"Snipes, Wesley." *Current Biography*, Sep. 1993.
Who's Hot: Wesley Snipes. RAY ZWOCKER. Dell, 1993.
"Woody and. . . ." MELINA GEROSA. *Entertainment Weekly*, Apr. 10, 1992.
"Hot shots." JERRY LAZAR. *Us*, Apr. 1992.
"Wesley Snipes. . . ." LAURA RANDOLPH. *Ebony*, Sep. 1991.
"Wesley fever. . . ." RALPH RUGOFF. *Premiere*, July 1991.

Sondheim, Stephen Joshua (1930–) A new Sondheim revue made its Broadway debut in 1993. Julie Andrews starred in *Putting It Together*, which opened for a limited run at the Manhattan Theater Club on March 2, with a cast that also included Stephen Collins, Christopher Durang, Michael Rupert, and Rachel York. The show received mixed reviews, although Andrews was well received in her return to the Broadway stage after more than 30 years.

Sondheim's work was also seen on television in 1993, in the television film *Gypsy*, a redo of the 1959 Jule Styne-Stephen Sondhem Broadway hit musical, starring Bette Midler in title role, in a cast that included Peter Riegert, Cynthia Gibb, and Edward Asner; Emile Ardolino directed. On the other coast, Carol Burnett and Patrick Cassidy starred in a Long Beach Civic Light Opera revival of Sondheim's 1970 hit musical *Company*. Forthcoming was a new Sondheim musical, written in collaboration with James Lapine.

New York City-born Sondheim emerged as a leading American musical-theater lyricist in the late 1950s with the lyrics for *West Side Story* (1957) and *Gypsy* (1959), and then as a leading composer with both words and music for *A Funny Thing Happened on the Way to The Forum* (1962). As a composer and lyricist, he has won five Tonys, for *Company* (1970), *Follies* (1971), *A Little Night Music* (1973), *Sweeney Todd* (1979), and *Into the Woods* (1988), and a Pulitzer Prize for *Sunday in the Park with George* (1984). During 1990, he was Oxford University's first visiting professor of drama and musical theatre, resident at St. Catherine's College, a position funded by producer Cameron Mackintosh. Sondheim's 1950 B.A. was from Williams College.

FURTHER READING

Stephen Sondheim. MARTIN GOTTFRIED. Abrams, 1993.
Art Isn't Easy: The Theatre of Stephen Sondheim, rev. ed. JOANNE GORDON. Da Capo, 1992.
"Exploring along with Sondheim." HAP ERSTEIN. *Insight*, Aug. 28, 1989.
Sondheim & Co., 2nd ed. CRAIG ZADAN. Harper, 1988.

Sontag, Susan (1933–) Continuing in a fictional/historical line, Susan Sontag in 1933 published a new play, *Alice in Bed: A Play in Eight Scenes*; it focuses on the life of Alice James (1848–92), sister of the novelist Henry and psychologist William. Though regarded as brilliant, Alice suffered from depression, and in the play (as in her adult life) she was largely bedridden or at least housebound. Sontag the dramatist overcame this major obstacle in various ways, not least by having her commune with notable women of the past, at one point in a ghostly tea party. The play has been produced in Germany and Austria, but had so far appeared only in book form in the United States.

Sontag the director and political activist undertook an unusual free production in August 1993; with an all-volunteer cast and crew, she staged Samuel Beckett's *Waiting for Godot* in a candle-lit theater only 1000 feet from the front lines in Sarajevo, Bosnia. In November 1993, she acted as a "foil" for controversial and death-threatened Salman Rushdie; for security reasons, his appearance at Massachusetts Institute of Technology was billed publicly as a reading of Sontag's own works; he joked that she was "his beard."

Sontag attended the University of California

at Berkeley, the University of Chicago, and Harvard University, where she received M.A.'s in English literature and philosophy. Her first published work was *The Benefactor* (1963). With her 1964 *Partisan Review* essay "Notes On Camp," followed by her 1965 essay "On Style," and her 1966 essay collection *On Interpretation*, she emerged as one of the most notable literary essayists of her generation. Among her published works are *Death Kit* (1967), *Styles of Radical Will* (1969), *On Photography* (1977), *Illness as Metaphor* (1978), *Under the Sign of Saturn* (1980), and *AIDS and Its Metaphors* (1989). In a remarkable change of pace, she also wrote a best-selling historical novel *The Volcano Lover: A Romance* (1992), a retelling of the love story involving Admiral Horatio Nelson and Emma Hamilton. Sontag has also written and directed the films *Duet for Cannibals* (1970) and *Brother Carl* (1971), and written the films *Promised Lands* (1974) and *Unguided Tour* (1983).

FURTHER READING

"Susan Sontag. . . ." LESLIE GARIS. *New York Times Magazine*, Aug. 2, 1992.
"Sontag, Susan." *Current Biography*, Feb. 1992.
"Education of the heart." HARRIETT GILBERT. *New Statesman & Society*, Mar. 29, 1991.
Susan Sontag: The Elegiac Modernist. SOHNYA SAYRES. Routledge, 1990.

Souter, David Hackett (1939–) In his third Supreme Court term, Justice Souter was considerably less a "swing" figure within the Court, instead dissenting from the conservative majority on several key isssues. He wrote the dissenting opinions in *St Mary's Honor Center v. Hicks*, ruling that workers must provide proof of specific discrimination against them to claim protection of civil rights laws and *Shaw v. Reno*, which made it possible to challenge "bizarrely" shaped voting districts formed to provide minority representation as unconstitutional. He also wrote a concurring dissent in *Alexander v. Reno*, which ruled that the First Amendment did not protect $25 million of books and movies destroyed, many of them not obscene, after a seller had been convicted as a pornographer, and joined the minority in *Herrera v. Collins*, which sharply limited the ability of those on death row to gain stays of execution on the basis of alleged later discovery of new evidence, and *Zobrest v. Catalina Foothills School District*, ruling that lo-

cal governments could pay for special services to the disabled in parochial schools, as compliance with federal equal educational opportunities for the disabled laws. Souter joined the majority in *Church of the Lukumi Babalu Aye v. City of Hialeah*, ruling unconstitutional three city ordinances banning ritual animal sacrifice; *Harris v. Forklift Systems*, in which the Court ruled unanimously that workers need not prove that they had suffered psychological damage or were unable to perform their tasks to successfully charge sexual harassment, instead applying the rule of "workplace equity;" *Sale v. Haitian Centers Council*, which ruled that Haitian refugees could be intercepted in international waters and forcibly returned to Haiti without violating American and international law; *Bray v. Alexandria Women's Health Clinic*, which allowed abortion protestors to legally block abortion clinics; *Wisconsin v. Mitchell*, ruling that states could prescribe increased sentences for hate-motivated crimes; and *Lamb's Chapel v. Center Moriches Union Free School District*, in which the Court ruled unanimously that religious groups had equal access to school facilities with other organizations in the community.

Massachusetts-born Souter moved up in the New Hampshire attorney-general's office (1968–76) and became state attorney-general (1976–78). He was a state court judge (1978–83) and a state Supreme Court justice (1983–89) until his appointment by George Bush to the U.S. Supreme Court. Souter's 1961 B.A. was from Harvard, as was his 1966 LL.B; he was also a Rhodes scholar.

FURTHER READING

"Poetic justice. . . ." JEFFREY ROSEN. *New Republic*, Mar. 8, 1993.
Turning Right: The Making of the Rehnquist Supreme Court. DAVID G. SAVAGE. Wiley, 1993.
David Souter. BOB ITALIA. Abdo & Daughters, 1992.
"A new day in court." LAUREN TARSHIS and JAMES EARL HARDY. *Scholastic Update*, Nov. 1, 1991.
"Souter, David Hackett." *Current Biography*, Jan. 1991.
"Naturally right. . . ." JEFF ROSEN. *New Republic*, Sep. 24, 1990.
"A retiring Yankee judge. . . ." BILL HEWITT. *People*, Aug. 6, 1990.
"An 18th century man. . . ." MARGARET CARLSON. *Time*, Aug. 6, 1990.
"In search of Souter." DONALD BAER. *U.S. News & World Report*, Aug. 6, 1990.
"An old-fashioned judge." *Economist*, July 28, 1990.

Spader, James (1960–) Actor James Spader starred in 1993 in the American Playhouse television film *The Music of Chance*, directed by Philip Haas and co-starring Mandy Patinkin, Charles Durning, Joel Grey, and M. Emmet Walsh. Spader, a drifter, is drawn into a "sure thing" high stakes poker game with rich "marks" Durning and Grey, with unanticipated consequences. Forthcoming was a starring role in the film *Wolf*, directed by Mike Nichols and co-starring Jack Nicholson, Michelle Pfeiffer, Kate Nelligan, and Richard Jenkins. Still forthcoming was a starring role opposite Theresa Russell in Nicolas Roeg's *Chicago Loop*, adapted for the screen by Paul Theroux from his own novel.

Boston-born Spader made his film debut in *Endless Love* (1981), and went on to play in such popular films as *Tuff Turf* (1985), *The New Kids* (1985), *Pretty in Pink* (1986), *Mannequin* (1987), *Baby Boom* (1987), *Wall Street* (1987), *Less Than Zero* (1987), *sex, lies, and videotape* (1989), *Bad Influence* (1990), *White Palace* (1990), *True Colors* (1991), and *Storyville* (1992). Spader studied at the Michael Chekhov Studio. He and his wife, Victoria Spader, have one son.

FURTHER READING

"James Spader." JAMIE DIAMOND. *Entertainment Weekly*, June 25, 1993.
"Actor James Spader's image. . . ." SHEILA BENSON. *Interview*, Apr. 1993.

Spielberg, Steven (1947–) Steven Spielberg in 1993 created yet another worldwide hit, the blockbuster film *Jurassic Park*, about modern genetically engineered dinosaurs that break free from a theme park and become a danger to humanity. The special effects science fiction film, which exploited humanity's deepest fears about science gone mad, while at the same time being a very appealing special effects triumph, became a worldwide commercial hit and the highest grossing film ever released. Directed by Spielberg, with screenplay by Michael Crichton and David Koepp, based on Crichton's novel, the film starred Sam Neill, Jeff Goldbum, Laura Dern, and Richard Attenborough.

Scoring a double triumph, Spielberg in 1993 also entered a new phase of his life and career,

FURTHER READING

Steven Spielberg: The Man, His Movies, and Their Meaning, rev. ed. PHILLIP M. TAYLOR. Continuum, 1994.
Meet Steven Spielberg. THOMAS CONKLIN. Knopf, 1994.
"After the survivors." JONATHAN ALTER, MARK MILLER, and LAURA SHAPIRO. *Newsweek*, Dec. 20, 1993.
"Spielberg's obsession." DAVID ANSEN. *Newsweek*, Dec. 20, 1993.
"Myths in the park." BRIAN D. JOHNSON. *Maclean's*, June 14, 1993.
"Steven Spielberg. . . ." SKIP PRESS. *Boys' Life*, July 1992.
"The panning of. . . ." HENRY SHEEHAN. *Film Comment*, May-June 1992.
"Peter pandemonium." FRED SCHRUERS. *Premiere*, Dec. 1991.
"Stephen Spielberg." MAURA J. MACKOWSKI. *Ad Astra*, July-Aug. 1991.
The Future of the Movies: Interviews with Martin Scorsese, George Lucas, and Steven Spielberg. ROGER EBERT and GENE SISKEL. Andrews & McMeel, 1991.
Icons: Intimate Portraits. DENISE WORRELL. Atlantic Monthly, 1989.
The Picture Life of Steven Spielberg. MICHAEL LEATHER. Watts, 1988.
Steven Spielberg: Amazing Filmmaker. JIM HARGROVE. Childrens, 1988.
The Fantastic Films of Steven Spielberg-Master Filmmaker. ROBERT G. MARRERO. RGM Publications, 1987.

by directing and producing the film *Schindler's List*, a classic and immediately acclaimed fact-based fictional treatment of the Holocaust, set in Nazi-occupied Poland during World War II. Liam Neeson starred as Oscar Schindler, a German Catholic businessman from the Sudetenland (occupied Czechoslovakia), who comes to Poland to make money by using slave labor, but who ultimately saves 1,100 Polish Jews from the German gas chambers. The large cast includes Ben Kingsley, Ralph Fiennes, Caroline Goodall, Jonathan Sagalle, and Embeth Davidtz. The film was voted the best film of 1993 by the New York Film Critics' Circle.

Spielberg directed and in several instances produced many of the most successful action-adventure and science fiction spectacles of the 1970s and 1980s, including *Jaws* (1975), *Close Encounters of a Third Kind* (1977; he also co-authored), *1941* (1979), *Raiders of the Lost Ark* (1981), *E.T.* (1982; he also produced), *Indiana Jones and the Temple of Doom* (1984), *The Color Purple* (1985; he also produced), *Indiana Jones and the Last Crusade* (1989; the third in the series), and *Always* (1989; a remake of *A Guy Named Joe)*. He also wrote and produced *Poltergeist* (1982) and co-produced *Back to the Future* (1985). Spielberg attended California State College. Formerly married to actress Amy Irving, Spielberg married actress Kate Capshaw in 1991. He has five children, three of them with Capshaw.

Stallone, Sylvester Enzio (1946–) For

the 1993 summer season, action film hero Sylvester Stallone starred in the mountain rescue film *Cliffhanger*, set in the Rockies; written by Michael France and Stallone, based on a France story, and directed by Renny Harlin. Co-starring were Janine Turner and, in a cast that included Michael Rooker and Rex Linn.

For the autumn-winter season, Stallone starred in the film *Demolition Man*, directed by Marco Brambilla, and co-starring Wesley Snipes and Sandra Bullock. In the science-fiction special effects thriller, Stallone plays a Los Angeles police officer who winds up 70 years in the future, along with a psychopathic mass murderer, played by Snipes; Bullock plays a police officer of that future time.

Forthcoming were starring roles in the film *The Specialist*, co-starring Sharon Stone and James Woods, and in *Judge Dredd*, directed by Danny Cannon.

In 1976, New York City-born Stallone starred in *Rocky*; he also wrote the screenplay. The movie won a best film Oscar, was a worldwide hit, and Stallone was immediately an international star. He did four sequels: *Rocky II* (1979; he wrote the screenplay and directed); *Rocky III* (1982); *Rocky IV* (1985; he directed); and *Rocky V* (1990). He also starred as Rambo in *First Blood* (1982), *Rambo: First Blood Part II* (1985), and *Rambo III* (1988), and in such other films as *F.I.S.T.* (1978), *Paradise Alley* (1978), *Nighthawks* (1981), *Rhinestone* (1984), *Cobra* (1986), *Over the Top* (1987), *Lock Up* (1989), *Tango and Cash* (1989), *Oscar* (1991), and *Stop! Or My Mom Will Shoot* (1992). Stallone attended the American College of Switzerland and Miami University. He has been married twice and has two children.

FURTHER READING

"Sly's body electric." ZOE HELLER. *Vanity Fair*, Nov. 1993.
"Regrets, he's. . . ." GREGG KILDAY. *Entertainment*, June 4, 1993.
"Rocky road." GREGG KILDAY. *Entertainment*, June 4, 1993.
"Stallone on the range." GRAYDON CARTER. *Vogue*, Dec. 1991.
"The shaping of an icon. . . ." DAVID KLINGHOFFER. *Insight*, May 20, 1991.
"Rocky: the article. . . ." FRANZ LIDZ. *Sports Illustrated*, Nov. 12, 1990.
"Move over, Rambo. . . ." LAURA MORICE. *Mademoiselle*, Feb. 1990.

"Sly Stallone's rocky road. . . ." LEO JANOS. *Cosmopolitan*, Jan. 1990.
"Requiem for a heavyweight. . . ." CAMERON STAUTH. *American Film*, Jan. 1990.
Rocky and the Films of Sylvester Stallone. ED GROSS. Movie Publications Services, 1990.

Stark, Freya Madeleine (1893–1993) British traveler and writer Freya Stark lived with her family in England and in several other countries during her highly mobile childhood. Her formal education consisted of two years at Bedford College before World War I and later courses at the London School of Oriental Studies. She saw service as a nurse during World War I. In 1927, she traveled to Lebanon, Syria, Palestine, and Egypt, beginning the series of sojourns in southwest Asia and the Mediterranean that would provide the basis for her very popular, history-laden travel books, among them *The Valley of the Assassins* (1934), *The Southern Gates of Arabia* (1938), *Letters From Syria* (1942), *The Lycian Shore* (1956), *Alexander's Path* (1958), and *Rome on the Euphrates* (1966). She also wrote a four-volume autobiography (1951–61). There were no survivors. (d. Asolo, Italy; May 9, 1993)

FURTHER READING

"Bon voyage madame." CAROLINE MOOREHEAD. *Conde Nast Traveler*, Aug. 1993.
Obituary. *The Times* (of London), May 11, 1993.
Obituary. *New York Times*, May 11, 1993.
"A hundred years of wanderlust." MOLLY IZZARD. *Observer*, Jan. 31, 1993.

Steenburgen, Mary (1953–) Film star Mary Steenburgen became a stage star as well in 1993, starring on Broadway in a very well received Roundabout Theater Company revival of George Bernard Shaw's *Candida*; Gloria Muzio directed. On screen, she appeared in a strong supporting role in the AIDS discrimination story *Philadelphia*, directed by Jonathan Demme and starring Tom Hanks as the rising young attorney fired for alleged incompetence but in fact for having AIDS, Denzel Washington as Hanks's own lawyer in the discrimination case brought by Hanks against his old law firm, and Jason Robards as a leading member of the

old firm; Steenburgen was Robards's assistant. She also starred opposite Johnny Depp and Juliette Lewis in *What's Eating Gilbert Grape*, a story set in American rural life; Lasse Hallstrom directed. She was also one of the celebrity actors who did readings for Bill Couterie's environmentalist film *Earth and the American Dream*.

Forthcoming were starring roles in the films *Pontiac Moon*, directed by Peter Medak, and co-starring Ted Danson; and *A Summer Story*, directed by Bob Clark and co-starring Charles Grodin and Kieran Culkin.

Arkansan Steenburgen made her film debut in *Goin' South* (1978), and went on to such films as *Ragtime* (1981), *Time After Time* (1979), *Melvin and Howard* (1980; she won a best supporting actress Oscar), *Cross Creek* (1983), *Dead of Winter* (1987), *End of the Line* (1987). *Parenthood* (1989), *Back to the Future Part III* (1990), and *The Butcher's Wife* (1991). She also produced and played a bit role in *The Whales of August* (1987). In addition, she appeared in such telefilms as *Tender Is the Night* (1985) and *The Attic: The Hiding of Anne Frank* (1988). Steenburgen attended Hendricks College and studied at New York's Neighborhood Playhouse. She has two children from her previous marriage to actor Malcolm McDowell.

FURTHER READING

"The players." ANDREW CORSELLO and AMY DONOHUE. *Philadelphia Magazine*, Dec. 1993.

"After years. . . ." MARY H.J. FARRELL. *People*, Aug. 28, 1989.
"Mary, Mary, quite contrary." TIM APPELO. *Savvy Woman*, May 1989.

Stegner, Wallace Earle (1909–93) Iowa-born Wallace Stegner taught English at the University of Utah after receiving his doctorate from the University of Iowa in 1935. He began his long career as a novelist, short story writer, and essayist with the story "Remembering Laughter," winner of a 1937 Little, Brown writing contest. He emerged as a popular novelist of the American west with *The Big Rock Candy Mountain* (1943), also writing *The Preacher and the Slave* (1950), a biographical novel about labor martyr Joe Hill, and *The Gathering of Zion: The Story of the Mormon Trail* (1964). Stegner won a 1972 Pulitzer Prize for the novel *Angle of Repose*, and a 1977 National Book Award for his novel *The Spectator Bird*. He also received several National Book Critics Circle nominations, including one for his most recent book, the essay collection *Where the Bluebird Sings to the Lemonade Spring: Living and Writing in the West* (1992). Among his other works are *Recapitulation* (1986), *On the Teaching of Creative Writing* (1989) and *Collected Stories of Wallace Stegner* (1990). He was survived by his wife, Mary, and a son, novelist Page Stegner. (d. Santa Fe, New Mexico; April 13, 1993)

FURTHER READING

"Wallace Stegner. . . ." *Audubon*, July-Aug. 1993.
Obituary. T.H. WATKINS. *Wilderness*, Summer 1993.
Obituary. *Current Biography*, June 1993.
"The dean of Western letters. . . ." MALCOLM JONES, JR. *Newsweek*, Apr. 26, 1993.
Obituary. *The Times* (of London), Apr. 21, 1993.
Obituary. *New York Times*, Apr. 15, 1993.
"A vision of the West." ALVIN P. SANOFF. *U.S. News & World Report*, Mar. 16, 1992.
"Prairie patriarch. . . ." KENNETH WHYTE. *Saturday Night*, Apr. 1991.
Wallace Stegner: A Descriptive Bibliography. JAMES R. HEPWORTH and NANCY COLBERG, eds. Confluence Press, 1991.
Conversations with Wallace Stegner: On Western History and Literature, rev. ed. WALLACE STEGNER and RICHARD W. ETULAIN. University of Utah Press, 1990.

Steinbrenner, George Michael, III

(1930–) The big, bad boss was back in 1993. Barred from day-to-day activities of his New York Yankees team in late 1990 by former baseball commissioner Fay Vincent, himself later ousted, Steinbrenner was allowed to return to active participation in running his team as of March 1, 1993. By September, Steinbrenner was back in his usual form, maligning the character and talent of his team, at the time in a tight American League pennant race, by implication putting at jeopardy the position of manager Buck Showalter.

During the season, Steinbrenner also publicly explored the possibility of moving the Yankees out of the Bronx, a move strongly opposed by New Yorkers, including Governor Mario Cuomo, and left undecided at year's end. Also in 1993, Steinbrenner brought in Yankee legend Reggie Jackson to be his special advisor; Jackson's number was retired during the season.

Ohio-born Steinbrenner is a leading shipbuilding company executive, who has since 1967 run the American Ship Building Company, cofounded by his grandfather. He bought a controlling interest in the New York Yankees in 1973, and quickly became a highly controversial figure, who hired and fired managers again and again, with 18 managerial changes from 1973 to 1992, and engaged in widely publicized feuds with key players. The Yankees won the World Series in 1977 and 1978 and won the American League pennant in 1981, but the following decade was a troubled time for the team. Steinbrenner was banned from day-to-day active participation in the management of the Yankees in 1990, because of his payments to a gambler as part of what were judged improper attempts to interfere with a trade of then-Yankee Dave Winfield. Steinbrenner's 1952 B.A. was from Williams College. He married Elizabeth Joan Zieg in 1956; they have four children.

FURTHER READING

"I, Reggie. . . ." MIKE LUPICA. *Esquire*, June 1993.
"Will the boss behave himself?" JILL LIEBER. *Sports Illustrated*, Mar. 1, 1993.
The Wit and Wisdom of George Steinbrenner. FRANK COFFEY. NAL-Dutton, 1993.
"Welcome to hardball city." MIKE LUPICA. *Esquire*, June 1991.
"George Steinbrenner. . . ." JEFFREY KLUGER. *Playboy*, May 1991.

"The many woes. . . ." TOM CALLAHAN. *U.S. News & World Report*, Aug. 6, 1990.
Damned Yankees: A No-Holds-Barred Account of Life with "Boss" Steinbrenner. BILL MADDEN and MOSS KLEIN. Warner, 1990.

Sten, Anna

(Annel Stenskaja Sudakevich; 1908–93) Kiev-born Anna Sten began her long acting career on stage, in Constantin Stanislavsky's Moscow Art Theater. She appeared in several Soviet films during the 1920s, including *The Girl in the Hatbox* (1927) and Vsevoled I. Pudovkin's classic *Storm Over Asia* (*The Heir of Genghis Khan*) (1928). In Weimar Germany, she starred as Grushenka in the film *The Brothers Karamazov*. She was brought to Hollywood in the early 1930s by Samuel Goldwyn, who hoped to turn her into a major star, but failed. He starred her in a 1934 version of *Nana*; opposite Fredric March in *We Live Again*, a Hollywood version of Leo Tolstoy's *Resurrection*; and opposite Gary Cooper in *The Wedding Night* (1935), but was unable to recreate the superb, delicate actress as a Hollywood star. Among her later films was *So Ends Our Night* (1941). There were no survivors. (d. New York City; November 12, 1993)

FURTHER READING

Obituary. *Variety* Nov. 24, 1993.
Obituary. *The Times* (of London), Nov. 22, 1993.
Obituary. *New York Times*, Nov. 15, 1993.

Stephanopoulos, George Robert

(1961–) George Stephanopoulos began 1993 in the visible job of White House Director of Communications, carrying over his presidential campaign and transition role. He was President Bill Clinton's chief spokesperson during the often-difficult early months of the new administration. But he found it difficult to handle the aggressive and independent White House press corps, and sharp criticism of administration lack of openness and attempts to "manage" the news soon developed, with Stephanopoulous at the center of a growing storm. After several highly publicized and embarrassing incidents, which included a huge press outcry over the price of a presidential haircut, and massive press criticism of the White House travel office firings, Clinton brought in David Gergen as White House Direc

tor of Communications, moving Stephanopolos into a less visible role, as a still-close senior White House advisor on strategy and policy.

Stephanopoulos has spent almost all of his brief career in politics. He received his 1982 B.A. from Columbia University, and in that year worked for the Carnegie Endowment for International Peace. He was a congressional aide to Representative Edward Feighan (1983–84), then a Rhodes Scholar at Oxford University (1984–86), returning to his work with Feighan (1986–88). During the 1988 presidential campaign, he was a deputy communications director for Michael Dukakis. He then returned again to Congress, this time as an aide to Representative Richard Gephardt (1989–91).

Stephanopoulos began the 1992 presidential campaign as candidate Bill Clinton's assistant communications director, but soon became a key political advisor and main organizer of the day-to-day campaign, as well as Clinton's chief spokesperson throughout the entire electoral process. He continued on as communications director through the transition period.

FURTHER READING

"The importance of being. . . ." FRED BARNES. *New Republic*, Sep. 6, 1993.
"Socks, underwear, action!" HILARY MACKENZIE. *Maclean's*, Feb. 8, 1993.
"Clinton's boy wonder." MATTHEW COOPER. *U.S. News & World Report*, Dec. 7, 1992.
"Riding shotgun." JOE TREEN. *People*, Oct. 26, 1992.

Stern, David Joel (1942–) In 1993, the National Basketball Association (NBA) and its commissioner, David Stern, were reeling from a series of losses. Larry Bird and Earvin "Magic" Johnson-the two stars who had done so much to build the sport's popularity-had retired, one in 1992 because of a bad back, the other in 1991 because of infection with HIV, the virus that causes AIDS. Two young stars died tragically in 1993: Reggie Lewis of a heart ailment and Drazen Petrovic of injuries suffered in a car crash. Then the sport's reigning superstar, Michael Jordan, suffering his own loss of his father and troubled by allegations of gambling, suddenly retired at the top of his career. How basketball would fare with the loss of so many key players was an open question. Stern continued expand his league's influence around the world, sending various teams and players as emissaries for the sport. *NBA Jam Session: A Photo Salute to the NBA Dunk* (1993) was published under his name.

Another focus was a series of legal concerns, notably to prevent teams from structuring player contracts in ways that undermine the salary cap, which Stern has stressed is vital to protect the NBA from financial anarchy, and to prevent the televising of games nationwide on "superstations," which undermines local teams' ability to sell tickets and to survive. The league voted to add a new team in Toronto as of 1995; a decision to add a second new team was tabled in November 1993, though Vancouver seemed likely. Meanwhile, with a year to go on their existing $600 million contract, the NBA and NBC negotiated an extension to the 1997–98 season for a minimum of $750 million, with an innovative revenue-sharing plan above that amount.

Stern was also in the process of restructuring the lottery, which was intended to give teams that failed to make the playoff the top picks in the college draft, but had by a quirk of chance allowed the Orlando Magic to get two consecutive number one picks, in 1992 and 1993. Stern and the NBA were also making a significant attempt to curb violence during games, with increased penalties, especially for flagrant fouls, involving ejections and suspensions, where warranted.

New York-born Stern received his B.A. from Rutgers University in 1963 and his LL.B. from Columbia University. He was associated with the NBA's law firm, Proskauer Rose Goetz &

Mendelsohn (1966–78), before being named NBA general counsel in 1978. He became the NBA's executive vice president for business and legal affairs (1980), then NBA commissioner (1984–   ). He has also served as adjunct professor of law at New York's Cardozo Law School (1983–   ). Stern married Dianne Bock in 1963; they have two sons.

FURTHER READING

"Stern, David Joel." *Current Biography*, Apr. 1991.

Stern, Howard

Stern, Howard (1954–   ) He describes himself variously as the "King of all Media" and "the nicest, sweetest, most sentimental radio personality on the planet." Whatever his claim to the former, few others would apply the latter description to Howard Stern, who is most notable for his scabrous ramblings on sex and bodily functions, and for his bitter attacks on women, minorities, and a series of other targets, at a level aimed to shock and titillate his listeners. His tactics have certainly won him attention. His New York-based radio talk show has millions of fans, officially estimated at 4 million, but perhaps as large as 16 million; it is broadcast on 14 stations nationwide, generally in early morning.

During his nationwide publicity tour for a new book, Stern was sometimes mobbed. At Pasadena, an estimated 10,000 people showed up for a Stern book-signing, which turned into a 7-hour affair requiring police for crowd control; in Manhattan, likewise, a book-signing drew another 10,000 people, spilling onto Fifth Avenue and blocking noontime traffic. The book was *Private Parts*, a print version of his commentaries, which shot to the top of the best-seller list and had one million copies in print by late 1993. Some book suppliers found the book so offensive that they refused to carry it. In addition to his book and radio show, Stern had an interview show on cable's E! channel, and he was scheduled to host a New Year's Eve pay-per-view special.

As has been true throughout his career, Stern continued to spark government attempts to control commentary deemed offensive, with Federal Communication Commission (FCC) fines totaling more than $1.2 million levied against Infinity Broadcasting, Stern's employer. In 1993, some stations broadcasting the show also admitted to editing the show somewhat before airing, sparking charges of censorship from both fans and foes. In late November, a government ban intended to prohibit broadcasting of "indecent" material between 6 A.M. and midnight was struck down as in violation of the free-speech guarantee of the First Amendment. In late December, the FCC upped the ante, delaying Infinity's proposed $170 million purchase of three large stations, which could result in multi-million-dollar losses and possible license revocation; that conflict, too, seemed headed for the Supreme Court.

Long Island-born Stern began his radio career as a disc jockey at WRNW, Briarcliff Manor, N.Y. (1976–78), then working at WCCC, Hartford, Connecticut (1978–79), and WWWW, Detroit (1979–80). He emerged as a rather popular and highly controversial figure at WWDC, Washington, D.C. (1980–82). After being fired from that job, he went to work at WNBC, New York City (1982–85), broadcasting along the same lines and again building a following. Fired from that job, as well, he moved to WXRK with his "Howard Stern Show" (1986–   ), there building a national following by pursuing the same tactics, despite FCC fines and widespread condemnation. He also hosted weekly cable television interview shows on WWOR-TV (1990–92) and E! Entertainment Television (1992–   ). Stern received his B.S. from Boston University, where he met his wife, Alison Berns; they have three daughters.

FURTHER READING

"Big mouths." KURT ANDERSEN. *Time*, Nov. 1, 1993.
"Blow Hard." BRUCE FRETTS. *Entertainment*, Oct. 15, 1993.
Howard Stern: Big Mouth. JEFF MENELL. Windsor (NY), 1993.
"Bad mouth. . . ." JEANIE KASINDORF. *New York*, Nov. 23, 1992.
"Howard Stern." BENJAMIN SVETKEY. *Entertainment*, Aug. 21, 1992.
"I love myself. . . ." BARBARA KRUGER and REBECCA JOHNSON. *Esquire*, May 1992.

Stevens, John Paul

Stevens, John Paul (1920–   ) Although voting with the conservative majority in some instances, Supreme Court Justice John Paul Stevens was, with Harry Blackmun, again distinctly in the minority in the conservative Rehnquist court. He wrote dissenting opinions in *Bray*

v. *Alexandria Women's Health Clinic*, which allowed abortion protestors to legally block abortion clinics, and *Shaw v. Reno*, which made it possible to challenge "bizarrely" shaped voting districts formed to provide minority representation as unconstitutional. He also dissented in several other key cases, including *Herrera v. Collins*, which sharply limited the ability of those on death row to gain stays of execution on the basis of alleged later discovery of new evidence; *Zobrest v. Catalina Foothills School District*, ruling that local governments could pay for special services to the disabled in parochial schools, as compliance with federal equal educational opportunities for the disabled laws; *St Mary's Honor Center v. Hicks*, ruling that workers must provide proof of specific discrimination against them to claim protection of civil rights laws; and *Alexander v. Reno*, which ruled that the First Amendment did not protect $25 million of books and movies destroyed, many of them not obscene, after a seller had been convicted as a pornographer.

He wrote the majority opinion in *Sale v. Haitian Centers Council*, which ruled that Haitian refugees could be intercepted in international waters and forcibly returned to Haiti without violating American and international law; and joined the majority in *Church of the Lukumi Babalu Aye v. City of Hialeah*, ruling unconstitutional three city ordinances banning ritual animal sacrifice; *Harris v. Forklift Systems*, in which the Court ruled unanimously that workers need not prove that they had suffered psychological damage or were unable to perform their tasks to successfully charge sexual harassment; *Lamb's Chapel v. Center Moriches Union Free School District*, in which the Court ruled unanimously that religious groups had equal access to school facilities with other organizations in the community; and *Wisconsin v. Mitchell*, ruling that states could prescribe increased sentences for hate-motivated crimes.

Chicago-born Stevens practiced law for two decades before being appointed to the Seventh Circuit U.S. Court of Appeals in 1970. President Gerald Ford appointed him to the Supreme Court in 1975. Stevens was thought to be a moderate conservative at the time of his appointment, as was Ford; the estimate was right, for Stevens often functioned as a middle force between the conservative and liberal wings of the court in the years that followed. But in later years, as the court turned sharply to the right,

he was more often seen as a moderate liberal, in most instances agreeing with Justices Blackmun, Marshall, and Brennan, the latter two since retired. Stevens's 1941 B.A. was from the University of Chicago, and his 1947 LL.B. from Northwestern. He has been married twice, last to Maryan Mulholland Simon in 1979, and has four children.

FURTHER READING

John Paul Stevens. BOB ITALIA and PAUL DEEGAN. Abdo & Daughters, 1992.
"A new day in court." LAUREN TARSHIS and JAMES EARL HARDY. *Scholastic Update*, Nov. 1, 1991.
"A voice of reason. . . ." *American Legion Magazine*, June 1990.
Eight Men and a Lady. HERMAN SCHWARTZ et al. National Press, 1990.
John Paul Stevens and the Constitution: The Search for Balance. ROBERT J. SICKELS. Pennsylvania State University Press, 1988.

Stewart, Rod (1945–) Resuming his place as a major current figure in popular music, Rod Stewart in 1993 issued the hit album *Unplugged . . . and Seated*, a studio-setting collection of many of his 1970s standards, among them "Tonight's the Night," "People Get Ready," "Maggie May," "Hot Legs," "Reason to Believe," and "Have I Told You Lately," the last two also issued as hit singles. He toured in support of the album for much of the year, backed by a two-dozen-strong musical ensemble. At the 1993 World Music Awards, Stewart received an award for lifelong contribution to the rock industry. For 1993, he was Billboard's No. 3 hot adult contemporary artist, and "Have I Told You Lately" was No. 5 hot adult contemporary single.

London-born Stewart sang with the Jeff Beck Group (1968–69) and Faces (1969–75). He began his solo recording career with the album *An Old Raincoat Won't Let You Down* (1969), and in the 1970s became one of the most popular recording artists of the era. Among his best known albums are *Every Picture Tells a Story* (1971), *Never a Dull Moment* (1972), *Smiles* (1974), *Atlantic Crossing* (1975), and *A Night on the Town* (1976). He continued to compose and tour throughout his career, into the mid-1990s. Stewart is married to model Rachel Hunter.

FURTHER READING

Rod Stewart: A Biography. TIM EWBANK and STAFFORD HILDRED. Trafalgar, 1992.
Rod Stewart: The Visual Documentary. STEVE HOLMES and JOHN GRAY. Omnibus (NY), 1992.
"Some guys have all the luck." BILL ZEHME. *Rolling Stone*, July 11, 1991.

Sting (Gordon Matthew Sumner; 1951–   ) A new Sting album is a considerable event in popular music. In 1993, Sting issued his fourth solo album *Ten Summoner's Tales*, which quickly moved to near the top of the charts, overall becoming Billboard's 21st-rated album of the year, with the album's single "Fields of Gold" the 7th-rated hot adult contemporary single, and Sting himself ranked 4th on the hot adult contemporary artist list. The songs "If I Ever Lose My Faith In You" and "Nothing 'Bout Me," both from the album, were issued as singles and became hits.

Sting also issued a music video version of *Ten Summoner's Tales*, which won an MTV video award nomination as best male video, and the hit single "Demolition Man," the theme song from the 1993 Sylvester Stallone-Wesley Snipes action film. Sting also toured widely for much of the year, including in his itinerary several benefit appearances for environmental causes.

Sting, a former grade school schoolteacher, became a major rock star in the early 1980s, as lead singer of the Police, formed in 1977 with Andy Summers and Bill Copeland. He went on his own in the late 1980s, recording such albums as *The Dream of the Blue Turtles* (1985) and *Nothing Like the Sun* (1987). He also developed a substantial film and stage career; his films include *Quadrophenia* (1978), *Brimstone and Treacle* (1982), *Dune* (1984), *Plenty* (1985), and *Rosencrantz and Guildenstern Are Dead* (1989). In November 1989, he made his Broadway debut as Mack the Knife in a revival of *The Threepenny Opera*. He and Trudie Styler have three children; he also has two children from a former marriage.

FURTHER READING

"Yoga with Sting at the Ritz." DOUG STANTON. *Esquire*, Mar. 1993.
Sting: The Illustrated Lyrics. ROBERTO GILGROV. IRS Books, 1991.
"Twisting Mack the Knife. . . ." JOHN ISTEL. *Mother Jones*, Nov. 1989.
"Sting." RUDY MAXA. *Washingtonian*, Sep. 1989.
"Sting speaks." ART LANGE. *Down Beat*, Sep. 1989.

Stone, Oliver (1946–   ) In 1993, celebrated writer, director, and producer Oliver Stone issued the third of his Vietnam War films, this one *Heaven and Earth*, based on two autobiographical works by Le Ly Hayslip: *When Heaven and Earth Changed Places*, written with Jay Wurts, and *Child of War, Woman of Peace*, written with James Hayslip, together covering a period stretching from the 1950s through the

1980s, from her days as a guerrilla soldier in Vietnam to her later life in America as the wife of a soldier she met in Vietnam. Hie Thi Le plays Hayslip and Tommy Lee Jones her husband, in a cast that included Joan Chen, Haing S. Ngor, and Dustin Nguyen. The screenplay, by Michael Singer, was also published as a book.

Stone also produced the film *The Joy Luck Club*, based on the Amy Tan novel and directed by Wayne Wang, and the ABC miniseries "Wild Palms." Forthcoming was the film *Noriega*, about the Panamanian dictator, which Stone is to direct. Also reportedly forthcoming was a film version of *Evita*, the Andrew Lloyd Webber-Tim Rice stage musical, which Stone is slated to adapt and direct.

On the personal side, Elizabeth Cox Stone brought divorce proceedings against Stone.

New York-born Stone fought in Vietnam (1965–66), an experience that has deeply affected some of his most notable work. He has won three Oscars. His first was for his *Midnight Express* (1978) screenplay. His second was for his direction of *Platoon* (1986), a film that he also wrote and that won a best picture Oscar. His third was as best director for *Born on the Fourth of July* (1989), filmed from the Oscar-nominated screenplay by Stone and Ron Kovic, based on Kovic's autobiography; Stone himself appeared in a small role in the film, which also won several other awards. Stone also co-wrote and directed such films as *Scarface* (1983), *Wall Street* (1987), *Talk Radio* (1988), and *The Doors*

(1991), and his controversial, classic *JFK* (1992). He attended Yale University; his 1971 B.F.A. was from the New York University Film School. He has been married twice, first to Najwa Sarkis, with whom he had a son, then in 1981 to former nurse Elizabeth Cox. Their son, Sean, at age six, played the young Jim Morrison in *The Doors*.

FURTHER READING

Oliver Stone. FRANK BEAVER. Twayne/Macmillan, 1994.
"Oliver Stone." MAHMOUD HUSSEIN and REGIS DEBRAY. *UNESCO Courier,* July-Aug. 1993.
"Oliver Stone." STUART FISCHOFF. *Psychology Today,* Sep.-Oct. 1993.
"Splinters to the brain." NATHAN GARDELS and LEILA CONNERS. *New Perspectives,* Spring 1992.
"Heart of stone." JEFF YARBROUGH. *Advocate,* Apr. 7, 1992.
"Ollie uber Alles. . . ." PETER COLLIER. *American Spectator,* Apr. 1992.
"Camera obscura." STEVE DALY. *Entertainment,* Jan. 17, 1992.
"The man who shot 'JFK.' " JENNET CONANT. *GQ-Gentleman's Quarterly,* Jan. 1992.
"Plunging into the labyrinth." *Time,* Dec. 23, 1991.
"What does. . . ." DAVID ANSEN. *Newsweek,* Dec. 23, 1991.
"Can Hollywood solve. . . ." MARK SEAL. *Texas,* Dec. 1991.
"Riders on the storm." ROBERT HORTON. *Film Comment,* May-June 1991.
"60s something. . . ." STEPHEN TALBOT. *Mother Jones,* Mar.-Apr. 1991.
"Oliver Stone. . . . " DAVID BRESKIN. *Rolling Stone,* Apr. 4, 1991.
"Unorthodox behaviour. . . ." *Economist,* Mar. 16, 1991.
"Stone unturned." MARK ROWLAND. *American Film,* Mar. 1991.
"Oliver Stone." JOHN CLARK. *Premiere,* Feb. 1990.
Icons: Intimate Portraits. DENISE WORRELL. Atlantic Monthly, 1989.

Streep, Meryl (Mary Louise Streep; 1949–) As her 1992 Hollywood-set hit film *Death Becomes Her* moved from theatrical release to its 1993 release in home video, Streep was filming a vastly different kind of work. In the forthcoming *The River Wild*, directed by Curtis Hanson and co-starring David Strathairn and Joe Mazzello as her husband and son, Streep starred as a woman who takes her family river

STREISAND, BARBRA

Meryl Streep (right) and Goldie Hawn

rafting as means of fostering closeness. The film was completed only after a protracted but finally amicably settled disagreement with environmental groups over shooting some scenes in Oregon's protected Rogue River country.

Also forthcoming was a starring role in the film version of Isabel Allende's novel *House of the Spirits*. Set in Chile, the movie co-stars Jeremy Irons, Glenn Close, Winona Ryder, and Anthony Banderas. Streep is also slated to co-narrate, with George Winston, the children's story "The Velveteen Rabbit," for Mel Gibson's upcoming "Rabbit Ears Radio" show. Streep was awarded Denmark's 1993 Rungstedlund Prize, named after the home of Karen Blixen, whom she played in *Out of Africa*.

New Jersey-born Streep was quickly recognized as a major dramatic star in the late 1970s; her work includes such films as *The Deer Hunter* (1978), *Manhattan* (1979), *Kramer vs. Kramer* (1980; she won a best supporting actress Oscar), *Sophie's Choice* (1982; she won a best actress Oscar), *Silkwood* (1983), *Out of Africa* (1985), *Ironweed* (1987), *She-Devil* (1989), *Postcards from the Edge* (1990), and *Defending Your Life* (1991). Streep's B.A. was from Vassar in 1971; her M.F.A. from Yale in 1975. She married sculptor Donald J. Gummer in 1978; the couple have four children.

FURTHER READING

"Serious lady with a comic touch." RICHARD BROOKS. *Observer*, Oct. 18, 1992.
"Hope I die before I get old." TERESA CARPENTER. *Premiere*, Sep. 1992.
"Winning Streep." DAVID HANDELMAN. *Vogue*, Apr. 1992.
"Queen for a decade." MARC ELIOT. *California*, Sep. 1991.
"Getting the skinny. . . ." MICHAEL SEGELL. *Cosmopolitan*, May 1991.
"Meryl Streep. . . ." WENDY WASSERSTEIN. *Saturday Evening Post*, July-Aug. 1989.
"Ms. Streep goes. . . ." BONNIE JOHNSON. *People*, Mar. 20, 1989.
Meryl Streep: A Critical Biography. EUGENE E. PFAFF, JR., and MARK EMERSON. McFarland, 1987.

Streisand, Barbra (Barbara Joan Streisand; 1942–) Legendary and very live singer, actress, director, and producer Streisand in 1993 issued the new hit album *Back To Broadway*, a collection of classic and current musical theater songs. She had also had a hit single, "I've Got a Crush on You," her duet with Frank Sinatra, from his *Duets* album. She also made her first concert appearances in 27 years, with much-in-demand December 31, 1993 and January 1, 1994 performances at the opening of the 15,000-seat Grand Garden Theater as the Las Vegas MGM Grand hotel in Las Vegas.

In development was a starring role as artist Lee Krasner opposite Robert De Niro as her husband, artist Jackson Pollack. Also in development was her first television film production, an NBC film autobiography of Col. Margarethe Cammermeyer, expelled from the armed forces after 26 years of service after stating that she was a lesbian; Glenn Close was slated to star and co-produce.

Active in the 1992 Clinton-Gore campaign, Streisand found herself welcome at the Clinton White House during the first year of the new administration. She also continued to be active in social causes, and in November donated her 24-acre Malibu property, valued at $15 million, to the Santa Monica Mountains Conservancy.

Brooklyn-born Streisand is one of the great popular music stars of the modern period, whose work also includes several very notable film, stage, and television credits. Her breakthrough roles came on stage in musical theater, in *I Can Get It for You Wholesale* (1962) and as Fanny Brice in *Funny Girl* (1964), a role for which she won a best actress Oscar in the 1968 film version. She became a worldwide recording star in the mid-1960s for such Grammy-winning songs as "People" (1964) and "Evergreen" (1977; also an Oscar winner), and such Grammy-winning albums as *The Barbra Streisand Album* (1963) and *My Name is Barbra* (1965). A six-time best vocalist Grammy-winner, she issued many old, but many new, songs in the four-CD *Just for the Record* (1991). She also starred in such films as *Hello Dolly* (1969), *On a Clear Day You Can See Forever* (1970), *The Owl and the Pussycat* (1971), *The Way We Were* (1973), *Funny Lady* (1975), and *Nuts* (1987). She produced and starred in *A Star is Born* (1976); directed, produced, and starred in *Yentl* (1983); and directed and starred in *The Prince of Tides* (1991). Her 1965 television special, *My Name is Barbra*, won five Emmys. She was formerly married to the actor Elliott Gould, and has one child.

FURTHER READING

"The unguarded Barbra." JULIA REED. *Vogue*, Aug. 1993.

"President Streisand." JAMIE MALANOWSKI. *Us*, Aug. 1993.

"Woman of the hour. . . ." KRISTINA JOHNSON et al. *People*, May 31, 1993.

Her Name is Barbra: An Intimate Portrait of the Real Barbra Streisand. RANDALL RIESE. Birch Lane/Carol, 1993.

Barbra Streisand: A Biography. PETER CARRICK. Ulverscroft, 1993.

"Streisand, Barbra." *Current Biography*, Sep. 1992.

"Barbra Streisand." JOHN CLARK. *Premiere*, Dec. 1991.

"The triumph of. . . ." JOE MORGENSTERN. *Cosmopolitan*, Oct. 1991.

"Queen of Tides." KEVIN SESSUMS. *Vanity Fair*, Sep. 1991.

Barbra—An Actress Who Sings, The Unauthorized Biography of Barbra Streisand. JAMES KIMBRELL. Branden, Vol. I, 1989; Vol. II, 1992.

Styron, William (William Clark Styron, Jr.; 1925–) In 1993, William Styron published his first book of fiction in over a decade, *A Tidewater Morning: Three Tales From Youth*. Originally published in *Esquire* (1978–1987) and well-received on their publication in book form, the semi-autobiographical tales are all told from the perspective of a single Virginia boy, Paul, remembering three notable moments in his life: preparing for the assault on Okinawa (as did the young Styron); childhood memories of an elderly former slave coming to his birthplace for death and burial; and his and his father's attempt to deal with the death of his mother from cancer.

A featured speaker at the American Booksellers Association convention in Miami in May 1993, Styron was also one of several authors courageous enough to supply some juvenile writings for a collection called *First Words: Earliest Writings from 42 Favorite American Authors*, edited by Paul Mandelbaum. He also contributed to *The Rushdie Letters: Freedom to Speak, Freedom to Write*. Also his *Inheritance of Night: Early Drafts of "Lie down in Darkness"* was published in a special edition. Styron was among those awarded the National Medal of Arts by President Bill Clinton in October.

With his first novel, *Lie Down in Darkness* (1951), Virginia-born Styron was recognized as a leading American author. His *The Confessions of Nat Turner* (1967), a fictional re-creation of the celebrated 19th-century American slave revolt, won a Pulitzer Prize. His *Sophie's Choice* (1979) won an American Book Award; in the film version, Meryl Streep won an Academy Award as his European refugee in postwar New York. Other writings include the novella *The Long March* (1953), an essay collection *This Quiet Dust and Other Writings* (1982), and *Darkness Visible: A Memoir of Madness* (1990), describing his mid-1980s painful, near-suicidal experience with depression. Styron's B.A. and Litt.D. were from Duke University, in 1947 and 1968. He married Rose Burgunder in 1953; they have four children.

FURTHER READING

" 'It was an anguish.' " LYNN KARPEN. *New York Times Book Review*, Sep. 12, 1993.
"William Styron." BAHGAT ELNADI and ADEL RIFAAT. *UNESCO Courier*, Apr. 1992.
"Itchy feet and pencils. . . ." RUSSELL BANKS et al. *New York Times Book Review*, Aug. 18, 1991.
William Styron Revisited. SAMUEL COALE. Twayne/Macmillan, 1991.
"William Styron." *People*, Dec. 31, 1990.
"William Styron. . . ." KIM HUBBARD. *People*, Aug. 27, 1990.
"Out of his system." LAUREL GRAEBER. *New York Times Book Review*, Aug. 19, 1990.
"Trading on pain. . . ." PHILIP GOLD. *Insight*, Sept. 17, 1990.
William Styron. JUDITH RUDERMAN. Ungar, 1987.

Sulzberger, C(yrus) L(eo) (1912–93)

New York City-born C.L. Sulzberger, a nephew of Arthur Hays Sulzberger and cousin of Arthur Ochs Sulzberger, both publishers of the *New York Times*, began his long newspaper career in 1935, as a reporter for Scripps-Howard's *Pittsburgh Press*. He joined the *New York Times* as a foreign correspondent in 1939, reporting on World War II during its early years. As chief correspondent for the *Times* (1944–54) and as a widely syndicated columnist with the *Times*, he had open access to most of the world's leaders, as well as a widely recognized reputation for discretion, which helped make him one of the most noted journalist-interviewers of his time. Sulzberger's many books included *The Big Thaw* (1956), his memoir *A Long Row of Candles*

(1969), and the autobiographical *Seven Continents and Forty Years* (1977). He won a Pulitzer Prize citation in 1951 for a jail interview with Archbishop Stepinac of Yugoslavia. He was survived by a daughter and a son. (d. Paris; September 20, 1993)

FURTHER READING

"Sulzberger, Cyrus Leo." *Current Biography*, Nov. 1993.
Obituary. *The Times* (of London), Sep. 22, 1993.
Obituary. *New York Times*, Sep. 21, 1993.

Sun Ra: See Ra, Sun.

Sutherland, Donald McNichol

(1934–) Canadian film star Donald Sutherland appeared in *Six Degrees of Separation*, the 1993 film version of the hit John Guare play, with screenplay by Guare, and directed by Fred Schepisi; Stockard Channing recreated her Broadway role, in a cast that also included Will Smith, Ian McKellen, and Mary Beth Hurt.

In 1993, Sutherland also appeared in the film *Shadow of the Wolf*, directed by Jacques Dorfmann and co-starring Lou Diamond Phillips, Toshiro Mifune, and Jennifer Tilly, set in an Eskimo culture in the mid-1930s Canadian north. A third appearance was a starring role in the psychological thriller *Benefit of the Doubt*, opposite Amy Irving, he as a convicted killer paroled after 25 years in prison, she as the daughter whose testimony had helped convict him; Jonathan Heap directed. Sutherland also narrated the eight-hour documentary *The Prize: Epic Quest for Oil, Money and Power*, which appeared as a television series.

Sutherland began his film career in the mid-1960s, and emerged as a star playing Korean War surgeon Benjamin Franklin "Hawkeye" Pierce in the original film *M*A*S*H* (1970). He went on to a wide variety of dramatic roles, many of them chosen primarily for their quality, in such films as *Klute* (1971), *The Day of the Locust* (1975), *1900* (1976), *Casanova* (1976), *Ordinary People* (1980), *Eye of the Needle* (1981), *Gaugin* (1986), *A Dry White Season* (1989), *Lock Up* (1989), *Eminent Domain* (1991), *Backdraft* (1991), *JFK.* (1992), *The Railway Station Man* (1992), and *Buffy the Vampire Slayer* (1992). On television, he starred in the Canadian miniseries *Bethune: The Making of a Hero*. Sutherland attended the University of Toronto. He has been married three times, and has five children, including actor Kiefer Sutherland.

FURTHER READING

"Donald Sutherland and. . . ." GERMANO CELAND and BRIGITTE LACOMBE. *Interview*, Sep. 1990.

Sutherland, Kiefer (1966–) In 1993, Kiefer Sutherland starred as Athos in *The Three Musketeers*, directed by Stephen Herek; co-starring were Charlie Sheen as Aramis, Chris O'Donnell as D'Artagnan, Oliver Platt as Porthos, Tim Curry as Cardinal Richelieu, and Rebecca De Mornay as Milady. Sutherland also starred in the thriller *The Vanishing*, directed by George Sluizer and co-starring Jeff Bridges, Nancy Travis, and Sandra Bullock. In a change of pace, he directed and starred as a condemned killer in the anti-death-penalty television film *Last Light*, co-starring Forest Whitaker. Forthcoming was the science fiction thriller *Natural Selection*, which Sutherland was producing for television.

London-born Sutherland made his theater debut as a child, in *Throne of Straw* (1977), and his film debut in *Max Dugan Returns* (1983). His breakthrough role came in *Stand By Me* (1986). Among his films were *The Lost Boys* (1987), *Bright Lights, Big City* (1988), *Young Guns* (1988), *Renegades* (1989), *Flatliners* (1990), *Young Guns II* (1990), *Article 99* (1991), *Twin Peaks: Fire Walk With Me* (1992), and *A Few Good Men* (1992).

He has also played in several television films. He was previously married, and has two children. He is the son of actor Donald Sutherland.

FURTHER READING

"Kiefer madness." LOU HARRY. *Philadelphia*, Apr. 1992.
"Miss Roberts regrets." LOUISE LAGUE. *People*, July 1, 1991.
"20 questions. . . ." PAUL ENGLEMAN. *Playboy*, Oct. 1990.
"His father's shadow." DON GILLMOR. *Saturday Night*, Dec. 1990.
"You asked for them. . . ." *Teen Magazine*, Mar. 1989.

Swayze, Patrick (1954–) Although Swayze's 1992 Calcutta-set film *City of Joy* did not do very well at the box office in 1992, it did find audiences in home video release, extending into 1993. Swayze starred in 1993 in the film *Father Hood*, directed by Darrell James Roodt and co-starring Halle Berry, Sabrina lloyd, and Brian Bonsall. The story line of the chase movie had Swayze, as a small-time criminal who had rescued his two small children from an institution, evading pursuit as he and the children fleeing across the countryside, building their family relationship as they go on the run together. Forthcoming was a starring role in the film *Tall Tale*, directed by Jeremiah Chechik.

Trained for ballet, Swayze began his career as a dancer, and danced and acted a lead in *Grease* for two years on Broadway before emerging as a leading film player late in the 1980s. His breakthrough role was as Johnny Castle in *Dirty Dancing* (1987). It was followed by a starring role opposite his wife, Lisa Niemi, in the fantasy-action film *Steel Dawn* (1987); and by starring roles in *Road House* (1989); *Next of Kin* (1989), *Ghost* (1990), and *Point Break* (1991). Swayze also appeared in the television miniseries "North and South" (1990), and in several other television films.

FURTHER READING

"Patrick Swayze." *Playboy*, June 1992.
"Patrick Swayze. . . ." STEPHANIE MANSFIELD. *GQ-Gentleman's Quarterly*, Feb. 1992.

"Body and soul." JEANNIE PARK. *People*, Aug. 26, 1991.

"From here to maturity. . . ." *Seventeen*, July 1991.

"Patrick Swayze." *People*, Dec. 31, 1990.

"Patrick Swayze. . . ." KATHRYN CASEY. *Ladies Home Journal*, Aug. 1990.

"A wild and Swayze guy." BILL ZEHME. *Cosmopolitan*, Aug. 1989.

"Going Swayze." LAURA MORICE. *Mademoiselle*, June 1989.

Patrick Swayze. MITCHELL KRUGEL. St. Martin's, 1988.

The New Breed: Actors Coming of Age. KAREN HARDY and KEVIN J. KOFFLER. Holt, 1988.

Sydow, Max von

Sydow, Max von (Carl Adolf von Sydow; 1929–) Swedish actor Max von Sydow in 1993 starred as Swedish literature teacher Martin Lamm opposite Mai Zetterling and Marika Lagercrantz in the Swedish film *Morfars Resa (Grandfather's Journey)*. The film was written and directed by Staffan Lamm, set in 1945, and based on his own recollections of his grandfather, the subject of the work.

Von Sydow also starred in the film *Needful Things*, written W. D. Richter, based on the Stephen King novel, and directed by Fraser C. Heston. He played Leland Gaunt, new shopowner in a small town, who from his shop, called "Needful Things," devilishly sets the people of the town against each other. The cast included Ed Harris, Bonnie Bedelia, Amanda Plummer, and J.T. Walsh. The horror film was received with distaste by many critics, while proving appealing to King's many fans. Forthcoming were starring roles in Dan Petrie's *A Dog In Flanders* and John Irving's adaptation of his own novel, *Cider House Rules*.

The classic Ingmar Bergman films in which von Sydow made his greatest impact include *The Seventh Seal* (1957), *The Magician* (1958), *The Virgin Spring* (1960), *Through a Glass Darkly* (1961), and *Winter Light* (1962). He also starred on television and in later theatrical release in two linked sagas of 19th-century Scandinavian-American immigration: *The Emigrants* (1969) and *The New Land* (1969). His later work included such films as *Three Days of the Condor* (1975), *Hannah and Her Sisters* (1985), *Pelle the Conqueror* (1986), *Until the End of the World* (1991), *The Best Intentions* (1992), *The Silent Touch* (1992), *The Ox* (1992), and *Zentropa* (1992). He played a Catholic priest working in Hiroshima in the television film *Hiroshima: Out of the Ashes*, which premiered on August 6, 1990, the 45th anniversary of the atom bombing of city.

Von Sydow has long been recognized as one of Sweden's leading stage actors. He attended Stockholm's Royal Dramatic Theatre School, and has been associated with that theater since 1960. He married Christina Olin in 1951, and has two children.

FURTHER READING

"In step with. . . ." JAMES BRADY. *Parade*, Oct. 25, 1992.

T

Tagliabue, Paul John (1940–) After five years of negotiation, and under threat of court settlement, a new seven-year labor agreement between the football players and owners was created in January 1993, encompassing a massive set of changes for the sport, and a major testament to the effectiveness of National Football League (NFL) commissioner Paul Tagliabue. Incorporating elements mandated by a September 1992 court decision, the new agreement provided free agency for veteran players, except for a single "franchise" player on each team, as long as that player's salary meets or exceeds the average of the top five players at that position, and except for a right of first refusal for two other players, again with salary protections. The new agreement also called for a salary cap, limitations on rookies' salaries, and fewer rounds in the college draft, to compensate teams for losses through free agency. Though the salary cap would not take effect until the 1994 season, its effects were already seen during 1993, as teams made long-term contracts with the cap in mind.

However, in December 1993, it became clear that the caps would be a little higher than anticipated. That is because Tagliabue negotiated an enormously favorable set of new television contracts, starting with the 1994 season. Rupert Murdoch's Fox Network, seeking parity with the "big three" networks, bid an astonishing $395 million for National Football Conference (NFC) television rights, outbidding longtime NFC network CBS by $100 million. American Football Conference (AFC) rights remained with NBC, while ABC maintained Monday Night Football and ESPN and TBS continued to split Sunday night games. Late in 1993, Tagliabue announced that two new franchises would be added to the league in 1995, in Charlotte and Jacksonville.

Among the other questions still facing Tagliabue and football were artificial turf and its potential to cause injuries; injuries overall, but especially neck and spine injuries, which sparked NFL programs stressing to players "See what you hit"; and the possible return of instant replay. Whatever results, the owners clearly have confidence in Tagliabue; in May, even before the network renegotiations, they extended his current contract, which would expire November 1994, through the year 2000, at an average $1 million a year.

After graduating from law school in 1965, Tagliabue worked at the defense department in Washington until 1969, and then for twenty years as a lawyer at Covington and Burling, becoming a partner in 1974. He became commissioner of the National Football League in 1989. Tagliabue's 1962 B.A. was from Georgetown University, where he played basketball; his 1965 J.D. was from New York University. He is married and has two children.

FURTHER READING

"The face of. . . ." RICK TELANDER. *Sports Illustrated*, Sep. 10, 1990.
"NFL commish's torch passed. . . . " *Sporting News*, Feb. 18, 1990.
"Tagliabue. . . ." PAUL ATTNER. *Sporting News*, Feb. 12, 1990.

"Tagliabue plans. . . ." STEVE HUBBARD. *Sporting News*, Dec. 4, 1989.
"A new quarterback. . . ." *U.S. News & World Report*, Nov. 6, 1989.
"In a blink. . . ." VITO STELLINO. *Sporting News*, Nov. 6, 1989.
"The NFL's new boss." PETER KING. *Sports Illustrated*, Nov. 6, 1989.

Tambo, Oliver (1917–93) A militant South African equal rights activist from his student days at the University College of Fort Hare, Oliver Tambo joined the African National Congress (ANC) in 1943, was with Nelson Mandela a founder of its youth league, and in 1949 became an executive committee member of the ANC. He and Mandela practiced law together in Johannesburg in 1952. He and the rest of the ANC leadership were arrested and unsuccessfully charged with treason in 1956. In 1960, after the Sharpeville Massacre, Tambo escaped the mass arrests of the ANC leadership, and went abroad to organize a guerrilla war against the South African government, and did so during the three following decades, ultimately becoming a world figure. He became acting president of the ANC in 1967, and full president in 1978. Tambo suffered a stroke in August 1989, was flown to Britain and then to Sweden for treatment, and therefore saw the historic freeing of Nelson Mandela and other key political prisoners, the legalization of the ANC, and the full ceasefire agreement of August 7, 1990 from afar. He returned home to South Africa in late 1990.

Among his written works are *Oliver Tambo Speaks: Preparing for Power* (1988) and *No Easy Walk to Freedom* (1990), written with Nelson Mandela. He was survived by his wife, anti-apartheid activist Adelaide Tambo, two daughters, and a son. (d. Johannesburg; April 24, 1993)

FURTHER READING

Obituary. *Current Biography*, June 1993.
Obituary. *The Times* (of London), Apr. 25, 1993.
Obituary. *New York Times*, Apr. 24, 1993.
Mandela, Tambo, and the African National Congress: The Struggle Against Apartheid, a Documentary Study, 1948–1990. SHERIDAN JOHNS and R. HUNT DAVIS, JR., eds. Oxford University Press, 1991.
"Return of the native son." *Time*, Dec. 24, 1990.

The Struggle: A History of the African National Congress. HEIDI HOLLAND. Braziller, 1990.
"Bound by blood." ROGER WILKINS. *Mother Jones*, May 1989.
Oliver Tambo and the Struggle Against Apartheid. E.S. REDDY. Apt Books, 1988.

Tan, Amy Ruth (1952–) Amy Tan's 1989 best-selling novel *The Joy Luck Club* came to the screen in 1993. Directed by Wayne Wang, the film told the interlocking stories of four women—all American immigrants born in 1920s China, who gather over weekly mah-jongg games—and their very American daughters. With its no-big-name ensemble playing, the film won wide praise, in particular for its clear-eyed, powerful view of the characters and their lives-as one reviewer put it, "Three hankies; no sentimentality." Tan's own role was not just that of novelist, but also co-screenwriter, with Ron Bass, and co-producer, with Oliver Stone and others; Tan and Bass also played bit roles, as the first guests seen in the party that opens the film. By the time *Joy Luck* opened, Tan, Wang, and Bass were developing a script of Tan's second novel, *The Kitchen God's Wife*, for future production.

In May, Tan also went on an eight-city Massachusetts-to-Miami bus tour with an all-author rock band called the Rock Bottom Remainders, including Stephen King, Dave Barry, Barbara Kingsolver, Robert Fulghum, and Tan on vocals. The authors were publishing a book about the group, *Mid-Life Confidential*, due in 1994.

Born in Oakland, California, of Chinese immigrant parents, Tan received a B.A. and M.A. in linguistics and English from California's San Jose State University in 1974 and 1976. She worked as a specialist in language development for the Alameda County Association for the Mentally Retarded, in Oakland (1976–80), and as project direct for M.O.R.E. in San Francisco (1980–81), then becoming a freelance writer. In addition to numerous short stories and essays, her book-length works include the novels *The Joy Luck Club* (1989), *The Kitchen God's Wife* (1991), and *The Moon Lady* (1992), a children's book based on a chapter in *Joy Luck*. Tan married Louis M. DeMattei in 1974.

FURTHER READING

"Fresh voices. . . ." JOHN F. BAKER and CALVIN REID. *Publishers Weekly*, August 9, 1993.

Writers Dreaming-Dreamers Writing: 25 Writers Discuss Dreams and the Creative Process. NAOMI EPEL. Crown, 1993.
"Amy Tan." *Bon Appetit*, Oct. 1992.
"Tan, Amy." *Current Biography*, Feb. 1992.
"Joy, luck, and literature." ANITA MERINA. *NEA Today*, Oct. 1991.
"Cosmo talks to. . . ." JOAN CHATFIELD-TAYLOR. *Cosmopolitan*, Nov. 1989.
"The Joy Luck Club. . . ." KIM HUBBARD. *People*, Apr. 10, 1989.

Tanaka, Kakuei (1918–93) Former Japanese Prime Minister Kakuei Tanaka was an extrepreneur, who founded a construction company in the late 1930s. Invalided out of military service in 1941, he built his business into a major company during World War II. He went into politics in 1946, winning election to the lower house of Parliament in 1947, and holding the seat in the decades that followed. Tanaka rose through a series of ministerial posts in the 1950s and 1960s simultaneously becoming a major force within the ruling Liberal Democratic Party. He became Prime Minister in 1972 and was forced to resign in 1974 because of persistent corruption charges. In 1976, he was formally charged with having taken millions of dollars in bribes from the Lockheed Corporation while Prime Minister. During the seven years in which the charges were pending, he remained one of the most powerful of Japanese politicians, often described as a behind-the-scenes "kingmaker." Even after his conviction in 1983, he retained great power. He was survived by his wife, Hana Sakamoto, and a daughter. (d. Tokyo; December 16, 1993)

FURTHER READING

Obituary. *The Times* (of London), Dec. 17, 1993.
Obituary. *New York Times*, Dec. 17, 1993.

Tandy, Jessica (1909–   ) American television audiences had the rare privilege of seeing Hume Cronyn and Jessica Tandy, both now in their mid-80s, create yet another joined set of roles 1993. Hailed as America's leading theatrical couple, the British actress and Canadian actor, partners on stage and screen for more than four decades, starred in the acclaimed television film *To Dance with the White Dog*, she on screen as his wife, who dies, he on screen throughout as her survivor, attempting to deal with loss and pain by conjuring up an imaginary white dog, whom nobody else can see, which he insists is a reincarnation of his dead wife.

Tandy was also seen on television on an NBC presentation of her 1991 film *Fried Green Tomatoes*; an index of her popularity was that the rerun's rating were the best enjoyed by a theatrical film since *Star Wars* was first shown in 1984. Forthcoming were starring roles in the film *Nobody's Fool*, written and directed by Robert Benton and co-starring Paul Newman, Melanie Griffith, and Bruce Willis; and *Camilla*, directed by Deepa Mehta and co-starring Bridget Fonda and Howie Mandell.

London-born Tandy appeared in London and New York during the 1930s, though mainly in London and in the classics, most notably as Ophelia to John Gielgud's *Hamlet* (1934). On the Broadway stage, she created the Blanche Du Bois role in Tennessee Williams's *A Streetcar Named Desire* (1947). After she and Hume Cronyn married in 1942, they created a lasting theater partnership, appearing together in such plays as *The Fourposter* (1951), *A Delicate Balance* (1966), and *Foxfire* (1982; and the 1987 television version). She appeared in strong character roles in several films, before emerging very late in her career as a film star in her best actress Oscar-winning role in *Driving Miss Daisy* (1989). Tandy and Cronyn were awarded the 1990 National Medal of the Arts. Cronyn wrote about their life and work together in his *A Terrible Liar: A Memoir* (1991). Tandy attended the Ben Greet Academy of Acting (1924–27). Her first husband was British actor Jack Hawkins, with whom she had a daughter. She and Cronyn have two children, one of them the actress Tandy Cronyn.

FURTHER READING

The Magic of Theater. DAVID BLACK. Macmillan, 1993.
"Jessica Tandy." JOHN CLARK. *Premiere*, Feb. 1992.
"He drives Miss Daisy. . . ." EVE DROBOT. *Saturday Night*, Oct. 1991.
"Jessica Tandy. . . ." CINDY ADAMS. *Ladies Home Journal*, Apr. 1991.
Jessica Tandy: A Bio-Bibliography. MILLY S. BARRANGER. Greenwood, 1991.
"Two lives, one ambition. . . ." GERALD CLARKE. *Time*, Apr. 2, 1990.

"Happily ever after." JEANNE MARIE LASKAS. *Life*, Apr. 1990.
"She oughta be in pictures. . . ." NINA DARNTON. *Newsweek*, Jan. 1, 1990.
"Driving Miss Daisy. . . ." ROBERT SEIDENBERG. *American Film*, Jan. 1990.
"Two for the road." MARK MATOUSEK. *Harper's Bazaar*, Jan. 1990.

Taylor, Elizabeth (1932–)

Twice a best actress Oscar-winner, Taylor was honored with a far more meaningful Oscar in 1993. For her work in the fight against AIDS, she was awarded a Jean Hersholt Humanitarian Award; for the first time, the Academy voted two such awards, the other posthumously to Audrey Hepburn for her work with the world's children, through UNICEF. Taylor continued to be one of the world's leading figures in the fight against AIDS, through fundraising and public awareness programs, including the American Foundation for AIDS Research and the Elizabeth Taylor AIDS Foundation. She also again appeared in the Arsenio Hall-Paula Abdul AIDS television special *In a New Light*.

Making a step back toward acting, she stars opposite John Goodman, Elizabeth Perkins, Rick Moranis, and Rosie O'Donnell in the forthcoming film *The Flintstones*, a live-actor version of the classic television animated series.

On the personal side, Taylor and her husband, Larry Fortensky, flew to Singapore in late August to appear at the side of their friend, singer Michael Jackson, accused of child molestation, and stayed with him as media attacks mounted.

London-born Taylor began her film career as a young teenager with *Lassie Come Home* and *Jane Eyre*, both in 1943, and became a star at the age of 12 in *National Velvet* (1944). She went on to star in such films as *A Place in the Sun* (1951), *Giant* (1956), *Raintree Country* (1957), *Cat on a Hot Tin Roof* (1958), *Suddenly Last Summer* (1959), *Butterfield 8* (1960; she won a best actress Oscar), *Cleopatra* (1962), *Who's Afraid of Virginia Woolf?* (1966, and a second best actress Oscar), *Under Milk Wood* (1971), and *The Blue Bird* (1975). She has starred on Broadway in revivals of *The Little Foxes* (1979) and *Private Lives* (1983). Taylor has been married eight times, twice to actor Richard Burton, and has four children. She was married to Larry Fortensky in 1991. Her other husbands were socialite Nicky Hilton, actor Michael Wilding, producer Mike Todd, singer Eddie Fisher, and Senator John Warner.

FURTHER READING

"Elizabeth shows off. . . ." *Good Housekeeping*, Nov. 1993.
"Liz's AIDS odyssey." NANCY COLLINS. *Vanity Fair*, Nov. 1992.
"Elizabeth at sixty." VERNON SCOTT. *Good Housekeeping*, Feb. 1992.
"Living with Liz." BRAD DARRACH and HARRY BENSON. *Life*, Feb. 1992.
"Elizabeth Taylor. . . ." SALLY OGLE DAVIS. *Ladies Home Journal*, Nov. 1991.
"He does, she does. . . ." JEANNIE PARK. *People*, Oct. 21, 1991.
"Liz: she's survived. . . ." GEORGINA HOWELL. *Vogue*, June 1991.
"Elizabeth." ALEXANDER WALKER. *Cosmopolitan*, Jan. 1991.
All About Elizabeth: Elizabeth Taylor, Public and Private. CAROLINE LATHAM and JEANNIE SAKOL. NAL-Dutton, 1991.
Elizabeth: The Life of Elizabeth Taylor. ALEXANDER WALKER. Grove-Weidenfeld, 1991.
Five for Hollywood: Their Friendship, Their Fame, Their Tragedies. JOHN PARKER. Carol, 1991.
Elizabeth Taylor: A Celebration. SHERIDAN MORLEY. Viking Penguin, 1990.
The Films of Elizabeth Taylor. JERRY VERMILYE and MARK RICCI. Carol, 1989.
The New Elizabeth. MARIANNE ROBIN-TANI. St. Martin's, 1988.

Taylor, Harold Alexander (1914–93)

Toronto-born Harold Taylor, a leading educator, received his doctorate in philosophy at the University of London in 1938, and taught philosophy at the University of Wisconsin before becoming president of Sarah Lawrence College (1949–59). While at Sarah Lawrence, he emerged as a major figure in progressive education, his innovations prefiguring practices that would become common in later years, including a no-grades approach, the development of individual independent courses of study, student self-government, and informal campus dress. A progressive in the wider world, as well, he pressed for integration on and off campus, and, in a period when McCarthyism was very strong, powerfully defended democratic rights. He later taught at the New School for Social Research and City University, hosted television's "Meet the Professor" (1961–62), was a leader in peace and human rights movements, was active in support of the performing arts, and wrote prolifically on educational change. He was survived by two daughters and a sister. (d. New York City; February 9, 1993)

FURTHER READING

Taylor, Harold Alexander. *Current Biography*, Apr. 1993.
Obituary. *The Times* (of London), Feb. 20, 1993.
Obituary. *New York Times*, Feb. 10, 1993.

Thatcher, Margaret (Margaret Hilda Roberts; 1925–) Former British Conservative Prime Minister Margaret Thatcher, now Baroness Thatcher, continued to oppose the European Community Maastricht Treaty and to harshly criticize the Conservative government of her successor, Prime Minister John Major during 1993. In July, her move to force a national referendum on the Maastricht issue was defeated in the House of Lords, while her supporters within the party continued to score Major's economic policies, thought to be somewhat more moderate than Thatcher's.

In October, Thatcher published the first volume of her autobiography, *The Downing Street Years*, focusing on her years in power. Prepublication "leaks" revealed substantial criticisms of Major; her formal statement of support for him did little to soften the impact of her criticisms. Forthcoming was the second volume of her autobiography.

Thatcher was a chemist and then barrister before her 1959 election as a Conservative Member of Parliament. She became Conservative education spokesperson in 1969, and when her party came to power again was education and science minister (1970–74). In 1975, she succeeded Edward Heath as Conservative leader, becoming the first woman to lead any major British political party, and in 1979 became Britain's first woman prime minister; she was ultimately Britain's longest-serving prime minister of the 20th century, in office until 1990. Her era was marked by wide-scale privatization, the 1982 Falklands war, and the continuing civil wars in Northern Ireland; she personally survived several IRA assassination attempts. She attended Somerville College, Oxford. She married Denis Thatcher in 1951; they have two children.

FURTHER READING

"The grandees and the grocer's daughter." IAN AITKEN. *New Statesman & Society*, Oct. 22, 1993.
"Scarlet lady." *New Yorker*, June 14, 1993.
The Anatomy of Thatcherism. SHIRLEY R. LETWIN. Transaction, 1993.
Margaret Thatcher: A Bibliography. FAYSAL MIKDADI. Greenwood, 1993.
" 'It just won't do'. . . ." ROBERT LENZNER. *Forbes*, Oct. 26, 1992.
"Birth of a she-devil." SHIRLEY ROBIN LETWIN. *New Statesman & Society*, Oct. 2, 1992.
The Thatcher Era: And Its Legacy, 2nd ed. PETER RIDDELL. Blackwell, 1992.
Margaret Thatcher: In Victory and Downfall, 1987 and 1990. E. BRUCE GEELHOED. Praeger/Greenwood, 1992.
Margaret Thatcher: A Bibliography. FAYSAL H. MIKDADI. Meckler, 1992.
" 'That woman'. . . ." GEOFFREY WHEATCRAFT. *Atlantic*, Dec. 1991.
"Maggie's big problem." MAUREEN ORTH. *Vanity Fair*, June, 1991.
"A Woman for Four Seasons." OWEN HARRIES. *National Review*, Apr. 15, 1991.
Margaret Thatcher: The Woman Within. ANDREW THOMSON. Isis (NY), 1991.
Reagan and Thatcher. GEOFFREY SMITH. Norton, 1991.
Maggie: An Intimate Portrait of a Woman in Power. CHRIS OGDEN. L.J. Kaplan, 1990.
Margaret Thatcher: Britain's Prime Minister. DOROTHY HOLE. Enslow, 1990.

Margaret Thatcher: First Woman Prime Minister of Great Britain. LEILA M. FOSTER. Childrens, 1990.

Margaret, Daughter of Beatrice: A Politician's Psychobiography of Margaret Thatcher. LEO ABSE. Random, 1990.

Margaret Thatcher. MARIETTA D. MOSKIN. Messner, 1990.

Madame Prime Minister: A Biography of Margaret Thatcher. LIBBY HUGHES. Dillon, 1989.

The Iron Lady. HUGO YOUNG. Farrar, Straus & Giroux, 1989.

Theremin, Leon (Lev Sergeyevich Termen; 1896–1993) St. Petersburg-born Leon Theremin-of French ancestry, he was known as Theremin in the West-became one of the founders of electronic music, through his 1926 invention of the theremin (first called the etherophone), a device that through the use of oscillators and antennae created a cello-like tone, and was played by moving the player's hands in the air near the antennae, without touching the machine. In essence, the theremin was the first synthesizer. Theremin perfected the device in the Soviet Union, displayed and patented it in the West, sold manufacturing rights to RCA, and settled in New York, where at his Theremin Laboratory he created a series of related and unrelated inventions in electronics. In 1938, he returned to the Soviet Union, perhaps kidnapped by Soviet agents, and was then sentenced to a Siberian prison, from which he was freed during World War II to do secret war research. He reportedly invented a miniature "bugging" device for the KGB in this period. After the war, he continued to work for the KGB, until in 1964 becoming a professor of acoustics at the Moscow Conservatory. But he later gave an interview to a foreign correspondent, and was dismissed, then working only as an electronic technician, while apparently continuing to work on new inventions. During the 1930s, Theremin married dancer Lavinia Williams. He later married again in the Soviet Union, and was survived by two daughters of that marriage. (d. Moscow; November 3, 1993)

FURTHER READING

Obituary. *Billboard*, Nov. 20, 1993
Obituary. *The Times* (of London), Nov. 17, 1993.
Obituary. *New York Times*, Nov. 9, 1993.

Thomas, Clarence (1948–) In his second full year on the Supreme Court, conservative Justice Thomas generally voted with Chief Justice Rehnquist and Justice Scalia. He voted with the majority in many key cases, including *Herrera v. Collins*, which sharply limited the ability of those on death row to gain stays of execution on the basis of alleged later discovery of new evidence; *Zobrest v. Catalina Foothills School District*, ruling that local governments could pay for special services to the disabled in parochial schools, as compliance with federal equal educational opportunities for the disabled laws; *Bray v. Alexandria Women's Health Clinic*, which allowed abortion protestors to legally block abortion clinics; *Church of the Lukumi Babalu Aye v. City of Hialeah*, ruling three city ordinances banning ritual animal sacrifice unconstitutional; *Harris v. Forklift Systems*, in which the Court ruled unanimously that workers need not prove that they had suffered psychological damage or were unable to perform their tasks to successfully charge sexual harassment, instead applying the rule of "workplace equity;" *Sale v. Haitian Centers Council*, which ruled that Haitian refugees could be intercepted in international waters and forcibly returned to Haiti without violating American and international law; *Shaw v. Reno*, which made it possible to challenge "bizarrely" shaped voting districts formed to provide minority representation as unconstitutional; *St. Mary's Honor Center v. Hicks*, ruling that workers must provide proof of specific discrimination against them to claim protection of civil rights laws; *Lamb's Chapel v. Center Moriches Union Free School District*, in which the Court ruled unanimously that religious groups had equal access to school facilities with other organizations in the community; *Wisconsin v. Mitchell*, ruling that states could prescribe increased sentences for hate-motivated crimes, and *Alexander v. Reno*, which ruled that the First Amendment did not protect $25 million of books and movies destroyed, many of them not obscene, after a seller had been convicted as a pornographer.

Savannah-born Thomas was from early in his career a protégé of John Danforth, currently U.S. senator from Missouri. Thomas was Missouri assistant attorney general (1974–77), when Danforth was state attorney general. Thomas was a corporate lawyer for the Monsanto Company (1977–79), a legislative assistant to Senator Danforth (1979–81), assistant secretary for civil rights in the federal Education Department (1981–82), and chairman of the U.S. Equal Opportunity Employment Commission (1982–89), before being named by President Ronald Reagan to the U.S. Court of Appeals for the District of Columbia in 1989. Thomas's 1971 B.A. was from Holy Cross, and his 1974 J.D. from Yale Law School. His second wife is the former Virginia Lamp, a lawyer at the U.S. Labor Department, and formerly at the U.S. Chamber of Commerce. Thomas has one son, from a former marriage.

FURTHER READING

Strange Justice: The Selling of Clarence Thomas. JUNE MAYER. Houghton Mifflin, 1994.

"Her word against his." DAVID BROCK. *National Review*, May 10, 1993.

Critical Judicial Nominations and Political Change: The Impact of Clarence Thomas. CHRISTOPHER E. SMITH. Greenwood, 1993.

Clarence Thomas: Supreme Court Justice. WARREN J. HALLIBURTON. Enslow, 1993.

Turning Right: The Making of the Rehnquist Supreme Court. DAVID B. SAVAGE. Wiley, 1993.

The Real Anita Hill: The Untold Story. DAVID BROCK. Free Press, 1993.

"One year later. . . ." RONALD M. DWORKIN. *New York Times Book Review*, Oct. 25, 1992.

"Never mind. . . ." JEFF ROSEN. *New Republic*, Sep. 21, 1992.

Clarence Thomas. PAUL DEEGAN. Abdo & Daughters, 1992.

Clarence Thomas: Confronting the Future. L. GORDON CROVITZ, ed. Regnery Gateway, 1992.

Court of Appeal: The Black Community Speaks Out on the Racial and Sexual Politics of Thomas vs. Hill. ROBERT CHRISMAN and ROBERT ALLEN, eds. Ballantine, 1992.

Capitol Games: Clarence Thomas, Anita Hill, and the Behind-the-Scenes Story of a Supreme Court Nomination. TIMOTHY M. PHELPS and HELEN WINTERNITZ. Disney, 1992; HarperCollins, 1993.

Advice and Consent: The Senators and the Justices. PAUL SIMON. National Press, 1992.

"Breaking silence." VIRGINIA LAMP THOMAS. *People*, Nov. 11, 1991.

"The lesson of. . . ." STEVE ALLEN. *America*, Nov. 9, 1991.

"A question of character." RICHARD LACAYO. "An ugly circus." NANCY GIBBS. *Time*, Oct. 21, 1991.

"Thomas and Hill. . . ." ELOISE SALHOLZ. "Anatomy of a debacle." DAVID A. KAPLAN. "A moment of truth." *Newsweek*, Oct. 21, 1991.

"Judging Thomas." GLORIA BORGER. "Asking the questions. . . ." DONALD BAER. *U.S. News & World Report*, Oct. 21, 1991.

"Thomas and Benedict. . . ." GEORGE KANNAR. *New Republic*, Oct. 14, 1991.

"The pain of being black." JACK E. WHITE. *Time*, Sep. 16, 1991.

"Supreme mystery." DAVID A. KAPLAN. *Newsweek*, Sep. 16, 1991.

"The crowning Thomas affair." STEVEN V. ROBERTS. *U.S. News & World Report*, Sep. 16, 1991.

Thomas, Frank Edward (1968–)

When it came to selecting the most valuable player of baseball's American League, it was no contest. Every single member of the Baseball Writers Association named Chicago White Sox first baseman Frank Thomas as their first choice for MVP, making him only the eighth AL player and tenth baseball professional ever to be selected unanimously. The honor was especially sweet because he had been third in the voting in 1991, his first year in the major leagues, but a surprising eighth in 1992, and because a late-season arm injury had kept him from posting even stronger numbers than his team record 41 home runs, .317 batting average, 128 RBI's, and 77 extra-base hits, breaking a 1920 club record set by Joe Jackson. He led his team into a pennant race, but lost to the Toronto Blue Jays, who went on to win the World Series. Thomas also had the best ranking at any position in the statistical rankings kept by the Elias Sports Bureau for use in determining compensation for free agents; with the "ideal" being 1.0, Thomas had 1.6, while the runner-up was National League MVP Barry Bonds, with a 2.0. A *Sporting News* poll of players also named Thomas player of the year.

The White Sox acknowledged Thomas's value by signing a new four-year contract extension worth $29 million, the second-richest in baseball, slightly behind Bonds. The contract includes a no-trade provision through 1996, and provides that after that, he can be traded to certain teams only with his permission. Reebok also signed Thomas to a substantial contract for baseball.

Born in Columbus, Georgia, Thomas attended Auburn University, originally playing tight end in football but later switching to baseball, and being named to the *Sporting News* All-Star Collegiate All-American Team (1989). Named *Baseball America*'s minor league player of 1990 for his play with the Birmingham Barons, he joined the Chicago White Sox in 1990, and in 1991 was named to the *Sporting News* All-Star Team and received the Silver Slugger award. He played a cameo role in the film *Mr. Baseball* (1992). Thomas married Elise Silver and has a son.

FURTHER READING

"First thing's first." JEROME HOLTZMAN et al. *Sporting News*, Oct. 11, 1993.
"No doubting Thomas." STEVE RUSHIN. *Sports Illustrated*, Sep. 16, 1991.

Thomas, Lewis (1913–93) New York City-born Lewis Thomas, a doctor, poet, and essayist, had a long and distinguished career as an educator and administrator, as a professor of medicine at several colleges and universities, Dean of the New York University School of Medicine (1966–69), Dean of the Yale School of Medicine (1972–73), and as President of the Memorial Sloan-Kettering Cancer Center (1973–80), later becoming president emeritus of Sloan-Kettering. He is best known by far as a writer and humanist, the author of very popular essays, on a wide range of topics, though many focusing on scientific and medical matters; many of these were published in collections such as the best-selling National Book Award-winning *The Lives of A Cell* (1974), *The Medusa and the Snail*

(1979), *The Youngest Science* (1983), *Late Night Thoughts on Listening to Mahler's Ninth Symphony* (1983), *Could I Ask You Something?* (1984), *Et Cetera, Et Cetera* (1990), and *The Fragile Species* (1992). Thomas was survived by his wife, Beryl Dawson, and three daughters. (d. New York City; December 3, 1993)

FURTHER READING

Obituary. *New York Times*, Dec. 4, 1993.
Lewis Thomas. ANDREW J. ANGYAL. Twayne/Macmillan, 1989.
Inventing the Truth: The Art and Craft of Memoir. WILLIAM ZINSSER, ed. Houghton Mifflin, 1988.

Thompson, E(dward) P(almer)
(1924–93) English historian E.P. Thompson grew up in Oxford and attended Cambridge University, there becoming a Marxist and a member of the Communist Party. He remained a Marxist historian for several decades, but decisively left the Communist Party and movement after the 1956 Soviet crushing of the Hungarian Revolution. He taught at Leeds University (1948–65) and at the University of Warwick (1965–71). Thompson's first major work was a massive biography of William Morris (1955), and his second the work for which he is by far best known: *The Making of the British Working Class* (1963). He later became a major figure in the British antinuclear movement. He was survived by his wife, historian and teacher Dorothy Towers, a daughter, and two sons. (d. Worcester; August 28, 1993)

FURTHER READING

"A revolutionary. . . ." PAUL BUHLE. *Tikkun*, Nov.-Dec. 1993.
Obituary. *The Times* (of London), Aug. 30, 1993.
Obituary. *New York Times*, Aug. 30, 1993.
E.P. Thompson: Critical Debates. HARVEY J. KAYE and KEITH MCCLELLAND. Temple University Press, 1990.

Thompson, Emma (1959–) For her performance in *Howard's End*, actress Emma Thompson was greatly honored by her peers in 1993, winning the best actress Oscar, British Academy of Film and Television Arts, Golden

Globe, and National Society of Film Critics awards.

Thompson continued to emerge as a major world film figure, with starring roles in three highly regarded films. She starred, again opposite Anthony Hopkins, in the film *The Remains of the Day*, directed by James Ivory, and written by Ruth Prawer Jhabvala, based on the novel by Kazuo Ishiguro, in a cast that included James Fox, Christopher Reeve, Peter Vaughan, Hugh Grant, Michael Lonsdale, and Tim Pigott-Smith.

She also starred opposite unjustly imprisoned Daniel Day-Lewis, playing his lawyer in the Northern Ireland-set film *In the Name of the Father*, a fact-based film adapted from Conlon's book *Proved Innocent*, by Terry George and Jim Sheridan, and directed by Sheridan. Her third starring role was as Beatrice in Shakespeare's *Much Ado about Nothing*, adapted, directed, co-produced, and starring Kenneth Branagh, her husband, as Benedick; Denzel Washington as Don Pedro and Michael Keaton as Dogberry co-starred.

After playing small roles in British theater and television in the early 1980s, Thompson's breakthrough came with a starring role in the musical *Me and My Girl* (1985). After playing in the television comedy series "Tutti Frutti," she found another starring role, in the television miniseries "The Fortunes of War," opposite Kenneth Branagh, whom she later married. She won a British best television actress award for the role. Her films include *Henry V* (1989), *Im-promptu* (1991), and *Dead Again* (1991). She attended Newnham College, Cambridge.

FURTHER READING

"Thompson's turn." GEORGINA HOWELL. *Vogue*, June 1993.
"Emma Thompson's. . . ." RUSSELL MILLER. *New York Times Magazine*, Mar. 28, 1993.
"Much ado about Emma." CHRIS HEATH. *US*, Mar. 1993.
"Classy sassy. . . ." DAVID GRITTEN. *Cosmopolitan*, Jan. 1993.
"All the world's a stage. . . ." GARY ARNOLD. *Insight*, Sep. 9, 1991.
"Riding high. . . ." SUSAN SCHINDEHETTE. *People*, Sep. 9, 1991.

Todd, Ann (1909–93) Cheshire-born Ann Todd, on stage in the 1920s, made her film debut in several small roles in 1931, and played in supporting roles until her sudden emergence as a star opposite James Mason and Herbert Lom in *The Seventh Veil* (1945). She went on to star in several Hollywood films, including *So Evil My Love* (1946) and *The Paradine Case* (1947). Her third husband, David Lean, directed her in *The Passionate Friends* (1948), *Madeleine* (1949), and *The Sound Barrier* (1952). Her film career sagged after the early 1950s, and she returned to the stage in several roles with the Old Vic company. During the 1960s, she became a highly regarded documentary filmmaker. Her autobiography was *The Eighth Veil* (1980). She was survived by a daughter and a son. (d. London; May 7, 1993)

FURTHER READING

Obituary. *Variety*, May 17, 1993.
Obituary. *New York Times*, May 8, 1993.
Obituary. *The Times* (of London), May 7, 1993.

Tomlin, Lily (1939–) Lily Tomlin was honored by her peers in 1993, with an Emmy nomination for best performance in variety or music program in her one-woman show *The Search for Signs of Intelligent Life in the Universe*, which had won a Tony on Broadway. In 1993, she appeared in Robert Altman's well-received film *Short Cuts*, based on eight stories and a poem by Raymond Carver, as adapted for

film by Altman and Frank Barhydt. The large cast also included Tim Robbins, Fred Ward, Anne Archer, Robert Downey, Jr., Jennifer Jason Leigh, Jack Lemmon, Andie MacDowell, Matthew Modine, and Tom Waits.

Tomlin also appeared in the film *And The Band Played On*, Arnold Schulman's screen adaptation of Randy Shilts's book about AIDS; directed by Roger Spottiswoode, in a cast that included Matthew Modine, Phil Collins, David Dukes, Richard Gere, Glenne Headly, Anjelica Huston, Swoosie Kurtz, Steve Martin, and Ian McKellen. A third film role was as Miss Hathaway in *The Beverly Hillbillies*, directed by Penelope Spheeris. One of her many benefit performances was in the AIDS-awareness television special *In a New Light*, hosted by Arsenio Hall and Paula Abdul.

Detroit-born Tomlin became a leading comedian during her years in television's "Laugh-In" (1969–72), and moved into a wide range of theater and film roles, also building her career as a singer and variety entertainer. Her film debut came in *Nashville* (1975; she won a New York Film Critics award). Her films also include *The Late Show* (1977), *Moment by Moment* (1978), *The Incredible Shrinking Woman* (1981), *Nine to Five* (1980), *All of Me* (1984), *Big Business* (1988), and *Shadows and Fog* (1992). Tomlin won a special Tony award for her one-woman Broadway show *Appearing Nitely* (1977), and a best actress Tony and several other awards for *The Search for Intelligent Life in the Universe*

(1986). She attended Wayne State University.

FURTHER READING

"Lily Tomlin. . . ." Louise Bernikow. *TV Guide*, Aug. 15, 1992.
"In search of. . . ." Donna Minkowitz. *Advocate*, Nov. 5, 1991.
Lily Tomlin: Woman of a Thousand Faces. Jeff Sorensen. St. Martin's, 1989.
TV Sirens. Michael McWilliams. Putnam, 1987.

Townsend, Robert (1957–) In 1993, Robert Townsend wrote, directed, and starred in the film *The Meteor Man*, a Washington D.C.-set fable about schoolteacher Jefferson Reed, who is struck by a meteor and gains superhuman powers, enabling him to successfully battle the gang that is running his neighborhood. The fantasy-with-a-purpose, aiming to provide African-American children with a role model, co-starred Marla Gibbs, Robert Guillaume, James Earl Jones, and Luther Vandross. It was moderately well received, perhaps most of all for its purposes and for Mr. Townsend, an enormously appealing performer. Townsend also ventured into new territory, as co-producer, co-director, and star of a new comedy-variety television series, "Townsend Television," which had a short life late in 1993.

Chicago-born Townsend made his film debut in *Cooley High* (1974), and played in supporting film and television roles during the 1980s, also working as a standup comedian. His major breakthrough came entirely on his own: he co-wrote, produced, directed, and starred in the low-budget, very highly regarded film *Hollywood Shuffle* (1987), a comedy-satire about the trials of a discriminated-against African-American actor. Gaining a studio contract and support, he made his second (and first reasonably financed) film, *The Five Heartbeats* (1991). He also directed the film *Eddie Murphy Raw* (1987). Townsend attended Illinois State University and Hunter College, and also studied at the Negro Ensemble Company and the Second City comedy workshop.

FURTHER READING

"Robert Townsend. . . ." Lester Sloan. *American Visions*, Feb.-Mar. 1993.
"Robert Townsend. . . ." Aldore Collier. *Ebony*, June 1991.

"Robert Townsend. . . ." VERONICA WEBB. *Interview*, Feb. 1991.

Townshend, Peter (1945–)

After a decade of relative obscurity, rock composer Peter Townshend leapt back into the limelight, with a hit Broadway revival and adaptation of his 1969 rock opera *Tommy* (*The Who's Tommy*), co-conceived by Townshend and director Des McAnuff. At the Tony awards in June, *Tommy* brought Townsend the best score award, which because of the first-ever tie in Tony voting, he shared with John Kander and Fred Ebb for their *The Kiss of the Spider Woman*. Director McAnuff also took home a Tony, as did light designer Chris Parry, scenic designer John Arnone, and choreographer Wyne Cilento, In all, the play, starring Michael Cerveris, took five out of its eleven Tony nominations. The musical was accompanied by the book *The Who's Tommy: The Musical*, written by Townshend and McAnuff. In 1993, Townshend premiered his new album *Psychoderelict*, a story-and-song cycle that included Townshend singing 11 of his new songs. He also appeared on the two-hour concert video *Pete Townshend Live*.

Townshend, Keith Moon, Roger Daltry, and John Entwhistle formed the British rock band *The Who* in 1964; for two decades it was a leading rock music band, on tour and recordings, with such Townshend songs as "My Generation" (1965), "Happy Jack" (1966; title song of an album), and such other albums as *The Who Sell Out* (1967), *Magic Bus* (1970), *Who's Next* (1971), *The Who By Numbers* (1975), *Who Are You?* (1978), *Face Dances* (1981), and *It's Hard* (1982). In 1969, Townshend's rock opera *Tommy* was a highly innovative hit show, as was their concert album of the opera and Ken Russell's Oscar-nominated 1975 film adaptation. Townshend's second rock opera was *Quadrophenia* (1973). Townshend has also recorded several solo albums, including *Secret Policeman's Ball* (1980), *Empty Glass* (1980), *All the Best Cowboys Have Chinese Eyes* (1982), and *White City* (1985). His musical *Iron Man* (1989) is an adaptation of the Ted Hughes's children's story. He also published the short story collection *Horse's Neck* (1985).

FURTHER READING

"Psychodrama. . . ." CHRIS GILL. *Guitar Player*, Sep. 1993.
"Pete, we can hear you." JANICE C. SIMPSON. *Time*, July 12, 1993.
" 'Tommy's' next stage." JOHN HEILPERN. *Vogue*, May 1993.
"Who's on Broadway?" DAVID WILD. *Rolling Stone*, Mar. 18, 1993.
Rock Lives: Profiles and Interviews. TIMOTHY WHITE. Holt, 1990.
"Godhead revisited. . . ." MATT RESNICOFF. *Guitar Player*, Sep. 1989.
"Flailing your way. . . ." MATT RESNICOFF. *Guitar Player*, Oct. 1989.
"The Who. . . ." STEVE POND and ELLIOT MURPHY. *Rolling Stone*, July 13, 1989.

Tritt, Travis (1963–)

In 1993, Travis Tritt and Marty Stuart were awarded a Grammy for the best country vocal collaboration for their hit single "The Whiskey Ain't Workin'." Tritt issued the hit singles "Looking Out For Number One," co-written with Troy Seals, and "Worth Every Mile." Tritt also issued the documentary music video *A Celebration: A Musical Tribute To The Spirit Of The American Disabled Veteran*, as a benefit for that organization. In a change of pace, Tritt starred opposite Kenny Rogers and Naomi Judd in the television western *Rio Diablo*. An autobiography, tentatively titled *Ten Foot Tall and Bulletproof* and written with Michael Bane, was scheduled for 1994 publication.

Georgia-born Tritt emerged as a popular coun-

try music singer and songwriter in the early 1990s, with the hit albums *Country Club* (1990), *It's All About to Change* (1991), *T-R-O-U-B-L-E* (1992), and *A Travis Tritt Christmas: Loving Time of the Year* (1992). He was named Billboard's top new male country artist in 1990.

FURTHER READING

"Country hunks." MARJIE McGRAW. *Ladies Home Journal*, Oct. 1992.
"Travis Tritt. . . ." JOHN MORTHLAND. *Country Music*, May-June, 1992.
"Introducing Travis Tritt." PATRICK CARR. *Country Music*, Sep.-Oct. 1990.

Tully, Alice Bigelow (1902–93) Born in Corning, New York, Alice Tully grew up in New York City. She studied voice in New York and Paris in the mid-1920s, making her professional debut in recital in 1927 in Paris, and her operatic debut in 1933 as Santuzza in a New York City Salmaggi Opera producton of *Cavalleria Rusticana*. She sang in recital and opera until her retirement in 1950. In 1958, she inherited a substantial fortune, and became the main contributor responsible for the construction of what became Lincoln Center's Alice Tully Hall, which opened on September 11, 1969, her 67th birthday. Tully received many awards, including an American National Medal of Arts and the

French Legion of Honor. There were no survivors. (d. New York City; December 10, 1993)

FURTHER READING

Obituary. *The Times* (of London), Dec. 22, 1993.
Obituary. *New York Times*, Dec. 11, 1993.

Turner, Kathleen (1954–) Stage and screen star Kathleen Turner starred in 1993 opposite Tommy Lee Jones in the film *House of Cards*, written and directed by Michael Lessac. Turner plays widow Ruth Matthews, whose 6-year-old daughter has stopped speaking, after the untimely death of her father; Jones is a child psychiatrist. The film, its release postponed in 1992, received mixed reviews. Turner also starred in the New Orleans-set comedy-action film *Undercover Blues*, opposite Dennis Quaid; they play Jeff and Jane Blue, he as an independent-minded, fun-loving CIA spook, she as his equally fun-loving wife.

Forthcoming was a starring role in the film *Serial Mom*, written and directed by John Waters and co-starring Sam Waterston and Rickie Lake. Still forthcoming was a starring role in Daniel Algrant's film *Naked in New York*, co-starring Timothy Dalton, Whoopi Goldberg, Eric Stolz, and Mary Louise Parker;

Missouri-born Turner moved from the theater into films in the early 1980s, and quickly emerged as a leading movie star, in such films as *Body Heat* (1981), *Romancing the Stone* (1984), *Prizzi's Honor* (1985), *The Jewel of the Nile* (1985), *Peggy Sue Got Married* (1986), *Switching Channels* (1988), *The Accidental Tourist* (1988), *The War of the Roses* (1989), and *V.I. Warshawski* (1991). She also starred in a 1989 New York revival of Tennessee Williams's *Cat on a Hot Tin Roof*, and was the voice of the sexy cartoon figure, Jessica, in *Who Framed Roger Rabbit* (1988). Turner attended Southwest Missouri State University and received her M.F.A. from the University of Maryland. She married Jay Weiss in 1984; they have one child.

FURTHER READING

"The ups and downs. . . ." CHRIS CHASE. *Cosmopolitan*, July 1993.
"Kathleen Turner. . . ." MALCOLM MacPHERSON. *Premiere*, Nov. 1989.
Kathleen Turner. REBECCA STEFOFF. St. Martin's, 1987.

Turner, Ted (Robert Edward Turner, III; 1938–) During 1993, Ted Turner decisively turned his attention toward films, while at the same time beginning to position himself for growth in the emerging new multimedia world communications system. As owner of the Atlanta Braves baseball and Atlanta Hawks basketball teams, he also continued to be a major figure in American sports.

Turner made it clear that what he wanted was no less than ownership of a major studio, side by side with his ownership of major television properties. Far short of that goal, but on the way, on August 17 Turner Broadcasting announced agreement to acquire two film studios, New Line Cinema and Castle Rock Entertainment, for a total of $600 million. He also focused on the creation of film and multimedia programming by Turner Broadcasting, including a $60 million multimedia project on American Indian history and culture, which began to air in early December, with the two-hour television film *Geronimo*, and was slated to include 14 hours of original films, 6 hours of documentaries, and a 20-part television news series. He also acquired the 4-hour film *Gettysburg*, opening it in theatrical release. Restricted in his acquisition activities by the terms of agreements with his financial partners, he took no part during 1993 in the media acquisition mania that swept the world communications industry, but was expected by many to soon move in that direction, as well.

Turner began building what ultimately became a set of major enterprises in the 1960s, and emerged as a leading American industrial and sports figure during the 1970s. After encountering serious financial problems in the mid-1980s, Turner in the late 1980s emerged as a world communications industry leader at the head of the Turner Broadcasting System (TBS), the Cable News Network (CNN), and Turner Network Television (TNT). TNT began broadcasting its combination of old movies, sports, original television movies, and a potpourri of other programming in October 1988, and quickly grew into a major asset. From 1989, CNN grew into a worldwide broadcast news network, with hundreds of millions of viewers, through its 24-hour coverage of such massive events as the Tiananmen Square demonstrations and massacre, the San Francisco and Los Angeles earthquakes, the tearing down of the Berlin Wall, the continuing events in Eastern Europe and the former Soviet Union, the Palestinian uprising, and the Persian Gulf War.

A leading yachtsman, Turner won the America's Cup in 1977. He sponsored the Goodwill Games at Moscow in 1986 and at Atlanta in 1990. Turner attended Brown University. Before marrying actress Jane Fonda in 1991, he had been married twice previously, and has five children.

FURTHER READING

It Ain't As Easy As It Looks: The Story of Ted Turner and CNN. PORTER BIBB. Crown, 1993.
Ted Turner. DAVID M. FISCHER. Rourke, 1993.
"What new worlds . . .?" SUBRATA N. CHAKRAVARTY. *Forbes*, Jan. 4, 1993.
"Prince of the global village." "The taming of Ted Turner." PRISCILLA PAINTON. "History as it happens." WILLIAM A. HENRY, III. "Inside the world of CNN." RICHARD ZOGLIN. *Time*, Jan. 6, 1992. "Man of the Year" issue.
Ted Turner: Television's Triumphant Tiger. REBECCA STEFOFF. Garrett, 1992.
"Ted Turner turns it on." BRUCE STUTZ. *Audubon*, Nov.-Dec. 1991.
"Jane and Ted's. . . ." JERRY ADLER. *Esquire*, Feb. 1991.
"Terrible Ted. . . ." IVOR DAVIS. *Los Angeles Magazine*, Aug. 1990.
"Captain planet. . . ." JOHN MOTAVALLI. *Interview*, June 1989.
"Ted Turner. . . ." GREG DAWSON. *American Film*, Jan.-Feb. 1989.
The Alexander Complex: Six Businessmen and the Empires They Built. MICHAEL MEYER. Random, 1989.

The Corporate Warriors. DOUGLAS K. RAMSEY. Houghton Mifflin, 1987.

Turner, Tina (Annie Mae Bullock; 1938–) Rock star Tina Turner saw her life pass before her on the screen in 1993, with the release of a new biographical film, named after Turner's 1984 hit song "What's Love Got to Do With It," with Angela Bassett playing Tina and Laurence Fishburne as her former husband and partner, Ike Turner. Turner herself went on a cross-country concert tour, performing songs old and new, including her recent hits "I Don't Wanna Fight" and the 1993 single, "Why Must We Wait Until Tonight?," from the film's soundtrack. She was also the subject of a music video, *The Girl From Nutbush,* dubbed a "rockumentary," featuring performances of hits such as "Steamy Windows," "Proud Mary," "Private Dancer," and-naturally-"What's Love . . ." as well as interviews with Turner and many others, including David Bowie, Mick Jagger, Eric Clapton, Bryan Adams, Ann-Margret, longtime manager Roger Davies, and photographer Herb Ritts. In June, she was honored at the 1993 World Music Awards for her lifelong contribution to the music industry. In Billboard's 1993 rankings, she was eleventh on the list for hot adult contemporary artists. Turner's ex-husband, Ike, had been sentenced to four years in prison over drug problems in 1990; in 1993 interviews, he sharply complained about the negative view of him given in the film and documentary about Tina.

Tennessee-born Turner joined Ike Turner's band in 1956; the couple were married in 1958, and after her hit recording of "A Fool in Love" (1960), emerged as leading rock figures of the 1960s and early 1970s. After their parting, in the mid-1970s, Tina Turner went on to become a very popular soloist of the 1980s, with such albums as *Private Dancer* (1984), *Break Every Rule* (1986), and *Foreign Affairs* (1989), which included "Steamy Windows" and "The Best." She was among the many who sang "We Are the World" (1985), in the USA for Africa benefit. She has also appeared in several films, including *Tommy* (1975) and *Mad Max Beyond Thunderdome* (1985). In 1986, she published *I, Tina,* written with Kurt Loder. She has four children.

FURTHER READING

"Tina Turner." HAL RUBENSTEIN. *Interview,* Aug. 1993.

" 'What's Love Got To Do With It.' " ALDORE COLLIER. *Ebony,* July 1993.

"What becomes . . .?" AUDREY EDWARDS. *Essence,* July 1993.

"Aye, Tina." RICHARD CORLISS and RICHARD ZOGLIN. *Time,* June 21, 1993.

"Will it work out fine?" DAVID GATES. *Newsweek,* June 21, 1993.

"Angela Bassett takes on. . . ." THERESA STURLEY. *Interview,* June 1993.

"The sixth Essence awards." AUDREY EDWARDS. *Essence,* May 1993.

"The lady has legs." MAUREEN ORTH. *Vanity Fair,* May 1993.

"Tina Turner at 52 . . ." EDNA GUNDERSEN. *Ebony,* Jan. 1992.

"Rich, free and in control. . . ." LYNN NORMENT. *Ebony,* Nov. 1989.

Picture Life of Tina Turner. GENE BUSNER. Watts, 1987.

Turow, Scott F. (1949–) In 1993, best-selling novelist Scott Turow was back in his own fictional Kindle County for his third novel, *Pleading Guilty.* But this new book had a very different feel. The inside of a courtroom was nowhere to be seen; instead the story focused on the inner workings of a corporate law firm, the main character being Mack Malloy, ex-cop and

low-status lawyer in a high-status firm. His search for a missing law partner and missing millions from the firm's main corporate client, and his encounters with people like his vengeful ex-police partner Pigeyes and his sexually-adventurous law firm associate Brushy keep the story moving along, and helped drive the book onto the best-seller lists. The legal thriller was a main selection of both the Book-of-the-Month Club and Quality Paperback Book Club, and was also scheduled to appear as a Franklin Library First Edition, a Time-Life condensed book, an audio book, a large print book, and an electronic book. Film rights for the book were also sold, with Jon Avnet scheduled as producer and probably director.

Chicago-born Turow was an assistant U.S. attorney in Chicago (1978–86), then going into private practice with Soonscheim Carlin Nath and Rosenthal. His early work included *One L.: An Inside Account of Life in the First Year at Harvard Law School* (1977). He emerged as a best-selling popular novelist with *Presumed Innocent* (1987), which was adapted into the 1990 film, directed by Alan J. Pakula and starring Harrison Ford, Brian Dennehy, Raul Julia, and Bonnie Bedelia. His second, also best-selling novel was *The Burden of Proof* (1990). His B.A. was from Amherst College, his M.A. from Stanford University, and his J.D. from Harvard Law School. Turow is married to Annette Weisberg, and has three children.

FURTHER READING

"Turow, Scott." *Current Biography*, Aug. 1991.
"Going to extremes." MARCIA FROELKE COBURN. *Chicago*, July 1990.
"Out with another. . . ." KEN GROSS. *People*, June 11, 1990.
"Burden of success. . . ." PAUL GRAY. *Time*, June 11, 1990.
"Scott Turow." BRENDAN LEMON. *Interview*, June 1990.

Twitty, Conway (Harold Jenkins; 1933–93) Mississippi-born Conway Twitty, began his singing career in 1947, with The Rockhousers, an Arkansas country group. He became a rock-and-roll songwriter in the early 1950s, and made his first singles records in 1957. His first hit, which he wrote and recorded, was "It's Only Make Believe"; its millions of sales very quickly made him a major star of the rock-and-roll era. He followed it with recordings of "Mona Lisa" and "Lonely Blue Boy," and other less popular rock-and-roll songs. Twitty also appeared in several youth-oriented films of the period. He switched to country music in the mid-1960s, in the decades that followed becoming a country music star, with more than 50 top songs to his credit, as well as scores of records. Twitty also went into several businesses, among them Twitty City. He was survived by his wife, Dee, two daughters, two sons, and his mother. (d. Springfield, Missouri; June 5, 1993)

FURTHER READING

Obituary. RICH KIENZLE. *Country Music*, Sep.-Oct. 1993.
Obituary. DON McLEESE. *Rolling Stone*, Aug. 5, 1993.
Obituary. *The Times* (of London), June 7, 1993.
Obituary. *New York Times*, June 6, 1993.

Tyson, Laura D'Andrea (1947–) Chairwoman of the Council of Economic Advisors Laura D'Andrea Tyson helped President Bill Clinton chart a considerably altered economic course for the United States during 1993. An advocate of balanced, rather than unrestricted international free trade, her thinking clearly influenced the Clinton administration's early stress on the encouragement, and to some extent the protection, of high-technology American industries-the managed-trade approach. A strong proponent of opening up closed Japanese markets by ending Japanese discriminatory protectionist policies-so strong that she has been called by some a "Japan-basher"-Tyson also played an important advisory role in developing a far more aggressive American approach to Japanese trade negotiators. She was also a key figure in developing the American position in the GATT (General Agreement on Tariffs and Trade) negotiations. Throughout the year, Tyson continued to be attacked as a "protectionist," who traveled outside the mainstream of free market economic thinking; but her thinking was clearly entirely consonant with that of President Clinton.

New Jersey-born Tyson's B.A. was from Smith College, and her Ph.D. from the Massachusetts Institute of Technology. At the time of her appointment, Tyson was a professor of economics and business administration at the University of California at Berkeley, where she also served as the director of the Institute of International Studies and research director of the Berkeley Roundtable on International Economy. She was an economic advisor to the Clinton/Gore campaign. Among her works are *American Industry in International Competition: Government Policies and Corporate Strategies* (1983; edited with John Zysman) and *The Dynamics of Trade and Politics and Productivity: The Real Story of How Japan Works* (1989; edited with Chalmers Johnson and John Zysman). Among her other works are *The Yugoslav Economic System and Its Performance in the 1970s* (1980), *The Impact of International Economic Disturbances on the Soviet Union and Eastern Europe* (1980; edited with Egon Neuberger), *Power, Purpose and Collective Choice: Economic Strategy in Socialist States* (1986; edited with Ellen Comisso), *Can Gorbachev's Reforms Succeed?* (1990; with various co-editors), and *Who's Bashing Whom? Trade Conflict in High Technology Industries* (1992). She is married to writer Eric Tarloff; they have one child.

FURTHER READING

"A woman of influence." SUSAN DENTZER and ERIK TARLOFF. *Working Woman*, Aug. 1993.
"Practicing what. . . ." SUSAN DENTZER. *U.S. News & World Report*, June 14, 1993.
"Rougher trade. . . ." JOHN B. JUDIS. *New Republic*, May 31, 1993.
"Far from Berkeley. . . ." MAGGIE MAHAR. *Barron's*, May 24, 1993.
"Straight talk from. . . ." ANN REILLY DOWD and CARLA RAPOPORT. *Fortune*, May 3, 1993.
"Econoclast. . . ." MICHAEL LEWIS. *New Republic*, Feb. 1, 1993.
"Whatever you call it. . . ." PAUL MAGNUSSON. *Business Week*, Dec. 28, 1992.
"Tyson's trade treatment." VIVIAN BROWNSTEIN. *Fortune*, Dec. 28, 1992.
"No longer home alone." *Time*, Dec. 21, 1992.
"Teaching Washington. . . ." DAVID HAGE. *U.S. News & World Report*, Dec. 14, 1992.

Tyson, Mike G. (1966–) Former heavyweight boxing champion Mike Tyson continued to try for his freedom in 1993. With the aid of Harvard Law School professor and celebrity lawyer Alan Dershowitz, he was appealing his February 1992 rape conviction; Miss Black America contestant Desiree Washington had accused Tyson of raping her in his hotel room in Indianapolis in July 1991, while Tyson said they had consensual sex. An August appeal for review of the case, on the grounds that the lower court refused to let three defense witnesses testify or to allow evidence about Washington's sexual past, was denied by the Indiana Supreme Court. But in December, the Indiana Court of Appeals granted Tyson a hearing. Late in 1992, Tyson reached an out-of-court settlement in Washington's $100 million civil suit against him, though he still faced other civil suits.

In September, then-champion Riddick Bowe visited Tyson in the Plainfield, Indiana, prison where he is serving his six-year term (actually ten years, with four suspended) for a rape conviction; among his other visitors have been Spike Lee, Whitney Houston, and Hammer. In October, Tyson said that he might settle in Africa to escape America's racism against Blacks; he would be eligible for parole in 1995, his stay lengthened by 30 days in March 1993 for allegedly disobeying a prison officer. In February, NBC aired a two-hour documentary on Tyson's life, *Fallen Champ: The Untold Story of Mike Tyson*, by Oscar-winning director Barbara Kopple.

Brooklyn-born Tyson turned professional in 1985, and quickly became a leading heavyweight title contender. From 1986 to 1988, he successively defeated several boxers, the last of them Michael Spinks in June 1988, and united the three boxing titles to become sole world heavyweight champion, the youngest ever. He held the title until his unexpected defeat, his first as a professional, by James "Buster" Douglas in February 1990. Tyson was formerly married, to actress Robin Givens. After a 1991 suit, he acknowledged paternity of a daughter.

FURTHER READING

"Tale of the tapes." *Sports Illustrated*, Apr. 26, 1993.

"Tyson's appeal ignites. . . ." BEN McINTYRE. *Times*, Feb. 15, 1993.

Down for the Count: The Shocking Truth Behind the Mike Tyson Rape Trial. MARK SHAW. Sagamore, 1993.

"The lost boy." PETER BOYER. *Vanity Fair*, Mar. 1992.

"Judgment day." JOE TREEN. *People*, Feb. 24, 1992.

"Destined to fall." RICHARD HOFFER. *Sports Illustrated*, Feb. 17, 1992.

"Lawyers to their corners." TOM CALLAHAN. *U.S. News & World Report*, Feb. 3, 1992.

"Tyson." KEITH BOTSFORD. *Independent*, Jan. 11, 1992.

"Mike Tyson. . . ." PHIL BERGER. *M.*, Jan. 1992.

Mike Tyson: Money Myth Betrayal. MONTEIL ILLINGWORTH. Carol 1991.

Mike Tyson. JOHN HENNESSEY. Smithmark, 1990.

Bad Intentions: The Mike Tyson Story. PETER HELLER. NAL-Dutton, 1990.

Blood Season: Tyson and the World of Boxing. PHIL BERGER. Morrow, 1989.

Fire and Fear: The Inside Story of Mike Tyson. JOSE TORRES. Warner, 1989.

U

Ullman, Tracey (1959–) Stage, screen, and television star Tracey Ullman focused on the screen forms in 1993. She starred in the film *Household Saints*, directed by Nancy Savoca and produced by Jonathan Demme, and co-starring Vincent D'Onofrio, Lili Taylor, and Judith Malina. The film was a multigenerational family drama set in New York City's Little Italy.

Ullman also starred in the well-received television film *Tracey Ullman Takes on New York*, directed by Don Scardino and consisting of three intertwined stories set in New York. Ullman starred in all three, successively opposite Dan Castellaneta; Michael Williams; and Blythe Danner and John Cunningham, in a large cast that included Michael York, Robert Joy, Jill Eikenberry, James Lally, and Josh Mostel. Ullman won a 1993 Emmy as best guest actress in a comedy series for her appearance on "Love and War."

Forthcoming was a starring role in film, untitled at year's end, written and directed by Woody Allen and co-starring John Cusack, Mary-Louise Parker, Jennifer Tilly, Chazz Palmintieri, Dianne Wiest, Carl Reiner, Alan Arkin, and Jack Warden.

Ullman has been on stage since the mid-1970s, and emerged as a star in British television comedy in the early 1980s. She became a comedy star in American television in her own "The Tracey Ullman Show" (1987–90); the series won a best comedy series Emmy in 1989. She also won a 1990 Emmy, for best individual performance in a variety or musical program, in *The Best of the "Tracey Ullman Show"*; the show received a total of 13 Emmy nominations. Ullman also appeared in supporting roles in several films, including *Plenty* (1985), and starred opposite Kevin Kline in Lawrence Kasdan's film *I Love You to Death* (1990). In 1990, she also played Katherine to Morgan Freeman's Petruchio in a New York stage production of *The Taming of the Shrew*; and recorded the album *You Broke My Heart in Several Places*, with its hit single "They Don't Know." Ullman is married to Allan McKeown; the couple have two children, the second a son born in August 1991.

FURTHER READING

"Tracey Ullman. . . ." Jerry Lazar. *New York Times Magazine*, Oct. 15, 1989,
"Tracking Tracey." Michael Dare and Matthew Rolston. *Interview*, Jan. 1989.

Updike, John Hoyer (1932–) Literary luminary John Updike took a long look at his poetic work and, in 1993, published his *Collected Poems 1953–1993*. The gathering of over 300 poems, from throughout his career, was well-received, drawing as it does from the whole range of life and experience, and was praised for its sparkle and clarity. An Updike short story was also anthologized in *The Literary Lover: Great Contemporary Stories of Passion and Romance* (1993), edited by Larry Dark. A new novel, *Brazil*, was scheduled for 1994 publication. A television miniseries based on his quartet of "Rabbit" novels was also forthcoming.

Pennsylvania-born Updike, a novelist and essayist, is best known for his "Rabbit" cycle—*Rabbit Run* (1960), *Rabbit Redux* (1977), *Rabbit Is Rich* (1981), and *Rabbit at Rest* (1990), which won the Pulitzer Prize and the National Book Award. Among his other novels are the National Book Award-winning *The Centaur* (1963), *Couples* (1968), *Bech: a Book* (1970; and its 1972 sequel), *The Witches of Eastwick* (1984), and *Memories of the Ford Administration* (1992). He has also written short stories, many of them first published in *The New Yorker*, as well as essays, poetry, and a play. His recent work also includes the autobiography *Self-Consciousness: Memoirs* (1990) and the collection *Odd Jobs: Essays and Criticism* (1990). Updike's 1954 B.A. was from Harvard University. Formerly married to Mary Pennington, he married Martha Bernhard in 1977, and has four children.

FURTHER READING

Conversations with John Updike. JAMES PLATH, ed. University Press of Mississippi, 1994.
John Updike: A Bio-Bibiliography, 1967–1993. JACK DE BELLIS, ed. Greenwood, 1993.
"Personally speaking." *Vogue*, Sep. 1992.
John Updike. JUDIE NEWMAN. St. Martin's, 1988.
John Updike. HAROLD BLOOM, ed. Chelsea House, 1987.

V

Valvano, Jim (James Thomas Valvano; 1946–93) New York City-born Jim Valvano, child of a basketball family, played for his father's Seaford, Long Island high school basketball team and for Rutgers before moving into coaching, which became his life's work. After a year as an assistant coach at Rutgers, he coached at several small colleges, and had a very successful five years at Iona College. He moved into very "big time" college basketball as the coach of North Carolina State in 1980, his team winning a 1983 national championship. He also became a very active and well-paid speaker, and product endorser, his income estimated to be in the $500,000 per year range. However, a series of ethical problems involving North Carolina players surface in 1989 and 1990; although he was not personally involved, North Carolina went into a period of probation, and he stepped down, first from his athletic director's post and then from his coaching job. He then successfully began a new career as a sportscaster, which was cut short by the cancer that took his life. He published the autobiographical *Valvano: They Gave Me a Lifetime Contract and Then They Declared Me Dead* (*Valvano: My Side*) (1991), written with Curry Kirkpatrick. He was survived by his wife, Pam, and three daughters. (d. Durham, North Carolina; April 28, 1993)

FURTHER READING

Obituary. *New York Times*, Apr. 29, 1993.
"As time runs out." GARY SMITH. *Sports Illustrated*, Jan. 11, 1993.
"Jimmy V's brave war. . . ." JIM BAKER. *TV Guide*, Dec. 19, 1992.
"Tarnished Valvano. . . ." CHUCK STOGEL. *Sporting News*, Nov. 26, 1990.
"The Wolfpack held. . . ." ALEXANDER WOLFF. *Sports Illustrated*, Mar. 12, 1990.
" 'I'm just a spectator'. . . ." TOM CALLAHAN. *Newsweek*, Mar. 12, 1990.
" 'The darker side' of. . . ." MIKE DOUCHANT. *Sporting News*, Aug. 21, 1989.
"Foul play by the book. . . ." HARRY F. WATERS. *Newsweek*, Aug. 14, 1989.
"The ordeal of. . . ." JOHN FEINSTEIN. *Sports Illustrated*, Jan. 30, 1989.

Vidal, Gore (1925–) After four decades as an *enfant terrible*, Gore Vidal was lauded by the literary world for his mammoth collection, *United States: Essays 1951–1992*, containing no fewer than 114 essays from throughout his career, including his trademark biting criticism of works, notables, political concerns, and his own personal interests, notably the movies. The collection was very well received and, in November, was a surprise winner of the National Book Award for non-fiction. In a benefit for the Actors Studio in February, Vidal-predictably playing the devil-joined several other literary figures in a reading of George Bernard Shaw's *Don Juan in Hell*.

Born at West Point, New York, Vidal is one of the most prolific novelists, satirists, and social critics of the last four decades. His celebrated series of novels on American historical themes includes *Burr* (1972), *Lincoln* (1984), *Empire* (1987), and *Hollywood: A Novel of America in the 1920s* (1989). He has also written several novels set in the Greco-Roman world, including *Julian* (1964), *Myron* (1974), and *Creation* (1981). His many other works include the novel *Myra Breckenridge* (1968), the satirical time-traveling novel *Live From Golgotha* (1992), the plays *Visit to a Small Planet* (1957) and *The Best Man* (1960), several screenplays, occasional non-fiction works such as *Vidal in Venice* (1987), and a wide range of essays, reviews, and letters, including *Screening History, The Decline and Fall of the American Empire* (1992). Under the pseudonym Edgar Box, the young Vidal wrote several mysteries, some of which were in the 1990s reprinted in special editions, including *Death in the Fifth Position* (1952), *Death Before Bedtime* (1953), and *Death Likes It Hot* (1954). As an actor, he appeared as Senator Brickley Paiste in Tim Robbins's satirical film *Bob Roberts* (1992). A liberal, he was twice an unsuccessful candidate for public office, and was head of the short-lived New Party (1971–72). He graduated from Philips Exeter Academy in 1943.

FURTHER READING

"The importance of being Gore." ANDREW KOPKIND. *Nation*, July 5, 1993.
"Rebel, rebel." NUALA BOYLAN. *Harper's Bazaar*, Jan. 1993.
Gore Vidal: Writer Against the Grain. JAY PARINI, ed. Columbia University Press, 1993.
"Gospel according to Gore." DAVID HUTCHINGS. *People*, Nov. 2, 1992.
"A gadfly . . . ." MARTHA DUFFY. *Time*, Sep. 28, 1992.
"Gore's lore." ARTHUR LUBOW. *Vanity Fair*, Sep. 1992.
" 'J.F.K.' is not. . . ." MICHAEL ANDERSON. *New York Times Book Review*, Aug. 30, 1992.
"Mailer and Vidal. . . ." CAROLE MALLORY. *Esquire*, May 1991.
"Through the looking glass." HOWARD MEANS. *Washingtonian*, Feb. 1990.
"Tug of war." COLIN WRIGHT. *New Statesman & Society*, Nov. 3, 1989.

Villechaise, Herve (1943–93)

Paris-born Herve Villechaise began his career as a painter, becoming an actor after moving to New York. He played in a wide range of supporting roles during the 1960s and 1970s, successfully resisting all efforts to typecast him because of his height; he was 3 feet and 11 inches tall. He became a familiar face on American television in the role of Tattoo, opposite Ricardo Montalban in the series "Fantasy Island" (1978–83) He also played Nick Nack in *The Man with the Golden Arm* (1974). During his later years, he encountered career and health problems; he indicated that the latter were the cause of his suicide. There were no survivors. (d. Los Angeles; September 4, 1993)

FURTHER READING

"Laying down the burden." TOM GLIATTO. *People*, Sep. 20, 1993.
Obituary. *Variety*, Sep. 20, 1993.
Obituary. *The Times* (of London), Sep. 6, 1993.
Obituary. *New York Times*, Sep. 5, 1993.

von Sydow, Max: See Sydow, Max von

Wachtler, Sol (1930–) Formerly Chief Judge of New York State's Court of Appeals, Wachtler in the spring of 1992 began a bizarre set of moves that were to destroy his career and send him to prison. In the summer of 1991, he and Joy A. Silverman, a socialite and Republican Party figure, ended a four-year affair. By the spring of 1992, Ms. Silverman had developed a companionship with New Jersey lawyer David Samson. Wachtler, for no immediately apparent reason, began a 13-month-long campaign of harassment aimed at Ms. Silverman and her daughter, then 13 years old, which included obscene anonymous calls and letters, threats generated by Wachtler posing as a fictional private investigator, and attempted extortion, all of these finally traced to Wachtler. On November 7, 1992, Wachtler was arrested on harassment, extortion, and attempted kidnapping charges. He resigned from the Court of Appeals three days later, and was then placed under house arrest. He was indicted in February 1993, pleaded guilty to a single charge of threatening to kidnap Ms. Silverman's daughter, and on September 9 was sentenced to a 15-month prison term.

New York City-born Wachtler was until his troubles surfaced a highly regarded and much honored judge and scholar, whose career had developed through an unbroken string of successes. He was Town of North Hempstead councilman (1963–65), and then concurrently town chief executive and a member of the Nassau County Board of Surpervisors (1965–67). In 1968, he was appointed to the State Supreme Court, in 1972 stepped up to become a judge of

the State Court of Appeals, and in 1985 stepped up again, to become chief judge of that court, the highest judicial position in New York State. During his entire tenure on the judiciary, he was a guest lecturer in the United States and abroad, active in professional affairs, and in every visible respect a pillar of judiciary and community. He is married to Joan Wolosoff, and has four children.

FURTHER READING

"Crazy for you. . . ." ERIC POOLEY. *New York*, Dec. 14, 1992.
"Sol Wachtler. . . ." ROB GURWITT. *Governing*, Jan. 1992.

Wagner, Robert F(erdinand), Jr. (1944–93) Actually, the third to bear his name, Wagner was the son of three-time New York Democratic mayor Robert Wagner, Jr., and grandson of four-time U.S. Democratic Senator Robert Wagner, architect of the 1930s New Deal Wagner Act (National Labor Relations Act). A lawyer and New York City political figure, Wagner served as a Councilman at Large in 1973, and was a deputy mayor during the Koch era. He had also been chairman of the New York City Planning Commission, head of the Board of Education, and head of the Health and Hospitals Corporation. A lifelong Democrat, he had recently supported Republican-Liberal candidate Rudolf Giuliani in his winning campaign for the

New York City mayoralty, and was a senior policy advisor for Giuliani. He was survived by a brother and a stepmother. (d. San Antonio, Texas; November 15, 1993)

FURTHER READING

"Remembering Bobby. . . ." *New Yorker*, Dec. 6, 1993.
Obituary. *New York Times*, Nov. 17, 1993.

Waite, Terry (Terence Hardy Waite; 1939–)

As the Archbishop of Canterbury's personal envoy, seeking to gain the freedom of other Westerners held hostage in Lebanon, Terry Waite was himself taken hostage, on January 20, 1987. So began a confinement of almost five years, the first four in solitary, made more difficult by physical torture and by his questionable health, especially asthma; he joined fellow hostages only for the last year, until his release after 1763 days on November 18, 1991. Describing those terrible days in a new book published in 1993, *Taken on Trust*, Waite explored how he tried to handle his ordeal by analyzing his life, both as child and adult, and examining deeper philosophical questions about his life and work, including his status as a political prisoner, writing in his head the book that he would later write on paper. But the trauma was severe. He described how, even nearly two years after his release from captivity, he was having difficulty adjusting to normal life, and continued to live largely alone, in rooms provided by Cambridge University, apart from his family and most other people.

After his release, rumors suggested that his negotiations were involved in the Reagan administration's arms-for-hostages trading. Waite denied that he was knowingly involved, and when, during a 1993 publicity tour, he met Oliver North, a key man in that attempt, Waite seemed upset that he had inadvertently been used to cover American attempts to free the hostages; it was his association with Americans that had been the focus of interrogation by his captors, and perhaps a trigger for the kidnapping itself.

The publication of Waite's book, in September, was timed to coincide with the showing of a BBC documentary on the Lebanon hostages.

Waite was writing a sequel to *Taken on Trust*, and also a novel.

Born in Bollington, Cheshire, Waite was educated at London's Church Army College, then beginning work as an advisor to Anglican church officials, at Bristol (1964–68) and in Uganda, Rwanda, and Burundi (1968–71); as liaison with the Roman Catholic Church (1972–79); then as advisor to the Archbishop of Canterbury on Anglican Communion Affairs (1980–92), also carrying out several special missions, relating to the Iranian hostages (1981) and Libyan hostages (1985). He received the Radar Award as the United Kingdom's Man of the Year (1985). In 1992, he founded Friends of Victim Support. Waite married (Helen) Frances Watters in 1964; they have four children.

FURTHER READING

Terry Waite. TREVOR BARNES. Bethany House, 1992.
"The faces. . . ." CARLA ANNE ROBBINS. *U.S. News & World Report*, Dec. 2, 1991.
"Terry Waite's endgame." ANTHONY HADEN-GUEST. *Vanity Fair*, Mar. 1991.
Terry Waite and Ollie North: The Untold Story of the Kidnapping and the Release. GAVIN HEWITT. Little, Brown, 1991.
"Hostages to terror." *Maclean's*, Apr. 30, 1990.
"God in the chaos." SANDRA P. ALDRICH. *Christian Herald*, Nov.-Dec. 1989.
"Not again. . . ." RICHARD LACAYO. *Time*, Aug. 14, 1989.
Terry Waite: Man with a Mission. TREVOR BAINES. Eerdmans, 1987.

Waits, Tom (Thomas Alan Waits; 1949–)

Versatile singer, composer, and actor Tom Waits won a best alternative music album Grammy in 1993, for his album *Bone Machine*. His major release of the year was a new album, *The Black Ryder*, based on his score for the 1990 opera *The Black Rider*, with libretto by William S. Burroughs, which had been produced by Robert Wilson in Hamburg. Late in 1992, Waits and Wilson had again collaborated on a new musical, *Alice in Wonderland*, also produced in Hamburg.

Waits also appeared in 1993 in Robert Altman's film *Short Cuts*, based on eight Raymond Carver stories and a poem, in a large cast that included Andie MacDowell, Jack Lemmon, Matthew Modine, Bruce Davison, Julianne Moore,

FURTHER READING

Small Change: A Life of Tom Waits. PATRICK HUMPHRIES. St. Martin's, 1990.

Walcott, Derek Alton (1930–) In 1993,
Nobel laureate Derek Walcott announced plans to establish, in cooperation with the government of his homeland, St. Lucia, an international arts center and retreat for artists, writers, and economists, on three-acre, uninhabited Rat Island, off northwest St. Lucia. He formed the Rat Island Foundation to develop the small villages and studios envisioned. Meanwhile, Walcott saw his play, *The Odyssey,* based on Homer's epic poem, move to London in 1993, to considerable acclaim; it had originally been produced by Britain's Royal Shakespeare Company at Stratford in 1992. In addition to *The Odyssey,* he also saw published his *Antilles: Fragments of Epic Memory* and *Selected Poetry.*

Walcott was a featured guest at the Hay-on-Wye Festival of Literature in late May and early June. A major new project is a coming collaboration with singer-songwriter Paul Simon to create a Broadway musical.

Born in St. Lucia, Walcott received his 1953 B.A. from the University of the West Indies, at Kingston, Jamaica. Though today best-known as a poet, much of his early work was for the theater, and, in the late 1950s, he was a founder of the Trinidad Theatre Workshop, which produced his works and those of other West Indian playwrights. His poetic works include *In A Green Night* (1962), *Selected Poems* (1964), *Castaway* (1965), *The Gulf* (1969), *Another Life* (1973), *Sea Grapes* (1976), *The Star-Apple Kingdom* (1979), *The Fortunate Traveler* (1982), *Midsummer* (1984), *Collected Poems 1948–84* (1986), *The Arkansas Testament* (1987), and *Omeros* (1989). His plays include *Henri Christophe* (1950), *Drums and Colors* (1958), *The Sea at Dauphin* (1960), *Six in the Rain* (1969), *In a Fine Castle* (1972), *Dream on Monkey Mountain* (1970), *Ti-Jean and His Brothers* (1971), *The Charlatan* (1974), *The Joker of Seville* (1978), *O Babylon* (1978), *Remembrance* (1980), *Pantomime* (1980), *The Isle Is Full of Noises* (1982), *The Last Carnival* (1986), and *The Odyssey* (1992). He was awarded the 1992 Nobel Prize for Literature. He has taught at several U.S. colleges and universities, including Harvard University, Columbia University, Yale University, and most

Anne Archer, Fred Ward, Jennifer Jason Leigh, Robert Downey, Jr., Tim Robbins, and Lily Tomlin.

On the business side, the U.S. Supreme Court let stand a $2.5 million award to Waits in his suit against Frito-Lay, over their unauthorized use of a "sound-alike" singer in commercials. Waits also sued his music publisher, alleging that they licensed his songs for foreign use without his consent; that suit was pending.

California-born Waits became a popular singer and composer with his first album *Closing Time* (1973), and went on to compose and sing 12 more albums, including *The Heart of Saturday Nite* (1974), *Nighthawks at the Diner* (1975), *Small Change* (1976), *Foreign Affairs* (1978), *Heartattack and Vine* (1980), *Swordfishtrombones* (1983), *Rain Dogs* (1985), *Anthology* (1985), *Frank's Wild Years* (1987), *Big Time* (1988), and *Bone Machine* (1992). He has also composed the scores for the films *One From the Heart* (1982; he received an Oscar nomination), *Streetwise* (1985), and *Night on Earth* (1991); the scores of the operas *The Black Rider* (1990) and *Alice in Wonderland* (1992); and songs for *Night On Earth* (1991), co-written with Kathleen Brennan. He made his film acting debut in *Paradise Alley* (1978); among his other films were *Rumble Fish* (1983), *The Cotton Club* (1984), *Ironweed* (1987), *At Play in the Fields of the Lord* (1991), and *Bram Stoker's Dracula* (1992). He is married to Kathleen Patricia Brennan; they have two children.

recently Boston University. His 1953 B.A. was from the University of the West Indies, at Kingston, Jamaica. His third wife is Norlin Metiver; he has three children.

FURTHER READING

Derek Walcott, rev. ed. ROBERT HAMNER. Twayne/Macmillan, 1993.
Critical Perspectives on Derek Walcott. ROBERT HAMNER, ed. Three Continents, 1993.
"Derek Walcott's. . . ." JERVIS ANDERSON. *New Yorker*, Dec. 21, 1992.
Art of Derek Walcott. STEWART BROWN. Dufour, 1992.
Derek Walcott's Poetry: American Mimicry. REI TERADA. New England University Press, 1992.
"The mango and the oak." *Economist*, Oct. 27, 1990.

Walesa, Lech (1943–) Polish President

Lech Walesa in 1993 led a country encountering increasing economic problems, even as it was being hailed as a model of post-communist free enterprise by many in the West. With foreign debts of more than $12 billion, a growing foreign trade deficit, and functioning within a continuing world recession, Polish voters rejected further cuts in social services, instead turning out the government of Premier Hanna Suchocka. On October 14, Walesa appointed Polish Peasant Party (SLD) leader Waldemar Pawlak premier, succeeding Suchocka; Pawlak headed a government of the left, in coalition with the Democratic Left Alliance (SLD); together, the two parties held 303 seats in the 460-seat Polish parliament (*Sejm*). Pawlak promised social services and a continuing commitment to a market economy, but it was clear that the new government meant to soften the impact of privatization, focusing on restoration of social services. Another major question facing the new government was that of abortion. The Catholic Church had won a significant victory in February, with passage of an abortion-limitation law; but the national debate on the matter was far from over.

The last Russian troops left Poland in September; but the rise of fascism and nationalism in Russia, as signaled by the electoral showing of fascist Vladimir Zhirinovsky, coupled with the rise of Naziism in Germany, stirred new Polish fears, and a newly urgent turn toward military alliance with the West late in 1993.

Walesa became an electrician at the Lenin Shipyard in Gdansk in 1966; fired after leading the 1970 strike, he continued to organize Poland's developing labor movement. In 1980, he led the successful Lenin Shipyard strike, which sparked a nationwide series of largely successful strikes, and, in September 1980, he was a founder and first president of the Polish trade union confederation, Solidarity. He was imprisoned for a year after Solidarity was outlawed in 1981, but continued to serve as underground leader of the union and movement. As the Gorbachev era developed, he and Solidarity emerged openly once again, and Solidarity was legalized under his leadership in 1989. He led in the negotiations that resulted in the Polish turn toward democracy, and to the free elections of June 1989, won by Solidarity. Walesa refused the Polish presidency at that point, instead supporting Tadeusz Mazowiecki, but in June 1990 decided to run, then defeating Mazowiecki and Stanislaw Tyminski in a three-way vote, and in the December runoff defeating Tyminski by a margin of 3–1. Walesa was awarded the 1983 Nobel Peace Prize. In 1987, he published *A Way of Hope: An Autobiography*. He married Danuta Walesa in 1969; they have eight children.

FURTHER READING

The Struggle and the Triumph. LECH WALESA; FRANKLIN PHILLIP and HELEN MAHUT, eds. Arcade, 1994.
Lech Walesa. CAROLINE E. LAZO. Dillon/Macmillan, 1993.
Lech Walesa: Democrat or Dictator? JAROSLAW KURSKI. Westview, 1993.
"Walesa's poisoned chalice." NICHOLAS BETHELL. *Observer*, Aug. 16, 1992.
"L'état, c'est Lech. . . ." *Economist*, May 2, 1992.
Lech Walesa. ANN ANGEL. Gareth Stevens, 1992.
Lech Walesa: The Road to Democracy. REBECCA STEFOFF. Fawcett, 1992.
"Lech-luster. . . ." VICTORIA POPE. *New Republic*, Dec. 3, 1990.
"Walesa answers. . . ." MARTIN POLLACK. *World Press Review*, Aug. 1990.
Lech Walesa: The Leader of Solidarity and Campaigner for Freedom and Human Rights in Poland. MARY CRAIG. Gareth Stevens, 1990.
"A symbol of hope." PHIL SUDA. *Scholastic Update*, Oct. 20, 1989.
"The struggle for solidarity. . . ." BARRY CAME. *Maclean's*, Apr. 17, 1989.
Lech Walesa. TONY KAYE. Chelsea House, 1989.
Crystal Spirit: Lech Walesa and His Poland. MARY CRAIG. ABC-CLIO, 1987.
Lech Walesa and His Poland. MARY CRAIG. Continuum, 1987.

Walken, Christopher (1943–) In 1992,
Christopher Walken again starred opposite
Glenn Close, in the television film *Skylark*, a
sequel to their very successful 1991 television
film *Sarah, Plain and Tall*, he as Kansas farmer
Jacob Wittig, she as his New England mail order
bride.

Walken also appeared in the film *Wayne's
World 2*, directed by Stephen Surjik and co-
starring Mike Myers, Dana Garvey, Tia Carrere,
and Kim Basinger. A third film was the thriller
True Romance, directed by Tony Scott, with a
cast that included Christian Slater, Patricia Arquette, Dennis Hopper, Gary Oldman, Brad Pitt,
and Val Kilmer.

Forthcoming were starring role in the films *A
Business Affair*, directed by Charlotte Brandstrom and co-starring Carole Bouquet and
Jonathan Pryce, and *God's Army*, written and
directed by Gregory Widen.

New York City-born Walken gained his early
experience in a wide range of regional theater
and New York stage roles, making his 1959
Broadway debut in *J.B.* His early work also included a notable appearance in *The Lion in Winter* (1966), and his later work a New York
Shakespeare Festival appearance in *Coriolanus*
(1988). He made his film debut in *The Anderson
Tapes* (1972), played substantial roles in *Next
Stop Greenwich Village* (1976), *Roseland* (1977),
and *Annie Hall* (1977), and had a breakthrough
role in *The Deer Hunter* (1978), winning a best
supporting actor Oscar. He went on to major
roles in such films as *The Dogs of War* (1980),
Heaven's Gate (1980), *Pennies from Heaven*
(1981), *The Milagro Beanfield War* (1988), *Biloxi
Blues* (1988), *Communion* (1989), *McBain*
(1991), *The Comfort of Strangers* (1991), *Batman Returns* (1992), and *Day of Atonement*
(1992). Walken attended Hofstra University. He
is married to casting director Georgianne
Walken.

FURTHER READING

"Out there on a visit." GAVIN SMITH. *Film Comment*,
July-Aug. 1992.
"Walken, Christopher." *Current Biography*, Oct.
1990.

Walker, Alice Malsenior (1944–) In
her 1992 novel, *Possessing the Secret of Joy*, Alice Walker found more than a subject for fiction;
she found a cause: the ritual operation traditionally called female circumcision but more properly called genital mutilation, which has been
performed on an estimated 100 million women
today, in African and Asian countries, especially
in Muslim communities, and in immigrant communities around the world. Turning to new
forms, Walker teamed up with London-based
feminist filmmaker Pratibha Parmar, born in
Kenya of Indian descent, to make a film about
the practice; called *Warrior Marks*, it opened at
New York's Town Hall in November 1993. The
duo also produced a companion book, *Warrior
Marks: Female Genital Mutilation and the Sexual Blinding of Women*, also published in late
1993. Perhaps partly because of Walker's work,
governments in several Western countries were
in 1993 taking legal action against immigrant
women who had had their female children mu-
tilated in this way. A Walker short story was
also anthologized in *The Literary Lover: Great
Contemporary Stories of Passion and Romance*
(1993), edited by Larry Dark. Also new in 1993
was *Her Blue Body Everything We Know: Earth-
ling Poems, 1965–1990 Complete* and a children's work *To Hell with Dying*.

Georgia-born Walker is a leading African-
American writer and feminist-or "womanist," as
she calls it-whose work largely focuses on sex-
ism and racism. Her novels include *The Third
Life of Grange Copeland* (1970), *Meridian*
(1976), *The Temple of My Familiar* (1989), and

her best-selling and Pulitzer Prize-winning *The Color Purple* (1982), the story of an African-American Southern woman, which was adapted into Steven Spielberg's 1985 film, starring Whoopi Goldberg. Among Walker's other publications are several volumes of poems, including *Once* (1968) and *Revolutionary Petunias* (1973); a biography of Langston Hughes; and several volumes of essays, including *In Search of our Mother's Gardens* (1983) and *Living By the Word* (1991). Her 1966 B.A. was from Sarah Lawrence College. She was previously married, to lawyer Melvyn Leventhal, and has one child.

FURTHER READING

Alice Walker. TONY GENTRY. Chelsea House, 1993.
Alice Walker: Critical Perspectives Past and Present. HENRY L. GATES, JR., and K.A. APPIAH. Amistad, 1993.
"Alice Walker's appeal." PAULA GIDDINGS. *Essence*, July 1992.
"Alice Walker. . . ." CHARLES WHITAKER. *Ebony*, May 1992.
Alice Walker. TONY GENTRY. Chelsea House, 1992.
"The craft of survival." ALVIN P. SANOFF. *U.S. News & World Report*, June 3, 1991.
Double Stitch: Black Women Write about Mothers and Daughters. PATRICIA BELL-SCOTT, ed. Beacon, 1991, HarperCollins, 1993.
Alice Walker. HAROLD BLOOM, ed. Chelsea House, 1990.
"Alice Walker." ALEXIS DE VEAUX. *Essence*, Sep. 1989.
"Alice Walker. . . . " CLAUDIA DREIFUS. *Progressive*, Aug. 1989.
"I dream a world." BRIAN LANKER and MAYA ANGELOU. *National Geographic*, Aug. 1989.
"Living by the word. . . ." GREGORY JAYMES. *Life*, May 1989.
"Alice Walker." *U.S. News & World Report*, Feb. 13, 1989.
Alice Malsenior Walker: An Annotated Bibliography. L.H. PRATT and DARNELL D. PRATT. Greenwood; Series 1, 1987; Series 2, 1988.

Walker, Edwin Anderson (1909–93)

Texas-born Edwin Walker graduated from West Point in 1931. During World War II, he commanded joint American-Canadian special forces units that saw action in Italy and France, and ultimately became a regimental commander. During the Korean War, he was also a regimental commander, and was later an American armed forces advisor to Chiang Kai-shek on Taiwan. In 1957, he commanded federal troops ordered out by President Dwight D. Eisenhower to suppress antischool integration rioting in Little Rock, Arkansas. A far-right-wing conservative, Walker in 1961, while a serving officer in Germany, publicly called Eleanor Roosevelt, former President Harry Truman, and former Secretary of State Dean Acheson all "definitely pink," and praised the right-wing John Birch Society to troops under his command. Reprimanded, he resigned, refused his retirement benefits, and became an active opponent of desegregation in the South. He was arrested but not indicted on charges of insurrection and seditous conspiracy in 1962, for his allegedly central role in inciting the riots generated around the admission of African-American James Meredith to the University of Mississippi. Walker was allegedly fired on and missed by Lee Harvey Oswald in 1963. Walker was personally discredited in 1976, after being arrested, pleading no contest, and being fined for allegedly making sexual advances to a male police officer in Dallas. He was survived by a nephew. (d. Dallas; October 31, 1993)

FURTHER READING

Obituary. *The Times* (of London), Nov. 5, 1993.
Obituary. *New York Times*, Nov. 2 , 1993.
"The old soldier." GARY CARTWRIGHT. *Texas Monthly*, Feb. 1991.

Wanamaker, Sam (1919–93)

Seattle-born Sam Wanamaker began his acting career in Chicago before World War II. After World War II service, he emerged as a leading player on Broadway, most notably starring opposite Ingrid Bergman in *Joan of Lorraine* (1946). He also made his film debut in *My Girl Tisa* (1948) and played in several other films before being blacklisted during the McCarthy era. Wanamaker then emigrated to Britain, where he developed a full-scale acting, directing, and producing career, making his stage debut opposite Michael Redgrave and Googie Withers in Clifford Odets's *Winter Journey* (1952), which Wanamaker also directed. He went on to appear in and direct many plays, and in 1957 became artistic director of Liverpool's New Shakespeare theater. After the McCarthy period ended, he also played again in American films and theater, though remaining based in Britain. He is best known to wide audiences for his film appearances, as in *The Concrete Jungle* (1960), *The Spy Who Came in From the Cold* (1965), and *Voyage of the Damned* (1976). Wanamaker was very highly regarded in Britain for his two-decades-long campaign to build a replica of Shakespeare's Globe Theater. He was survived by his wife, Charlotte, and three daughters, one of them actress Zoë Wanamaker. (d. London; December 19, 1993)

FURTHER READING

Obituary. *Variety*, Dec. 20, 1993.
Obituary. *The Times* (of London), Dec. 20, 1993.
Obituary. *New York Times*, Dec. 19, 1993.

Wang Zhen (1908–93) Hunan-born Wang Zhen joined the Communist Party of China at the age of 19, in 1927, the year the Chinese Civil War began. Wang was to fight with the Red Army for the entire 22-year-long war, and against the Japanese invaders of China through the parallel Sino-Japanese War. He survived the Long March (1934–35), and was a much-decorated frontline commander and political commissar. He became a general and held cabinet-level positions after the communists took power in 1949, was out of power during the Cultural Revolution of the late 1960s, and moved back into power in the mid-1970s, as an ally of Deng Xiaoping. He joined the Politburo in 1978 and became a vice president in 1986. A hardliner, he was one of those responsible for the Tienanmen Square massacre of 1989, and the wave of repression that followed. No information was available on survivors. (d. Mar. 12, 1993)

FURTHER READING

Obituary. *The Times* (of London), Mar. 13, 1993.
Obituary. *New York Times*, Mar. 13, 1993.

Ward, Charlie (1970–   ) The culmination of quarterback Charlie Ward's college football career could not have been sweeter. In 1993, he led the Florida State Seminoles to an 11–1 record, a number one national ranking, and victory over the Nebraska Cornhuskers in the Orange Bowl, for the national championship. A

scrambler who operates primarily from the shotgun formation, Ward completed 264 of 380 passes for 3032 yards during the 1993 regular season, for an Atlantic Coast Conference (ACC) record completion percentage, at 69.5, and threw an ACC season record 27 touchdowns, with only 4 interceptions. For his performance, he received over twenty post-season awards, including Player of the Year from UPI, *Sporting News*, and other organizations and was an All-American on numerous lists. Most notably, he won the Heisman trophy with a record 93.6 percent of all first-place votes (740 of 790 ballots); his winning margin-2310 points over runner-up Heath Shuler's 688-was the largest since O.J. Simpson's 1750-point margin in 1968.

Though recruited by Florida State as a football player, Ward is one of those rare two-sport players, in his case, as leading playmaker on the basketball court as well, expert at distributing the ball to his teammates. During the 1993 season, he averaged 7.8 points and 5.5 assists while leading his team to a 40–9 record. Going into the 1994 season, he was also only ten-shy of breaking the FSU all-time record for number of steals. At year's end he had not yet decided which sport to pursue professionally, and had announced that he would choose before football's college draft in April 1993.

Georgia-born Ward attended Florida State University, where he was elected vice president of the student body in 1992. Among his college career records in the Atlantic Coast Conference football are highest completion percentage, at

62.3 percent, and highest average yards per play (total offense), at 7.13.

FURTHER READING

"Don't dare doubt him." PAUL ATTNER and CHRIS MORTENSEN. *Sporting News*, Dec. 13, 1993.
"Great expectations." ALAN SCHMADTKE. *Sporting News*, Aug. 23, 1993.

Washington, Denzel (1954–)

For his title role in Spike Lee's 1992 film *Malcolm X*, Denzel Washington was nominated as best actor at the Academy Award and Golden Globe awards. For his role in *Mississippi Marsala*, he received an NAACP Image Award. In 1993, Washington starred as newspaper reporter Gray Grantham opposite Julia Roberts as law student Darby Shaw, who uncovers damning assassination evidence, in *The Pelican Brief*, written and directed by Alan Pakula, based on John Grisham's best-selling novel about assassination and intrigue in high places. The cast included Hume Cronyn, John Lithgow, Sam Shepard, John Heard, and Robert Culp.

Washington also starred as the lawyer representing Tom Hanks in the AIDS-discrimination case brought by Hanks against his old law firm in the film *Philadelphia*, directed and produced by Jonathan Demme. He also starred as Don Pedro in Kenneth Branagh's film version of *Much Ado about Nothing*, opposite Branagh, Emma Thompson, and Keanu Reeves.

Washington emerged as a strong stage player from the mid-1970s at the New York Shakespeare Festival and in several off-Broadway plays, one of them the Negro Ensemble Company's *A Soldier's Play*, recreating his role in the 1984 film *A Soldier's Story*. He starred in the title role of *Richard III* (1990) at the New York Shakespeare Festival in Central Park. Washington became a television star in the 1980s as Dr. Otis Chandler in "St. Elsewhere" (1982–88). His films include *Cry Freedom* (1987), as South African Black leader Steve Biko, *For Queen and Country* (1989), *The Mighty Quinn* (1989), *Heart Condition* (1989), *Glory* (1989; he won the 1990 best supporting actor Oscar), *Mo' Better Blues* (1990), *Ricochet* (1991), *Mississippi Masala* (1991), and *Malcolm X* (1992). Washington attended Fordham University and studied at San Francisco's American Conservatory Theater. He is married to singer Paulette Pearson; they have two children.

FURTHER READING

"The players." ANDREW CORSELLO and AMY DONOHUE. *Philadelphia Magazine*, Dec. 1993.
Who's Hot!: Denzel Washington. EVAN KEITH. Dell, 1993.
"Denzel Washington." *People*, Dec. 28, 1992.
"Denzel Washington. . . ." LAURA B. RANDOLPH. *Ebony*, Dec. 1992.
"Denzel Washington." CLAUDE REED. *US*, Dec. 1992.
"Denzel on Malcolm." JOE WOOD. *Rolling Stone*, Nov. 26, 1992.
"Denzel Washington." JOHN CLARK. *Premiere*, Nov. 1992.
"Playing with fire. . . ." LENA WILLIAMS. *New York Times Magazine*, Oct. 25, 1992.
"Washington, Denzel." *Current Biography*, July 1992.
"The mo' better Denzel." ELVIS MITCHELL. *California*, Sep. 1990.
"Days of glory. . . ." PHOEBE HOBAN. *New York*, Aug. 13, 1990.
"Denzel delivers." SHARI ROMAN. *Video Magazine*, Aug. 1990.
"Denzel in the Swing." THULANI DAVIS. *American Film*, Aug. 1990
"Denzel Washington." VERONICA WEBB AND HERB RITTS. *Interview*, July 1990.

Waterston, Sam (1940–)

Sam Waterston's highly regarded prime-time television series "I'll Fly Away" was canceled for low ratings by NBC after 38 episodes, in May 1993. PBS picked it up for reruns of all 38 episodes, plus a final 2-hour show, wrapping up the stories of all its main characters. For his work on the series, Waterston received a best actor Emmy nomination in 1993.

Waterston also starred on stage in 1993, in a well-received New York Lincoln Center revival of the 1938 Robert Sherwood play *Abe Lincoln in Illinois*, in which he recreated and reinterpreted the Lincoln role originated by Raymond Massey; Gerald Gutierrez directed.

On screen, he opened in the film *A Captive in the Land*, set in northern Siberia; he played an American meteorologist, who rescues a Russian air crash survivor, played by Aleksandr Potapov; John Berry directed, with screenplay by Lee Gold, based on the James Aldridge novel. Forthcoming was a starring role in the film *Serial Mom*, written and directed by John Waters and co-starring Kathleen Turner and Rickie Lake.

Massachusetts-born Waterston spent much of his early career on the New York stage; his work in Shakespeare includes roles in *Hamlet*, *The Tempest*, *Measure for Measure*, and *Much Ado About Nothing*, and his later stage work includes *A Walk in the Woods* (1988). His breakthrough film role was as Nick Carroway in *The Great Gatsby* (1975); among his other films are *Rancho Deluxe* (1976), *Interiors* (1978), *The Killing Fields* (1984), *Hannah and Her Sisters* (1986), *Welcome Home* (1989), and *The Man in the Moon* (1991). He has also starred in several television films, among them *The Glass Menagerie* (1975), *Friendly Fire* (1978), *Oppenheimer* (1982), and in the miniseries "Gore Vidal's Lincoln" (1988). Waterston's B.A. is from Yale University. He is married to Lynn Louisa Woodruff, and has four children.

FURTHER READING

Sam Waterston goes South. SAMUEL G. FREEDMAN. *New York Times*, Nov. 17, 1991.

Watson, Thomas, Jr. (1914–93) A major figure in American industry, Thomas Watson, Jr., was largely responsible for building IBM (International Business Machines) into a huge multinational corporation and by far the largest company in the computer industry. Watson's father had taken over IBM in 1914, and developed the company as a punched-card manufacturer.

The younger Watson, who joined the company in 1946 after World War II service, and became company president in 1952, promoted the then-new computer technology within IBM; he so aggressively and successfully marketed IBM computers as to drive several competitors out of the computer business, and emerged as a major figure during the late 1950s and the 1960s, at the head of a worldwide near-monopoly. Watson retired from IBM in 1971, then turning to social and political issues. He was a strong advocate of nuclear disarmament. A lifelong Democrat, he was ambassador to the Soviet Union (1979–81) during the Carter administration. Watson published *Father, Son & Co.: My Life at IBM and Beyond* (1990). He was survived by his wife, Olive Field Cawley, and six children. (d. Greenwich, Connecticut; December 31, 1993)

FURTHER READING

Obituary. *New York Times*, Jan. 1, 1994.
"The secret of IBM's success." DAVID R. BROUSELL. *Datamation*, Mar.15, 1991.
"True confessions. . . ." RICHARD BLOW. *Business Month*, Aug. 1990.
"The ties that bind. . . ." GARY COHEN. *U.S. News & World Report*, July 9, 1990.
"Thomas J. Watson Jr. . . ." *Life*, Fall 1990.
The Hero's Farewell: What Happens When CEOs Retire. JEFFREY SONNENFELD. Oxford University Press, 1988.

White, Byron Raymond (1917–) During his final term on the Court, Justice Byron White was in agreement with the conservative majority far more than the liberal minority. He spoke for a unanimous Court in *Lamb's Chapel v. Center Moriches Union Free School District*, ruling that religious groups had equal access to school facilities with other organizations in the community; and concurred in *Herrera v. Collins*, which sharply limited the ability of those on death row to gain stays of execution on the basis of alleged later discovery of new evidence. He also took the majority position on several other key cases, including *Church of the Lukumi Babalu Aye v. City of Hialeah*, ruling unconstitutional three city ordinances banning ritual animal sacrifice; *Harris v. Forklift Systems*, in which the Court ruled unanimously that workers need not prove that they had suffered psychological damage or were unable to perform

their tasks to successfully charge sexual harassment, instead applying the rule of "workplace equity;" *Sale v. Haitian Centers Council*, which ruled that Haitian refugees could be intercepted in international waters and forcibly returned to Haiti without violating American and international law; *Zobrest v. Catalina Foothills School District*, ruling that local governments could pay for special services to the disabled in parochial schools, as compliance with federal equal educational opportunities for the disabled laws; *Wisconsin v. Mitchell*, ruling that states could prescribe increased sentences for hate-motivated crimes; and *Alexander v. Reno*, which ruled that the First Amendment did not protect $25 million of books and movies destroyed, many of them not obscene, after a seller had been convicted as a pornographer.

White wrote a dissenting opinion in *Shaw v. Reno*, which made it possible to challenge as unconstitutional "bizarrely" shaped voting districts formed to provide minority representation; and also dissented in *Bray v. Alexandria Women's Health Clinic*, which allowed abortion protestors to legally block abortion clinics; and *St. Mary's Honor Center v. Hicks*, ruling that workers must provide proof of specific discrimination against them to claim protection of civil rights laws.

Justice White announced his retirement from the Court on March 19, 1993, effective on the choice of successor, Ruth Bader Ginsburg, who was confirmed on June 14.

Colorado-born White was football star "Whizzer" White in the late 1930s. After World War II, he practiced law in Denver until 1960. He campaigned for John F. Kennedy in 1960; as president, Kennedy appointed him a deputy attorney general in 1961 and then a Supreme Court Justice in 1962. White's 1938 B.A. was from the University of Colorado, and his 1945 LL.B. from Yale. He is married to Marion Stearns; they have two children.

FURTHER READING

Byron White. Bob Italia. Abdo & Daughters, 1992.
"A new day in court." Lauren Tarshis and James Earl Hardy. *Scholastic Update*, Nov. 1, 1991.
"Byron White leads. . . ." David A. Kaplan. *Newsweek*, Apr. 30, 1990.
Eight Men and a Lady. Herman Schwartz et al. National Press, 1990.

Whitman, Christine Todd (1947–)

On November 2, 1993, Republican challenger Whitman upset incumbent Democratic governor Jim Florio in a close New Jersey gubernatorial race, becoming the first woman to be elected governor of New Jersey. She won with a very strong antitax message, capitalizing on Florio's unpopular 1990 state sales and personal income tax measures.

On November 9, Whitman's campaign manager, longtime Republican political professional Ed (Edward J.) Rollins, publicly stated to reporters at a breakfast meeting that the Whitman campaign had made cash donations of up to $500,000 to African-American ministers and campaign workers to discourage a pro-Florio African-American turnout on Election Day. A storm immediately arose, as Whitman angrily denied that any such thing had happened, many African-American ministers reacted with outrage, and national figures in both parties reacted with sharp disapproval. President Bill Clinton called such practices "terribly wrong" if true. The Democratic Party filed a civil suit, and federal and state attorney generals began probes. Rollins then made a complete about-face, claiming that he had made it all up. He was met by widespread skepticism. In late November, the Democratic Party withdrew its suit, stating inability to prove the charges.

The daughter of a political family, whose mother was Republican national committeewoman Eleanor Schley Todd and father Republican state chairman Webster B. Todd, Whitman worked for the Republican National Office before her election to the Somerset County Board (1982). She was appointed chairman of the New Jersey Board of Public Utilities in 1985, and made a surprisingly strong senatorial run against Bill Bradley in 1990.

Her B.A. was from Wheaton College. She is married to John Whitman, and has two children.

FURTHER READING

Governor's Race: A TV Reporter's Chronicle of the 1993 Florio-Whitman Campaign. Michael Aron. Rutgers University Press, 1994.

Williams, Archie (1915–93) Winner of the 400 meters race at the 1936 Berlin Olympics, Archie Williams was, with Jesse Owens, one of the African-American athletes whose perfor-

mance gave the lie to Adolf Hitler's attempt to assert White, or "Aryan" supremacy during the run-up to World War II. An engineering student at the University of California at Berkeley, Williams graduated in 1939 to become the victim of American racism; unable to get a job as an engineer because of his race, he became a pilot instead, and became a flight instructor at Tuskegee Institute, before serving with the armed forces (1942–64), retiring as a lieutenant colonel. He later became a high school mathematics and computer science teacher, then returning to flying. He was survived by his wife, Vesta. and two sons. (d. Fairfax, California; June 24, 1993)

FURTHER READING

Obituary. *The Times* (of London), June 28, 1993.
Obituary. *New York Times*, June 26, 1993.

Robin Williams

Williams, Robin (1952–) For the third year in a row, film star and comedian Robin Williams scored a massive fall-and-Christmas season success, in 1993 with the smash cross-dressing hit *Mrs. Doubtfire*, directed by Chris Columbus and co-starring Sally Field, Pierce Brosnan, and Harvey Fierstein. Williams plays an actor whose wife (Field) has just ejected him from their home, who returns disguised as a nanny, and lives with his wife in their home disguised as a woman. The absurdist situation appealed to large audiences, very willing to suspend disbelief and treat the film as an engaging

fantasy. Williams and Ry Cooder were slated to read the classic children's story "Pecos Bill" in Mel Gibson's new American Public Radio show "Rabbit Ears Radio." With Whoopi Goldberg and Billy Crystal, Williams has been a prime mover in the *Comic Relief* benefits for the homeless, with a new show scheduled for early 1994.

Chicago-born Williams began his career as a comic in cabaret, playing many West Coast clubs, and then moved into television, in variety and then as a star in "Mork and Mindy" (1978–82). He became a leading film star of the 1980s, in such movies as *The World According to Garp* (1982), *Moscow on the Hudson* (1984), *Good Morning, Vietnam* (1987), *The Adventures of Baron Munchausen* (1989), *Dead Poets Society* (1989; he received a best actor Oscar nomination), *Cadillac Man* (1989), *Awakenings* (1990), *Dead Again* (1991), *Hook* (1991), *The Fisher King* (1991), *Aladdin* (1992) and *Toys* (1992). In 1989, he published *To Be Somebody*. Williams attended Claremont College, Marin College, and the Juilliard School. Formerly married to Valerie Velardi, he married Marsha Garces in 1989; he has three children. (For additional photo, see Field, Sally.)

FURTHER READING

"Robin Williams's. . . ." JESSE KORNBLUTH. *New York*, Nov. 22, 1993.
"Mr. and Mrs. Williams." LILLIAN ROSS. *New Yorker*, Sep. 20, 1993.
"Playboy interview. . . ." *Playboy*, Jan. 1992.
"A Peter Pan for yuppies." KURT ANDERSEN. *Time*, Dec. 16, 1991.
"Peter pandemonium." FRED SCHRUERS. *Premiere*, Dec. 1991.
"Robin Williams. . . ." JEFF GILES and MARK SELIGER. *Rolling Stone*, Feb. 21, 1991.
"Awake and sing." FRED SCHRUERS. *Premiere*, Jan. 1991.
"Talking with. . . ." CARSON JONES. *Redbook*, Jan. 1991.
"Robin Williams. . . ." JOE MORGENSTERN. *New York Times Magazine*, Nov. 11, 1990.
"Robin Williams has. . . ." LISA GRUNWALD. *Esquire*, June 1989.
"Actor. . . ." *Life*, Spring 1989.

Willis, Bruce (1955–) Although no longer as "bankable" an action film superstar as he was, Willis continued to attract audiences, in 1993 starring in the film *Striking Distance*, as a demoted Pittsburgh detective hunting a serial

killer. Rowdy Herrington directed and Sarah Jessica Parker co-starred in a cast that included Dennis Farina and Tom Sizemore. Forthcoming was a starring role in the film *Nobody's Fool*, written and directed by Robert Benton and co-starring Paul Newman, Jessica Tandy and Melanie Griffith. Also forthcoming was a starring role in the film *North*, directed by Rob Reiner and co-starring Elijah Wood, Jon Lovitz, and John Candy. A third forthcoming film was *Color of Night*, directed by Richard Rush and co-starring Jane March, Ruben Blades, Lesley Ann Warren, and Scott Bakula. At year's end, Willis and his wife, Demi Moore, were expecting their third child.

German-born Willis worked in the New York theater from the late 1970s, and appeared in several small film roles in the early 1980s. He emerged as a television star in the long-running series "Moonlighting" (1985–89), and, with *Blind Date* (1987), moved into starring roles in films. He starred in *Sunset* (1988), *Die Hard* (1988; and its 1989 sequel), *In Country* (1989), *The Bonfire of the Vanities* (1990), *Hudson Hawk* (1991), *Mortal Thoughts* (1991), *The Last Boy Scout* (1991), and *Death Becomes Her* (1992). He was also the featured voice of baby Mikey in *Look Who's Talking* (1989) and *Look Who's Talking Too* (1990). Willis attended Montclair State College. He and Demi Moore married in 1987; they have two daughters.

FURTHER READING

"Demi's big moment." NANCY COLLINS and ANNIE LEIBOVITZ. *Vanity Fair*, Aug. 1991.
"Bruce on the loose." ANTHONY HADEN-GUEST. *Vanity Fair*, Jan. 1991.
"Bruce Willis. . . ." FRED ROBBINS. *McCall's*, June 1989.
"Bruce Willis. . . ." *Video Review*, Feb. 1989.

Wilson, John Tuzo (1908–93) Ottawa-born John Tuzo Wilson, a leading geophysicist, worked with Geological Survey of Canada after receiving his doctorate from Princeton University in 1936. After World War II military service, he began his teaching career at the University of Toronto in 1946, soon contributing to the body of work that in the 1960s led to general acceptance of the plate tectonics theory: that Earth's crust is composed of plates, some continent-size, that float atop a molten mantle, with earthquakes and volcanos caused by plates scraping against or sliding under each other, new crust forming at rifts, and the plates moving apart in sea floors. Wilson led in the development of the International Geophysical Year (1957–58). He was founding president of Erindale College at the University of Toronto (1967–74), and director-general of the Ontario Science Center (1974–85). He was survived by his wife, Isabel Dickson, and two daughters. (d. Toronto; April 15, 1993)

FURTHER READING

"Pioneering scientists made. . . ." *Canadian Geographic*, July-Aug. 1993.
"The great divide. . . ." JOHN FRASER. *Saturday Night*, July-Aug. 1993.
Obituary. *New York Times*, May 30, 1993.
Obituary. *The Times* (of London), May 3, 1993.

Wind, Timothy E.: See King, Rodney.

Winfrey, Oprah (1954–) As evidence of the impact of Oprah Winfrey's afternoon talk show, consider the week of July 12, 1993, which she devoted to one-on-one conversations with five authors she personally admired: Deepak Chopra, Maya Angelou, M. Scott Peck, Elie Wiesel, and Andrew Vachss. Within a week, sales of new and old books for all five authors jumped significantly, in Chopra's case landing his just-published *Ageless Body, Timeless Mind* at the top of the best-seller lists. Booksellers also credit her with giving the initial boost to Robert James Waller's phenomenally successful *The Bridges of Madison County*. Winfrey herself was to have published her autobiography; it was one of the hottest of the projected fall books at the American Bookseller's Association convention in May, where Winfrey was a featured guest; but in June, she suddenly postponed the work indefinitely.

In February, Winfrey had scored a notable coup, conducting the first live interview with Michael Jackson from his ranch north of Los Angeles, which aired worldwide as a 90-minute prime-time special. In October, she also had the first interview with Michael Jordan after his surprise retirement from basketball. Winfrey's show even figured in Barbara Kingsolver's 1993 best-selling novel *Pigs in Heaven*, whose main characters appear on the show, gaining unwanted celebrity. Winfrey also continued to produce the children's series "ABC Afternoon Specials," as she has since mid-1992.

In November, Winfrey starred in the television film *There Are No Children Here*, based on Alex Kotlowitz's 1991 book; she played LaJoe Rivers, a welfare mother raising her children in a Chicago housing project, with Angelou as her mother Lelia Mae. Winfrey had earlier devoted a program to Kotlowitz's book and had bought the film rights herself; her $500,000 acting fee (matched by ABC) was donated to the children of the project. In 1993 estimated by *Forbes* to be the world's highest-paid entertainer, with a two-year income of approximately $98 million, Winfrey has given money to numerous other organizations, especially those to help battered women and abused children, to fight AIDS, and to support education, including in 1993 $1 million to Chicago's innovative Providence-St. Mel High School; her fiancé Stedman Graham serves on the school's board of trustees.

Mississippi-born Winfrey attended Tennessee State University. She began her broadcasting career in 1972, as a reporter for WVOL radio while still in school and then for WTVF-TV (both in Nashville), before moving to Baltimore's WJZ-TV as co-anchor in 1976. Becoming co-host of the station's morning show, she entered a new career, scoring a major success as the host of "AM Chicago" for Chicago's WLS-TV, which was renamed "The Oprah Winfrey Show" in 1984, and became a nationally syndicated hit show. She also starred in the 1989 television miniseries *The Women of Brewster Place*, later developing the role in the short-lived television prime-time series, "Brewster Place," and narrated *Scared Silent*, a program about child abuse within families, shown simultaneously on three networks and the fourth two days later (1992). She has appeared in several films, including *The Color Purple* (1985) and *Native Son* (1986), and was the voice of Elizabeth Keckley on the documentary *Lincoln* (1992).

FURTHER READING

Oprah Winfrey: Entertainer. LOIS NICHOLSON. Chelsea House, 1994.

"Oprah sets. . . ." JILL BROOKE COINER. *McCall's*, Nov. 1993.

"Oprah opens up. . . ." LAURA B. RANDOLPH. *Ebony*, Oct. 1993.

"Understanding Oprah." JACKIE ROGERS. *Redbook*, Sep. 1993.

Meet Oprah Winfrey. AUDREEN BUFFALO. Random, 1993.

Oprah Winfrey: Media Success Story. ANNE SAIDMAN. Lerner, 1993.

Oprah Winfrey: Television Star. STEVE OTFINOSKI. Blackbirch, 1993.

"The mystery of. . . ." KATHRYN CASEY. *Ladies Home Journal*, Nov. 1992.

"Her man Stedman." ELIZABETH SPORKIN. *People*, Nov. 23, 1992.

"The prime time of. . . ." DAVID RENSIN. *TV Guide*, May 16, 1992.

"The companies they keep." FRED GOODMAN. *Working Woman*, Dec. 1991.

"Oprah Winfrey. . . ." ALAN EBERT. *Good Housekeeping*, Sep. 1991.

"Next on Oprah." BILL BRASHLER. *Ladies Home Journal*, Aug. 1991.

"Walking in the light." PEARL CLEADGE. *Essence*, June 1991.

Oprah Winfrey. GERALDINE WOODS. Dillon, 1991.

Oprah Winfrey: TV Talk Show Host. MARGARET BEATON. Childrens, 1990.

Oprah Winfrey: Talk Show Host and Actress. LILLIE PATTERSON and CORNELIA H. WRIGHT. Enslow, 1990.

Everybody Loves Oprah!: Her Remarkable Life Story. NORMAN KING. Morrow, 1988.

Oprah! ROBERT WALDRON. St. Martin, 1987.

Winger, Debra

Winger, Debra (Mary Debra Winger; 1955–) In a major 1993 role, Debra Winger starred as Joy Gresham opposite Anthony Hopkins as C. S. Lewis in the film *Shadowlands*.

William Nicholson adapted his own hit play for film; Richard Attenborough directed and produced. The acclaimed film, its director, and both of its stars were immediately thought by many to be in the running for Academy Awards.

In a second, quite different major role, Winger starred opposite Barbara Hershey and Gabriel Byrne in the title role of the film *A Dangerous Woman*, directed by Stephen Gyllenhaal. Winger played Martha Horgan, a truth-telling, somewhat disengaged, and apparently harmless semi-dropout, who lives in a guest cottage on a ranch owned by her aunt, played by Hershey.

In contrast to these two films, *Wilder Napalm*, Winger's third film release of the year, cast her as the wife of a part-time fireman (Arliss Howard), whose estranged brother (Dennis Quaid) returns to their hometown, the brothers then fighting over Winger. Both brothers have the ability to create fires by willing them, complicating the otherwise simple, standard plot.

Cleveland-born Winger began her career in television, most notably in the series "Wonder Woman" (1976–77), and then moved into films. She emerged as a highly regarded dramatic actress in such films as *French Postcards* (1979), *Urban Cowboy* (1980), *Cannery Row* (1982), *An Officer and a Gentleman* (1982), *Terms of Endearment* (1983), *Legal Eagles* (1986), *Black Widow* (1987), *Betrayed* (1988), *The Sheltering Sky* (1990), *Everybody Wins* (1990), and *Leap of Faith* (1992). Winger attended California State University. She was formerly married to actor Timothy Hutton; she has one child.

FURTHER READING

"Confessions of. . . ." TOM ROBBINS. *Esquire*, Feb. 1993.
"Debra Winger." STEVE POND. *Harper's Bazaar*, June 1992.

Wood, Walter Abbott (1908–93) A leading American geographer, mountain climber, and explorer, Walter Wood began his career with a 1929 expedition to the Himalayas. He was a graduate of the American Geographical Society surveying school in 1932, and during the 1930s climbed and mapped in many areas, including Alaska, the Yukon, Greenland, and Central America. He saw service as a mountain and alpine troops trainer during World War II. Long associated with the American Geographical Society, he became its president (1957–61). He was also president of New York's Explorers Club (1967–71). Wood was survived by his wife, Renée Menassa, and a son. (d. West Palm Beach, Florida; May 18, 1993)

FURTHER READING

Obituary. *New York Times*, May 20, 1993.

Woodward, Joanne (1930–) For her powerful portrayal of Congresswoman Nell Harrington in the television film *Blind Spot*, Joanne Woodward received an Emmy nomination as best lead actress in miniseries or special. Woodward played a strong, sure public figure, who unexpectedly found herself facing a very private drug addiction problem at home, and also found herself to be part of the problem. Michael Toshiyuki Uno directed and Laura Linney and Fritz Weaver co-starred. Woodward also starred opposite Brian Dennehy in the television film *Foreign Affairs*, she as a university professor researching a book in Britain, he as an involuntarily retired Oklahoma sewage engineer, they ultimately becoming a pair, for however long.

Woodward also played a cameo in Jonathan Demme's AIDS discrimination movie, *Philadelphia*, starring Tom Hanks and Denzel Washington. She was also the narrator in the film *The Age of Innocence*, one of the high points of the year. Martin Scorsese directed the adaptation of the Edith Wharton novel, set in New York high society in the 1870s; Daniel Day-Lewis, Michelle Pfeiffer, and Winona Ryder starred.

Georgia-born Woodward has been a leading actress for over three decades, since her best actress Oscar-winning role in *The Three Faces of Eve* (1957); she went on to star in such films as *The Long Hot Summer*, (1958), *The Sound and the Fury*, (1959), *The Fugitive Kind* (1960), *The Stripper* (1963), *A Fine Madness*, (1965), *Rachel, Rachel* (1968), *Summer Wishes, Winter Dreams* (1973), *The Drowning Pool* (1975), *The Glass Menagerie* (1987), and *Mr. and Mrs. Bridge* (1990). She has also played in some notable television films, such as *Do You Remember Love* (1985). She married Paul Newman in 1958; the couple have three children. She attended Louisiana State University (1947–49) and studied at the Neighborhood Playhouse.

FURTHER READING

"Joanne Woodward. . . ." Steve Vineberg. *American Film*, Nov.-Dec. 1991.
"Paul Newman and. . . ." Maureen Dowd. *McCall's*, Jan. 1991.
"Mr. and Mrs. Bridge." Graham Fuller. *Interview*, Nov. 1990.
"Joanne Woodward. . . ." Beth Weinhouse. *Redbook*, Jan. 1990.
Paul and Joanne: A Biography of Paul Newman & Joanne Woodward. Joe Morella and Edward Z. Epstein. Delacorte, 1988.

Wouk, Herman (1915–) One of the mid-20th century's most notable writers of big historical novels, Herman Wouk had a new offering in 1993: *The Hope*, a saga set in Israel, from the establishment of modern Israel through the Six-Day War (1948–67), the title being the English translation of the Israeli national anthem "Hatikvah." The book's main fictional character-the equivalent of *Wind of War*'s Pug Henry-is Zev Barak, a military commander turned diplomat, who shares the grand canvas with many historical characters, including Golda Meir, David Ben Gurion, Moshe Dayan, Ariel Sharon, Menahem Begin, and Itzhak Rabin. The book was well received, with some reviewers noting with approval that Wouk did not paint Arabs as villains, nor did he routinely whitewash Israeli actions. Not surprisingly, given his previous track record, *The Hope* quickly landed on the best-seller lists, and was the main selection of the Book-of-the-Month Club, which also offered various of his earlier works (several reissued in 1992 in anticipation of this new work), in book and film form.

Born in New York City of Russian immigrant parents, Wouk received his A.B. with general honors from Columbia University in 1934, from 1935 working as a scriptwriter for various radio comedians, notably Fred Allen (1936–41). After serving briefly as consultant to the U.S. Treasury (1941), he served in the U.S. Naval Reserve as executive officer on the *U.S.S. Southard* (1942–46). His first novel, *Aurora Dawn* (1947), was followed by many others, notably *The City Boy* (1948), *Slattery's Hurricane* (1949), the Pulitzer Prize-winning *The Caine Mutiny* (1951), *Marjorie Morningstar* (1955), the semi-autobiographical *Youngblood Hawke* (1962), *Don't Stop the Carnival* (1965), *The Winds of War* (1971), its sequel *War and Remembrance* (1978), and the Washington Book award-winning *Inside, Outside* (1985). He has also written several plays, including *The Traitor* (1949), *The Caine Mutiny Court-Martial* (1953), and *Nature's Way* (1957), and the non-fiction work *This Is My God: The Jewish Way of Life* (1959). He also wrote the screenplays, based on his novels, for the successful television miniseries of *The Winds of War* (1983) and *War and Remembrance* (1986). Wouk married Betty Sarah Brown in 1945; he had three sons, one of them deceased.

FURTHER READING

Herman Wouk. Laurence W. Mazzeno. Twayne/Macmillan, 1994.
Jewish American Fiction Writers: An Annotated Bibliography. Gloria L. Cronin. Garland, 1991.

Wynonna: See **Judd, Wynonna.**

X-Y-Z

Yeltsin, Boris Nikolayevich (1931–)

During 1993, the continuing conflict between Russian President Boris Yeltsin and the conservative leaders of the Russian parliament grew even sharper, the pace of reform in Russia ground slowly to a halt, and the continuing economic crisis deepened even further. A major confrontation came on March 28, when the full Congress of People's Deputies refused to impeach Yeltsin, while also attempting to further limit his powers.

A second confrontation came in the nationwide referendum of April 25, with Yeltsin winning personal approval from 58 percent of those voting, and his policies receiving 53 percent approval. But conservative forces, led by Vice President Alexandr Rutskoi, who then broke with Yeltsin, and by parliamentary speaker Ruslan Khasbulatov, charged electoral fraud; the struggle continued, while Yeltsin drafted a new constitution.

The final confrontation began on September 21, when Yeltsin dissolved parliament, and announced December 11–12 elections for a new parliament. The parliament declared his action a coup, formally deposed him, and named Rutskoi acting president. President Bill Clinton, Prime Minister John Major, and many other Western leaders openly supported Yeltsin in the crisis that then came. On October 3, an estimated 5,000 marchers broke through riot police lines to gather before the Russian White House (parliament building), going over to armed insurrection en route, with small military forma-

tions in the line of march opening automatic weapons fire on the police during the breakthrough. Ruskoi, addressing the crowd, urged them to form military units and seize the Moscow broadcasting center, the mayor's office, and the Kremlin. Previously prepared formations, swelled by new recruits, stormed and took the mayor's office and attacked the broadcasting center. On October 4, the armed forces responded on behalf of the government; armored infantry and airborne units surrounded, shelled, and forced the surrender of rebel forces at the Russian White House, in an action that took 12 hours. Yeltsin's forces arrested the rebel leaders, while Yeltsin decisively reasserted and increased his power.

On December 12, 1993, Russian voters approved Yeltsin's constitution, while at the same time voting in large numbers for his nationalist and communist opponents. Although the reform parties won enough seats to form a government, their weakness was widely interpreted as sharp nationwide reaction to Yeltsin's continuing failure to reverse or even halt Russia's deepening economic catastrophe.

Yeltsin worked as an engineer (1955–68), then going into Communist Party work in his home city of Sverdlovsk. During the early 1980s, he strongly supported and was close to Mikhail Gorbachev; Yeltsin moved into far higher party positions in 1985, when Gorbachev came to power. He was mayor of Moscow (1985–87) and secretary of the Communist Party central committee (1985–86). He moved into opposition in

1987, becoming a leader of those who felt that reform was not proceeding quickly enough; he was for some years a "maverick" in Soviet politics, who was not taken very seriously, and whose relations with Gorbachev were often abrasive.

In 1989, Yeltsin won the Moscow elections to the Congress of People's Deputies by an overwhelming majority, and became an opposition leader in the Soviet parliament. In March 1990, he refocused, winning election as a delegate to the Russian Federation's Supreme Soviet. On May 29, 1990, he was elected president of the Russian Federation, and began a campaign to secure greater Russian autonomy from the central government. In July 1990, he also resigned from the Communist Party.

On August 19, 1991 Gorbachev was placed under house arrest while vacationing in the Crimea, and a right-wing Communist coup began. Yeltsin became the center of opposition to the coup, gathering huge unarmed crowds and then key capital military units around him at the White House, the Russian parliament building in Moscow. On August 21st, the aborted coup collapsed, Yeltsin was a national hero, and a second, democratic Russian Revolution quickly swept away the remnants of Soviet communism and the Soviet state. Gorbachev on his return to Moscow was unable to hold the Soviet state together, or in the following period to resist the rise of Yeltsin to effective power in the Russian Republic.

During the balance of 1991 and throughout 1992, Yeltsin gambled much on crash market economy reforms, without much success and encountering growing conservative opposition, which was able to blame him for the continuing economic disaster, while itself greatly contributing to it by blocking major elements of the reform program. On December 14, 1992, conservatives in the Russian Congress voted to derail many of Yeltsin's economic reform programs, and to replace Premier Yegor T. Gaidar, chief architect of those programs, with conservative Viktor S. Chernomyrdin, who called himself an advocate of reform, but clearly spoke for those who wanted to slow and perhaps reverse Yeltsin's programs, setting the stage for the confrontation that came in 1993.

Yeltsin has published an autobiography, *Against the Grain* (1990); forthcoming was his book on the August 1991 events. He attended the Urals Polytechnic Institute. Little is known of his personal life, except that he is married to Naina Yeltsin.

FURTHER READING

"Reforming Russia's economy. . . ." *Economist*, Dec. 11, 1993.
"Make them truly. . . ." BORIS KAGARLITSKY et al. *Nation*, Dec. 6, 1993.
"The last best chance. . . ." BRUCE W. NELAN. *Time*, Oct. 18, 1993.
"What Yeltsin must do." PETER GALUSZKA et al. *Business Week*, Oct. 18, 1993.
"Yeltsin in dubious battle." DANIEL SINGER. *Nation*, Oct. 11, 1993.
"Yeltsin regrets." *Economist*, Oct. 9, 1993.
"The war against democracy." JOHN PILGER. *New Statesman & Society*, Oct. 8, 1993.
"The West's reaction." *Economist*, Sep. 25, 1993.
"Russia votes yes." CARL YOUNG. *American Spectator*, July 1993.
"Yeltsin's next gamble. . . ." MARK HOPKINS. *New Leader*, May 3, 1993.
"I am Boris Yeltsin. . . ." *Economist*, May 1, 1993.
" 'The president is. . . .' " JOHN KOHAN and YURI ZARAKHOVICH. *Time*, Apr. 26, 1993.
"The softest coup. . . ." MARTIN MALIA. *New Republic*, Apr. 19, 1993.
"Yeltsin rolls the dice." JAMES SHERR. *National Review*, Apr. 12, 1993.
"Yeltsin's big gamble." GEORGE J. CHURCH. *Time*, Mar. 29, 1993.
"Stalin or Yeltsin." *Economist*, Mar. 27, 1993.
"Apocalypse not. . . ." MARTIN MALIA. *New Republic*, Feb. 22, 1993.
"Boris the bunny. . . ." *Economist*, Feb. 13, 1993.
World Leaders-Boris Yeltsin. SHLOMO LAMBROZA. Rourke, 1993.
Boris Yeltsin. KATE S. SCHECTER. Chelsea House, 1993.
"What makes Boris tick?" JONATHAN STEELE. *Guardian*, Dec. 21, 1992.
"Holding Russia's fate. . . ." JOHN KOHAN. *Time*, Dec. 7, 1992.
"One nation under Boris." STEPHEN SESTANOVICH. *New Republic*, June 29, 1992.
" 'Yeltsin. . . .' " PAUL KLEBNIKOV. *Forbes*, June 8, 1992.
Boris Yeltsin: A Political Biography. VLADIMIR SOLOVYOV and ELENA KLEPIKOVA. Putnam, 1992.
Gorbachev-Yeltsin: The Fall of Communism. STUART A. KALLEN. Abdo & Daughters, 1992.
Gorbachev, Yeltsin and the Last Days of the Soviet Empire. NEIL FELSHMAN. Thomas Dunne/St. Martin's, 1992.
Boris Yeltsin: Man of the People. ELEANOR H. AYER. Dillon/Macmillan, 1992.
Boris Yeltsin: Russia's First President. JOHN MORRISON. NAL-Dutton, 1991.

Young, Steve (Jon Steven Young; 1961–)
Even being the National Football League's top-rated quarterback two years running did not make Steve Young entirely secure in his position as San Francisco 49ers' starting quarterback-not while the great Joe Montana was still on the team. Coach George Seifert had stressed during the 1992 season that, with Montana injured, the 49ers were now Young's team, but in early January 1993, when Montana returned for the last two quarters of an essentially meaningless game, San Francisco, the media, and football fans went wild. That reignited the controversy over who should be the starting quarterback. Montana wanted to play, and when in early 1993 he said he would leave San Francisco to do so, Seifert offered him the starting position. But in the end, Montana went to Kansas City, and the 49ers finally *were* Young's team.

In the 1993 season, Young led the 49ers to a division-winning record of 10–6, despite being bothered by a broken thumb on his throwing hand, especially during the first few games of the season. He ended with the highest quarterback pass rating in the league for the third year running, at 101.5, his career pass rating only a shade behind Montana's. During 1993, Young also led the league in average total yards per pass, at 8.7, and number of touchdown passes, at 29, and gained 4023 yards passing, second by a whisker only to Denver's John Elway. At the turn of the year, the 49ers were advancing toward the Super Bowl. Unfortunately, San Francisco was defeated by the Dallas Cowboys in the Conference playoffs in January 1994, as they had been in January 1993. Dallas both times went on to win the Super Bowl, while Young and the 49ers could only look forward to another try next season.

A great-great-great-grandson of the Mormon leader Brigham Young, Steve Young was born in Salt Lake City and attended high school in Greenwich, Connecticut. At Brigham Young University, he was a consensus All-American and runner-up for the Heisman Trophy, capped by an extraordinary senior year in which he completed 306 of 429 passes, for 3902 yards and 33 touchdowns, setting a then-record pass percentage of .713, and winning 11 of 12 games, passing for over 300 yards in all but two. In 1991, *Sports Illustrated* made a statistical analysis of college quarterback records-their personal statistics and team winning percentage-and found

that Young led the list. After playing briefly for the L.A. Express of the U.S. Football League in 1984, when he became the first professional football player ever to rush for 100 yards and pass for 300 yards in the same game, Young moved to the Tampa Bay Buccaneers in 1985. Acquired by the San Francisco 49ers in 1987, he saw only sporadic playing time until 1991, when Montana was injured. Young was the highest-rated quarterback in the National Football League three seasons running (1991–93), all three times with over a 100-point rating, and was named the NFL's most valuable player in 1992. Young completed law school at BYU in the off-season in 1992.

FURTHER READING

"Young, Steve." *Current Biography*, Oct. 1993.
"Steve Young." Mark Fainaru. *Sport*, Aug. 1993.
"The proof is in the playoffs." Ira Miller. *Sporting News*, Jan. 11, 1993.
"There's no killing. . . ." Chris Mortensen. *Sporting News*, Sep. 14, 1992.
"Quarterbacks quantified." Douglas S. Looney. *Sports Illustrated*, Fall 1991.
"The Young 49ers." Rick Reilly. *Sports Illustrated*, Sep. 30, 1991.
"Young and rich." Peter King. *Sports Illustrated*, Sep. 16, 1991.
"49ers reserve is. . . ." *Sporting News*, Feb. 5, 1990.

Zappa, Frank (Francis Vincent Zappa; 1940–93) Baltimore-born Frank Zappa grew up in California, and began his recording career in the early 1960s. He joined Ray Collins's Soul Giants band in 1964; in 1966 the band began recording as The Mothers of Invention (1964–77). The group's hit albums included *Freak Out!* (1966), *Absolutely Free* (1967), and *200 Motels* (1971; and the 1971 film). On his own, Zappa made such records as *Hot Rats* (1969), *Apostrophe* (1974), and *Joe's Garage* (1979). His hit singles include "Don't Eat the Yellow Snow" (1974), "Dancin' Fool" (1979), and "Valley Girl" (1982), in which he teamed up with his daughter Moon Unit, then only 14. Zappa's most notable later work joined jazz and classical music, on such albums as *Boulez Conducts Zappa* (1982; 1987), *The Perfect Stranger and Other Works* (1985), *Make a Jazz Noise Here* (1991), *The Greatest Band You Never Heard in Your Life* (1991), and *You Can't Do That on Stage Anymore* (1992). In 1989, Zappa published *A Mother of Necessity:*

The Real Frank Zappa Book, written with Peter Occhiogrosso. Zappa was survived by his wife, Gail, and their four children. (d. Los Angeles; December 4, 1993)

FURTHER READING

"The duke of prunes. . . ." MICHAEL WALSH. *Time*, Dec. 20, 1993.
" 'Night, mother." TOM SINCLAIR. *Entertainment*, Dec. 17, 1993.
"Absolutely free. . . ." *Economist*, Dec. 11, 1993.
Obituary. *Billboard*, Dec. 18, 1993.
Obituary. *Variety*, Dec. 7, 1993.
Obituary. *The Times* (of London), Dec. 7, 1993.
Obituary. *New York Times*, Dec. 7, 1993.
"Frank Zappa." *Playboy*, Apr. 1993.
"Frank Zappa stricken. . . ." KIM NEELY. *Rolling Stone*, Jan. 9, 1992.
"Frank Zappa makes. . . ." MICHAEL DAVIS. *Down Beat*, July 1991.
"Frank Zappa-trading partner." DAVID CORN. *Nation*, Mar. 19, 1990.
"Zappa, Frank." *Current Biography*, Feb. 1990.
"Frank Zappa. . . ." TIM SCHNECKLOTH. *Down Beat*, Sep. 1989.
"Frank Zappa. . . ." STEVE DOUGHERTY. *People*, May 22, 1989.

Zhirinovsky, Vladimir Volfovich

(1946–) In the December 11, 1993 Russian elections, a chilling development for Russian democrats and for the entire world was the emergence of the fascist and ultra-nationalist Liberal Democratic Party, led by Vladimir Zhirinovsky, which won the single largest proportion of the popular vote, variously reported as in the 18–25 percent range, though it won far less parliamentary seats, and could not form a government. Democratic parties, though splintered, formed a coalition government, and made a major reapprochement, given the threat of fascism posed by Zhirinovsky and his followers.

Though he denied it after the election, Zhirinovsky was very clearly running as a fascist and ultra-nationalist. During the election campaign, he among other things threatened to use use nuclear weapons against Japan; demanded the return of Alaska, with compensation; made thinly veiled anti-Jewish threats; attacked and threatened the United States and Germany for interfering in Russian internal affairs; and threatened reprisals against the countries of the former Soviet Union for alleged discrimination against Russians. He and his views were condemned by American President Bill Clinton, Vice President Al Gore, and a wide range of other world leaders. Zhirinovsky's showing was viewed with great concern in Russia and throughout the world, because of the continuing existence of the Russian nuclear arsenal, a daily menace to the continued existence of humanity and the rest of the earth's beings, but feared especially so in his or other fascist and nationalist hands. During 1993, Zhirinovsky also published the autobiography *The Last Play for the South*.

Kazakhstan-born Zhirinovsky reportedly saw some military service before working as a lawyer for Mir Publications (1983–89). He was a founder of the Liberal Party of the Soviet Union in 1990. He attended Moscow State University. He is married, and has two children.

FURTHER READING

"The laughing fascist." CARROLL BOGERT and DORINDA ELLIOTT. *Newsweek*, Dec. 27, 1993.
"Flying circus: Russia's David Duke." PAUL QUINN-JUDGE. *New Republic*, Nov. 11, 1991.
"The coup next time." VLADIMIR KLIMENKO. *Mother Jones*, Nov.-Dec. 1991.

PHOTO CREDITS

Abdul, Paula. Virgin Records (Photo: Alberto Tolot 0991)

Aikman, Troy. Dallas Cowboys

Allende, Isabel. HarperCollins (Photo: © Marcia Lieberman)

Altman, Robert. © 1993 Fine Line Features (Photo: Joyce Rudolph)

Anderson, Terry. Crown Publishers

Angelou, Maya. Random House (Photo: © Steve Dunwell)

Atwood, Margaret. Doubleday (Photo: Anthony Loew)

Aylwin Azócar, Patricio. Embassy of Chile

Azinger, Paul. Copyright © 1993 PGA (Professional Golfers' Association) Tour

Baird, Zoë. Presidential Transition Press Office.

Baldwin, Alec. Copyright © 1992 Twentieth Century Fox (Photo: Herb Ritts)

Barkley, Charles. Phoenix Suns.

Barry, Dave. The Miami Herald

Bates, Kathy. Copyright © 1992 Twentieth Century Fox (Photo: Don Smetzer)

Bentsen, Lloyd. Presidential Transition Press Office

Berenger, Tom. Turner Pictures © 1993 New Line Cinema (Photo: Merrick Morton)

Bergman, Ingmar. Arcade Publishing (Photo: Bengt Wanselius)

Billington, James H. Library of Congress

Bolton, Michael. Copyright © 1990 Sony Music, Columbia (Photo: Timothy White)

Bowe, Riddick. Swanson Communications.

Bridges, Jeff. Copyright © 1993 Warner Bros. (Photo: Merrick Morton)

Broderick, Matthew. Copyright © Universal City Studios, Inc. (Photo: Elliott Marks)

Brooks, Garth. Liberty® (Photo: Beverly Parker 8/93A)

Brooks, Mel. Copyright © 1993 Twentieth-Century Fox (Photo: Peter Sorel)

Brown, Ronald H.. U.S. Department of Commerce

Brown, Rosellen. Farrar, Straus and Giroux (Photo: Copyright © 1992 Keith Carter)

Browner, Carol. Environmental Protection Agency

Butler, Robert Olen. Henry Holt (Photo: Gray Little)

Caan, James. Copyright © 1993 Paramount Pictures (Photo: Lorey Sebastian)

Cage, Nicolas. Copyright © 1993 Castle Rock Entertainment (Photo: Jim Bridges)

Campbell, Kim. Canadian Embassy

Capriati, Jennifer. International Management Group (Photo: Michael Baz)

Carey, Mariah. Columbia/Horizon Entertainment Management Group © 1993 Sony Music (Photo: Daniela Federici)

Carter, Jimmy. The Carter Center

Charles, Prince. British Information Service

Charles, Ray. © 1993 Warner Bros (Photo: Mark Hanauer)

Chavis, Benjamin. NAACP

Chrétien, Jean. Canadian Embassy

Clapton, Eric. Warner Bros. © 1992 (Photo: Carl Studna)

Clinton, Bill. The White House

Clinton, Hillary Rodham. The White House

Collins, Phil. Atlantic Records (Photo: Alastair Thain)

Costner, Kevin. Copyright © 1991 Warner Bros.

Courier, Jim. International Management Group (Photo: Sygma)

Cruise, Tom. Copyright © 1992 Castle Rock Entertainment (Photo: Sidney Baldwin)

Crystal, Billy. Copyright © 1992 Castle Rock Entertainment ® (Photo: Bruce McBroom)

Culkin, Macaulay. Copyright © Twentieth Century Fox (Photo: Don Smetzer)

Cuomo, Mario. St. Martin's Press

Dafoe, Willem. Copyright © 1992 New Line Cinema (Photo: Steve Sands)

Danson, Ted. Copyright © 1993 Regency Enterprises V.O.F. and Le Studio Canal

Davis, Ossie. Copyright © 1993 Warner Bros. (Photo: Ron Phillips)

Day-Lewis, Daniel. Universal Pictures Copyright © 1993 (Photo: Andrew MacPherson)

Deighton, Len. HarperCollins (Photo: Bebop Deighton)

De Niro, Robert. Copyright © 1992 Universal City Studios (Photo: Patrick Demarchelier)

DeVito, Danny. Copyright © 1993 Twentieth Century Fox (Photo: Melinda Sue Gordon)

Dillon, Matt. Copyright © 1993 Warner Bros. (Photo: Timothy White)

Dole, Robert. U.S. Senate

Douglas, Michael. Copyright © 1993 Warner

Downey, Robert, Jr. Copyright © 1993 Universal City Studios (Photo: Bruce Talamon)

Dreyfuss, Richard. Copyright © 1993 Columbia Pictures

Dylan, Bob. Columbia © 1993 Sony Music (Photo: Randee St. Nicholas)

Eastwood, Clint. © 1993 Columbia Pictures/© 1993 Castle Rock Entertainment

Elders, Joycelyn. Public Health Service

Elizabeth II. British Information Service

Estefan, Gloria. Epic ©1993 Sony Music (Photo: Alberto Tolot)

Ewing, Patrick. New York Knicks (Photo: George Kalinsky)

Field, Sally. Copyright © 1993 Twentieth Century Fox (Photo: Phil Bray)

Ford, Harrison. Paramount Pictures, Copyright © 1992 (Photo: John Seakwood)

Freeh, Louis. Federal Bureau of Investigation.

Freeman, Morgan. Copyright © 1992 Warner Bros.

Fulghum, Robert. Villard Books (Photo Copyright © 1991 Dan Lamont/Matrix)

Gaston, Cito. Toronto Blue Jays.

Gerstner, Louis V., Jr. I. B. M.

Gibson, Mel. Copyright © 1992, Warner Bros. Inc.

Gill, Vince. MCA® Nashville (Photo: Victoria Pearson 8/93)

Ginsburg, Ruth Bader. U.S. Supreme Court

Giuliani, Rudolph. Office of the Mayor, New York City (Photo: Sender Schwartz)

Glover, Danny. Copyright © 1992 Warner Bros. Inc.

Goldberg, Whoopi. Copyright © 1993 Regency Enterprises V.O.F. and Le Studio Canal

Goodman, John. Copyright © Universal City Studios (Photo: Dean Williams).

Gore, Al. The White House

Gossett, Louis, Jr. Copyright © 1992 Metro-Goldwyn-Mayer (Photo: Richard Foreman)

Hackman, Gene. Copyright © 1992 Warner Bros.

Hanks, Tom. Copyright © 1992 Columbia Pictures

Hershey, Barbara. Universal Pictures, Copyright © 1992 (Photo: Ben Glass)

PHOTO CREDITS

Hijuelos, Oscar. Farrar, Straus and Giroux (Photo: Robert Koch © 1993)

Holyfield, Evander. Main Events

Hosokawa, Morihiro. Embassy of Japan

Houston, Whitney. Arista/Nippy, Inc.

Hurley, Bobby. Duke University

Hutchison, Day Bailey. U.S. Senate

Ice-T. Copyright © 1991 Sire Records Company (Photo: Harrison Funk)

Irons, Jeremy. Copyright © 1993 Geffen Pictures (Photo: Takashi Seida)

Jackson, Bo. Chicago White Sox

Jackson, Janet. Virgin (Photo: Yuri Elizondo 11/93)

Jackson, Michael. Epic ©1991 MJJ Productions (Photo: Sam Emerson)

Jackson, Phil. Chicago Bulls

Jagger, Mick. Atlantic (Photo: Paul Cox © 1992)

Janzen, Lee. © 1993 PGA Tour

Joel, Billy. Columbia Records

Johnson, Jimmy. Dallas Cowboys

Jones, James Earl. Dale Olsen & Associates

Jones, Tommy Lee. Warner Bros. Copyright © 1993 (Photo: Roland Neveu)

Jordan, Michael. Chicago Bulls.

Jordan, Richard. © New Line Cinema Corp. (Photo: Merrick Morton)

Judd, Wynonna. Curb™/MCA® (Photo: Randee St. Nicholas 04993A)

Kennedy, Ted. U.S. Senate

Kidman, Nicole. Copyright © 1992 Universal City Studios

King, Larry. Harcourt Brace (Photo: Dirck Halstead)

Lehrer, Jim. MacNeil/Lehrer Productions (Photo: Christopher Little)

Lemmon, Jack. Copyright © 1993 Warner Bros. (Photo: Ron Phillips)

Limbaugh, Rush. Pocket Books (Photo: E.J. Camp/Outline)

Lucas, John. San Antonio Spurs

McEntire, Reba. Starstruck, MCA® Nashville (Photo McGuire 0991A)

McKellen, Ian. Brooklyn Academy of Music, Boneau/Bryan-Brown (Photo: John Haynes)

McMillan, Terry. Viking Penguin (Photo: Marion Ettlinger)

MacNeil, Robert. MacNeil/Lehrer Productions (Photo: ©Eddie Adams)

Madonna. Copyright © 1992 Sire Records Company

Major, John. British Information Service

Malkovich, John. Copyright © 1993 Columbia Pictures/© 1993 Castle Rock Entertainment

Matlin, Marlee. Copyright © 1993 Twentieth Century Fox (Photo: Merrick Morton)

Matthau, Walter. © 1993 Warner Bros. (Photo: Marsha Blackburn) Caption: Walter Matthau (left) and Mason Gamble

Michener, James. Random House (Photo: © John Kings)

Midler, Bette. PMK (Photo: Greg Gorman)

Mitterrand, François. Embassy of France

Modine, Matthew. © 1993 Fine Line Features (Photo: Joyce Rudolph)

Montana, Joe. Kansas City Chiefs

Moore, Demi. Copyright © 1992 Castle Rock Entertainment (Photo: Sidney Baldwin)

Murdoch, Iris. Viking Penguin (Photo: Tom Blau)

Murphy, Eddie. Copyright © 1992 Paramount Pictures (Photo: Bruce W. Talamon)

Murray, Bill. Copyright © 1992 Universal City Studios (Photo: Charles Hodes)

Naruhito, Crown Prince. Embassy of Japan

Masako, Crown Princess. Embassy of Japan

Navratilova, Martina. World Tennis Association (Photo: © Carol L. Newsom/Virginia Slims)

Neeson, Liam. © 1993 Universal City Studios (Photo: David James)

Nelson, Willie. Columbia ©1993 Sony Music (Photo: Frank Ockenfels)

Nicholson, Jack. Copyright © 1992 Castle Rock Entertainment (Photo: Sidney Baldwin)

Nicklaus, Jack. © 1993 PGA Tour

Norman, Greg. © 1993 PGA Tour

Nunn, Sam. U.S. Senate

Oates, Joyce Carol. Dutton/William Abrahams Books (Photo: Norman Seeff).

O'Brien, Conan. Baker, Winokur, Ryder Public Relations

Olajuwon, Hakeem. Houston Rockets

Oldman, Gary. © 1991 Warner Bros. Inc., Regency Enterprises V.O.F. and Le Studio Canal

O'Leary, Hazel. U.S. Department of Energy.

Pacino, Al. Universal City Studios, Copyright © 1992 (Photo: Myles Aronowitz)

Panetta, Leon. Office of Management and Budget, The White House

Parton, Dolly. Columbia ©1993 Sony Music (Photo: Randee St. Nicholas)

Price, Nick. © 1993 PGA Tour

Prince. Copyright © 1992 Warner Bros. (Photo: Jeff Katz)

Quaid, Dennis. Copyright © 1993 Paramount Pictures (Photo: Lorey Sebastian)

Quindlen, Anna. Random House (Photo Credit © Joyce Ravid)

Redford, Robert. Copyright © 1992 Columbia Pictures Industries, Inc.

Reich, Robert. Presidential Transition Press Office

Reiner, Rob. © 1992 Castle Rock Entertainment.

Reno, Janet. U.S. Department of Justice

Reynolds, Burt. Copyright © 1992 Universal City Studios (Photo: Peter Steve Schapiro)

Riley, Pat. New York Knicks (Photo: George Kalinsky)

Rivers, Larry. Aaron Asher Books/HarperCollins

Robbins, Tim. © 1993 Fine Line Features (Photo: Joyce Rudolph)

Roberts, Julia. Warner Bros. Copyright © 1993 (Photo: Ken Regan/Camera 5)

Rostenkowski, Dan. U.S. House of Representatives

Roth, Philip. Simon & Schuster (Photo: Nancy Crampton)

Ruehl, Mercedes. Copyright © 1993 Columbia Pictures

Rushdie, Salman. Viking Penguin (Photo: © Jerry Bauer)

Sampras, Pete. ProServ (Photo: Gus Bower)

Schroeder, Pat. U.S. House of Representatives

Sendak, Maurice. Candlewick Press (Photo: Chris Callis)

Sessions, William. Federal Bureau of Investigation

Seth, Vikram. HarperCollins (Photo: Aradhana Seth)

Shalala, Donna. Presidential Transition Press Office

Shalikashvili, John. U.S. Department of Defense

Sheen, Martin. Copyright © 1993 Twentieth Century Fox (Photo: Merrick Morton)

Simon, Paul. Copyright © 1991 Warner Bros. Records (Photo: Edie Baskin)

Smith, Emmitt. Dallas Cowboys

Snipes, Wesley. Copyright © 1993 Warner Bros. (Photo: Andrew Cooper)

Spielberg, Steven. © 1993 Universal City Studios (Photo: David James)

Stallone, Sylvester. Copyright © 1993 Warner Bros. (Photo: Andrew Cooper)

Steenburgen, Mary. Copyright © Paramount Pictures (Photo: Peter Iovino)

Stephanopoulous, George. The White House

Stewart, Rod. © 1993 Warner Bros. Records (Photo: Robert Matheu)

Sting. A & M Records (Photo: Brian Airs 4/93)

Stone, Oliver. Warner Bros. Copyright © 1993 (Photo: Elizabeth Stone)

Streep, Meryl. Copyright © 1992 Universal City Studios (Photo: Deana Newcomb)

Streisand, Barbra. Columbia ©1993 Sony Music (Photo: Firooz Zahedi)

Styron, William. Random House (Photo Credit © Peter Simon)

Sutherland, Kiefer. Copyright © 1993 Twentieth Century Fox (Photo: Ralph Nelson)

Thatcher, Margaret. Harper Collins.

Thomas, Frank. Chicago White Sox

Thompson, Emma. Sony Pictures

Tomlin, Lily. © 1993 Fine Line Features (Photo: Joyce Rudolph)

Townshend, Peter. Atlantic Records (Photo: © Andrew Eccles)

Tritt, Travis. © 1992 Warner Bros. Records (Photo: Randee St. Nicholas)

Turner, Ted. Copyright © 1989 Turner Broadcasting System

Turner, Tina. Virgin (Photo: Herb Ritts 5/93)

Turow, Scott. Farrar, Straus and Giroux (Photo: Skrebniski © 1993)

Waits, Tom. © 1993 Fine Line Features (Photo: Joyce Rudolph)

Walken, Christopher. Copyright © 1993 Paramount Pictures (Photo: Elliott Marks)

Ward, Charlie. Florida State University

Washington, Denzel. Copyright © 1992 Warner Bros. Inc. (Photo: David Lee/ Warner Bros.)

Williams, Robin. Copyright © 1993 Twentieth Century Fox (Photo: Arthur Grace)

Willis, Bruce. Copyright © 1992 Universal City Studios (Photo: Deana Newcomb)

Cumulative Alphabetical Index

For ease of access, we have here provided a cumulative alphabetical index of all those who have appeared in any edition of **People in the News.** For each individual, the index gives the year of any edition in which he or she appears, and (after the colon) the page number where the entry begins. So for Pete Sampras, who appears in three of the first four editions, the index entry reads:

Sampras, Pete **'94:331** / **'92:310** / **'91:281**

Note that this 1994 edition of **People in the News** also includes a cumulative index by occupation beginning on page 427.

Scorsese, Martin '94:336 / '93:351 / '92:316 / '91:287
Scott, George C. '94:337 / '92:317 / '91:287
Scott, William George '91:288
Scowcroft, Brent '93:352 / '92:317 / '91:288
Seale, Arthur '93:353
Seale, Irene. See Seale, Arthur
Seinfeld, Jerry '94:338
Seles, Monica '94:338 / '93:353 / '92:318
Selig, Bud '94:339
Selleck, Tom '93:354 / '92:319 / '91:288
Selznick, Irene Mayer '91:289
Sendak, Maurice '94:340 / '91:289
Sergeyev, Constantin '93:355
Serkin, Rudolf '92:319
Sessions, William '94:341
Seth, Vikram '94:341
Seton, Anya '91:289
Seurat, Michel. See Lebanon hostages
Seuss, Dr. (Theodore Geisel) '92:320 / '91:290
Sevareid, Eric '93:355
Seyrig, Delphine '91:290
Shalala, Donna '94:342 / '93:355
Shalikashvili, John '94:343
Shamir, Yitzhak '93:356 / '92:321 / '91:290
Shannon, Del '91:291
Sharaff, Irene '94:343
Sharon, Ariel '93:356 / '92:321 / '91:291
Shatner, William '94:344
Shawcross, Arthur '92:322
Shawn, William '93:357
Sheehan, George '94:344
Sheen, Martin '94:345 / '93:357 / '92:322 / '91:292
Sheets, Robert C. '93:358
Shell, Art '91:292
Shevardnadze, Eduard '94:345 / '93:359 / '92:323 / '91:293
Shilts, Randy '94:346
Shirer, William L. '94:347
Shirley, Anne '94:347
Shula, Don '94:348
Shuster, Joseph '93:359
Siegel, Don '92:324
Siegmeister, Elie '92:324
Sihanouk, Norodom '94:348 / '93:360 / '92:324 / '91:293
Silber, John Robert '91:294
Simon, Kate '91:295
Simon, Neil '94:349 / '93:360 / '92:325 / '91:295
Simon, Norton W. '94:350
Simon, Paul '94:350 / '93:361 / 92:326 / '91:296
Sinatra, Frank '94:351 / '93:362 / '92:326 / '91:296

Singer, Isaac Bashevis '92:327
Singh, Vishwanath Pratap '91:297
Singleton, John '93:363
Sirica, John J. '93:363
Siskind, Aaron '92:328
Sisulu, Notsikelelo Albertina. See Sisulu, Walter
Sisulu, Walter '93:363 / '92:328 / '91:298
Skinner, B. F. '91:298
Skinner, Samuel K. '93:364 / '92:329 / '91:298
Slayton, Deke '94:352
Smallwood, Joey '92:329
Smart, Pamela Wojas '92:330
Smiley, Jane Graves '93:364
Smith, Alexis '94:352
Smith, Emmitt '94:352
Smith, Maggie '94:353 / '93:365 / '92:330 / '91:299
Smith, William French '91:299
Smith, William Kennedy '92:331
Smoot, George F. '93:366
Snelling, Richard Arkwright '92:331
Snipes, Wesley '94:354
Snyder, Mitch '91:299
Solzhenitsyn, Alexander '93:366 / '92:332 / '91:300
Sondheim, Stephen '94:354 / '93:367 / '92:332 / '91:301
Sontag, Susan '94:355 / '93:367
Soupault, Philippe '91:301
Soustelle, Jacques '91:302
Souter, David '94:355 / '93:368 / '92:333 / '91:302
Spacek, Sissy '93:369 / '92:334
Spader, James '94:356 / '93:370 / '92:334
Speck, Richard '92:335
Spessivtseva, Olga '92:335
Spewack, Bella Cohen '91:302
Spielberg, Steven '94:356 / '93:370 / '92:335 / '91:303
Springsteen, Bruce '93:371 / '91:303
Stallone, Sylvester '94:357 / '93:372 / '92:336 / '91:304
Stanwyck, Barbara '91:304
Stark, Freya '94:358
Starr, Ringo '93:372 / '91:305
Starzl, Thomas '93:373 / '91:305
Steber, Eleanor '91:306
Steen, Alann. See Lebanon hostages
Steenburgen, Mary '94:358 / '93:374 / '92:337 / '91:306
Stegner, Wallace '94:359
Steinbrenner, George '94:360 / '93:374 / '92:337 / '91:307
Sten, Anna '94:360
Stephanopolous, George '94:360 / '93:375

Stern, David '94:361 / '93:375 / '92:337
Stern, Howard '94:362
Stern, Philip '93:376
Stevens, John Paul '94:362 / '93:376 / '92:338 / '91:307
Stewart, Rod '94:363
Stigler, George '92:339
Sting '94:364 / '93:377 / '92:340 / '91:308
Stirling, James Frazer '93:378
Stone, Oliver '94:364 / '93:378 / '92:340 / '91:308
Strand, Mark '91:309
Streep, Meryl '94:365 / '93:379 / '92:341 / '91:309
Streisand, Barbra '94:366 / '93:380 / '92:341
Strout, Richard Lee '91:310
Struebig, Heinrich. See Lebanon hostages
Stuart, Carol DiMaiti. See Stuart, Charles
Stuart, Charles '91:310
Sturges, John '93:381
Styron, William '94:367 / '91:311
Sullivan, Louis Wade '93:381 / '92:342 / '91:311
Sulzberger, C(yrus) L(eo) '94:368
Sununu, John '93:381 / '92:343 / '91:312
Sutherland, Donald '94:368 / '93:382 / '92:344 / '91:313
Sutherland, Kiefer '94:369
Sutherland, Thomas. See Lebanon hostages
Sutton, Denys Miller '92:344
Swanberg, William A. '93:382
Swayze, Patrick '94:369 / '93:383 / '92:345 / '91:313
Swenson, May '91:314
Sydow, Max von '94:370 / '93:383 / '92:345 / '91:314
Syms, Sylvia '93:384
Tagliabue, Paul '94:371 / '93:385 / '92:347 / '91:315
Tal, Mikhail '93:386
Tamayo, Rufino '92:348
Tambo, Oliver '94:372 / '91:316
Tan, Amy '94:372
Tanaka, Kakuei '94:373
Tandy, Jessica '94:373 / '93:386 / '92:348 / '91:316
Tanenbaum, Marc Herbert '93:387
Tayback, Vic '91:317
Taylor, A. J. P. '91:317
Taylor, Elizabeth '94:374 / '93:387 / '92:349 / '91:317
Taylor, Harold '94:374
Taylor, Lawrence '92:350 / '91:318
Terkel, Studs '93:388
Terris, Norma '91:318

Cumulative Index by Occupation

For ease of access, we have here indexed by occupation or other area of news interest those individuals profiled in **People in the News**. Under the appropriate headings, such as "Law and Court Cases" or "Stage and Screen," readers will find volume and page references for all who have appeared in any edition of **People in the News**.

For each person, the index gives the year of any editions in which he or she appears, and (after the colon) the page number where the entry begins. So for Pete Sampras, who appears in three of the first four editions, the index entry is found under the heading "Sports and Games" and reads:

Sampras, Pete **'94:331 / '92:310 / '91:281**

Note that some people are listed under more than one heading, such as Barbra Streisand, who appears under both "Music" and "Stage and Screen." The headings are:

Business and FinanceDance   Politics
Education   ReligionScience, Technology, and Medicine
Journalism and Publishing   Social Activism
Law and Court Cases   Social Sciences
Literature   Sports and Games
Military   Stage and Screen
Miscellaneous   Visual Arts
Music

The main body of each edition of **People in the News** is, of course, self-indexed, with individuals listed alphabetically. However, the second and succeeding volumes also contain a cumulative alphabetical index, in this edition beginning on page 415.

Visual Arts